FUNDAMENTALS
OF SELLING

McGraw-Hill/Irwin Series in Marketing

NINTH EDITION

FUNDAMENTALS OF SELLING

CUSTOMERS FOR LIFE THROUGH SERVICE

CHARLES M. FUTRELL
TEXAS A&M UNIVERSITY

McGraw-Hill
Irwin

Boston   Burr Ridge, IL   Dubuque, IA   Madison, WI   New York   San Francisco   St. Louis Bangkok
Bogotá   Caracas   Kuala Lumpur   Lisbon   London   Madrid   Mexico City   Milan   Montreal
New Delhi   Santiago   Seoul   Singapore   Sydney   Taipei   Toronto

McGraw-Hill
Irwin

FUNDAMENTALS OF SELLING: CUSTOMERS FOR LIFE THROUGH SERVICE

Published by McGraw-Hill/Irwin, a business unit of The McGraw-Hill Companies, Inc., 1221 Avenue of the Americas, New York, NY, 10020. Copyright © 2006, 2004, 2002, 1999, 1996, 1993, 1990, 1988, 1984 by The McGraw-Hill Companies, Inc. All rights reserved. No part of this publication may be reproduced or distributed in any form or by any means, or stored in a database or retrieval system, without the prior written consent of The McGraw-Hill Companies, Inc., including, but not limited to, in any network or other electronic storage or transmission, or broadcast for distance learning.

Some ancillaries, including electronic and print components, may not be available to customers outside the United States.

This book is printed on acid-free paper.

2 3 4 5 6 7 8 9 0 DOW/DOW 0 9 8 7 6 5

ISBN   0-07-296210-0

Editorial director: *John E. Biernat*
Publisher: *Andy Winston*
Sponsoring editor: *Barrett Koger*
Editorial coordinator: *Scott Becker*
Executive marketing manager: *Dan Silverburg*
Media producer: *Benjamin Curless*
Project manager: *Kristin Puscas*
Lead production supervisor: *Michael R. McCormick*
Designer: *Kami Carter*
Senior photo research coordinator: *Jeremy Cheshareck*
Photo researcher: *Robin Sand*
Senior media project manager: *Rose M. Range*
Supplement producer: *Gina F. DiMartino*
Developer, Media technology: *Brian Nacik*
Typeface: *10/12 Times*
Compositor: *SR Nova Pvt Ltd, Bangalore, India*
Printer: *R. R. Donnelley*

Library of Congress Cataloging-in-Publication Data

Futrell, Charles.
  Fundamentals of selling : customers for life through service / Charles M. Futrell.—9th ed.
    p. cm.—(The McGraw-Hill/Irwin series in marketing)
  Includes bibliographical references and index.
  ISBN 0-07-296210-0 (alk. paper)
  1. Selling. I. Title. II. Series.
HF5438.25.F87 2006
  658.85—dc21

                                                                                      2004060957

www.mhhe.com

To my Father!

Charles M. Futrell is the Federated Professor of Marketing in the Mays Business School at Texas A&M University in College Station, Texas. Texas A&M University has approximately 44,000 students with 6,000 business majors and 800 marketing majors. Dr. Futrell has a B.B.A., M.B.A., and Ph.D. in marketing. Dr. Futrell is a former salesperson turned professor. Before beginning his academic career, Professor Futrell worked in sales and marketing capacities for eight years with the Colgate Company, The Upjohn Company, and Ayerst Laboratories.

Dr. Futrell serves as a frequent reviewer for several academic journals. He is on the editorial board of *The Journal of Personal Selling & Sales Management* and the editorial advisory board of *The Journal of Marketing Theory and Practice.* His research in personal selling, sales management, research methodology, and marketing management has appeared in numerous national and international journals, such as the *Journal of Marketing* and the *Journal of Marketing Research.* An article in the summer 1991 issue of *The Journal of Personal Selling & Sales Management* ranked Charles as one of the top three sales researchers in America. He was also recognized in *Marketing Education,* Summer 1997, as one of the top 100 best researchers in the marketing discipline. His work has earned him several research awards.

Professor Futrell served as the American Marketing Association's Chair of the Sales and Sales Management Special Interest Group (SIG) for the 1996–97 Academic year. He was the first person elected to this position. Charles was elected Finance Chair for the Sales SIG's 1998–99 term. In 1999, The Association of Former Students awarded him the Lowry Mays College and Graduate School of Business Distinguished Teaching Award. Mu Kappa Tau, the National Marketing Honor Society, recognized Charles for exceptional scholarly contributions to the sales profession in 2000. This is only the fourth time this recognition has been bestowed since its creation in 1988.

In the spring of 2001, Dr. Futrell was chosen as a Fish Camp (Texas A&M University's Freshman Orientation Camp) Namesake. Fish Camps are named after faculty members who have made a significant impact on Texas A&M, and nominations for the award are made by students, which makes it a very prestigious honor for instructors.

Dr. Futrell has written or co-written eight successful books for the college and professional audience. Three of the most popular books are *Sales Management: Teamworks, Leadership, and Technology,* sixth edition, South-Western Thomson Learning College Publishers; *Fundamentals of Selling: Customers for Life through Service* eighth edition, and *ABC's of Relationship Selling through Service,* ninth edition, both published by McGraw-Hill/Irwin. These books are used in hundreds of American and international schools. Over 300,000 students worldwide have learned from Professor Futrell's books.

In 1997 Dr. Futrell began using his Web site and group e-mails in his sales classes that at that time often had 100 students in each section. Students sign up for both a lecture period and lab time. In each semester's six labs, students are videotaped in activities such as making a joint sales call, panel interview, selling oneself on a job interview, product sales presentations, and various experiential exercises.

TAMU's College of Business Administration and Graduate School of Business is one of the largest business programs in America, with more than 6,000 full-time business majors. Approximately 50 percent of the Marketing Department's 800 majors are in Charles's personal selling and/or sales management classes at various times. He has worked with close to 10,000 students in sales-related classes.

Professor Futrell's books, research, and teaching are based on his extensive work with sales organizations of all types and sizes. This broad and rich background has resulted in his being invited to be a frequent speaker, researcher, and consultant to industry.

Preface

Your textbook title includes the word *service*. Service refers to making a contribution to the welfare of others. Why? It is time to make the bold statement that salespeople exist to help others.

In recent years we have seen the worst of American business. Gallup (one of America's leading pollsters) has found that some categories of salespeople's jobs are the lowest-rated job categories for perceived honesty and ethical standards. Chances are, the majority of students have a negative attitude about salespeople.

We can correct this image by illustrating the wonderful things professional salespeople do. This edition emphasizes helping others through the application of the Golden Rule of Personal Selling. This simple sales philosophy is based upon treating others unselfishly, as you would like to be treated.

Fundamentals of Selling is written by a salesperson turned teacher. For eight years I worked in sales with Colgate, Upjohn, and Ayerst. As an academic, I have taught selling to thousands of college students, businesspeople, and industry sales personnel, developing and using the strategies, practices, and techniques presented in this textbook. Moreover, each year I continue to spend time in fieldwork with sales personnel. In my classes and programs, I stress "learning by doing" examples and exercises and videotape role playing of selling situations. This book is the result of these experiences.

When students ask me why I moved out of sales, I always reply, "I really haven't. I'm just selling a different product in a different industry." We are all selling, whether it's a product, an idea, our parents, a friend, or ourselves—as when interviewing for a job.

Fundamentals' Approach

Fundamentals of Selling was conceived as a method of providing ample materials that allow readers to construct their own sales presentations after studying the text. This allows the instructor the flexibility of focusing on the "how-to-sell" approach within the classroom. Covering the basic foundations for understanding the concepts and practices of selling in a practical, straightforward, and readable manner, it provides students with a guide to use in preparing sales presentations and role-playing exercises.

The Philosophy behind This Book

The title should help you understand the philosphy of this book. A student of sales should understand the fundamentals—the basics—of personal selling. All of them. I do not advocate one way of selling as the best route to success! There are many roads to reaching one's goals.

I *do* feel a salesperson should have an assortment of selling skills and should be very knowledgeable, even an expert, in the field. Based on the situation, the salesperson determines the appropriate actions to take for a particular prospect or customer. No matter what the situation, however, the basic fundamentals of selling can be applied.

There is no place in our society for high-pressure, manipulative selling. The salesperson is a problem solver, a helper, and an advisor to the customer. If the customer has no need, the salesperson should accept that and move on to help another person or firm. If the customer has a need, however, the salesperson should and must go for the sale. All successful salespeople I know feel that once they determine that the customer is going to buy someone's product—and that their product will satisfy that customer's needs—it is their job to muster all their energy, skill, and know-how to make that sale. That is what it's all about!

It is my sincere hope that after the reader has studied this book, he or she will say, "There's a lot more to selling than I ever imagined." I hope many people will feel that this material can help them earn a living and that selling is a great occupation and career.

At the end of the course, I hope all the students will have learned how to prepare and give a sales presentation by visually, verbally, and nonverbally communicating their message. I know of no other marketing course whose class project is so challenging and where so much learning takes place.

Finally, I hope each student realizes that these new communication skills can be applied to all aspects of life. Once learned and internalized, selling skills will help a person be a better communicator throughout life.

Basic Organization of the Book

The publisher and I worked hard to ensure that *Fundamentals of Selling* would provide students with the basic foundation for understanding all major aspects of selling. The 17 chapters in the text are divided into four parts:

- **Selling as a Profession.** Emphasizes the history, career, rewards, and duties of the professional salesperson and illustrates the importance of the sales function to the organization's success. It also examines the social, ethical, and legal issues in selling.

- **Preparation for Relationship Selling.** Presents the background information salespeople use to develop their sales presentations.

- **The Relationship Selling Process.** At the heart of this book, this part covers the entire selling process from prospecting to follow-up. State-of-the-art selling strategies, practices, and techniques are presented in a "how-to" fashion.

- **Managing Yourself, Your Career, and Others.** The importance of the proper use and management of one's time and sales territory is given thorough coverage. Two chapters cover the fundamentals of managing salespeople. For many students, this is their only exposure to what a sales manager does in this challenging job.

In This Edition

Expanded Emphasis. Unselfish and ethical service to the customer underscores the Golden Rule of Personal Selling—a sales philosophy of unselfishly treating others as you would like to be treated without expecting reciprocity. This is how to build long-term relationships with customers.

The Tree of Business Life Icon. Beginning with Chapter 3, The Tree of Business Life icon is used to remind the reader of one of the main themes of the book. This theme emphasizes that by providing ethical service you build true relationships. This section was developed in hopes of having the reader consider how a salesperson would incorporate ethical service into the chapter's topic.

The Golden Rule Icon. The Golden Rule icon appears in each chapter to help reinforce the Tree of Business Life. The combination of the Golden Rule and the "Tree" guidelines for business and selling form the core theme of this textbook. Unselfishly treating prospects/customers as you would like to be treated without expecting something in return results in ethical service which builds true long-term relationships. If you think about it, this is how you build true personal friendships. Why not build your business relationships on this rock?

Comprehensive Cases. At the end of the book are comprehensive sales cases. These cases approach sales from the broader sales management perspective.

Video Cases. Cases 3-1, 3-2, 5-3, 6-5A, 8-3, 11-3, 13-4, 14-3 can be used independently or with eight of the videos accompanying this book. Each of the eight cases highlights a tough ethical dilemma often faced by sales personnel in today's competitive marketplace. Use any or all of these cases to emphasize ethics in your sales class.

Sales Call Role-Plays and Videos. The first three of the four role-plays in Appendix A have videos created incorporating our selling process. The two people featured in the three role-plays

completed my selling course. The professional selling materials in Chapters 8, 9, 10, 11, 12, and 13 do a great job in illustrating. Actually used in my classes by hundreds of students, these role-plays are created from information used by today's top sales forces.

Sell Yourself on a Job Interview. This all-time favorite role-play is in Appendix B with other experiential exercises. For years I have used this student pleaser in both my personal selling and sales management classes. When students see themselves on video they quickly realize what needs to be done for a professional interview. You have to try this exercise one time!

ACT! Customer Contact. Using software to maintain contact with customers and prospects is a necessity in the 21st century.

Student Application Learning Exercises (SALES). Chapters directly related to creating the role-play have SALES that aid students in better understanding how to construct this popular class project. These were first used in Professor Futrell's classes in the fall of 1997. Students unanimously felt they were great in helping them correctly construct their role-plays.

Sales Careers. Career information has been expanded throughout so students will better understand that there are sales jobs in *all* organizations—business, service, and nonprofit.

Selling Experiential Exercises. These end-of-chapter exercises help students to better understand themselves and/or the text material. Many can be done in class or completed outside and discussed in class.

Selling Globally Appendix. Many of these new box items were written by friends and colleagues from countries around the world.

Technology in Selling. A central theme within each chapter shows the use of technology and automation in selling and servicing prospects and customers.

Text and Chapter Pedagogy

Many reality-based features are included in the ninth edition to stimulate learning. One major goal of this book is to offer better ways of using it to convey sales knowledge to the reader. To do this, the book includes numerous special features:

Photo Essays. The book features many photographs accompanied by captions that describe sales events and how they relate to chapter materials.

Chapter Topics and Objectives. Each chapter begins with a clear statement of learning objectives and an outline of major chapter topics. These devices provide an overview of what is to come and can also be used by students to see whether they understand and have retained important points.

Sales Challenge/Solution. The text portion of each chapter begins with a real-life challenge sales professionals face. The challenge pertains to the topic of the chapter and will heighten students' interest in chapter concepts. The challenge is resolved at the end of the chapter, where chapter concepts guiding the salespersons' actions are highlighted.

Making the Sale. These boxed items explore how salespeople, when faced with challenges, use innovative ideas to sell.

Selling Tips. These boxes offer the reader additional selling tips for use in developing their role-plays.

Artwork. Many aspects of selling tend to be confusing at first. "What should I do?" and "How should I do it?" are two questions frequently asked by students in developing their role-plays. To enhance students' awareness and understanding, many exhibits have been included throughout the book. These exhibits consolidate key points, indicate relationships, and visually illustrate selling techniques.

Chapter Summary and Application Questions. Each chapter closes with a summary of key points to be retained. The application questions are a complementary learning tool that enables students to check their understanding of key issues, to think beyond basic concepts, and to determine areas that require further study. The summary and application questions help students discriminate between main and supporting points and provide mechanisms for self-teaching.

Key Terms for Selling/Glossary. Learning the selling vocabulary is essential to understanding today's sales world. This is facilitated in three ways. First, key concepts are boldfaced and completely defined where they first appear in the text. Second, each key term, followed by the page number where it was first introduced and defined, is listed at the end of each chapter. Third, a glossary summarizing all key terms and definitions appears at the end of the book for handy reference.

Ethical Dilemma. These challenging exercises provide students an opportunity to experience ethical dilemmas faced in the selling job. Students should review Chapter 3's definition and explanation of ethical behavior before discussing the ethical dilemmas.

Further Exploring the Sales World. These projects ask students to go beyond the textbook and classroom to explore what's happening in the real world. Projects can be altered or adapted to the instructor's school location and learning objectives for the class.

Cases for Analysis. Each chapter ends with brief but substantive cases for student analysis and class discussion. These cases provide an opportunity for students to apply concepts to real events and to sharpen their diagnostic skills for sales problem solving. Comprehensive cases are found in the back of the book.

As you see, the publisher and I have thoroughly considered how best to present the material to readers for maximizing their interest and learning. Teacher, reviewer, and student response to this revision has been fantastic. They are pleased with the readability, reasonable length, depth, and breadth of the material. You will like this edition better than the previous one.

Teaching and Learning Supplements

McGraw-Hill/Irwin has spared no expense to make *Fundamentals of Selling* the premier text in the market today. Many instructors face classes with limited resources, and supplementary materials provide a way to expand and improve the students' learning experience. Our learning package was specifically designed to meet the needs of instructors facing a variety of teaching conditions and for both the first-time and veteran instructor.

ProSelling Video. Several hours of student role-plays, exercises, examples of selling techniques, and industry sales training programs show students how to prepare their role-plays and how course content relates to the sales world.

Inc. Business Resources Video Package. A new feature from Inc. demonstrates key features of relationship selling.

Instructor's Manual. Loaded with ideas on teaching the course, chapter outlines, commentaries on cases, answers to everything—plus much more—the *Instructor's Manual* is a large, comprehensive time-saver for teachers.

Test Bank. The most important part of the teaching package is the *Test Bank.* We gave the *Test Bank* special attention during the preparation of the ninth edition because instructors desire test questions that accurately and fairly assess student competence in subject material. Prepared by Dr. Thomas K. Pritchett, Dr. Betty M. Pritchett of Kennesaw State College and myself, the *Test Bank* provides hundreds of multiple-choice and true/false questions. Professor Tom Pritchett also uses the book for his selling classes. Each question is keyed to chapter learning objectives, has been rated for level of difficulty, and is designated either as factual or application so that instructors can provide a balanced set of questions for student exams.

Instructor CD-Rom: A course preparation CD including:

- **A PowerPoint Presentation.** A state-of-the-art program offering hundreds of lecture slides. These slides can be customized for any course. They are great!
- **Computerized Test Bank.** The Computerized Test Bank allows instructors to select and edit test items from the printed Test Bank and to add their own questions. Various versions of each test can be custom printed.

■ **Electronic Version of the Instructor's Manual.**

Course Web Site. At **http://www.mhhe.com/futrell,** you can access downloadable versions of instructor support materials, as well as a student tutorial and student self-assessment quizzes.

ACT! Express Software. For many businesspeople, staying in touch with prospects, customers, clients, vendors, and suppliers—people outside the company—is critical to success. And that success depends on managing those contacts for highly productive business relationships.

Included with this textbook is ACT!™ Express, a tool that will help students entering the business world. Based on the best-selling ACT! contact management system, ACT! Express shows students how to become more productive—resulting in better business relationships and greater business opportunities.

Whether in sales, a small or start-up company, a consulting practice, a professional services firm, or another business setting, students will become more proficient at effectively managing their contacts.

But what *is* a contact manager?

A contact manager will help the student manage all of the tasks and information critical to building effective business relationships such as these:

■ Finding and contacting prospects.

■ Following up with prospects and clients.

■ Sending product information, proposals, and quotes.

■ Scheduling meetings.

■ Generating correspondence.

■ Managing customers' postsale activities and requests.

■ Keeping a history of previous customer interactions.

■ Generating reports of activities and client/account status.

Effective contact management means making the most of contacts with prospects, customers, clients, vendors, and suppliers.

ACT! Express includes the following features:

■ *Complete contact and calendar managment.* Seventy predefined fields for contact information, notes, tasks, schedules, history, and more.

■ *Search capabilities.* Quickly locate any information in the database by name, ZIP code, phone number, or keyword.

■ *Groups.* Sort contacts into groups by company, interests, or other commonalities.

■ *Activity reminders.* Set alarms for upcoming activity reminders.

■ *Basic e-mail functions.* Send and track e-mail correspondence—and attach e-mails directly to specific contact records.

■ *Basic contact reporting.* Easily generate basic reports such as Activity History, Task List, Source of Referrals, and more.

■ *Built-in word processor.* Includes prewritten letters that can be easily personalized.

■ *Data synchronization with Palm Powered™ Handhelds.* Take contact information, notes, and history anywhere.

Students who become proficient with ACT! Express may want to explore more advanced functions available in the full ACT! contact management system.

Students desiring more information about either ACT! Express or ACT! are encouraged to visit **www.act.com/students.**

Acknowledgments

Working with the dedicated team of professionals at McGraw-Hill/Irwin, who were determined to produce the best personal selling book ever, was a gratifying experience.

In overseeing this revision, Sponsoring Editor Barrett Koger and Editorial Coordinator Scott Becker offered ideas for improvements to the ninth edition package. Jeremy Chesharck and Robin Sand oversaw the selection of new photographs for this edition. Project Manager Kristin Puscas ably guided the manuscript and page proofs through the production process.

Another group of people who made a major contribution to this text were the sales experts who provided advice, reviews, answers to questions, and suggestions for changes, insertions, and clarifications. I want to thank these colleagues for their valuable feedback and suggestions: Katrece Albert, *Southern University;* Jon M. Hawes, *University of Akron;* Raymond Wimer, *Syracuse University.*

I also want to again thank those people who contributed to earlier editions, because their input is still felt in this ninth edition. They were Ramon A. Avila, *Ball State University;* Duane Bachmann, *Central Missouri State University;* Ames Barber, *Adirondack Community College;* John R. Beem, *College of DuPage;* Dawn Bendall-Lyon, *University of Montevallo;* Milton J. Bergstein, *Pennsylvania State University;* Chris Brandmeir, *Highline Community College;* Michael Cicero, *Highline Community College;* Marjorie Cooper, *Baylor University;* Norman Cohn, *Milwaukee Tech;* Gerald Crawford, *University of North Alabama;* William H. Crookston, *California State University—Northridge;* Gary Donnelly, *Casper College;* Sid Dudley, *Eastern Illinois University;* Dennis Elbert, *University of North Dakota;* Earl Emery, *Baker Junior College of Business;* O.C. Ferrell, *Colorado State University;* Myrna Glenny, *Fashion Institute of Design and Merchandising;* Ric Gorno, *Cypress College;* Kevin Hammond, *Community College of Allegheny County;* John Hawes, *University of Akron;* Deborah Jansky, *Milwaukee Area Technical College;* Albert Jerus, *Northwestern College;* Donna Kantack, *Elrick & Lavidge;* Dennis Kovach, *Community College of Allegheny County;* Deborah Lawe, *San Fransicsco State University;* James E. Littlefield, *Virginia Polytechnic Institute & State University;* Lynn J. Loudenback, *New Mexico State University;* Leslie E. Martin, Jr., *University of Wisconsin–Whitewater;* Brian Meyer, *Mankato State University;* Ken Miller, *Kilgore College;* Harry Moak, *Macomb Community College;* Dick Nordstrom, *California State University–Fresno;* James Ogden, *Kutztown University;* Becky Oliphant, *Stetson University;* Roy Payne, *Purdue University;* Robert Piacenza, *Madison Area Technical College;* Alan Rick, *New England Institute of Technology;* John Ronchetto, *University of San Diego;* Jeff Sager, *University of North Texas;* Donald Sandlin, *East Los Angeles College;* Camille P. Schuster, *Xavier University;* Richard Shannon, *Western Kentucky University;* Dee Smith, *Lansing Community College;* Robert Smith, *Illinois State University;* Ed Snider, *Mesa Community College;* William A. Stull, *Utah State*

University; Robert Tangsrud, Jr., *University of North Dakota;* Ruth Taylor, *Southwest Texas State University;* Albert J. Taylor, *Austin Peay State University;* James L. Taylor, *University of Alabama;* Robert Thompson, *Indiana State University;* Rollie Tilman, *University of North Carolina at Chapel Hill;* John Todd, *University of Tampa;* Glenna Urbshadt, *British Columbia Institute of Technology;* Bruce Warsleys, *Trend Colleges;* Dan Weilbaker, *Northern Illinois University;* Timothy W. Wright, *Lakeland Community College;* and George Wynn, *James Madison University.*

I would also like to thank the many Texas A & M students who have used the book in their classes and provided feedback. Thanks also to the many instructors who call me each year to discuss the book and what they do in their classes. While we have never met face-to-face, I feel I know you. Your positive comments, encouragement, and ideas have been inspirational to me.

In addition, salespeople and sales managers have provided photographs, selling techniques, answers to end-of-chapter exercises and cases, and other industry materials that enrich the reader's learning experience. They include the following:

Kim Allen, *McNeil Consumer Products Company;* Alan Baker, *Noxell Corporation;* Michael Bevan, *Parbron International of Canada;* Richard Ciotti, *JC Penney Company;* John Croley, *The Gates Rubber Company;* Terry and Paul Fingerhut, *Steamboat Party Sales, Inc., Tupperware;* Bill Frost, *AT&T Communications;* Steve Gibson, *Smith Barney;* Gary Grant, *NCR;* Jerry Griffin, *Sewell Village Cadillac—Sterling, Dallas;* Martha Hill, *Hanes Corporation;* Debra Hutchins, *Sunwest Bank of Albuquerque;* Mike Impink, *Aluminum Company of America (ALCOA);* Bob James, *American Hospital Supply Corporation;* Morgan Jennings, *Richard D. Irwin, Inc.;* Patrick Kamlowsky, *Hughes Tool Company;* Cindy Kerns, *Xerox Corportion;* Alan Killingsworth, *FMC Corporation;* Santo Laquatra, *SmithKline Beecham;* Stanley Marcus;* Gerald Mentor, *Richard D. Irwin, Inc.;* Jim Mobley, *General Mills, Inc.;* George Morris, *The Prudential Insurance Company of America;* Vikki Morrison, *First Team Walk-In Realty, California;* Greg Munoz, *The Dow Chemical Company;* Kathleen Paynter, *Campbell Sales Company;* Bruce Powell, *Richard D. Irwin, Inc.;* Jack Pruett, *Bailey Banks and Biddle;* Emmett Reagan, *Xerox Corporation;* Bruce Scagel, *Scott Paper Company;* Linda Slaby-Baker, *The Quaker Oats Company;* Sandra Snow, *The Upjohn Company;* Matt Suffoletto, *International Business Machines (IBM);* Ed Tucker, *Cannon Financial Group, Georgia.*

For the use of their selling exercises and sales management cases, I am especially grateful to these people:

- Gerald Crawford, Keith Absher, Bill Stewart, *University of North Alabama*
- Zarrell V. Lambert, *Southern Illinois University at Carbondale*
- Fred W. Kniffin, *University of Connecticut*
- Dick Nordstrom, *California State University–Fresno*
- Jeffrey K. Sager, *University of North Texas*
- James L. Taylor, *University of Alabama*
- George Wynn, *James Madison University*

Finally, I wish to thank the sales trainers, salespeople, and sales managers who helped teach me the art of selling when I carried the sales bag full time. I hope I have done justice to their great profession of selling.

I hope you learn from and enjoy the book. I enjoyed preparing it for you. Readers are urged to forward their comments on this text to me. I wish you great success in your selling efforts. Remember, it's the salesperson who gets the customer's orders that keeps the wheels of industry turning. America cannot do without you.

Charles M. Futrell
c-futrell@tamu.edu
http://futrell-www.tamu.edu

Contents

PART II

PREPARATION FOR RELATIONSHIP SELLING 109

PART III
THE RELATIONSHIP SELLING PROCESS 223

CHAPTER 7
Prospecting—The Lifeblood of Selling 224

CHAPTER 11

Elements of a Great Sales Presentation 340

CHAPTER 12

Welcome Your Prospect's Objections 374

CHAPTER 13

Closing Begins the Relationship 410

CHAPTER 14

Service and Follow-Up for Customer Retention 444

PART IV

MANAGING YOURSELF, YOUR CAREER, AND OTHERS 473

CHAPTER 15

Time, Territory, and Self-Management: Keys to Success 474

CHAPTER 16

Planning, Staffing, and Training Successful Salespeople 500

CHAPTER 17

Motivation, Compensation, Leadership, and Evaluation of Salespeople 532

PART I

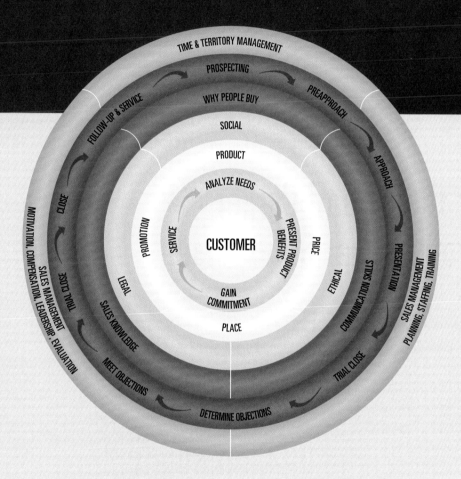

TIME & TERRITORY MANAGEMENT
PROSPECTING
PREAPPROACH
WHY PEOPLE BUY
FOLLOW-UP & SERVICE
SOCIAL
APPROACH
PRODUCT
ANALYZE NEEDS
CLOSE
PROMOTION
SERVICE
CUSTOMER
PRESENT PRODUCT BENEFITS
PRICE
MOTIVATION, COMPENSATION, LEADERSHIP, EVALUATION
SALES MANAGEMENT
TRIAL CLOSE
LEGAL
GAIN COMMITMENT
ETHICAL
PRESENTATION
SALES MANAGEMENT PLANNING, STAFFING, TRAINING
SALES KNOWLEDGE
PLACE
COMMUNICATION SKILLS
MEET OBJECTIONS
TRIAL CLOSE
DETERMINE OBJECTIONS

SELLING AS A PROFESSION

Part 1 provides an overview of the sales profession. Chapter 1 examines the sales job and introduces the 10-step selling process used throughout the book. Chapter 2 explains how personal selling fits into a firm's marketing program. Chapter 3 illustrates the impact of social, ethical, and legal issues on a firm's operations.

A central theme of your book involves how sales personnel analyze needs of the customers, present benefits, gain commitment for purchase, and provide service after the sale. The sales firm provides the product to sell, sets price, determines how the customer can receive the product, and promotes the product. All of the activities must take into consideration the many social, ethical, and legal issues that affect how the organization operates.

As you study the three chapters in Part 1, continually refer back to the exhibit. It will help you remember each chapter's core contents and their relationships.

1 CHAPTER

The Life, Times, and Career of the Professional Salesperson

LEARNING OBJECTIVES

This chapter introduces you to the professional and rewarding career of selling. After studying this chapter, you should be able to

- Define and explain the term *selling*.
- Explain why everyone sells, even you.
- Explain the relationship between the definition of personal selling and the Golden Rule of Personal Selling.
- Discuss the reasons people might choose a sales career.
- Enumerate some of the various types of sales jobs.
- Describe the job activities of salespeople.
- Define the characteristics that salespeople believe are needed for success in building relationships with customers.
- List and explain the 10 steps in the sales process.

Debra Hutchins majored in French, with a minor in English literature, at Washington University in St. Louis. After graduation she began work as a secretary in the marketing department at Sunwest Bank in Albuquerque, New Mexico.

"I had never considered a sales job while in school and sales didn't appeal to me when I began work at the bank. I always felt you would have to be an extrovert. I'm more the shy, intellectual type. I don't see myself in the role of a salesperson.

"Someday I *do* want a more challenging job. I'm a very hard worker; long hours don't bother me. I've always had a need to achieve success. One of the things I like about being a secretary is helping customers when they call the bank. It is important to carefully listen to their problems or what they want in order to provide good customer service. Maybe one day I'll find a job that has more challenge, professionalism, and reward."

If you were in Debra's position, what would you do? What types of jobs would you recommend she consider?

*Nothing happens
until someone sells
something.*

Debra Hutchins is like many people in that while she was in school a career in sales did not seem like the thing to do. Most people are unfamiliar with what salespeople do.

As you learn more about the world of sales, a job selling goods or services may become appealing. The salesperson makes valuable contributions to our quality of life by selling goods and services that benefit individuals and industry. Red Motley, former editor of *Parade* magazine, once said, "Nothing happens until somebody sells something." Selling brings in the money and causes cash registers across the country to ring. For centuries, the salespeople of the world have caused goods and services to change hands.

More than ever, today's salespeople are a dynamic power in the business world. They generate more revenue in the U.S. economy than workers in any other profession. The efforts of salespeople have a direct impact on such diverse areas as these:

- The success of new products.
- Keeping existing products on the retailer's shelf.
- Constructing manufacturing facilities.
- Opening businesses and keeping them open.
- Generating sales orders that result in the loading of trucks, trains, ships, airplanes, and pipelines that carry goods to customers all over the world.

The salesperson is engaged in a highly honorable, challenging, rewarding, and professional career. In this chapter, you are introduced to the career, rewards, and duties of the salesperson. The chapter begins by defining selling and examining why people choose sales careers.

WHAT IS SELLING?

Many people consider *selling* and *marketing* synonymous terms. However, selling is actually only one of many marketing components, as we will see in Chapter 2. In business, a traditional definition of personal selling refers to the personal communication of information to persuade a prospective customer to buy something—a good, service, idea, or something else—that satisfies that individual's needs.

In personal selling, a salesperson can tailor a presentation to the needs of an individual customer.

This definition of selling involves a person helping another person. The salesperson often works with prospects or customers to examine their needs, provide information, suggest a product to meet their needs, and provide after-the-sale service to ensure long-term satisfaction.

The definition also involves communications between seller and buyer. The salesperson and the buyer discuss needs and talk about the product relative to how it will satisfy the person's needs. See, for example, Exhibit 1.1. If the product is what the person needs, then the salesperson attempts to persuade the prospect to buy it.

Unfortunately this explanation of personal selling does not explain the best selling philosophy for the 21st century. Why?

PERSONAL SELLING TODAY

In the early 2000s the worst side of American business became obvious. Corporate corruption, misstated financials, and the personal profit of chief executives as their companies went out of businesses all contributed to the public's negative attitude toward most, if not all, business professions.[1] Unethical business practices resulted in bankruptcies, which in turn led to massive layoffs across the country. This had an impact on all Americans and their families, leaving no person or organization untouched.

How Some Salespeople Are Viewed

Each year, from 1977 to 2001, Gallup (one of America's leading pollsters) has found that insurance salespeople, advertising practitioners, and used car salespeople are the three lowest-rated job categories on perceived honesty and ethical standards. Which of the three would you say rated the lowest each year? Yes, it was the used car salesperson![2] Unfortunately, people tend to generalize from such research findings that most salespeople are not honest or ethical, which is not the case.

A sheep in wolf's clothing.

I know used car salespeople with the highest of ethical standards. Be careful in making a hasty decision about a salesperson. You cannot judge a book by its cover. You may be dealing with a sheep in wolf's clothing.[3]

What about You?

How do you view the honesty and ethical standards of today's businesses and salespeople? For the last several years, at the beginning of my classes, I have asked sales students the following three questions on a poll found on my Web site:

1. What does the general public think about salespeople? Only 9 percent of the over 1,500 respondents had a positive attitude.
2. What do you think about salespeople? Thirty-five percent had a positive attitude.
3. After graduation, would you accept a sales job? Forty-four percent said "yes."

What is your answer to the poll questions?

These percentages do not represent high marks from my students. What are your answers to these three questions? Please take a few minutes to answer the poll at **http://futrell-www.tamu.edu.**

What would you say is the number one reason for salespeople's low ratings on honesty and ethics? It is trust. Many people feel they may not be able to trust a salesperson. Why? Greed is often the answer! The love of money is the root of all kinds of problems. From the least of us to the greatest, we all seem to be greedy to some extent, and greed can make some people blind to all else around them. Given all that has gone on in America as we are revising this textbook, we will use a different definition of selling in your book from the traditional view. This difference is very important given the present status of business in America and the public's— maybe even your—view of salespeople.

A NEW DEFINITION OF PERSONAL SELLING

The new definition inserts the word *unselfish* into the traditional definition discussed earlier. It is that simple! **Personal selling** refers to the personal communication of information to unselfishly persuade a prospective customer to buy something—a good, a service, an idea, or something else—that satisfies that individual's needs.

This definition of selling involves the many things we discussed before, such as a person helping another person through selling. However, when the word *unselfishly* is added to the definition, it makes a big difference in how someone might look at selling. The word *unselfish* tells salespeople to be caring toward customers and to serve—help—the person or organization without expecting to get something in return. If you are still wondering about the "unselfish" approach to selling, think of the analogy of selling to your grandmother.

Think of Your Grandmother

"Would you mistreat your grandmother in a sales transaction?"

Think of your, or your best friend's, grandmother. Would you treat her in a selfish manner? Would you sell her something just to make a sale? No way! You would not take advantage of granny (grandmother). Salespeople should handle their customers with unselfish and ethical service. How are you going to build a long-term relationship with customers unless you treat them unselfishly by placing their interests first?

Tell the truth about what the product will do, give the best price on the best product for the need, deliver on time, and provide outstanding follow-up service to make sure the customer is delighted with the purchase. If it is not the right product for the need expressed, tell the customer. If she or he still wants to buy—sell it to them! After all, you, the salesperson, may be wrong.

THE GOLDEN RULE OF PERSONAL SELLING

When asked, "What would you like to learn in this course?" Steven Osborne, a student in my personal selling class, said "I would like to know how to believe in a profession that many people do not trust." I sincerely hope you will be a believer in the value of sales integrity at the end of this sales course and be able to give Steven a positive perspective.

Part of your answer will involve your understanding the definition of personal selling discussed earlier and the Golden Rule of Personal Selling. A **rule** is a prescribed guide for conduct or action. The **Golden Rule of Personal Selling** refers to the sales philosophy of unselfishly treating others as you would like to be treated. Reciprocity is not expected. Read the short essay at the back of this chapter in Appendix A titled "The Golden Rule of Personal Selling as Told by a Salesperson." This short story illustrates the importance of helping people through our jobs and our lives.

Exhibit 3.7 in Chapter 3 provides examples of how people around the world view the Golden Rule. As you study the various statements of the Golden Rule in Exhibit 3.7, be sure to note that all are phrased negatively except for one—the last one. The negative form would teach behavior in this way: If you do not like to get cheated in a purchase, don't cheat others. The positive form, on the other hand, would say that if you like to receive the best price, then offer the best price to your customers.

To help you understand the concept better, consider how the Golden Rule applies to a litter of kittens. One child watched in delight as the tiny kittens snuggled together, in the cardboard box where her cat had just delivered the litter. "Aw, isn't that cute?" she exclaimed. "They love each other so much that they're trying to keep each other warm." "Well not exactly," replied her mother. "Actually they're trying to keep themselves warm." The Golden Rule is all about trying to keep somebody else warm, even if it means that we get cold in the process.[4] Stop a minute and think about how this applies to your life and the business world. This important concept will be applied to personal selling throughout the textbook. It is especially effective in explaining differences in salespeople and why so many people may have a negative view of some salespeople and a positive view of other salespeople.

Salesperson Differences

Garry Smith, a former consumer goods sales manager, and your author illustrate some of the differences between salespeople's approaches to personal selling today. In general, Exhibit 1.2 shows that differences can be explained by the extent of the person's self-interest. As Gallup's survey poll of Americans indicates, people view traditional salespeople as having their self-interest as a priority.[5] This type of salesperson is preoccupied with his or her own well-being—usually defined in terms of making money—and thus is selfish and cannot be trusted.

The salesperson following the Golden Rule of Personal Selling, however, places the interests of others before self-interest. Professional salespeople fall somewhere in between the traditional and Golden Rule salesperson in terms of how they view prospects and customers. As Exhibit 1.2 illustrates, as interest in serving others improves, a person's self-interest lessens. The more the salesperson considers the customer's interest, the better the customer service.

EVERYBODY SELLS!

If you think about it, everyone sells. From an early age, you develop communications techniques for trying to get your way in life. You are involved in selling when you want someone to do something. For example, if you want to get a date, ask for a pay increase, return merchandise, urge your professor to raise your grade, or apply

EXHIBIT 1.2

Interest in serving the customer improves as our self-interest decreases.

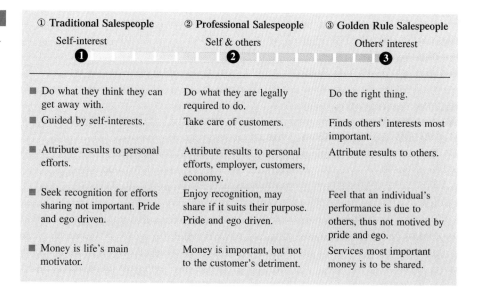

① Traditional Salespeople Self-interest ❶	② Professional Salespeople Self & others ❷	③ Golden Rule Salespeople Others' interest ❸
■ Do what they think they can get away with.	Do what they are legally required to do.	Do the right thing.
■ Guided by self-interests.	Take care of customers.	Finds others' interests most important.
■ Attribute results to personal efforts.	Attribute results to personal efforts, employer, customers, economy.	Attribute results to others.
■ Seek recognition for efforts sharing not important. Pride and ego driven.	Enjoy recognition, may share if it suits their purpose. Pride and ego driven.	Feel that an individual's performance is due to others, thus not motived by pride and ego.
■ Money is life's main motivator.	Money is important, but not to the customer's detriment.	Services most important money is to be shared.

for a new job, you are selling. You use personal communication skills to persuade someone to act. Your ability to communicate effectively is a key to success in life.

This is why so many people take sales courses. They want to improve their communication skills to be more successful in both their personal and business lives. The skills and knowledge gained from a selling course can be used by a student who plans to go into virtually any field, such as law, medicine, journalism, the military, or his or her own business.

Selling is not just for salespeople; it is a must for everyone. In today's competitive environment, where good interpersonal skills are so valued, the lack of selling capability can put anyone at a disadvantage. So as you read this book and progress through the course, think about how you can use the material both personally and in business.

WHAT SALESPEOPLE ARE PAID TO DO

In the short term, on a day-to-day, week-to-week basis, salespeople are paid to sell—that is their job. When a sales manager sees one of her salespeople, the question is always, "Did you sell anything today?" Salespeople need to sell something "today" to meet the performance goals for

- Themselves, in order to serve others, earn a living and keep their jobs.
- Their employer, because without the generation of revenues the company fails.
- Their customers, because their products help customers fulfill their needs and help their organizations to grow.

In the long run—month to month, year to year—salespeople must build positive long-term relationships with their customers. Why? Because they know, and now you know, that up to 80 percent or more of the future sales of many organizations come from present customers and customer referrals.

Salespeople need to close sales and at the same time maintain a great relationship with the buyer. Think about that last sentence. It is a very important thing to understand and learn. Salespeople want to sell to their present customers today, more tomorrow, and even more the day after that. How do you sell someone something and remain his or her business friend? You need to know how the Golden Rule of Personal Selling applies to the sales job. That is what this textbook is about.

WHY CHOOSE A SALES CAREER?

Six major reasons for choosing a sales career are (1) the opportunity to provide service to others; (2) the wide variety of sales jobs available; (3) the freedom of being on your own; (4) the challenge of selling; (5) the opportunity for advancement in a company; and (6) the rewards from a sales career (see Exhibit 1.3).

Service: Helping Others

When asked what she will look for in a career after graduating from college, a student of your author's, Jackie Pastrano, said "I'd like to do something that helps other people." The sales career provides the opportunity for service and an emotional purpose in life gained from helping others. That is why this book's central core value is "service." Service is a major reason for choosing a sales career! For many, service is the number one reason.

Service refers to making a contribution to the welfare of others. All of us want to do what Jackie hopes to do—help others! Would you like to help others? There are millions of sales jobs and thus many opportunities to help people and organizations.

A Variety of Sales Jobs Are Available

As members of a firm's sales force, salespeople are a vital element in the firm's effort to market goods and services profitably. Personal selling accounts for major expenditures by most companies and presents a large number of career opportunities. There are millions of sales jobs, and the probability that at one time during your life you will have a sales job is high.

There are also hundreds, maybe thousands, of different types of sales positions. Think about this! Almost every good or service you know of has a salesperson who sells it to one or more people in order to get the product to the final user. That is why so many sales jobs are available.

Types of Sales Jobs—Which Is for You?

Although there are numerous specific types of sales jobs, most salespeople work in one of three categories: as a retail salesperson, a wholesaler's salesperson, or a manufacturer's sales representative. These categories are classified according to the type of products sold and the salesperson's type of employer.

Selling in Retail. A **retail salesperson** sells goods or services to consumers for their personal, nonbusiness use. Retail selling is so important to a society that this book has numerous examples of it. Three common types of sellers who sell at retail are the (1) in-store salesperson, (2) direct seller who sells face-to-face away from a fixed store location, and (3) telephone salesperson.

EXHIBIT 1.3

Six major reasons for choosing a sales career.

Service to others	Variety of sales jobs	Freedom	Challenge	Advancement	Rewards

EXHIBIT 1.4

Retail salespeople are becoming well-rewarded professionals.

Look back at the definition of a retail salesperson. Think of all the different types of retail organizations selling something—retailers such as bakeries, banks, caterers, hotels, video stores, and travel agents, and stores selling clothes, electronics, flowers, food, and furniture (see Exhibit 1.4). Each customer contact person takes your money and provides a good or service in return. **Customer contact person** is another name for a salesperson. Although the title may be different their job is the same—to help you buy.

Direct sellers sell face-to-face to consumers—typically in their homes—who use the products for their personal use.[6] An organization could have one salesperson or 3 million salespeople, like Amway.

As in any type of job—including accountants, mechanics, and politicians—some retail salespeople do very little to help their customers. However, many retail salespeople are highly skilled professionals, commanding exceptionally high incomes for their ability to service their customers. I personally know retail salespeople earning $40,000 a year selling shoes; $80,000 selling furniture; $110,000 selling jewelry; and $150,000 selling automobiles.

Selling for a Wholesaler. Wholesalers (also called distributors) buy products from manufacturers and other wholesalers and sell to other organizations. A **wholesale salesperson** sells products to parties for

- Resale, such as grocery retailers buying items and selling to consumers.
- Use in producing other goods or services, such as a home builder buying electrical and plumbing supplies.
- Operating an organization, such as your school buying supplies.

Firms engaged in wholesaling are called wholesaling middlemen. Classifying wholesaling middlemen is difficult because they vary greatly in (1) the products they sell, (2) the markets to which they sell, and (3) their methods of operation. As there are so many different types, the discussion of types of wholesalers is beyond the scope of this book.

This pharmaceutical rep must service and meet the needs of technicians, physicians, and buyers in hospitals that use her company's products.

Selling for a Manufacturer. Manufacturers' salespeople work for organizations producing the product. The types of **manufacturer's sales representative** positions range from people who deliver milk and bread, to the specialized salesperson selling highly technical industrial products. The salesperson working for a manufacturer may sell to other manufacturers, wholesalers, retailers, or directly to consumers. There are five main types of manufacturer sales positions:

1. An account representative calls on a large number of already established customers in, for example, the food, textile, and apparel industries. This person asks for the order.
2. A detail salesperson concentrates on performing promotional activities and introducing new products rather than directly soliciting orders. The medical detail salesperson seeks to persuade doctors, the indirect customers, to specify a pharmaceutical company's trade name product for prescriptions. The actual sale is ultimately made through a wholesaler or directly to pharmacists and hospitals who fill prescriptions.
3. A sales engineer sells products that call for technical know-how and an ability to discuss technical aspects of the product. Expertise in identifying, analyzing, and solving customer problems is another critical factor. This type of selling is common in the oil, chemical, machinery, and heavy equipment industries because of the technical nature of their products.

   Greg Munoz, a sales engineer for the Dow Chemical Company, says,

   > Our sales technique typically takes the team approach. Several of Dow's finest staff (technical, production, marketing, and support) and I work in unison to address the customer's specific needs. I am responsible for building the business relationship with the customer and directing resources and information toward securing a customer's plastic-resin business. Market managers and district sales managers coordinate pricing and positioning as the customer relates to the industry as a whole. Dow technicians engineer materials to meet or exceed the requirements specified for the application and work with the customer's production department to see that they perform accordingly. Customer service representatives handle order placement and product-delivery logistics while servicing the customer's information needs. Once the sale is closed, I follow up and maintain our profile while serving as the first line of communication and interface for the customer.

4. An industrial products salesperson, nontechnical, sells a tangible product to industrial buyers. No high degree of technical knowledge is required. Packaging materials manufacturers and office equipment sales representatives are nontechnical salespeople.
5. A service salesperson, unlike the four preceding types of manufacturing salespeople, must sell the benefits of intangible or nonphysical products such as financial, advertising, or computer repair services. Services, like goods, are either technical or nontechnical in nature.

Selling services is ordinarily more difficult than selling tangibles. The salesperson can show, demonstrate, and dramatize tangible products; the salesperson of intangible products, cannot. Intangibles often are difficult for the prospect to

EXHIBIT 1.5

The complexity and difficulty of these seven sales job categories increase as they move left to right.

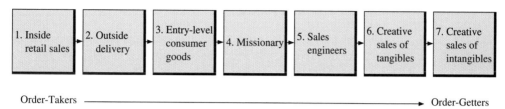

comprehend. People cannot feel, smell, see, hear, or taste intangible products. This makes them more challenging to sell.

Order-Takers versus Order-Getters. Sales jobs vary widely in their nature and requirements (see Exhibit 1.5). Some sales jobs require the salesperson only to take orders. **Order-takers** may ask what the customer wants or wait for the customer to order. They do not have a sales strategy and often use no sales presentation. Order-takers must be employed to bring in additional business that the employer probably would not obtain without their efforts. Many never attempt to close the sale. They perform useful services. However, few truly *create* sales.

On the other hand, the creative selling of tangible goods or intangible services in highly competitive lines (or where the product has no special advantages) moves merchandise that cannot be sold in equal volume without a salesperson. These people are **order-getters.** They get new and repeat business using a creative sales strategy and a well-executed sales presentation. The salesperson has an infinitely more difficult selling situation than that faced by the order-taker. In this sense, the individual is a true salesperson, which is why this person usually earns so much more than the order-taker.

This salesperson has two selling challenges. First, the salesperson must often create discontent with what the prospect already has before beginning to sell constructively. Second, the salesperson often has to overcome the most powerful and obstinate resistance. For example, the prospect may never have heard of the product and, at the outset, may have no desire whatsoever to purchase it. The prospect may even be prejudiced against it and may resent the intrusion of this stranger. In other instances, the prospect may want it but may want competing products more. Frequently, the prospect cannot afford it. To meet such sales situations successfully requires creative selling of the highest order.

Creative salespeople often are faced with selling to numerous people to get one order. This is the most difficult selling situation because the representative may have to win over not only the decision maker, the one who can say yes, but also other persons who cannot approve the order but who have the power to veto.

Freedom of Action: You're on Your Own   A second reason why people choose a sales career is the freedom it offers. A sales job provides possibly the greatest relative freedom of any career. Experienced employees in outside sales usually receive little direct supervision and may go for days, even weeks, without seeing their bosses.*

---

* Outside sales usually are conducted off the employer's premises and involve person-to-person contact. Inside sales occur on the premises, as in retail and telephone contact sales.

Job duties and sales goals are explained by a manager. Salespeople are expected to carry out their job duties and achieve goals with minimum guidance. They usually leave home to contact customers around the corner or around the world.

Job Challenge Is Always There

Working alone with the responsibility of a territory capable of generating thousands (sometimes millions) of dollars in revenue for your company is a personal challenge. This environment adds great variety to a sales job. Salespeople often deal with hundreds of different people and firms over time. It is much like operating your own business, without the burdens of true ownership.

Opportunities for Advancement Are Great

Successful salespeople have many opportunities to move into top management positions. In many instances, this advancement comes quickly.

A sales personnel **career path,** as Exhibit 1.6 depicts, is the upward sequence of job movements during a sales career. Occasionally, people without previous sales experience are promoted into sales management positions. However, 99 percent of the time, a career in sales management begins with an entry-level sales position. Firms believe that an experienced sales professional has the credibility, knowledge, and background to assume a higher position in the company.

Most companies have two or three successive levels of sales positions, beginning at the junior or trainee level. Beginning as a salesperson allows a person to

- Learn about the attitudes and activities of the company's salespeople.
- Become familiar with customer attitudes toward the company, its products, and its salespeople.
- Gain first-hand knowledge of products and their application, which is most important in technical sales.
- Become seasoned in the business world.

EXHIBIT 1.6

A sales personnel career path.

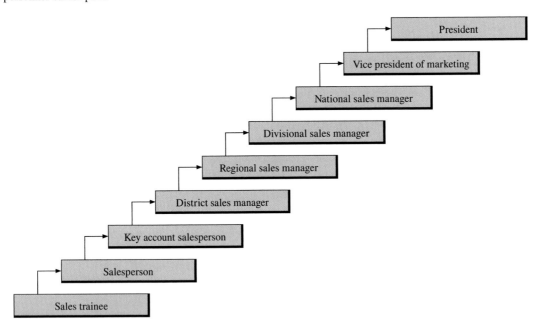

When asked why they like their jobs, first-line sales managers say it is because of the rewards. By rewards, they mean both financial rewards and nonfinancial rewards, such as the great challenge and the feeling of making a valuable contribution to their salespeople and the company. Managers also frequently mention that this position represents their first major step toward the top. They have made the cut and are on the management team. Instead of having responsibility for $1 million in sales, as a salesperson does, the manager is responsible for $10 million.

With success, various jobs throughout the sales force and in the corporate marketing department open up. This can include sales training, sales analysis, advertising, and product management. Frequently, traveling the upward career path involves numerous moves from field sales to corporate sales, back to the field, then to corporate, back to the field, and so on. However, sales experience prepares people for more responsible jobs in the company.

Success also creates financial rewards. The larger a company's revenues, the heavier the responsibility of the chief executive, and the larger the compensation. Today, it's common for a CEO of a large national corporation to receive compensation totaling more than $1 million annually.

Leaving aside compensation at the top echelons, both corporate and field sales managers typically receive higher salaries than others (such as production, advertising, product, or personnel managers) at the same organizational level. Salary is just one part of compensation. Many firms offer elaborate packages that include extended vacation and holiday periods; pension programs; health, accident, and legal insurance programs; automobiles and auto expenses; payment of professional association dues; educational assistance for themselves and sometimes for their families; financial planning assistance; company airplanes; home and entertainment expenses; and free country club membership. The higher the sales position, the greater the benefits offered. In addition to performance, salary typically is related to the following factors:

- Annual sales volume of units managed.
- Number of salespeople managed.
- Length of experience in sales.
- Annual sales volume of the firm.

Rewards: The Sky's the Limit

As a salesperson, you can look forward to two types of rewards—nonfinancial and financial.

Nonfinancial Rewards

Sometimes called psychological income or intrinsic rewards, nonfinancial rewards are generated by the individual, not given by the company. You know the job has been done well—for instance, when you have helped the buyer through the purchase of your product.

Successfully meeting the challenges of the job produces a feeling of self-worth. You realize your job is important. Everyone wants to feel good about their job, and a selling career allows you to experience these good feelings and intrinsic rewards daily. Salespeople often report that the nonfinancial rewards of their jobs are just as important to them as financial rewards.

After training, a salesperson is often given responsibility for a sales territory. The person then moves into a regular sales position. In a short time, the salesperson can earn the status and financial rewards of a senior sales position by contacting the larger, more important customers. Some companies refer to this function as a key account sales position.

There Are Two Career Paths

Don't let Exhibit 1.6 mislead you—many salespeople prefer selling over managing people. They want to take care of themselves rather than others. In some companies, a salesperson may even earn more money than the manager; even the firm's president.

Many companies recognize the value of keeping some salespeople in the field for their entire sales career. They do a good job, know their customers, and love what they are doing—so why promote them if they do not want to move up within the organization? However, many other people work hard to move into management.

You Can Move Quickly into Management

The first managerial level is usually the district sales manager's position. It is common for people to be promoted to this position within two or three years after joining the company. From district sales manager, a person may move into higher levels of sales management.

Financial Rewards

Many are attracted to selling because in a sales career financial rewards are commonly based solely on performance. Many professional salespeople have opportunities to earn large salaries. Their salaries average even higher than salaries for other types of workers at the same organizational level.

IS A SALES CAREER RIGHT FOR YOU?

It may be too early in life to determine if you really want to be a salesperson. The balance of this book will aid you in investigating sales as a career. Your search for any career begins with you. In considering a sales career, be honest and realistic. Ask yourself questions such as these:

- What are my past accomplishments?
- What are my future goals?
- Do I want to have the responsibility of a sales job?
- Do I mind travel? How much travel is acceptable?
- How much freedom do I want in the job?
- Do I have the personality characteristics for the job?
- Am I willing to transfer to another city? Another state?

Your answers to these questions can help you analyze the various types of sales jobs and establish criteria for evaluating job openings. Determine the industries, types of products or services, and specific companies in which you have an interest.

College placement offices, libraries, and business periodicals offer a wealth of information on companies as well as sales positions in them. Conversations with friends and acquaintances who are involved within selling, or have been in sales, can give you realistic insight into what challenges, rewards, and disadvantages the sales vocation offers. To better prepare yourself to obtain a sales job, you must understand what companies look for in salespeople.

A Sales Manager's View of the Recruit

The following discussion of what sales managers consider when hiring a sales person is based on a summary of a talk given by a sales manager to a sales class. It is reasonably representative of what companies look for when hiring salespeople.

> We look for outstanding applicants who are mature and intelligent. They should be able to handle themselves well in the interview, demonstrating good interpersonal skills. They should have a well-thought-out career plan and be able to discuss it rationally. They should have a friendly, pleasing personality. A clean, neat appearance is a must. They should have a positive attitude, be willing to work hard, be ambitious, and demonstrate a good degree of interest in the employer's business field. They should have good grades and other personal, school, and business accomplishments. Finally, they should have clear goals and objectives in life. The more common characteristics on which applicants for our company are judged are (1) appearance, (2) self-expression, (3) maturity, (4) personality, (5) experience, (6) enthusiasm, and (7) interest in the job.

People often consider sales careers because they have heard that salespeople can earn good salaries. They think anyone can sell. These people have not considered all the facts. A sales job has high rewards because it also has many important responsibilities. Companies do not pay high salaries for nothing. As you will see in this book, a sales career involves great challenges that require hard work by qualified individuals. Let us review the characteristics of a successful salesperson.

SUCCESS IN SELLING— WHAT DOES IT TAKE?

Over the years, I have asked many salespeople and sales managers the question, "What helps make a salesperson successful?" The answer is contained in the words *love, success,* and *person,* as in the phrase "a person who loves success." As these words will indicate, to be a good salesperson today it helps to be a good person.

As a student, I loved phrases and acronyms to help me remember. That is why I use them here to help you remember and better understand what selling in today's business environment requires. As Exhibit 1.7 shows, the eight most frequently mentioned characteristics necessary to be successful in sales can be found in the words *love* and *success.* To help remember, think of the word *ssuccess,* spelled with four s's.

S—Success Begins with Love

The successful salesperson is an individual who loves selling, finds it exciting, and is strongly convinced that the product being sold offers something of great value. Of the eight work characteristics for sales success, love of selling is clearly number one. Love is at the center of success. It has been said that if you find a job you love, you will never work again.

S—Service to Others

Today's salespeople make a contribution to the welfare of others through **service.** They are dream makers. They sell solutions to people's needs that make their dreams come true. Salespeople love to help others fulfill their needs through selling their products.

U—Use the Golden Rule of Selling

If salespeople do not know how to place the customer's needs first, how can they build a long-term relationship? People like to buy, not be sold. And they like to buy from people they know and trust. That is one reason today's salesperson needs to treat others as he or she would like to be treated.

EXHIBIT 1.7

Love of selling is at the heart of helping others. Spell success with four s's. Ssuccess

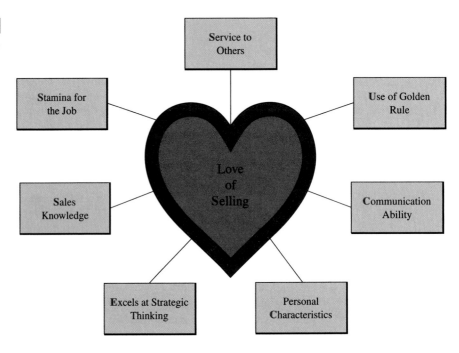

C—Communication Ability

Good salespeople are good communicators. Great salespeople are great communicators. Whether it involves nonverbal or verbal communications, as discussed in Chapter 5, top salespeople speak the other person's language.

C—Characteristics for the Job

Can anyone be a successful salesperson? It helps to reach that goal if you possess the personal characteristics needed for a sales career. These characteristics are discussed after the remaining work characteristics are introduced. Let's continue our discussion of those work characteristics now.

E—Excels at Strategic Thinking

The sixth work characteristic is that high-performing salespeople tend to be strategic problem solvers for their customers. They can match up their product's benefits with the customer's needs. Strategic customer sales planning is discussed more in Chapter 8.

S—Sales Knowledge at the M.D. Level

Top professional salespeople have mastered the basic competencies of selling, which include product knowledge (see Chapter 6) and selling skills. As goods and services become more complex, companies place greater emphasis on training their salespeople and on salespeople training themselves. Salespeople must be experts on everything involved with their products, as a medical doctor is an expert. Remember, however, that knowledge is power, but enthusiasm pulls the switch.

S—Stamina for the Challenge

Today's salesperson needs to be physically, mentally, and spiritually prepared to meet the daily challenges of a sales career. Body, mind, and soul play an important role in the level of a person's stamina. With physical preparedness comes mental strength. Exercise, for example, elevates your mood by increasing energy and simultaneously secreting adrenaline-like substances in the body that act as stimulants

MAKING THE SALE

Don't Quit

When things go wrong, as they sometimes will,
When the road you're trudging seems all uphill,
When the funds are low and the debts are high,
And you want to smile, but you have to sigh,
When care is pressing you down a bit—
Rest if you must, but don't you quit.
Life is queer with its twists and turns,
As every one of us sometimes learns,
And many a person turns about
When they might have won had they stuck it out.

Don't give up though the pace seems slow—
You may succeed with another blow.
Often the struggler has given up
When he might have captured the victor's cup;
And he learned too late
When the night came down,
How close he was to the golden crown.
Success is failure turned inside out—
So stick to the fight when you're hardest hit—
It's when things seem worst that you mustn't quit.[7]

and antidepressants, according to the medical community. This increased feeling of well-being transmits itself to the body and mind. In this stressed-out world we all need stress relief. Exercise can help!

Kenneth H. Cooper, M.D., often referred to as the Father of Aerobics, says "It is easier to maintain good health through proper exercise, diet, and emotional balance than to regain it once it is lost."[8] Exhibit 1.8 presents some aerobic, strength, and flexibility fitness exercise guidelines you can consider using. Take a few minutes and calculate your exercise target heart rate. Aerobics, strength training, and stretching are wonderful tools to reduce stress, help you feel better, focus better, and have more energy. If you are not actively using these techniques, try them for three months. Find out how exercise can help you! Be sure to check with your doctor before starting any exercise program, though.

For many people, personal spirituality or belief in a Supreme Being has a great impact upon physical and mental stamina and thus job performance. This is especially true if they feel their sales career is a calling. People's faith may direct everything they do on the job, ranging from how they treat customers to how ethically they act toward their employer.

C—CHARACTERISTICS FOR THE JOB EXAMINED

We skipped over the personal characteristics needed for a sales career earlier. Let's discuss them now. Certainly any discussion of what it takes to be successful in a sales job has to include the person's personal characteristics. As we have described selling, the salesperson wants to help people and thus build a long-term relationship. The question has been asked "How do you sell someone something and remain business friends?"

In the movie *Harry Potter and the Chamber of Secrets,* see Exhibit 1.9, his teacher tells Harry that it is not our abilities that show who we truly are but our choices. A salesperson can choose to be like the traditional salesperson we all disparage or the salesperson who is truly people oriented (refer again to Exhibit 1.2).

Aerobics

Aerobic exercise is any type of continuous, vigorous activity within your target heart rate zone (THR). To calculate your THR, use the following formula.

$$220 - \text{age} = \underline{\hspace{1cm}} \text{ Maximum heart rate (MHR)}$$
$$\text{MHR} \times .60 = \underline{\hspace{1cm}} \text{ Low end of aerobic zone}$$
$$\text{MHR} \times .85 = \underline{\hspace{1cm}} \text{ High end of aerobic zone}$$

Aerobic Activities	Nonaerobic Activities
■ Walking—treadmill or precor elliptical	■ Golf
■ Running—treadmill	■ Basketball
■ Step aerobics	■ Weight training
■ Cycling	■ Yoga
■ Swimming	

Strength Training

One set of 8 to 12 repetitions per exercise for each muscle group performed at least two days per week is recommended. All major muscle groups should be utilized starting with the larger groups and working down to the smaller groups. Muscle groups to be worked include legs, chest, back, arms, shoulders, and abdominals.

Flexibility

A static stretching regimen should be performed at least three days a week, with three to five repetitions of each stretch (held 30–60 seconds each) for all the major muscle groups. You can stretch while watching TV, right before you go to sleep at night, or in the morning right after you get up.[9]

Caring, Joy, and Harmony

Today's salesperson needs personal characteristics that allow for true caring for customers. Through caring comes the joy of helping others. Customers recognize when a person clearly cares. The caring attitude helps to create harmony in the

EXHIBIT 1.9

Harry Potter and you have something in common. You both have the freedom to choose the type of person you want to be and thus how you will treat others.

relationship. Thus salespeople need to have the personal characteristic that allows them to place the customer first. Some people's pride and egos, however, get in the way.

Patience, Kindness, and Moral Ethics

Salespeople are often under pressure to make the sale today! They need to be able to handle the pressure to sell *now* through demonstrating patience in their working relationship with the customer. Let the customer decide when to buy instead of pressuring for a quick decision. The salesperson's job is to present the necessary information for the buyer to make an educated decision. Patience in closing the sale goes a long way toward building a long-term relationship. Buyers do not like to be pressured into making a quick decision. Do you!?

Your actions speak louder than your words. Having patience with the customers shows that the salesperson understands the customer's needs and wants to help (kindness), not solely make the sale. When salespeople show that the customer comes first, people are more likely to trust them. The salesperson's actions show that she or he is a morally ethical (good) person.

Faithful, Fair, Self-Controlled

A person who cares, likes the job, is good to work with and is patient, kind, and morally ethical is certainly someone who will be faithful in taking care of customers. The salesperson will spend the time necessary to help, not just make the sale and never be heard from again until the next sales call. We all want to be thought of as ethical. Faithfulness is an ethical virtue. It shows the employer, customers, and competitors that the salesperson is loyal and trustworthy. Customers can trust this person.

Now we come to self-control, which is the most difficult trait for a salesperson to develop. This is why we discuss it last. Self-control concerns our emotions, passions, and desires. How do salespeople control themselves by being patient in closing the sale, for example? Remember, the salesperson must sell to make a living and keep the job. This is a considerable impetus for the salesperson to use pressure, even unethical practices, to compel the customer to buy something that may not be needed.

Self-Control Involves Discipline

Self-control also refers to the needed discipline to rise early, work late, and prepare for the next day in the evening. Often the biggest challenge to success is not out there in the sales territory; it is within us. We can not achieve unless we are willing to pay the price—discipline.

What comes first in your life?

Discipline also includes creating time for family—spouse and children. So often we are caught up in the American way of wanting to be rich and famous that we forget about the others in our life. Instead we must discipline ourselves to set priorities. What comes first, your job or your family? For me, it should always be family before job. Setting priorities requires willpower many of us do not have. Do you ever wonder why there are so many divorces in America and so many children raised in one-parent homes? Misplacing priorities by not putting family first is the number one contributor to the breakdown of American families. Self-control and discipline are thus very important personal characteristics for all of us, no matter what our careers.

As you see in Exhibit 1.10, the list of personal characteristics needed to be a good salesperson in today's marketplace is a long one. No doubt your instructor will add to this list, and you undoubtedly will think of other characteristics as well. These characteristics make salespeople good citizens in the business world. However, sadly, it seems that all of us do not have the ability or desire to place the customer first.

EXHIBIT 1.10

Personal characteristics needed to sell for building long-term relationships.

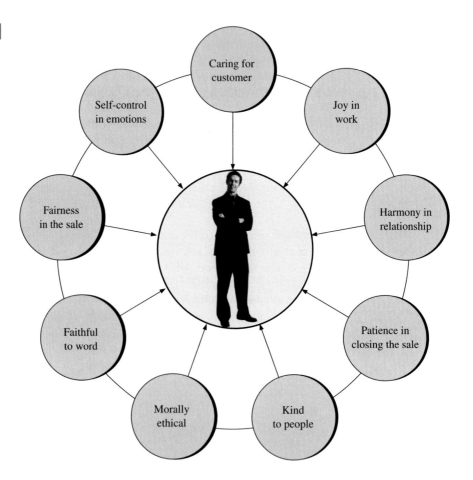

Many years ago a man named John Wesley, known as one of the kindest men who ever walked on earth, talked about a simple rule of life. Wesley said he tried to "Do all the good he can by all the means he can in all the places he can at all the times he can to all the people he can as long as ever he can."[10] How would you like to deal with a salesperson that followed both Wesley's rule of life and the Golden Rule? Me too!

DO SUCCESS CHARACTERISTICS DESCRIBE YOU?

What do you think? Do these success characteristics describe you? Are you willing to incorporate them into your life? You may have to go beyond your normal limits. Only your self-imposed limitations can hold you back. If you fail to realize success or if your success is limited, your own preconceptions may be the cause by throwing an invisible barrier across your path. The following puzzle illustrates how perception can hold you back. The challenge is to connect all nine dots with four straight lines, without lifting your pencil from the paper. Try it!

● ● ●

● ● ●

● ● ●

It seems impossible to intersect all nine dots with four straight lines. How do you move something from the impossible to the possible? *Go beyond the limits.*

When you go beyond the limits, the impossible becomes possible. When you go beyond the limits, you can connect all nine dots with four straight lines.

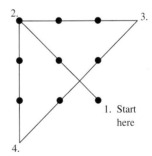

Successful salespeople break through their self-imposed limitations. No one said when you drew four straight lines that they couldn't go beyond the dots. That was a limitation you imposed. When you impose limitations, the puzzle becomes unsolvable. You can break away from self-imposed limits when you think bigger following the Golden Rule.

RELATIONSHIP SELLING

Salespeople are no longer adversaries who manipulate people for personal gain. They want to be consultants, partners, and problem solvers for customers. Their goal is to build a long-term relationship with clients. Salespeople seek to benefit their employer, themselves, and customers.

EXHIBIT 1.11

EXHIBIT 1.11

The customer is at the center of the sales solar system.

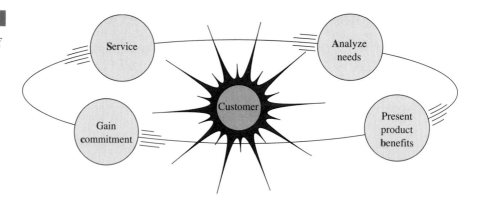

In recent years, the distinction between a salesperson and a professional has blurred because the salesperson of today is a pro. Many salespeople know more about their field and product than the buyer. This expertise enables the seller to become the buyer's partner, a counselor on how to solve problems. Today's salesperson professionally provides information that helps customers make intelligent actions to achieve their short- and long-term objectives. Service and follow-up are then provided to ensure satisfaction with the purchase. This builds *customer loyalty*—a relationship.

Exhibit 1.11 shows the four main elements in the customer relationship process used by salespeople to build long-term relationships. To help you remember these four elements the letters **ABCS** stand for **a**nalyze, **b**enefits, **c**ommitment, and **s**ervice. Salespeople analyze customer needs, present product benefits and gain commitment for the purchase. They provide excellent service in order to maintain and grow the relationship. Customer product and service satisfactions give the salesperson the opportunity to restart the sales cycle by continuing to analyze customer needs.

SALES JOBS ARE DIFFERENT

As you can see, sales jobs are different from other jobs in several ways. Here are some major differences:

- Salespeople represent their companies to the outside world. Consequently, opinions of a company and its products are often formed from impressions left by the sales force. The public ordinarily does not judge a firm by its office or factory workers.
- Other employees usually work under close supervisory control, whereas the outside salesperson typically operates with little or no direct supervision. Moreover, to be successful, salespeople must often be creative, persistent, and show great initiative—all of which require a high degree of motivation.
- Salespeople probably need more tact, diplomacy, and social poise than other employees in an organization. Many sales jobs require the salesperson to display considerable emotional and social intelligence in dealing with buyers.
- Salespeople are among the few employees authorized to spend company funds. They spend this money for entertainment, transportation, and other business expenses.

MAKING THE SALE

What Is a Customer?

- Customers are the most important people in any business.
- Customers are not dependent on us. We are dependent on them.
- Customers are not an interruption of our work. They are the purpose of it.
- Customers do us a favor in doing business with us. We aren't doing customers a favor by waiting on them.
- Customers are part of our business—not outsiders. Customers are not just money in the cash register. Customers are human beings with feelings, and they deserve to be treated with respect.

- Customers are people who come to us with needs and wants. It is our job to fill them.
- Customers deserve the most courteous attention we can give them.
- Customers are the lifeblood of this and every business. Customers pay your salary. Without customers we would have to close our doors.
- Don't ever forget it![11]

- Some sales jobs frequently require considerable traveling and time spent away from home and family. At times, salespeople deal with customers who seem determined not to buy the sellers' products. These challenges, coupled with the physical demands of long hours and traveling, require mental toughness and physical stamina rarely demanded in other types of jobs.

Selling is hard work! It requires intelligence, the desire to achieve, and the ability to overcome difficulties.

WHAT DOES A PROFESSIONAL SALESPERSON DO?

The salesperson's roles or activities can vary from company to company, depending on whether sales involve goods or services, the firm's market characteristics, and the location of customers. For example, a salesperson selling Avon products performs similar, but somewhat different, job activities than the industrial salesperson making sales calls for General Electric.

Most people believe that a salesperson only makes sales presentations, but there is much more to the job than person-to-person selling. The salesperson functions as a **territory manager**—planning, organizing, and executing activities that increase sales and profits in a given territory. A sales territory comprises a group of customers often assigned within a geographical area. Exhibit 1.12 indicates a few typical activities of a salesperson. As manager of a territory, the salesperson performs the following nine functions:

1. **Creates New Customers.** In order to increase sales and replace customers that will be lost over time, many types of sales jobs require a salesperson to prospect. Prospecting is the lifeblood of sales because it identifies potential customers. Salespeople locate people and/or organizations that have the potential to buy their products. The salespeople need the ability to close, or make, the sale.
2. **Sells More to Present Customers.** Tomorrow's sales come from selling to new customers and selling to present customers again . . . and again . . . and again.
3. **Builds Long-Term Relationships with Customers.** Earning the opportunity to sell a present customer more product means the salesperson must have a positive, professional business relationship with people and organizations who trust the salesperson and the products purchased.

EXHIBIT 1.12

A professional salesperson . . .

. . . helps meet the needs and solve the problems of the customer.

. . . makes presentations to new and current customers.

. . . sells to wholesalers and distributors.

. . . handles customer complaints.

4. **Provides Solutions to Customers' Problems.** Customers have needs that can be met and problems that can be solved by purchasing goods or services. Salespeople seek to uncover potential or existing needs or problems and show how the use of their products or services can satisfy needs or solve problems.

5. **Provides Service to Customers.** Salespeople provide a wide range of services, including handling complaints, returning damaged merchandise, providing samples, suggesting business opportunities, and developing recommendations on how the customer can promote products purchased from the salesperson.

If necessary, salespeople may occasionally work at the customer's business. For example, a salesperson selling fishing tackle may arrange an in-store demonstration of a manufacturer's products and offer to repair fishing reels as a service to the retailer's customers. Furthermore, a manufacturer may have its salespeople sell to distributors or wholesalers. Then, the manufacturer's representative may make sales calls with the distributor's salespeople to aid them in selling and providing service for the distributor's customers.

6. **Helps Customers Resell Products to Their Customers.** A major part of many sales jobs is for the salesperson to help wholesalers and retailers resell the products that they have purchased. The salesperson helps wholesale customers sell products to retail customers and helps retail customers sell products to consumers.

   Consider the Quaker Oats salesperson selling a product to grocery wholesalers. Not only must the wholesaler be contacted but also grocery retailers must be called on, sales made, and orders written up and sent to the wholesaler. In turn, the wholesaler sells and delivers the products to the retailers. The Quaker Oats salesperson also develops promotional programs to help the retailer sell the firm's products. These programs involve supplying advertising materials, conducting store demonstrations, and setting up product displays.

7. **Helps Customers Use Products after Purchase.** The salesperson's job is not over after the sale is made. Often, customers must be shown how to obtain full benefit from the product. For example, after a customer buys an IBM computer system, technical specialists help the buyer learn how to operate the equipment.

8. **Builds Goodwill with Customers.** A selling job is people oriented, entailing face-to-face contact with the customer. Many sales are based, to some extent, on friendship and trust. The salesperson needs to develop a personal, friendly, businesslike relationship with everyone who may influence a buying decision. This ongoing part of the salesperson's job requires integrity, high ethical standards, and a sincere interest in satisfying customers' needs.

9. **Provides Company with Market Information.** Salespeople provide information to their companies on such topics as competitors' activities, customers' reactions to new products, complaints about products or policies, market opportunities, and their job activities. This information is so important for many companies that their salespeople are required to send in weekly or monthly reports on activities of the firm's competition in their territory. Salespeople are a vital part of their employers' information retrieval system.

Reflect Back   Review the nine functions shown in Exhibit 1.13 to see what they mean and if you could do any or all of them. Carefully think about the second and third functions. To be successful, a salesperson must close sales and build relationships with the same person and/or organization in order to sell more. To do both is challenging to any person. It requires the salesperson to do the other functions: solve problems, provide service, help resell, teach how to use the purchase, build goodwill, and keep your employer up-to-date on customers' needs and feelings toward product and service.

EXHIBIT 1.13

What does a professional salesperson do? Here are nine of the most important job functions.

1. Creates new customers.
2. Sells more to present customers.
3. Builds long-term relationships with customers.
4. Provides solutions to customers' problems.
5. Provides service to customers.
6. Helps customers resell products to their customers.
7. Helps customers use products after purchase.
8. Builds goodwill with customers.
9. Provides company with market information.

A Typical Day for a Xerox Salesperson

You are responsible for sales coverage, time, and budget. Help is available and you'll have plenty of marketing and service support; but you're expected to work independently, without constant direction.

Your day is devoted primarily to customer contact. Potential customers may phone the branch and ask to see a Xerox representative. More likely, however, you will acquire customers by making appointments or by visiting businesses to meet the decision-makers, discuss their needs, and offer solutions to their problems. As part of your position, you'll make product presentations, either at the Xerox branch office or at the customer's office. You will also spend a fair amount of time on the telephone following up leads, arranging appointments, and speaking with managers in a variety of businesses and organizations.

In working with customers, you'll need to solve a number of problems. What Xerox product best fits the customer's

needs? How do Xerox products compare with the competition? Should the machine be purchased or leased? What's the total cash outlay—and per-copy cost—for the machine and its service? How should the product be financed? Where should the machine be placed for maximum efficiency? What training is needed for employees? How can Xerox products meet future office needs?

You'll also be engaged in a number of customer support activities, such as expediting product deliveries, checking credit, writing proposals, and training customer employees in the use of the product. You also might refer customers to other Xerox sales organizations and make joint calls with representatives from these organizations.

Each day will bring you new challenges to face and problems to solve. Your days will be busy and interesting.[12]

Your book is about these nine functions and much more. When combined and properly implemented, these nine job activities produce increased sales for the organization and more rewards for the salesperson. An example of how a salesperson integrates these activities will help you better understand the sales job. See the box, "A Typical Day for a Xerox Salesperson."

THE FUTURE FOR SALESPEOPLE

One final thought: In an uncertain and rapidly changing world, how do you learn to be a salesperson? More specifically, how does a course in selling prepare you to become a salesperson ready to face the 21st century?

Learning Selling Skills

Selling is an art and a science.

Selling is both an art and a science. It is an art because many skills cannot be learned from a textbook. Selling takes practice, just like golf or tennis. Studying a book helps, but it is not enough. Many skills—such as understanding buyers' nonverbal communication messages, listening, handling objections, and closing—take practice. These skills are learned through experience.

Selling is also a science because a growing body of knowledge and objective facts describes selling. Becoming a successful salesperson requires a blend of formal learning and practice, of science and art. Practice alone used to be enough to learn how to sell, but no longer. Formal course work in sales can help a salesperson become more competent and be prepared for the challenges of the future. The study of selling helps people see and understand things about sales that others cannot. Training helps salespeople acquire the conceptual, human, and technical skills necessary for selling; this asset results in a salesperson earning more income over a lifetime.

As we see throughout this book, because a salesperson's job is diverse and complex, it requires a range of skills. Although some authors propose a long list of skills, the necessary skills can be summarized in three categories that are especially important: conceptual, human, and technical.

Conceptual Skills

Conceptual skill is the cognitive ability to see the selling process as a whole and the relationship among its parts. Conceptual skill involves the seller's thinking and planning abilities. It involves knowing where one's product fits into the customer's business or how the beginning of a sales presentation relates to asking for the order. Conceptual skills allow the seller to think strategically—to understand the product, presentation, buyer, and purchaser's organization.

Although all sellers need conceptual skills, they are especially important for the creative order-getters. They must perceive significant elements in a situation and broad, conceptual patterns.

Human Skills

Human skill is the seller's ability to work with and through other people. Salespeople demonstrate this skill in the way they relate to other people, including customers or people within their own organizations. A seller with human skills likes other people and is liked by them. Sellers who lack human skills often are abrupt, critical, and unsympathetic. Pushy and arrogant, they are not responsive to others' needs.

Technical Skills

Technical skill is the understanding of and proficiency in the performance of specific tasks. Technical skill includes mastery of the methods, techniques, and equipment involved in selling—such as presentation skills and uses for one's products. Technical skill includes specialized knowledge, analytical ability, and the competent use of tools and techniques to solve problems in that specific discipline.

Preparing for the 21st Century

Over the next few years, new forces will shape sales careers. Salespeople will continue to rely heavily on their technical, human, and conceptual skills; however, they will apply them in different ways. Major changes occurring today will continue to occur in the distant future and require salespeople to be knowledgeable in areas they didn't need to know about only a few years ago. These include (1) international/global selling, (2) diversity of salespeople and customers, (3) customer partnerships, (4) ethical and professional behavior, and (5) technology.

International/Global Selling

Salespeople need to think globally because companies are enmeshed with foreign competitors, suppliers, and customers. Successful salespeople of tomorrow will be able to cross borders, speak other languages, and understand cultural differences. Right now executive recruiting organizations are searching worldwide for salespeople to take assignments in global organizations. Global experience is a prized asset of the salespeople of tomorrow.

EXHIBIT 1.14

The American sales force is becoming diversified. Millions of sales jobs provide room for everyone in a sales career!

Diversity of Salespeople and Customers

In the future, organizations mapping long-range strategies will have to reckon with the changing demographics of the sales force (see Exhibit 1.14). As the general population becomes more diverse, so does the workforce. Thus, a growing percentage of new sales hires are nonwhite males. In addition, women, blacks, Hispanics, and Asians are proving to be outstanding salespeople and providing opportunities for others to enter the sales field.

With more diversity in the workplace comes more diversity in the seller's customers. Will this have an impact on the sales force? Yes, it will! Purchasing agents, for example, are becoming a more diverse group of people. The nonwhite males who are now industrial purchasing agents want to see sellers of all types calling on them. Studies show that women buy 50 percent—and influence the purchase of 80 percent—of American cars, yet less than 5 percent of car salespeople are female. This is beginning to change.

Customer Partnerships

Finding a new customer is much harder than keeping an old one. Organizations are finally realizing what Carl Sewell, the Dallas Cadillac-Lexus car dealer, knew years ago: "If cars are $50,000 apiece, 12 cost $600,000. That's how many a customer can buy in a lifetime. If we treat the customer fairly on the car they buy and do a good job servicing the car today, we have a better chance of getting the person's future business.

"There is also the rock-in-the-pool theory to explain why you should treat customers this way," says Sewell. "That word-of-mouth advertising is stronger than anything we can do on television. In fact our advertising line is, 'Ask the person who drives one.' If people ask our customers about what it's like to do business with us, we have a much better chance of getting them to become customers themselves.

"And, every car we can sell to a friend represents another potential $600,000 in business. So you can see that while I truly believe in treating customers as you would a spouse, parent, or friend, it's not all altruism. We are all motivated by self-interest. We do think about 'What's in it for me?' And if we treat people in a positive, comfortable way, we're going to do more business than if we rough them up and bounce them around. The folks who feel comfortable roughing them up don't care if the customer comes back."[13]

Why is customer retention important?

Customer-oriented thinking, as described by Sewell, requires a company to define customer needs from its customers' point of view. Every buying decision involves trade-offs, and management cannot know what these are without researching customers. Why is it important to satisfy the target customer? Basically because a company's sales each period come from two groups: *new customers* and *repeat customers*. It always costs more to attract new customers than to retain current customers. Therefore, customer retention is more critical than customer attraction. The key to customer retention is *customer satisfaction.*

The satisfied customer buys more from the seller and stays loyal longer. The customer listens to the seller but pays less attention to the seller's competition. The buyer also benefits because the seller knows the customer's business. It becomes less costly for the buyer to purchase from the same seller because transactions are routinized. The buyer and seller know each other, trust each other, and realize that by working together both benefit.

Ethical and Professional Behavior

Salespeople are learning the necessity of dealing with customers in an ethical and professional manner. Bill Gardner, a retired 23-year IBM veteran, remarked, "I sold systems that people didn't want, didn't need, and couldn't afford." Not so long ago, many salespeople might have regarded Gardner's admission as the mark of a colleague at the top of his game, one so skilled he could persuade people to act against their own interests. Today, such a dubious achievement is more often seen as embarrassing, unenlightened, counterproductive, and under some new compensation systems, even a shortcut to a smaller bonus. Merely "pushing metal," as IBM insiders call it, or "slamming boxes," as Xerox salespeople describe the act of closing a copier deal, won't carry a sales force in the 21st century. Companies now measure success not only by units sold but also by the far more rigorous yardstick of customer satisfaction. If you anticipate what your customers need and then deliver it beyond their expectations, order flow takes care of itself.

As it happens, IBM knows better than most the dollars-and-cents argument for a more professional, customer-conscious sales approach. Robert LaBant, senior vice president in charge of IBM's North American sales and marketing, says every percentage point variation in customer satisfaction scores translates into a gain or loss of $500 million in sales over five years. What's more, he says, developing new business costs Big Blue three to five times as much as maintaining the old.[14]

E-Selling: Technology Used by Salespeople

To better do their jobs and service customers, salespeople are going high tech. Talking computers, e-mail, cellular phones, faxes, satellites, and automated maps with driving directions are products rapidly becoming part of salespeople's selling

EXHIBIT 1.15

Technology is enabling
salespeople to do a better job
selling and servicing their
customers.

arsenals (see Exhibit 1.15). Throughout this book, you learn about technology used
by salespeople. Here's one example:

Imagine walking into a sales call with every piece of information needed to introduce a product to a customer: a record of the customer's sales history, up-to-date
information about the customer's industry and competitors, detailed product spec
sheets, current price sheets, and all the other information needed to close the sale.
One way to do this would be to bring along a team of experts, each lugging cases
filled with printed information. Another way would be to make a series of calls to
the support team at the home office.

Or you could walk into the call carrying a two-pound notebook computer containing all of the information just listed and with the capability of making a wireless real-time connection to data stored at the home office. This is state-of-the-art
sales force automation.

Sales force automation is not a new concept. What makes it of interest today are
the powerful information and communication tools now available. These include
portable computers with an enormous amount of information capacity, high-speed
modems, cellular and radio data networks that allow for wireless communication,
and software that allows computers to easily share information.

**Selling Is for
Large and Small
Organizations**

Many textbook examples are from big business. This is typically because readers
recognize Ford Motor Company or McDonald's. Even though America's large
organizations are easily recognizable and extremely important to our prosperity, it is
easy to overestimate the importance of big business because of its greater visibility.
Small firms, even though less conspicuous, are a vital component of our economy.

Small business contributes significantly to our economy. The Small Business
Administration classifies approximately 98 percent of all business in the United
States—sole proprietorships, partnerships, corporations, part-time businesses, and
unincorporated professional activities—as small businesses.

Small enterprises run the gamut from a corner news vender to a developer of op-
tical fibers. Small business people sell gasoline, flowers, and coffee to go. They pub-
lish magazines, haul freight, teach languages, and program computers. They make

crafts, motion pictures, and high-fashion clothes. They build new homes and restore old ones. They repair plumbing, fix appliances, recycle metals, and sell used cars. They drive taxicabs, run cranes, and fly helicopters. They drill for oil, quarry sand and gravel, and mine exotic ores. They forge, cast, weld, photoengrave, electroplate, and anodize. They also invent antipollution devices, quality control mechanisms, energy-saving techniques, microelectronic systems—a complete list would go on for volumes.

Often, small business entrepreneurs cannot compete head-to-head with giant firms. However, most large firms started small, and then prospered by using many of the concepts, ideas, and practices discussed in this textbook. Because of this fact, we use small business as examples throughout this textbook.

THE PLAN OF THIS TEXTBOOK

Personal selling and the sales job are much more than you might have imagined. The plan of your textbook provides you with the *fundamentals* of what selling is all about. Some of the major topics you will study include these:

- The role of the sales force in the firm's marketing efforts.
- The social, ethical, and legal issues in selling.
- Why people and organizations buy what they do.
- Verbal and nonverbal communications.
- The importance of knowing your and your competition's products.
- An in-depth discussion of the selling process.
- Self-, time, and sales territory management.
- Important functions of sales management.

Salespeople are managers of the sales generated from their customers. There is much to know if you want to be a successful sales professional. There is even more to know once you are promoted to the sales manager's job. Sometime before your course is over, be sure to review the last two chapters of this book. They provide you with an overview of the sales manager's job.

BUILDING RELATIONSHIPS THROUGH THE SALES PROCESS

Much of your course will revolve around the sales process. The **sales process** refers to the salesperson's sequential series of actions that leads toward the customer taking a desired action and ends with a follow-up to ensure purchase satisfaction. This desired action by a prospect is usually buying, which is the most important action. Such desired actions also can include advertising, displaying, or reducing the price of the product.

Although many factors may influence how a salesperson makes a presentation in any situation, following a logical, sequential series of actions can greatly increase the chances of making a sale. This selling process involves 10 basic steps as briefly listed in Exhibit 1.16. The following chapters discuss each of these steps in greater detail.

Before a sales presentation is attempted, several important preparatory activities should occur. This involves prospecting and planning the sales presentation. Steps 3 through 9 make up the sales presentation itself. Step 10 involves the important follow-up phase of the selling process to ensure customer satisfaction.

Before discussing the selling process, Chapter 2 presents the big picture to show where selling fits into a firm's marketing effort. Chapter 3 considers the social, ethical, and legal issues in selling. With this background, we are ready to examine what is involved in preparing to meet the customer, followed by an in-depth discussion of how to develop the sales presentation.

ETHICAL DILEMMA

Mexico Here I Come

As you come to the end of your presentation, you realize one of your best customers—John Adams—may not buy. John and you have become friends over the last three years. Losing this sale will result in your missing out on a $500 bonus, forfeiting a chance to win a trip to Mexico, and failing to reach your sales quota for the year.

When you finish, John says, "We can't buy." You then explain your situation to John. He says, "Well, why don't you ship the merchandise to me. After the contest is over but before it's time to pay for it, I will ship it back to your company or you can transfer it in small quantities to several of your customers. That way you'll get credit for the sale." You know that your boss will not mind because if you reach your sales quota he will also look good and be rewarded.

What do you do? In selecting your action, consider the discussion of ethical behavior in Chapter 2.

1. Accept John's offer without consulting your boss and send the merchandise to his store—in turn, receiving a $500 bonus, a trip to Mexico, and praise from your boss for making the sale and reaching your sales quota.
2. Talk to your boss about the situation and explain John's offer. Let your boss be the ultimate decision maker (taking responsibility instead of you), knowing that he will tell you to take the "sale" from John.
3. Thank John for trying to be a supportive friend but decline his offer because it would not be right to falsify sales for your own benefit.

EXHIBIT 1.16

Ten important steps in the customer relationship selling process.

1. *Prospecting.* Locating and qualifying prospects.
2. *Preapproach.* Obtaining interview; determining sales call objective; developing customer profile, customer benefit program, and sales presentation strategies.
3. *Approach.* Meeting prospect and beginning customized sales presentation.
4. *Presentation.* Further uncovering needs; relating product benefits to needs using demonstration, dramatization, visuals, and proof statements.
5. *Trial close.* Asking prospect's *opinions* during and after presentation.
6. *Objections.* Uncovering objections.
7. *Meet objections.* Satisfactorily answering objections.
8. *Trial close.* Asking prospect's *opinion* after overcoming each objection and immediately before the close.
9. *Close.* Bringing prospect to the logical conclusion to buy.
10. *Follow-up and service.* Serving customer after the sale.

SUMMARY OF MAJOR SELLING ISSUES

Personal selling is an old and honorable profession. It has helped improve this country's standard of living and provided benefits to individual buyers through the purchase of products. Millions of people have chosen sales careers because of the opportunity to serve others, the availability of sales jobs, the personal freedom sales provides, the challenge, the multitude of opportunities for success, and the nonfinancial and financial rewards.

A person can become a successful salesperson through company and personal training and by properly applying this knowledge while developing skills and abilities that benefit customers. Also important are believing in the product or service being sold, working hard, wanting to succeed, and maintaining a positive outlook toward both selling and oneself. In addition, a successful salesperson should be knowledgeable, able to plan, and efficient in using selling time. Effective salespeople are good listeners who provide service to customers. En route to success, salespeople develop a range of skills through study and practice, enhancing their ability to think strategically, relate to others, and understand the technical aspects of their business.

For the future, salespeople will need to be well versed in diverse international markets, able to ethically develop customer partnerships, and ready to utilize technology. The remainder of this book expands on these topics to provide you with the background either to improve your present selling ability or to help you decide if a sales career is right for you.

MEETING A SALES CHALLENGE

As a secretary in Sunwest Bank's marketing department, Debra Hutchins worked closely with the bank's outside salespeople and sales manager. When a sales job opened up, both Alex Romero, the director of marketing, and Rick Mather, the sales manager, asked her if she wanted the job. Debra had seen what salespeople do, so she said, "OK, I'll give it a shot."

Debra was so good as a salesperson she was promoted and now is sales manager, managing three men and one woman. "It's the best decision I've ever made," she says. "If you have not considered a sales career, I highly recommend it."

KEY TERMS FOR SELLING

personal selling   5
rule   6
Golden Rule of Personal Selling   6
service   8
retail salesperson   8
customer contact person   9
direct sellers   9
wholesale salesperson   9
manufacturer's sales representative   10

order-taker   11
order-getter   11
career path   12
territory manager   23
conceptual skill   27
human skill   27
technical skill   27
sales process   31

SALES APPLICATION QUESTIONS

1. The term *salesperson* refers to many types of sales jobs. What are the major types of sales jobs available?
2. Chapter 1 described characteristics of several successful salespeople currently selling goods and services for national companies. Describe those characteristics and then discuss whether or not those same characteristics also are needed for success in other types of jobs.
3. People choose a particular career for many reasons. What are the reasons someone might give for choosing a sales career?
4. What is meant by the term *career path?* What are the various jobs to which a salesperson might be promoted in a company?
5. Describe the Golden Rule of Personal Selling and how it relates to the work characteristics of successful salespeople and the personal characteristics needed to sell while building long-term relationships.

FURTHER EXPLORING THE SALES WORLD

1. Interview one or more salespeople and write a brief report on what they like and dislike about their jobs; why they chose a sales career; what activities they perform; and what they believe it takes to succeed in selling their products.

2. Contact your college placement office and report on what staff members believe firms recruiting people for sales positions look for in applicants.

SELLING EXPERIENTIAL EXERCISE

Are You a Global Traveler?

Our global environment requires that American sales personnel learn to deal effectively with people in other countries. The assumption that foreign business leaders behave and negotiate in the same manner as Americans is false. How well prepared are you to live with globalization? Consider the following items, writing the numbers reflecting your views on another sheet of paper.

Are you guilty of:	Definitely No				Definitely Yes
1. Being impatient? Do you think "Time is money" or "Let's get straight to the point"?	1	2	3	4	5
2. Having a short attention span or bad listening habits, or being uncomfortable with silence?	1	2	3	4	5
3. Being somewhat argumentative, sometimes to the point of belligerence?	1	2	3	4	5
4. Being ignorant about the world beyond your borders?	1	2	3	4	5
5. Having a weakness in foreign languages?	1	2	3	4	5
6. Placing emphasis on short-term success?	1	2	3	4	5
7. Believing that advance preparations are less important than negotiations themselves?	1	2	3	4	5
8. Being legalistic and believing a deal is a deal, regardless of changing circumstances?	1	2	3	4	5
9. Having little interest in seminars on the subject of globalization, failing to browse through international topics in libraries or magazines, or not interacting with foreign students or employees?	1	2	3	4	5

Total Score _____

Add up your score. If you scored less than 27, congratulations. You have the temperament and interest to do well in a global company. If you scored more than 27, it's time to consider a change. Regardless of your score, go back over each item and make a plan of action to correct deficiencies indicated by answers of 4 or 5 to any question.[15]

CHAPTER 1

The Life, Times and Career of the Professional Salesperson

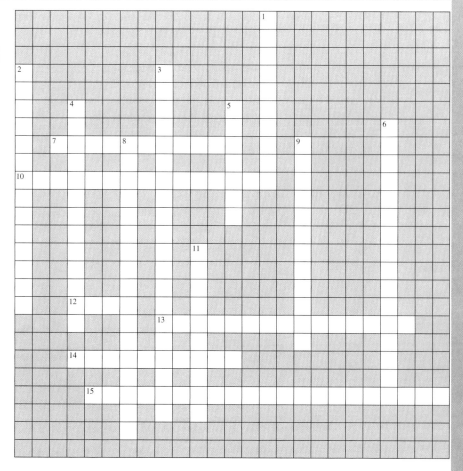

Across

7. Salespeople who get new and repeat business by using a creative sales strategy and a well-executed sales presentation.
10. The ability to see the selling process as a whole and the relationship among its parts.
12. A prescribed guide for conduct or action.
13. Personal communication of information to unselfishly persuade a prospective customer to buy something—a good, service, idea, or something else—that satisfies that individual's needs.
14. The upward sequence of job movements during a sales career.
15. Another name for a salesperson.

Down

1. The seller's ability to work with and through other people.
2. The understanding of and proficiency in the performance of specific tasks.
3. A person who sells products to parties for resale, use in producing other goods or services, or operating an organization.
4. Sellers who sell face-to-face to consumers—typically in their homes—who use products for their personal use.
5. Making a contribution to the welfare of others.

6. A person who plans, organizes, and executes activities that increase sales and profits in a given territory.

8. This individual sells goods or services to customers for their personal, nonbusiness use.

9. A sequential series of actions by the salesperson that leads toward the

prospect taking a desired action and ends with follow-up to ensure purchase satisfaction.

11. Salespeople who only take orders by asking what the customer wants or waiting for the customer to order. They have no sales strategy and use no sales presentation.

CASE 1-1
What They Didn't Teach Us in Sales Class*

Rick Lester was depressed. He was cold and damp from the rain as he sat in his van in the parking lot of a Food World supermarket. He had just telephoned the Nabisco division sales office and talked with Helen, the office secretary. Rick had asked her, "What are we supposed to do when it rains like this?" Rick could hear her repeat the question to Mr. Brown, the division sales manager, who just happened to be in the office. Rick could hear the reply in the background, "Tell him to buy a raincoat!" When Helen repeated the response, Rick replied to her, "OK, have a nice day" with a slightly embarrassed tone in his voice. As he hung up the pay phone and sat back in his van he thought, "What a heck of a way to make a living."

As a new salesman, it was clear that Rick had much to learn. He had only been on the job for one month, but he had about decided that it was no "piece of cake." It had all seemed so much easier when he watched Mr. Brown make calls during his two-week on-the-job training period. Now that he was making calls on his own, it was quite different and much more difficult. Interestingly, the sales class Rick had taken at the University of Alabama at Birmingham the previous year had covered many reasons to go into selling, but few disadvantages of pursuing a career in sales. Rick was now learning about these firsthand.

Rick's family—his parents and two younger sisters—had lived in Birmingham for many years. Mr. Lester was a salesman, and Mrs. Lester was a homemaker. Rick was an average student in high school, where he really majored in athletics and cheerleaders. After high school he accepted a partial athletic scholarship to Northwest Mississippi Junior College. His grades in college were about average overall but were low in basic math classes. The chief reason he selected business as his major was that it required no algebra. Following two years in Mississippi, Rick transferred to the University of Alabama at Birmingham and continued to work toward a B.S. degree in marketing. He met a nice girl there, and they later married when he graduated from UAB. There had been three specific job opportunities, all in sales, but he chose the job with Nabisco because it was a big company with many benefits. He also thought highly of Mr. Brown, the local recruiter and division sales manager.

Rick started to work on September 1. The first week was spent reviewing sales training manuals and completing employment paperwork. He also stocked his new van with merchandise, advertising materials, and displays. The following two weeks were spent "working the trade" with Mr. Brown, who made most of the calls while Rick learned by observing. Toward the end of the third week of employment, Rick was starting to make the sales presentations while Mr. Brown observed. They would discuss each call after they returned to the van. During the fourth week, Rick worked

* This case was written by Gerald Crawford and R. Keith Absher, Professors of Marketing, and William S. Stewart, Professor of Management, University of North Alabama, Florence, Alabama 35632.

alone. The present week had been difficult . . . there was so much he didn't know. On Friday it rained, and this was not helpful. It was about two o'clock when he called the office and was told to buy a raincoat.

As he sat in the van waiting for the rain to let up, he began thinking about the situation in which he now found himself, and it was depressing. The rain was not the only reason for his low morale. He thought about his wife and how she had told her friends that Rick was in public relations rather than sales. Although they had not discussed it, Rick assumed that she did not particularly like the title *salesman.* Somewhere in the back of Rick's thoughts, there was clearly an image that selling has low occupational status. Maybe it came from his father. He couldn't remember. Another troublesome aspect of the new job was the calloused way that some retailers treat all salespeople. Others simply try to brush them off or avoid them altogether. This job, Rick thought, certainly does not build up one's ego.

There are other negative aspects of being in sales. One is that selling is physically demanding. It is a requirement to carry the sales bag into all calls. Properly loaded, Rick's sales bag weighed 38 pounds and contained advertising materials, new products, sample merchandise, a stapler, and the selling portfolio. In addition, in some calls, salespeople must transport cases of merchandise from the storage area to the shelves. A great deal of bending and lifting is simply a part of the routine workday. By quitting time each day, Rick's clothing was wrinkled and damp from perspiration. Yesterday he had snagged a hole in the trousers of his new suit.

At the end of each day, Rick had to prepare reports and mail them to the home office. It was also necessary to reorganize and restock the van for the next day's work. Sometimes there were telephone calls that had to be made. By the time these chores were completed, it was almost bedtime. There was not much time left to spend with his new wife, and she had mentioned this a time or two.

The last annoying concern involved the knowledge that a good part of his success, or lack of it, depended on events over which he had no control. In several calls this week, a competitor had persuaded dealers to reduce shelf space for Nabisco products. These dealers reported that the competitor had a special promotion going on and the deal was just too good to pass up. There was no way that Rick could recover the lost shelf space in those calls. This did not look good on the salesperson's daily report.

As the rain continued to come down, Rick felt very alone. Mr. Brown was not there to help or provide answers. The physical and emotional obstacles just seemed too big to overcome. The only way out of this mess, it seemed, was to quit this job and try to find another one that was not this depressing. "Maybe I could get a job in a bank, where customers are always nice and the work is easier," Rick thought. As he started his van and drove away toward the division office, he felt relieved that he would soon be free of this impossible responsibility.

Questions

1. Should Rick Lester "turn in his keys"?
2. How should Mr. Brown handle this situation? What should he say to Rick?
3. How can firms reduce high turnover among new sales personnel?
4. What can firms do to increase salesperson status?
5. What can professors do to better prepare students in sales classes?

Appendix: The Golden Rule of Personal Selling as Told by a Salesperson

Some time ago your present job was offered to you. You researched the company and its products, decided you liked what you found, and became a salesperson. You had heard good and bad things about salespeople. However, these things seem to occur in all occupations.

Your employer produces worthwhile products that will help people. It does not produce things that feed the world's desires. You feel people must always be more important than products, money, or you. You have found an outlet for your life's mission and philosophical goals since you accepted this opportunity.

THE GOLDEN RULE OF SELLING

You chose to base your sales philosophy on unselfishly treating others as you would like to be treated. This is what you fondly refer to as the "Golden Rule of Selling." Customer needs come before your needs. So each time you make a sales call you ask yourself, "Do I want to build a friendly relationship with this person because I need something from her/him?" You want to help people without expecting something in return. If you do not know how to put other people's needs first, how can you build a true relationship with them?

OTHERS INCLUDES COMPETITORS

Although you love making a sale, you feel the Golden Rule of Selling especially applies to your relationship with competitors. In fact, applying the Golden Rule of Selling to the competition is one of the main reasons you like sales. For if your customers or prospects do not feel your products will fulfill their needs, you discuss and, if possible, recommend a competitor's product. You prefer to lose your commission in order to be faithful to a relationship and do what is right for your customer. This experience gives you a real sense of joy and peace because, after all, it is your personal mission to help all people.

SALES IS YOUR CALLING TO SERVE

You really do not think of your occupation as work. It's what you do. It defines who you are. It's something you look forward to each day. Going to your job isn't work; it's a chance to be with your friends, because you are all in this together. You want to see your employer's business prosper because it employs many people who use their salary to support their families and the economy. Other people, such as the vendors you buy supplies from, prosper as your company experiences improved sales and profits.

You enjoy business relationships and work wholeheartedly at your job. Yet you enjoy time off from sales to be with your family and to do things within your community. Your family is very important in your life. They are second in your life in importance, just behind your faith, and career is number three in your life.

When pressure is on to sell, you remember the story of a person who also loved his job and talked about how his family was important in his life. Then one Saturday he took his young son to work with him. The boy asked "Daddy is this where you live?" Shocked at first, he thought about all the days he leaves home before the child wakes and gets home after the boy is in bed. His behavior revealed what he truly valued? This was a life-changing question coming from a five-year-old child.

You learned long ago that what you do and how you live, more than anything you say, reveals what you truly believe, value, and are in your life and your relationships with others. Your life's goal of helping others includes your family, friends, boss, co-workers, and community.

What is the purpose of your life?

You want to do something worthwhile in your life, and your occupation is one of the things that fills that need. This is where you feel you are meant to be in your life. It is your calling. You were put on this earth to do what you're doing. Some time ago, you stopped to ask yourself, "What is the purpose of my life?" The answer you have discovered is serving others. Service, to you, means making a contribution to the welfare of others.[16] You want to "make a difference!" And you do make a difference in customers' lives. That is one reason you love sales! You have the opportunity to be with so many people each day. Each day brings wonderful opportunities to improve others' lives.

You have realized that only through service can you find fulfillment in your job and life.[17] Serving others provides you with an emotional purpose in life that helps to sustain enthusiasm for getting up each day. Service gives you this daily excitement for life within your heart. But one of the first things you realized in your sales job was that to truly serve others you had to know what you were talking about.

TO SERVE, YOU NEED KNOWLEDGE

After much training and experience, you are considered an expert on your industry, competitors, products, and the application of both your products and those of your competitors to customers' needs. Being knowledgeable on products and selling skills is extremely important to you. It allows you to provide a high level of customer service, which can aid you in properly helping your customers fulfill their needs. This knowledge is also valuable in helping your fellow salespeople. In sales, however, you quickly learned people don't care how much you know until they know how much you care.[18]

CUSTOMERS NOTICE INTEGRITY

While it did not happen overnight, your customers love to see you! They trust that you are looking out for their best interest because you are a person of integrity and self-control. But to you, integrity is who you are when no one is looking.[19]

A sincere desire motivates you to help others by having them purchase your products, and you believe in what you sell. Since your first day of contacting customers, you have realized that they want to buy, not be sold. You have gained genuine happiness from seeing how your products help solve the needs of other people. Because of your gentleness, kindness, and patience, people view you as a role model. Work provides a sense of fulfillment for you, a personal satisfaction from knowing that you are doing something purposeful, meaningful, and worthwhile.

PERSONAL GAIN IS NOT YOUR GOAL

Pursuing sales for the sake of self-interest and gain is not your goal. Helping others is. You are never concerned about sales goals, only customers. Take care of customers, and customers will take care of you. Your productivity is really not in your hands. Results come in direct proportion to your level of customer service.

It is clear to you that diligence—the willingness to work hard and do your best—is a vital part of your life. You work hard, not to become rich, famous, or admired, although those may be by-products of such a lifestyle, but to help and serve others. Financial rewards result from helping others. You use the rewards gained from aiding others to meet your needs and to contribute to the needs of the less fortunate, besides saving some money for your retirement. You have seen others lose their health to make money, then lose their money to restore their health.[20] But you are secure and content with what you have been given. Financial reward is not, nor will ever be, your idol.

You are proud of what you do. Your intention in life is to accomplish business, sales, and personal goals, such as supplying a better life for your family, selling a quality product, providing good value to the customer, and building and strengthening your community through fair business practices and increased employment.[21]

OTHERS COME FIRST

You have even built up a reputation as a volunteer in your community by giving your time, money, and effort to projects that help people. Like your job, working for society's benefit provides you with great joy. It is a chance to bring goodness into the community.

While you occasionally think about taking credit, you honestly feel you have had little, if any, direct influence on your accomplishments. You are not a self-made person. Your faith, father and mother, relatives, schoolteachers, friends, spouse, managers, peers, customers, company trainers, and the products you sell are just some of the factors that have molded your life, allowing you to make contributions to the sales growth of your company. This realization of how so many others have helped you over the years has caused you to be aware of how small you are compared to others. Others have provided the means for you and your family to have a wonderful life. For that reason you have a strong affection for every person in your life. Their interests come before yours. That is why you never compare yourself to others; you can let the boss do that.

THE FRUITS OF THE SELLING SPIRIT

This in turn brings you back around to your life's philosophy based upon the Golden Rule of Selling—to unselfishly treat others as you would like to be treated. What has been the effect of applying the Golden Rule of Selling to work and life? It has resulted in an abundantly productive, or fruitful, life. The by-products of dedicating your life to others have been love, joy, peace, patience, kindness, goodness, faithfulness, gentleness, and self-control. These nine fruits of the selling spirit have given your life purpose. As you tell others, "Practicing the Golden Rule of Selling has resulted in my being blessed by unmerited kindness from others!"

2 CHAPTER

Relationship Marketing: Where Personal Selling Fits

LEARNING OBJECTIVES

The sales force is but one part of an organization's marketing effort; you should understand the role and importance of the sales force in a firm's total marketing effort. After studying this chapter, you should be able to

■ Define and explain the terms *marketing* and *marketing concept*.

■ Describe the evolution of customer orientation in the United States.

■ Answer the question, Why is marketing important to an organization?

■ Illustrate how the firm's product, price, distribution, and promotion efforts are coordinated for maximum sales success.

■ Explain why an organization should listen to its customers.

■ Discuss the role of personal selling in the firm's marketing relationship efforts.

■ Understand a salesperson's roles when practicing consultative selling.

Do you know what is involved in marketing? Imagine you were Larry Cunningham who several years ago started Aggieland Screen Printing (ASP) in College Station, Texas. ASP produces and sells such products as T-shirts, sweats, bumper stickers, caps, jackets, and signs. Larry graduated from Texas A & M University with a bachelor's degree in architecture. Because he was an excellent artist, he decided to open his own business. At the end of his first year, he employed four part-time workers to run all of the printing equipment. The Bryan–College Station area has 100,000 people, plus about 43,000 students enrolled at Texas A & M. Larry felt this was a good business area, even though he had 10 competitors.

Sales, however, have been so slow that Larry may have to quit or try to sell the business. Larry loves the creative side of the business, but admits he knows nothing about marketing. He cannot afford any advertising, including the Yellow Pages.

If you were in Larry Cunningham's position, what would you do?

Firms of all sizes face the dilemma of how to increase sales. Many organizations are good at developing goods or services, but know very little about marketing their products. This chapter introduces the purpose and components of a firm's marketing efforts, along with the role and importance of the sales force in a firm's total marketing effort. Let's begin by answering the question, "What is the purpose of business?"

WHAT IS THE PURPOSE OF BUSINESS?

The purpose of business is to increase the general well-being of humankind through the sale of goods and services. This requires making a profit in order to operate the business and provide beneficial products to the marketplace. Profit is a means to an end. Reduced to basics, businesses have two major functions: *production* of goods or creation of services and *marketing* those goods and services.[1]

WHAT IS MARKETING?

To be successful in today's competitive marketplace, people in business realize that they must first determine people's needs and wants, then produce goods and services to satisfy them. A company, whether it is Ford Motor Company or a small retailer, is in business to create want-satisfying goods and services for its customers. In today's competitive business environment, the success of goods and services is determined by the consumers who buy them. Goods and services that do not satisfy consumers are forced from the market, since consumers do not buy them.

If you asked the general public what the term *marketing* means, many would say that it means *selling*. Selling, in turn, usually implies advertising and personal selling to the public. Yet the act of selling is only one part of a firm's marketing activities.

Marketing's Definition

There are numerous definitions of marketing. Your book will use the American Marketing Association's definition:

> **Marketing** is an organizational function and a set of processes for creating, communicating and delivering value to customers and for managing customer relationships in ways that benefit the organization and its stakeholders.[2]

This definition of marketing is the most widely accepted by marketing educators and practitioners. It indicates that there is more to marketing than advertising or personal selling. Marketing involves a diverse set of activities directed at a wide range of goods, services, and ideas. These activities involve the development, pricing, promotion, and distribution of want-satisfying goods and services to consumers and industrial users. Marketing activities are therefore very important both to the individual company and to our economy as a whole.

Marketing's Not Limited to Business

Marketing is not limited to business. Whenever you try to persuade somebody to do something—donate to the Salvation Army, fasten a seat belt, lower a stereo's noise during study hours in the dorm, vote for your candidate, accept a date with you (or maybe even marry you)—you are engaging in a marketing activity. So-called nonprofit organizations that are really in business but don't think of themselves as businesspeople also engage in marketing. Their *product* may be a vacation place they want you to visit like Florida; a social cause or an idea they want you to support, such as "don't drink and drive"; or an institution they want you to attend such as a church, school, or zoo. Whatever the product is, the organization is engaging in marketing.

Exchange and Transactions

The definition of marketing indicates that people have needs and wants and can place value on products. When people decide to satisfy needs and wants through exchange, marketing is involved. Exchange is the defining concept underlying marketing. **Exchange** refers to the act of obtaining a desired product from someone by offering something in return.

The exchange takes place between two parties. When an exchange occurs, a transaction takes place, as transactions are the basic unit of exchange. A **transaction** is a trade of values between two parties; it forms a relationship between buyer and seller. Once the transaction has occurred, the exchange is complete. The sale is made whether it involves buying a stereo or voting for a political candidate.

CUSTOMER ORIENTATION'S EVOLUTION

American business has gone through many changes of philosophy and direction. These changes were largely caused by the ultimate realization that organizations must be customer oriented. However, this has not always been the viewpoint of business. Several major nonconsumer marketing phases existed prior to the emergence of today's customer-oriented attitude.

The Production Concept

Before the Great Depression of the 1930s, a common saying in industry was, "Build a better mousetrap, and the world will beat a path to your door." Companies were basically production oriented. "We know what people want—they want our product," or "I like this product and so will others" were phrases often used by corporate presidents.

In those days, few firms had marketing departments, and many did not even have a formal sales department. An engineer would develop a product, have the production department make it, and then simply put it in the catalog and wait for people to order. Production and engineering shaped the company's objectives and planning. Products were sold at a price determined by production and financial executives. Henry Ford, for example, said that customers could have any color automobile they wanted as long as it was black. The automobile was a new, exciting product that consumers needed. America bought what was produced.[3]

The Selling Concept

By the early 1940s, it became clear that the attitude and needs of the consumer had changed. The military requirements of World War II created a shortage of goods and services. This wartime deprivation resulted in a strong consumer demand when the war was over.

A few years after the war, consumers had many products to choose from and firms found they had to go to the consumer, instead of waiting for consumers to buy. Companies still produced goods with little regard for the consumer's needs. However, they recognized that personal selling and advertising were important selling methods. In the postwar era, firms placed most emphasis on advertising their product, expecting salespeople to contact customers and take their orders.

Salespeople, armed with very unsophisticated selling techniques, were asked to contact potential customers, show them their products, and take their orders. Training for salespeople consisted mainly of providing them with product knowledge. They had to rely on natural ability for developing and giving sales presentations. Few companies recognized the value of training their salespeople in selling techniques. However, as time passed, businesses found that they had to become market-oriented rather than sales-oriented.

The Marketing Concept

Beginning in the 1950s, marketing, rather than selling, became the focus of business sales activities. As businesspeople recognized that marketing was vitally important to the success of a firm, an entirely new way of business thinking—a new philosophy—began to evolve. The *marketing concept* has three fundamental beliefs:

- All company planning and operations should be *customer-oriented*.
- The goal of the firm should be *profitable sales volume* and not just volume for the sake of volume alone.
- All marketing activities in a firm should be *organizationally coordinated*.

The **marketing concept** is a business philosophy that says the customers' want-satisfaction is the economic and social justification for a firm's existence. Consequently, all company activities should be devoted to determining customers' wants and then satisfying them, while still making a profit.

Difference between Selling and Marketing Concepts

Unfortunately, many people, including some business executives, still do not understand the difference between selling and marketing. In fact, many people think the terms are synonymous. Instead, these concepts have opposite meanings as Exhibit 2.1 illustrates.[4]

EXHIBIT 2.1

The difference between selling and marketing concepts.

Selling Concept	Marketing Concept
1. Emphasis is on the product.	1. Emphasis is on customers' wants.
2. Company first makes the product and then figures out how to sell it.	2. Company first determines customers' wants and then figures out how to make and deliver a product to satisfy those wants.
3. Management is sales-volume-oriented.	3. Management is profit-oriented.
4. Planning is short-run, in terms of today's products and markets.	4. Planning is long-run, in terms of new products, tomorrow's markets, and future growth.
5. Stresses needs of seller.	5. Stresses wants of buyers.

Under the selling concept, a company makes a product and then uses various selling methods to persuade customers to buy the product. In effect, the company is bending consumer demand to fit the company's supply. Just the opposite occurs under the marketing concept. The company determines what the customer wants and then develops a product to satisfy that want and still yield a profit. Now, the company bends its supply to the will of consumer demand.

For a business enterprise to realize the full benefits of the marketing concept, that philosophy must be translated into action. This means (1) marketing activities must be fully coordinated and well managed, and (2) the chief marketing executive must be accorded an important role in company planning.

MARKETING'S IMPORTANCE IN THE FIRM

Marketing considerations should be the most critical factor guiding all short-range and long-range planning in any organization. Too often, unfortunately, American business has been oriented toward production. Products have been designed by engineers, manufactured by production people, priced by marketers, and then given to sales managers to sell. That procedure generally won't work in today's environment of intense competition and constant change. Just building a good product will not result in a company's success. The product must be marketed to consumers before its full value is realized.

As shown in Exhibit 2.2, the marketing group is the link between customers and the organization. Salespeople are part of marketing. They are in direct contact with customers.

Marketing people typically have these four basic objectives to accomplish:

1. Maximize the sales of existing products in existing markets.
2. Develop and sell new products.
3. Develop new markets for existing or new products.
4. Provide the quality of service necessary for customers to be satisfied with their transactions and to continue doing business with the organization.

EXHIBIT 2.2

The marketing group is the link between customers and the organization.

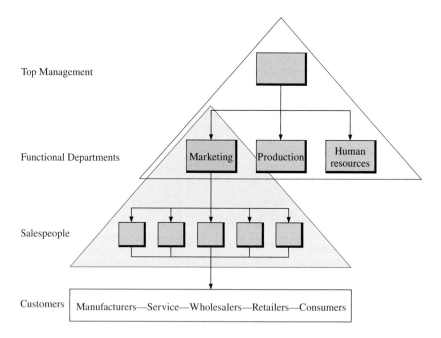

Marketing Generates Sales

As you can see from the first three objectives, the main role of marketing in an organization is basically to generate revenues. The money marketing generates is managed by the financial people and used by the production people in creating goods and services. Marketing activities are therefore very important to the organization because it must generate sales to stay in business.

Marketing Provides Quality Customer Service

Marketing personnel also help make sure customers are satisfied with their purchases. Marketing provides more to the marketplace than a needed product; it helps generate sales by providing the quality of service customers expect.

Excellent service pays off because it creates true customers—customers who are glad they selected a product because of the organization and its service. True customers are like annuities—they keep pumping revenue into the firm's coffers.

It is the performance of service that creates true customers: customers who buy more and who influence others to buy. Quality service thus helps the organization to maximize sales.

ESSENTIALS OF A FIRM'S MARKETING EFFORT

The essentials of a firm's marketing effort include their abilities (1) to determine the needs of their customers and (2) to create and maintain an effective marketing mix that satisfies customer needs. As shown in Exhibit 2.3, a firm's **marketing mix** consists of four main elements—product, price, distribution or place, and promotion—a marketing manager uses to market goods and services. It is the marketing manager's responsibility to determine how best to use each element in the firm's marketing efforts.

Product: It's More Than You Think

A **good** is a physical object that can be purchased. A radio, a house, and a car are examples of a good. A **service** is an action or activity done for others for a fee. Lawyers, plumbers, teachers, and taxicab drivers perform services. The term *product* refers to both goods and services.

Salespeople have gone from selling goods, to selling goods and services, to now selling goods, services, and value-added services. **Value-added** refers to benefits received that are not included in the purchase price of the individual good or service. A retailer may offer customers free financing, great store locations, free gift-wrapping, loaner cars, and well-trained salespeople. Exhibit 2.4 gives several examples of business-to-business value-adding practices. That is why it is often said salespeople are selling more than just a good or service. They sell products.

EXHIBIT 2.3

Four elements to the marketing mix and four promotion activities.

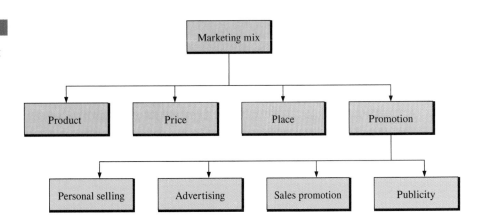

EXHIBIT 2.4

Examples of business-to-business value-adding.

Help customer reduce process costs.
- Improve yields.
- Reduce waste (through recycling, etc.).
- Reduce rework.
- Reduce direct labor.
- Reduce indirect labor (inspection, handling).
- Reduce energy costs.

Help customer reduce inventory.
- Consignment.
- Just-in-time delivery.
- Reduced cycle time.

Help customer reduce administrative costs.
- Simplify billing.
- Improve traceability.
- Use electronic data interchange.

Improve safety for customer and his employees.
- Reduce price to the customer.
- Substitute certain product components.
- Improve company processes and supplier processes.

So, what is a product? When you think of a product, most likely you imagine some tangible object you can touch, such as a radio, or automobile. However, there is more to a product than you think.

What image does your dress and grooming reflect?

A **product** is a bundle of tangible and intangible attributes, including packaging, color, and brand, plus the services and even the reputation of the seller. People buy more than a set of physical attributes. They buy want-satisfaction such as what the product will do, its quality, and the image of owning the product. Take a Polo shirt, for example. What is the difference (besides price) in a Polo shirt and a nonbranded shirt bought at Wal-Mart? Both shirts perform the same function of clothing someone. So why does one buy a Polo? For many people, image plays an important part in the decision to purchase the Polo shirt. So a seller of a product is selling more than what a product will do for people.

There are two general types of products. **Consumer products** are produced for, and purchased by, households or end consumers for their personal use. **Industrial products** are sold primarily for use in producing other products.

Today, firms spend enormous amounts of time and money creating the products they sell. They carefully research what customers want before developing a product. They consider the product and its package design, trademarks, warranties, and service policies.

Research and development and strategies for selling new products are major corporate marketing department activities. Often, sales personnel have little input on what products should be produced. Their involvement in selling the product begins after the product has been produced.*

Price: It's Important to Success

The corporate marketing department also determines each product's initial price. This process involves establishing each product's normal price and possible special discount prices. Since product price often is critical to customers, it is an important part of the marketing mix. **Price** refers to the value or worth of a product that attracts the buyer to exchange money or something of value for the product.

* Product, price, and distribution are discussed further in Chapter 6.

Companies develop varied pricing techniques and methods for their salespeople to use. For example, General Motors, Chrysler, and Ford have offered consumers cash rebates to increase automobile sales. Companies such as Quaker Oats, Kraft, and Lever Brothers send out discount coupons to consumers and offer special price reductions to retailers on their products so that retailers reduce their prices. Some salespeople use offers of price reductions in their sales presentations to entice the retailer to purchase large quantities of the product. Getting large shipments to retailers and other types of customers leads to another element of the marketing mix.

Distribution: It Has to Be Available

The marketing manager also determines the best method of distributing the product. **Distribution** refers to the channel structure used to transfer products from an organization to its customers. It is important to have the product available to customers in a convenient and accessible location when they want it.

Distribution Moves Products to Customers

Customers can be individuals and/or organizations. Several examples of distribution channels for consumer and industrial products are shown in Exhibit 2.5. Customers fall into one of three groups: (1) households, (2) firms, and (3) governments.

A **household** refers to a decision-making unit buying for personal use. Every individual in the economy belongs to a household. Some households consist of a single person whereas others consist of families or of groups of unrelated individuals, such as two or three students sharing an apartment.

A **firm** is an organization that produces goods and services. All producers are called firms, no matter how big they are or what they produce. Car makers, farmers, banks, and insurance companies are all firms. Firms can be for-profit like General Electric or nonprofit like the American Heart Association.

A **government** is an organization that has two functions: the provision of goods and services to households and firms and the redistribution of income and wealth. Examples of the goods and services supplied by the government are national defense, law enforcement, public health, transportation, and education. Government buys billions of dollars each year of all types of products. Thus, a firm and a government are both organizations.

EXHIBIT 2.5

Examples of distribution channels for consumer and industrial products.

Consumer Products

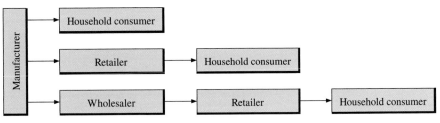

Industrial Products

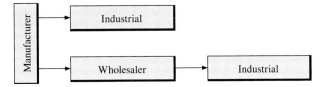

Distribution Uses Resellers

Many organizations sell directly to resellers. **Resellers,** such as wholesalers or retailers, purchase products and then sell to organizations and/or individuals. The wholesaler buys goods in large quantities, reselling them—usually in smaller quantities—to retailers or to industrial or business users. The retailer buys goods from others and sells them to ultimate consumers for their personal use.

Two main distribution channels for manufacturers of industrial products are selling directly to the industrial user, such as another manufacturer, or selling to a wholesaler, who in turn sells to another manufacturer or industrial user of products.

Promotion: You Have to Tell People about It

Nothing else ruins the truth like stretching it.

Promotion, as part of the marketing mix, increases company sales by communicating product information to potential customers. The four basic parts of a firm's promotional effort are (1) **personal selling,** (2) **advertising,** (3) **publicity,** and (4) **sales promotion.** These are briefly explained in Exhibit 2.6. The company's sales force is one segment of the firm's promotional effort.

In addition to informing people about a product's existence, promotion also educates consumers about the product's features, advantages, and benefits; tells them where to buy it; and makes them aware of its price versus value. The question arises as to "What are the best promotional elements to use in selling a product?" This decision is made only after consideration of the type of product and the customers who will buy it.

The marketing manager determines what proportion of the firm's budget will be allocated to each product and how much emphasis on each of the promotional variables will be given to each product. Firms typically spend more money on their sales force than on advertising and promotion. Organizations selling in industrial markets spend a higher percentage of the promotion budget on their sales force than manufacturers of consumer goods. This is because industrial purchasing agents do not see advertisements for their products on television. Salespeople keep them informed.

The Goal of a Marketing Mix

The goal of designing a marketing mix is simple. The organization's marketing group strives to create a marketing mix containing the right product, at the right price, at the right time, with the right promotional effort.

EXHIBIT 2.6

Promotion activities.

- *Personal selling.* Personal communication of information to unselfishly persuade a prospective customer to buy something—a good, service, idea, or something else—that satisfies an individual's needs.
- *Advertising.* Nonpersonal communication of information paid for by an identified sponsor such as an individual or an organization. Modes of advertising include television, radio, direct mail, catalogs, newspapers, and outdoor advertising such as billboards.
- *Publicity.* Nonpersonal communication of information that is not paid for by an individual or organization. Information appears in media such as television, radio, and newspapers.
- *Sales promotion.* Involves activities or materials used to create sales for goods or services. The two types of sales promotion are consumer and trade sales promotion. Consumer sales promotion includes free samples, coupons, contests, and demonstrations to consumers. Trade sales promotion encourages wholesalers and retailers to purchase and to sell aggressively using devices such as sales contests, displays, special purchase prices, and free merchandise.

EXHIBIT 2.7

Examples of each marketing
mix element.

Product	Price	Place	Promotion
■ Brand name	■ Credit terms	■ Business partners	■ Advertising
■ Features	■ Discounts	■ Channels	■ Coupons
■ Image	■ List price	■ Distributors	■ Customer service
■ Packaging	■ Promotional allowances	■ Inventory	■ Direct mail
■ Quality level		■ Locations	■ Direct sales
■ Returns		■ Retailers	■ Internet
■ Services		■ Transportation	■ Public relations
■ Sizes		■ Wholesalers	■ Telemarketing
■ Warranties			■ Telesales
			■ Trade shows

Coordination Is Important

No matter what marketing mix activities are used, they must be coordinated with the marketing elements shown in Exhibit 2.7. The most effective marketing effort considers the needs of customers and coordinates activities from all four elements.

Manufactured by 3M, Post-it Notes is a perfect example of a product that nearly failed under an ineffective marketing mix. Originally tested in several medium-size markets, results were drab. Post-it Notes were successful only after 3M redesigned the marketing strategy to incorporate essential activities from all four marketing mix elements. Concentrating on the Boise, Idaho, test market, management decided the flaw in the original marketing program was too little promotion and no demonstration of how the notes worked or what they were designed to do. The redesigned strategy joined five activities from the original marketing mix with two more activities to increase the promotional element. The original components were, first, *product:* 3M recognized that a large market existed for note pages that could be peeled off and attached easily. Second, they capitalized on the pad's unique *feature,* a "totally imperfect" adhesive. Third, 3M made the pads available in a variety of *sizes.* Fourth, the company offered special promotional *prices.* And fifth, *place:* 3M had local dealers available through which businesses could place orders. 3M added two components to increase promotion in the campaign: sixth, *nonpersonal promotion:* 3M took out eight two-color inserts in the *Boise Statesman* newspaper illustrating the use of Post-it Notes; and seventh, 3M increased the power of personal selling through a combined use of *free samples* and *demonstration.* 3M hired Manpower Temporary Services personnel to go from office to office in the Boise business section, demonstrating the pads and leaving samples. Local dealers then dispatched salespeople to close the sales.

Following this campaign, Post-it Notes immediately caught on. Within four years they went into national production and were the most successful product in 3M's history. By overlooking the promotional element, 3M almost had a failure on hand. Adding promotional activities coordinated the marketing plan and enabled Post-it Notes to succeed. You can see that coordination of all major elements is essential.

RELATIONSHIP MARKETING

Organizations today have targeted new and present customers. The emphasis is shifting from selling customers *today* to creating customers for *tomorrow.* Thus, business is thinking more long term than short term.

Relationship marketing is the creation of customer loyalty. Organizations use combinations of products, prices, distribution, promotions, and service to achieve this goal. Relationship marketing is based on the idea that important customers need continuous attention.

An organization using relationship marketing is not seeking a simple sale or transaction. It has targeted a major customer that it would like to sell to now and in the future. The company wants to demonstrate to the customer that it has the capabilities to serve the account's needs in a superior way, particularly if a *committed relationship* can be formed. The type of selling needed to establish a long-term collaborative relationship is complex. General Motors, for example, prefers suppliers who can sell and deliver a coordinated set of goods and services to many locations, who can quickly solve problems that arise in their different locations, and who can work closely with them to improve products and processes.

Most companies, unfortunately, are not set up to meet these requirements. Today, the level of customer relationships varies. Many organizations still sell to customers and then forget them. Other organizations develop a close relationship—even a partnership—with their customers.

RELATIONSHIP MARKETING AND THE SALES FORCE

A major issue in an organization's relationship marketing program is the role of the sales force. Firms use salespeople in many ways. However, these four basic questions are guidelines that define the role of the sales force:

1. How much selling effort is necessary to gain and hold customers?
2. Is the sales force the best marketing tool, compared to advertising and other sales promotion methods, in terms of cost and results?
3. What type of sales activities—for example, technical assistance, frequent or infrequent sales calls—will be necessary?
4. Can the firm gain strength relative to its competition with its sales force?

The answers to these questions come largely from an analysis of competition, the target markets, and the firm's product offerings. This helps determine (1) sales force objectives, (2) the level of resources—such as personnel and money—allocated to sales force activities, and (3) the importance of personal selling in the marketing mix.

When selling business to business, IBM, for example, used a variety of marketing and sales activities for the introduction of one of their new midsized computers. As shown in Exhibit 2.8, IBM used its direct sales force to develop a proposal, demonstrate the equipment, and close the sale. It used other marketing methods for the various sales tasks shown across the top of Exhibit 2.8. Other sellers may use the marketing methods in a different way, depending on the answers to the above four questions.

Personal Selling Builds Relationships

Personal selling is an essential element of any organization's marketing mix. The main functions of personal selling are to generate revenue and provide service to help make customers satisfied with their purchases. This builds relationships and is the key to success in today's competitive marketplace.

EXHIBIT 2.8

Examples of various marketing and sales methods used to sell midsized computers business to business.

Marketing / Sales Tasks

Marketing Method / Channel	Awareness	Inquiry generation	Lead qualification	Proposal development	Trial or demonstration	Close	Postsale activity
Public relations							
Advertising							
Direct mail							
Telemarketing							
Internet							
Trade shows							
Telesales							
Distributors / Business partners							
Direct sales							
Customer service							

Salespeople Generate Revenue

Once a product has been developed, it must be sold. To generate profitable sales, the product has to be promoted. In today's competitive marketplace, a firm has to make personal selling a main promotional method for selling the product.

Think about this! Virtually every product you see in any factory, office, school, or retail store was sold to that organization by a salesperson. The next time you are in a grocery store, stop and look around at the thousands of products you can buy. Salespeople are responsible for making those products available for you.

Because they are involved in person-to-person discussions, salespeople can customize their sales presentations to the individual needs of specific people and organizations. Salespeople can see a customer's reaction to a sales approach and make needed adjustments immediately. Advertising cannot do this.

It's true that advertising attracts the consumer's attention and arouses desire; however, ads don't close any sales. Personal selling does. In many cases, personal selling ends in an actual sale.

MAKING THE SALE

Salespeople Have Made America Great!

He came on muleback, dodging outlaws as he went, with a pack full of better living and a tongue full of charms. For he was the great American salesman, and no man ever had a better thing to sell.

He came by rickety wagon, one jump behind the pioneers, carrying axes for the farmer, fancy dress goods for his wife, and encyclopedias for the farmer's ambitious boy. For he was the great practical democrat, spreader of good things among more and more people.

He came by upper berth and dusty black coupe, selling tractors and radios, iceboxes and movies, health and leisure, ambition and fulfillment. For he was America's emissary of abundance, Mr. High-Standard-of-Living in person.

He rang a billion doorbells and enriched a billion lives. Without him there would be no American ships at sea, no busy factories, and fewer jobs. For the great American salesman is the great American civilizer, and everywhere he goes he leaves people better off.

The promotional method of selling is, however, costly. The high cost is due to the expense of developing and operating a sales force. Yet this drawback is compensated for by salespeople being able to contact specific individuals.

Organizations need a good personal selling effort to compete in today's marketplace. Salespeople help make companies successful. Many of us feel salespeople have made America great!

Salespeople Provide Service

If an organization wants a customer to return—to be satisfied—it must provide an excellent level of service quality. **Service quality** is a subjective satisfaction assessment that customers arrive at by comparing the service level they believe an organization ought to deliver to the service level that they perceive being delivered.

Some customers may get the product they want but become unhappy because of poor service. In fact many consumers feel they never really get service anymore. Take this story, for example. "Mom," the little girl said, "do all fairy tales begin with 'Once upon a time'?" "No dear," her mother said. "Sometimes they begin with, 'The couch you ordered has arrived at our warehouse and should be delivered within five working days.'"

Where is service today? is a question frequently asked by customers. An organization's salespeople can help ensure that the organization's service standards are higher than customers' expectations.

Salespeople Implement Relationship Marketing

Who better to help develop a relationship marketing program than the personnel constantly in contact with customers—salespeople. Relationship marketing and the marketing concept are based on the philosophy of being customer oriented. Organizations following this philosophy rely on their sales personnel to help implement customer contact programs. Salespeople sell customers products; when customers are unhappy, the salespersons take care of the problems.

Marketing links the organization with the customer. Salespeople are in direct contact with customers; those who help customers find just the right products to satisfy their particular requirements are providing good service. Salespeople who are knowledgeable, who listen well and come up with answers, and who stand by their customers after the sales are made are providing good service. Sales and service are inseparable.

LEVELS OF RELATIONSHIP MARKETING

What type of relationships should an organization have with its customers? Is the cost of keeping a relationship worth it? To answer these questions, let's define the three general levels of selling relationships with customers:

- **Transaction selling:** customers are sold to and not contacted again.
- **Relationship selling:** the seller contacts customers after the purchase to determine if they are satisfied and have future needs.
- **Partnering:** the seller works continually to improve its customers' operations, sales, and profits.

Most organizations focus solely on the single transaction with each customer. When you go to McDonald's and buy a hamburger, that's it. You never hear from them again unless you return for another purchase. The same thing happens when you go to a movie, rent a video, open a bank checking account, visit the grocery store, or have your clothes cleaned. Each of these examples involves low-priced, low-profit products. Also involved are a large number of customers who are geographically dispersed. This makes it very difficult and quite costly to contact customers. The business is forced to use transactional marketing.

Relationship marketing focuses on the transaction—making the sale—along with follow-up and service after the sale. The seller contacts the customer to ensure satisfaction with the purchase. The Cadillac Division of General Motors contacts each buyer of a new Cadillac to determine the customer's satisfaction with the car. If that person is not satisfied, General Motors works with the retailer selling the car to make sure the customer is happy.

Partnering is a phenomenon of the 1990s. Businesses' growing concern over the competition not only in America but also internationally revitalized their need to work closely with important customers. The familiar **80/20 principle** states that 80 percent of sales often come from 20 percent of a company's customers. Organizations now realize the need to identify their most important customers and designate them for their partnering programs. The organization's best salespeople are assigned to sell and service these customers. Let's take a closer look at partnering since it is becoming so important to organizations.

PARTNERING WITH CUSTOMERS

The ultimate outcome of relationship marketing is the building of a partnership between the seller and the buyer. The seller's company works continuously to help the customer. As the customer prospers, so does the seller. The customer is not sold and then forgotten. Nor is the customer sold and much later asked, "How did you like it?" The seller continues to work with the buyer and the company after the sale to ensure the customer's satisfaction with the product's quality and value.

Partnering encourages both buyer and seller to share information such as marketing research findings and production cost data. Their goal is to share risks and profits together. When two businesses create partnership plans, each accepts a redefinition of its goals. Each accepts an implicit contract to stimulate the other's growth. As illustrated in Exhibit 2.9, they become relatively more dependent on one another.

When this occurs, they become distinctly different species than when they started. They're no longer a buyer and a seller—one striving for the lowest possible cost, the other aiming for the highest possible margin. They're no longer opponents, but two companies working toward an objective.

EXHIBIT 2.9

Dependence increases as
relationships become more
important.

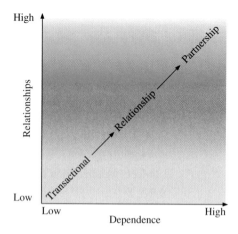

Both are now in the business of enriching the other, not getting rich at the
other's expense. They're not concerned with growth simply by conquest and
market penetration. They're not concerned with simply planning in private, each
using its own resources. They now share objectives with a partner committed to
achieving them.

Partnering gives a whole new meaning to customer focus. Companies that put
partnering into practice find they reduce or eliminate conflicts of interest between
themselves and their clients. Those who work at partnering find that very quickly
their sensitivity and responsiveness improve significantly. They begin to anticipate
trends in their customers' businesses. They begin to know their customers' requirements almost before the customers do.

Once a company defines its own business as growing the business of its partner,
it can begin thinking along completely new lines. It can break loose from archaic
planning and accept the idea that growth is something partners do together.

Criteria for building partnerships are shown in Exhibit 2.10.[5] Think about each
of the eight criteria for a few minutes. If you were CEO of a company, would you
be willing to become partners with one of your suppliers or customers?

EXHIBIT 2.10

Eight criteria for building
partnerships.

1. *Individual excellence:* Both partners add value, and their motives are positive (to pursue opportunity) rather than negative (to mask weakness).
2. *Importance:* Both partners want the relationship to work because it helps them meet long-term strategic objectives.
3. *Interdependence:* The partners need each other; each helps the other reach its goal.
4. *Investment:* The partners devote financial and other resources to the relationship.
5. *Information:* The partners communicate openly about goals, technical data, problems, and changing situations.
6. *Integration:* The partners develop shared ways of operating; they teach each other and learn from each other.
7. *Institutionalization:* The relationship has formal status with clear responsibilities.
8. *Integrity:* Both partners are trustworthy and honorable.

THE NEW CONSULTATIVE SELLING

Not too long ago, the typical sales presentation was a *pitch* focused on a specific product and tightly controlled by the salesperson. Today, the best sales calls are highly interactive dialogues between a salesperson and a customer working toward a common goal. The sales call is a balanced exchange of information, based on trust and focused on achieving a mutually beneficial agreement.

Salespeople have gone from selling goods, to selling goods and services, to selling goods, services, and value-added services. Customer needs have become more complex, which makes customers want to do business with sales organizations that can help them meet those needs. Sales executives feel the critical skill salespeople need is the ability to develop customer relationships over time. This is usually referred to as consultative selling. **Consultative selling** is the process of helping the customer achieve strategic short- and long-term goals through the use of the seller's good and/or service. The term *consultative selling* is not a new one, but sales managers are redefining it to reflect the values of today's more sophisticated customers and sales forces.

Three Roles of Consultative Selling

The roles of a salesperson center around what customers want from him or her. Typically customers want three things. First, they want salespeople who are committed to helping them succeed. To ensure the success of a long-term relationship, salespeople must help their customers achieve short- and long-term objectives. Next, they want salespeople who will stay involved with them over time—even if there is not an immediate sales opportunity. Finally, customers want the salesperson always to focus on their needs when developing recommendations and suggesting products to the buyer. These three needs of the customer require the salesperson to take on the roles of team leader, business consultant, and long-term ally.

The Team Leader Role

For many of today's sales organizations, salespeople do not work alone—they are not "Lone Rangers." They work on multifunctional teams just as many organizations have set up buying teams. **Buying teams** are composed of multifunctional specialists who ensure that their organizations accurately convey their complex needs to the seller and thoroughly assess the accuracy of the supplier's recommendations.

In the role of **team leader** the salesperson coordinates all of the information, resources, and activities needed to support customers before, during, and after the sale. The team leader works to bring together all of the organization's resources for the customer. As illustrated in Exhibit 2.2, the salesperson serves as the primary contact between the buyer's and seller's organizations and makes the customer aware of the network of resources that stand behind the salesperson.

The salesperson knows who within the company can best create a unique solution for a customer. This often requires the salesperson to form a team. **Team selling** brings together the appropriate people and resources needed to make the sales call. The sales call may take place over the phone, in person, and/or by video teleconference. The customer can be quickly provided with a wide range of information, advice, ideas, and even decisions.

As digital video and audio technology make video calling widely available, you will see more of **E-sales calls** (see Exhibit 2.11). The salesperson, or team, will be positioned in front of the computer interacting with the buyer or buying team. The

Compassion is difficult to give away because it keeps coming back.

EXHIBIT 2.11

E-sales calls allow a supplier's sales team to make a presentation to any buyer group at locations around the world.

salesperson will need the competencies of making both the face-to-face, or one-on-one sales call, plus the group and telephone presentation.

Top-to-Top. Eastman Chemical frequently uses sales teams, including top executives. Eastman's CEO, Ernie Deavenport, is assigned several of the company's top customers, as is its executive vice-president, Wiley Bourne, and Worldwide Sales Division President George Trabue. They call on accounts—in conjunction with the local sales rep—several times a year. The seller's top executive talking with the buyer's top executive, **top-to-top,** has proven to be very beneficial to both organizations. When needed, an engineer, a chemist, an accountant, or other specialist is present to work with his or her customer's counterparts. The salesperson is responsible for following up on any commitments made during the sales call.

The Business Consultant Role

As a **business consultant,** the salesperson gives advice and service. The salesperson uses internal and external resources to gain an understanding of the customer's business and marketplace.

Customers are under great pressure to grow their sales and profits. Their time is valuable. Often prospective customers do not have time to educate salespeople about their organization. Today they expect salespeople to arrive at the very first meeting prepared to discuss some of the deeper issues surrounding the customer's organization and its needs. Because customers have many suppliers wanting to sell to them, they are impatient with salespeople who are unable to quickly demonstrate that they are knowledgeable business professionals and not simply persuasive "peddlers."

This is one of the greatest challenges salespeople face today. To add value for their customers, salespeople need to know a significant amount about the customer's business at the start of every sales interaction. They have to be prepared when they first walk in the prospective customer's door.

Would you hand a stranger your wallet or purse and let him or her go through your personal items? Would you show a stranger your bank statement? Would you tell the stranger all about your personal finances? Would you let a stranger come into your home or apartment and go through everything? That is what many salespeople face when just starting to sell a customer. They often must collect confidential information and data before being able to make purchase recommendations. Several of the things that help salespeople become business consultants are

1. Demonstrating and refining their understanding of the customer's big picture.
2. Creating an atmosphere of trust, integrity, reliability, and professionalism that fosters the exchange of information and ideas.
3. Continually strengthening their business knowledge.
4. Following the Golden Rule.

Today's salespeople need to be experts on a wide range of topics in order to be considered a business consultant by their customers. This requires information.

The Long-Term Ally Role

In the role of **long-term ally,** the salesperson acts as a helper in meeting the customer's needs. The salesperson's goal is to create a "win–win" situation. As the customer's sales and profits grow, so do the salesperson's. Thus, the salesperson presents goods and services honestly and turns down business that is not in the customer's long-term interest. The salesperson "goes to bat" for customers with the seller's employer whenever necessary and helps customers carry out fact-finding missions within the customer's company.

The ability of a salesperson to fulfill the role of long-term ally is a pivotal factor in determining whether a sales interaction is just a *transaction* or the beginning of a relationship. This is a dramatic change from the past, when many salespeople considered their job completed after closing the sale.

It seems to be human nature for a salesperson's interest in the customer to decline after the sale. This difference between the salesperson's pre- and postsale concern for the customer is referred to as the **relationship gap.** Yet the customer's interest in using the product increases rapidly after the purchase. This is one of the reasons service after the sale is so important to the long-term relationship.

Salespeople who fulfill the role of long-term ally work to eliminate the relationship gap by ensuring that the customer is receiving the level of support and service that meets expectations now and throughout the duration of the customer relationship process.

E-SELLING: TECHNOLOGY AND INFORMATION BUILD RELATIONSHIPS

In this chapter you were introduced to the importance that knowledge plays in helping the salesperson fulfill the role of business consultant and how customers expect salespeople to be more knowledgeable than ever before. This creates a tremendous challenge for the salesperson in that the information and knowledge needed to properly sell and service perhaps several hundred customers within the sales territory have expanded well beyond what any individual could possibly know. Salespeople need more information about goods, services, customers, and competitors than ever before.

Video conferencing is excellent for presentations and training.

Often the need to gather and organize information lengthens the sales process. Also, the growing emphasis on team selling and group buying makes it critical to share information quickly and accurately among a wide variety of people who influence the customer's buying decision.

The good news is that technology has exploded the boundaries of today's knowledge frontiers. Salespeople have access to almost any conceivable piece of information or data. Technology is making it possible to improve a person's sales and service performance. (See Exhibit 2.12.) Desktop and laptop computers, video-cassette recorders, CD-ROM videodiscs, automatic dialers, electronic mail, fax machines, and teleconferencing are quickly becoming popular sales tools. The salesperson has truly gone high tech. Not only is sales and inventory information transferred much faster, but also specific computerized decision support systems have been created for sales managers and sales representatives.

The goal is to help salespeople increase the speed with which they can find and qualify leads, gather information prior to a customer presentation, reduce their paperwork, report new sales to the company, and service customers after the sale. Computer technology has provided the answer.

Technology is expensive. Hardware, software, and training take a large investment. Yet companies believe it is worth the cost because of decreased travel and paperwork, more productive sales calls, and better customer service. Chapter 5 has further discussions on the technology salespeople use to build relationships.

WHAT'S A SALESPERSON WORTH?

You have learned the importance of salespeople in selling and servicing customers for their organizations. However, are salespeople worth their cost? Why not rely on such marketing tactics as advertising, direct mail, and telephone salespeople to sell customers and create new ones? Why not have telephone service advisors take care of problems?

ETHICAL DILEMMA

Who Is Correct?

One of the great things about working for your company is the material provided for you in developing your sales presentations. This allows you to spend time selling rather than doing your own research on the economy, industry, and competitive products. However, you do not totally rely on this information. You subscribe to eight industry publications and routinely attend educational conferences to stay abreast of the current technology.

Before attending next week's sales meeting, all salespeople have been asked to develop a sales presentation on a new high-tech medical product using the information supplied by the company. Each of the five salespeople will be asked to role-play their presentation. Then the group will take the best ideas and develop a presentation everyone can use companywide. In developing your presentation, you notice that the data and the methods used to collect it appear to be unreliable according to a past article in one of your magazines. The results may mislead your customers. Your boss tells you the company information is correct and to use it.

What do you do? In selecting your action, consider the discussion of ethical behavior in Chapter 3.

1. Use the information provided by your company to do the best presentation possible—it isn't that big of a deal to mislead customers. After all, every other salesperson will be using the same information.
2. Use the information provided by your company during the "role play" presentation but substitute what you believe to be the more accurate information when you are with your customers. You don't mind what the other salespeople use with their customers—you just want to be sure that your customers have the best information possible.
3. Talk to your boss and explain how helpful the company-supplied materials are to the salespeople. Show him or her your research and offer to help update the company's information. Tell your boss that you are uncomfortable participating in the presentations until accurate data is provided.

Get weary in your work, not weary of your work.

So what is a salesperson worth? Of course, it depends. It depends on what the salesperson costs, how much she sells, and the profit margin on the products sold. Chapter 15 discusses this fully. For now, let's look at what a salesperson can do for an organization.

David Greene sells paper—cash register rolls and other total-commodity papers—for AT&T Global Information Solutions (AT&TGIS), formerly NCR Corporation. The industry profit margins are small for that type of product, perhaps 5 to 10 percent. Although the production of paper is a high fixed-cost endeavor, sales swing widely due to cyclical usage, while output is remarkably flat (except when a major plant starts up or shuts down). So it's hard to estimate a gross profit margin. Let's err on the conservative side and say that the profit on each additional dollar of sales revenue is about 7.5 cents.

Greene increased the sales in his district from $300,000 to $1.5 million. In doing so, he added an incremental $1.2 million in business to AT&TGIS's revenues. Using the conservative estimate of 7.5 percent profit margin on incremental sales, those sales are worth $90,000 per year to the firm in pure profit—that is, after accounting for the cost of David Greene himself!

Of course, this estimate completely ignores the fact that customers tend to become less price-sensitive when they become accustomed to dealing with a salesperson and receiving great service. While this doesn't mean that Greene can gouge his customers, he may be able to maintain a reasonable price when a particular competitor lowballs prices in his market in an effort to gain market share. Needless to say, that improves the margin on Greene's total basket of business and may push it above the 7.5 percent level we have estimated for the entire country. With total sales of $1.5 million, an increase of a single percentage point in profitability is worth $15,000—nothing to sneeze at.[6]

As you learn more about sales you will find salespeople make a valuable contribution to the success of their employer. Selling closes the deals. It generates the revenue to keep the organization in business.

THE KEY TO SUCCESS

Companies cannot survive today by simply doing a good job. They must do an excellent job if they are to succeed in the increasingly competitive global marketplace. Consumer and business buyers face an abundance of suppliers seeking to satisfy their every need. The key to profitable company performance is knowing and satisfying target customers with competitively superior products and service. Marketing is the company function that defines not only customer targets but also the best way to satisfy their needs and wants competitively and profitably.

Marketing's main customer contacts are salespeople. Because salespeople know how to produce sales, profits, and customer satisfaction, they are critical to being successful in today's fierce competitive battles in the marketplace.

Exhibit 2.13 helps to summarize this chapter. The **four Ps of marketing** (product, price, place, and promotion) aid the salesperson's selling efforts. The salesperson's organization provides the product to sell, at a price and place to be delivered or for pickup. Often a company's promotions inform the buyers about the product. The salesperson personally contacts the buyer to analyze needs, present product benefits, and gain commitment or close the sale, and to provide service to ensure customer satisfaction. Together marketing and personal selling provide the needed service for customers to build long-term relationships.

EXHIBIT 2.13

Marketing and personal selling provide service to customers.

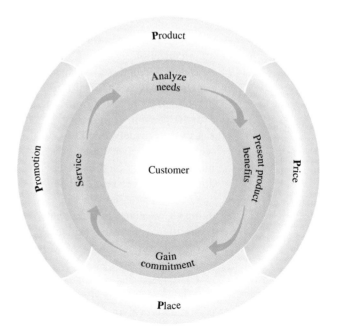

SUMMARY OF MAJOR SELLING ISSUES

Most people today associate marketing with selling. Yet, the act of selling is only one part of the overall marketing activities of the firm. The task of providing products that satisfy consumers' wants forms the basis for our current marketing systems. Marketing is an exchange process between buyers and sellers, the purpose of which is to satisfy the buyer's needs and wants through the purchase of the seller's products.

This marketing concept evolved over the years, developing as American business matured. Initially, production-oriented American business assumed that people would buy whatever was efficiently produced. This concept gradually evolved into a sales-oriented approach in which firms generally depended on effective sales approaches to stimulate consumer demand for a product. Today's marketing-oriented philosophy focuses on a firm's desire to increase sales while anticipating and satisfying consumer needs. Progressive businesses today are much more consumer oriented than firms have been in the past.

The marketing mix consists of four variables—product, price, distribution (or place), and promotion. The product variable encompasses its physical attributes. Pricing involves the marketing manager, who establishes each product's price as well as overall pricing policies. Getting that product to the right place at the right time is the distribution variable. The promotion variable increases demand by communicating information to potential customers via personal selling, advertising, publicity, and sales promotion.

Firms must carefully consider the role of the sales force in their promotional program or promotional aspect of the marketing mix. A firm has to decide if a sales force is a viable direct-marketing tool; and if so, which types of selling activities optimally promote its products. The different levels of relationship marketing (transaction selling, relationship selling, and partnering) allow salespeople to create customer loyalty. In this manner, they can keep today's customers while generating new customers for tomorrow.

The new consultative selling requires the salesperson to take on the roles of a team leader, business consultant, and long-term ally. By performing these three roles the salesperson can reduce the relationship gap so the customer is satisfied with doing business with the seller.

MEETING A SALES CHALLENGE

You might suggest to Larry that he develop a prospect list of organizations that could purchase his products. By telephone and in person he could contact organizations such as churches, high schools, little league baseball teams, sororities, and fraternities.

During the day Larry could make sales calls. Nights and weekends he could design, produce, bill and ship orders. He must make sure his prices are competitive.

As soon as possible, Larry could hire one university student to contact organizations at Texas A&M University. The student could be paid on a straight commission or a small hourly salary and commission. As sales and profits increased he could advertise in the Yellow Pages. Larry could also start to sponsor several charity events.

Larry could hire another salesperson to contact his customers and prospect for new customers. He might continue to telephone customers. With salespeople, Larry could reduce the hours he works and concentrate on the production side of the business. Can you see how the phrase "Nothing happens until someone sells something" applies to this situation?

SALES APPLICATION QUESTIONS

1. Discuss the role of personal selling as it relates to a firm's marketing effort.
2. Explain the difference between the production, sales, and marketing stages in the evolution of marketing management.
3. Discuss the four elements of a firm's marketing mix. Give several examples of how companies today have developed a marketing mix to compete in their industry.
4. Assume that the XYZ company has hired you. One of the first things you are asked is what you believe is the relationship between the sales quota your manager gives you and sales objectives expected of the entire sales force. What would you say?
5. What type of coordination is needed between the firm's sales force and its advertising department to have a coordinated selling effort?

FURTHER EXPLORING THE SALES WORLD

Visit a local company and determine the marketing mix it uses in selling its products or services. Determine what the company expects of its salespeople and how the company helps them sell its goods and services.

SELLING EXPERIENTIAL EXERCISE

What Should Your Children's College Majors Be?

You are the parent of 10 children and have just used your inheritance to acquire a medium-size pharmaceutical company. Last year's sales were down 18 percent from the previous year. In fact, the past three years have been real losers. You want to clean house of current managers over the next 10 years and bring your children into the business. Being a loving parent, you agree to send your children to college to educate each of them in one functional specialty. The 10 children are actually five sets of twins exactly one year apart. The first set begins college this fall, followed by the remaining sets during the next four years. The big decision is which specialty each child should study. You want to have the most important functions taken over by your children as soon as possible, so you will ask the older children to study the most important areas.

Your task right now is to rank the functions to which your children will be assigned in order of priority and develop reasons for your ranking. Write this list on a separate sheet of paper. These are the functions:

_____ Distribution
_____ Manufacturing
_____ Market research
_____ New product development
_____ Human resources
_____ Product promotion
_____ Quality assurance
_____ Sales
_____ Legal and governmental affairs
_____ Controller

Analyze your reasons for how functional priority relates to the company's environmental/strategic needs. Now rank the functions as part of a small group. Discuss the problem until group members agree on a single ranking. How does the group's reasoning and ranking differ from your original thinking?[7]

CHAPTER 2

Relationship Marketing: Where Professional Selling Fits

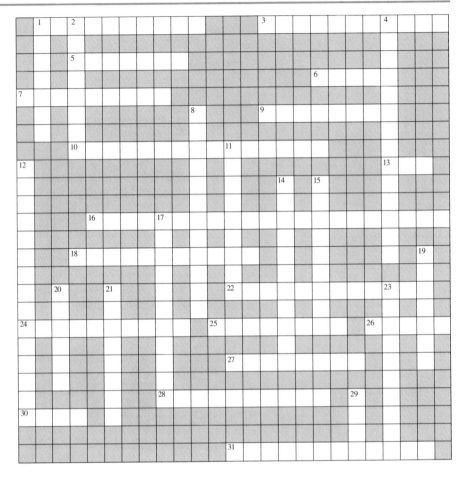

Across

1. When the seller works continually to improve the customer's operations, sales, and profits.

3. The nonpersonal communication of information paid for by an identified sponsor, for example, an individual or organization.

5. The product which is an action or activity done for others for a fee.

6. The value or worth of a product.

7. The nonpersonal communication of information that is not paid for by an individual or organization.

9. The top executives from the seller's company meet with the customer's or prospect's top executives.

10. The difference between the buyer and the seller's postsale level of concern for each other.

13. The four main elements used by a marketing manager to market goods and services. These elements are product, price, distribution or place, and promotion. This is known as the marketing ____.

16. A principle in which a few key or large accounts bring in 80 percent of profitable sales although they represent only 20 percent of total accounts.

18. A trade of values between two parties.

22. The channel structure used to transfer products from an organization to its customers.

24. A sales call in which the seller and the customer interact using an electrical device, such as a computer.

25. The act of obtaining a desired product from someone by offering something in return.

26. Value _____ benefits are not included in the purchase price of the individual good or service.

27. _____ products are produced for and purchased by, households or end consumers for their personal use.

28. An organization that provides goods and services to households and firms, and that redistributes income and wealth.

30. A physical object for sale.

31. A salesperson who helps customers reach long-term sales goals.

Down

1. One of the four main elements of the marketing mix. It is a bundle of tangible and intangible attributes, including packaging, color, and brand, plus the services and even the reputation of the seller.

2. Resellers purchase products and sell to organizations and/or individuals.

4. Activities and materials used to create sales of goods and services.

8. The process of helping the customers achieve strategic short- and long-term goals through the use of the seller's good or service is known as _____ selling.

11. A decision-making unit buying for their personal use.

12. Personal communication of information to unselfishly persuade a prospective customer to buy something—a good, service, idea, or something else—that satisfies that individual's needs.

14. Composed of multifunctional specialists who ensure that their organizations accurately convey their complex needs to the seller and thoroughly assess the accuracy of supplier's recommendations.

15. The process of planning and executing the conception, pricing, promotion, and distribution of goods, services, and ideas to create exchanges that satisfy individual and organizational objectives.

17. Brings together the appropriate people and resources needed to make the sales call.

19. The marketing _____ is a philosophy of business maintaining economic and social reason for a firm's existence and that the firm should therefore direct its activities toward fulfilling those needs and wants, yielding, at the same time, long-term profitability.

20. In team selling, the team _____ coordinates all of the information, resources, and activities needed to support the customers before, during, and after the sale.

21. A _____ consultant gives advice and service.

23. _____ products are sold primarily for use in producing other products.

29. An organization that produces goods and services.

CASE 2-1

Reynolds & Reynolds

TEAM SELLING

In the past, warranty work accounted for as much as 70 percent of an auto dealership's service load.[8] That number is steadily dropping to around 30 percent. Because of this large decline, dealerships must now proactively target service retention and loyalty among new car buyers. That's where the sales team of Reynolds & Reynolds comes in.

Reynolds helps dealerships become more effective at retaining new car buyers as service customers and building loyalty among the customers to keep them coming back. They help dealers to better understand their customer base, figure out who their most profitable customers are, and then target them with focused incentives to get the customers back into the dealerships when service is needed.

The Opportunity

Bob Sherman, a Minneapolis-area sales associate with Reynolds, and his regional sales manager, Tim O'Neill, along with Chuck Wiltgen, marketing specialist, met with representatives from Ben Frothingham's American Ford Dealership. American Ford was in need of a new retention plan to boost service sales, and Reynolds provided them with one. The group effectively presented their marketing strategies and tied up the deal successfully.

Sherman established the contact with American Ford's service department and discussed their options. His next call was more promising and he talked with them more about a new initiative from Ford called "Quality Care Maintenance." They gave him negative feedback, so he suggested that they meet with his boss, Tim O'Neill. By the close of the third meeting, American Ford agreed to have reports run on their customer retention rate and their database system.

Precall Planning

Before the call, Sherman, O'Neill, and Wiltgen discussed details of the opportunity, roles each would play, and any possible concerns that they anticipated. They decided that Sherman would discuss the reports with the customer, and Chuck would be the implementation guy. Tim would be there for backup. Because they had been working together so long, they basically already knew how to present their information.

Stage 1: Report

After two reports were run to determine just who the dealership's customer base was, the three met with Carol Bemis, the dealership's new parts and service director, and Brad Greenberg, service manager. Sherman opened the meeting by recapping the set of mutual expectations and handing out copies of the reports. Sherman had calculated that in the previous year, the dealership lost $144,000 from customers who did not return for service. Sherman calls this the "lost opportunity" for that year. He explained that if American Ford had done business with every one of its new car customers from the past five years, the service department would have brought in an additional $1.3 million. O'Neill and Wiltgen confirmed these figures, and Tim recommended that the company run these reports every 90 days to use as a diagnostic tool.

Stage 2: Analysis

Sherman then shared the database information with Bemis and Greenberg. He discussed with them the number of customers they have on the database that were considered active, meaning that they had been in for service in the previous six months. The report also divided the customers into where they come from, broken down into area codes and the top nine nearby ZIP codes.

They discussed problems they were having with their marketing strategies, and they all came to the conclusion that the dealership needed service reminders. In response to specific questions, the Reynolds sales team explained that (1) with more than 100 different coupons, mailers could be easily customized to suit changing needs; (2) mailings to customers could be sorted by area code, American Ford service advisor, or ZIP code; (3) the American Ford logo could be placed on the new mailers; and (4) copies of all the coupons available for use could be made available for Bemis and Greenberg to review.

Stage 3: Program

The Reynolds team then helped them to figure out the best way to implement a "Preferred Customer Card" program. Sherman explained that in other dealerships with the program, they generally have the service advisors ask the customers up front if they have the card. If they do, the advisor knows that the customer is already in the database and does not need to be added to the list. Reynolds calls this "data hygiene," meaning they are helping companies cleanse their databases so that their service reminder program really hits the mark.

Stage 4: Returns

The team then presented Bemis and Greenberg with Reynolds's "Direct Drive" program. This program allows the dealership to customize its mailings for the customers who are active and those who are inactive. It also sorts customers by vehicle so that each customer will receive a mailing that is specifically designed for his or her needs.

This suggestion rolled the conversation over to the topic of cost. Sherman went over the monthly fees for the Direct Drive program and the costs per mailer and phone call for service reminders. Greenberg and Bemis discovered that they were spending about the same amount on the poor results they were getting from their current vendor. Sherman then calculated that if the dealership did implement the program, they could gain $30,750 of additional business in a single month with only a 5 percent response rate.

Stage 5: Close

After Greenberg looked over the figures, he showed genuine enthusiasm for what Reynolds could do for American Ford. O'Neill added that his company's programs cover all angles of the customer base—the actives, inactives, and new customers. Bemis and Greenberg agreed to move forward with the service reminder program for the entire database of active customers. They also decided to go with the Direct Drive program to target their inactive customers. This was more progress than the Reynolds team had expected from the account. The meeting closed with Greenberg and Wiltgen hammering out the fine print of the agreement, while O'Neill, Sherman, and Bemis set up a timetable for the next step in the process.

Questions

1. How is the effectiveness of team selling demonstrated by the Reynolds team, and what are some of the disadvantages to this method in this particular case?
2. How did the Reynolds team successfully execute the following critical roles in sales: client access, client education/persuasion, and fulfillment?

Ethics First . . . Then Customer Relationships

LEARNING OBJECTIVES

This chapter is one of the most important in this book. Social, ethical, and legal issues for sales personnel are often personal and technical in nature, yet they are essential for understanding how to be an outstanding professional. After studying this chapter, you should be able to

- Describe management's social responsibilities.

- Explain what influences ethical behavior.

- Define management's ethical responsibilities.

- Discuss ethical dealings among salespeople, employers, and customers.

- Describe the international side of ethics.

- Explain what is involved in managing sales ethics.

- Write a short essay on the components of the Business Tree of Life and how the Tree relates to sales ethics.

As the sales manager of a printing company, you are about to invest in a car leasing program that involves 18 company cars for your sales staff. Together with your comptroller, you have examined several leasing programs. You have narrowed down your selection to two leasing companies that offer very similar terms. You are meeting with the president of Equilease, a company with which you have never done business before. You know from your own prospect files that one of your sales representatives has tried to call on the purchasing manager of Equilease before to get some of their printing business; however, he could not sell the account.

As you meet with the president for lunch, you gently steer the conversation in the direction of printing services. Since he is very knowledgeable about printing services and prices, you ask him about ballpark prices charged by his existing supplier. You believe you could provide his company with higher-quality service at a better price.

Since the president of Equilease is in a good mood, you think about setting up a win–win situation. You are considering making this offer: Let's make this a double win. I'll give you 100 percent of our leasing business if you'll consider giving us 50 percent of your printing business. Fair enough?

Is there an ethical conflict in this situation? Would it be ethical to propose such a deal?

Sales personnel constantly are involved with social, ethical, and legal issues. Yet if you think about it, everyone is—including you. If you found a bag full of $100 bills lying on the side of the road, would you keep it? Would you say you were sick to get extra time off work? Would you use the company car to run a personal errand? Have you ever broken the speed limit? Have you ever gone home with one of your employer's pens in your purse or jacket pocket?

These sorts of questions may be difficult for the average person to answer. Some people will respond with an unequivocal yes or no. Others may mull it over awhile. Still others may feel compelled to say "it depends" and qualify their response with a "yes, but . . ." or a "no, but . . ." Maybe that was what you did with the Sales Challenge feature.

Newspapers, radio, and television frequently have news stories of individuals and organizations involved in both good and bad practices. This chapter addresses many of the important social, ethical, and legal (SEL) issues in selling. It begins by discussing management's social responsibilities. Then it examines ethical behavior followed by the ethical issues involved in dealing with salespeople, employers, and consumers. The chapter ends by presenting ways an organization can help its sales personnel follow ethical selling practices.

SOCIAL, ETHICAL, AND LEGAL INFLUENCES

An organization's environment is a major influence on how the firm sells its products. As pictured in Exhibit 3.1, social, ethical, and legal (SEL) influences and considerations surround the firm's product, price, place, and promotion.

Due to the environmental turmoil in the world of commerce, this chapter is arguably the most important in the entire book. Let's begin by asking, "Does an organization have any responsibilities to society?"

EXHIBIT 3.1

Social, ethical, and legal (SEL) influences have a powerful influence on an organization's marketing program!

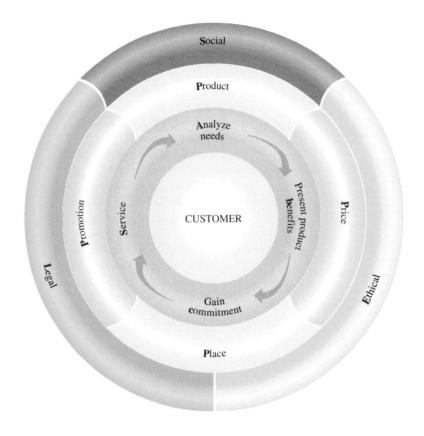

MANAGEMENT'S SOCIAL RESPONSIBILITIES

In one sense, the concept of corporate social responsibility is easy to understand; it means distinguishing right from wrong and doing right. It means being a good corporate citizen. The formal definition of **social responsibility** is management's obligation to make choices and take actions that contribute to the welfare and interests of society as well as to those of the organization.

As straightforward as this definition seems, social responsibility can be a difficult concept to grasp because different people have different opinions as to which actions improve society's welfare. To make matters worse, social responsibility covers a range of issues, many of which have ambiguous boundaries between right and wrong.

Organizational Stakeholders

One reason for the difficulty in understanding social responsibility is that managers must confront the question, "responsibility to whom?" The organization's environment consists of several sectors both inside and outside the organization. From a social responsibility perspective, enlightened organizations view the internal and external environment as a variety of stakeholders.

A **stakeholder** is any group within or outside the organization that has a stake in the organization's performance. Each stakeholder has a different interest in the organization.

Exhibit 3.2 illustrates eight important stakeholders. These are represented by the acronym **CCC GOMES.**[1] The first *C* refers to customers and the last *S* refers to suppliers. Owners', creditors', and suppliers' interests are served by managerial

EXHIBIT 3.2

Major stakeholders in the organization's performance: CCC GOMES.

efficiency—that is, the use of resources to achieve profits. Managers and salespeople expect work satisfaction, pay, and good supervision. Customers are concerned with decisions about the quality and availability of goods and services.

Other important stakeholders include the government and the community. Most corporations exist under the proper charter and licenses and operate within the limits of laws and regulations imposed by the government, including safety laws and environmental protection requirements. The community includes local government, the natural and physical environments, and the quality of life provided for residents. Socially responsible organizations pay attention to all stakeholders affected by their actions.

An Organization's Main Responsibilities

Once a company is aware of its stakeholders, what are its main responsibilities to them? Companies have four types of responsibility: (1) economic, (2) legal, (3) ethical, and (4) discretionary. See Exhibit 3.3.

Economic Responsibilities

The business institution is, above all, the basic economic unit of society. Its responsibility is to produce the goods and services that society wants and to maximize profits for its owners and shareholders.

Quite often, corporations are said to operate solely to maximize profits. Certainly, profits are important to a firm, just as a grade point average is important to a student. Profit provides the capital to stay in business, to expand, and to compensate for the risks of conducting business. Businesses have a responsibility to make a profit to serve society. Imagine what would happen to our society if large corporations (e.g., AT&T, General Motors) did not make a profit and went out of business. Thousands of people and the U.S. economy would be affected. This has happened in the last few years!

Legal Responsibilities

All modern societies lay down ground rules, laws, and regulations that organizations are expected to follow. Legal responsibility defines what society deems as important with respect to appropriate corporate behavior. Organizations are expected to fulfill their economic goals within the legal framework. Legal requirements are imposed by local town councils, state legislators, and federal regulatory agencies.

EXHIBIT 3.3

An organization's main
responsibilities.

Ethical Responsibilities

Ethical responsibility includes behaviors that are not necessarily codified into law
and may not serve the corporation's direct economic interests. To be ethical, organizational decision makers should act with equity, fairness, and impartiality; respect
the rights of individuals; and provide different treatment of individuals only when
relevant to the organization's goals and tasks. Unethical behavior occurs when
decisions enable an individual or company to gain at the expense of society.

Discretionary Responsibilities

Discretionary responsibility is purely voluntary and guided by a company's desire
to make social contributions not mandated by economics, law, or ethics. Discretionary activities include generous philanthropic contributions that offer no monetary return to the company and are not expected.

Discretionary responsibility is the highest criterion of social responsibility, because it goes beyond societal expectations to contribute to the community's welfare.
For example, Baxter International, a manufacturer and marketer of medical products, is using its environmental knowledge to help its customers set up pollution-
reduction and recycling programs. Baxter has even set up an alliance with Waste
Management to better assist customers in handling environmental problems. Baxter
also has studied its own products and packing to find ways to reduce waste. By
reducing the waste created by its products, Baxter reduces the environmental
problems of its customers.[2]

**How to
Demonstrate
Social
Responsibility**

A corporation can demonstrate social responsibility in numerous ways, including these:

1. Taking corrective action before it is required.
2. Working with affected constituents to resolve mutual problems.
3. Working to establish industrywide standards and self-regulation.
4. Publicly admitting mistakes.
5. Getting involved in appropriate social programs.

6. Helping correct environmental problems.
7. Monitoring the changing social environment.
8. Establishing and enforcing a corporate code of conduct.
9. Taking needed public stands on social issues.
10. Striving to make profits on an ongoing basis.

Economic, legal, ethical, and discretionary responsibilities to stakeholders are important concerns organizations must face. Society is demanding more responsible action of organizations, particularly regarding their ethical conduct.

WHAT INFLUENCES ETHICAL BEHAVIOR?

Organizations are composed of individuals. These individuals' morals and ethical values help shape those of the organization. Critical to making decisions in an ethical manner is the individual integrity of the organization's managers, especially those in top management positions. Thus, two major influences on the ethical behavior of sales personnel are employees and the organization itself.

The Individual's Role

All of us, employees and managers alike, bring certain beliefs about the world to a job. These beliefs direct our daily decisions. This "big picture" view of life that directs our behavior is based upon our core belief system. It often is referred to as a person's "worldview."

Personality, religious background, family upbringing, personal experiences, and the situation faced are examples of factors shaping our core belief system. This is why you hear, "no two people are alike." Each one views the world differently than someone else. Your parents probably view many things differently than you do, for example.

Because people have different beliefs about the world around them, referred to as a person's **worldview,** they tend to have different views on ethics and morality.[3] From an early age, you begin a journey down a road to higher moral development. Research has shown that individuals grow or progress in their ability to understand the "truth" or the ability to know what is right or wrong. People's **morals** are their adherence to right or wrong behavior and right or wrong thinking. As one thinks, one does! That includes you and me.

As one thinks, one does!

Over time moral development gradually matures in many people. With moral maturity many individuals—but not all—adhere to more truthful or stringent moral principles. Often a person's current moral development can be placed into one of the levels shown in Exhibit 3.4.

- **Level One: Preconventional.** At the **preconventional moral development level,** an individual acts in his or her own best interest and thus follows rules to avoid punishment or receive rewards. This individual would break moral and legal laws. In making an ethical or moral decision, a salesperson at this level might ask, "What can I get away with?"
- **Level Two: Conventional.** At the **conventional moral development level,** an individual conforms to the expectations of others, such as family, friends, employer, boss, society and upholds moral and legal laws. A salesperson at this level might ask, "What am I legally required to do?" when making an ethical or moral decision.
- **Level Three: Principled.** At the **principled moral development level,** an individual lives by an internal set of morals, values, and ethics regardless of punishments or majority opinion. The individual would disobey orders, laws,

EXHIBIT 3.4

What is your level of moral development?

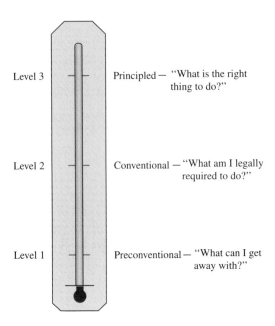

Level 3 — Principled — "What is the right thing to do?"

Level 2 — Conventional — "What am I legally required to do?"

Level 1 — Preconventional — "What can I get away with?"

and consequences to follow what he or she believes is right. When making an ethical or moral decision a salesperson at this level might ask, "What is the right thing to do?"

The majority of sales personnel, as well as people in general, operate at the conventional level. However, a few individuals are at level one, and it is estimated that less than 20 percent of individuals reach level three.

As shown in Exhibit 3.5, the majority (60 to 80 percent) of sales personnel, as well as people in general, behaves at the conventional level—level 2. However, approximately 10 to 20 percent of the people behave at each of the other two levels—levels 1 and 3. Within each level, there is a lower and higher level of moral development behavior. Some people at level 2, for example, have behavior closer to level 1 people or level 3 people.

The Organization's Role

If the vast majority of people in our society are at the preconventional or conventional levels, it seems that most employees in an organization would feel they must "go along to get along," in other words, they acquiesce to questionable ethical standards to keep their jobs. At most, they only follow formal policies and procedures.

How will sales personnel handle ethical dilemmas? What if there are no policies and procedures pertaining to some sales practices and a superior directs the salesperson to do something that appears unethical? It is no wonder that radio, television, and newspaper reports frequently feature unethical business practices. Following the hear no evil, see no evil, speak no evil philosophy can create a preconventional or conventional organizational climate.

ARE THERE ANY ETHICAL GUIDELINES?

The development of sales personnel's moral character can be crucial to a company. The Golden Rule of Selling requires people whose personal character is at level 3, who have caring attitudes and recognize the rights of others, and who act based on personal, independently defined universal principles of justice and values.

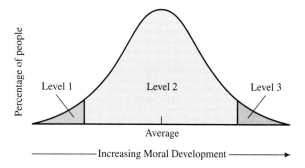

EXHIBIT 3.5

People's levels of moral development differ, as does the number of people at each level of moral development. Where are you on your moral development journey?

What Does the Research Say?

The question is, "What should an individual base her or his values upon?" In a February 12, 2002, national poll, American adults said by a 3-to-1 margin that truth is always relative to a person's situation. People are most likely to make their moral and ethical decisions on the basis of whatever feels right or comfortable in a situation.[4]

What Does One Do?

Do you face different situations regularly? If the situation is always changing how do you make a decision over an ethical dilemma? For example, if you found $125,000 in cash that had fallen out of the armored truck of a local bank, would you return it to the bank? But if you found someone's wallet in a parking lot, would you feel compelled to turn it in to a lost-and-found or the police? Why would you decide to keep the $125,000, when you would most likely be willing to turn in the wallet without taking any money from it? Out of class, is it all right to copy someone's homework assignment even when the course syllabus states you have to do your own work? What keeps you from copying on an exam when your professor is out of the room? With your boss's approval, is it all right to offer a customer a $10,000 trip if the customer purchases a $3 million order, even though it is against company policy? Why would you not even question doing so if a $20 lunch was associated with the purchase?

Is Your Conscience Reliable?

Almost every day you have to decide what is the correct thing to do in situations. We all have an internal ultimate moral standard we use to measure good and evil, right and wrong. Some people call that their "conscience." Most of us know we should return the $125,000 or wallet, not copy, or not give someone a bribe. But what would we actually do in these situations?

A person in these situations may feel there is no way to get caught. You could ask the boss about the $10,000, and she might say, "That's what you have to do to get the business. Everyone is doing it." Does that make it all right? Or your college friends cheat. What does it hurt if everyone does it?

What if a person's value system is at the level 2 stage of moral development? This person makes decisions based upon the "situation" and what others, such as friends, family, boss, or competitors, say or do. A person may do the right thing in one situation after talking it over with her mother, yet take the wrong action in some other situation after talking with the boss. Usually people internally rationalize their actions by saying, for example, "I will only copy the homework this one time."

Many people are so used to doing things unethically that they think nothing of it. For example, a woman received a telephone call from her husband's sales manager complaining that he was taking home company office supplies. In a rage his

EXHIBIT 3.6

How do you know which fork in the road to take? You need a moral compass!

wife replied, "I don't believe that! Why does he do that? He knows I bring enough office supplies home from my job for the both of us."

Yogi Berra, the retired great baseball player, is famous for saying, "When you come to a fork in the road, take it."[5] As shown in Exhibit 3.6, when you come to a fork in the road, how do you know which road is the ethical one? Are your feelings about a situation an accurate measure of its rightness or wrongness? At times, I am not a good judge of what is best to do in a situation because the outcome involves something I want. Thus, I cannot always trust my conscience.

> *"When you come to a fork in the road, take it."*
> YOGI BERRA

Sources of Significant Influence

Think about this next question for a moment before reading on. What do you use to resolve ethical or moral dilemmas that occur in your life? In the margin, make a list of two or three factors that influence your choices when faced with an ethical or moral issue. What do you base your decisions upon? Do your decision factors include your friends, family, or things you see on television or in the movies? Do their thoughts on what is ethical sometimes change from day to day?

Barna Research is conducting an ongoing study of sources influencing American's ethical and moral decision-making processes. In early returns, Barna found the leading influencers in American society to be movies, television, the Internet, books, music, public policy and law, and family.[6]

Wouldn't it be nice to be able to base your decisions on something that never changes, something that can always be depended upon to provide the correct answer in any situation?

It is said that Satan greets people in hell by saying, "You'll find that there's no right or wrong here, just what works for you!"[7] Can business and salespeople make ethical choices based on whatever works for them—decisions unique to each situation? We have nothing to help us determine what is really right or wrong no matter what situation you, a businessperson, or a salesperson faces. Or do we?

Three Guidelines for Making Ethical Decisions

What do you need to make a decision about the right or wrong action to take in any situation? You need a never-changing fixed point of reference that is separate from you so you, or anyone else, cannot influence it.[8] The three guidelines to look for in a standard for making ethical decisions, then, are that it never changes, offers a fixed point of reference, and is separate. What does that mean?

A **fixed point of reference** refers to something that provides the correct action to take in any situation and never gets tailored to fit an occasion. This fixed point of reference must be separate from you; otherwise you will be changing the rules based upon your best interest in various situations. This is why your conscience is usually not your best guide to making moral and ethical decisions.

Let's say you are on one of the survivor television shows popular in the early 2000s. You and your teammate are blindfolded, placed in a boat, and set down in the ocean. You are provided a sextant, which is an instrument for measuring angular distances used in navigation to observe altitudes of celestial bodies, such as stars. Your survivor host tells you there is an island directly south of you at a certain latitude and longitude. And luckily, your teammate knows how to work the sextant.

How do you know exactly how to reach this island? You have to have a fixed point of reference that never changes and is 100 percent reliable to point you south to the island. Plus, it cannot connect with you, your teammate, or the boat. What fits these requirements for making the correct decision? The position of the stars fits these three requirements. Stars are fixed points of reference that never change and are separate from the two of you.

Using the sextant and stars allows you to sail directly to the island. The stars have the same fixed location today that they had 2000 years ago and that they will have in the future. The unchanging star locations offer a good example of a fixed point of reference.

How does this relate to a person making ethical, moral decisions in real life? As in the examples of the money, class, and bribe, people need a fixed point of reference separate from them that always provides the same correct ethical answer. What do most people of the world have that fits these three criteria for making the correct decisions in any situation?

Sextant

Will the Golden Rule Help?

Many people of the world make basic right and wrong decisions based upon their religious principles or faith. All the major religious faiths of the world provide their followers with written doctrine. When these doctrines are compared it is interesting to find out that similar faith-based principles appear in all religions despite the differences among the various religions. Exhibit 3.7 provides examples of how Christians, Jews, Hindus, Buddhists, and Confucius' followers view the Golden Rule.[9]

EXHIBIT 3.7

World religions embrace the Golden Rule.

Religious doctrines from around the globe have been reciting the same moral principle for centuries. The Hindu *Mahabharata* 5:1517 reads: "This is the sum of duty do naught unto others what you would not have them do to you." Confucius' *Analects* 12:2 states, "Do not do to others what you would not like yourself." The Buddhist *UdanaVarga* 5:1 mandates, "Hurt not others in ways that you yourself would find hurtful," "Rabbi Hillel famously told the cynic who demanded that the sage teach him all the Torah while he stood on one foot, 'That which is hateful to you do not do unto your neighbor. The rest is commentary.'"*The Christians' Jesus simplified it in the parable of the Great Assizes (Matthew 25:31–46): love of neighbor counts as love of God (Romans 13:8–10). Our love of God is demonstrated by our love of neighbor. Those who like rules need memorize only one. "Do to others as you would have them do to you" (Matthew 7:12). This is often referred to as the Golden Rule.

Because of the universality of such a simple concept, the Golden Rule can be applied to any person and is sure to be appreciated and respected no matter one's faith, or lack thereof, around the globe.

*Essential Judaism, p. 235.

EXHIBIT 3.8

What is your moral compass
in life?

The key to understanding the Golden Rule from the perspectives of the religions mentioned in Exhibit 3.7 is to realize that the aspect the Golden Rule they hold in common is that it does not involve reciprocity. Reciprocity says if you do for me, I will do for you. Many people think of this as a use of the Golden Rule. It is not!

As described in Chapter 1, the Golden Rule means doing for others without expecting something in return. When studying Exhibit 3.7 think in terms of unselfishly treating others as you would like to be treated.

In her textbook *Perspectives in Business Ethics,* Laura Hartman asks this question, "Could the Golden Rule serve as a universal, practical, helpful standard for the businessperson's conduct?"[10] What do you think?

President George W. Bush seems to agree with Professor Hartman's inference that the Golden Rule can guide business decisions. In his April 2002 remarks on faith-based initiatives in America, President Bush talked about people heeding a great call. "A call to love your neighbor just like you'd like to be loved yourself. It's a universal call, and it's a call that has been applicable throughout history. It's really needed right now."[11]

Do you think faith-based perspectives can help people make decisions in an ethical manner? Would you consider your faith a fixed point of reference that never changes and is separate from you? Could your faith's teachings be your moral compass in both your business and personal life? See Exhibit 3.8.

MANAGEMENT'S ETHICAL RESPONSIBILITIES

The concept of ethics, like that of social responsibility, is easy to understand. However, ethics is difficult to define in a precise way. In a general sense, **ethics** are the codes of moral principles and values that govern the behaviors of a person or a group with respect to what is right or wrong. Ethics set standards for what is good or bad in conduct and decision making.[12]

Many companies and their sales personnel get into trouble by making the mistaken assumption that if it's not illegal, it must be ethical. Ethics and moral values are a powerful force for good that can regulate behaviors both inside and outside the sales force. As principles of ethics and social responsibility are more widely recognized, companies can use codes of ethics and their corporate cultures to govern behavior, thereby eliminating the need for additional laws governing right and wrong.

What Is Ethical Behavior?

Sales personnel are frequently faced with ethical dilemmas. **Ethical behavior** refers to treating others fairly. Specifically, it refers to

- Being honest and truthful.
- Maintaining confidence and trust.
- Following the rules.
- Conducting yourself in the proper manner.
- Treating others fairly.
- Demonstrating loyalty to company and associates.
- Carrying your share of the work and responsibility with 100 percent effort.

The definition of ethical behavior, while reasonably specific and easy to understand, is difficult to apply in every situation. In real life, there are always conflicting viewpoints, fuzzy circumstances, and unclear positions. Though difficult, it is critically important to cut through the smoke screen that sometimes exists in such a situation and use 20/20 vision to make an ethical choice.

What Is an Ethical Dilemma?

Because ethical standards are not classified, disagreements and dilemmas about proper behavior often occur. An ethical dilemma arises in a situation when each alternative choice or behavior has some undesirable elements due to potentially negative ethical or personal consequences. Right or wrong cannot be clearly identified. Consider the following examples:

- Your boss says he cannot give you a raise this year because of budget constraints, but because of your good work this past year, he will look the other way if your expense accounts come in a little high.
- Stationed at the corporate headquarters in Chicago, you have 14 salespeople in countries all over the world. A rep living in another country calls to get approval to pay a government official $10,000 to OK an equipment purchase of $5 million. Such payoffs are part of common business practice in that part of the world.
- An industrial engineer, who is your good friend, tells you three of your competitors have submitted price bids on his company's proposed new construction project. He suggests a price you should submit and mentions certain construction specifications his boss is looking for on the job.

Managers must deal with these kinds of dilemmas and issues that fall squarely in the domain of ethics. Because of their importance, an Ethical Dilemma feature appears at the end of Chapters 1 through 17. In answering the questions at the end of these features, refer both to this chapter and to the chapter in which the feature appears.

Now let's turn to the three main ethical areas sales personnel face most frequently. These involve

1. Salespeople.
2. Employer.
3. Customers.

Although not all-inclusive, our discussion gives you a feel for some of the difficult situations sales personnel encounter.

ETHICS IN DEALING WITH SALESPEOPLE

Sales managers have both social and ethical responsibilities to sales personnel. Salespeople are a valuable resource; they are recruited, carefully trained, and given important responsibility. They represent a large financial investment and must be treated in a professional manner. Yet, occasionally a company may place managers and/or salespeople in positions that force them to choose among compromising their ethics, not doing what is required, or leaving the organization. The choice depends on the magnitude of the situation. At times, situations arise wherein it is difficult to say whether a sales practice is ethical or unethical. Many sales practices are in a gray area somewhere between completely ethical and completely unethical. Five ethical considerations sales managers face are the level of sales pressure to place on a salesperson, decisions concerning a salesperson's territory, whether or not to be honest with the salesperson, what to do with the ill salesperson, and employee rights.

Level of Sales Pressure

What is an acceptable level of pressure to place on salespeople? Should managers establish performance goals that they know a salesperson has only a 50–50 chance of attaining? Should the manager acknowledge that goals were set too high? If circumstances change in the salesperson's territory—for example, a large customer goes out of business—should the manager lower sales goals? (See Exhibit 3.9.)

These are questions all managers must consider. There are no right or wrong answers. Managers are responsible for group goals. They have a natural tendency to place pressure on salespeople to reach those goals. Some managers motivate their people to produce at high levels without applying pressure whereas others place tremendous pressure on salespeople to attain sales beyond quotas. However, managers should set realistic and obtainable goals. They must consider individual territory situations. If they do so fairly and sales are still down, then pressure may be applied.

Decisions Affecting Territory

Management makes decisions that affect sales territories and salespeople. For example, the company might increase the number of sales territories, which often necessitates splitting a single territory. A salesperson may have spent years

EXHIBIT 3.9

How much pressure should a manager place on salespeople to increase sales?

building the territory to its current sales volume only to have customers taken away. If the salesperson has worked on commission, this would mean a decrease in earnings.

Consider a situation of reducing the number of sales territories. What procedures would you use? See if the real-world examples in this section follow the Golden Rule. Several years ago, a large manufacturer of health and beauty aids (shaving cream, toothpaste, shampoo) reduced the number of territories to lower selling costs. So, for example, three territories became two. Here is how one of their salespeople described it:

> I made my plane reservation to fly from Dallas to Florida for our annual national meeting. Beforehand, I was told to bring my records up to date and bring them to the regional office in Dallas; don't fly, drive to Dallas. I drove from Louisiana to Dallas with my bags packed to go to the national meeting. I walked into the office with my records under my arm. My district and regional managers were there. They told me of the reorganization and said I was fired. They asked for my car keys. I called my wife, told her what happened, and then caught a bus back home. There were five of us in the region that were called in that day. Oh, they gave us a good job recommendation— it's just the way we were treated. Some people had been with the company for five years or more. They didn't eliminate jobs by tenure but by where territories were located.

Companies must deal with their employees in a fair and straightforward manner. It would have been better for managers of these salespeople to go to their home-towns and explain the changes personally. Instead, they treated the salespeople unprofessionally.

One decision affecting a territory is what to do with extra-large customers, some-times called *key accounts*. Are they taken away from the salesperson and made into house accounts? Here, responsibility for contacting the accounts rests with some-one from the home office (house) or a key account salesperson. The local salesper-son may not get credit for sales to this customer even though the customer is in the salesperson's territory. A salesperson states the problem:

> I've been with the company 35 years. When I first began, I called on some people who had 1 grocery store. Today, they have 208. The buyer knows me. He buys all of my regular and special greeting cards. They do whatever I ask. I made $22,000 in commissions from their sales last year. Now, management wants to make it a house account.

Here, the salesperson loses money. It is difficult to treat the salesperson fairly in this situation. The company does not want to pay large commissions, and 90 percent of the 208 stores are located out of the salesperson's territory. Management should carefully explain this to the salesperson. Instead of taking the full $22,000 away from the salesperson, they could pay a one-time bonus as a reward for building up the account.

To Tell the Truth?   Should salespeople be told they are not promotable, that they are marginal per-formers, or that they are being transferred to the poorest territory in the company so that they will quit? Good judgment must prevail. Sales managers prefer to tell the truth.

Do you tell the truth when you fire a salesperson? If a fired employee has tried and has been honest, many sales managers will tell prospective employers that the person quit voluntarily rather than being fired. One manager put it this way: "I feel he can do a good job for another company. I don't want to hurt his future."

**The Ill
Salesperson**

How much help do you give to an alcoholic, drug-addicted, or physically or mentally ill salesperson? Many companies require salespeople to seek professional help for substance abuse. If they improve, companies offer support and keep them in the field. Yet, there is only so far the company can go. The firm cannot have an intoxicated or high salesperson calling on customers. Once the illness has a negative effect on business, the salesperson is taken out of the territory. Sick leave and workers' compensation often cover expenses until the salesperson recovers. The manager who shows a sincere, personal interest in helping the ill salesperson greatly contributes to the person's chances of recovery.

Employee Rights

The sales manager must be current on ethical and legal considerations regarding employee rights and must develop strategies for the organization in addressing those rights. Here are several important questions that all managers should be able to answer:

- Under what conditions can an organization fire sales personnel without committing a violation of the law?
- What rights do and should sales personnel have regarding the privacy of their employment records and access to them?
- What can organizations do to prevent sexual and racial harassment and other forms of bias in the workplace?

Employee rights are rights desired by employees regarding their job security and their treatment by employers while on the job, irrespective of whether those rights are currently protected by law or collective bargaining agreements of labor unions. Let's briefly examine three employee-rights questions.

Termination-at-Will

Early in the 20th century, many courts were adamant in strictly applying the common law rule to terminate at will. For example, the **termination-at-will rule** was used in a 1903 case, *Boyer v. Western Union Tel. Co.* [124 F 246, CCED Mo. (1903)], in which the court upheld the company's right to discharge its employees for union activities and indicated that the results would be the same if the company's employees were discharged for being Presbyterians.

Later on, in *Lewis v. Minnesota Mutual Life Ins. Co.* [37 NW 2d 316 (1940)], the termination-at-will rule was used to uphold the dismissal of the life insurance company's best salesperson—even though no apparent cause for dismissal was given and the company had promised the employee lifetime employment in return for his agreement to remain with the company.

In the early 1980s, court decisions and legislative enactments moved the pendulum of protection away from the employer and toward the rights of the individual employee through limitations on the termination-at-will rule.

Although many employers claim that their rights have been taken away, they still retain the right to terminate sales personnel for poor performance, excessive absenteeism, unsafe conduct, and poor organizational citizenship. It is crucial, however, for employers to maintain accurate records of these events for employees and to inform employees about where they stand. To be safe, it is also advisable for employers to have an established grievance procedure for employees to ensure that due process is respected. These practices are particularly useful in discharge situations that involve members of groups protected by Title VII, the Rehabilitation Act, or the Vietnam Era Veterans Act.

MAKING THE SALE

The EEOC and Sexual Harassment

Sexual harassment in the workplace wasn't recognized as a legal issue until the 1970s. In 1980, the Equal Employment Opportunity Commission (EEOC) guidelines identified two types of sexual harassment: The first type is quid pro quo; in which an employee who refuses to submit to a superior's sexual advances is threatened with dismissal or other sanctions. The second type is hostile environment harassment; it occurs when jokes, graffiti, and other behavior are directed at persons of the opposite sex. The landmark ruling came in 1986, when the Supreme Court held unanimously that sexual harassment violates Title VII of the 1964 Civil Rights Act if it is unwelcome and "sufficiently severe or pervasive to alter the conditions of the victim's employment and create an abusive working environment."

Some executives believe the courts are being unreasonable about their definitions of sexual harassment. The issue is often awkward or embarrassing to discuss, and no clearcut definitions of what constitutes offensive behavior exist. For example, a comment about clothing might be considered a compliment by the giver but harassment by the receiver. For these and other reasons, some companies are unwilling to spend time or money educating employees about this issue.

The problem continues to be serious. In 1990, the EEOC received about 5,600 sexual harassment complaints. And new forms of harassment, such as obscene software on company computers and suggestive electronic mail and answering machine messages, keep appearing.

Fortunately, DEC, Honeywell, Corning, CBS, and a number of other companies have long been concerned about sexual harassment. They distribute booklets that describe inappropriate behavior to employees. They hire consultants or conduct in-house training sessions that include films and role playing. The EEOC has published guidelines to help people understand liability. A key factor in determining liability is whether the employer has an effective internal grievance procedure that allows employees to bypass immediate supervisors (who are often the offenders).[13]

Privacy

Today it is more important than ever to keep objective and orderly personnel files. They are critical evidence that employers have treated their employees fairly and with respect, and have not violated any laws. Without these files, organizations may get caught on the receiving end of a lawsuit.

Although several federal laws influence recordkeeping, they are primarily directed at public employers. However, many private employers are giving employees the right to access their personnel files and to prohibit the file information from being given to others without their consent. In addition, employers are casting from their personnel files any non–job-related information and ending hiring practices that solicit such information.

Sexual Harassment

Cooperative acceptance refers to the right of employees to be treated fairly and with respect regardless of race, sex, national origin, physical disability, age, or religion while on the job (as well as in obtaining a job and maintaining job security). Not only does this mean that employees have the right not to be discriminated against in employment practices and decisions, but it also means that employees have the right to be free of sexual and racial harassment.

Today, the right to not be discriminated against is generally protected under Title VII, the Age Discrimination in Employment Act, the Rehabilitation Act, the Vietnam Era Veterans Readjustment Assistance Act, and numerous court decisions and state and local government laws. Though the right to be free of sexual harassment is found explicitly in fewer laws, it has been made a part of the 1980 EEOC guidelines, which state that sexual harassment is a form of sex discrimination. The designation of sexual harassment as a form of sex discrimination under Title VII also is found in numerous court decisions.

Employers must prevent racial and sexual harassment, which they can do with top management support, grievance procedures, verification procedures, training for all employees, and performance appraisal and compensation policies that reward antiharassment behavior and punish harassment.

Companies realize that sexual harassment can be expensive. For example, in a landmark decision, a federal judge in Madison, Wisconsin, approved a damages award of $196,500 to a man who said he was demoted because he resisted the sexual advances of his female supervisor. This was the first time a man ever won a sexual harassment case against a woman. The man also received $7,913 in back pay and $21,726 in attorney's fees in addition to the damages award approved by U.S. Judge John Shabaz.[14]

Companies must recognize these important strategic purposes served by respecting employee rights:

- Providing a high quality of work life.
- Attracting and retaining good sales personnel. This makes recruitment and selection more effective and less frequent.
- Avoiding costly back-pay awards and fines.
- Establishing a match between employee rights and obligations and employer rights and obligations.

Both organizations and employees benefit from antibias measures. Organizations benefit from reduced legal costs, since not observing employee rights is illegal; and their image as a good employer increases, resulting in enhanced organizational attractiveness. This makes it easier for the organization to recruit a pool of qualified applicants. And, although it is suggested that expanded employee rights, especially job security, may reduce needed management flexibility and profitability, it may be an impetus for better planning, resulting in increased profitability.

Increased profitability also may result from the benefits employees receive when their rights are observed; employees may experience feelings of being treated fairly and respectfully, increased self-esteem, and a heightened sense of job security. Employees who have job security may be more productive and committed to the organization than those who do not. As employees begin to see the guarantees of job security as a benefit, organizations also gain through reduced wage-increase demands and greater flexibility in job assignments.

SALESPEOPLES' ETHICS IN DEALING WITH THEIR EMPLOYERS

Both salespeople and sales managers, may occasionally misuse company assets, moonlight, or cheat. Such unethical practices can affect co-workers and need to be prevented before they occur.[15]

Misusing Company Assets

Company assets most often misused are automobiles, expense accounts, samples, and damaged-merchandise credits. All can be used for personal gain or as bribes and kickbacks to customers. For example, a salesperson can give customers valuable product samples or a credit for damaged merchandise when there has been no damage.

EXHIBIT 3.10

The salesperson can easily download company data and take it with him to his next employer.

Moonlighting Salespeople are not closely supervised and, consequently, they may be tempted to take a second job—perhaps on company time. Some salespeople attend college on company time. For example, a salesperson may enroll in an evening M.B.A. program but take off in the early afternoon to prepare for class.

Cheating A salesperson may not play fair in contests. If a contest starts in July, the salesperson may not turn in sales orders for the end of June and lump them with July sales. Some might arrange, with or without the customer's permission, to ship merchandise that is not needed or wanted. The customer holds the merchandise until payment is due and then returns it to the company after the contest is over. The salesperson also may overload the customer to win the contest.

Affecting Other Salespeople Often, the unethical practices of one salesperson can affect other salespeople within the company. Someone who cheats in winning a contest is taking money and prizes from other salespeople. A salesperson also may not split commissions with co-workers or may take customers away from co-workers.

Technology Theft Picture this. A salesperson or sales manager quits, or is fired, and takes the organization's customer records to use for his or her or a future employer's benefit. (See Exhibit 3.10.) How is that possible? Well, it's getting easier to do these days because more and more companies provide their sales personnel with computers, software, and data on their customers.

ETHICS IN DEALING WITH CUSTOMERS "We have formal, ethical policies called business conduct guidelines," says FMC's Alan Killingsworth. "These guidelines thoroughly discuss business conduct and clearly state what is proper conduct and how to report improper conduct. All sales personnel review them and even sign a statement that they understand the guidelines."

Numerous ethical situations may arise in dealing with customers, and sales organizations may create specific business conduct guidelines like FMC's to deal with them. Some common problems sales personnel face include bribes, misrepresentation, price discrimination, tie-in sales, exclusive dealership, reciprocity, and sales restrictions.

MAKING THE SALE

Keep Your Sense of Humor

"It was my first call as a district manager in Washington, D.C.," says Alan Lesk, senior vice president of sales and merchandising at Maidenform. "One of the major department stores was not doing a lot of business with Maidenform, and we were looking for more penetration in the market. Surprisingly, the sale took only two sales calls.

"The first person I approached was a buyer. He was completely uncooperative. On the way out of the store, I popped my head into his boss's office and we set up a meeting with some higher level executives later in the week.

"So there I was, a young kid facing a committee of nine tough executives, and I had to make my presentation. I was in the middle of my pitch when the executive vice president stopped me. He told me that this was going to be a big program, about $500,000, and asked me point blank how much of a rebate I was willing to give him to do business with their store, over and above the normal things like co-op ad money. He was actually asking me for money under the table!

"I had to make a decision fast. I stood up and said, 'If this is what it takes to do business here, I don't want anything to do with it.' I then turned to walk out the door, and the guy started cracking up. I guess he was just testing me to see what lengths I'd go to in order to get my sales program into the store.

"This one incident taught me some very important things: You can't compromise your integrity, and you can't let people intimidate you. Most importantly, don't lose your sense of humor. Needless to say, we got the program into the store, and today we do more than $2 million worth of business a year with them."[17]

Bribes   A salesperson may attempt to bribe a buyer.[16] By offering money, gifts, entertainment, and travel opportunities. At times, there is a thin line between good business and misusing a bribe or gift. A $10 gift to a $10,000 customer may be merely a gift, but how do we define a $4,000 ski trip for buyers and their spouses?

Many companies forbid their buyers to take gifts of any size from salespeople. However, bribery does exist. The U.S. Chamber of Commerce estimates that bribes and kickbacks account for $27 billion of the annual $50 billion in white-collar crime.

Buyers may ask for cash, merchandise, or travel payments in return for placing an order with the salesperson. Imagine that you are a salesperson working on a 5 percent commission. The buyer says, "I'm ready to place a $20,000 order for office supplies with you. However, another salesperson has offered to pay my expenses for a weekend in Las Vegas in exchange for my business. You know, $500 tax-free is a lot of money." You quickly calculate that your commission is $1,000. You still make $500. Would it be hard to pass up that $500?

Many large companies have taken steps to control giving and receiving gifts. Bull H. N. Information Systems, a Massachusetts computer manufacturer, prohibits employees from accepting "money, favors, or anything of significance." This does not include, however, bar bills, meals, entertainment, or other small items given as tokens of appreciation.[18]

Misrepresentation   Today, even casual misstatements by salespeople can put a company on the wrong side of the law. Most salespeople are unaware that they assume legal obligations—with accompanying risks and responsibilities—every time they approach a customer. However, we all know that salespeople sometimes oversell. They exaggerate the capabilities of their products or services and sometimes make false statements just to close a sale.

MAKING THE SALE

Is This Man Really Dying to Make a Sale?

"He made his sales pitch over the phone, and he was good. There existed a little-known but glistening investment opportunity, and if I got into it early I could make an awesome profit.

"Then I said, 'Sounds good to me. I will buy several million shares.' There was a gasp from the other end of the line. 'How many?' he said. 'Several million,' I said, in my coolest manner. By now he was panting. And I felt guilty. He was just trying to make a living.

"On the other hand, he was trying to gouge me out of my net worth. So I offered him a deal. 'I will go for it if you will sign a paper.' 'What kind of paper?' he asked. 'I would like you to sign a piece of paper saying that if this investment fails, you will kill yourself. Or, if you can't fulfill your end of it, I can terminate you.'

"He sounded stunned. 'You expect me to kill myself?' 'It seems reasonable to me,' I said. 'You are asking me to risk the food on my family's table, the roof over their heads. So it seems to me that if this is a foolproof investment, the least you can do is put your life on the line.'

"The man actually stuttered. You don't hear many stutterers these days. He said, 'You have to be kidding.' I told him, in a most grave tone: 'No, I am not kidding. It seems reasonable to me that if this is a good deal and if I can't lose money on it, and if you are so kind as to offer this opportunity to a total stranger rather than to your friends and loved ones, the least you can do is stake your life on it.'

"There was a long pause on the other end. Then he said, 'That's the most ridiculous thing I've ever heard.' Now my feelings were hurt. Here was a man trying to persuade me to put my blood, meaning the rewards of my labors, into an investment, and he was quibbling over a petty deal.

"'You won't agree to kill yourself?' I asked. 'That is ridiculous,' he said. 'So is your pitch,' I said. He hung up. I knew he wasn't sincere. Odds are that he didn't ask his grandmother to put her dough into that stock. So my advice to any potential investors is this: Ask them if they will leap off a bridge if you lose money. If they refuse, it isn't a good deal."[20]

A liar has to have a good memory.

Often, buyers depend heavily on the technical knowledge of salespeople, along with their professional integrity. Yet, sales managers and staff find it difficult to know just how far they can go with well-intentioned sales talk, personal opinion, and promises. They do not realize that by using certain statements they can embroil their companies in a lawsuit and ruin the business relationship they are trying to establish.

When a customer relies on a salesperson's statements, purchases the product or service, and then finds that it fails to perform as promised, the supplier can be sued for **misrepresentation** and **breach of warranty.** Companies around the United States have been liable for million-dollar judgments for making such mistakes, particularly when their salespeople sold high-ticket, high-tech products or services.

You can avoid such mistakes, however, if you're aware of the law of misrepresentation and breaches of warranty relative to the selling function, and if you follow strategies that keep you and your company out of trouble. Salespeople must understand the difference between sales puffery (opinions) and statements of fact—and the legal ramifications of both. There are preventive steps to follow; salespeople must work closely with management to avoid time-consuming delays and costly legal fees.[19]

What the Law Says

Misrepresentation and breach of warranty are two legal causes of action, that is, theories on which an injured party seeks damages. These two theories differ in the proof required and the type of damages awarded by a judge or jury. However, both

Conflict of Interest?

The real estate salesperson assured the young couple that she would work hard to find them the right house. "Consider me your scout," she said. "I'll find you the best house for the least money." The couple was reassured, and on the way home they talked about their good fortune. They had a salesperson working just for them. With prices so high, it was nice to think they had professional help on their side.

The family selling the house felt the same way. They carefully chose the broker because, they observed, with home prices all over the lot these days, they hoped a good salesperson might win them several thousand dollars more. They had another reason to choose carefully: At today's prices, the 6 percent sales commission is a lot of money. "If we have to pay it," they reasoned, "we're better off paying it to the best salesperson."

It happens all the time, and it can have serious consequences. How can both parties expect the best deal? How can a salesperson promise the seller the most for the money and then make the same promise to the buyer?

In the same vein, how can a salesperson whose commission rises or falls with the price of the house being sold be expected to cut into her income? Isn't her total allegiance with the person paying her?

Confusion of this sort has existed in the marketplace for so long that critics are sometimes confounded that regulators haven't made greater efforts to clarify matters.

Two explanations are sometimes offered. First, it is more a human than a legal problem; even if warned, buyers will continue to assume that salespeople work solely for them, rather than for the seller, who pays the salesperson a commission.

Second, a good salesperson sometimes can come close to serving the desires of both parties. The point is arguable, but the justification offered is that the salesperson's compromises may be necessary to save a sale from falling through.

A somewhat similar situation exists in the stock market, where many small investors view their stockbroker as a confidant and adviser.[21]

theories arise in the selling context and are treated similarly for our purposes. Both situations arise when a salesperson makes erroneous statements or offers false promises regarding a product's characteristics and capabilities.

Not all statements have legal consequences, however. When sales personnel loosely describe their product or service in glowing terms ("Our service can't be beat; it's the best around"), such statements are viewed as opinions that the customer, supplier, or wholesaler generally cannot rely on. Thus, a standard defense lawyers use in misrepresentation and breach of warranty lawsuits is that a purchaser cannot rely on a salesperson's puffery because it's unreasonable to take these remarks at face value.

Be a person of 100% truth, not 99% truth. Your proof is in your word.

When a salesperson makes claims or promises of a factual nature regarding a product's or service's inherent capabilities (that is, the results, profits, or savings that will be achieved; what it will do for a customer; how it will perform; etc.), the law treats these comments as statements of fact and warranties.

There is a subtle difference between sales puffery and statements of fact; they can be difficult to distinguish. No particular form of words is necessary; each case is analyzed according to its circumstances. Generally, the less knowledgeable the customer, the greater the chances that the court will interpret a statement as actionable. The following is an actual recent case that illustrates this point:

An independent sales rep sold heavy industrial equipment. He went to a purchaser's construction site, observed his operations, then told the company president that his proposed equipment would "keep up with any other machine then being used," and that it would "work well in cooperation with the customer's other machines and equipment."

The customer informed the rep that he was not personally knowledgeable about the kind of equipment the rep was selling, and that he needed time to study the rep's report. Several weeks later, he bought the equipment based on the rep's recommendations.

After a few months, he sued the rep's company, claiming that the equipment didn't perform according to the representations in sales literature sent prior to the execution of the contract and to statements made by the rep at the time of sale. The equipment manufacturer defended itself by arguing that the statements made by the rep were nonactionable opinions made innocently by the rep, in good faith, with no intent to deceive the purchaser.

The court ruled in favor of the customer, finding that the rep's statements were "predictions" of how the equipment would perform; this made them more than mere sales talk. The rep was held responsible for knowing the capabilities of the equipment he was selling; his assertions were deemed statements of fact, not opinions. Furthermore, the court stated that it was unfair that a knowledgeable salesperson would take advantage of a naive purchaser.[22]

Suggestions for Staying Legal

The following suggestions cover ways that management and sales staff can minimize exposure to costly misrepresentation and breach of warranty lawsuits. Salespeople must always do the following:

1. Understand the distinction between general statements of praise and statements of fact made during the sales pitch (and the legal consequences). For example, the following statements, taken from actual cases, were made by salespeople and were determined legally actionable as statements of fact:

   - This refrigerator will preserve foods in the warmest weather.
   - This tractor has live power-take-off features.
   - Feel free to prescribe this drug to your patients, doctor. It's nonaddicting.
   - This mace pen is capable of instantaneous incapacitation for a period of 15 to 20 minutes.
   - This is a safe, dependable helicopter.

2. Thoroughly educate all customers before making a sale. Salespeople should tell as much about the specific qualities of the product as possible. The reason is that when a salesperson makes statements about a product in a field in which his or her company has extensive experience, the law makes it difficult for the salesperson to claim it was just sales talk.

   This is especially true for products or services sold in highly specialized areas to unsophisticated purchasers who rely entirely on the technical expertise of the salesperson. However, if the salesperson deals with a customer experienced in the trade, courts are less likely to find that the salesperson offered an expressed warranty, since a knowledgeable buyer has a duty to look beyond the assertions of a salesperson and investigate the product individually.

3. Be accurate when describing a product's capabilities. Avoid making speculative claims, particularly with respect to predictions concerning what a product will do.

4. Know the technical specifications of the product. Review all promotional literature to ensure that there are no exaggerated claims. Keep abreast of all design changes as well. The salesperson shown in Exhibit 3.11, for example, must carefully and honestly explain the technical aspects of her product to her industrial buyers.

The scales of justice can be harsh to those not following the Golden Rule

EXHIBIT 3.11

This salesperson must be careful about the claims made in the sales presentation. If she says, "This equipment will increase production 2 percent," and it doesn't, the salesperson and her company may find themselves in court.

5. Avoid making exaggerated claims about product safety. The law usually takes a dim view of such affirmative claims, and these remarks can be interpreted as warranties that lead to liability.

   For example, the Minnesota Court of Appeals ruled that a salesperson's assurances that a used car had a rebuilt carburetor and was a "good runner" constituted an expressed warranty of the vehicle's condition. Someone had bought the car based on the salesperson's assurance of its good quality. The carburetor jammed, causing the car to smash into a tree and injuring the purchaser, who recovered sizable damages.[23]

6. Know federal and state laws regarding warranties and guarantees.

7. Know the capabilities and characteristics of your products and services.

8. Keep current on all design changes and revisions in your product's operating manual.

9. Avoid offering opinions when the customer asks what results a product or service will accomplish unless the company has tested the product and has statistical evidence.

   Statements such as, "This will reduce your inventory backlog by 40 percent" can get the company in trouble if the system fails to achieve the promised results. Stay away from that kind of statement. If you don't know the answer to a customer's question, don't lead her on. Tell her you don't know the answer but will get back to her promptly with the information.

10. Never overstep authority, especially when discussing prices or company policy. Remember, a salesperson's statements can bind the company.

   One final point: It's generally easy for customers to recover damages on the grounds of misrepresentation and breach of warranty. In many states, this holds even when a salesperson's statement is made innocently.

Price Discrimination

Some customers may receive price reductions, promotional allowances, and support while others do not, even though, under certain circumstances, this violates the **Robinson-Patman Act** of 1936. The act allows sellers to grant what are called *quantity discounts* to larger buyers based on savings in manufacturing costs.

Individual salespeople or managers may practice **price discrimination** to improve sales. *Price discrimination* refers to selling the same quantity of the same product to different buyers at different prices. This can be illegal if it injures or reduces competition. It is certainly unethical and no way to treat customers.

Tie-in Sales

To buy a particular line of merchandise, a buyer may be required to buy other, unwanted products. This is called a **tie-in sale** and is prohibited under the **Clayton Act** when it substantially lessens competition. For example, the salesperson of a popular line of cosmetics tells the buyer, "I have a limited supply of the merchandise you want. If all of your 27 stores will display, advertise, and push my total line, I may be able to supply you. That means you'll need to buy 10 items that you have never purchased before." Is this good business? No—it's illegal.

Exclusive Dealership

When a contract requires that a wholesaler or retailer purchase products from one manufacturer, it is an *exclusive dealership*. If it lessens competition, it is prohibited under the Clayton Act.

Reciprocity

The salesperson says, "I can get my company to buy all of our office supplies from your company if you buy lighting fixtures, supplies, and replacement parts from us." Is this a good business practice?

Reciprocity refers to buying a product from someone if the person or organization agrees to buy from you. The Federal Trade Commission and the Department of Justice consider such a trade agreement illegal if it results in hurting or eliminating competition. Most purchasing agents find this practice offensive. Because reciprocal sales agreements may be illegal, if not unethical, buyers often are afraid to even discuss this with sellers.

Sales Restrictions

To protect consumers against the sometimes unethical sales activities of door-to-door salespeople, there is legislation at the federal, state, and local levels. The Federal Trade Commission and most states have adopted **cooling-off laws.** They provide a cooling-off period (usually three days) in which the buyer may cancel the contract, return any merchandise, and obtain a full refund. The law covers sales of $25 or more made door-to-door. It also states that the buyer must receive from the seller a written, dated contract and/or receipt of the transaction and be told there is a three-day cancellation period.

Many cities require persons selling directly to consumers to be licensed by the city in which they do business if they are not residents and to pay a license fee. A bond also may be required. These city ordinances often are called **Green River ordinances** because the first legislation of this kind was passed in Green River, Wyoming, in 1933. This type of ordinance protects consumers and aids local companies by making it more difficult for outside competition to enter the market.

Both the cooling-off laws and the Green River ordinances were passed to protect consumers from salespeople using unethical, high-pressure sales tactics. These statutes and others were necessary because some salespeople used unethical practices in sales transactions.

THE INTERNATIONAL SIDE OF ETHICS

Often guidelines for conducting international business are not the same as ours and, in many cases, are nonexistent.* The laws are quite different, and you could find yourself competing with foreign companies allowed to do things considered unethical by U.S. standards.

It is a serious mistake to think that laws for U.S. companies end at our borders. Each and every employee of a U.S. company is subject to U.S. law regardless of the country in which the business takes place. Even the agents or the distributors are subject to U.S. law, and you are responsible, as a manager, for their actions. It's important to be up to date on the law and aware of how authorized representatives are conducting business.

The American position on business ethics is well known throughout the business world. FMC's Alan Killingsworth says:

> In my tenure internationally, I never lost an order because we refused to compromise our ethics. I will say we had to sell a little harder in some cases and had to continue to focus the customer on the benefits and features of our product, services, and company. We sold to an organization and not to an individual. This limited any attempt by an individual making a purchasing decision to evaluate FMC on anything but our features and benefits.
>
> Don't let these statements mislead you. The vast majority of international companies you will deal with have high ethical standards. The ones that don't cannot be defined by geographic location or culture. Awareness of your customer will lead you, early on, to feel comfortable in dealing with the people making the buying decisions. You'll learn to recognize quickly if you are being treated fairly and evaluated on the merits of your company.
>
> Ethics relating to employees and community are often more difficult to understand. We have to remember we are guests in a country and not there to impose our ideas on their culture. Often, we are confronted with situations that seem strange and unfair. All we can do in such cases is to lead by example. We should treat our international community and personnel with the same respect we give people back in the good old U.S.A.

MANAGING SALES ETHICS

Over the years, a number of surveys to determine managers' views of business ethics have found the following:

- All managers feel they face ethical problems.
- Most managers feel they and their employers should be more ethical.
- Managers are more ethical with their friends than with people they do not know.
- Even though they want to be more ethical, some managers lower their ethical standards to meet job goals.
- Managers are aware of unethical practices in their industry and company ranging from price discrimination to hiring discrimination.
- Business ethics can be influenced by an employee's superior and by the company environment.

Organizations are concerned about how to improve their social responsiveness and ethical climate. Managers must take active steps to ensure that the company stays on ethical ground. Management methods for helping organizations to be more

---

* This section was written by Alan Killingsworth of FMC's petroleum equipment group. He has spent more than 20 years in sales overseas.

EXHIBIT 3.12

Top-level management sets the climate for ethical behavior in its sales force.

responsive include (1) top management taking the lead, (2) carefully selecting leaders, (3) establishing and following a code of ethics, (4) creating ethical structures, (5) formally encouraging whistle-blowing, (6) creating an ethical sales climate, and (7) establishing control systems.

Follow the Leader

The organization's chief executive officer, president, and vice presidents should clearly champion the efforts for ethical conduct. (See Exhibit 3.12.) Others will follow their lead. Their speeches, interviews, and actions need to constantly communicate the ethical values of the organization. The Business Roundtable, an association of chief executives from 250 large corporations, issued a report on ethics policy and practice in companies such as Boeing, Chemical Bank, General Mills, GTE, Xerox, Johnson & Johnson, and Hewlett-Packard. The report concluded that no point emerged more clearly than the crucial role of top management in guiding the social and ethical responsibilities of their organization.

Leader Selection Is Important

Since so few individuals are at the principled level of moral development, it is critical to carefully choose managers. Only people who have the highest level of integrity, standards, and values should assume leadership positions.

Establish a Code of Ethics

A **code of ethics** is a formal statement of the company's values concerning ethics and social issues. It states those values or behaviors that are expected and those that are not tolerated. These values and behaviors must be backed by management's action. Without top management support, there is little assurance that the code will be followed.

The two types of codes of ethics are principle-based statements and policy-based statements. Principle-based statements are designed to affect corporate culture, define fundamental values, and contain general language about company responsibilities, quality of products, and treatment of employees. General statements of principle are often called *corporate credos.* Examples are GTE's "Vision and Values," Johnson & Johnson's "The Credo," and Hewlett-Packard's "The HP Way."

Policy-based statements generally outline the procedures to be used in specific ethical situations. These situations include marketing practice, conflicts of interest, observance of laws, proprietary information, political gifts, and equal opportunities. Examples of policy-based statements are Boeing's "Business Conduct Guidelines,"

ETHICAL DILEMMA

The Boss Told Me to Do It!

The prospect must have delivery of the product in four weeks to meet a national advertising rollout. The company has big bucks invested in the ad campaign. After beating the production people about the head and shoulders, the best delivery your company can promise is six weeks. The boss orders you to promise the customer delivery within a four-week deadline. What is the most ethical action to take?

1. Tell your boss that you do not believe that it is right to lie to the customer. State that you will not pass the

four-week lead time along but you would be more than happy to tell the customer the true six-week lead time. Tell your boss that you cannot support dishonesty within the company.

2. Do as your boss says and promise the four-week deadline, even though you know there is no possibility of meeting this deadline.

3. Tell your boss to pass the information to the customer himself. That way you do not have to actually lie.

Chemical Bank's "Code of Ethics," GTE's "Code of Business Ethics" and its "Anti-Trust and Conflict of Interest Guidelines," and Norton's "Norton Policy on Business Ethics."

Create Ethical Structures

An **ethics committee** is a group of executives appointed to oversee company ethics. The committee provides rulings on questionable ethical issues. The ethics committee assumes responsibility for disciplining wrongdoers. This responsibility is essential if the organization is to directly influence employee behavior. An **ethics ombudsman** is an official given the responsibility of corporate conscience who hears and investigates ethics complaints and informs top management of potential ethics issues. For example, companies like IBM, Xerox, and Procter & Gamble have ethics committees reporting directly to the CEO.

Encourage Whistle-Blowing

Employee disclosure of illegal, immoral, or illegitimate practices on the employer's part is called *whistle-blowing*. Companies can provide a mechanism for whistle-blowing as a matter of policy. All employees who observe or become aware of criminal practices or unethical behavior should be encouraged to report the incident to their superiors, to a higher level of management, or to an appropriate unit of the organization, such as an ethics committee. Formalized procedures for complaining can encourage honest employees to report questionable incidents. For example, a company could provide its employees with a toll-free number that they may call to report unethical activities to top management. This silent witness program could be successful because it allows employees to report incidents without actually having to confront personnel. This program is especially valuable if the employee's own manager is involved in unethical practices. However, with programs such as these, careful verification then becomes necessary to guard against the use of such means to get even with managers or other employees.

Create an Ethical Sales Climate

The single most important factor in improving the climate for ethical behavior in a sales force is the action taken by top-level managers. Sales managers must help develop and support their codes of ethics. They should publicize the code and their opposition to unethical sales practices to their subordinate managers and their salespeople. A stronger level of ethical awareness can be achieved during sales meetings, training sessions, and when contacting customers while working with salespeople.[24]

Establish Control Systems

Finally, control systems must be established. Methods should be employed to determine whether salespeople give bribes, falsify reports, or pad expenses. For example, sales made from low bids could be checked to determine whether procedures have been followed correctly. Dismissal, demotion, suspension, reprimand, and withholding of sales commissions would be possible penalties for unethical sales practices.

Overall, management must make a concerted effort to create an ethical climate within the workplace to best serve customer and organizational goals.

ETHICS IN BUSINESS AND SALES

This chapter was a condensed introduction to the subject of social, ethical, and legal issues in selling. There is so much to learn about these three topics. A person can get a law degree or a Ph.D. specializing in each of these three subjects.

From your viewpoint, however, did you learn anything about how an organization might make moral and ethical decisions each day? What about factors you might consider in making the right decisions that guide your life?

Consider this: Take some time now and each day for one week to write down in a diary or journal what guides your thinking and actions, especially those related to moral and ethical issues. Make your journal entries throughout the day and review at the end of each day. Your goal is to see what guides your choices. For example, do you make your moral and ethical decisions based upon

■ Whatever will bring you the most pleasing or satisfying results.
■ What will make other people happy or minimize interpersonal conflict.
■ Values taught by your family.
■ Religious principles and teaching or Bible content.
■ Something other than the above four reasons.

The most interesting question is, "What is a moral or ethical issue for you?" It is said, "Different strokes for different folks." What's ethical to you may not be ethical to someone else. If you drive five miles per hour over the speed limit, is that all right? What about my telling my wife I like her meat loaf when I do not? What about downloading music from the Internet?

Using the three levels of moral development discussed earlier in the chapter, score each ethical or moral decision you make this week one, two, or three according to the definitions of preconventional, conventional, and principled levels of moral development. Do you have a pattern of using different moral development levels for different decisions, or do you use the same level for each decision?

Helpful Hints to Making Career Decisions

As you look at your basic pattern of making moral and ethical decisions, think about this question: Does your personal belief system lend itself to the business or sales profession? This is an important question to answer for your future. As we discussed in Chapter 1, how can you believe in a profession that not many people trust? Here are a few ideas that may help you make a decision about a business or sales career:

■ Be involved in businesses/organizations that provide worthwhile products— not just things that feed the world's desires.

- Do what is right according to your beliefs no matter what the cost.
- Do not compromise on your beliefs.
- Remember that people must always be more important than products, finances, fame, power, and position.
- Recognize that good people are desperately needed in all types of businesses/organizations.

This last point is very important. All occupations need people with good personal integrity, character, and values. You can make a difference by being a role model for others, as a person who wants to unselfishly help other people.

Do Your Research!   Be sure to research any organization in which you are considering a job. Annual reports and the Internet allow you to quickly learn a little about an organization. Talking to people who work there and working for a day with a salesperson also helps you get to know about a company. However, you really have to work for the organization to truly know it. Exhibit 3.13 might provide hints on what to look for when researching an organization.

Exhibit 3.13 shows a hypothetical organization with the slogan of "Preparing People for the 21st Century." The firm's mission is to serve others using the Golden Rule as its vision. The foundation upon which the organization is built is service. Integrity, trust, and character provide the upright support for the firm's substructure of values.[25]

Integrity, Trust, and Character

A person with **integrity** is honest without compromise or corruption. Ethics begins at the individual level of the organization. An organization filled with ethical people is an ethical organization. The people and organization possess a firm adherence to a code of moral values. From integrity flows confidence that one can **trust** the other. The organization and its salespeople have the attributes and characteristics with which one likes to do business.

Character is who you are when no one is looking!

Integrity and trust form the attributes that make up and distinguish the organization and salesperson, often referred to as **character.** Think of character as who you are when no one is looking and what you are willing to stand for when someone is looking.[26]

Character is developed and revealed by tests, and all of life is a test. Major changes in your life, delayed promises, impossible problems, undeserved praise or criticism, senseless tragedies or good fortunes, choices between what is right or wrong and the results of the choices, forgiveness, overcoming temptations, hard and good times are examples of tests we experience in life. Life's testing forms one's character. I have a lot of character. How about you?

Integrity, trust, and character help form the **values** or moral code of conduct toward others. Respect for the dignity of the individual is at the heart of the universal moral code referred to as "the Golden Rule" by most people of the world. Please refer back to Exhibit 3.7. This is why salespeople with integrity, trustworthiness, character, and values are so sought after and needed in today's business world.

People who use the Golden Rule as their moral compass practice and speak the truth. They are **true** to their word and reflect the best of mankind. Truth is consistent with fact or reality.

EXHIBIT 3.13

What do you look for in an employer?

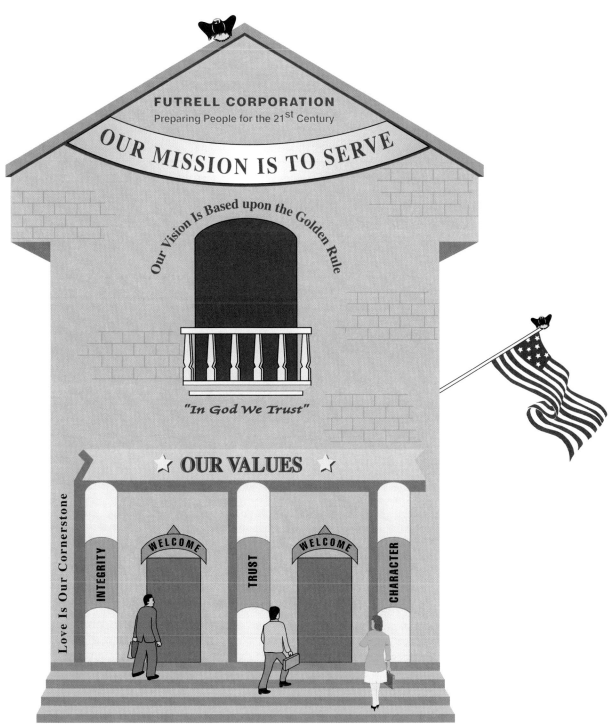

The Foundation and Cornerstone

Again look at Exhibit 3.13. Although this firm's foundation is based upon service, its **cornerstone** (the essential part of a building's foundation) is love. **Love** is the strong affection, desire, or devotion to people. Who are the people? They are the stakeholders referred to at the beginning of this chapter that can be described by the acronym **CCC GOMES.**

We can be proud to be a part of one of the greatest professions in the world for providing service to people—that of a sales career! Making a contribution to others, **CCC GOMES,** is how you sell someone and remain friends, plus keep good employees and be a force for good in our country and the world.

THE TREE OF BUSINESS LIFE

As a reminder that the Golden Rule of Personal Selling should apply to all aspects of business, marketing, and sales, the Tree of Business Life was grown. The Tree will appear at various locations in your book to emphasize how the chapter's topic relates to the materials you have just read in Chapter 3. Please refer back to this chapter to refresh your memory as to why this book proclaims ethical service builds true relationships.

Exhibit 3.14 shows that the Tree with the Ts standing for truth framed by ethical service builds relationships. The Tree is grounded by its roots of integrity, trustworthiness, and character. The center of business life is truth. The **truth** refers to the facts needed to make ethical and moral decisions.

EXHIBIT 3.14

Ethical service builds true relationships.

The Tree of Business Life's
Roots and Frame Based Upon Truth

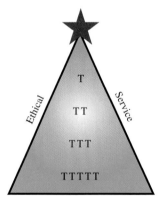

The Tree is rooted in:
- **Integrity** is being honest without compromise or corruption.
- From integrity flows confidence that one can **trust** the other.
- Integrity and trust form the attributes often referred to as **character**.

Framed by:
- Ethical service builds true relationships

Shown with Ts standing for:
- **Truth**: facts needed to make ethical and moral decisions.

Absolute truth sets standards.

The best facts are those that do not change. The best facts are the same yesterday, today, and tomorrow. The best facts are fixed standards, or absolute truths, by which to measure all other facts needed to make any moral or ethical decision. You might want to look over the three guidelines for making ethical decisions again to better understand this term called "truth." You cannot separate personal life from business life. People do, but it is folly. Separation of moral behavior from personal and business life will not work in an individual. Something within the person quietly whispers what is right or wrong in life and business. Service, ethics, relationships, integrity, trustworthiness, and character based upon the truth are at the heart of a person's, and the organization's, moral behavior. So look for the Tree of Business Life, reflect upon it, rest under it, live by it.

Ethics Rule Business

Both ethical behavior and The Golden Rule refer to treating others fairly. Take a moment to look back at their specific definitions. Then review once again this section's discussion of the Tree of Business Life.

Notice the title of this brief but important section of this book—ethics rule business. The word "ethics" comes from ethical behavior. The word "rule" comes from the Golden Rule. And the word "business" comes from the Tree of Business Life. What a powerful phrase—simple but profound. Ethics rule business. While not always true today, hopefully when you are a business leader ethics will rule your business and guide your life.

SUMMARY OF MAJOR SELLING ISSUES

Ethics and social responsibility are hot topics for managers. Ethical behavior pertains to values of right and wrong. Ethical decisions and behavior are typically guided by a value system. For an individual manager, the ability to make correct ethical choices will depend on both individual and organizational characteristics. An important individual characteristic is one's level of moral development. Corporate culture is an organizational characteristic that influences ethical behavior.

Corporate social responsibility concerns a company's values toward society. How can organizations be good corporate citizens? The model for evaluating social performance uses four criteria: economic, legal, ethical, and discretionary.

Social responsibility in business means profitably serving employees and customers in an ethical and lawful manner. Extra costs can accrue because a firm takes socially responsible action, but this is a part of doing business in today's society, and it pays in the long run.

What should an individual base her or his values upon? Could the Golden Rule serve as a universal, practical, helpful standard for salespeople's conduct? What about your ethical and moral conduct?

Salespeople and managers realize that their business should be conducted in an ethical manner. They must be ethical in dealing with their salespeople, their employers, and their customers. Ethical standards and guidelines for sales personnel must be developed, supported, and policed. In the future, ethical selling practices will be even more important to conducting business profitably. Techniques for improving social responsiveness include leadership, codes of ethics, ethical structures, whistle-blowing, and establishing control systems. Finally, research suggests that socially responsible organizations perform as well as—and often better than—organizations that are not socially responsible.

MEETING A SALES CHALLENGE

In essence, the sales manager was seeking reciprocity. The contemplated deal is clearly unethical. In some cases, such a deal may even be unlawful. Companies aware of their legal and ethical responsibilities protect themselves and their employees from unnecessary exposure.

For example, IBM marketing representatives are urged to follow the specific steps set forth in IBM's "Business Conduct Guideline"—a policy-based code of ethics—which states, "You may not do business with a supplier of goods or services." Reasonable? *Yes.* Important? *Absolutely.*

Remember that your career and the future of your company depend on creating values that last. This objective depends on making decisions we can live with tomorrow, not on what we might get away with today.

KEY TERMS FOR SELLING

social responsibility   72
stakeholder   72
CCC GOMES   72
discretionary responsibility   74
worldview   75
morals   75
preconventional moral development level   75
conventional moral development level   75
principled moral development level   76
fixed point of reference   79
ethics   80
ethical behavior   81
employee rights   84
termination-at-will rule   84
cooperative acceptance   85
misrepresentation   89
breach of warranty   89
Robinson-Patman Act   92

price discrimination   93
tie-in sale   93
Clayton Act   93
reciprocity   93
cooling-off laws   93
Green River ordinances   93
code of ethics   95
ethics committee   96
ethics ombudsman   96
integrity   98
trust   98
character   98
values   98
true   98
cornerstone   100
love   100
truth   100

SALES APPLICATION QUESTIONS

1. Which of the following situations represent socially responsible actions by firms?
   a. Creating recreation facilities for sales personnel.
   b. Paying for college courses associated with an M.B.A. program.
   c. Allowing sales personnel to buy company products at a discount.
   Do managers feel business ethics can be improved? Describe ethical situations that sales managers may face in dealing with salespeople.
2. Imagine that you are being encouraged to inflate your expense account. Do you think your choice would be most affected by your individual moral development or by the cultural values of the company for which you worked? Explain.
3. Have you ever experienced an ethical dilemma? Evaluate the dilemma with respect to its impact on other people.
4. Discuss the difference between sales puffery and misrepresentation and how to avoid making mistakes that may prove costly to the firm.
5. Lincoln Electric considers customers and employees to be more important stakeholders than shareholders. Is it appropriate for management to define some stakeholders as more important than others? Should all stakeholders be considered equal?

6. Do you think a code of ethics combined with an ethics committee would be more effective than leadership alone implementing ethical behavior? Discuss.

FURTHER EXPLORING THE SALES WORLD

Talk to a sales manager about the social, ethical, and legal issues involved in the job. Does the manager's firm have

a. A code of ethics?
b. An ethics committee?
c. An ethics ombudsman?
d. Procedures for whistle-blowing?

Get a copy of any materials relating to topics discussed in this chapter. Report on your findings.

SELLING EXPERIENTIAL EXERCISES

On a separate sheet of paper answer the following questions by writing down the number that best describes an organization for which you have worked:

Ethical Work Climates

	Disagree				Agree
1. Whatever is best for everyone in the company is the major consideration here.	1	2	3	4	5
2. Our major concern is always what is best for the other person.	1	2	3	4	5
3. People are expected to comply with the law and professional standards over and above other considerations.	1	2	3	4	5
4. In this company, the first consideration is whether a decision violates any law.	1	2	3	4	5
5. It is very important to follow company rules and procedures here.	1	2	3	4	5
6. People in this company strictly obey company policies.	1	2	3	4	5
7. In this company, people are mostly out for themselves.	1	2	3	4	5
8. People are expected to do anything to further the company's interests, regardless of the consequences.	1	2	3	4	5
9. In this company, people are guided by their own personal ethics.	1	2	3	4	5
10. Each person in this company decides for himself or herself what is right and wrong.	1	2	3	4	5

Total Score_____

Add up your score. These questions measure the dimensions of an organization's ethical climate. Questions 1 and 2 measure caring for people, questions 3 and 4 measure lawfulness, questions 5 and 6 measure rules adherence, questions 7 and 8 measure emphasis on financial and company performance, and questions 9 and 10 measure individual independence. Questions 7 and 8 are reverse scored. (That is, if you answered "five," your actual score to write down is "one"; a "four" is really a "two," etc.) A total score above 40 indicates a very positive ethical climate. A score from 30 to 40 indicates an above-average ethical climate. A score from 20 to 30 indicates a below-average ethical climate, and a score below 20 indicates a very poor ethical climate.

Go back over the questions and think about changes that you could have made to improve the ethical climate in the organization. Discuss with other students what you could do as a manager to improve ethics in future companies you work for.[27]

How Ethical Are You? How ethical are you? It has been written that people must be honest with themselves before they can be honest with others. A person who is not honest with himself or herself presents a hopeless case.[28] Answer the following question:

	Never ethical	Seldom ethical	Somewhat ethical	Mostly ethical	Always ethical
I am:	_____	_____	_____	_____	_____

What is your answer? Think about your answer. Why did you answer the way you did? My guess is you placed yourself in the "always" or "mostly" group. Most people do even if their ethics need improving.[29]

CHAPTER 3

**Ethics First . . .
Then Customer
Relationships**

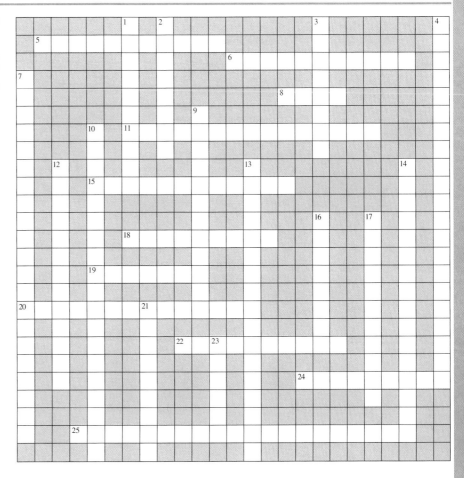

Across

5. An agreement by which a person or organization buys a product if the person or organization selling the product also buys a product from the first party.

6. Any group within or outside the organization that has a stake in the organization's performance.

8. Strong affection, desire, or devotion to people.

11. The first level of an individual's moral development, known as _____ moral development. At this level, an individual acts in his or her own best interest and thus follows rules to avoid punishment or receive rewards. This individual would break moral and legal laws.

15. A formal statement of the company's values concerning ethics and social issues.

18. An ethics _____ consists of a group of executives appointed to oversee company ethics.

19. The _____ Act prohibits the practice of tie-in sales when they substantially lessen competition.

20. Laws that provide a cooling-off period during which the buyer may cancel the contract, return any merchandise, and obtain a full refund.

22. The _____ _____ ordinance protects consumers and aids local firms by making it more difficult for outside competition to enter the market.

24. Prohibited under the Clayton Act, it occurs when a buyer is required to buy other, unwanted products in order to buy a particular line of merchandise.
25. The responsibility to profitably serve employees and customers in an ethical and lawful manner.

Down

1. The third level of an individual's moral development, known as ____ moral development. At this level, an individual lives by an internal set of morals, values, and ethics, regardless of punishments or majority opinion.
2. Acronym for the eight important stakeholders of an organization: customers, community, creditors, government, owners, managers, employees, suppliers.
3. Ethical ____ demonstrates a willingness to treat others fairly, shows one to be honest and trustworthy, and exhibits loyalty to company, associates, and the work for which one is responsible.
4. Something that provides the correct action to take in any situation and never gets tailored to fit an occasion.
7. The right of employees to be treated fairly and with respect regardless of race, sex, national origin, physical disability, age, or religion, while on the job.
9. The second level of an individual's moral development, known as ____ moral development. At this level, an individual conforms to the expectations of others, such as family, employer, boss, and society,

and upholds moral and legal laws.
10. The act of selling the same quantity of the same product to different buyers at different prices.
12. ____ responsibility refers to actions taken by a company that are purely voluntary and guided by its desire to make social contributions not mandated by economics, law, or ethics.
13. A legal cause of action on which an injured party seeks damages. It arises when a salesperson makes erroneous statements or offers false promises regarding a product's characteristics and capabilities.
14. Another name for the misrepresentation of truth by a salesperson.
16. ____ rights are desired by employees regarding their job security and the treatment administered by their employers while on the job, irrespective of whether those rights are currently protected by law or collective bargaining agreements of labor unions.
17. The essential component of a building's foundation which for the organization is love of others.
21. An ethics ____ is an official given the responsibility of corporate conscience who hears and investigates ethical complaints and informs top management of potential ethical issues.
23. Principles of right or good conduct, or a body of such principles, that affect good and bad business practices.

CASE 3-1

Ethical Selling at Perfect Solutions: The Case of the Delayed Product

Scott Patterson is a salesperson for Perfect Solutions, a chemical manufacturing firm. He sells to distributors, sometimes called wholesalers. Distributors buy in large quantities from various manufacturers and sell in smaller quantities to other businesses. Larry Ingram, the CEO of one of Scott's best distributors, called Scott into his office to discuss some concerns he has regarding their business relationship.

Ingram's company has been distributing Perfect Solutions products for over 10 years. In addition, Ingram's company has been the top seller for Perfect Solutions products two of the past three years. However, Scott seems to be doing things that may affect Ingram's sales. Mr. Ingram is very upset!

Scott Signs Competitor

Video

Case

Scott recently signed up Barber Distributing to distribute and sell his company's products. Barber Distributing is a competitor of Ingram's. Ingram found out about this relationship when Scott's new client, Barber Distributing, sold to one of Ingram's customers at a price 10 percent under Ingram's normal list price to get the DIS project. Ingram had cut their prices to the bone and still did not win the bid. "Did PS give Barber special price deals?" asks Mr. Ingram. Scott says, "No." Ingram wants to know if Barber will bid for the "plant" business coming up. He wants Scott to get him their bid price. Ingram places pressure on Scott to get him the best price for the bid or lose his business.

Ingram feels that his company has been very valuable to Perfect Solutions and demands that Patterson reveal the prices he sold products to Barber Distributors. Patterson then promises Ingram that Perfect Solutions has fixed prices that are never altered. Scott told Ingram that he and Barber pay the same price for a particular product.

The Customer Is Upset!

This does not satisfy Ingram and he lets Patterson know that the Dymotzue's Company, a competitor of Scott and Perfect Solutions, has quoted Ingram better prices. The price sheets are on Ingram's desk. Ingram says he will not hesitate to leave Patterson for Dymotzue if Scott does not take care of him. Scott asks Ingram what he could do to help ease Ingram's frustration. Ingram says he wants to buy about two truckloads of Bond-do-Perm that Scott promised him but has not yet delivered.

While the Cat Is Away

Ingram is called out of the office. While Ingam is out of his office Patterson calls his manufacturing plant and talks with Jack, the manager. Jack tells him the Bond-do-Perm has some manufacturing problems and will not be available for two months. The company does not want to ship a bad product. Scott gets off the phone as Ingram walks back into his office. Patterson promises Ingram one truckload of the Bond-do-Perm within a few weeks knowing it cannot be delivered at that time. Ingram says he can sell one truckload to his customers as soon as the Bond-do-Perm arrives.

About this time, one of Ingram's salespeople comes into the distribution center's main office and says that Barber Distributing, Ingram's competitor, has just made an offer to sell LubeExcel to one of Ingram's customers at a price 5 percent lower than that of Ingram's price. Ingram is furious, yelling at Scott to do something about this! To help Ingram meet the price, Patterson offers a free drum of LubeExcel to Ingram. Scott is only authorized to give free samples to new customers.

When Ingram leaves the office, Scott decides to look at the Dymotzue price list on Mr. Ingram's desk.

Questions

1. Describe the situation faced by both Scott Patterson and Larry Ingram.
2. What would you do if you were Scott Patterson?
3. What would you do if you were Larry Ingram?
4. What are the ethical considerations, if any, in this case?
5. What level of moral development are Patterson and Ingram operating at in this business relationship?

CASE 3-2

Sales Hype: To Tell the Truth or Stretch It, That Is the Question

Video

Case

Sally Bateman and Kara McAfree have recently begun working as trainees selling furniture for a large department store. Sally has a very aggressive style, whereas Kara strongly believes in giving the customer the best information possible and then selling them a product that best fits their needs.

Sally Tries to Steal Kara's Customer

One day, one of Kara's customers came in shopping for furniture. Sally told the customer Kara was out of the store. After Sally determined they were shopping for a new dining table and chairs, she showed them a certain style and told the couple it was brand new. The customer left the store.

Kara happened to overhear the conversation and approached her co-worker with some concerns. Sally initially thought Kara was frustrated because the couple was Kara's customer and she wanted to make sure she got credit for the sale. Kara's main concern, however, was that Sally lied to the customer about the table being new when it was in fact a year old. Sally told Kara that everyone uses "hype" to make sales and if she wants to make her sales figures, she will have to do it too.

Kara Is Concerned about Her Performance

Performance appraisals are quickly approaching and Kara knows she is getting a poor review because her sales pale in comparison to Sally's. She talks to a co-worker about the review process and asks him if she should tell management that Sally's high numbers are the result of her stealing customers and lying about products. He tells Kara he thinks that would be a bad idea because it might make her look like she is making excuses. He makes it sound as if management may condone the use of sales hype.

Questions

1. Describe the situation faced by Kara.
2. What would you do if you were Kara?
3. What are the ethical considerations, if any, in this case?
4. What level of moral development are Sally and Kara operating at in this business situation?

PART II

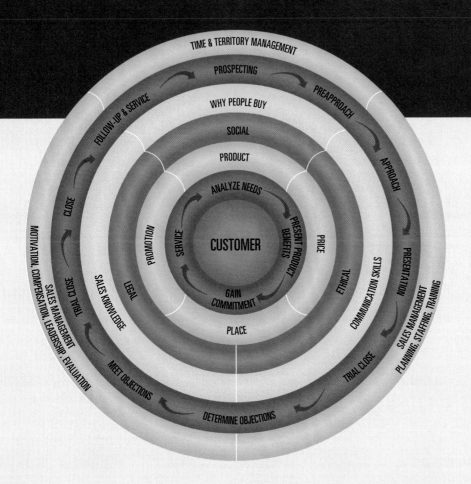

TIME & TERRITORY MANAGEMENT
PROSPECTING
PREAPPROACH
WHY PEOPLE BUY
FOLLOW-UP & SERVICE
SOCIAL
APPROACH
PRODUCT
ANALYZE NEEDS
CLOSE
PROMOTION
SERVICE
PRESENT PRODUCT BENEFITS
CUSTOMER
PRICE
GAIN COMMITMENT
LEGAL
ETHICAL
COMMUNICATION SKILLS
PRESENTATION
SALES KNOWLEDGE
PLACE
SALES MANAGEMENT PLANNING, STAFFING, TRAINING
TRIAL CLOSE
SALES MANAGEMENT MOTIVATION, COMPENSATION, LEADERSHIP, EVALUATION
MEET OBJECTIONS
DETERMINE OBJECTIONS
TRIAL CLOSE

PREPARATION FOR RELATIONSHIP SELLING

Part 2 focuses on the main sales knowledge that salespeople need. Chapter 4 discusses buyer behavior. It begins the discussion of the communication techniques you will use in your sales presentation—salespeople must be excellent communicators. Chapter 5 introduces you to basic verbal and nonverbal communications techniques used by today's salespeople. Chapter 6 provides an overview of sales knowledge required to call on customers. Salespeople use knowledge of buyer behavior, communication skills, and sales knowledge to effectively analyze customer needs, select the proper product benefits to present, gain commitment from the buyer, and provide exceptional service, allowing the opportunity to sell again in the future.

CHAPTER 4

The Psychology of Selling: Why People Buy

MAIN TOPICS

The Tree of Business Life: Benefits

Why People Buy—The Black Box Approach

Psychological Influences on Buying

A *FAB*ulous Approach to Buyer Need Satisfaction

How to Determine Important Buying Needs—a Key to Success

The Trial Close—a Great Way to Uncover Needs and SELL

SELL Sequence

Your Buyer's Perception

Perceptions, Attitudes, and Beliefs

The Buyer's Personality Should Be Considered

Adaptive Selling Based on Buyer's Style

You Can Classify Buying Situations

Technology Provides Information

View Buyers as Decision Makers

Satisfied Customers Are Easier to Sell to

To Buy or Not to Buy—a Choice Decision

LEARNING OBJECTIVES

What do people really buy? They buy the benefits of a product. This chapter examines why and how individuals buy. It emphasizes the need for salespeople to stress benefits in their presentations. After studying this chapter, you should be able to

- Explain the difference between a feature, an advantage, and a benefit.
- Be able to construct a SELL Sequence.
- Know when and how to use a trial close.
- Explain why people buy benefits rather than features or advantages.
- Enumerate techniques for determining a customer's needs.
- List factors that influence the customer's buying decision.
- Show why buying is a choice decision.

Five years ago John Salley graduated with a computer science degree from MIT. One year later, he earned his MBA from Texas A&M University with a perfect "A" average. John was on every campus recruiter's list as an outstanding applicant. He had the brains, personality, looks, and motivation of a winner. IBM convinced him to take a sales job.

John was at the top of his class in the IBM sales-training program. However, his first two years in sales resulted in an average performance. He could not understand why, because his knowledge of the products was outstanding. John could discuss in great depth the most technical aspects of his products. He was not used to being average. John loved sales but felt things had to change.

If you were in John's position, what would you do?

John Salley is like many people who do everything it takes to be successful in sales. Yet for some reason, they never reach their maximum performance potential. To be successful, salespeople need to be knowledgeable, even experts, on everything discussed in Part II, "Preparation for Relationship Selling."

Chapter 4 examines why and how an individual buys. Numerous influences determine why people buy one product over another. We discuss these reasons and apply them to the various steps in the customer's buying process. This chapter presents selling techniques that will aid you later in developing your sales presentation. They also can help John Salley in his efforts to improve his sales performance. He needs to know why people buy.

THE TREE OF BUSINESS LIFE: BENEFITS

As you learn about the psychology of selling, why people buy, and emphasize benefits in your sales presentation in this chapter, keep the Golden Rule in mind. Customers want to trust you! They depend upon you to tell the truth. Use your selling skills learned in this chapter to help people by being a better communicator. Periodically asking a person about what you have just said is a great way to find out what they think about your talk. Do the right thing for the person, even if it means a "no sale." After all, you are with the person to unselfishly help that person make the correct buying decision for his or her need, not your need to make a sale. Ethical service builds relationships and is based upon the truth.

WHY PEOPLE BUY—THE BLACK BOX APPROACH

The question of why people buy has interested salespeople for many years. Salespeople know that some customers buy their product after the presentation, yet they wonder what thought process resulted in the decision to buy or not to buy. Prospective buyers are usually exposed to various sales presentations. In some manner, a person internalizes or considers this information and then makes a buying decision. This process of internalization is referred to as a **black box** because we cannot see into the buyer's mind—meaning that the salesperson can apply the stimuli (a sales presentation) and observe the behavior of the prospect but cannot witness the prospect's actual decision-making process.

EXHIBIT 4.1

Stimulus–response model of
buyer behavior.

The classic model of buyer behavior shown in Exhibit 4.1 is called a **stimulus–response** model. A stimulus (sales presentation) is applied, resulting in a response (purchase decision). This model assumes that prospects respond in some predictable manner to the sales presentation. Unfortunately, it does not tell us why they buy or do not buy the product. This information is concealed in the black box.

Salespeople seek to understand as much as they can about the mental processes that yield the prospects' responses. We do know

■ That people buy for both practical (rational) and psychological (emotional) reasons.

■ That salespeople can use specific methods to help determine the prospects' thoughts during sales presentations.

■ That buyers consider certain factors in making purchase decisions.

This chapter introduces these three important topics. Each topic emphasizes the salesperson's need to understand people's behavior.

PSYCHOLOGICAL INFLUENCES ON BUYING

Since personal selling requires understanding human behavior, each salesperson must be concerned with a prospective customer's motivations, perceptions, learning, attitudes, and personality. Furthermore, the salesperson should know how each type of behavior might influence a customer's purchase decision.

Motivation to Buy Must Be There

Human beings are motivated by needs and wants. These needs and wants build up internally, which cause people to desire to buy a product—a new car or a new duplicating machine. People's **needs** result from a lack of something desirable. **Wants** are needs learned by the person. For example, people *need* transportation—but some *want* a BMW while others *prefer* a Ford Mustang.

This example illustrates that both practical or rational reasons (the need for transportation) and emotional or psychological reasons (the desire for the prestige of owning a BMW) influence the buying decision. Different individuals have different reasons for wanting to buy. The salesperson must determine a prospect's needs and then match the product's benefits to the particular needs and wants of the prospect (see Exhibit 4.2).

Economic Needs: The Best Value for the Money

Economic needs are the buyer's need to purchase the most satisfying product for the money. Economic needs include price, quality (performance, dependability, durability), convenience of buying, and service. Some people's purchases are based primarily on economic need. However, most people consider the economic implications of all their purchases along with other reasons for buying.

Many salespeople mistakenly assume that people base their buying decision solely on price. This is not always correct. A higher product price relative to competing goods often can be offset by such factors as service, quality, better performance, friendliness of the salesperson, or convenience of purchase.

EXHIBIT 4.2

Product plus: A product is more than a product.

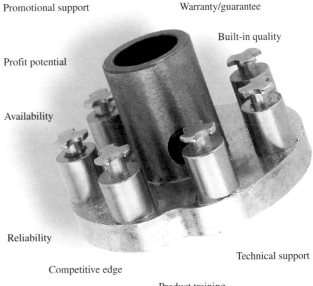

Promotional support

Warranty/guarantee

Built-in quality

Profit potential

Availability

Reliability

Technical support

Competitive edge

Product training

Whatever a person's need might be, it is important for a salesperson to uncover it. Once you determine the individual's need, you are better prepared to develop your sales presentation in a manner relating your product's benefits to that particular need. This is not always easy to do because people may not be fully aware of their needs.

Awareness of Needs: Some Buyers Are Unsure

You have seen that people purchase products to satisfy various needs. Often, however, these needs are developed over such a long period that people may not be fully conscious of their reasons for buying or not buying a product. The buying decision can be complicated by their level of need awareness. Three levels of need awareness have been identified—conscious, preconscious, and unconscious.

At the first level, the **conscious need level,** buyers are fully aware of their needs. These are the easiest people to sell to because they know what products they want and are willing to talk about their needs. A customer might say to the salesperson, "I'd like to buy a new car and I want a BMW loaded with accessories. What can you show me?"

At the second level, the **preconscious need level,** buyers may not be fully aware of their needs. Needs may not be fully developed in the conscious mind. They know what general type of product they want but may not wish to discuss it fully. For example, a buyer may want to buy a certain product because of a strong ego need yet be hesitant about telling you. If you don't make a sale and ask why, this buyer may present false reasons, such as saying your price is too high, rather than revealing the real motivation. Falsification is much easier than stating the true reasons for not buying your product—thus getting into a long conversation with you, arguing with you, or telling you that your product is unsatisfactory. You must avoid this brush-off by determining a buyer's real needs first and then relating your product's benefits to these needs.

At the third level, the **unconscious need level,** people do not know why they buy a product—only that they do buy. When people say, "I really don't know what I want to buy," it may be true. Their buying motives might have developed years earlier and may have been repressed. In this case, the salesperson needs to determine the needs that are influential. Often, this is accomplished by skillful questioning to draw out prospective buyers' unconscious needs. An awareness of the types of needs that buyers may have will allow you to present your product as a vehicle for satisfaction of those needs. Several methods of presenting a product's benefits are available.

A *FABULOUS* APPROACH TO BUYER NEED SATISFACTION

A most powerful selling technique used by successful salespeople today is **benefit selling.** In benefit selling, the salesperson relates a product's benefits to the customer's needs using the product's features and advantages as support. This technique is often referred to as the *FAB* **selling technique** (*F*eature, *A*dvantage, and *B*enefit).* These key terms are defined as follows:

- A product **feature** is any *physical characteristic* of a product.
- A product **advantage** is the *performance characteristic* of a product that describes how it can be used or will help the buyer.
- A product **benefit** is a favorable *result* the buyer receives from the product because of a particular advantage that has the ability to satisfy a buyer's need.

The Product's Features: So What?

All products have features or physical characteristics such as the following:

■ Size	■ Terms	■ Packaging
■ Color	■ Quantity	■ Flavor
■ Taste	■ Price	■ Service
■ Quality	■ Shape	■ Uses
■ Delivery	■ Ingredients	■ Technology

Descriptions of a product's features answer the question, What is it? Typically, when used alone in the sales presentation, features have little persuasive power because buyers are interested in specific benefits rather than features.

When discussing a product's features *alone,* imagine the customer is thinking, "So what? So your product has this shape or quality; how does it perform and how will it benefit me?" That is why you have to discuss the product's advantages as they relate to the buyer's needs.

The Product's Advantages: Prove It!

Once a product feature is presented to the customer, the salesperson normally begins to discuss the advantages that product's physical characteristics provide. This is better than discussing only its features. Describing the product's advantages, how a product can be used, or how it will help the buyer increase the chances of making a sale. Examples of product advantages (performance characteristics) follow:

- It is the fastest-selling soap on the market.
- You can store more information and retrieve it more rapidly with our computer.
- This machine will copy on both sides of the pages instead of only one.

How does the prospective customer know that your claims for a product are true? Imagine a prospect thinking, "Prove it!" Be prepared to substantiate any claims you make.

---

* Some companies train their salespeople using only features and benefits. They see an advantage and benefit as one and the same. Most companies use FAB. This section plus the trial close and SELL Sequence sections are very important for you to learn and use in your sales presentation.

EXHIBIT 4.3

Discuss benefits to fulfill people's needs and to increase sales.

Industrial salespeople work closely with customers to design products and systems that fit their needs.

Consumer goods salespeople can show customers how to increase sales by setting up strategic merchandise displays.

Companies typically train their salespeople thoroughly on the product's physical and performance characteristics. A salesperson may have excellent knowledge of the product yet be unable to describe it in terms that allow the prospect to visualize the benefits of purchasing it. This is because many salespeople present only a product's features and advantages—leaving the buyer to imagine its benefits.

While your chances of helping the customer increase when you discuss both the features and the advantages of your product, you must learn how to stress product benefits that are important to the prospect in your presentation. Once you have mastered this selling technique, your sales will increase.

The Product's Benefits: What's in It for Me?

People are interested in what the product will do for them. Emphasizing benefits appeals to the customer's personal motives by answering the question, What's in it for me? In your presentation, stress how the person will benefit from the purchase rather than the features and advantages of your product as shown in Exhibit 4.3.

To illustrate the idea of buying benefits instead of only features or advantages, consider four items: (1) a diamond ring, (2) camera, (3) STP motor oil, and (4) movie tickets. Do people buy these products or services for their features or advantages? No; people buy the product's benefits such as these:

- A diamond ring—image of success, investment, or to please a loved one.
- Camera—memories of places, friends, and family.
- STP motor oil—engine protection, car investment, or peace of mind.
- Movie tickets—entertainment, escape from reality, or relaxation.

As you can see, people are buying benefits—not a product's features or advantages. These benefits can be both practical, such as an investment, and psychological, such as an image of success. The salesperson needs to discuss benefits to answer the prospect's question, What's in it for me?

EXHIBIT 4.4

Match the buyer's needs to the product's benefits and emphasize them in the sales presentation.

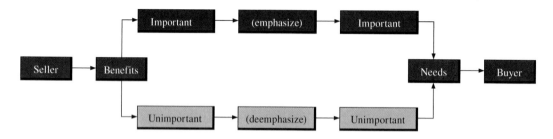

EXAMPLE:

Vacuum-cleaner salesperson to householder: "This vacuum cleaner's high speed motor (**feature**) works twice as fast (**advantage**) with less effort (**advantage**), which saves you 15 to 30 minutes in cleaning time (**benefit**) and the aches and pains of pushing a heavy machine (**benefit**)."

Sporting goods salesperson to customer: "With this ball, you'll get an extra 10 to 20 yards on your drives (**advantage**), helping to reduce your score (**benefit**) because of its new solid core (**feature**)."

Salesperson to buyer of grocery store health and beauty aids: "Prell's economy size (**feature**) sells the best of all brands (**advantage**) in stores like yours. You can increase store traffic 10 to 20 percent (**benefit**) and build your sales volume by at least 5 percent (**benefit**) by advertising and reducing its normal price (**feature**) in next Wednesday's ad."

New salespeople frequently are not accustomed to using feature, advantage, and benefit phrases. To use them regularly in your sales conversation, a standardized *FAB Sequence* can be used as follows:

The . . . (**feature**) . . . means you . . . (**advantage**) . . . with the real benefit to you being . . . (**benefit**) . . . .

The FAB Sequence allows you to easily remember to state the product's benefit in a natural, conversational manner. For example, "*The* new solid core center of the Gunshot Golf Ball *means you* will have an extra 10 or 20 yards on your drives, *with the real benefit to you being* a lower score." You can substitute any features, advantages, and benefits between these transition phrases to develop FAB sequences. Several sequences can be used one after another to emphasize your product's benefits.

Try it. Out loud, read the golf ball FAB Sequence. Then do it again using your own phrasing. Create several variations until finding one you would feel comfortable using in a conversation.

Why should you emphasize benefits? There are two reasons (see Exhibit 4.4). First, by emphasizing benefits customers can better understand if your product will satisfy their need(s). Your primary purpose is to help the person. Second, stressing benefits in your presentation, rather than features or advantages, will bring success. You will satisfy more people's needs and thus your sales will increase.

Given that people make a buying decision based on whether they believe a product's benefits will satisfy their needs, how can you uncover a buyer's needs?

HOW TO DETERMINE IMPORTANT BUYING NEEDS—A KEY TO SUCCESS

Sell the sizzle, not the steak!

Your initial task when first meeting the customer is to differentiate between important buying needs and needs of lesser or no importance. Exhibit 4.5 illustrates the concept that buyers have both important needs and needs that are not major reasons for buying a product (relatively unimportant buying needs).

Determine buyers' important needs and concentrate on emphasizing product benefits that will satisfy those needs. Benefits that would satisfy buyers' unimportant needs should be deemphasized in the sales presentation. Suppose your product had benefits involving service, delivery, time savings, and cost reductions. Is the buyer interested in all four benefits? Maybe not. If you determine that delivery is not important, concentrate on discussing service, time savings, and cost reductions. This selling strategy is important to your success in helping the buyer.

Elmer Wheeler, a famous sales speaker, said, "Sell the sizzle, not the steak!" Wheeler is saying that people buy for reasons other than what the product will actually do or its price. They have both practical (rational) and psychological (emotional) reasons for buying. Customers may not buy the product to solve the rational need that the salesperson perceives as important. They may buy to satisfy an emotional need not easily recognized. It is important to understand this sales concept and learn to determine the buyer's important buying needs. A list of common psychological buying needs includes these:

- Fear
- Vanity (keep up with the Joneses)
- Desire for gain
- Security
- Love of family

- Personal pleasure
- Desire to succeed
- Comfort or luxury
- Self-preservation
- Prevention of loss

You must determine the buying needs that are most important to the customer. How can you do this? Several methods are frequently used to uncover important needs. These methods create the acronym **L-O-C-A-T-E:**

Listen: Prospects may drop leading remarks like, "I wish I had a television like this one."

Observe: Look at prospects; study their surroundings. Experienced salespeople can determine much about people by observing the way they dress or where they live and work.

Combine: A skillful salesperson may talk to others, listen to a prospect, probe with questions, make careful observations, and empathize—all in an effort to uncover the prospect's needs.

Ask questions: Questions often bring out needs that the prospect would not reveal or does not know. The salesperson asks, "Is a quiet ceiling fan important to you?" "Yes, it is," says the buyer. "If I could provide you with the quietest ceiling fan on the market, would you be interested?"

Talk to others: Ask others about a prospect's needs. For instance, ask an office manager's secretary about the manager's satisfaction with a copy machine.

Empathize: Look at the situation from the customer's point of view.[1]

Once you determine the major buying need, you are ready to relate the person's needs to your product's benefits. Like the television camera that transmits images to the television receiver, buyers picture desired products in their minds. Before they focus the picture, buyers often need to be turned on and tuned in. Once you find their real reasons for wanting a particular product or identify major problems that they want to solve, you have uncovered the key to helping them.

Determine needs to fulfill needs!

Uncovering these important buying needs is pushing the button that turns on a machine. You have just pushed the customer's hot button. You have awakened a need, and customers realize that you understand their problems. *Basically, this is what selling is all about—determining needs and skillfully relating your product's benefits to show how its purchase will fulfill customers' needs.*

This is not always easy. As we have seen, people have a multitude of different needs and may not understand or see their unconscious needs or problems. In this situation, your challenge is to convert customers' apparently unconscious needs into recognized and understood needs. One of the best ways to uncover needs is to ask questions at certain times during the sales presentation. This question is referred to as a trial close.

THE TRIAL CLOSE—A GREAT WAY TO UNCOVER NEEDS AND SELL

The **trial close** is one of the best selling techniques to use in your sales presentation. It checks the pulse or attitude of your prospect toward the sales presentation. The trial close should be used at these four important times:

1. After making a strong selling point in the presentation.
2. After the presentation.
3. After answering an objection.
4. Immediately before you move to close the sale.

The trial close allows you to determine (1) whether the prospect likes your product's feature, advantage, or benefit; (2) whether you have successfully answered the objection; (3) whether any objections remain; and (4) whether the prospect is ready for you to close the sale. It is a powerful technique to induce two-way communication (feedback) and participation from the prospect. The Selling Tips box gives examples of trial closes. Learn these—you'll use them throughout the course.

If, for example, the prospect says little while you make your presentation, and if you get a "no" when you come to the close, you may find it difficult to change the prospect's mind. You have not learned the real reasons why the prospect says no. To avoid this, salespeople use the trial close to determine the prospect's attitude toward the product throughout the presentation.

The trial close seeks an opinion.

The trial close asks for the prospect's *opinion,* not a decision to buy. It is a direct question that can be answered with few words.* Look at the trial close examples shown in Selling Tips.

Remember the prospect's positive reactions. Use them later to help overcome objections and in closing the sale. Also remember the negative comments. You may need to offset the negatives with the positives later in the presentation. Generally, however, you will not discuss the negative again.

Here is an example of using the prospect's positive comments to ask for the order. Assume that during the presentation you have learned from the prospect that she likes the product's profit margin, fast delivery, and credit policy. You can summarize these benefits in a positive manner such as this:

Salesperson: Ms. Stevenson, you say you like our profit margin, fast delivery, and credit policy. Is that right? [Summary and trial close.]

* See Chapter 10 for other uses and examples of direct questions.

Using Trial Closes

The trial close is an important part of the sales presentation. It asks for the prospect's opinion concerning what you have just said. The trial close does not ask the person to buy directly. Here are examples:

- How does that sound to you?
- What do you think?
- Are these the features you are looking for?
- That's great—isn't it?
- Is this important to you?

- Does that answer your concern?
- I have a hunch that you like the money-saving features of this product. Did I guess right?
- It appears that you have a preference for this model. Is this what you had in mind?
- I can see that you are excited about this product. On a scale from 1 to 10, how do you feel it will fit your needs?
- I notice your smile. What do you think about . . . ?
- Am I on the right track with this proposal?

Prospect: Yes, I do.

Salesperson: With the number of customers coming into your store and our expected sales of the products due to normal turnover, along with our marketing plan, I *suggest you buy* . . . . [State the products and their quantities.] This will provide sufficient quantities to meet customer demand for the next two months, plus provide you with the profit you expect from your products. I can have the order to you early next week. [Now wait for her response.]

Note that the prospect has said there are three things she likes about what you are selling. If the prospect responds favorably to your trial close, then you are in agreement or you have satisfactorily answered an objection. Thus, the prospect may be ready to buy. However, if you receive a negative response, do not close. Either you have not answered some objection or the prospect is not interested in the feature, advantage, or benefit you are discussing. This feedback allows you to better uncover what your prospect thinks about your product's potential for satisfying needs.

SELL SEQUENCE

One way to remember to incorporate a trial close into your presentation is the **SELL Sequence.** Exhibit 4.5 shows how each letter of the word *sell* stands for a sequence of things to do and say to stress benefits important to the customer. By remembering the word *sell*, you remember to *show the feature, explain the advantage, lead into the benefit, and then let the customer talk by asking a question about the benefit (trial close).*

EXAMPLE:
Industrial salesperson to industrial purchasing agent: "This equipment is made of stainless steel **[feature]**, which means it won't rust **[advantage].** The real benefit is that it reduces your replacement costs, thus saving you money **[benefit]!** That's what you're interested in—right **[trial close]?**"

Talk a while, then ask a question, listen!

EXHIBIT 4.5

The SELL Sequence: Use it throughout your presentation.

S	E	L	L
Show feature	Explain advantage	Lead into benefit	Let customer talk

EXAMPLE:
Beecham salesperson to consumer goods buyer: "Beecham will spend an extra $1 million in the next two months advertising Cling Free fabric softener **[feature].** Plus, you can take advantage of this month's $1.20 per dozen price reduction **[feature].** This means you will sell 15 to 20 percent more Cling Free in the next two months **[advantage],** thus making higher profits and pulling more customers into your store **[benefits].** How does that sound **[trial close]?**"

Once you use a trial close, carefully listen to what the customer says and watch for nonverbal signals to determine if what you said has an impact. If you receive a positive response to your trial close, you are on the right track.

Remember, the trial close does not ask the customer to buy or make any type of purchase decision. It asks only for an opinion. The trial close is a trial question to determine the customer's opinion toward the salesperson's proposition to know if it is time to close the sale. Thus, its main purpose is to induce feedback from the buyer.

Exhibit 4.6 presents six examples of SELL Sequences composed of features, advantages, benefits, and trial closes of products. The first column lists features or product characteristics such as size, shape, performance, and maintenance data. The second column shows advantages that arise from respective features. These are the performance characteristics or what the product will do. The third column contains benefits to the customer from these features and advantages.

SELL Sequences sell.

The last column shows a question—or trial close—related to what the salesperson said. The trial close acts as a feedback method to determine the buyer's opinion about the feature, advantage, and/or benefit. It helps uncover what is important, and what is not important, to the other person. Try using the trial close in your everyday conversations with friends, co-workers, and family members. It works!

EXHIBIT 4.6

Examples of features, advantages, benefits, and trial closes that form the SELL Sequence.

Features (physical characteristics)	Advantages (performance characteristics)	Benefits (result from advantage)	Trial Closes (feedback questions)
1. Nationally advertised consumer product	1. Will sell more product	1. Will make you a high profit	1. What do you think?
2. Air conditioner with a high energy-efficiency rating	2. Uses less electricity	2. Saves 10 percent in energy costs	2. Is this important to you?
3. Product made of stainless steel	3. Will not rust	3. Reduces your replacement costs	3. How does that sound to you?
4. Supermarket computer system with the IBM 3651 Store Controller	4. Can store more information and retrieve it rapidly by supervising up to 24 grocery checkout scanners and terminals and look up prices on up to 22,000 items	4. Provides greater accuracy, register balancing, store ordering, and inventory management	4. That's great—isn't it?
5. Five percent interest on money in bank checking NOW account	5. Earns interest that would not normally be received	5. Gives you one extra bag of groceries each month	5. Do you want to earn extra money?
6. Golf club head made of aerodynamically designed titanium steel	6. Increased club head speed, longer drives	6. Lower scores	6. And that's what counts—right?

For each major product feature, you should develop the resulting advantage and benefit. Then create a trial close to induce feedback for the buyer. You should use the SELL Sequences throughout your presentation.

YOUR BUYER'S PERCEPTION

Why would two people have the same need but buy different products? Likewise, why might the same individual at different times view your product differently? The answers to both questions involve how the person perceives your product.

Perception is the process by which a person selects, organizes, and interprets information. The buyer receives the salesperson's product information through the senses: sight, hearing, touch, taste, and smell. These senses act as filtering devices that information must pass through before it can be used.

Each of the three perception components (selection, organization, and interpretation) plays a part in determining buyers' responses to you and to your sales presentation. Buyers often receive large amounts of information in a short period, and they typically perceive and use only a small amount of it. They ignore or quickly forget other information because of the difficulty of retaining large amounts of information. This process is known as **selective exposure** because only a portion of the information an individual is exposed to is selected to be organized, interpreted, and allowed into awareness.

Why does some information reach a buyer's consciousness while other information does not? First, the salesperson may not present the information in a manner that ensures proper reception. For example, the salesperson may provide too much information at one time. This causes confusion, and the buyer tunes out. In some cases, information may be haphazardly presented, which causes the buyer to receive it in an unorganized manner (see Exhibit 4.7).

Sight, smell, hearing, taste, feeling.

A sales presentation that appeals to the buyer's five senses helps to penetrate perceptual barriers. It also enhances understanding and reception of the information as you present it. Selling techniques such as asking questions, using visual aids, and

EXHIBIT 4.7

Visual aids help this pharmaceutical salesperson present complex medical information in a simple, organized manner. What human senses is this salesperson appealing to?

demonstrating a product can force buyers to participate in the presentation. This helps determine if they understand your information.

Second, buyers tend to allow information to reach consciousness if it relates to needs they recognize and wish to fulfill. If, for example, someone gives you reasons for purchasing life insurance and you do not perceive a need for it, there is a good chance that your mind will allow little of this information to be perceived. However, if you need life insurance, chances are you will listen carefully to the salesperson. If you are uncertain about something, you will ask questions to increase your understanding.

A buyer's perceptual process also may result in **selective distortion** or the altering of information. It frequently occurs when a person receives information that is inconsistent with existing beliefs and attitudes. When buyers listen to a sales presentation on a product that they perceive as low quality, they may mentally alter the information to coincide with that belief, thereby reinforcing themselves. Should buyers believe that the product is of high quality, even when it is not, they may change any negative information about the product into positive information. This distortion can substantially lessen the intended *effect* of a salesperson attempting to compare a product to the product currently used by the individual.

Selective retention can also influence perception. Here, buyers may remember only information that supports their attitudes and beliefs, and forget what does not. After a salesperson leaves, buyers may forget the product's advantages the salesperson stressed because they are not consistent with their beliefs and attitudes.

These perceptions help explain why a buyer may or may not buy. Buyers' perceptual processes act as a filter by determining what part of the sales message they hear, how they interpret it, and what product information they retain. Therefore, two different sales messages given by two different salespeople, even though they concern similar products, can be received differently. A buyer can tune out one sales presentation, tune in the other presentation, and purchase the perceived product.

Although you cannot control a buyer's perceptions, often you can influence and change them. To be successful, you must understand that perceptual barriers can arise during your presentation. You must learn to recognize when they occur and how to overcome them.

PERCEPTIONS, ATTITUDES, AND BELIEFS

You make a sales presentation concerning a product's features, advantages, and benefits. Your goal is to provide information that makes the buyer knowledgeable enough to make an educated purchase decision. However, a person's perceptual process may prevent your information from being fully utilized. Understanding how people develop their perceptions can help you be more successful in selling (see Exhibit 4.7).

Perceptions are learned. People develop their perceptions through experience. This is why **learning** is defined as acquiring knowledge or a behavior based on past experiences.

Successful salespeople must help buyers learn about them and their products. If buyers have learned to trust you, they listen and have faith in what you say, thereby increasing the chance of making sales. If your products perform as you claim they will, buyers will repurchase them more readily. If your presentation provides the information necessary to make a decision, your probability of making the sale increases. Product knowledge influences the buyer's attitudes and beliefs about your product.

"The wisest mind has something yet to learn."

GEORGE SANTAYANA

MAKING THE SALE

Find the F's

Count the number of F's in the sentence below. How many did you find the first time you read the sentence?

> FEATURE FILMS ARE
> THE RESULT OF YEARS
> OF SCIENTIFIC STUDY
> COMBINED WITH THE
> EXPERIENCE OF YEARS.

We often miss what may be right under our noses, such as buying signals. How many F's are there? There are six, but three are part of the word *of* which has a different sound. You would be surprised at the number of people who miss the answer.

A person's **attitudes** are learned predispositions toward something. These feelings can be favorable or unfavorable. If a person is neutral toward the product or has no knowledge of the product, no attitude exists. A buyer's attitude is shaped by past and present experience.

Creating a positive attitude is important, but it alone does not result in your making the sale. To sell a product to someone, you also must convert a buyer's belief into a positive attitude. A **belief** is a state of mind in which trust or confidence is placed in something or someone. The buyer must believe your product will fulfill a need or solve a problem. A favorable attitude toward one product over another comes from a belief that one product is better.

Also, a buyer must believe that you are the best person from whom to buy. If they do not trust you as the best source, people will not buy from you. Assume, for example, that someone decides to buy a 19-inch portable RCA color television. Three RCA dealers are in the trading area and each dealer offers to sell at approximately the same price. Chances are that the purchaser will buy from the salesperson she believes to be the best, even though there is no reason not to trust the other dealers.

If buyers' perceptions create favorable attitudes that lead them to believe your product is best for them and that they should buy from you, you make sales. Often, however, people may not know you or your product. Your job is to provide information about your product that allows buyers to form positive attitudes and beliefs. Should their perception, attitudes, and beliefs be negative, distorted, or incorrect, you must change them. As a salesperson, you spend much of your time creating or changing people's learned attitudes and beliefs about your product. This is the most difficult challenge a salesperson faces.

**Example of
a Buyer's
Misperceptions**

Assume, for example, that a woman is shopping for a ceiling fan for her home. The three main features of the product she is interested in are price, quality, and style. While shopping around, she had seen two brands, the Hunter and the Economy brand. The information she received about these two brands has caused her to conclude that all ceiling fans are basically alike. Each brand seems to offer the same features and advantages. Because of this attitude, she has formed the belief that she should purchase a low-price fan, in this case, the Economy ceiling fan. Cost is the key factor influencing this purchase decision.

She decides to stop at one more store that sells Casablanca fans. She asks the salesperson to see some lower-priced fans. These fans turn out to be more expensive than either the Hunter or Economy models. Noting their prices, she says to the salesperson, "That's not what I had in mind." She walks away as the salesperson says, "Thanks for coming by."

What should the salesperson have done? When the customer walked into the store, the salesperson knew her general need was for a ceiling fan. However, the customer had wrongly assumed that all brands are alike. It was the salesperson's job to first ask fact-finding questions of the customer such as: "Where will you use the fan?" "What color do you have in mind?" "Is there a particular style you are interested in?" "What features are you looking for?" and "What price range would you like to see?" These questions allow the salesperson to determine the customer's specific needs and her attitudes and beliefs about ceiling fans.

Learning the answers to these questions enables the salesperson to explain the benefits of the Casablanca fan as compared to the Hunter and Economy brands. The salesperson can show that fans have different features, advantages, and benefits and explain why there are price differences among the three fans. The buyer can then make a decision as to which ceiling fan best suits her specific needs. Knowledge of a buyer's learned attitudes and beliefs can make sales; with this information, a salesperson can alter the buyer's perceptions or reinforce them when presenting the benefits of the product.

THE BUYER'S PERSONALITY SHOULD BE CONSIDERED

People's personalities also can affect buying behavior by influencing the types of products that fulfill their particular needs. **Personality** can be viewed as the individual's distinguishing character traits, attitudes, or habits. Although it is difficult to know exactly how personality affects buying behavior, it is generally believed that personality has some influence on a person's perceptions, attitudes, and beliefs, and thus on buying behavior.

Self-Concept

One of the best ways to examine personality is to consider a buyer's **self-concept,** the view of one's self. Internal or personal self-evaluation may influence a buyer's attitude toward the products desired or not desired. Some theorists believe that people buy products that match their self-concept. According to self-concept theory, buyers possess four images:

1. The **real self**—people as they actually are.
2. The **self-image**—how people see themselves.
3. The **ideal self**—what people would like to be.
4. The **looking-glass self**—how people think others regard them.

How do you view yourself?

As a salesperson, you should attempt to understand the buyer's self-concept, because it may be the key to understanding the buyer's attitudes and beliefs. For example, if a man is apparently unsatisfied with his self-image, he might be sold through appeals to his ideal self-image. You might compliment him by saying, "Mr. Buyer, it is obvious that the people in your community think highly of you. They know you as an ideal family man and good provider for your family [looking-glass self]. Your purchase of this life insurance policy will provide your family with the security you want [ideal self]." This appeal is targeted at the looking-glass self and the ideal self. Success in sales is often closely linked to the salesperson's knowledge of the buyer's self-concept rather than the buyer's real self.

ADAPTIVE SELLING BASED ON BUYER'S STYLE

While it is important to know a buyer's self-concept, you also should attempt to uncover any additional aspects of the prospect's personality that might influence a decision to buy so that you can further adjust your sales approach. One way to do this is through the study of personality types.

Personality Typing

Carl Gustav Jung (1875–1961), with Sigmund Freud, laid the basis for modern psychiatry. Jung divided human awareness into four functions: (1) feeling, (2) sensing, (3) thinking, and (4) intuiting.* He argued that most people are most comfortable behaving in one of these four groups. Each group, or personality type, has certain characteristics formed by past experiences.

Exhibit 4.8 provides some guidelines you can use to identify someone's personality style. You can determine styles by identifying the key trait, focusing on time orientation, and identifying the environment, and by what people say. Imagine that four of your buyers say the following things to you:

a. "I'm not interested in all of those details. What's the bottom line?"
b. "How did you arrive at your projected sales figure?"
c. "I don't think you see how this purchase fits in with our whole operation here."
d. "I'm not sure how our people will react to this."

How would you classify their personality styles?[†]

Adapt Your Presentation to the Buyer's Style

The major challenge is to adapt your personal style to best relate to the people you deal with. For example, if you consider the customer (or person) that you best relate to, the one that you find it easiest to call on, the odds are that his or her primary personality style is similar to yours. The other side of the coin states that the person hardest for you to call on usually has a primary style that differs from yours.

The objective is to increase your skill at recognizing the style of the people you deal with. Once you recognize the basic style of a buyer, for example, it is possible to modify and adapt your presentation to the buyer's style to achieve the best results. Although this method is not foolproof, it does offer an alternative way of presenting material if you are not succeeding. Let's examine a suggested tailored selling method based on the prospect's personality type preferences.

The Thinker Style

This person places high value on logic, ideas, and systematic inquiry. Completely preplan your presentation with ample facts and supporting data and be precise. Present your material in an orderly and logical manner. When closing the sale be sure to say, "Think it over, Joe, and I'll get back to you tomorrow," whenever the order does not close on the spot.

---

* There are numerous methods of personality typing, each of which is due to the method's conceptual theory. Currently, personality typing is a popular sales training technique. I use Jung's classification because of his scientific reputation.

[†] Answers: (*a*) Senser, (*b*) Thinker, (*c*) Intuitor, and (*d*) Feeler.

EXHIBIT 4.8

Guidelines to identifying personality style.

Guideline	Thinker	Intuitor	Feeler	Senser
How to describe this person	A direct, detail-oriented person. Likes to deal in sequence on *his/her time*. Very precise, sometimes seen as a nitpicker. Fact-oriented.	A knowledgeable, future-oriented person. An innovator who likes to abstract principles from a mass of material. Active in community affairs by assisting in policy making, program development, etc.	People-oriented. Very sensitive to people's needs. An emotional person rooted in the past. Enjoys contact with people. Able to read people very well.	Action-oriented person. Deals with the world through his/her senses. Very decisive and has a high energy level.
The person's strengths	Effective communicator, deliberative, prudent, weighs alternatives, stabilizing, objective, rational, analytical, asks questions for more facts.	Original, imaginative, creative, broad-gauged, charismatic, idealist, intellectual, tenacious, ideological, conceptual, involved.	Spontaneous, persuasive, empathetic, grasps traditional values, probing, introspective, draws out feelings of others, loyal, actions based on what has worked in the past.	Pragmatic, assertive, directional results-oriented, technically skillful, objective–bases opinions on what he/she actually sees, perfection seeking, decisive, direct and down to earth, action-oriented.
The person's drawbacks	Verbose, indecisive, overcautious, overanalyzes, unemotional, nondynamic, controlled and controlling, overserious, rigid, nit-picking.	Unrealistic, far-out, fantasy-bound, scattered, devious, out-of-touch, dogmatic, impractical, poor listener.	Impulsive, manipulative, overpersonalizes, sentimental, postponing, guilt-ridden, stirs up conflict, subjective.	Impatient, doesn't see long range, status-seeking, self-involved, acts first then thinks, lacks trust in others, nit-picking, impulsive, does not delegate to others.
Time orientation	Past, present, future	Future	Past	Present
Environment				
Desk	Usually neat	Reference books, theory books, etc.	Personal plaques and mementos, family pictures	Chaos
Room	Usually has a calculator and computer output, etc.	Abstract art, bookcases, trend charts, etc.	Decorated warmly with pictures of scenes or people. Antiques.	Usually a mess with piles of papers, etc. Action pictures or pictures of the manufacturing plant or products on the wall.
Dress	Neat and conservative.	Mod or rumpled.	Current styles or informal.	No jacket; loose tie or functional work clothes.

The Intuitor Style

This person places high value on ideas, innovation, concepts, theory, and long-range thinking. The main point is to tie your presentation into the buyer's big picture or overview of this person's objectives. Strive to build the buyer's concepts and objectives into your presentation whenever possible. In presenting your material, be sure you have ample time.

In closing the sale, stress time limitations on acting. A good suggestion is to say, "I know you have a lot to do—I'll go to Sam to get the nitty-gritty handled and get this off the ground."

The Feeler Style

This person places high value on being people oriented and sensitive to people's needs. The main point to include in your presentation is the impact your idea will have on people. The feeler likes to small talk with you, so engage in conversation and wait for this person's cue to begin your presentation. The buyer will usually ask, "What's on your mind today?" or something similar. Use emotional terms and words, such as, "We're *excited* about this!"

In your presentation, start with something carried over from your last call or contact. Keep the presentation on a personal note. Whenever possible, get the buyer away from the office (lunch, snack, etc.) on an informal basis; this is how this person prefers to do business. Force the close by saying something such as, "OK, Joe, if there are no objections, let's set it up for next week." Even if the buyer says "No," you are not dead. The key with a feeler is to push the decision.

The Senser Style

This person places high value on *action.* The key point with a senser is to be brief and to the point. Graphs, models, and samples help the senser visualize your presentation. With a senser, verbal communication is more effective than written communication.

In presenting, start with conclusions and results and have supporting data to use when needed. Suggest an action plan—"Let's move *now*"—the buyer has to feel you know what to do.

In closing, give one best way. Have options, but do not present them unless you have to. An effective senser close is, "I know you're busy; let's set this up right *now.*"

Watch for Clues

Exhibit 4.9 shows two buyers' environments. Look at the environment guidelines listed in Exhibit 4.8 to identify each buyer's personality style.

The neatness of the desk and dress of the buyer on the left indicates she may be a thinker, whereas the buyer on the right appears to be a senser. The salesperson should alternate the presentation to fit each person's style. However, determining a buyer's personality style is not always as easy as the example shown in Exhibit 4.9.

Determining Style Can Be Difficult

Each of the four styles is present, in some degree, in all of us. However, one primary style is usually dominant, and another complementary style is used as a back-up. The primary style an individual employs often remains the same in both normal and stress situations, whereas the secondary style is likely to vary.

Some individuals do not have a primary or secondary style, but have a personal style comprising all four types. Dealing with this individual requires strong rapport to isolate the prospect's predominant personal likes and dislikes.

What Is Your Style?   What is your personality style? It only takes a few minutes to find out by completing the short questionnaire "What's My Style" in Appendix B.

EXHIBIT 4.9

Environment provides clues to the buyer's style. What are the personality styles of the buyers who sit at these desks?

YOU CAN CLASSIFY BUYING SITUATIONS

Some people may appear to make up their minds quickly and easily either to buy or not to buy. This is not always the case. The quickness and ease of deciding the product to buy typically depends on the buying situation. Purchasing a gallon of milk is quite different from buying an automobile. People have more difficulty in selecting, organizing, and interpreting information when purchasing an automobile. Also, their attitudes and beliefs toward the automobile may not be well formed.

True, a few people have the type of personality (and resources) that allows them to quickly purchase an expensive product such as an automobile, but this is unusual. When purchasing some types of products, most people carefully compare competing brands. They talk to salespeople. As they collect information, they form attitudes and beliefs toward each product. People must decide which product has the most desirable features, advantages, and benefits. When considering several brands, people may seek information on each one. The more information they collect, the greater the difficulty they may have in deciding which product to buy.

Purchase decisions can usually be classified as to the difficulty involved in deciding which product to buy. The purchase decision is viewed as a problem-solving activity falling into one of three classifications shown in Exhibit 4.10. These are routine decision making, limited decision making, and extensive decision making.

Some Decisions Are Routine

Many products are purchased repeatedly. People are in the habit of buying a particular product. They give little thought or time to the routine purchase; they fully realize the product's benefits. These are called low-involvement goods because they involve a routine buying decision. People's attitudes and beliefs toward the product are already formed and are usually positive. Milk, cold drinks, and many grocery items often are purchased through **routine decision making.**

For a customer making a routine purchase decision, reinforce that this is the correct buying decision. It is important to have the product in stock. If you do not have it, the customer may go to another supplier.

For someone not currently using your product, the challenge is to change this person's product loyalty or normal buying habits. The features, advantages, and benefits of your product should be directly compared to the buyer's preferred brand. Of course, not all purchase decisions are routine.

EXHIBIT 4.10

The three classes of buying situations.

Low Involvement — Routine decision making → Limited decision making → Extensive decision making — High Involvement

Some Decisions Are Limited

When buyers are unfamiliar with a particular product brand, they seek more information when making a purchase decision. In this case, there is **limited decision making**—a moderate level of actual buyer involvement in the decision. Buyers know the general qualities of goods in the product class, but they are not familiar with each brand's features, advantages, and benefits. For example, they may perceive that Xerox, 3M, and Canon copiers are the same in performance.

These buyers have more involvement in buying decisions in terms of shopping time, money, and potential dissatisfaction with the purchase than in the routine purchase decision. They seek information to aid them in making the correct decision. The sales presentation should provide buyers with the necessary knowledge to make brand comparisons and increase their confidence that the purchase of your product is the correct decision. Occasionally, the purchase of some products requires prospective buyers to go one step further and apply extensive decision making.

Some Decisions Are Extensive

Buyers seeking to purchase products such as insurance, a home, or an automobile are highly involved in making the buying decision. They may be unfamiliar with a specific brand or type of product and have difficulty in making the purchase decision. This kind of purchase requires more of an investment in time and money than the limited decision. This situation demands **extensive decision making** and problem-solving activities.

In making extensive decisions, buyers believe that much more is at stake relative to other buying decisions. They may become frustrated during the decision-making process, especially if a large amount of information is available. They may become confused—not knowing what product features they are interested in because of unfamiliarity with the products. Buying an automobile or a life insurance policy, for example, entails potentially confusing purchase decisions.

Determine all possible reasons why buyers are interested in a product. Then, in a simple, straightforward manner, present only enough information to allow the buyer to make a decision. At this time, you can make product comparisons, if necessary. You also can help the buyer evaluate alternative products.

In summary, your challenge is to *provide buyers with product knowledge that allows them to know if your products fulfill their needs.* Determining what type of decision process a buyer is using is critical to helping the person or organization.

TECHNOLOGY PROVIDES INFORMATION

Technology provides information for customer decision making and service. With enormous amounts of data and sophisticated computer programs at their fingertips, salespeople can serve customers faster and better.

The salesperson shown in Exhibit 4.11, for example, looks at the architect's specifications while reviewing his products on a laptop computer to see which best meet the customer's needs. At the same time, he is talking to his warehouse to determine inventory status and product cost. Once satisfied that the salesperson's product satisfies his needs and is available at a reasonable cost, the construction foreman approves the purchase.

EXHIBIT 4.11

This salesperson has seen automation increase his quality of service to his customers.

The salesperson asks his warehouse when the product would arrive at the construction site and then tells the warehouse to ship it. Technology allows the salesperson to sell his customer the right product, at the right price, in the quantity needed and to have it delivered in a timely manner.

VIEW BUYERS AS DECISION MAKERS

Buyers, whether individuals or industrial purchasing agents, are constantly exposed to information about various products. What steps do people go through in making a purchase decision?

Typically, the buying decision involves the five basic steps shown in Exhibit 4.12. Buyers recognize a need, collect information provided by the salesperson, evaluate that information, decide to buy, and after the purchase determine whether they are satisfied. This sequence reveals that several events occur before and after the purchase, all of which the salesperson should consider.

As Exhibit 4.12 shows, numerous forces influence a consumer's buying behavior. Rich people or older people, for example, often view purchases differently than lower-income or younger consumers. Psychological factors such as past experience with a salesperson—good or bad—certainly influence buying decisions. Have you ever had a friend or family member cause you to buy one product rather than another? We all have. Thus, whether we realize it or not, numerous factors influence why someone buys something.

Need Arousal

Remember from the first part of this chapter that buyers may experience a need, or the need can be triggered by the salesperson; this is called **need arousal.** It could be psychological, social, or economic; it could be a need for safety, self-actualization, or ego fulfillment. You must determine a person's needs to know what product information to provide. This information should relate the product's benefits to the person's needs.

Collection of Information

If buyers know which product satisfies a need, they buy quickly. The salesperson may need only approach them; they already want to buy the product.

EXHIBIT 4.12

Personal, psychological, and social forces that influence consumers' buying behavior.

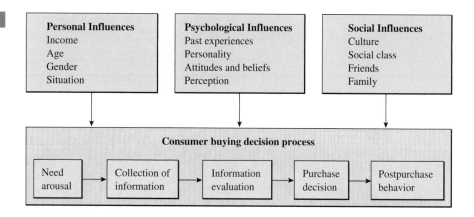

Personal Influences	**Psychological Influences**	**Social Influences**
Income	Past experiences	Culture
Age	Personality	Social class
Gender	Attitudes and beliefs	Friends
Situation	Perception	Family

Consumer buying decision process

Need arousal → Collection of information → Information evaluation → Purchase decision → Postpurchase behavior

However, when buyers are faced with limited or extensive problem solving, they may want to **collect information** about the product. They might visit several retail stores and contact several potential suppliers. They may talk with a number of salespeople about a product's price, advantage, size, and warranty before making a decision.

Information Evaluation

A person's product **information evaluation** determines what will be purchased. After mentally processing all the information about products that will satisfy a need—and this may or may not include your product—a buyer matches this information with needs, attitudes, and beliefs, as discussed earlier, in making a decision. Only then will a **purchase decision** be made.

This evaluation process includes rating preferences on factors such as price, quality, and brand reputation. Attitudes on different products are based on either psychological or rational reasons.

At this stage, a salesperson can be effective. Providing information that matches product features, advantages, and benefits with a buyer's needs, attitudes, and beliefs increases the chances of selling the person the correct product. So, the salesperson is responsible for uncovering the person's needs, attitudes, and beliefs early in the discussion to match the product with the person's needs.

One way to get such information is to determine not only needs, beliefs, and attitudes but also the type of information a person needs before making a decision. Here are some questions you need to know how to answer:

- Which product attributes are important in this decision—price, quality, service?
- Of these attributes, which are *most* important?
- What are the prospect's attitudes toward your products?
- What are the prospect's attitudes toward your competitor's products?
- Which level of satisfaction is expected from buying the product?

This type of questioning not only tells you about the customer's needs but also involves the customer in the presentation and may convey the idea that you are truly interested in his or her needs. This attitude toward you is enough to create positive attitudes about your product.

Armed with this knowledge about the customer, the salesperson is in a better position to provide the information necessary for a decision and also to help the customer evaluate information in favor of your product. The information should be provided simply, clearly, and in a straightforward manner. It should seek to correct any misinformation about your product. Matching information with a customer's needs may enable you to

- Alter the person's beliefs about your product, for example, by convincing the customer that your product is priced higher than the competition because it is a quality product.
- Alter the person's beliefs about your competitor's products.
- Change the amount of importance a person attaches to a particular product attribute, for example, by having the customer consider quality and service rather than price alone.
- Show unnoticed attributes of your product.
- Change the search for the ideal product into a more realistic pursuit, such as by substituting a $100,000 home for a $200,000 home, or showing a man who is 6 feet 10 inches tall a midsize car rather than a compact.

A company has no better promotional device than having its sales force help prospects and customers to evaluate products on the market—and not merely their own products. The two-way communication between buyer and seller is exceptionally effective in providing the information needed to make the sale on the one hand, and to evaluate the product on the other. Salespeople provide knowledge to aid people in their decision-making process. In many respects, salespeople are teachers (professors, if you will) who provide helpful information.

Purchase Decision   Is the sale made once the prospect states an intention to buy? No. Do not consider the sale final until the contract is signed or until you have the buyer's money, because there is still a chance for a change of mind. Even after a customer has selected a product, purchase intentions can be changed by these four basic factors:

1. The attitude of significant others, such as a relative, spouse, friend, or boss. Consider both the intensity of another person's attitude and the level of motivation the buyer has to comply with or to resist this other person's attitude (see Exhibit 4.13).
2. The perceived risk of buying the product—will it give a return on the money?
3. Uncontrollable circumstances, such as not being able to finance the purchase of a house or to pass the physical examination for a large life insurance policy.
4. The salesperson's actions after the decision has been reached—sometimes it is unwise to continue to talk about a product after this point; something could change the customer's mind.

The third factor, uncontrollable circumstances, is self-explanatory. However, how can attitudes of others influence a sale? A man may want to buy a dark, conservative business suit, whereas his wife wants him to buy a sport coat and slacks. The buyer's original favorable attitude toward the business suit may have been changed by his wife. In industrial selling, others in the buyer's firm can influence the sale. Be sure to tell your story.

Since buyers may not always be sure that they will be satisfied with a purchase, they may perceive a risk; they may experience tension and anxiety after buying your product. Haven't we all asked ourselves, Have I made the correct decision? The levels of tension and anxiety people experience are related to their perceptions of and attitudes about the products they had to choose from. Uncertainty about differences between your product and those of your competitors can create anxiety, especially if both products' benefits appear similar, or if your product is more expensive yet

EXHIBIT 4.13

Other people can influence the prospect's decision to purchase.

This pharmaceutical rep must service and meet the needs of technicians, physicians, and buyers in hospitals that use his company's products.

This salesperson should sell to both people in the discussion. Otherwise, one person could talk the other out of buying the product.

promises better benefits. Prospects might see little difference between products or may like them all—and thus can fairly easily change their minds several times before buying.

Finally, many sales have been lost after a buyer has said, "I will buy," and the salesperson continues to talk. Additional information sometimes causes buyers to change their minds. It is important to finalize the sale as quickly as possible after the buyer makes a decision. Once the prospect decides, stop adding information, pack up your bag, and leave.

Postpurchase

This is how you follow the Golden Rule of Personal Selling.

No, the decision process does *not* end with the purchase—not for the buyer at least! A product, once purchased, yields certain levels of satisfaction and dissatisfaction. **Purchase satisfaction** comes from receiving benefits expected, or greater than expected, from a product. If buyers' experiences from the use of a product exceed expectations, they are satisfied, but if experiences are below expectations, customers are dissatisfied.

The buyer can experience **purchase dissonance** after the product's purchase. Dissonance causes tension over whether the right decision was made in buying the product. Some people refer to this as *buyer's remorse.* Dissonance increases with the importance of the decision and the difficulty of choosing between products. If dissonance occurs, buyers may get rid of a product by returning it or by selling it to someone else. Alternatively, they may seek assurance from the salesperson or friends that the product is a good one and that they made the correct purchase decision (positively reinforcing themselves).

You can help the buyer to be satisfied with the product and lower the level of dissonance in several ways. First, if necessary, show the buyer how to use the product properly, as shown in Exhibit 4.13. Second, be realistic in making claims for the product. Exaggerated claims may create dissatisfaction. Third, continually reinforce buyers' decisions by reminding them how well the product actually performs and fulfills their needs. Remember, in some situations buyers can return the product to the seller after purchase. This cancels your sale and hurts your chances of making future sales to this customer. Fourth, follow up after the sale to determine if a problem exists. If so, help correct it. This is a great way to increase the likelihood of repeat business.

In summary, seek to sell a product that satisfies the buyer's needs. In doing so, remember that the sale is made only when the actual purchase is complete and that you should continue to reinforce the buyer's attitudes about the product at all times, even after the sale. This practice reduces the perceived risk of making a bad buy, which allows buyers to listen to and trust your sales message even though some of your proposals may be out of line with their purchase plans. It also can reduce the buyers' postpurchase dissonance. Buyers who have developed a trust in your product claims believe that you will help them properly use the product.

SATISFIED CUSTOMERS ARE EASIER TO SELL TO

It is easier to sell to a customer than to a stranger—especially a satisfied customer! That's why building a relationship—keeping in touch after the sale—is so important to a salesperson's success. Sally Fields of California Office Supply says:

> It took me five tough years to build up my customer base. Now selling is easy and fun. But the first months were terrible. Calling only on strangers got old, but I hung in there. I was going to succeed—no matter how hard I had to work.
>
> The more strangers I sold, the more friends (customers) I had. It is easy to sell a friend. So in the mornings I contacted possible new customers and in the afternoons I visited customers to make sure they were happy with their purchases and sell them more office supplies. Today, 80 percent of my monthly sales come from existing customers. I still make cold calls to keep sharp. By next year my goal is to have 95 percent sales come from these customers. To do that I must do all I can to make sure customers are happy plus find new customers. The relationships I build today will take care of my tomorrow!

Fields owes her success to doing everything she can to ensure her customers are happy with their purchases and her organization's service. Her yearly income is now more than $100,000. She has built her business through hard work, selling, and service. More on follow-up and service later in the book.

TO BUY OR NOT TO BUY—A CHOICE DECISION

Salespeople realize that people buy a product because of a need, and that need can be complex due to the influence of perceptions, attitudes, beliefs, and personality. Furthermore, perceptions, attitudes, and beliefs may differ from one purchase situation to another. How is it possible to state why people buy one product and not another?

Salespeople do not have to be psychologists to understand human behavior. Nor do they need to understand the material covered in courses taken by a psychology major. Furthermore, the average salesperson cannot know all that is involved in the psychological and practical processes that a buyer goes through in making a purchase decision.

ETHICAL DILEMMA

Sock It to Her!

Selling new cars often was difficult, but Linda Martin felt she had a new Cadillac sold. A woman called and said she wanted to buy a new Cadillac exactly like the one parked outside of Linda's office. Linda had another one the same color, but it was fully loaded with the latest high-tech equipment and cost $6,000 more.

The buyer, a 68-year-old widow, listened as Linda described both cars, emphasizing the higher-priced Cadillac. The buyer seemed to become confused over how to work options such as the disc stereo system and cellular telephone. Suddenly the buyer said, "Linda, you seem like a nice person. Which car do you think I should buy?"

What would be the most ethical action to take?

1. Tell the customer to buy the more expensive model. She probably has enough money and you will get more commission.

2. Advise the customer that you think she would be happier with the less expensive model—she does not seem to need or want all of the high-tech gadgets in the more expensive car. Offer to call other dealers in town to see if they have one in stock. You might lose the commission, but at least you have a satisfied customer.

3. Advise the customer that both are equally good options and let her make the decision herself. But do tell her that you only have the more expensive model in stock and that the other car would take six to eight weeks to deliver.

What the salesperson *does* need to understand are the various factors that can influence the buying decision, the fact that buyers actually examine various factors that influence these decisions, that buyers actually go through various steps in making decisions, and how to develop a sales presentation that persuades buyers to purchase the product to satisfy needs. To do this, the salesperson should consider the following questions before developing a sales presentation:

- What type of product is desired?
- What type of buying situation is it?
- How will the product be used?
- Who is involved in the buying decision?
- What practical factors may influence the buyer's decision?
- What psychological factors may influence the buyer's decision?
- What are the buyer's important buying needs?

Again, it seems necessary to know a great deal about a person's attitudes and beliefs to answer these questions. Can this be made simpler? Yes. Simply stated, to buy or not to buy is a choice decision. The person's choice takes one of two forms: First, a person has the choice of buying a product or not. Second, the choice can be between competing products. The question salespeople should ask themselves is, "How can I convince a person to choose my product?" The answer to this question involves five things; each is necessary to make the sale. People will buy if

1. They perceive a need or problem.
2. They desire to fulfill a need or solve a problem.
3. They decide there is a high probability that your product will fulfill their needs or solve their problems better than your competitor's products.
4. They believe they should buy from you.
5. They have the resources and authority to buy.

What do you do if you know your product can reduce a prospect's manufacturing costs, saving the firm $5,000 a year, for a cost of $4,000, and the prospect says, "No thanks, I like my present equipment"? This buyer does not perceive a need, and will not buy. Suppose you make your point about reducing operating costs, but for some reason the prospect seems uninterested in reducing costs. Chances are, this person will not buy no matter how persuasively you present your product's benefits—because the prospect does not see high costs as an important problem.

Furthermore, even customers who want to solve a problem, but do not like your product, will not buy. But if you have convinced them, if they want to solve a problem, and if they perceive your product as solving this problem, the question remains, Will these customers buy from you? They will, if they believe you represent the best supplier. If they would rather buy from another supplier, you have lost the sale. Your job is to provide the necessary information so that customers meet each of the five conditions for sale listed above.

SUMMARY OF MAJOR SELLING ISSUES

As a salesperson, be knowledgeable about factors that influence your buyer's purchase decision. You can obtain this knowledge, which helps to increase the salesperson's self-confidence and the buyer's confidence in the salesperson, through training and practice.

A firm's marketing strategy involves various efforts to create exchanges that satisfy the buyer's needs and wants. The salesperson should understand the characteristics of the target market (consumer or industrial) and how these characteristics relate to the buyer's behavior to better serve and sell to customers.

The individual goes through various steps or stages in the three buying situations of routine decision making, limited decision making, and extensive decision making. Uncover who is involved in the buying decision and the main factors that influence the decision. These factors include various psychological and practical buying influences.

Psychological factors include the buyer's motives, perceptions, learning, attitudes, beliefs, and personality—all of which influence the individual's needs and result in a search for information on what products to buy to satisfy them. Established relationships strongly influence buying decisions, making satisfied customers easier to sell to than new prospects. Customers evaluate the information, which results in the decision to buy or not to buy. These same factors influence whether the buyer is satisfied or dissatisfied with the product.

Realize that all prospects will not buy your products, at least not all of the time, due to the many factors influencing their buying decisions. You need to uncover buyers' needs, solve buyers' problems, and provide the knowledge that allows them to develop personal attitudes toward the product. These attitudes result in positive beliefs that your products fulfill their needs. Uncovering prospects' needs is often difficult because they may be reluctant to tell you their true needs or may not really know what and why they want to buy. You can usually feel confident that people buy for reasons such as to satisfy a need, fulfill a desire, and obtain a value. To determine these important buying needs, you can ask questions, observe prospects, listen to them, and talk to their associates about their needs.

MEETING A SALES CHALLENGE

John Salley took the advice of Joe Gandolfo who has reportedly sold more life insurance than any other person in the world. Joe's philosophy is that "selling is 98 percent understanding human beings and 2 percent product knowledge." Do not let that statement mislead you, for Joe holds the Charter Life Underwriter (CLU) designation as a member of the American College of Life Underwriters. He is extremely knowledgeable about insurance, tax shelters, and pension plans. In fact, he spends several hours a day studying recent changes on pensions and taxation. "But," Joe says, "I still maintain that it's not product knowledge but understanding of human beings that makes a salesperson effective."

John had his sales region's training director work with him two days a week for a month. The director analyzed John's sales presentations and found that they concentrated almost entirely on the technical features and advantages of the products. The training director contacted six of John's customers. Each said they often did not understand him because he was too technical. John immediately began emphasizing benefits and discussing features and advantages in nontechnical terms. Slowly his sales began to improve. Today, John Salley is a true believer in the phrase, "It's not what you say, but how you say it."

KEY TERMS FOR SELLING

black box   111
stimulus–response   112
needs   112
wants   112
economic needs   112
conscious need level   113
preconscious need level   113
unconscious need level   113
benefit selling   114
FAB selling technique   114
feature   114
advantage   114
benefit   114
L-O-C-A-T-E   117
trial close   118
SELL Sequence   119
perception   121
selective exposure   121
selective distortion   122

selective retention   122
learning   122
attitudes   123
belief   123
personality   124
self-concept   124
real self   124
self-image   124
ideal self   124
looking-glass self   124
routine decision making   128
limited decision making   129
extensive decision making   129
need arousal   130
collect information   131
information evaluation   131
purchase decision   131
purchase satisfaction   133
purchase dissonance   133

SALES APPLICATION QUESTIONS

1. What three types of buying situations may the buyer be in when contacted by a salesperson? Briefly describe each type.
2. What are the psychological factors that may influence the prospect's buying decision?
3. While you do not have to be a psychologist or understand exactly how the buyer's mind works, you do need to uncover the buyer's motives.
   a. What techniques can be used to uncover the buyer's motives?
   b. The prospect's intention to buy can be influenced by several things. What information does the salesperson need to obtain concerning the prospect's buying intentions before developing a sales presentation?

4. In the following statements, write down each idea that is a benefit:
   a. Counselor talking to a student: "To improve your science grade, Susie, you must establish better study habits."
   b. Construction supervisor talking to a worker: "That job will be a great deal easier, Joe, and you won't be as tired when you go home nights if you use that little truck over there."
   c. Father talking to his son: "You will make a lot of friends, Johnny, and be respected at school, if you learn how to play the piano."
   d. Banker talking to customer: "If you open this special checking account, Ms. Brown, paying your bills will be much easier."

5. In the following statements, determine what parts of each statement are features, advantages, or benefits.
   a. Hardware sales representative to homeowner: "Blade changing is quick and easy with this saw because it has a push-button blade release."
   b. Consumer sales representative to grocery store buyer: "The king-size package of Tide will bring in additional profits because it is the fastest selling, most economical size."
   c. Clothing salesperson to customer: "For long wear and savings on your clothing costs, you can't beat these slacks. All the seams are double-stitched and the material is 100 percent Dacron."

6. Indicate which of the following statements is a feature, advantage, or benefit. Write your answer on a sheet of paper.
   a. Made of pure vinyl.
   b. Lasts twice as long as competing brands.
   c. It's quick-frozen at 30° below zero.
   d. Available in small, medium, and large sizes.
   e. New.
   f. No unpleasant aftertaste.
   g. Saves time, work, and money.
   h. Approved by Underwriters' Laboratory.
   i. Gives 20 percent more miles to the gallon.
   j. Contains XR-10.
   k. Baked fresh daily.
   l. Includes a one-year guarantee on parts and labor.
   m. Is packed 48 units or eight six-packs to the case.
   n. Guaranteed to increase your sales by 10 percent.
   o. Adds variety to your meal planning.

7. Consider the following information:

   The DESKTOP XEROX 2300 copier is a versatile model that delivers the first copy in six seconds. It is also the lowest-priced new Xerox copier available. The 2300 is designed as a general purpose office copier and occupies less than half the top of a standard desk. The new unit copies on a full range of office materials as large as 8½ by 14 inches. A special feature is its ability to reproduce 5½ by 8½-inch billing statements from the same tray used for letter-size or legal-size paper. Selling price of the 2300 will be as low as $3,495 and rentals as low as $60 a month on a two-year contract without a copy allowance.

   What are the features, advantages, and benefits of the DESKTOP XEROX 2300 Copier? List two additional features, advantages, and benefits that a Xerox salesperson could use in presenting the new copier to a prospective buyer.

8. Several features of a car are listed below. Match each feature with its corresponding benefit(s):

   a. Low hoodline:
   (1) Better visibility.
   (2) Economy.
   (3) Quick start-up.

   b. Tinted glass:
   (1) Reflects sunlight.
   (2) Reduces eyestrain.
   (3) Reduces glare from sun.

   c. Rear window defroster:
   (1) Clears rear windshield and thus reduces the danger of driving on a cold, foggy day.
   (2) Rear windshield can be deiced or defogged automatically so you do not have to do it yourself.
   (3) Increases the cost of the car by $250.

   d. Whitewall tires:
   (1) Provide better handling and a more stable ride.
   (2) More appealing to the eye.
   (3) Increase the life of your tires.

9. To convince the customers that your product's benefits are important, show how the product benefits will meet their needs. Suppose the customer says: "I need some kind of gadget that will get me out of bed in the morning." Which of the following statements best relates your product feature, the GE clock radio's snooze alarm, to this customer's need?

   a. "Ms. Jones, this GE radio has a snooze alarm that is very easy to operate. See, all you do is set this button and off it goes."

   b. "Ms. Jones, the GE radio is the newest radio on the market. It carries a one-year guarantee and you can trade in your present radio and receive a substantial cut in the price."

   c. "Ms. Jones, since you say you have trouble getting up in the morning, you want an alarm system that will make sure you wake up. Now, GE's snooze alarm will wake you up no matter how often you shut the alarm off. You see, the alarm goes off every seven minutes until you switch off the special 'early bird' knob."

10. A salesperson says: "You expect a pencil sharpener to be durable. Our sharpener is durable because it's constructed with titanium steel bearings. Because of these bearings, our sharpener will not jam up and will last a long time."

    a. In this example, the titanium steel bearings are a (an)
    (1) Benefit.
    (2) Feature.
    (3) Need.
    (4) Advantage.

    b. "Will not jam up" is a (an):
    (1) Benefit.
    (2) Feature.
    (3) Need.
    (4) Advantage.

    c. In the statement, "will not jam up," the salesperson has
    (1) Converted a product feature into an advantage.

(2) Converted benefits into a product feature.
(3) Related a product feature to the customer's need via benefits.
(4) Numbers (1) and (2) are correct.
(5) Numbers (1) and (3) are correct.
  d. The statement, "will last a long time," is a (an):
    (1) Benefit.
    (2) Feature.
    (3) Need.
    (4) Advantage.
11. For each of the following products, determine a potential benefit based on their advantages:

Product	Feature	Advantage
a. Diet Coke	a. Only one calorie per 16-oz. serving	a. Will not increase your body weight when you drink it
b. Bic erasable ink pen	b. Erasable ink	b. Can erase mistakes
c. Ceiling fan	c. Hangs from ceiling, high efficiency	c. Out of the way uses less electricity
d. Sheer panty hose	d. No dark patches	d. Looks like real skin
e. Drilling an oil well	e. One of our engineers for the entire job	e. Better service
f. Hefty trash bags	f. 2-ply	f. Puncture proof, can overstuff them

12. As a salesperson for Procter & Gamble's soap division, you have been asked by your sales manager to determine the features, advantages, and benefits of Tide detergent and to discuss using Tide's benefits in a sales presentation at the next sales meeting. You have determined the following four features of Tide; listed underneath each feature are your ideas of factors that might interest retail grocery buyers. For each feature, determine the benefit that you would emphasize:

  a. Number one selling detergent:
    (1) Best traffic-pulling detergent.
    (2) Great brand loyalty.
    (3) High percent of market share.
  b. Four sizes:
    (1) Increases your total detergent sales.
    (2) Boxes are standard sizes.
    (3) Case cost is the same.
  c. Heaviest manufacturer-advertised detergent:
    (1) Continue to attract new customers to your store.
    (2) More customers remember this brand's advertising.
    (3) Produces high repeat business.
  d. Distinctive, colorful package:
    (1) Speeds shopping—easy for shoppers to locate on shelves.
    (2) High visual impact stimulates impulse purchases when on special display.
    (3) Familiar package design easy to recognize in store ads.

FURTHER EXPLORING THE SALES WORLD

1. Keep a diary of your purchases for two weeks. Select five or more of the products you purchased during that period and write a short report on why you purchased each product and what you feel are the features, advantages, and benefits of each product.
2. This week examine the television advertisement of three different products or services and report on the features, advantages, and benefits the commercial uses to persuade people to buy each product.
3. Shop for a product costing over $100. Report on your experience. Find out if the salesperson is on a commission pay plan.

STUDENT APPLICATION LEARNING EXERCISES (SALES)

At the end of appropriate chapters beginning with Chapter 4, you will find Student Application Learning Exercises (SALES). SALES are meant to help you construct the various segments of your sales presentation. SALES build on one another so that after you complete them, you will have constructed the majority of your sales presentation.

Sale 1 of 7— Chapter 4

Now you are ready to begin developing your sales presentation. To make **Sale 1:**

1. State what you will sell.
2. Briefly describe the individual and/or organization to which you will sell.
3. List three features of your product, including each feature's main advantage and benefit. Refer back to page114 for FAB definitions. FABs should discuss your product, not your marketing plan or business proposition. We'll do that later.

Feature	Advantage	Benefit
a.	a.	a.
b.	b.	b.
c.	c.	c.

4. Now create a SELL Sequence for each FAB (see pages 119–120). Label each of the components of the SELL Sequence using brackets as shown on page 119.

SELLING EXPERIENTIAL EXERCISE

You have learned much about selling in this course. Let's find out how much, and at the same time better understand your attitude toward selling. *Three* of the following 10 statements are false. Which are the false statements? Please first cover answers.

Is Organizational Selling for You?

1. Dealing with customers is less exciting than the work involved in most other jobs.
2. Selling brings out the best in your personality.
3. Salespeople are made, not born; if you don't plan and work hard, you'll never be exceptional at selling.
4. Attitude is more important in selling positions than most other jobs.
5. Those good at selling often can improve their income quickly.
6. Learning to sell now will help you succeed in *any* job in the future.

7. In your first sales job, what you learn can be more important than what you earn.
8. Selling is less demanding than other jobs.
9. You have less freedom in most selling positions.
10. A smile uses fewer muscles than a frown.[2]

False statements: 1, 8, and 9.

CHAPTER 4

The Psychology of Selling: Why People Buy

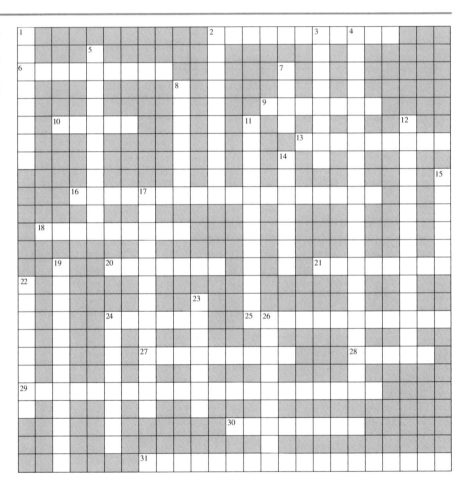

Across

2. A person's distinguishing character traits, attitudes, or habits.

6. The act of remembering only the information that supports one's attitudes and beliefs is referred to as selective _____.

9. Any physical characteristic of a product.

10. Needs that are learned by a person.

13. The person one would like to be.

16. The process by which buyers visit retail stores, contact potential suppliers, or talk with salespeople about a product's price, size, advantage, and warranty before making a decision regarding buying.

18. Buyers who are fully aware of their needs have a _____ need level.

20. A salesperson has triggered need _____ by demonstrating a psychological, social, or economic need in the buyer.

21. People as they actually are.

24. An acronym for methods to uncover important needs: listen, observe, combine, ask questions, talk to others, empathize.

25. Purchase _____ is expressed as gratification based on a product that supplies expected, or greater than expected, benefits.

27. _____ decision making is a characteristic of buyers who are unfamiliar with a specific product and who must therefore become highly involved in the decision-making process.

28. Self _____ or how a person sees himself or herself.

29. The process of being in the habit of buying a particular product so that attitudes and beliefs toward the product are already formed and are usually positive.

30. The unobservable, internal process taking place within the mind of the prospect as he or she reaches a decision whether or not to buy.

31. Tension on the part of a buyer regarding whether the right decision was made in purchasing a product.

Down

1. A buyer has made a _____ decision when he purchases something.

2. The process by which a person selects, organizes, and interprets information.

3. A person's learned predisposition toward something.

4. A process that determines what will be purchased as the buyer matches this information with needs, attitudes, and beliefs in making a decision.

5. An _____ need level at which people do not know why they buy a product.

7. The desire for something a person feels is worthwhile.

8. Self _____ is a person's view of himself or herself.

11. The level at which needs are not fully developed in the conscious mind, or _____ need level.

12. A method of selling by which a salesperson relates a product's benefits to the consumer's needs using the product's features and advantages as support.

14. _____ decision making is a characteristic of a buyer who invests a moderate level of energy in the decision to buy because, although the buyer is not familiar with each brand's features, advantages, and benefits, the general quality of the good is known to him or her.

15. A state of mind in which trust or confidence is placed in something or someone.

17. The buyer's need to purchase the most satisfying product for the money.

19. A sequence of things to do and say to stress benefits important to the customer: show the feature, explain the advantage, lead into the benefit, and let the customer talk by asking a question about the benefit.

22. Selective _____ is the process of allowing only a portion of the information revealed to be organized, interpreted, and permitted into awareness.

23. A favorable result the buyer receives from the product because of a particular advantage that has the ability to satisfy a buyer's need.

24. Acquiring knowledge or behavior based on past experiences.

26. The performance characteristic of a product that describes how it can be used or will help the buyer.

As a salesperson for Economy Ceiling Fans, you have been asked to research and determine customers' attitudes and beliefs toward your brand of ceiling fans. With this information you will determine if your company has the correct product line and suggest selling points for the company's salespeople when discussing fans with customers who come into their chain of retail stores.

You decide to hold an open house on a Sunday in one of your typical stores located in an upper-income neighborhood and advertise your special prices. During that time, you ask everyone to be seated, thank them for coming, and ask them to discuss their attitudes toward your company and ceiling fans.

Some people felt that they should shop for ceiling fans without considering brands, but once they selected a brand, they should go to the stores carrying that particular brand and buy from the store with the best price. Most people had collected information on fans from personal sources (such as friends), commercial sources (such as advertising, salespeople, company literature), and public sources (such as consumer rating organizations). Sixty percent had narrowed their choice to fans from Hunter, Casablanca, and Economy, and they seemed to look for three things in a ceiling fan: price, quality, and style.

Question

Given this information about why people buy ceiling fans, what should salespeople be instructed to do when a customer enters their store?

The used car salesperson for McDonald's Ford, John Alexander, approaches a woman, June Miller, in the car lot:

Seller: Can I help you?

Buyer: 20,000 miles on this one—I'll bet a little old lady owned this lemon! What was it, really, before you set it back?

Seller: That is the actual mileage. Hi, I'm John Alexander and you are . . . . [*He waits for reply.*]

Buyer: June Miller.

Seller: June, what can I help you with?

Buyer: Oh, I don't know. Something that runs and will get me around.

Seller: Do you travel out of town or just drive back and forth to work?

Buyer: I drive everywhere! I'm even getting in a car pool with my boss.

Seller: Good mileage is important then.

Buyer: Sure is. [*She walks over and looks at a full-size, four-door Ford.*] Say, I like this one! $6,500! You have to be kidding.

Seller: Do you need that much room?

Buyer: Not really, there is just me.

Seller: June, are you saying you need a car that is dependable, gets good gas mileage, not too big, and not too expensive?

Buyer: How did you guess?

Seller: Follow me . . . . [*He shows her five cars that he feels have those features. Then he asks:*] Which one of these do you like?

Buyer: Well, they are OK, but I really don't like them. Thanks for your time. I'll shop around a little more. Give me your card and I'll get back to you later.

Questions

1. Describe the situation and the buyer's apparent needs.
2. What should the seller do now that the buyer has said no to the cars he has shown her and is about to leave the car lot?

5
CHAPTER

Communication for Relationship Building: It's Not All Talk

MAIN TOPICS

The Tree of Business Life: Communication

Communication: It Takes Two

Nonverbal Communication: Watch for It

Communication through Appearance and the Handshake

Body Language Gives You Clues

Barriers to Communication

Master Persuasive Communication to Maintain Control

LEARNING OBJECTIVES

The ability to effectively communicate both verbally and nonverbally is crucial to sales success. This chapter introduces this important sales skill. After studying this chapter, you should be able to

■ Present and discuss the salesperson–buyer communication process.

■ Discuss and illustrate the importance of using nonverbal communication when selling.

■ Define and recognize acceptance, caution, and disagreement nonverbal signals.

■ Review barriers to effective sales communication.

■ Explain ways of developing persuasive communication.

Amos Skaggs, purchasing agent, stands as a salesperson enters his office. "Hi, Mr. Skaggs," the salesperson says, offering his hand. Skaggs returns a limp, one-second handshake and sits down behind his desk. He begins to open his afternoon mail, almost as though no one else was in the room.

The salesperson sits down and begins his canned sales talk by saying, "Mr. Skaggs, I'm here to show you how your company can lower manufacturing costs by 10 percent." Skaggs lays his mail down on his desk, leans back in his chair, crosses his arms, and with a growl says: "I'm glad to hear that. You know something, young fellow, pretty soon it won't cost us anything to manufacture our products." "Why is that?" the salesman mumbles, meekly looking down to the floor. "Well, you are the ninth person I've seen today who has offered to save us 10 percent on our costs."

Skaggs stands up, leans over the table, and while peering over his glasses says slowly, "I believe I've heard enough sales pitches for one day." The initially enthusiastic salesperson now apologetically says, "If this is not a good time for you, sir, I can come back at a later date."

The problem facing this salesperson is common. The buyer has been seeing salespeople all day. Basically, they say the same thing: "Buy from me and I'll save you money." The buyer has communicated his feelings toward the salesperson both verbally and nonverbally. What message has Skaggs sent to the salesperson? If you were the salesperson, what might you do now?

Although many other factors are crucial to sales success, the ability to communicate effectively is of prime importance. To convincingly convey this important sales skill, this chapter directly applies a basic communication model to the buyer–seller interaction. We describe several factors influencing communication, along with possible barriers to effective communication. We also examine the often ignored—though always critical—topic of nonverbal communication. The balance of this chapter relates some techniques to improve sales communication.

THE TREE OF BUSINESS LIFE: COMMUNICATION

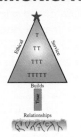

What if you could read someone's mind? What if you could tell what he or she is thinking? Wow, wouldn't that be cool! How would you use the knowledge of what is going on in a person's mind about what you are saying—for helping or selling purposes? For the other person's best interest or your best interest? People have ears, but cannot hear. People have eyes, but cannot see. People have two ears and one mouth but do more talking than listening. What are your answers for these four questions? How do the three "People have . . ." sayings relate to your life?

This chapter, and the last chapter, provides several of the little known secrets about how to read people's minds. Body language, coupled with asking questions periodically as you talk with someone and listening to their replies are a great way to better understand what is going on in someone's mind. Questions, watching nonverbals, listening, talking as needed are secrets to successfully helping others in a sales situation. It also works in your everyday like. Try them! Use these secrets of effective communication for building long-term relationships based upon the Golden Rule of Selling. Ethical service builds relationships and is based upon the truth.

EXHIBIT 5.1

What did you say? What did I hear?

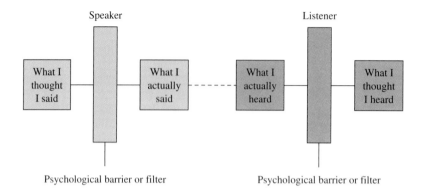

COMMUNICATION: IT TAKES TWO

Communication, in a sales context, is the act of transmitting verbal and nonverbal information and understanding between seller and buyer. This definition presents communication as an exchange process of sending and receiving messages with some type of response expected between seller and buyer.

This sounds simple, right? But have you ever had someone talk to you and realize you did not hear what was said? "You have eyes but do not see; you have ears but do not hear," is a saying that dates back thousands of years. This wise saying is important to all of us, including salespeople, in our daily living. Salespeople have to understand the many ways people communicate with them.

Communication channels during the sales presentation take many forms. Ideas and attitudes can be effectively communicated by media other than language. Actually, in a normal two-person conversation, less than 35 percent of the social meaning utilizes verbal components. Said another way, much of the social meaning in a conversation is conveyed nonverbally. Furthermore, what you say verbally is not always what you actually mean. Exhibit 5.1 expands on this point by illustrating the psychological thought processes of both the speaker and the listener.

Research has found that face-to-face communication is composed of *verbal*, *vocal*, and *facial* communication messages. One equation presents the total impact of communicated messages as equal to 7 percent verbal, 38 percent tone of voice, and 55 percent nonverbal expressions.[1] If one recognizes these findings as reasonable approximation of the total communicative process, then uninformed salespeople actually ignore a major part of the communication process that occurs during buyer–seller interaction. How the sales message is given can be as important to making the sale as what is said. Thus, nonverbal communications are important in communication between buyer and seller. An awareness of nonverbal communication is a valuable tool in successfully making a sale.

People have eyes but do not see. People have ears but do not hear.

Vocal communication includes such factors as voice quality, pitch, inflection, and pauses. Radio newscaster Paul Harvey is famous for how he broadcasts the news. He uses vocal pauses and inflections masterfully to obtain and hold the attention of his radio audience. A salesperson's use of vocal factors can aid in sales presentation, too. Along with verbal, vocal, and nonverbal communication, many other elements also are involved in sales communication.

Salesperson–Buyer Communication Process Requires Feedback

A basic communication model that depicts how the salesperson–buyer communication process works is shown in Exhibit 5.2. Basically, communication occurs when a sender transmits a message through some type of medium to a receiver

EXHIBIT 5.2

The basic communication model has eight elements.

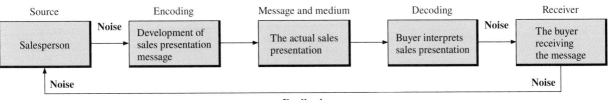

Feedback

who responds to that message. Exhibit 5.2 presents a model that contains eight major communication elements. These elements are defined as follows:

- **Source.** The source of communication (also called the communicator); in our case, it's the salesperson.
- **Encoding process.** The salesperson's conversion of ideas and concepts into the language and materials used in the sales presentation.
- **Message.** The information intended to be conveyed in the sales presentation.
- **Medium.** The form of communication used in the sales presentation and discussion; most frequently words, visual materials, and body language.
- **Decoding process.** Receipt and translation (interpretation) of the information by the receiver (prospective buyer).
- **Receiver.** The person the communication is intended for; in our case, it's the prospect or buyer.
- **Feedback.** Reaction to the communication as transmitted to the sender. This reaction may be verbal, nonverbal, or both.
- **Noise.** Factors that distort communication between buyer and seller. Noise includes barriers to communication, which we will discuss later.

"You can observe a lot by watching."

YOGI BERRA

This model portrays the communication process. A salesperson should know how to develop a sales presentation (encoding) so that the buyer obtains maximum understanding of the message (decoding). The salesperson should use communication media that most effectively communicate a specific sales message. Clear verbal discussion, visual aids such as pictures or diagrams, and models or samples of the product are several types of media a salesperson might use in communicating a sales message.

Studies have shown that people retain 10 percent of what they read, 20 percent of what they see, 30 percent of what they hear, and 50 percent of what they hear and see. If possible, it is important to incorporate into your presentation communication that appeals to all five senses (sight, hearing, smell, feel, taste). This is challenging to do!

One-way communication occurs when the salesperson talks and the buyer only listens. The salesperson needs a response or feedback from the buyer to know if communication occurs. Does the buyer understand the message? Once feedback or interaction and understanding between buyer and seller exist in a communication process, two-way communication has been established.

Two-way communication is essential to make the sale. The buyer must understand your message's information to make a buying decision. Two-way communication enables the salesperson the ability to present a product's benefits, instantly receive buyer reactions, and answer questions. Buyers usually react both verbally and nonverbally to your presentation.

Say What You Mean

At least six messages are involved in the communication process:

1. What you mean to say.
2. What you really say.
3. What the other person hears.
4. What the other person thinks is heard.
5. What the other person says about what you said.
6. What you think the other person said about what you said.

It gets complicated, doesn't it? Sue and I were looking at a gorgeous moon together under romantic circumstances. As we shared the moment, how was I actually feeling? I was feeling romantic. If we followed the six messages, that incident would have looked something like this:

1. What you mean to say   ("The moon puts me in a romantic mood.")
2. What you really say   ("Isn't that a brilliant moon?")

3. What the other person hears   ("The moon is bright.")
4. What the other person thinks she hears   ("Yes, it's bright enough for a walk.")
5. What the other person says about what you said.   ("Yes, it's bright enough to hit a golf ball by.")
6. What you think the other person said about what you said.   ("I don't feel romantic.")

We can miss each other's wavelengths completely by the time the six messages are completed without even realizing what has happened. All of us are constantly in the process of encoding and decoding messages.

We need to learn to ask questions or restate the point to clarify meaning. To say what we mean straightforwardly must be our constant goal in order for those around us to discard all decoding devices.[2]

NONVERBAL COMMUNICATION: WATCH FOR IT

Recognition and analysis of nonverbal communication in sales transactions is relatively new. Only in the past 10 to 15 years has the subject been formally examined in detail. The presence and use of nonverbal communication, however, has been acknowledged for years. In the early 1900s, Sigmund Freud noted that people cannot keep a secret even if they do not speak. A person's gestures and actions reveal hidden feelings about something.

People communicate nonverbally in several ways. Four major **nonverbal communication** channels are the physical space between buyer and seller, appearance, handshake, and body movements.

Concept of Space

The concept of **territorial space** refers to the area around the self that a person will not allow another person to enter without consent. Early experiments in territorial space dealt with animals. These experiments determined that higher-status members of a group often are afforded a freedom of movement that is less available to those of lower status. This idea has been applied to socially acceptable distances of space that human beings keep between themselves in certain situations. Territorial space can easily be related to the selling situation.

Space considerations are important to salespeople because violations of territorial space without customer consent may set off the customer's defense mechanisms and create a barrier to communications. A person (buyer) has four main types of distances to consider—intimate (up to 2 feet); personal (2 to 4 feet); social (4 to 12 feet); and public (greater than 12 feet).

Intimate space of up to 2 feet, or about arm's length, is the most sensitive zone, since it is reserved for close friends and loved ones. To enter intimate space in the buyer–seller relationship, for some prospects, could be socially unacceptable—possibly offensive.

During the presentation, a salesperson should carefully listen and look for signs that indicate the buyer feels uncomfortable—perhaps that the salesperson is too close. A buyer may deduce from such closeness that the salesperson is attempting to dominate or overpower the buyer. This feeling can result in resistance to the salesperson. If such uneasiness is detected, the salesperson should move back, which reassures the customer.

Personal space is the closest zone a stranger or business acquaintance is normally allowed to enter. Even in this zone, a prospect may be uncomfortable. Barriers, such as a desk, often reduce the threat implied when someone enters this zone.

Social space is the area normally used for a sales presentation. Again, the buyer often uses a desk to maintain a distance of 4 feet or more between buyer and seller. Standing while facing a seated prospect may communicate to the buyer that the salesperson seems too dominating. Thus, the salesperson should normally stay seated to convey a relaxed manner.

A salesperson should consider beginning a presentation in the middle of the social distance zone, 6 to 8 feet, to avoid the prospect's erecting negative mental barriers. This is especially true if the salesperson is not a friend of the prospect.

Public space can be used by the salesperson making a presentation to a group of people. It is similar to the distance between teacher and student in a classroom. People are at ease, and thus easy to communicate with, at this distance because they do not feel threatened by the salesperson.

Space Threats

The territorial imperative causes people to feel that they should defend their space or territory against **space threats.** The salesperson who pulls up a chair too close, takes over all or part of the prospect's desk, leans on or over the desk, or touches the objects on the desk runs the risk of invading a prospect's territory. Be careful not to create defensive barriers. However, should you sense a friendliness between yourself and the prospect, use territorial space to your benefit.

Space Invasion

The prospect who allows you to enter or invade personal and intimate space is saying, "Come on into my space; let's be friends." Now you can use space to your advantage.

In most offices, the salesperson sits directly across the desk from the prospect. The prospect controls the space arrangement. This defensive barrier allows the prospect to control much of the conversation and remain safe from **space invasion.** Often, seating is prearranged and it could be a space threat if you moved your chair when calling on a prospect for the first time.

However, if you have a choice between a chair across the desk or beside the desk, take the latter seat, as shown in Exhibit 5.3. Sitting beside the prospect lowers the desk communication barrier. If you are friends with the buyer, move your chair to the side of the desk. This helps create a friendly, cooperative environment between you and the buyer.

EXHIBIT 5.3

Office arrangements and
territorial space.

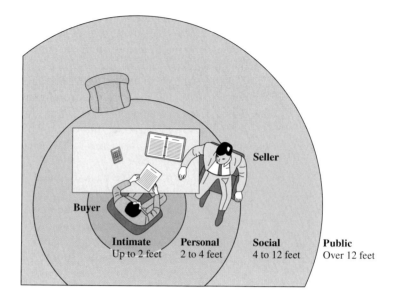

Intimate	Personal	Social	Public
Up to 2 feet	2 to 4 feet	4 to 12 feet	Over 12 feet

Communication through Appearance and the Handshake

Other common methods of nonverbal communication are signals conveyed by a person's physical appearance and handshake. Once territorial space has been established, general appearance is the next medium of nonverbal communication a salesperson conveys to a customer. Appearance not only conveys information such as age, sex, height, weight, and physical characteristics, but it also provides much data on personality. For instance, hairstyle is one of the first things a buyer notices about a salesperson.

Style Hair Carefully

Hairstyle traditionally has been important in evaluating personal appearance. Today's salespeople must consider the type of customer they call on and adjust their hairstyles accordingly. Both male and female salespeople should visit a hairstylist.

Though recently decreasing somewhat in popularity, some salesmen wear facial hair. Salespeople should carefully consider their grooming and its impact on customers' perceptions. Some companies ask male salespersons to be clean shaven and wear conservative haircuts. Their female salespersons are asked to choose a simple, businesslike, shoulder-length hairstyle. Other companies leave grooming up to each individual. Your grooming objective is to eliminate communication barriers. Your grooming can convey a favorable first impression. Should your company not have a policy on grooming, examine your customers' grooming before deciding on your style.

Dress as a Professional

Wardrobe has always been a major determinant of sales success, and today it is emphasized as never before. A variety of books and articles have appeared on proper dress for businesspeople. These books espouse the doctrine that men and women sales representatives should wear conservative, serious clothing that projects professionalism, just the right amount of authority, and a desire to please the customer. Sporty clothing is believed to accentuate sales aggressiveness, which can place a purchasing agent on the defensive and result in lost sales.

Many companies believe that decision rules exist for every major clothing item and accessory, but these are derivatives of one basic commandment—dress in a simple, elegant style. Xerox, IBM, and other large companies have incorporated these ideas into their sales training and daily policies. These firms encourage sales personnel to wear dark, conservative clothing. This practice is designed to project a conservative, stable corporate image to both customers and the general public.

Exhibit 5.4 illustrates several key considerations for appropriate dress and grooming. If you are uncertain about what to do, visit several retailers. Make sure at least one retailer is a specialty store. They will have the latest styles and spend time with you. Tell the salespeople what you are looking for and see what they say. Think of this as an investment in yourself because it is expensive to build a wardrobe. However, you are worth it!

You only have one chance to make a favorable first impression.

Clothes, accessories, and shoes are important, but do not forget personal grooming, such as skin care and hairstyle, as noted above. Learn to recognize image symbols in business dress and use them to your advantage. Be cautious in becoming too individualistic—the unspoken message in most companies is that freedom in dress may be a privilege of rank. Remember, too, that these guides for dress, including the remainder of the chapter, also apply to selling yourself in job interviews.

The nonverbal messages that salespeople emit through appearance should be positive in all sales situations. Characteristics of the buyer, cultural aspects of a sales territory, and the type of product being sold all determine a mode of dress. In considering these aspects, create a business wardrobe that sends positive, nonverbal messages in every sales situation. Before reading on, look over the "Dress for Success Appendix" at the end of this chapter to better prepare you for the business world.

Shake Hands Firmly and Look People in the Eye

Once you have determined appropriate dress and hairstyle, the next nonverbal communication channel to consider is your contact with a prospect through the handshake. The handshake is said to have evolved from a gesture of peace between warriors. By joining hands, two warriors were unable to bear arms against one another (assuming that a shield—not a weapon—was held in the other hand).

Today, a handshake is the most common way for two people to touch one another in a business situation, and some people feel that it is a revealing gesture. A firm handshake is more intense and is indicative of greater liking and warmer feelings. A prolonged handshake is more intimate than a brief one, and it could cause the customer discomfort, especially in a sales call on a new prospect. A loosely clasped, cold, or limp handshake is usually interpreted as indicating that someone is aloof and unwilling to become involved. This cold fish handshake is also perceived as unaffectionate and unfriendly.

General rules for a successful handshake include extending your hand first—if appropriate (see Exhibit 5.5).[3] Remember, however, a few people may be uncomfortable shaking hands with a stranger. At times, you may want to allow your customer to initiate the gesture. Maintain eye contact with the customer during the handshake, gripping the hand firmly. These actions allow you to initially establish an atmosphere of honesty and mutual respect—starting the presentation in a positive manner.[4]

EXHIBIT 5.4

To look sharp, be sharp, and feel sharp the correct clothes, grooming, attitude, and physical conditioning are required.
This applies to your career, to interviewing, and to your life.

Choose a suit that means business.

Natural fibers, a good fit, and current styles are important.

Physical conditioning produces the stamina and positive mental attitude necessary to be a success.

First impressions are crucial. Remember that you are representing your organization—and your customer's perception of that organization begins with you.

Body Language Gives You Clues

From birth, people learn to communicate their needs, likes, and dislikes through nonverbal means. The salesperson can learn much from a prospect's raised eyebrow, a smile, a touch, a scowl, or reluctance to make eye contact during a sales presentation. The prospect can communicate with you literally without uttering a word. An ability to interpret these signals is an invaluable tool to the successful sales

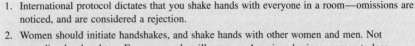

EXHIBIT 5.5

Five tips for international handshaking.

1. International protocol dictates that you shake hands with everyone in a room—omissions are noticed, and are considered a rejection.
2. Women should initiate handshakes, and shake hands with other women and men. Not extending her hand to a European male will cause an American businesswoman to lose credibility.
3. Western and Eastern Europeans reshake hands whenever they're apart for even a short period of time (e.g., lunch).
4. French and Japanese businesspeople shake hands with one firm gesture. In Japan, the handshake may be combined with a slight bow, which should be returned.
5. In Arab countries, handshakes are a bit limp and last longer than typical American handshakes. Latin Americans also tend to use a lighter, lingering handshake. In all cases, don't pull your hand away too soon; such a gesture will be interpreted as a rejection.

professional. In conjunction with interpretation of body language, the salesperson's skillful use and control of physical actions, gestures, and overall body position also are helpful.

The buyer can send nonverbal signals via five communication modes. They are the body angle, facial expression, arm movement or position, hand movements or position, and leg position. (Exhibit 5.6 shows examples.) These modes generally send three types of messages: (1) acceptance, (2) caution, and (3) disagreement.

Acceptance signals indicate that your buyer is favorably inclined toward you and your presentation. These signals give you the green light to proceed. While this may not end in a sale, at the least the prospect is saying, "I am willing to listen." What you are saying is both acceptable and interesting. Some common acceptance signals include these:

- *Body angle.* Leaning forward or upright at attention.
- *Face.* Smiling, pleasant expression, relaxed, eyes examining visual aids, direct eye contact, positive voice tones.
- *Hands.* Relaxed and generally open, perhaps performing business calculations on paper, holding on as you attempt to withdraw a product sample or sales materials, firm handshake.
- *Arms.* Relaxed and generally open.
- *Legs.* Crossed and pointed toward you or uncrossed.

Salespeople frequently rely only on facial expressions as indicators of acceptance. This practice may be misleading since buyers may consciously control their facial expressions. Scan each of the five key body areas to verify your interpretation of facial signals. A buyer who increases eye contact, maintains a relaxed position, and exhibits positive facial expressions gives excellent acceptance signals.

Acceptance signals indicate that buyers perceive that your product might meet their needs. You have obtained their attention and interest. You are free to continue with your planned sales presentation.

Caution signals should alert you that buyers are either neutral or skeptical toward what you say. Caution signals are indicated by these characteristics:

- *Body angle.* Leaning away from you.
- *Face.* Puzzled, little or no expression, averted eyes or little eye contact, neutral or questioning voice tone, saying little, and then only asking a few questions.
- *Arms.* Crossed, tense.
- *Hands.* Moving, fidgeting with something, clasped, weak handshake.
- *Legs.* Moving, crossed away from you.

EXHIBIT 5.6

Which of the five communication modes can a salesperson look for with these customers?

Caution signals are important for you to recognize and adjust to for two main reasons. First, they indicate blocked communication. Buyers' perceptions, attitudes, and beliefs regarding your presentation may cause them to be skeptical, judgmental, or uninterested in your product. They may not recognize that they need your product or that it can benefit them. Even though you may have their attention, they show little interest in or desire for your product.

Second, if caution signals are not handled properly, they may evolve into disagreement signals, which causes a communication breakdown and makes a sale difficult. Proper handling of caution signals requires that you

- Adjust to the situation by slowing down or departing from your planned presentation.
- Use open-ended questions to encourage your buyers to talk and express their attitudes and beliefs. How might we improve the efficiency of your workforce? or What do you think about this benefit? are examples of open-ended questions.
- Carefully listen to what buyers say, and respond directly.
- Project acceptance signals. Be positive, enthusiastic, and smile. Remember, you are glad to be there to help buyers satisfy their needs. Refrain from projecting caution signals even if a buyer does so. If you project a positive image in this situation, there is greater probability that you will change a caution light to a green one and make the sale.

Your objective in using these techniques is to change the yellow caution signal to the green go-ahead signal. If you continue to receive caution signals, proceed carefully with your presentation. Be realistic and alert to the possibility that the buyer may begin to believe that your product is not beneficial and begin sending disagreement or red-light signals.

Disagreement signals tell you immediately to stop the planned presentation and quickly adjust to the situation. Disagreements, or red-light signals, indicate that you are dealing with a person becoming uninterested in your product. Anger or hostility may develop if you continue the presentation. Your continuation can cause a buyer to feel an unacceptable level of sales pressure, resulting in a complete communication breakdown. Disagreement signals may be indicated by these signs:

- *Body angle.* Retracted shoulders, leaning away from you, moving the entire body back from you, or wanting to move away.
- *Face.* Tense, showing anger, wrinkled face and brow, little eye contact, negative voice tones, or sudden silence.
- *Arms.* Tense, crossed over chest.
- *Hands.* Motions of rejection or disapproval, tense and clenched, weak handshake.
- *Legs.* Crossed and away from you.

You should handle disagreement signals as you did caution signals, by using open-ended questions and projecting acceptance signals. There are four additional techniques to use. First, stop your planned presentation. There is no use in continuing until you have changed disagreement signals into caution or acceptance signals. Second, temporarily reduce or eliminate any pressure on the person to buy or to participate in the conversation. Let the buyer relax as you slowly move back to your presentation. Third, let your buyer know you are aware that something upsetting has occurred. Show that you are there to help, not to sell at any cost. Finally, use direct questions to determine a buyer's attitudes and beliefs such as, "What do you think of . . . ?" or "Have I said something you do not agree with?"

Body Guidelines

Over time, you will know customers well enough to understand the meaning of their body movements. Although a prospect may say no to making a purchase, body movements may indicate uncertainty. As Richard Dreyfuss says in the movie *The Goodbye Girl,* "Your lips say *no, no, no,* but your eyes say *yes, yes, yes!*" This phrase sometimes holds true for selling.

Exhibit 5.7 relates some common nonverbal signals that buyers may project.[5] The interpretation of most body language is obvious. Be cautious in interpreting an isolated gesture, such as assuming that little eye contact means the prospect is displeased with what you are saying. Instead, concentrate on nonverbal cues that are part of a cluster or pattern. Let's say your prospect begins staring at the wall. That is a clue that may mean nothing. You continue to talk. Now, the prospect leans back in the chair. That is another clue. By itself, it may be meaningless, but in conjunction with the first clue, it begins to take on meaning. Now, you see the prospect turn away, legs crossed, brow wrinkled. You now have a cluster of clues forming a pattern. It is time to adjust or change your presentation.

In summary, remember that nonverbal communication is well worth considering in selling. A salesperson ought to

- Be able to recognize nonverbal signals.
- Be able to interpret them correctly.
- Be prepared to alter a selling strategy by slowing, changing, or stopping a planned presentation.
- Respond nonverbally and verbally to a buyer's nonverbal signals.

EXHIBIT 5.7

What nonverbal signals are these buyers giving to you?

1. When you mention your price, this purchasing agent tilts her head back, raises her hands, and assumes a rigid body posture. What nonverbal signals is she communicating, and how would you move on with the sale?

2. As you explain your sales features, this buyer looks away, clasps his hands, and crosses his legs away from you. What nonverbal signals is he communicating, and how would you move on with the sale?

3. As you explain the quality of your product, this company president opens his arms and leans toward you. What nonverbal signals is he communicating, and how would you move on with the sale?

Answers
1. Your buyer is sending red signals. That means you are facing nearly insurmountable barriers. You've got to stop what you are doing, express your understanding, and redirect your approach.
2. This buyer is sending yellow signals that warn you to exercise caution. Your own words and gestures must be aimed at relaxing the buyer or the prospect may soon communicate red signals.
3. This buyer is sending green signals that say everything is "go." With no obstacles to your selling strategy, simply move to the close.

Effective communication is essential in making a sale. Nonverbal communication signals are an important part of the total communication process between buyer and seller. Professional salespeople seek to learn and understand nonverbal communication to increase their sales success.

BARRIERS TO COMMUNICATION

Like the high hurdler, a salesperson often must overcome a multitude of obstacles. These obstacles are more aptly called *barriers to communication.* Consider this example:

Salesperson Joe Jones heard that the XYZ Company buyer, Jake Jackson, was displeased with the company's present supplier. Jones had analyzed XYZ's operation and knew that his product could save the company thousands of dollars a year. Imagine Jones's surprise when Jackson terminated the visit quickly with no sale and no mention of a future appointment.

Jones told his boss about the interview: "Jackson kept asking me where I went to school, whether I wanted coffee, and how I liked selling while I was trying to

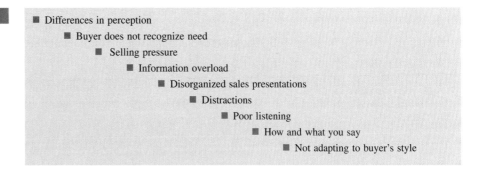

EXHIBIT 5.8

Barriers to communication which may kill a sale.

- Differences in perception
  - Buyer does not recognize need
    - Selling pressure
      - Information overload
        - Disorganized sales presentations
          - Distractions
            - Poor listening
              - How and what you say
                - Not adapting to buyer's style

In conversation, keep in mind that you're more interested in what you have to say than anyone else is.

ANONYMOUS

explain to him the features, advantages, and benefits of our product. Suddenly, Jackson stopped the interview." Jones asked the boss, "What did I do wrong? I know he needed our product."

The buyer was sending Jones signals that he likes doing business with people he knows. He was a "feeler," as discussed in Chapter 4. The buyer did not want to get down to business immediately. He wanted to visit for a while. No true communication was ever established between Jackson and Jones, which caused Jones to misread the customer and incorrectly handle the situation.

Salespeople, as illustrated in this example, often lose sales by failing to recognize communication barriers between buyer and seller. The main reasons communication breaks down in the sales situation include these (see Exhibit 5.8):

1. **Differences in perception.** If the buyer and seller do not share a common understanding of information contained in the presentation, communication breaks down. The closer a buyer's and seller's perceptions, attitudes, and beliefs, the stronger communication will be between them. Cultural differences are easily misperceived by buyers and sellers.

2. **Buyer does not recognize a need for product.** Communication barriers exist if the salesperson is unable to convince the buyer of a need, and/or that the salesperson represents the best supplier to buy from.

3. **Selling pressure.** There is a fine line between what is acceptable sales pressure or enthusiasm and what the buyer perceives as a high-pressure sales technique. A pushy, arrogant selling style can quickly cause the prospect to erect a communication barrier.

4. **Information overload.** You may present the buyer with an excess of information. This overload may cause confusion, perhaps offend, and the buyer will stop listening. For example, the engineer making a presentation to a buyer who is not an engineer may concentrate on the technical aspects of a product when the buyer only wants a small amount of information.

5. **Disorganized sales presentation.** Sales presentations that seem unorganized to the buyer tend to cause frustration or anger. Buyers commonly expect you to understand their needs or problems and to customize your sales presentation to their individual situations. If you fail to do this, communication can fall apart.

6. **Distractions.** When a buyer receives a telephone call or someone walks into the office, distractions occur. A buyer's thoughts may become sidetracked, and it may be difficult to regain attention and interest.

7. **Poor listening.** At times, the buyer may not listen to you. This often occurs if you do all or most of the talking—not allowing the buyer to participate in the conversation.

8. **How and what you say.** What we say probably affects more people than any other action we take. Here are four common speech patterns. The first two should be copied, and the last two should be avoided:

Why do you have one mouth and two ears?

   a. The Controlled Talk—those with this speech pattern think before speaking, know when silence is best, and give wise advice.
   b. The Caring Talk—those with this speech pattern speak truthfully while seeking to encourage.
   c. The Conniving Talk—those with this speech pattern are filled with wrong motive, gossip, slander, and a desire to twist truth.
   d. The Careless Talk—those with this speech pattern are filled with lies, salty language, and quick-tempered words—which can lead to self-destruction in sales.[6]

9. **Not adapting to buyer's style.** Sitting in on a sales call with a young salesperson selling high-priced industrial equipment, it became clear that the two were not communicating. The salesperson, who preferred telling to showing, kept talking about the product. But the visually oriented client wanted to see a picture of it. Eventually, the conversation deteriorated into a show versus tell confrontation. It was the classic sales miscommunication. Amazingly, the rep had product brochures in his briefcase. But he didn't bring them out because he was locked into his own form of communication. It is critical for salespeople to use different communication styles as discussed in Chapter 4. Most successful salespeople have learned to match their customers' communication styles. Remember the Golden Rule and adjust to the other person.

The nine barriers to communication just listed are not the only ones that may occur. As in the example of Joe Jones, the buyer may actually need the product and the salesperson may have excellent product knowledge and believe that the sales presentation was good, yet because of communication barriers, the buyer rejects the salesperson and the product. As a salesperson, constantly seek ways to recognize and overcome communication barriers, and identify and satisfy buyer needs through persuasive communication.

MASTER PERSUASIVE COMMUNICATION TO MAINTAIN CONTROL

To become a better communicator, consider two major elements of communication. First, always strive to improve the message and its delivery in the sales presentation. You need to be a capable encoder. Second, improve your ability to determine what the buyer is communicating to you. To do so, you need to be a good listener or decoder. A good sales communicator knows how to effectively encode and decode during a presentation.

Salespeople want to be good communicators to persuade people to purchase their products. **Persuasion** means the ability to change a person's belief, position, or course of action. The more effective you are at communicating, the greater your chances of being successful at persuasion.

The chapters on the selling process go into greater detail on specific persuasion techniques. For now, let's review several factors to develop persuasive communications. These factors relate to several components of the communication model shown in Exhibit 5.2: feedback, empathy, simplicity, listening, attitude, and proof statements.

SELLING TIPS

Don't Complicate Things

How can you simplify the following statements?

1. A mass of concentrated earthly material perennially rotating on its axis will not accumulate an accretion of bryophytic vegetation.
2. Individuals who are perforce constrained to be domiciled in vitreous structures of patent frangibility should on no account employ petrous formations as projectiles.
3. A superabundance of talent skilled in the preparation of gastronomic concoctions will impair the quality of a certain potable solution made by immersing a gallinaceous bird in embullient Adam's ale.

Answers

1. A rolling stone gathers no moss.
2. People who live in glass houses shouldn't throw stones.
3. Too many cooks spoil the broth.

Feedback Guides Your Presentation

Learn how to generate feedback to determine whether your listener has received your intended message. Feedback does not refer to any specific type of listening behavior by the buyer but rather to a recognizable response. A shake of the head, a frown, or an effort to say something are all signals to the salesperson. If the salesperson fails to notice or respond to these signals, no feedback can occur, which means faulty or incomplete communication. A salesperson's observation of feedback is like an auto racer's glances at the tachometer. Both aid in ascertaining a receiver's response.

Often, feedback must be sought openly because the prospect does not always give it voluntarily. By interjecting into the presentation questions that require the customer to give a particular response, you can stimulate feedback. Questioning, sometimes called probing, allows the salesperson to determine the buyer's attitude toward the sales presentation. **Probing** refers to gathering information and uncovering customer needs using one or more questions.

MCI Communications included this type of feedback in their sales training sessions. MCI sales trainers suggested to their salespeople that they use questions in their presentations. These were some of the questions:

- Do you think you are paying too much for telecommunications equipment?
- Are you happy with the service now being provided?
- Are you happy with the equipment your present supplier has installed for your company?

These questions were intended to draw negative responses from the customers concerning the relationship with their present supplier. They provided the MCI salespeople with a method of determining how the prospect felt about the competitor. These responses allow the salesperson to discuss the specific features, advantages, and benefits of MCI products relative to the products the prospect currently used. Future chapters will fully discuss questioning techniques to use during your presentation.

Remember the Trial Close

In planning your presentation, it is important to predetermine when and what feedback-producing questions to ask. Remember to use the trial close as part of your SELL Sequence, as discussed in Chapter 4. The use of a question after discussing a benefit is a great method of obtaining feedback. Another way to create positive feedback is through empathy.

Empathy Puts You in Your Customer's Shoes

"Try honestly to see things from the other person's point of view."

DALE CARNEGIE

Empathy is the ability to identify and understand the other person's feelings, ideas, and situation. As a salesperson, you need to be interested in what the buyer is saying—not just in giving a sales presentation. Many of the barriers to communication mentioned earlier can be overcome when you place yourself in the buyer's shoes. Empathy is saying to a prospect, "I'm here to help you," or "Tell me your problems and needs so I can help *you*." Empathy is also evidenced by a salesperson's display of sincerity and interest in the buyer's situation.

This may mean acknowledging at times that a prospect may not need your product. Take, for example, the Scott Paper Company salesperson who finds that the customer still has 90 percent of the paper towels purchased three months ago. There is no reason to sell this customer more paper towels. It is time to help the customer sell the paper towels now on hand by suggesting displays, price reductions, and formats for newspaper advertisements. It is always wise to adopt your customer's point of view to meet the customer's needs best.

Keep It Simple

The new salesperson was sitting in a customer's office waiting for the buyer. His boss was with him. As they heard the buyer come into the office, the sales manager said, "Remember, a **KISS** for him." No, he was not saying to give the buyer a kiss, but to use the old selling philosophy of **k**eep **i**t **s**imple, **s**alesperson.

The story is told of a little old lady who went into a hardware store. The clerk greeted her and offered her some help. She replied that she was looking for a heater. So the clerk said, "Gee, are you lucky! We have a big sale on these heaters, and a tremendous selection. Let me show you." So after maybe 30 or 45 minutes of discussing duothermic controls, heat induction, and all the factors involved with how a heater operates, including the features and advantages of each of the 12 models, he turned to the little old lady and said, "Now do you have any questions?" To which she replied, "Yes, just one, Sonny. Which one of these things will keep a little old lady warm?"

An overly complex, technical presentation should be avoided when it is unnecessary. Use words and materials that the buyer can understand easily. The skilled salesperson can make a prospect feel comfortable with a new product or complex technology through the subtle use of nontechnical information and a respectful attitude.

Three literary masterpieces, The Lord's Prayer, The Twenty-Third Psalm, and Mr. Lincoln's Gettysburg Address had few words and no long ones. Recall their phraseology:

Abraham Lincoln America's 16th president, 1861–1865

- Our Father who art in Heaven, hallowed be thy name
- The Lord is my shepherd; I shall not want
- Four score and seven years ago

Not a single three-syllable word; hardly any two-syllable words. All of the greatest things in human life are one-syllable things—love, home, child, wife, trust, faith. As part of your study, watch television, listen to the radio, and read magazine advertisements. All of the great advertisements, generally speaking, use simple, small words.[7] So keep it simple—KISS!

Creating Mutual Trust Develops Friendship

Salespeople who develop a mutual, trusting relationship with their customers cannot help being successful. This type of relationship eventually results in high source credibility and even friendship.

If a buyer realizes that in the past she was sold products that performed to expectations, the products were worth their price, and the salesperson did everything promised, she will trust the salesperson in the future. Building mutual trust is important to effective long-run communication.

MAKING THE SALE

Do You Have Any of These Listening Habits?

No one is perfect. We all have some bad listening habits that we get away with when we talk to our family and friends. In a business context, however, leave these bad habits behind and practice active listening. To gain insight into your listening habits, read through this list of common irritating listening habits and be honest with yourself; notice what you are guilty of and use this awareness to begin eliminating them:

1. You do all the talking.
2. You interrupt when people talk.
3. You never look at the person talking or indicate that you are listening.
4. You start to argue before the other person has a chance to finish.
5. Everything that is said reminds you of an experience you've had, and you feel obligated to digress with a story.
6. You finish sentences for people if they pause too long.
7. You wait impatiently for people to finish so that you can interject something.
8. You work too hard at maintaining eye contact and make people uncomfortable.
9. You look as if you are appraising the person talking to you, looking him or her up and down as if considering the person for a modeling job.
10. You overdo the feedback you give—too many nods of your head and "uh-huh's."

Listening Clues You In

Hearing refers to being able to detect sounds. **Listening** is deriving meaning from sounds that are heard. Everything you hear is not worth your undivided attention; for the salesperson, however, listening is a communication skill critical to success.

Salespeople often believe that their job is to talk rather than to listen. If they both talk *and* listen, their persuasive powers increase. Since people can listen (about 400 words per minute) roughly twice as fast as the average rate of speech, it is understandable that a person's mind may wander while listening to a salesperson's presentation or that the salesperson may tune out a prospect. To keep the buyer listening, ask questions, get the buyer involved in the conversation, and show visual aids. Once you ask a question, carefully listen to the response.

Listen to Words, Feelings, and Thoughts

This may seem obvious, but when someone speaks to you, the person is expressing thoughts and feelings. Despite the logic of this statement, most of us listen only to the words. Spoken language is an inexact form of communication, but it is the best we have in this stage of human evolution. If you come back 2,000 years from now, perhaps you will communicate with your prospects via mental telepathy. For now, given the limitations of words, look beyond them to hear the entire story.

Listen *behind* the words for the emotional content of the message. This is conveyed in the nuances of voice and body language. Some people, such as sensers (discussed in Chapter 4), give you little emotional information. That's all right, because you deal with them in a factual, business-only style. Feelers, on the other hand, reveal their emotions, and in turn, they appreciate your acknowledgement of their feelings. It is appropriate to discuss their feelings and treat them more as friends than as strict business associates.

"You can be a good conversationalist by being a good listener."

DALE CARNEGIE

Active listening is important to your sales success. Concentrate, take notes, look for clues, don't interrupt!

Silence creates:
- *Room for listening*
- *Freedom to observe*
- *Time to think*

You can hear the emotions behind the words in several ways. First, look for changes in eye contact. After establishing a comfortable and natural level of eye contact, any sudden deviations from the norm tip you off to emotional content in the message. People tend to look away from you when they talk about something embarrassing. When this happens, make a quick mental note of what it pertained to and treat that subject delicately. Also, give a person the courtesy of looking away momentarily yourself—as if you are saying, "I respect your privacy."

Listen *between* the words for what is not said. Some people reveal more in what they don't say. Part of this is due to the emotional content of the message and part is due to the information they give you. A story illustrates this point.

A salesperson was talking to the president of a large paper mill. "I simply asked him what kind of training he had for his salespeople. He went into a long discourse on all the seminars, training films, videotapes, and cassettes they had from the parent company, suppliers, industry associations, and in-house programs. I sat, listened, and took notes. At the end of his speech I said to him, 'I noticed you didn't mention anything about time management for salespeople.' He raised his voice and emphatically said, 'You know, just this morning I was talking to a guy and I told him we have to have some time-management training for our salespeople.'"

The lesson here is to get the prospect talking and listen actively—concentrate. Take notes, look for clues to emotions, and don't interrupt or start thinking about your next question (see Exhibit 5.9).

The Three Levels of Listening

Whenever people listen, they are at one of three basic levels of listening. These levels require various degrees of concentration by the listener. As you move from the first to the third level, the potential for understanding and clear communication increases.

Marginal Listening. Marginal listening, the first and lowest level, involves the least concentration, and typically listeners are easily distracted by their thoughts. During periods of marginal listening, a listener exhibits blank stares, nervous mannerisms, and gestures that annoy the prospect and cause communication barriers. The salesperson hears the message but it doesn't sink in. There is enormous room for misunderstanding when a salesperson is not concentrating on what is said. Moreover, the prospect cannot help but feel the lack of attention, which may be insulting and diminishes trust. It may be funny when family members continually patronize each other with, "Yes, dear," regardless of what is said. In real life, however, it is not funny:

> **Prospect:** What I need, really, is a way to reduce the time lost due to equipment breakdowns.

> **Salesperson:** Yeah, OK. Let's see, uh, the third feature of our product is the convenient sizes you can get.

Salespeople of all experience levels are guilty of marginal listening. Beginners who lack confidence and experience may concentrate so intensely on what they are supposed to say next that they stop listening. Old pros, by contrast, have heard it all before. They have their presentations memorized and want the prospect to hurry and finish talking so the important business can continue. These traditional salespeople forget that the truly important information lies in what the prospect says.

Evaluative Listening. Evaluative listening, the second level of listening, requires more concentration and attention to the speaker's words. At this level, the listener actively tries to hear what the prospect says but isn't making an effort to understand the intent. Instead of accepting and trying to understand a prospect's message, the evaluative listener categorizes the statement and concentrates on preparing a response.

The evaluative listening phenomenon is a result of the tremendous speed at which a human can listen and think. It is no surprise that evaluative listening is the level of listening used most of the time. Unfortunately, it is a difficult habit to break, but it can be done with practice.

> **Prospect:** What I need, really, is a way to reduce the time lost due to equipment breakdown.

> **Salesperson:** (defensively) We have tested our machines in the field, and they don't break down often.

In this example, the salesperson reacted to one aspect of the prospect's statement. Had the salesperson withheld judgment until the end of the statement, he could have responded more objectively and informatively.

In evaluative listening, it is easy to be distracted by emotion-laden words. At that point, you aren't listening to the prospect. Instead, you are obsessed with the offensive word and wondering what to do about it. This is a waste of time for both you and the prospect. It increases personal and relationship tension and throws your communication off course. To avoid the problems of marginal and evaluative listening, practice active listening.

Active Listening. Active listening is the third and most effective level of listening. The active listener refrains from evaluating the message and tries to see the other person's point of view. Attention is not only on the words spoken but also on the thoughts, feelings, and meaning conveyed. Listening in this way means the listener puts herself into someone else's shoes. It requires the listener to give the other person verbal and nonverbal feedback.

> **Prospect:** What I need is a way to reduce the time lost due to equipment breakdowns.

> **Salesperson:** Could you tell me what kind of breakdowns you have experienced?

SELLING TIPS

Listening Guidelines

Here are several things to do to improve your listening skills:

- Stop talking.
- Show the prospect you want to listen.
- Watch for nonverbal messages and project positive signals.

- Recognize feelings and emotions.
- Ask questions to clarify meaning.
- If appropriate, restate the prospect's position for clarification.
- Listen to the full story.

In this example, the salesperson spoke directly to the prospect's concerns—not around them. Her desire to make a presentation was deferred so she could accomplish a more important task—effectively communicating with the prospect.

Active listening is a skill that takes practice in the beginning, but after a while, it becomes second nature. The logic behind active listening is based on courtesy and concentration.

Active listening is sometimes difficult to do, especially for the novice salesperson. The novice may continue to talk about a particular situation or problem. However, the salesperson must *learn to listen*. It is a key to sales success. People like and appreciate a listener, as this poem says so well:

> His thoughts were slow,
> His words were few,
> And never made to glisten,
> But he was a joy
> Wherever he went.
> You should have heard him listen.
>
> *—Author Unknown*

Technology Helps to Remember

A distinction must be drawn between listening and remembering. Listening is the process of receiving the message the way the speaker intended to send it. **Memory** is recall over time. Listening and time have profound effects on memory. An untrained listener is likely to understand and retain only about 50 percent of a conversation. After 48 hours, the retention rate drops to 25 percent. Think of the implications. Memory of a conversation that occurred more than two days ago may be incomplete and inaccurate.

After you leave the prospect's office, take a few minutes to write down, or log in your computer, what occurred during the sales call (see Exhibit 5.10). This is valuable information for doing what you promised and planning the next sales call. Chapter 6 will discuss much more about the use of technology in communicating with customers.

Your Attitude Makes the Difference

Although a variety of methods and techniques exist in selling, truly effective sales persuasion is based on the salesperson's attitude toward the sales job and customers. The most important element of this attitude is the salesperson's degree of interest and enthusiasm in helping people to fulfill their needs. This is the foundation

EXHIBIT 5.10

Computers help you remember.

Computers are a great tool for recording what was discussed in the sales call.

> *"Do this and you'll be welcome anywhere— become genuinely interested in other people."*
>
> DALE CARNEGIE

for building effective communication techniques. **Enthusiasm** is a condition in which an individual is filled with excitement toward something. Excitement does not mean an aggressive attitude, but rather a positive view toward solving the customers' problems.

Sell yourself *on* yourself and on being a salesperson. The highly successful salesperson goes all out to help customers. Strive to make the buyer feel important. Show the buyer that you are there solely as a problem solver. Do this by developing methods of expressing true interest such as asking questions instead of talking at the buyer. This attitude will benefit you by allowing you to look at the sales situation from the buyer's viewpoint (empathy).

Proof Statements Make You Believable

Salespeople who have established **credibility** with their customers through continued empathy, willingness to listen to specific needs, and continual enthusiasm toward their work and customers' business can make claims that some customers may treat as gospel. Enthusiasm combined with proof statements greatly improves a salesperson's persuasive ability.

Salespeople have known for years that using highly credible sources can improve the persuasiveness of the sales presentation message. **Proof statements** are statements that substantiate the salesperson's claims. Pharmaceutical companies often quote research studies performed by outstanding physicians at prestigious medical schools to validate claims of product benefits. These proof statements add high credibility to a sales message.

Salespeople sometimes quote acknowledged experts in a field on the use of products. By demonstrating that other customers or respected individuals use the products, they encourage customer belief in the validity of information presented in a

It's Party Time!

You are part of a sales district containing six salespeople. At least once a month, everyone gets together for dinner and sometimes entertainment. This is an aggressive group, very spirited in their discussion of any topic.

Tonight you sit and listen to one of the salespeople maliciously and wrongfully attack your company and your boss. You can tell that this person is serious and has strong feelings about what is being said.

What would be the most ethical action to take?

1. Interject with your opinion. This might start a heated debate, but at least you did not compromise your ideas.
2. Interject with your opinion during dinner and leave dinner if the negative conversation continues. Sit down with your boss the next day and suggest that he bring the other salesperson in to discuss what the underlying problems are and how they might be resolved.
3. Let him talk. Everybody is entitled to his/her own opinions.

---

sales presentation. People place greater confidence in a trustworthy, objective source (particularly one not associated with the salesperson's firm) and are therefore more receptive to what the salesperson says.

SUMMARY OF MAJOR SELLING ISSUES

Communication is defined as transmission of verbal and nonverbal information and understanding between salesperson and prospect. Modes of communication commonly used in a sales presentation are words, gestures, visual aids, and nonverbal communication.

A model of the communication process is composed of a sender (encoder) who transmits a specific message via some medium to a receiver (decoder) who responds to that message. The effectiveness of this communication process can be hampered by noise that distorts the message as it travels to the receiver. A sender (encoder) can judge the effectiveness of a message and media choice by monitoring the feedback from the receiver.

Barriers, which hinder or prevent constructive communication during a sales presentation, may develop or already exist. These barriers may relate to the perceptional differences between the sender and receiver, cultural differences, outside distractions, or how sales information is conveyed. Regardless of their source, these barriers must be recognized and either overcome or eliminated if communication is to succeed.

Nonverbal communication has emerged as a critical component of the overall communication process within the past 10 or 15 years. Recognition of nonverbal communication is essential for sales success in today's business environment. Awareness of the prospect's territorial space, a firm and confident handshake, and accurate interpretation of body language are of tremendous aid to a salesperson's success.

Overall persuasive power is enhanced through development of several key characteristics. The salesperson who creates a relationship based on mutual trust with a customer by displaying true empathy (desire to understand the customer's situation and environment), a willing ear (more listening, less talking), and a positive attitude of enthusiastic pursuit of lasting solutions for the customer's needs and problems increases the likelihood of making the sale.

MEETING A SALES CHALLENGE

In this imaginary sales call, buyer and seller communicated both verbal and nonverbal messages. Here, nonverbal messages conveyed both parties' attitudes better than the actual verbal exchange. The salesperson's negative reactions served to increase Amos Skaggs's hostile attitude. He could sense that the salesperson did not understand his problem and was there only to sell him something—not to solve his problem. This impression caused a rapid breakdown in communication. The end result, as in this case, is usually **NO SALE.**

The salesperson may have reacted correctly to Skaggs. Since he is in a bad mood, coming back another day may be best. If the salesperson cannot come another day, then the salesperson needs to stop the planned presentation and let the buyer know he understands. He should show that he is there to help. But most of all, he must project a positive attitude and not be frightened by Skaggs.

KEY TERMS FOR SELLING

communication   148
source   149
encoding process   149
message   149
medium   149
decoding process   149
receiver   149
feedback   149
noise   149
nonverbal communication   150
territorial space   150
intimate space   151
personal space   151
social space   151
public space   151

space threats   151
space invasion   151
acceptance signals   155
caution signals   155
disagreement signals   157
persuasion   160
probing   161
empathy   162
KISS   162
hearing   163
listening   163
memory   166
enthusiasm   167
credibility   167
proof statements   167

SALES APPLICATION QUESTIONS

1. Draw the salesperson–buyer communication process. Describe each step in the process. Why is two-way communication important in this process?
2. This chapter outlined several forms of nonverbal communication.
   a. Give an example of a salesperson making a good first impression through the proper use of an introductory handshake.
   b. What signals should the salesperson look for from a buyer's body language? Give several examples of these signals.
3. A salesperson may spend hours developing a sales presentation and yet the buyer does not buy. One reason for losing a sale is that the salesperson and the buyer do not communicate. What barriers to communication may be present between seller and buyer during a sales presentation?
4. When two people are talking, they want the listener to understand what they are saying. They both want to be effective communicators. The same is true of the salesperson who wants the buyer to listen to a sales presentation. What can the salesperson do to help ensure that the buyer is listening?
5. You arrive at the industrial purchasing agent's office on time. This is your first meeting. After you have waited five minutes, the agent's secretary says, "She will see you." After the initial greeting, she asks you to sit down.

For each of these three situations determine:

a. What nonverbal signals is she communicating?

b. How would you respond nonverbally?

c. What would you say to her?

1. She sits down behind her desk. She sits up straight in her chair. She clasps her hands together and with little expression on her face says, "What can I do for you?"

2. She sits down behind her desk. She moves slightly backwards in her chair, crosses her arms, and while looking around the room says, "What can I do for you?"

3. She sits down behind her desk. She moves slightly forward in her chair, seems hurried, yet she is relaxed toward your presence. Her arms are uncrossed. She looks you squarely in the eye, and with a pleasant look on her face says, "What can I do for you?"

6. In each of the following selling situations determine:

a. What nonverbal signals is the buyer communicating?

b. How would you respond nonverbally?

c. What would you say?

1. The buyer seems happy to see you. Because you have been calling on him for several years, the two of you have become business friends. In the middle of your presentation, you notice the buyer slowly lean back in his chair. As you continue to talk, a puzzled look comes over his face.

2. As you begin the main part of your presentation, the buyer reaches for the telephone and says, "Keep going; I need to tell my secretary something."

3. As a salesperson with only six months' experience, you are somewhat nervous about calling on an important buyer who has been a purchasing agent for almost 20 years. Three minutes after you have begun your presentation, he rapidly raises his arms straight up into the air and slowly clasps his hands behind his head. He leans so far back in his chair that you think he is going to fall backward on the floor. At the same time, he crosses his legs away from you and slowly closes his eyes. You keep on talking. Slowly the buyer opens his eyes, uncrosses his legs, and sits up in his chair. He leans forward, placing his elbows on the desk top, propping his head up with his hands. He seems relaxed as he says, "Let me see what you have here." He reaches his hand out for you to give him the presentation materials you have developed.

4. At the end of your presentation, the buyer leans forward, his arms open, and he smiles as he says, "You really don't expect me to buy that piece of junk, do you?"

FURTHER EXPLORING THE SALES WORLD

Using questions is an effective method for a salesperson to obtain feedback from a buyer. This statement applies to conversation between two people. For the next two days, try using questions in your conversations with other people and report on your results. These questions should reflect an interest in the person you are conversing with and the topic being discussed. Use of the words *you* and *your* should increase feedback and create an atmosphere of trust.

For example, you can use questions such as "What do you mean?" "What do you think?" and "How does that sound?" in your conversation to have other people participate and to help determine how they feel toward the topic of conversation.

Asking people's opinions also can result in a positive response because they may feel flattered that you care about their opinion. Questions can help you guide the direction of topics discussed in conversation. Try to determine people's reactions to your questions and report your findings in class.

SELLING EXPERIENTIAL EXERCISE

Instructions: Read the following questions and write *yes* or *no* for each statement on a separate sheet of paper. Mark each answer as truthfully as you can in light of your behavior in the last few meetings or gatherings you attended.

Listening Self-Inventory

	Yes	No
1. I frequently attempt to listen to several conversations at the same time.	___	___
2. I like people to give me only the facts and then let me make my own interpretation.	___	___
3. I sometimes pretend to pay attention to people.	___	___
4. I consider myself a good judge of nonverbal communications.	___	___
5. I usually know what another person is going to say before he or she says it.	___	___
6. I usually end conversations that don't interest me by diverting my attention from the speaker.	___	___
7. I frequently nod, frown, or whatever to let the speaker know how I feel about what he or she is saying.	___	___
8. I usually respond immediately when someone has finished talking.	___	___
9. I evaluate what is being said while it is being said.	___	___
10. I usually formulate a response while the other person is still talking.	___	___
11. The speaker's delivery style frequently keeps me from listening to content.	___	___
12. I usually ask people's points of view.	___	___
13. I make a concerted effort to understand other people's points of view.	___	___
14. I frequently hear what I expect to hear rather than what is said.	___	___
15. Most people believe that I have understood their points of view when we disagree.	___	___

According to communication theory, the correct answers are as follows: No for questions 1, 2, 3, 5, 6, 7, 8, 9, 10, 11, 14; and Yes for questions 4, 12, 13, 15. If you missed only one or two questions, you strongly approve of your own listening habits, and you are on the right track to becoming an effective listener in your role as a salesperson. If you missed three or four questions, you have uncovered some doubts about your listening effectiveness, and your knowledge of how to listen has some gaps. If you missed five or more questions, you probably are not satisfied with the way you listen, and your friends and co-workers may not feel you are a good listener either. Work on improving your active listening skills.[8]

CHAPTER 5

Communication for Relationship Building: It's Not All Talk

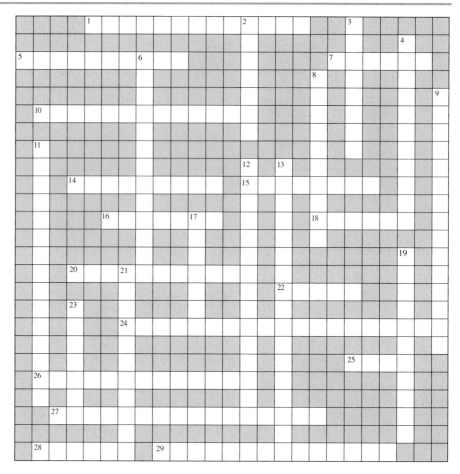

Across

1. An area 2 to 4 feet from a person; it is the closest zone a stranger or business acquaintance is normally allowed to enter.

5. Ability to change a person's belief, position, or course of action.

7. The form of communication used in the sales presentation and discussion; most frequently words, visual materials, and body language.

10. The act of transmitting verbal and nonverbal information and understanding between seller and buyer.

14. Ability to derive meaning from sounds that are heard.

15. The person a communication is intended for.

16. The ability to identify and understand another person's feelings, ideas, and circumstances.

18. The origin of a communication.

20. A situation in which a person threatens to invade another's spatial territory.

22. Factors that distort communication between buyer and seller, including barriers to communication.

24. Signs that the prospect does not agree with the presentation or does not think the product is beneficial.

25. A memory device standing for Keep It Simple, Salesperson.

26. A situation in which one person enters another person's personal or intimate space.

27. The area around oneself that a person will not allow another person to enter without consent.

28. The ability to recall information over time.

29. Signs that a buyer is neutral or skeptical toward what the salesperson says.

Down

2. The act of gathering information and uncovering customer needs by using one or more questions.

3. Verbal or nonverbal reaction to communication as transmitted to the sender.

4. Distances greater than 12 feet from a person.

6. A spatial zone up to two feet, about an arm's length, from a person's body that is reserved for close friends and loved ones.

8. A state of mind in which a person is filled with excitement toward something.

9. Receipt and translation of information by the receiver.

11. One of the eight elements of the communication process. This is the conversion by the salesperson of ideas and concepts into the language and materials used in the sales presentation.

12. Statements that substantiate claims made by the salesperson.

13. Signs that your buyer is favorably inclined toward you and your presentation.

17. The ability to detect sounds.

19. A zone that is 4 to 12 feet from a person and is the area normally used for sales presentations.

21. A salesperson's believability, established through empathy, willingness to listen to specific needs, and continual enthusiasm toward his or her work and the customer's business.

23. Information conveyed in the sales presentation.

CASE 5-1
Skaggs Manufacturing

John Andrews arrived promptly for his 10 A.M. meeting with Martha Gillespie, the buyer for Skaggs Manufacturing. At 10:15, when she hadn't arrived, John asked her secretary if she was out of the office for the morning. The secretary smiled and said, "She'll probably be a few minutes late." John resented this delay and was convinced that Martha had forgotten the appointment.

Finally, at 10:20, Martha entered her office, walked over to John, said hello, and promptly excused herself to talk to the secretary about a tennis game scheduled for that afternoon. Ten minutes later, Martha led John into her office. At the same time, a competing salesperson entered the office for a 10:30 appointment. With the door open, Martha asked John, "What's new today?" As John began to talk, Martha began reading letters on her desk and signing them. Shortly after that, the telephone began to ring, whereupon Martha talked to her husband for 10 minutes.

As she hung up, Martha looked at John and suddenly realized his frustration. She promptly buzzed her secretary and said, "Hold all calls." She got up and shut the door. John again began his presentation when Martha leaned backward in her chair, pulled her golf shoes out of a desk drawer, and began to brush them.

About that time, the secretary entered the office and said, "Martha, your 10:30 appointment is about to leave. What should I tell him" "Tell him to wait; I need to see him." Then she said, "John, I wish we had more time. Look, I think I have enough of your product to last until your next visit. I'll see you then. Thanks for coming by."

John quickly rose to his feet, did not shake hands, said "OK," and left.

Questions

1. What nonverbal cues did the salesperson, John Andrews, experience when contacting Martha Gillespie?
2. If you were John Andrews, how would you have handled the situation?

Judy Allison sells cellular telephones for Alabama Office Supply in Birmingham. Today she is calling on Bill Taylor, purchasing agent for a large manufacturing firm. Two weeks earlier, she had made her first sales call and had left a demonstrator for the company executives to try out. The previous evening, Bill had called Judy and asked her to come in so he could give her an order. After their initial hellos, the conversation continued:

Buyer: Judy, thanks for coming by today. Our executives really like your equipment. Here is an order for four phones. When can you deliver them?

Salesperson: Is tomorrow too soon?

Buyer: That is perfect. Leave them with Joyce, my secretary. Joyce [*Bill says over the intercom*], Judy will deliver the phones tomorrow. Joyce, I want you to go ahead and take them to Sally, Anne, and Sherri. Women sure understand the use of modern equipment.

Salesperson: Bill, thanks for your help.

Buyer: Forget it Judy, I wish I could have helped more. Your cellular phones can reduce the "telephone tag" we play with each other and customers. Customers are leaving us because they can't reach our salespeople when they are out on the road contacting customers.

Salesperson: You're right; many of my customers are going to them for that very reason.

Buyer: I know, but some executives still feel they don't want them. They don't want their phone to ring when they're in with a customer. Plus, the cancer scare has them worried. I wish the men in our company felt the same way the women do about using these things.

Question

Analyze and describe the conversation between Judy Allison and Bill Taylor. What should Judy do now?

Samantha Wells (Sam), a marketer at Vernex, is discussing shipping dates with Duke Stillwell, the shipping manager. Sam notices that Duke is shipping three hundred thousand HS200 fire alarm sensor circuits out of inventory. Sam asks Duke why the company is finally writing them off this inventory, especially before the merger is finalized. Duke informs Sam that Ed Naughton, the director of marketing, sold the sensor circuits to Executron, apparently at full price. Sam is confused by Executron's

Video

Case

purchase and also questions why Ed would charge them full price when the new HS300s are about to be introduced. Duke assures Sam that Ed knows what he is doing and comments that he is grateful for the much needed warehouse space.

Ed is talking with Carrie Ventana, the administrative manager, in the lobby when Sam joins them. Sam asks Carrie if she is going to attend the Dallas conference. Ed remarks that this is a conference they would not miss and that management has been going over the records carefully and should be announcing the merger and the new director of marketing then. Carrie tells Ed that he is a shoo-in for the job, especially since he just made the big Executron sale. Sam congratulates Ed on the sale and asks him why he did not notify her about it. Ed claims that he forgot and suggests a promotion for Sam if he becomes director of marketing.

After Ed leaves, Sam tells Carrie that she wanted to talk to her about the Executron sale. Sam asks Carrie whether Executron has ever bought sensor circuits from Vernex before. Carrie offers to go to her office to check the computer's central customer file. The computer verifies that this is the first time Executron has bought from this division. Sam explains that she is concerned because marketing overestimated the market for these circuits and now, suddenly, Ed sells the circuits to a company that appears to have no use for them. Carrie comments that the president of Executron is Ed's good friend so he would not do anything to hurt them. Carrie adds that she knows that Executron is doing well financially because Ed told her to invest in them years ago when he did, and now she regrets not following his advice. Sam still questions why Ed did not give Executron a discount for the old circuits. Carrie defends Ed's reputation and asks Sam why it is wrong for Ed to make himself look better, get rid of a liability, and beef up the bottom line. Sam admits nothing is wrong, if it is a legitimate sale. But what if Executron returns the circuits right after Ed's promotion?[9]

Questions

1. What are the main ethical issues, if any, in the Vernex, Inc. case?
2. What are Samantha (Sam) Wells's options?
3. How do the three levels of moral development relate to Sam's situation?
4. What would you do?

Appendix: Dress for Success . . . and to Impress for Business Professional and Casual Occasions!

You have only one chance to make a favorable first impression. Impressions of you are based upon your appearance. How you are dressed makes a first and lasting impression on those you meet in any situation. The following dress guidelines come from Texas A&M University's Center for Retailing Studies. For men and women you learn the basic guidelines for both business professional and business casual attire.

Men's

DRESS FOR SUCCESS
. . . and to impress!
brought to you by the Center for Retailing Studies

Business <u>Casual</u> Attire:

The Coat & Shirt:
Depending on the occasion, a sports coat with a nice solid or striped button-down shirt is appropriate. Be cautious not to pick anything too loud. Go with conservative colors. If you pick a striped shirt, be sure the stripes are subtle. The coat should be black, navy, gray or tweed.

The Slacks:
Choose a pair of slacks that is equally as professional as your suit pants. They should fit appropriately and coordinate with your shirt. They should be a neutral color such as black, brown, tan, grey or navy.

The Shoes:
Business casual shoes are similar to business professional shoes. They should match your outfit and preferably be leather. Although tie shoes are not necessary, be sure to pick a style that is conservative and still professional looking.

Accessories:
Accessories should always be used moderately. A tie is not necessary for business causal attire. The only jewelry you should wear is a gold or silver watch, a wedding band and/or a class ring. Also, always wear dark color socks and be sure the leather of your belt matches your shoes.

Tips to Remember:
The main difference between business casual and business professional is that you may not be wearing a suit jacket.
Even though it is called business casual, it is important to still look extremely professional.
Remember to avoid loud colors.
When in doubt, always dress up rather than down.

Men's

DRESS FOR SUCCESS

. . .and to impress!

brought to you by the Center for Retailing Studies

Business <u>Professional</u> Attire:

The Suit:

Choose a professional, conservative suit in charcoal or navy. It may be solid, stripped or have a subtle pattern. The suit should fit you properly and always be cuffed. The coat sleeve should show ¼ to ½ inches of your shirt sleeve. It is recommended that you wear a single breasted wool suit with two or three buttons. This suit is just an example of an appropriate one you may choose to wear.

The Shirt:

White, long sleeved button-down shirt. It should be very professional, fit you well and be nicely ironed.

The Shoes:

Choose a lace up shoe only in black or cordovan. It is recommended that they are leather and they should compliment your suit. Be sure they are clean and polished.

The Accessories:

Keep accessories to a minimum. Bring a portfolio or briefcase. Wear little or no cologne, trim fingernails and be sure your hair is nicely styled. Also, wear dark colored socks.

The Tie:

Wear a conservative silk tie with little or no pattern. A red or maroon color is recommended.

Tips to Remember:

First impressions are formed in the first seven seconds of a meeting
Avoid faddish styles and loud colors. You want the employer to focus on your skills and abilities, not your clothes.
It is better to be over dressed than under dressed.
The picture you create will greatly influence your chances of being hired.

Women's

DRESS FOR SUCCESS

...and to impress!

brought to you by the Center for Retailing Studies

Business <u>Casual</u> Attire:

The Shirt:

Choose a blouse or sweater that coordinates with your pants or skirt. It should be just as nice as a blouse you would wear with a business suit. Be sure it fits well and you will be comfortable wearing it without a jacket over it.

The Slacks or Skirt:

Choose a pair of slacks or skirt that is equally as professional as your suit bottoms. They should fit appropriately and coordinate with your blouse or sweater. They should be a neutral color such as black, brown, tan, grey or navy.

The Shoes:

Business casual shoes are similar to business professional shoes. They should match your outfit, be closed toed and preferable leather. It is recommended that they be closed in the back as well with a moderately low heel.

The Accessories

Accessories should always be used moderately. Bring a portfolio and a purse if desired and that it all you should need. Wear neutral hosiery and little jewelry. Belts, scarves and other accessories should be understated. You wanted them to remember you not your accessories.

Tips to Remember:

First impressions are formed in the first seven seconds of a meeting.
Avoid faddish styles and loud colors. You want the employer to focus on your skills and abilities, not your clothes.
Your nails should always be manicured.
It is better to be over dressed than under dressed.
The picture you create will greatly influence your chances of being hired.

CENTER
FOR
RETAILING
STUDIES

Women's

DRESS FOR SUCCESS

...and to impress!
brought to you by the Center for Retailing Studies

Business <u>Professional</u> Attire:

The Suit:
Choose a professional pant or skirt suit tailored to fit you just right. If you choose a skirt suit, be sure that the skirt falls at or just below your knees. These suits are just examples of appropriate ones you may choose to wear. Appropriate colors include black, navy or charcoal. For an interview it is best to wear a skirt suit.

The Shirt:
Choose a blouse that coordinates nicely with your suit, in a color that is subtle and professional, such as white or blue. Be sure the blouse fits you right and that it is not too low cut. It should be made of a nice material, such as silk or cotton. Some appropriate styles and cuts you may choose to wear are shown to the right. A button down shirt should be worn for an interview.

The Shoes:

For a professional look, choose a shoe that is conservative with a medium to low heel. The shoe should be closed toe and heel and should match the suit in color. Make sure your shoes are polished, with no scuff marks. Panty hose should *always* be worn and they should match the color of your skin. An example of an appropriate pair of shoes is shown to the left.

The Accessories:
Wear jewelry that compliments your outfit, and is simple and classy such as pearls or diamonds. Do not wear anything that is too flashy or gaudy. Also, do not wear a watch if you feel you will constantly be checking the time. Use perfume sparingly. Only wear one earring in each ear and one ring on each finger.

The Hair:
Be sure your hair is neatly brushed and clean. Keep it out of your face to avoid playing with it during an interview.

Tips to Remember:
First impressions are formed in the first seven seconds of a meeting.
Avoid faddish styles and loud colors. You want the employer to focus on your skills and abilities, not your clothes.
Your nails should always be manicured.
It is better to be over dressed than under dressed.
The picture you create will greatly influence your chances of being hired.

6 CHAPTER

Sales Knowledge: Customers, Products, Technologies

LEARNING OBJECTIVES

Successful salespeople are knowledgeable individuals. Many salespeople are experts in their field. After studying this chapter, you should be able to

- Explain why it is so important to be knowledgeable.

- Discuss the major body of knowledge needed for increased sales success.

- Illustrate how to use this knowledge during the sales presentation.

- Explain the main technologies used by salespeople.

You are proud of the products you sell and tell everyone they are the Cadillac of the industry, the best on the market, light years ahead of the competition. Of course you have only worked for the company two weeks. But the sales training course you took last week clearly convinced you that your products are much better than any others on the market. During one presentation on a new washing machine detergent, you concentrated on discussing the quality of the product: how well it cleans; its environmental safety factor; how much users like its pleasant scent on their clothes. The grocery store buyer said, "I could care less about the quality of your products."

Why did the buyer respond in a negative way to you? What is the buyer interested in?

Salespeople need to know many things. Features, advantages, and benefits are important to discuss, but which FABs are of interest to the buyer? The above situation is a sales challenge all salespeople face. The salesperson was apparently talking about the wrong things. What would be of interest to a retailer, wholesaler, manufacturer, or consumer? Chances are they are interested in similar, but also different, FABs. This chapter examines the basic body of knowledge essential to the success of all salespeople.

THE TREE OF BUSINESS LIFE: KNOWLEDGE

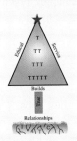

In Chapter 1 you learned salespeople need knowledge at the medical doctor, M.D., level. Salespeople must be experts on everything involved with their products. Although facts are needed to be learned, it is more important to have the wisdom necessary to apply the knowledge. Again, just as the medical doctor does when treating people for health problems, and just as you rely on the medical doctor to have the knowledge, wisdom, and skills needed to help you, so do customers rely on the help of salespeople. The salesperson may be the expert or have the most current information about a product or situation. The customer relies on the salesperson to provide information—truthfully.

This is why a person's integrity and character, as discussed in Chapter 3, are so important in building long-term relationships. Placing the customer's welfare before one's own welfare is key to having a successful sales career. Please remember, however, that people do not care how much you know until they know how much you care. They want you to follow the Golden Rule of Personal Selling, treat them as you would like to be treated by a salesperson. This is why one of the themes of your book as illustrated in the Tree of Business Life is that ethical service builds relationships and is based upon the truth.

SOURCES OF SALES KNOWLEDGE

Knowledge for selling is obtained in two ways: First, most companies provide some formal sales training that teaches information through preliminary training programs and sales meetings. Second, the salesperson learns by being on the job. Experience is the best teacher for the beginning salesperson.

Sales training is the effort an employer puts forth to provide the opportunity for the salesperson to receive job-related culture, skills, knowledge, and attitudes that result in improved performance in the selling environment.

Successful companies thoroughly train new salespeople and maintain ongoing training programs for their experienced sales personnel. Companies are interested in training primarily to increase sales volume, salesperson productivity, and profitability.

Like many professional careers, selling is a skill that is truly developed only through *experience.* Sales knowledge obtained through education, reading, formalized sales training, and word-of-mouth is helpful in enhancing overall sales ability, but actual experience is the critical source of sales knowledge. Some sales managers hire only experienced people to fill entry-level selling slots. Indeed, some corporations do not allow people to fill marketing staff positions unless they have had field sales experience with the company or a major competitor.

Sales experience improves a salesperson's abilities by showing how buyers perceive a product or product line, revealing unrecognized or undervalued product benefits or shortcomings, voicing a multitude of unanticipated protests and objections, showing a great number of prospect moods and attitudes over a short period, and generally providing a challenge that makes selling a skill that is never mastered, only improved.

No author or sales trainer can simulate the variety of situations that a salesperson confronts over the span of a career. Authors and trainers can provide only general guidelines as a framework for action. Only actual selling experience gives a person direct feedback on how to function in a specific selling situation. The sales knowledge gained through periodic sales training and actual experience benefits the salesperson, the firm, and the customers.

Only through possessing a high level of knowledge can the salesperson provide excellent service. This leads to "S–success" as discussed in Chapter 1. Knowledge is part of the Golden Rule of Personal Selling. Knowledge based upon wisdom and conveyed to the buyer truthfully builds relationships.

KNOWLEDGE BUILDS RELATIONSHIPS

Salespeople today must be knowledgeable to be effective in their jobs. Three important reasons for the salesperson to have selling knowledge are (1) to increase the salesperson's self-confidence, (2) to build the buyer's confidence in the salesperson, and (3) to build relationships through truly caring about the needs of others. These reasons are, for the salesperson, the major need for acquiring sales knowledge.

Knowledge Increases Confidence in Salespeople . . .

Salespeople who call on, for example, computer systems engineers, university professors, or aerospace experts may be at a disadvantage. In many cases, they have less education and experience than prospects in their fields of expertise.

Imagine making a sales call on Dr. Michael DeBakey, the distinguished heart surgeon. Can you educate him in the use of your company's synthetic heart valves? Not really, but you can offer help in supplying product information from your firm's medical department. This personal service, your product knowledge, and his specific needs are what will make the sale. Knowledge about your company, its market, and your buyer enables you to acquire confidence in yourself, which results in increased sales.

. . . and in Buyers

Furthermore, prospects and customers want to do business with salespeople who know their business and the products they sell. When a prospect has confidence in the salesperson's expertise, a sales presentation becomes more acceptable and believable to the prospect.

Strive to be the expert on all aspects of your product. Knowledge of your product and its uses also allows you to confidently answer questions and field objections that prospects raise. You can explain better how a product suits a customer's needs. But product knowledge alone may not be enough to convince every buyer.

Relationships Increase Sales

Often within minutes buyers can tell if salespeople know what they are talking about. You have experienced it yourself. You ask questions and quickly form an impression of a salesperson. A relationship begins to build; knowledge builds relationships and results in sales and money for the seller. Typically, the more knowledge you have and the more you care about the other person, the higher your sales.

KNOW YOUR CUSTOMERS

How can you match your product's benefits with a buyer's needs if you don't know your customers? If you are selling to someone you've never seen before—such as in a retail store—you have to ask about the buyer's needs. Business-to-business selling also requires asking numerous questions, sometimes spending weeks with a customer. There will be more on this important topic later in your book.

KNOW YOUR COMPANY

Knowledge of your firm usually helps you project an expert image to the prospect. Company knowledge includes information about the history, policies, procedures, distribution systems, promotional activities, pricing practices, and technology that have guided the firm to its current position.

The type and extent of company knowledge to use depends on the company, its product lines, and the industry (see Exhibit 6.1). In general, consumer-goods salespeople require less information about the technical nature of their products; however, selling high-technology products (computers, rocket-engine components, complex machinery, etc.) to highly knowledgeable industrial buyers requires extensive knowledge.

EXHIBIT 6.1

What would you need to know for selling . . .

. . . computers to consumers?

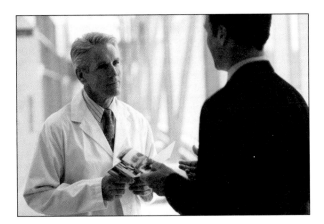

. . . pharmaceutical drugs to a physician?

General Company Information

All salespeople need to know the background and current operating policies of their companies. These policies are your guidelines, and you must understand them to do your job effectively. Information on company growth, policies, procedures, production, and service facilities is often used in sales presentations. Four examples follow.

Company Growth and Accomplishment

Knowledge of your firm's development since its origin provides you with promotional material and builds your confidence in the company. An IBM office products salesperson might say to a buyer:

> In 1952, IBM placed its first commercial electronic computer on the market. That year, our sales were $342 million. Currently, our sales are projected to be over $80 billion. IBM has reached these high sales figures because our advanced, technological office equipment and information processors are the best available at any price. This IBM "Star Trek I" system I am showing you is the most advanced piece of equipment on the market today. It is five years ahead of any other computer!

Policies and Procedures

To give good service, you should be able to tell a customer about policies: how an order is processed, how long it takes for orders to be filled, your firm's returned goods policy, how to open a new account, and what to do in the event of a shipping error. When you handle these situations quickly and fairly, your buyer gains confidence in you and the firm.

Production Facilities

Many companies require their new salespeople to tour their production facilities to give them a firsthand look at the company's operations. This is a good opportunity to gain product knowledge. For example, the Bigelow-Sanford Carpet Company salesperson can say, "When I was visiting our production plant, I viewed each step of the carpet-production process. The research and development department allowed us to watch comparison tests between our carpets and competitors' carpets. Our carpets did everything but fly . . . and they are working on that!"

Service Facilities

Many companies, such as Intel, Xerox, and 3M, have both service facilities and service representatives to help customers. Being able to say, "We can have a service representative there the same day you call our service center," strengthens a sales presentation, especially if service is important for the customer (as it is in the office copier and computer industries).

KNOW YOUR PRODUCT

Knowledge about your company's product and your competitors is a major component of sales knowledge. Become an expert on your company's products. Understand how they are produced and their level of quality. This type of product knowledge is important to the buyer. Product knowledge may include such technical details as

- Performance data.
- Physical size and characteristics.
- How the product operates.
- Specific features, advantages, and benefits of the product.
- How well the product is selling in the marketplace.

Many companies have their new salespeople work in the manufacturing plant (for example, on the assembly line) or in the warehouse (filling orders and receiving stock). This hands-on experience may cost the salesperson a lot of sweat and sore muscles for a couple of weeks or months, but the payoff is a world of product knowledge and help in future selling that could not be earned in any other way. International Paper, for example, has its new salespeople spend several weeks in a production plant. Often, new salespeople in the oil and gas industry roughneck and drive trucks for Exxon and Shell Oil during the first few months on the job. A sales representative for McKesson Chemical spends the first two or three weeks on the job in a warehouse unloading freight cars and flatbed trucks and filling 55-gallon drums with various liquid chemicals.

Salespeople also can learn much at periodic company sales meetings. At sales meetings, a consumer-goods manufacturer, such as Frito-Lay, may concentrate on developing sales presentations for the products to receive special emphasis during the coming sales period. Company advertising programs, price discounts, and promotional allowances for these products are discussed. Although little time is spent on the technical aspects of consumer products, much time is devoted to discussing the marketing mix for these products (product type, promotion, distribution, and price).

Sales managers for firms selling technical products, such as Merck, Alcoa, and Emerson Electric, might spend as much as 75 percent of a sales meeting discussing product information. The remaining time might be allotted to sales techniques.

KNOW YOUR RESELLERS

It is essential to understand the channel of distribution your company uses to move its products to the final consumer. Knowledge of each channel member (also called reseller or middleman) is vital. Wholesalers and retailers often stock thousands of products, and each one may have hundreds of salespeople from a multitude of companies calling on its buyers. Know as much about each channel member as possible. Some important information you will need includes the following:

- Likes and dislikes of each channel member's customers.
- Product lines and the assortment each one carries.
- When each member sees salespeople.
- Distribution, promotion, and pricing policies.
- What quantity of which product each channel member has purchased in the past.

Although most channel members will have similar policies concerning salespeople, keep abreast of the differences.

ADVERTISING AIDS SALESPEOPLE

Personal selling, advertising, publicity, and sales promotion are the main ingredients of a firm's promotional effort. Companies sometimes coordinate these promotional tools in a promotional campaign. The corporate marketing manager may ask a sales

EXHIBIT 6.2

Advertising and sales promotion information the salesperson provides the buyer.

1. **Massive Sampling and Couponing:**
   - There will be blanketing of the top 300 markets with 4.4-oz. samples plus 80-cents-off coupons. Your market is included.
   - There will be a 75 percent coverage of homes in the top 100 markets. Your market is included.

2. **Heavy Advertising:**
   - Nighttime network TV.
   - Daytime network TV.
   - Saturation spot TV.
   - Newspapers.
   - The total network and spot advertising will reach 85 percent of all homes in the United States five times each week based on a four-week average. This means that in four weeks, Fresh Mouth will have attained 150 million home impressions—130 million of these impressions will be women.
   - There will be half-page, two-color inserts in local newspapers in 50 markets, including yours. This is more than 20 million in circulation. Scheduled to tie in with saturation sampling is a couponing program.
   - $80 million will be spent on promotion to ensure consumer acceptance.

3. **TV Advertising Theme** (the salesperson would show pictures or drawings of the advertisement):
   - The commercial with POWER to sell!
   - "POWER to kill mouth odor—POWER to kill germs—POWER to give FRESH MOUTH."
   - The commercial shows a young man, about 20 years of age, walking up to a young woman saying, "Hi, Susan!" They kiss and she says, "My, you have a fresh mouth, Bill!" He looks at the camera with a smile and says, "It works!" The announcer closes the commercial by saying, "FRESH MOUTH—it has the POWER!"

4. **Display Materials:**
   - Shelf display tag.
   - Small floor stand for end-of-aisle display—holds 24 12-oz. bottles.
   - Large floor stand—holds 48 12-ounce bottles.

force to concentrate on selling Product A for the months of April and May. Meanwhile, Product A is simultaneously promoted on television and in magazines, and direct-mail samples or cents-off coupons for Product A are sent to consumers.

Keeping abreast of your company's advertising and sales promotion activities is a must. By incorporating these data into your sales presentation, you can provide customers with a world of information that they probably know little about and that can secure the sale. Exhibit 6.2 illustrates the type of advertising and sales promotion to use when making a sales presentation for a mouthwash called Fresh Mouth. Suppose Fresh Mouth is a new product that just emerged from the test market. As a lead-in to the information in Exhibit 6.2, you might say:

> Ms. Buyer, Fresh Mouth was a proven success in our Eastern test markets. Fresh Mouth had a 9.8 percent market share only nine months after the start of advertising. Laboratory tests proved that the Fresh Mouth formula is superior to the leading competition.
>
> Consumer panels significantly preferred Fresh Mouth to leading competing brands. There was a repurchase rate of 50 percent after sampling. The trade (retailers) gave enthusiastic support in the test-market areas.

Next, you would discuss the information contained in Exhibit 6.2.

Types of Advertising Differ

The development and timing of an advertising campaign for a product or service are handled by a firm's advertising department or by an outside advertising agency. The result of this effort is the television commercial, radio spot, print media (newspaper or magazine), or other form of advertisement (billboard, transit placard, etc.). Following development of the ad, the firm must establish and coordinate a plan for tying in sales force efforts with the new ad campaign. There are six basic types of advertising programs that a company can use: national, retail, cooperative, trade, industrial, and direct-mail advertising.

National advertising is advertising designed to reach all users of the product, whether consumers or industrial buyers. These ads are shown across the country. In some cases, national advertisers may restrict their expenditures to the top 100 markets. Top 100 refers to the 100 largest major metropolitan areas where most of the U.S. population is concentrated. Therefore, the advertiser gets more punch per ad dollar. Giant marketing companies like Procter & Gamble, IBM, Ford, Holiday Inn, and Coca-Cola commonly use national advertising.

Retail advertising is used by a retailer to reach customers within its geographic trading area. Local supermarkets and department stores regularly advertise nationally distributed brand products. National-brand advertising may be totally paid by the retailer or partially paid by the manufacturer.

Cooperative, or **co-op, advertising** is advertising the retailer conducts with the cost paid for by the manufacturer or shared by the manufacturer and retailer. It is an attractive selling tool for the salesperson to give the buyer an advertising allowance to promote a firm's goods. An advertising agreement between a retailer and a manufacturer often provides for these aspects:

- The duration of the advertisement. How long the advertisement will appear.
- The product(s) to be advertised.
- The amount of money paid to the retailer for advertising purposes.
- The type of advertising—radio, television, newspaper, magazine.
- Proof by the retailer that the product has been advertised as agreed upon (a copy of the advertisement).

Generally, national and retail advertising are aimed at the final consumers. Trade and industrial advertising are aimed at other members in the channel of distribution and other manufacturers.

Trade advertising is undertaken by the manufacturer and directed toward the wholesaler or retailer. Such advertisements appear in trade magazines serving only the wholesaler or retailer. (The Appendix Exhibit 6A.1 is an example of manufacturer advertising to retail pharmacies in the popular trade magazine *American Druggist.*)

Industrial advertising is aimed at individuals and organizations who purchase products used in manufacturing other products. General Electric may advertise small electric motors in magazines read by buyers employed by firms such as Whirlpool or Sears.

Direct-mail advertising is mailed directly to the consumer or industrial user; it is an effective method of exposing these users to a product or it reminds them that the product is available to meet a specific need. Often, trial samples or coupons accompany direct-mail advertising.

Direct-mail advertising can solicit a response from a current user of a product. For example, the user may be asked to fill out and mail in a questionnaire. In return, the manufacturer sends the user a sample of the product or information about the product.

Why Spend Money on Advertising?

Why would a company spend money on advertising? Companies advertise because they hope to

- Increase overall sales and sales of a specific product.
- Give salespeople additional selling information for sales presentations.
- Develop leads for salespeople through mail-ins, ad response, and so on.
- Increase cooperation from channel members through co-op advertising and promotional campaigns.
- Educate the customer about the company's products.
- Inform prospects that a product is on the market and where to buy it.
- Reduce cognitive dissonance over the purchase.
- Create sales or presell customers between a salesperson's calls.

Advertising serves various purposes depending on the nature of a product or industry. The majority of top advertisers are well-known manufacturers of consumer goods. This indicates that advertising dollars are lavished on consumer items. Because industrial advertising has more specified channels of communication (such as trade periodicals and trade shows) and a smaller number of potential customers, advertising costs tend to be lower. In either case, carefully employed advertising benefits both a firm and its sales force. Sales promotion is another potential aid to a company and its sales force.

SALES PROMOTION GENERATES SALES

Sales promotion involves activities or materials other than personal selling, advertising, and publicity used to create sales for goods or services. Sales promotion can be divided into consumer and trade sales promotion. **Consumer sales promotion** includes free samples, coupons, contests, and demonstrations to consumers. **Trade sales promotion** encourages resellers to purchase and aggressively sell a manufacturer's products by offering incentives like sales contests, displays, special purchase prices, and free merchandise (for example, buy 10 cases of a product and get 1 case free).

The company's promotional efforts can be a useful sales tool for an enterprising salesperson. Sales promotion offers may prove to the retailer or wholesaler that the selling firm will assist actively in creating consumer demand. This, in turn, improves the salesperson's probability of making the sale. Next, we discuss some popular sales promotion items: point-of-purchase displays, shelf positioning, and consumer and dealer premiums such as contests and sweepstakes.

Point-of-Purchase Displays: Get Them Out There

Point-of-purchase (POP) displays allow a product to be seen easily and purchased. A product POP display may include photographs, banners, drawings, coupons, a giant-sized product carton, aisle dumps, counter displays, or floor stands. POP displays greatly increase product sales. It is up to the salesperson to obtain the retailer's cooperation to allow the POP display in the store. People are attracted to displays. They catch the customer's attention and make products easy to purchase, which results in increased product sales.

In-store product demonstrations, sampling programs, and cross-merchandising are also popular. My Albertson's Grocery frequently has samples of food and drinks. They particularly like to cross-merchandise, such as by placing cookies in the dairy

EXHIBIT 6.3

Sales reps know that good shelf
positioning and shelf facings
boost sales.

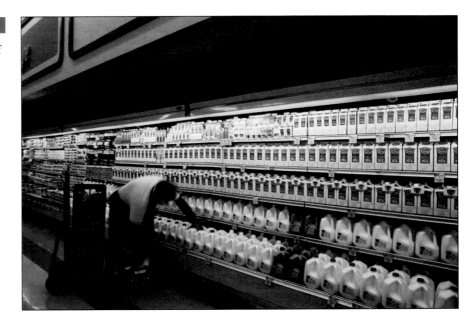

section. Employees at Neiman Marcus, Foley's, and Dillard's department stores offer
to spray men and women with fragrances as they shop. Each of these methods is an
effective way to sell products.

Shelf Positioning Is Important to Your Success

Another important sales stimulator is the shelf positioning of products. **Shelf positioning** refers to the physical placement of the product within the retailer's store.
Shelf facings are the number of individual products placed beside each other on the
shelf. Determine where a store's customers can easily find and examine your company's products and place products in that space or position with as many shelf
facings as the store allows (see Exhibit 6.3).

The major obstacle faced when attempting to obtain shelf space for products is
limited space. A retail store has a fixed amount of display space and thousands of
products to stock. You compete for shelf space with other salespeople and with the
retailer's brands.

It is often up to the salesperson to sell the store manager on purchasing different sizes
of a particular product. Also, the salesperson may want a product displayed at several
locations in the store. A Johnson & Johnson salesperson may want the company's baby
powder and baby shampoo displayed with baby products and adult toiletries.

Premiums

The premium has come a long way from being just a trinket in a Cracker Jack box.
Today, it is a major marketing tool. American businesses spend billions of dollars
on consumer and trade premiums and incentives. Premiums create sales.

A **premium** is an article of merchandise offered as an incentive to the user
to take some action. The premium may act as an incentive to buy, to sample the
product, to come into the retail store, or to stir interest so the user requests further
information. Premiums serve a number of purposes: to promote consumer sampling
of a new product, to introduce a new product, to encourage point-of-purchase displays, and to boost sales of slow products. Three major categories of premiums are
contests and sweepstakes, consumer premiums, and dealer premiums.

EXHIBIT 6.4

Examples of prices and discounts salespeople discuss in their sales presentations.

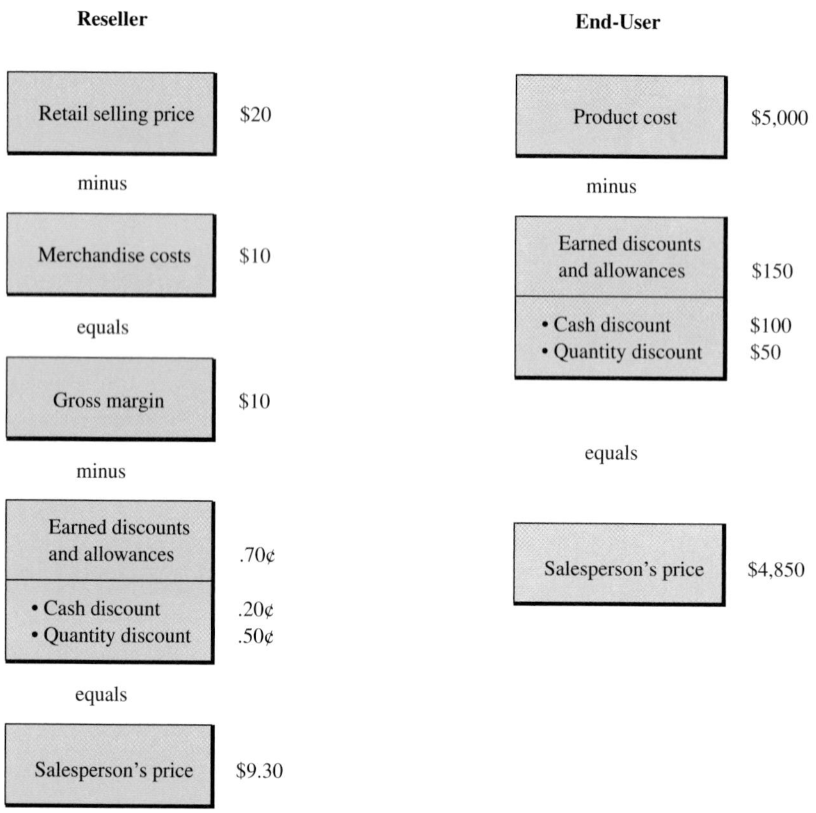

WHAT'S IT WORTH? PRICING YOUR PRODUCT

An important part of a comprehensive marketing strategy for a product is establishing its price. **Price** refers to the value or worth of a product that attracts the buyer to exchange money or something of value for the product. A product has some want-satisfying attributes for which the prospect is willing to exchange something of value. The person's wants assign a value to the item offered for sale. For instance, a golfer who wants to purchase a dozen golf balls already has conceived some estimated measure of the product's value. Of course, the sporting goods store may have set a price higher than estimated. This could diminish *want* somewhat, depending on the difference between the two. Should the golfer then find the same brand of golf balls on sale at a discount store, at a price more in line with a preconceived idea of the product's value, the want may be strong enough to stimulate a purchase.

Many companies offer customers various types of discounts from normal prices to entice them to buy. These discounts become an important part of the firm's marketing effort (see Exhibit 6.4). They are usually developed at the corporate level by the firm's marketing managers. Immediately before the sales period when the product's promotion begins, the sales force is informed of special discounts that they may offer to customers. This discount information becomes an important part of the sales presentation. It is important for salespeople to familiarize themselves with the company's price, discount, and credit policies so that they can use them as a competitive advantage and enhance their professional image with the buyer.[1]

At the back of this chapter is a further discussion of the various pricing issues salespeople should be able to explain to their buyers. The appendix, entitled "Sales Arithmetic and Pricing," has information useful to your developing a sales presentation for your class project role-play.

KNOW YOUR COMPETITION, INDUSTRY, AND ECONOMY

What would the retail salesperson shown in Exhibit 6.5 need to know about her competition? She needs to be knowledgeable about her products, her firm's service and credit policies, and the price of the products. She also needs to know what her competition is doing in each of these areas.

Today's successful salespeople understand their *competitors'* products, policies, and practices as well as their own. It is common for a buyer to ask a salesperson, "How does your product compare to the one I'm currently using?" If unable to confidently answer such a question, a salesperson will lose ground in selling. A salesperson needs to be prepared to discuss product features, advantages, and benefits in comparison to other products and confidently show why the salesperson's product will fulfill the buyer's needs better than competing products.

One method to obtain information on competitors is through advertisements. From a competitor's advertising, Joe Mitchell, a salesperson representing a small business machines firm, developed a chart for comparing the sales points of his machines against the competition. Joe does not do this for fun, nor does he name the competitive equipment on the chart. Instead, he calls them Machine *A*, Machine *B*, and Machine *C*. When he finds a claimed benefit in one of the other machines that his product does not have, he works to find a better benefit to balance it.

"Maybe the chart isn't always useful," Joe says, "but it certainly has prepared me to face a customer. I know just what other machines have—and what they do not have—that my prospect might be interested in. I know the principal sales arguments used in selling these machines and the benefits I must bring up to offset and surpass competition. Many times a prospect will mention an advertisement of another company and ask about some statement or other," Joe says. "Because I've studied those ads and taken the time to find out what's behind the claims, I can give an

EXHIBIT 6.5

What does this automotive salesperson need to know about her products and competition?

honest answer and I can demonstrate how my machine has the same feature or quality and then offer additional benefits. Of course, I never run down a competitor's product. I just try to run ahead of it."

The salesperson selling industrial goods and an industrial buyer work for different companies but are both in the same industry. The industrial buyer often seeks information from salespeople on the *industry* itself, and how economic trends might influence the industry *and* both of their companies. Thus, the salesperson should be well informed about the industry and the economy. The salesperson can find this information in the company records, newspapers, television, radio, *The Wall Street Journal,* industrial and trade periodicals, and magazines such as *Business Week* and *U.S. News & World Report.* The salesperson who is well informed is more successful than the poorly informed salesperson.

PERSONAL COMPUTERS AND SELLING

The use of personal computers (PCs) by sales personnel indicates the need to learn about computers and their use. To the nontechnical person the PC may cause an uncomfortable feeling at first. There is often apprehension about being able to use the PC and its software properly. However, computer manufacturers, software suppliers, and company training programs are quickly and effectively training people and providing easy-to-use computer software. For example, DuPont Merck Pharmaceutical has combated computer apprehension head-on by developing training programs that are humorous and easy to use. The interactive software incorporates games, allowing the users to work from their PC and move at their own pace.[2]

Sales personnel find PCs a valuable tool for increasing productivity within the sales force. The 10 most widely used applications of PCs are shown in Exhibit 6.6. Here are several major reasons for salespeople to use a PC:

- Provides more effective management of sales leads and better follow-through on customer contacts. Computerization provides a permanent lead file.
- Improves customer relations due to more effective follow-ups. This leads to greater productivity.
- Improves organization of selling time. PCs help reps monitor and organize everything.
- Provides more efficient account control and better time and territory management. There is a better awareness of each account's status, which provides more time for customer contacts.
- Increases number and quality of sales calls.
- Offers faster speed and improved accuracy in finishing and sending reports and orders to the company.
- Helps develop more effective proposals and persuasive presentations (see Exhibit 6.7).

If you have little knowledge about the computer, start learning! In your readings, look for how the computer is or can be used in your industry.

EXHIBIT 6.6

Top 10 PC applications.

PC applications are focused on the customer. Here are the top 10 applications in order of use:

1. Customer/prospect profile.	6. Sales presentation.
2. Lead tracking.	7. Time/territory management.
3. Call reports.	8. Order entry.
4. Sales forecasts.	9. Travel and expense reports.
5. Sales data analysis.	10. Checking inventory/shipping status.

EXHIBIT 6.7

The PC has numerous applications.

This salesperson uses his PC to analyze customer data while developing his sales presentation.

KNOWLEDGE OF TECHNOLOGY ENHANCES SALES AND CUSTOMER SERVICE

Computers are at the heart of salespeople's ability to provide top-quality customer service by receiving and sending out information.[3] Computers are impacting technology, advancing it at a rapid pace, and affecting people—including salespeople—in all aspects of their lives. Exhibit 6.8 shows how the use of technology to provide quality customer service is rapidly increasing salespeople's productivity.

Technology helps salespeople increase their productivity, effectiveness, and allows them to gather and access information more efficiently. You can use computer technology to improve communication to the home office, with others on your sales force, and with customers. Salespeople also use technology to create better strategies for targeting and tracking clients. Sales force automation breaks down into three broad areas of functionality covering (1) personal productivity, (2) communications, and (3) order processing and customer service.

Personal Productivity

Many programs can help a salesperson increase **personal productivity** through more efficient data storage and retrieval, better time management, and enhanced presentations. Remember that you do business with the one you trust and you trust the one you know. So keep in touch with customers. Let's discuss five of the most popular programs—beginning with contact management.

You do business with the one you trust and you trust the one you know. So keep in touch with your customers.

Contact Management

Contact management, such as ACT!, is a listing of all the customer contacts that a salesperson makes in the course of conducting business. This file is like an electronic Rolodex and should include such information as the contact's name, title, company, address, phone number, fax number, and e-mail address. It also may include additional information such as the particular industry, date of last order, name of administrative assistant, birthday, and so on.

Use technology to provide quality customer service and increase sales productivity.

Her laptop allows this salesperson to sell and service customers no matter what her location.

Calendar Management

As a salesperson, the most vulnerable asset you have to manage is time. Improvement of time management directly increases productivity. Electronic **calendar management,** as a part of sales force automation, can make time management easier and less prone to errors or oversights.

When a salesperson schedules appointments, telephone calls, or to-do lists on an electronic calendar, the system automatically checks for conflicts, eliminating the need for rescheduling. An electronic calendar can assign a relative priority to each item. It also can create an electronic link between a scheduled event and a particular contact or account so that the appointment or call information is accessible as part of the salesperson's calendar, and as part of the contact or account history. Once it can be viewed from different perspectives, the information contained in the calendar becomes much more useful.

For the sales manager, electronic calendar management automatically consolidates information concerning the whereabouts of the entire sales force. Weekly or monthly calendars, which quickly become outdated, have been improved. Now information can be automatically generated when salespeople schedule their appointments. The system also allows salespeople to instantly update their appointments and schedules directly from the field.

Automated Sales Plans, Tactics, and Ticklers

Sales strategies often fall in a sequence of events that can be identified and plotted. A traditional example involves a thank-you letter sent immediately after an initial sales call and a follow-up telephone call three days later. In the sales world, it may be difficult for busy salespeople to track all the details. As a result, important follow-up items sometimes get overlooked. If this happens, a salesperson's diligent prospecting efforts become wasted and valuable prospects are squandered.

MAKING THE SALE

The Salesperson's Business Card—Telephone, Fax, Beeper, E-Mail, and the Web

Today's business cards often show multiple phone numbers; many now have more than one address. The technology-driven trend has fax, cellular, and beeper numbers, as well as e-mail and Web addresses on many cards.

E-mail addresses already are standard fare in the high-tech, communication, and academic fields. Other professions are beginning to add them as more and more people sign on to national and international online services that offer e-mail at home or at the office.

Rocko Mitera, the marketing manager at Wace the Imaging Network, a graphics services company in Chicago, doesn't leave home without e-mail access or without the business cards that point the way to his electronic residence. "I've always maintained an electronic mail address," said Mitera, adding that it made him more accessible to business contacts and friends.

"When you travel, you can receive and respond to messages very quickly," said Mitera, who finds people respond faster to electronic mail.

Mitera uses a laptop to communicate with his office from out-of-town hotels; by using e-mail, he can send documents and file reports. Mitera believes that without e-mail, the minute you walk out the door, you lose your efficiency. E-mail beats phone tag, he contends, and predicts it will soon be a regular part of business communications.

While an e-mail address may be the next step in having a well-dressed business card, it's not without its detractors. Steven Buckman, a Chicago marketing consultant, has e-mail, but wouldn't use it for his professional contacts. "E-mail is recreational, the fax is professional," Buckman says, "I'm in sales; I have to talk to [clients]."[4]

A sales force automation system begins working as soon as the initial meeting is entered into the system. A few simple commands tell it to remind you to send a thank-you letter and schedule a follow-up phone call. It also can notify the sales manager if these follow-ups are not completed.

Another sales situation might call for a regular follow-up every year or two after the sale, depending on the sales cycle associated with your product. It is particularly easy for follow-up calls like this to be neglected because of the long lead time involved. The problem becomes more apparent if the salesperson who made the original sale leaves the company or is promoted. When that happens, the customer often falls through the cracks, becoming an orphan. Automated sales tactics and ticklers prevent this from happening.

Geographic Information Systems

A **geographic information system (GIS)** allows salespeople to view and manipulate customer and/or prospect information on an electronic map. This may be extremely useful if you are visiting an area for the first time. It also can be helpful in a familiar area. Customer information can be accessed directly from contact-management data and sorted accordingly, allowing you to plan sales calls geographically and make the most efficient use of your time. Also, a GIS may reveal customer buying patterns that otherwise may not be apparent.

Computer-Based Presentations

Computer-based presentations can be a powerful presentation tool. PowerPoint presentations with short product video clips provide a means of creating a customized dynamic video and sound discussion of the product.

Communications with Customers and Employer

As we begin the 21st century, a company's success hinges on its ability to deliver information quickly to customers and employees. Today's most popular sales force automation systems involve word processing, e-mail, and faxes.

Word Processing

Written communication plays a large part in the lives of most salespeople. Particularly important is the need for communication with customers. A thank-you letter mailed immediately after an initial sales call can often mean the difference between a favorable impression and one that is not as favorable. Sometimes it can make or break a sale. In spite of its potential impact, salespeople frequently overlook this simple task because they lack an easy way to get it done. There always seem to be other, more pressing things to do. A **word processing** system can abbreviate the time it takes to accomplish this task to no more than a minute or two, the time it takes to execute a few keystrokes.

Electronic Mail

Electronic mail (e-mail) allows messages to be sent electronically through a system that delivers them immediately to any number of recipients worldwide. If you truly want to be close to your customers, electronic mail can have a tremendous impact.

In creating an e-mail to customers, use the same professional writing skills you would in a business letter. Correct grammar, sentence structure, spelling and content are extremely important in building customer relationships. Also, make sure you send the e-mail to the correct person.

A couple from Chicago decided to escape the winter by enjoying a long weekend in South Texas, relaxing on the beach.[5] Due to their different work schedules, the husband decided to leave a day early, and his wife planned to meet him the next day in Texas. When the husband got to the hotel, he pulled out his laptop and sent his wife an e-mail back in Chicago. However, he accidentally left one letter off her e-mail address, and the e-mail went to another person, without his knowledge.

In Houston, a widow had just returned home from the funeral of her beloved husband. The widow checked her e-mail. Upon reading the first message, however, she fainted and fell to the floor. The widow's son heard the noise and rushed into the room. He turned and saw this message on the computer screen:

> To: My loving wife
>
> From: Your departed husband
>
> Subject: I've arrived!
>
> I've just arrived and have been checked in. Everything went very smoothly after my departure. I also verified that everything has been prepared for your arrival tomorrow. Looking forward to seeing you then! Hope your journey is as uneventful as mine was.
>
> PS: It sure is hot down here!

In the same way this widow received a startling, confusing message, an e-mail sent to the wrong customer may surprise and upset the customer. Take care in writing and sending e-mails.

Fax Capabilities and Support

The fax machine is the most important piece of communication equipment in business. Notebook computers equipped with fax modems offer salespeople unique time-savers while in the field. Options include the ability to prepare and fax a document—from your car perhaps—without having to print a hard copy. You can receive documents in the same manner. This represents a convenient, inexpensive way to handle the great majority of a salesperson's written communication from the road.

Customer Order Processing and Service Support

The process of obtaining, generating, and completing an order is much more complicated than it may actually sound. The many steps involved in a manual system may take several days or even weeks to complete and confirm. Automated systems shorten the sales-and-delivery cycle. While in the office with your customer, you can use the Internet to access information and make things happen more efficiently. You can check the inventory status of merchandise on the sales order, receive approval for your client's credit status, and begin the shipping process immediately. Salespeople's automated order entries directly update the company computer without having to be reentered at the home office.

Salespeople's Mobile Offices

Salespeople have begun installing small offices directly into their vehicles, such as minivans. For those salespeople who need to be constantly in touch with their clients, these minivans are a perfect solution for working through dead time. A vehicle can be equipped with a fully functional desk, swivel chair, light, computer, printer, fax machine, cellular phone, and satellite dish. In their **mobile offices,** salespeople can stay in constant contact with their customers even when driving between cities or states. Jeff Brown, an agent manager with U.S. Cellular, frequently uses a mobile office. "If I arrive at a prospect's office and they can't see me right away," Brown says, "then I can go outside to work in my office until they're ready to see me."[6]

GPS and PDA

Superhero Batman has his high-tech communication gadgets. Well, salespeople employ many of the same high-tech devices used by superheroes. Let's use 3M salesperson Bob Burr as an example of several gadgets used in sales. Exhibit 6.9 shows the inside of Bob's car. Headquartered in Houston, Texas, Bob's sales territory

EXHIBIT 6.9

3M's salesperson Bob Burr uses mobile technology to serve his customers.

is composed of seven states. He travels 25,000 miles by car each year and frequently flies by airplane, if the drive is greater than five hours. Bob, like many salespeople worldwide, relies on mobile technology. The three communication devices you see in Bob's car are the global positioning system (GPS) device, personal digital assistant (PDA), and cell phone. Bob could have a PDA with a built-in cell phone.

Global Positioning System. Trying to determine where you are and the directions to find someone's place of business can be a challenge to salespeople. Over the years a variety of technologies have tried to simplify the task. Finally, the U.S. Department of Defense spent $12 billion to create technology that changed navigation forever.

Constellation of Satellites circling earth

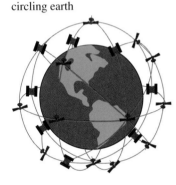

The **global positioning system** (GPS) is a worldwide radio-navigation system formed from a constellation of satellites circling the earth and their ground stations. GPS uses these "man-made stars" as reference points to calculate position accurate to a few feet or a meter. In a sense it's like giving every square foot or meter on the planet a unique address. Soon GPS will become almost as basic as the telephone, a universal utility.

Personal Digital Assistant. The **PDA** is a tiny fully functional computer that works as an extension of a desktop or laptop computer. Note Bob's PDA and cell phone in Exhibit 6.9. Both are easy to reach for Bob. In his mobile office he can use his:

- Cell phone with speaker phone, caller ID.
- Organizer with calendar, contact list memo pad, calculator.
- E-mail and text messaging.
- Color Web browser for the Internet.
- Camera to snap photos to store or send via e-mail.

Add a coffeepot and Bob has a home away from home—a true mobile office. Now I wonder if the back of Bob's front seat will recline for a nap?

SALES: INTERNET AND THE WORLD WIDE WEB

The Internet provides salespeople with access to research, data, people, and vast amounts of information. Currently there is so much to learn about the use of the Internet (Net) that its explanation is beyond the scope of this textbook. Sales organizations are spending millions of dollars on software, hardware, and training for their salespeople to use the Net. It is a great sales tool—if they can only learn how to fully use it. And the Net is constantly changing. You find a Web site you like one day and the next day it is gone—it has changed or someone is charging for its use. Let's briefly discuss the Internet.

The Internet

The **Internet,** often referred to as the Net, is a global network of computers. It is a worldwide, self-governed network, connecting thousands of smaller networks, and millions of computers and people, to megasources of information. Similar in some ways to the telephone system, it reaches every country in the world. Just as you can call people anywhere in the world, so too can you contact their computers as long as they are connected to the Net.

World Wide Web

The Internet and the World Wide Web are often thought of as the same—they are not. The Internet refers to the physical infrastructure of the interconnected global computer network. The Net is just a giant mass of cables and computers. The **World Wide Web** (more affectionately known as the Web or W3) is a part of the Internet

EXHIBIT 6.10

Web sites can provide valuable information to salespeople.

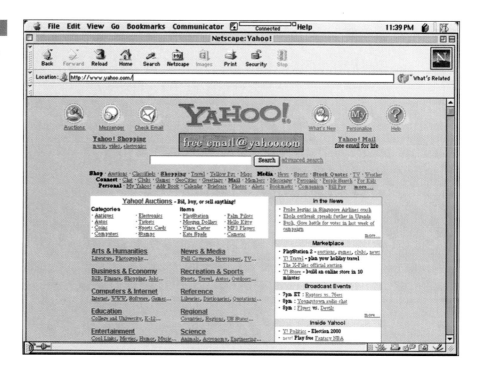

that houses "Web sites" that provide text, graphics, video, and audio information on millions of topics. Individuals, companies, government agencies, schools, or other types of organizations develop informational Web sites.

A distinctive characteristic of the Web is that every screenful of information (commonly called a **Web page**) has a number of links to other pages of information available on the Web (see Exhibit 6.10). These **links** are what give the Web its name; all of the links together form a web of information that spans the globe. **Surfing the Internet** is actually exploring the different sites found within this web of links.

At the back of this textbook, you will find Web exercises related to sales. Try them out. Get used to using the Web.

To learn, you need to read, study, and experience the activity. To learn—use the Web. Here are a few sites to visit:

- **http//www.weather.com** Find out the weather forecast for anywhere in the world.
- **http//www.mapquest.com** Get driving directions city to city.
- **http//www.yahoo.com** Locate people and businesses. Try finding yourself.

Over time, using the World Wide Web will become fun. It can be a great learning experience for you. There is no doubt that as a businessperson you need to know how to use sales technology such as the Web.

GLOBAL TECHNOLOGY PROVIDES SERVICE

The ability to access information is a valuable asset. We are in an era in which corporate strategy relies on efficiency; it can make or break a business. When salespersons travel far from home, the need for the right information, at the right time, in the right place becomes critical. Increased worldwide interaction requires access and exchange of data on a global basis.

ETHICAL DILEMMA

Advertising Will Close the Deal

Earl George is a new salesperson for a small specialty goods manufacturer, Aggie Novelty Company. One of his new products is a plastic toy car for children ages three to six. In the course of a sales call, the buyer for a small toy chain asks about the extent of advertising support the company would provide. In the past, the buyer has stressed the importance of advertising support in the chain's product line addition decisions. Because Aggie is small, it does very little TV advertising and no magazine advertising. If George tells the buyer this, he may lose the account. He knows they will buy if Aggie will advertise the product. George may get away with overstating the amount of TV advertising that Aggie will actually fund (the chain may not take the time to check the ads).

What would be the most ethical action for George to take?

1. Tell the customer that you currently have a small amount of TV advertising but that you are thinking of looking into expanding into magazines and radio. Technically, you would not be lying—it might never actually happen, but you can "look into" it.
2. Tell the customer what he wants to hear. A little exaggeration won't hurt and you will gain profit for your company.
3. Tell the customer that because you are a small company, you don't really have the resources to do a lot of advertising. Let him know that you do a small amount on TV and none in radio or magazines. Let the customer decide what he would like to do based on this information.

As technology solves problems, it presents new opportunities. For example, advances in mobile data collection and wireless data communications have dramatically increased the amount of data that need to be collected, managed, stored, and accessed. Organizations that harness this information can maximize the level of service they offer, resulting in increased sales.

A salesperson in Europe, for example, can send information to America by satellite transmission. The information is stored in the organization's main computer database. A salesperson in Florida has access to the information and can send additional data to the database. Even a Texas salesperson in a customer's office can send and receive information to and from the same database using a telephone modem transmission or wireless communication.

TECHNOLOGY ETIQUETTE

With so much technology available, salespeople have many options when it comes to communicating with customers and placing orders. For salespeople to use this technology properly, they must be aware of the proper etiquette that comes along with these various channels of communication.

Netiquette

Netiquette is the term used for etiquette on the Internet.[7] Since the Internet changes so rapidly, netiquette does also. No matter how quickly it changes, netiquette is still based on the "Golden Rule," or "do unto others as you would have done to you." In sales, the need for netiquette mostly arises when sending or distributing e-mail.

Many practices should be considered when sending an e-mail to a customer, prospect, or your manager. According to Mary Mitchell, author of *The Complete Idiot's Guide to Business Etiquette,* people seem to express rudeness a lot more than they used to—especially online. In her opinion, one of the reasons for increased rudeness is that electronic communication has reduced the amount of human-to-human contact. "This not only makes it easier to be rude, but we lose regular practice in being mannerly," says Mitchell.

Mitchell also believes that rudeness produces more rudeness. Since rudeness tends to multiply, each individual act of politeness also has a ripple effect. Here are some do's and don'ts when it comes to e-mail communication:[8]

Do:

- Be concise, but not too short.
- Respond as quickly to an e-mail as you would answer telephone messages.
- Avoid **flaming,** which is the equivalent of a verbal lashing in public on the Internet.
- Use clear, descriptive and current subject headings. If topics change, rewrite the subject line.
- Use dates, salutations, proper punctuation, and a friendly closing.

Don't:

- Make comments or requests in an e-mail that you would not make in person.
- Send repeat messages.
- Use all capital letters, which is the online equivalent of SHOUTING!
- Send the same message to a long distribution list.
- Send bad news via e-mail.

The best thing to remember in sending e-mail is to treat customers in the same courteous manner in which you would treat them in person. Your customers cannot see you through your e-mail, and the only way that they can judge you is by the way in which you represent yourself.

Cell Phones

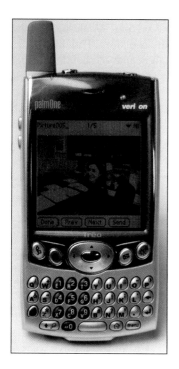

Hundreds of millions of people subscribe to wireless services worldwide, and almost half of these subscribers are in the United States, according to the Cellular Telecommunications Industry Association.[9] With the convenience that cell phones bring, including wireless service that allows you to check your e-mail and surf the Web from your phone, some problems emerge as well. When salespeople do not understand the courteous use of their phone, meetings and sales calls can be interrupted and ruined.

A salesperson can prevent distractions caused by his or her cell phone in many ways. These guidelines should be kept in mind at all times:[10]

- **The person you are with is the most important person to talk to.** Whether you are with a customer, potential buyer, or your supervisor, utilize the Caller ID feature for screening options. You may decide to let your voice mail take the call and return the call at a more appropriate time.
- **Use text messaging to simplify your life.** If you are expecting important information from a colleague but need to be in a public area, switch your phone to message mode and ask them to send a text message to your phone.
- **Turn off your phone during meetings, sales calls, and presentations.** Talking on the phone during any of these can be disruptive and violate basic courtesy. If you are expecting an important call, use text messaging.
- **Don't engage in cell yell.** Yelling on a cell phone can be offensive to a customer and unnecessary. Most phones have sensitive microphones that can pick up even a whisper. There is no need to speak louder on your cell phone than you would on any other phone.

Voice Mail

Voice mail is a convenient way for salespeople to receive messages in their office or on their cell phone when they are unavailable. It is important to always change your outgoing message to let your customers know where you are and your availability. It also lets them know when you will return their calls. You should always leave a contact name and the phone number of someone who can help in case a customer needs immediate assistance.

Please, please repeat your telephone number s-l-o-w-l-y!

It is also important to be courteous when leaving a voice message for someone else. You should say your name and phone number slowly at the beginning and ending of the message. This keeps the recipient from having to replay your message. You should also be specific and concise when leaving a message; you do not want to ramble. I frequently outline the key points in my message before the call. Standing while talking helps the message be like a natural conversation.

Faxes

As discussed earlier, fax machines are extremely important to salespeople. When faxing someone, salespeople should always remember to include a cover page with their fax number, the number of pages being sent, and a phone number where the recipient can reach them. They should always telephone or e-mail the person and let them know that a fax is coming, especially if it is time-sensitive material. As with any document, the spelling and grammar should be checked carefully before sending.

Speakerphones and Conference Calls

It may be necessary to conduct a meeting over the telephone through a conference call. This should be the only reason a salesperson uses a speakerphone in an office setting. This prevents private information from being heard. People participating in a conference call should identify themselves while speaking, and one person should act as the meeting leader to prevent confusion from people talking over one another.

SUMMARY OF MAJOR SELLING ISSUES

Company knowledge includes information about a firm's history, development policies, procedures, products, distribution, promotion, and pricing. A salesperson also must know the competition, the firm's industry, and the economy. This knowledge can even be used to improve one's self-concept. A high degree of such knowledge helps the salesperson build a positive self-image and feel thoroughly prepared to interact with customers.

Wholesalers and retailers stock thousands of products, which often makes it difficult to support any one manufacturer's products as the manufacturer would like. This situation may result in conflicts between members of the channel of distribution. To reduce these conflicts and aid channel members in selling products, manufacturers offer assistance in advertising, sales promotion aids, and pricing allowances. Additionally, many manufacturers spend millions of dollars to compel consumers and industrial buyers to purchase from channel members and the manufacturer.

National, retail, trade, industrial, and direct-mail advertising create demand for products and are a powerful selling tool for the salesperson in sales presentations. Sales promotion activities and materials are another potential selling tool for the salesperson to use in selling to consumer and industrial buyers. Samples, coupons, contests, premiums, demonstrations, and displays are effective sales promotion techniques employed to help sell merchandise.

Price, discounts, and credit policies are additional facts the salesperson should be able to discuss confidently with customers. Each day, the salesperson informs or answers questions customers pose in these three areas. Customers always want to know the salesperson's list and net price, and if there are any transportation charges. Discounts (quantity, cash, trade, or consumer) represent important buying incentives the manufacturer offers to the buyer. The buyer wants to know the terms of payment. The salesperson needs to understand company credit policies to open new accounts, see that customers pay on time, and collect overdue bills. See the appendix at the end of this chapter for additional discussions on pricing.

Finally, success in sales requires knowledge of the many technologies used to sell and service customers. Computers, word processing, e-mail, faxes, pagers, cellular phones, the Internet, and the World Wide Web have quickly become part of the professional's sales kit. Proper knowledge of the courteous manner in which these many technologies should be used is a necessity.

MEETING A SALES CHALLENGE

To be successful, salespeople need to be knowledgeable about many things. However, being an expert on the product is only part of what it takes to be a top performer. You also need to know how to use good communication and selling skills.

Sure, this grocery buyer wants to sell his customers a good product, but the reseller is possibly more interested in whether he can sell the product once he buys it, and how much money he will make. Resellers are "bottom-line" oriented; because they want to know what's in it for them, they concentrate on discussing return on investment.

KEY TERMS FOR SELLING

sales training   181
national advertising   187
retail advertising   187
cooperative (co-op) advertising   187
trade advertising   187
industrial advertising   187
direct-mail advertising   187
consumer sales promotion   188
trade sales promotion   188
point-of-purchase (POP) displays   188
shelf positioning   189
shelf facings   189
premium   189
price   190
personal productivity   193
contact management   193

calendar management   194
geographic information system (GIS)   195
computer-based presentations   195
word processing   196
electronic mail (e-mail)   196
mobile offices   197
global positioning system (GPS)   198
PDA   198
Internet   198
World Wide Web   198
Web page   199
links   199
surfing the Internet   199
netiquette   200
flaming   201

SALES APPLICATION QUESTIONS

1. A salesperson's knowledge needs to extend into many areas such as general company knowledge; product knowledge; knowledge of upcoming advertising and promotional campaigns; knowledge about company price, discount, and credit policies; and knowledge about the competition, the industry, and the economy. These are all vital for sales success. For each of these categories, explain how a salesperson's knowledge can lay the groundwork for successful selling.

2. How do salespeople generally acquire their sales knowledge?

3. Explain how a salesperson's knowledge can be converted into selling points used in the sales presentation. Give two examples.

4. A salesperson must have a good understanding of the competition, customers, and everything connected with the company. Why, however, should a salesperson take time to be up-to-date on facts about the economy and the industry?

5. What is the difference between a product's shelf positioning and its shelf facings? How can a salesperson maximize both shelf positioning and shelf facings? Why is this important?

6. Companies use numerous premiums in their efforts to market products. Why? What types of premiums do they use? How can a salesperson use a premium offer in a sales presentation to a wholesaler or a retailer?

7. What are the major types of advertising that a manufacturer might use to promote its products? How can a salesperson use information about the company's advertising in a sales presentation?

8. Before firms such as General Foods and Quaker Oats introduce a new consumer product nationally, they frequently place the product in a test market to see how it will sell. How can a salesperson use test information in a sales presentation?

9. What is cooperative advertising? Explain the steps involved.

10. Why do companies advertise?

11. Consumer sales promotion and trade sales promotion try to increase sales to consumers and resellers, respectively. Several promotional techniques follow; classify each item as a consumer or trade promotional technique and give an example for each one. Can any of the promotions be used for both consumers and the trade?

    a. Coupons on or inside packages.

    b. Free installation (premium).

    c. Displays.

    d. Sales contests.

    e. Drawings for gifts.

    f. Demonstrations.

    g. Samples.

12. What is *netiquette,* and when does the need for it mostly arise in sales?

13. Cell phones are a convenient way for salespeople to keep in touch with customers even when they are out of their office. Although cell phones are useful, they can be a distraction. List four things that salespeople can do to make sure that they are using their phones in a courteous manner.

FURTHER EXPLORING THE SALES WORLD

To complete this project, you will need to visit two places. First, visit your local library. Examine magazines such as *American Druggist, Incentive Marketing, Journal of the American Medical Association, Purchasing,* and *Sales & Marketing Management,* and report on the type of promotions companies offer their customers. Second, visit local retailers such as a supermarket and report on merchandising techniques used to promote individual products. Once you have collected information on several products, pick one product and describe how this information could become part of a sales presentation.

SELLING EXPERIENTIAL EXERCISE

You may think you have a good attitude for sales, but if you do not have the confidence to meet customers and prospects you do not know, all is lost. This exercise can help you measure your self-confidence. Read each statement and then, on a separate sheet of paper, write the number you believe best fits you.

How Is Your Self-Confidence?

	High				Low
I can convert strangers into friends quickly and easily.	5	4	3	2	1
I can attract and hold the attention of others even when I do not know them.	5	4	3	2	1
I love new situations.	5	4	3	2	1
I'm intrigued with the psychology of meeting and building a good relationship with someone I do not know.	5	4	3	2	1
I would enjoy making a sales presentation to a group of executives.	5	4	3	2	1
When dressed for the occasion, I have great confidence in myself.	5	4	3	2	1
I do not mind using the telephone to make appointments with strangers.	5	4	3	2	1
Others do not intimidate me.	5	4	3	2	1
I enjoy solving problems.	5	4	3	2	1
Most of the time, I feel secure.	5	4	3	2	1

Total Score _____

Add up the numbers to get your score. If you scored more than 40, you are self-confident enough to consider selling as a profession. If you rated yourself between 25 and 40, you need more experience in dealing with people. A score of less than 25 indicates that you need to build your self-confidence, and another type of job probably would be better for you.[11]

CHAPTER 6

Sales Knowledge: Customers, Products, Technologies

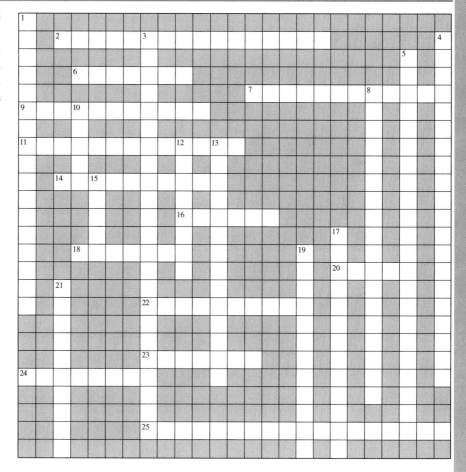

Across

2. The physical placement of the product within the retailer's store.

6. The equivalent of a verbal lashing on the Internet.

7. The number of individual products placed beside each other on the self.

9. _____ advertising is conducted by the retailer with costs paid for by the manufacturer or shared by the manufacturer and the retailer.

11. Vehicles converted to mobile offices.

14. Etiquette used on the Internet.

16. Advertising used by a retailer to reach customers within its geographic trading area is known as _____ advertising.

18. Each computer screen of information on the Internet.

20. Pointers to other pages of information on the World Wide Web.

22. _____ advertising is mailed directly to the customer or industrial user.

23. An article of merchandise offered as an incentive to the user to take some action.

24. _____ advertising is designed to reach all users of the product, whether consumers or industrial buyers.

25. Exploring the different sites found within World Wide Web links.

Down

1. Automated listing of all customer contacts a salesperson makes in the course of conducting business.

3. Displays that allow a product to be easily seen and purchased.

4. Technology to help a salesperson increase productivity through more efficient data storage and retrieval, better time management, and enhanced presentations.

5. A promotion that includes free samples, coupons, contests, and demonstrations to consumers.

8. Scheduling appointments, telephone calls, or "to do" lists.

10. The value or worth of a product.

12. A global network of computers.

13. Allows information to be sent electronically through a system that delivers the message immediately to any number of recipients.

15. _____ advertising is undertaken by the manufacturer and directed toward the wholesaler or retailer.

17. The effort put forth by an employer to provide the opportunity for the salesperson to acquire job-related attitudes, concepts, rules, and skills that result in improved performance in the selling environment.

19. The part of the Internet that houses Web sites—providing text, graphics, video, and audio information.

21. _____ advertising is aimed at individuals and organizations that purchase products for manufacturing or reselling other products.

Appendix A:
Sales Arithmetic and Pricing

Salespeople want to exchange something for something—usually their products for the customer's money. Organizations, consumers (and even you) want the answer to the question "How much is this going to cost?" Salespeople have to be prepared to discuss all aspects of costs and prices. Consequently, some knowledge of the rudiments of sales arithmetic and pricing is essential for you.

Since most students taking this course will create a sales presentation as their class project, this information will benefit you. Some students will have had a course in accounting, marketing, or retailing, and therefore this information is intended as a review. This appendix discusses sales arithmetic and pricing concepts that are useful in sales to (1) resellers, such as wholesalers and retailers, and (2) end-users, such as businesses and nonprofit organizations.

TYPES OF PRICES

Although a firm may engage in many pricing practices, all companies have a list price, net price, and prices based on transportation terms. Five of the most common types of prices are

- **List price**—the standard price charged to customers.
- **Net price**—the price after allowance for all discounts.
- **Zone price**—the price based on geographical location or zone of customers.
- **FOB shipping point**—FOB (free on board) means the buyer pays transportation charges on the goods—the title to goods passes to the customer when they are loaded on shipping vehicles.
- **FOB destination**—the seller pays all shipping costs.

These prices are established by the company. Normally, the salesperson is not involved in pricing the product. This type of pricing allows the salesperson to quote prices according to company guidelines.

Selling the same quantity of similar products at different prices to two different industrial users or resellers is illegal. Laws such as the Robinson-Patman Act of 1936 forbid price discrimination that injures competition in *interstate* commerce. Although the law does not apply to sales within a state (intrastate sales), a majority of states have similar laws.

A company can justify different prices if it can prove to the courts that its price differentials do not substantially reduce competition. Often, companies justify price differentials by showing the courts one of two things. First, take the case of one customer buying more of a product than another. For the customer purchasing larger quantities, a firm can manufacture and market the products at a lower cost. These lower costs are passed on to the customer in the form of reduced prices. Second, price differentials can be justified when a company must lower prices to meet competition. Thus, if justified, companies can offer customers different prices. They typically do this through discounts.

DISCOUNTS LOWER THE PRICE

Discounts are a reduction in price from the list price. In developing a program to sell a product line over a specified period, marketing managers consider discounts along with the advertising and personal selling efforts the firm engages in. The main types of discounts allowed to buyers are quantity, cash, trade, and consumer discounts.

Quantity Discounts: Buy More, Pay Less

Quantity discounts result from the manufacturer's saving in production costs because it can produce large quantities of the product. As Exhibit 6A.1 shows, these savings are passed on to customers who buy in large quantities using discounts. Quantity discounts are either noncumulative or cumulative.

One-time reduction in prices are **noncumulative quantity discounts,** which are commonly used in the sale of both consumer and industrial goods. For example, the list price for a computer might be $6,000. If a business buys 9 or less the price would be $5,800, 10 to 29 units $5,500 and any number of computers over 30 $5,000. The Schering salesperson might offer the buyer of Coricidin D a 16.6 percent price reduction. The Colgate salesperson may offer the retailer 2 dozen king-size Colgate tubes of toothpaste free for every 10 dozen purchased.

The salesperson is expected to use these discounts as inducements for the retailer to buy in large quantities. The sales goal is to have the prospect display and locally advertise the product at a price lower than normal. Ideally, the retailer's selling price should reflect the price reduction allowed because of the quantity discount.

Cumulative quantity discounts are discounts the customer receives for buying a certain amount of a product over a stated period, such as one year. Again, these discounts reflect savings in manufacturing and marketing costs.

To receive a 10 percent discount, a buyer may have to purchase 12,000 units of the product. Under the cumulative discount, buyers would not be required to purchase the 12,000 units at the same time—they could purchase 1,000 units each month, for example. As long as the agreed-on amount is purchased within the specified time, the 10 percent discount on each purchase applies. A cumulative discount allows the buyer to purchase the products as needed rather than in a single order.

EXHIBIT 6A.1

Various promotional allowances available to resellers.

Great New Deal!

Four double-strength sizes to strengthen your profits!

	Promotional Allowances				Promotional Support
Free-Goods Allowance*	**Plus Advertising Allowance†**		**Plus Merchandising Allowance**		
	Option A	Option B‡	Reduced Price Feature	Display	
12-oz liquid 8⅓% off invoice	Up to $1.25 per dozen	$1.00 per dozen	$.75 per dozen reduced price feature	$.75 per dozen floor or end cap display	Direct to consumer national TV promotion . . . 1.705 GRPs
5-oz liquid 8⅓% off invoice	Up to $.75 per dozen	$.50 per dozen	$.50 per dozen reduced price feature	$.50 per dozen floor or end cap display	88% reach 1.7 billion impressions
60s tablets 8⅓% off invoice	Up to $1.25 per dozen	$1.00 per dozen	$.75 per dozen reduced price feature	$.75 per dozen floor or end cap display	Year-round physician detailing and sampling
24s tablets 8⅓% off invoice	Up to $.75 per dozen	$.50 per dozen	$.50 per dozen reduced price feature	$.50 per dozen floor or end cap display	Major trade and medical journal advertising support

Also available—up to 2% billback allowance for four-color roto advertising or consumer coupon programs.

Unlimited purchases allowed for claiming billback allowances.

Retail buy-in period: July 15 through August 30, 2005.

Advertising performance period: July 15 through November 8, 2005.

Claim deadline: 45 days following appearance of ad.

Contact your representative for complete details.

*Through participating wholesaler.

†All ads should feature both liquid and tablets.

‡Provided advertising coverage is in at least 75% of the applicant's trading area.

Cash Discounts Entice the Customer to Pay on Time

Cash discounts are earned by buyers who pay bills within a stated period. For example, if the customer purchases $10,000 worth of goods on June 1 and the cash discount is $2/10$ net 30, the customer pays $9,800 instead of $10,000. Thus, $2/10$ net 30 translates into a 2 percent discount if the bill is completely paid within 10 days of the sale. If the payment is not made within 10 days, the full $10,000 is due in 30 days. Buyers should understand that 2 percent can mean extra money.

Trade Discounts Attract Channel Members' Attention

The manufacturer may reduce prices to channel members (middlemen) to compensate them for the services they perform. These are **trade discounts.** The trade discount is usually stated as a percentage off the list retail price. A wholesaler may be offered a 50 percent discount and the retailer offered a 40 percent discount off list price. The wholesaler's price to its retail customers is 10 percent above its cost or 40 percent off the list price. The wholesaler earns a 10 percent gross margin on sales to retail customers. Channel members are still eligible to earn the quantity and cash discounts.

Consumer Discounts Increase Sales

Consumer discounts are one-time price reductions the manufacturer passes on to channel members or directly to the consumer. Cents-off product labels are price reductions passed directly to the consumer. A package marked 15 cents off each product or $1.80 a dozen uses a consumer discount (see Exhibit 6A.2).

EXHIBIT 6A.2

Types and examples of discounts.

Types of Discounts	Discount Examples
Quantity discount	
Noncumulative (one-time)	■ Buy 11 dozen, get 1 dozen free.
	■ 20 percent off on all purchases.
	■ $5-off invoice for each floor-stand purchase.
Cumulative (yearly purchases)	■ 5 percent discount with purchase of 8,000 units.
	■ 8 percent discount with purchase of 10,000 units.
	■ 10 percent discount with purchase of 12,000 units.
Cash discounts	■ $2/10$ end-of-month.
	■ $2/10$ net 30.
Trade discounts	■ 40 percent off to retailers.
	■ 50 percent off to wholesalers.
Consumer discounts	■ 15 cents off regular price marked on product's package.
	■ 10-cents-off coupon.

EXHIBIT 6A.3

Example of markup on selling price in channel of distribution.

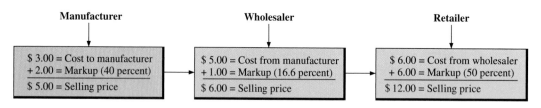

Manufacturer

| $ 3.00 = Cost to manufacturer |
| + 2.00 = Markup (40 percent) |
| $ 5.00 = Selling price |

Wholesaler

| $ 5.00 = Cost from manufacturer |
| + 1.00 = Markup (16.6 percent) |
| $ 6.00 = Selling price |

Retailer

| $ 6.00 = Cost from wholesaler |
| + 6.00 = Markup (50 percent) |
| $ 12.00 = Selling price |

The manufacturer expects channel members to reduce the price from their normal price. A mass merchandiser might normally sell a product with a list price of $2.50 for $1.98. The manufacturer would want salespeople to persuade the retailer to price the product 15 cents lower than the $1.98, or at a price of $1.83.

Cents-off coupons that the consumer brings to the retail store are another example of a temporary price discount. In both the cents-off label and coupon examples, the manufacturer ensures that the price reduction is passed on to the consumer. This occurs because channel members may not have promoted the product or reduced the price, keeping the quantity or off-invoice savings for themselves. The salesperson uses an offer of a cents-off product label and coupons to sell larger quantities to customers. For a summary of discounts and examples of each, see Exhibit 6A.2.

Resellers: Markup and Profit

Markup is the dollar amount added to the product cost to determine its selling price. Markup often is expressed as a percentage and represents gross profit, not net profit. **Gross profit** is the money available to cover the costs of marketing the product, operating the business, and profit. **Net profit** is the money remaining after the costs of marketing and operating the business are paid.

Exhibit 6A.3 presents an example of markup based on a product's selling price for each channel-of-distribution member. Each channel member has a different percentage markup. The product that costs the manufacturer $3 to produce eventually costs the consumer $12. The manufacturer's selling price represents the wholesaler's cost. Price markups enable the wholesaler to pay business operating costs, to cover the product's cost, and to make a profit. The wholesaler's selling price of $6 becomes the retailer's cost. In turn, the retailer marks up the product to cover its cost, the associated costs of doing business (such as stocking the product and allocation of fixed costs per square foot), and to maintain a desired profit level.

The percentage markup is based on either the product's selling price or its cost. It is important to know the method of determining markup. Using the manufacturer's cost of $3, a markup of $2, and a selling price of $5 shown in Exhibit 6A.3, the methods of determining percentage markup can have different results:

$$\text{Percentage markup on selling price} = \frac{\text{Amount added to cost}}{\text{Selling price}} = \frac{\$2.00}{\$5.00} = 40\,\text{percent}$$

$$\text{Percentage markup on cost} = \frac{\text{Amount added to cost}}{\text{Cost}} = \frac{\$2.00}{\$3.00} = 66.6\,\text{percent}$$

Channel members want to buy goods at low prices and establish selling prices at a competitive level that allows for a reasonable profit. Such objectives result in retailers having different markups on different goods. For example, a retailer may have markups of 10 percent on groceries, 30 percent on cameras, and 50 percent on houseware items. Based on the type of store (discount—high volume; specialty—low volume; department—high service), markups may vary greatly depending on the volume of sales and degree of service rendered.

In preparing the sales presentation for an individual customer, the salesperson should consider all the discounts available to suggest a promotional plan for the retailer. For example, the advertisement shown in Exhibit 6A–1 illustrates several of the discounts a retailer can receive with the purchase of three decongestants. The salesperson can use these discounts in the sales presentation by suggesting that the retailer advertise the products at a reduced price and place the promotional displays by each of the store's cash registers.

Markup and Unit Price

Sellers, especially consumer goods salespeople, like to talk in terms of the cost and profits earned from an individual unit. However, wholesalers and retailers do not buy one product at a time. Depending on the customer's size, manufacturers may sell resellers several dozens or thousands of dozens at a time. The cost and profits of an individual unit may not be useful for wholesalers, but it becomes extremely important to retailers because their customers buy the product one at a time.

Here is how it works: Assume you are selling a consumer product to a large chain of grocery stores. As shown in Exhibit 6A.4, each unit normally costs $1.80 and the retailer sells it for $2.19, 10¢ less than the manufacturer's $2.29 suggested selling price. This gives a normal profit of 39¢ or an 18 percent markup [($2.19 − $1.80 = 39¢) then divide by $2.19 (39¢ ÷ $2.19 = 18 percent)]. Subtracting the 53¢ promotional allowance gives a deal cost of $1.27.

The normal profit, or markup, is 18 percent. If the product is sold at $1.89 for an additional two weeks, the markup reflecting the 53¢ promotional allowance equals 33 percent. If the retailer buys the product and does not reduce the price, the manufacturer is throwing away 53¢ a unit or $6.36 a dozen.

What are the salesperson's objectives? To have the retailer (1) buy a larger quantity than normal; (2) reduce the price for a three-day $1.39 advertised promotion; and (3) run a two-week, in-store promotion at $1.89. The retailer's sale price of $1.39 would provide an 8.6 percent profit and the $1.89 produces a 33 percent profit margin. The manufacturer, retailer, and the retailer's customers all win in this deal.

EXHIBIT 6A.4	Consumer goods salespeople often break down costs and talk of unit costs and profits. Here is the arithmetic one salesperson used in her presentation:
Example of using unit cost.	

$1.80 = Regular cost of each unit

       = Special promotional allowance

$1.27 = Deal cost

$2.29 = Manufacturer's suggested selling price

$2.19 = Normal retail selling price

18% = Retailer's normal profit ($2.19 − $1.80 = 39¢ markup) (39¢ ÷ $2.19 = 18% markup)

$1.39 = 3-day special price suggested for retailer to advertise product.

8.6% = 3-day sale profit margin ($1.39 − $1.27 = 12¢) (12¢ ÷ $1.39 = 8.6% markup)

$1.89 = 2-week special price suggested for in-store promotion.

33% = After-sale profit margin ($1.89 − $1.27 = .62) (.62 ÷ $1.89 = 33% markup)

18% = Normal profit ($2.19 − 1.80 = 39¢) (39¢ ÷ $2.19 = 18%)

The above information (except for the arithmetic in parentheses) was on a sheet of paper with the buyer's company name at the top. The seller showed how the buyer could purchase a large quantity and make 9 percent profit by selling each item for $1.39 instead of the normal $2.19. The retailer's customers save 80¢ ($2.19 − $1.39 = 80¢). After the three-day sale, the retailer increases the price to $1.89 for two weeks and makes 33 percent instead of the 18 percent markup. Some numbers are rounded up.

EXHIBIT 6A.5

Profit forecaster for Granola Bars shown to buyer.

	3-Day Special	2-Week Special	Normal
Total stores	100	100	100
Deal dates	June 1 through June 30		
Regular cost per dozen	$21.60	$21.60	$21.60
Less allowance ($.53)			
Deal cost per dozen	$15.24	$15.24	$21.60
Feature price	1.39	1.89	2.19[f]
Cases purchased	500[a]	1,000	1,500
Total investment	$7,620[b]	$15,240	$32,400
Total gross sales	$8,340[c]	$22,680	$39,420
Total gross profit	$720[d]	$7,440	$7,020
Return on investment (ROI)	9.0%[e]	49%	22%[g]

[a]5 cases per store

[b]500 × 15.24 = $7,620

[c]500 × 12 = 6,000; 6,000 × $1.39 = $8,340

[d]$8,340 − $7,620 = $720

[e]$720 ÷ $7,620 = 9%

[f]$21.60 ÷ 12 @ case = $1.80 (regular cost)

[g]$7,020 ÷ $32,400 = 22%

Markup and Return on Investment

Consumer goods salespeople also can use return on investment (ROI) in their presentations. **Return on investment (ROI)** refers to an additional sum of money expected from an investment over and above the original investment. ROI is often expressed as a percentage; however, salespeople can also use a dollar return on investment. The information shown in Exhibit 6A.5 illustrates the actual ROI a salesperson used. Continuing the previous example shown, the salesperson wants the customer to have a three-day advertised special; offer a two-week, in-store price reduction; and buy a large quantity for normal stock. The purchasing agent buys for a chain of 100 grocery stores.

Normally, the chain averages selling 1,500 dozen during a six-week period. The salesperson feels the promotion and price reduction will increase sales to 3,000 dozen (500 + 1,000 + 1,500). As seen in Exhibit 6A.5, the salesperson asks the retailer to invest $45,720 ($7,620 + $15,240 + $22,860). Sales are projected to be $70,440 ($8,340 + $22,680 + $39,420) with profits of $24,720 ($720 + $7,440 + $16,560). The retailer's return on investment is 35 percent as shown here:

$70,440 = total gross sales

−45,720 = total investment

$24,720 = total gross profit

35% = ROI ($24,720 ÷ $70,440)

Discounts, payment plans, markups, unit prices, and return on investment are important for salespeople to understand thoroughly. Customers are extremely interested in listening to this information during the salesperson's presentation.

ORGANIZATIONS: VALUE AND ROI

Business salespeople often include a value analysis in the sales presentation. A **value analysis** determines the best product for the money. It recognizes that a high-priced product may sometimes be a better value than a lower-priced product. Many firms routinely review a value analysis before deciding to purchase a product (see Exhibit 6A.6).

The value analysis evaluates how well the product meets the buying company's specific needs. It addresses such questions as

■ How do your product's features, advantages, and benefits compare to the product currently being used?

■ Can your product do the same job as your buyer's present product at a lower price?

■ Does the buyer's current equipment perform better than required? (Is equipment too good for present needs?)

■ On the other hand, will a higher-priced, better-performing product be more economical in the long run?

As you can see from the examples in this chapter, frequently you must analyze the buyer's present operation carefully before suggesting how your product might improve efficiency, enhance the quality or quantity of the product produced, or save money.

EXHIBIT 6A.6

This copier salesperson uses a value analysis to help his customers determine the best buy for their investment.

In discussing how to present a value analysis to a buyer, Patrick Kamlowsky, who sells drilling bits for oil and gas wells, said this:

It's not as simple as it may appear to make a recommendation and have the oil company adhere to it. You must be thorough in the presentation and present the facts in an objective manner. After all, their money is at stake. The presentation must be logical and based on facts that are known; it must be made with as little speculation as possible.

What is difficult is presenting a recommendation to one who has spent 30 or more years in the oil field and has drilled all over the world. I am confronted with the challenge of explaining to this man that the methods he has employed for years may not be the best application where he is currently drilling. The presentation of the recommendation must therefore be thorough and to the point. When talking to him, I do not imply that his method is outdated or wrong, but that I believe I can help him improve his method. To be successful, I must establish two things very quickly—his respect and my credibility. Showing him my proposal and supporting evidence, and permitting him the time to evaluate it are vital. I don't wish to come on to him too strong, just show him that I genuinely want to help.

A salesperson can develop numerous types of value analyses for a prospective buyer. Three types frequently used are (1) product cost versus true value, (2) unit cost, and (3) return on investment.

Compare Product Costs to True Value

All buyers want to know about costs. The value analysis developed for a customer should present cost in a simple, straightforward manner. A product's costs are always relative to something else; thus, cost must be judged in value and results. The base cost of your product should never be the determining factor of the sale. Buying a product based solely on cost could cause a customer to lose money.

Never discuss costs until you have compared them to the *value* of a product. In this manner, the customer intelligently compares the true worth of the proposed investment in your product to its true monetary cost. In effect, a good purchase involves more than initial cost; it represents an investment and you must demonstrate that what you sell is a good investment.

Exhibit 6A.7 provides an example of how a salesperson might compare the cost of a copier (Product X) with a competitive copier (Product C). It illustrates how you can demonstrate to a buyer that your product is a better value than one would think from looking only at purchase price. Another value analysis technique is to further break down a product's price to its unit cost.

EXHIBIT 6A.7

Cost versus value of a small copier.

	Product C	Product X
Initial cost	$2,695	$3,000
Type of paper	Treated paper	Plain paper
Copy speed	12 copies per minute	15 copies per minute
Warm-up time	Instant	Instant
Cost of each copy	3¢ a copy	1¢ a copy
Monthly cost (assuming 10,000 copies)	$300	$100

Conclusion: The difference in the purchase price of the two copiers is $305 ($3,000 − $2,695). Product X saves $200 on monthly copy costs. The savings on monthly copy costs pays for the higher-priced Product X in one and one-half months. In 15 months, savings on the monthly copy equal the purchase price of Product X. Therefore, Product X is less expensive in the long run.

Sales reps often must show industrial buyers what return they will receive on their investment.

Unit Costs Break Price Down

One method of presenting a product's true value to a buyer is to break the product's total costs into several smaller units or the **unit cost.** Assume you sell a computer system that costs $1,000 per month and processes 50,000 transactions each month. The cost per transaction is only 2 cents.

Return on Investment Is Listened to

Return on investment refers to an additional sum of money expected from an investment over and above the original investment. Buyers are interested in knowing the percentage return on their initial investment. Since the purchase of many business products is an investment in that it produces measurable results, salespeople can talk about the percentage return that can be earned by purchasing their products (see Exhibit 6A.8).

Again, assume you sell computer equipment requiring a $10,000 per month investment. Benefits to the buyer are measured in hours of work saved by employees, plus the resulting salary savings. First, have the buyer agree on an hourly rate, which includes fringe benefit cost; let's say salaries average $5 an hour for employees. The hours saved are then multiplied by this hourly rate to obtain the return on investment. If hours saved amounted to 2,800 per month, the savings would be $14,000 per month (2,800 hours × $5 hourly rate). You could develop a table to show the potential return on investment:

Value of hours saved	$14,000 per month
Cost of equipment	−10,000 per month
Profit	$ 4,000 per month
Return on investment ($14,000 ÷ $10,000)	140 percent

Subtracting the $10,000 cost per month from the return of $14,000 per month provides a $4,000 a month profit or a 140 percent return on investment. This is taken one step further by considering return on investment after taxes—calculated like this:

$$\frac{\$14,000 \ (1 - \text{Tax rate})}{\$10,000}$$

This return on investment presents the buyer with a logical reason to buy. Remember to let the customer make the cost estimates. The buyer must agree with the figures used for this to be effective in demonstrating the real value of buying your product.

KEY TERMS FOR SELLING

list price   207
net price   207
zone price   207
FOB shipping point   207
FOB destination   207
noncumulative quantity discounts   208
cumulative quantity discounts   208
cash discounts   209

trade discounts   209
consumer discounts   209
markup   210
gross profit   210
net profit   210
return on investment (ROI)   212
value analysis   213
unit cost   215

SALES APPLICATION QUESTIONS

1. Many companies offer customers various discounts from their normal or list price to entice them to buy. Discuss the main types of discounts offered.

2. Should the salesperson mention a discount at the beginning, middle, or end of a sales presentation? Why?

3. It cost a company $6 to manufacture a product that it sold for $10 to a wholesaler who sold it to a retailer for $12. A customer of the retailer bought it for $24. What was the markup on selling price for each member of this product's channel of distribution?

4. Determine the markup of a product that costs your customer $1 with the following potential suggested resell prices: $1.25, $1.50, $2. How much profit would the wholesaler or retailer make selling your product at each of the three suggested resell prices?

5. Assume you sell hardware supplies to grocery, drug, and hardware retailers. Tomorrow, you plan to call on the ACE Hardware chain—your largest customer. To reach your sales quota for this year, you must get a large order. You know they will buy something; however, you want them to purchase an extra amount. Furthermore, you know they are 120 days overdue on paying for what you shipped them months ago, and your company's credit manager will not ship them more merchandise until they pay the bill. How would you handle the sales call? Include in your answer where you would discuss the overdue bill problem in your sales presentation. Also include what you would do if the buyer said, "I haven't paid for my last order yet! How can I buy from you today?"

6. List and define five commonly quoted types of prices.

7. The following examples are several types of discounts. In each situation: (*a*) explain what type of discount is used, (*b*) determine by what percentage the *cost* of the product has been reduced, as well as savings per unit, and (*c*) answer other questions asked for each situation.

   a. Bustwell Inc., a regional business computer firm, is attempting to sell a new computer-operated gasoline pump meter to a convenience store chain, Gas 'N' Go. The device will help reduce gasoline theft, give an accurate record of each sale, and aid in determining when Gas 'N' Go should order more gasoline. Gus Gas, of the convenience chain, seems interested in your initial proposal but believes the price may be too high. The cost of each computer is $1,000, but you could sell Gas 50 computers for $45,000. The Gas 'N' Go chain owns 43 stores and is building eight more that will open in about one month.

   b. The Storage Bin Warehouse in your territory has reported a number of breakins in the past three months. As a salesperson for No-Doubt Security Products, you believe your extensive line of alarm systems and locks could benefit the warehouse greatly. You make an appointment with the manager at the Storage Bin for early next week. During your preparation for the sales call, you discover that the warehouse currently uses poor-quality locks and has no security system. You plan to offer the manager a security package consisting of 150 Sure-Bolt dead-bolt locks (for their 150 private storage rooms) at a price of $10 each, and a new alarm system costing $5,000. The terms of the sale are $2/10$ net 30. How would the total cost change if the terms of the alarm system alone were changed to $5/10$ net 30 (and the locks remained $2/10$ net 30)? What is the cost of the security package if the Storage Bin takes 25 days to pay for the purchase?

   c. You are a salesperson for Madcap Arcade Games, selling video games and pinball machines. A local business wants to open an arcade, and would like to buy a new game about every two weeks. A new game costs $3,000. You can offer a 5 percent discount (an end-of-year rebate) if at least 25 games are purchased from you during the next year. What will the discount be in dollars?

   d. The XYZ company is having its year-end sales push. As a salesperson for XYZ, a manufacturer of consumer goods like toothpaste, shampoo, and razor blades, you have been instructed to give a "buy 11 get 1 free" discount to half of your accounts. The remainder of your accounts, because of their small volume, are offered 10 percent off on all purchases. Compare the two situations. Which is the better deal?

8. As a salesperson for the Electric Generator Corporation, you have decided to attempt to sell your EG 600 generator to the Universal Construction Corporation. The EG 600 costs about $70,000. You estimate that operating and maintenance costs will average $3,000 a year and that the machine will operate satisfactorily for 10 years. You can offer a $65,000 price to Universal if they purchase 10 to 20 machines. Should they purchase more than 21 machines, their cost would be $58,000 per generator. The generators currently used originally cost $65,000, have a life of seven years, and cost $5,000 each year to operate. As far as you know, their present supplier cannot offer them a quantity discount.

   a. Develop a value analysis table comparing the two generators.

   b. In your presentation, what are the selling points you would stress?

9. Value analysis is an effective sales tool. Define value analysis and describe its use in a selling situation.

STUDENT APPLICATION LEARNING EXERCISES (SALES)

At the end of appropriate chapters beginning with Chapter 4, you will find Student Application Learning Exercises (SALES). SALES are meant to help you construct the various segments of your sales presentation. SALES build on one another so that after you complete them, you will have constructed the majority of your sales presentation.

SALE 2 of 7— Chapter 6

An important part of your presentation is the discussion of price to your buyer. To make **SALE 2,** first review pages 207 to 215.

Your assignment is to construct one or more pages that show the prices you will discuss with your buyer. This page—or pages—will serve as a visual aid (as shown on pages 209, 212, and 214) that you show and discuss with your buyer during the business proposition phase of your sales presentation.

CHAPTER 6 APPENDIX

Sales Arithmetic and Pricing

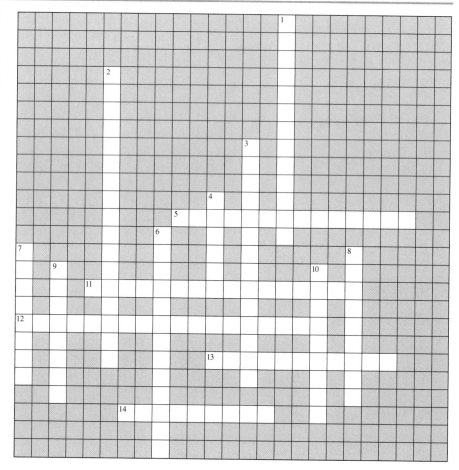

Across

5. Discounts on the list retail price offered to channel members.

11. The shipping process in which the buyer pays transportation charges for goods, the title for which passes to the customer when the goods are loaded onto the shipping vehicle.

12. The additional sum of money expected from an investment over and above the original investment.

13. Money available to cover the costs of marketing the product, operating the business, and profit.

14. The price based on geographic location or zone of customers.

Down

1. An investigation that determines the best product for the money.

2. One-time price reductions passed on from the manufacturer to channel members or directly to the customer.

3. The point at which the seller pays all shipping costs.

4. The dollar amount added to the product cost to determine its selling price.

6. Discounts earned by buyers who pay bills within a stated period.

7. The price after allowance for all discounts.

8. Money remaining after costs of marketing and operating the business are paid.

9. A small component price of a product's total cost.

10. A standard price charged to all customers.

CASE 6A-1

Claire Cosmetics

Jane Thompson was hired recently by a national cosmetics manufacturer. She just graduated from college. Having no previous work experience, she always felt nervous about making sales presentations. Her largest customers made her especially nervous. However, for the month she was in her territory, Jane only took orders, which relieved much of the pressure, and the salespeople whom Jane replaced did an excellent job; customers seemed to accept Jane because of this.

In today's mail, Jane receives information on products the company wants the sales force to emphasize next month. She is instructed to review the material and come to next week's sales meeting prepared to discuss the information. Of the four products to concentrate on, one product will receive special emphasis. Claire Super Hold hair spray will have the following sales promotion aids and price allowances:

- Floor stand containing 12 8-ounce and 36 12-ounce sizes.
- Counter display containing 6 8-ounce and 6 12-ounce sizes.
- $1 floor stand and counter display off-invoice allowance.
- 10 percent co-op advertising allowance requiring proof of advertising.
- 10 percent off-invoice discount for each dozen of each size purchased.

The 8-ounce size has a suggested retail price of $1.39 and has a normal invoice cost of 83 cents or $9.96 a dozen. The more popular 12-ounce size retails for $1.99 and costs $1.19 each or $14.28 a dozen. Jane knows that she, like each salesperson, will be called on at the meeting to give her ideas on how to sell this product in front of the 10 salespeople in her district. Her boss will be there and, it is rumored, the national sales manager will be in the area and may attend. This makes her really nervous.

Questions

1. What can Jane do to prepare herself for the meeting and reduce her nervousness?
2. If you were attending the meeting, what ideas would you present?

CASE 6A-2

McBath Women's Apparel

Getting a new, improved product into a chain of stores that has never carried her line of women's apparel is a new experience for Lynn Morris. Lynn has been promoted to key account sales representative for McBath Women's Apparel in the past month.

She has worked for McBath since graduating from college three years earlier. As a novice salesperson in a large metropolitan market, she inherited a sales territory where all of the major department stores in her area carried the popular McBath line. By displaying a service attitude, Lynn kept all her original accounts and managed to help several outlets increase sales of McBath products, but she was never given the opportunity to sell to new accounts.

Now, she has accepted the key account (a key account is one that generates a large volume of sales for the company) sales position in another region of the country. Also, she has the responsibility of selling to a large chain of department stores (Federale) that has never carried McBath products. Maurice Leverett, vice president of marketing at McBath, is counting heavily on adding the Federale chain because James McBath, the company's president, is intent on continuing McBath's rapid sales growth.

Lynn firmly believes that her products are the best on the market. She is concerned, however, about the sales interview she has scheduled with the chief purchasing agent at Federale, Mary Bruce. Despite McBath's high-quality image and its reputation for having a dependable, hard-working sales force, Mary Bruce has turned down other McBath salespeople several times over the past six years, saying, "We already stock four manufacturers' lingerie. We are quite happy with the lines we now carry and with the service their salespeople provide us. Besides, we only have so much floor space to devote to lingerie and we don't want to confuse our customers with another line."

Lynn has decided to make her company's new display system her major selling point for several reasons:

■ Several high-ranking McBath executives (including vice president of marketing Maurice Leverett) are strong supporters of the new display and want it in all retail outlets.
■ The stores currently using the display for test marketing purposes have shown an increase in sales for McBath products of 50 percent.
■ Federale will not have to set aside much space for the new system, and it can be installed, stocked, and ready for use in less than one hour.
■ The display will increase shopping convenience by allowing shoppers easy access to the well-known, trusted line of McBath products with the aid of clear, soft-shell plastic packaging and easy-to-understand sizing.
■ A new advertising campaign will start in a few weeks and will emphasize the revolutionary display. Other promotions, such as coupons and special introductory sales, will also be tried.

Questions

1. Lynn believes a good presentation will be critical for her to sell Bruce the new display. How should she structure her presentation? What are the key selling points to discuss?
2. Assume you are Maurice Leverett (vice president of marketing for McBath). Give an example of each of the four major types of discounts discussed in this chapter that your salespeople could use to help put the new display into retail stores. What type of discount will be most effective, and what will be least effective? Explain your reasoning.
3. How can Lynn use quantity (cumulative and noncumulative), cash, trade, and consumer discounts to her advantage?

CASE 6A-3
Electric Generator Corporation

The Electric Generator Corporation was founded in the early 1970s to develop and market electrical products for industrial and commercial markets. Recently, the company has developed a new electric generator, the EGI, with a revolutionary design. Although its initial cost is $2,000 higher than any competing generator, reduced maintenance costs will offset the higher purchase price within 18 months. The Electric Generator sales force has been instructed to concentrate all effort on selling this new generator, as the company believes it has a sales potential of $500 million.

Sandy Hart, the company's South Texas salesperson, has as her main customer the E. H. Zachary Construction Company of San Antonio, which is the largest nonunion construction firm in the world. Because of the importance of potential Zachary purchases of the EGI (estimated at $1 million), Sandy's boss asks her to take two days off and develop a plan for contacting and selling to Zachary. Monday morning, she is expected at the Houston regional sales office to present this plan to her boss, the regional sales manager, and the divisional sales manager. These two people will critique the presentation, and then the four of them will finalize a sales plan that Sandy will present to Zachary's buying committee.

Questions

1. If you were Sandy, what would be your suggested sales plan?
2. How would a value analysis enter into your presentation?

CASE 6A-4
Frank's Drilling Service

Frank's Drilling Service specializes in drilling oil and gas wells. Scott Atkinson, one of its salespeople, was preparing to contact the drilling engineer at Oilteck, an independent oil company. Scott has learned that Oilteck plans to drill approximately 12 new wells in the next six months.

Scott estimates that each oil well will require a drilling depth of approximately 10,000 feet. The drilling service the company currently uses charges 90 cents a foot, plus $1,200 per hour for personnel to operate the equipment. The service takes about 16 days to drill each well.

Frank's charges $1,200 per hour for personnel, and its costs are $1 a foot. Scott believes his drilling crews save customers time and money because they can drill a 10,000 foot well in 12 days.

Questions

1. Using the above information, develop a value analysis that Scott could use to sell to his customer.
2. What are several features, advantages, and benefits Scott should discuss with Oilteck's drilling engineer?

CASE 6A-5
FruitFresh, Inc.

Video

Case

Perry Ackerman, a product manager for FruitFresh, is visiting with his wife Dee, a member of the Town Recycling Committee, outside the local grocery store. Perry is upset because his new product line is losing market share to FruitFresh's major competitor, Cainer. Dee mentions that Cainer's new slogan "Nature Knows Best" is a good one, but Perry explains Cainer is not being truthful because they are using artificial coloring in its juice. Dee recalls that Cainer has previously been in trouble for inappropriately advertising its packaging as biodegradable and comments that maybe someone will report them again. Dee then asks Perry about progress on FruitFresh's plan to use recycled packaging materials. Perry explains that it is a very difficult and expensive process, but that there is a project team meeting on Tuesday that should give them some answers.

In the Tuesday meeting Perry tells the other employees on the team that people care about the environment and that they will spend their money to prove it. Lynn Samuels, the marketing director, agrees that the market exists and instructs Mike Stritch, from its advertising agency, to begin his presentation. Mike informs the group that the agency recommends building a campaign around recycled packaging. He goes on to explain that FruitFresh can make their cartons with better than 50 percent recycled products, the highest percentage that any company has been able to achieve, and suggest the slogan "FruitFresh. Good for you, good for your world." Lynn and the other employees like the idea, but Perry is concerned. Perry questions whether they would be misrepresenting its product by claiming that the container is recycled when only half of the packaging comes from recycled products.

Defending his idea, Mike comments that Cainer, FruitFresh's competitor would have no problem making such a claim. When Perry counters that Cainer might copy their campaign, Mike argues that the public may not believe them because of their previous record in the environmental area. Perry inquires why they do not publicize that Cainer is using artificial coloring in its "natural" juice. Mike does not think that this would have the same impact and stresses that they would have to be careful before they began making accusations. Lynn also stresses that FruitFresh has a sizable investment in this product line and explains that they cannot raise their prices enough to offset the increased manufacturing costs of going above 50 percent recycled material because of the tight market. She comments that she is interested in keeping plastics out of the waste stream, but that FruitFresh also needs to make a profit. Mike then assures Perry that he has done his research and that they have to determine what plastics are recycled in laminated products. Lynn reminds Perry that it is his decision since he is the brand manager. Perry contemplates his decision.[12]

Questions

1. What are the main ethical issues, if any, in the FruitFresh case? Describe each ethical issue.
2. What are Perry's options?
3. How do the three levels of moral development relate to Perry's situation?
4. What would you do?

PART III

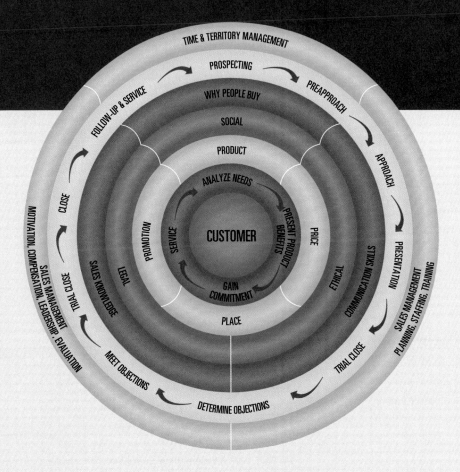

TIME & TERRITORY MANAGEMENT

PROSPECTING

PREAPPROACH

FOLLOW-UP & SERVICE

WHY PEOPLE BUY

SOCIAL

PRODUCT

APPROACH

CLOSE

ANALYZE NEEDS

PROMOTION

SERVICE

PRESENT PRODUCT BENEFITS

CUSTOMER

PRICE

PRESENTATION

SALES MANAGEMENT
MOTIVATION, COMPENSATION, LEADERSHIP, EVALUATION

TRIAL CLOSE

SALES KNOWLEDGE

LEGAL

GAIN COMMITMENT

ETHICAL

COMMUNICATION SKILLS

SALES MANAGEMENT
PLANNING, STAFFING, TRAINING

PLACE

MEET OBJECTIONS

TRIAL CLOSE

DETERMINE OBJECTIONS

THE RELATIONSHIP SELLING PROCESS

We are now prepared to study the selling skills that successful salespeople use. These skills help salespeople find prospects, analyze their needs, create a presentation that emphasizes benefits of the salesperson's products, and show how needs will be fulfilled. Successful salespeople address potential objections in order to gain commitment, in other words close the sale. They provide exceptional service to earn the privilege of repeating the cycle in order to help the customer in the long term. These salespeople follow the Golden Rule throughout the sales process in order to sell today and build a long-term business friendship.

223

7

CHAPTER

Prospecting—The Lifeblood of Selling

LEARNING OBJECTIVES

Here we begin to discuss the steps within the sales process. This chapter examines the first step—prospecting. After studying this chapter, you should be able to

■ Define the sales process, and list and describe its 10 steps in the correct sequence.

■ State why it is important to prospect.

■ Describe the various prospecting methods.

■ Ask for a referral anywhere during the referral cycle.

■ Make an appointment with a prospect or customer in person or by telephone.

Larry Long, John Alexander, and Kathryn Reece just sat down for their weekly sales meeting when Larry said, "Selling Apple's new Power Mac personal computer in our market will not be easy for us. The city has only 200,000 people; the county has 275,000. Yet there are 20 or more companies selling personal computers in the area. Radio Shack, IBM, Digital, and the others are tough competitors. I'm not sure where to begin."

"Larry, our best prospects and the ones to begin seeing this afternoon are our present customers—not only the ones presently using our Apple PCs, but customers who buy our equipment and office supplies," said John. "These people know us and already have accounts set up."

"That's OK for you," replied Kathryn; "however, many of my present customers already have PCs. So, I'm not sure I can count on selling many to them. I'm going to have to explore new territories, knock on doors, and dial-for-dollars to even come up with leads."

Larry broke in with, "Let's go after the IBM customers. IBM has the biggest market share in our area. We need to hit them head-on."

"No way," replied John, "we could get creamed if we got into a war by attacking IBM or any of our other competitors."

"But with all of our advertising," Larry continued, "the company's service, and our fair price on a state-of-the-art PC, we can regain our market share."

"Hold it, hold it," Kathryn said. "Let's start over and develop a plan that will allow us to uncover as many prospects as quickly as we can. After all, we need to push this new product and get the competitive edge before competition knows what hit 'em."

If you were one of these salespeople, how would you respond? What would be your sales plan?

The first two parts of this book give much of the background a salesperson needs for making an actual presentation. However, you can be the most knowledgeable person on topics such as buyer behavior, competitors, and product information, yet still have difficulty being a successful salesperson unless you are thoroughly prepared for each part of the sales call. Part III of this book examines the various elements of the sales process and sales presentation. It begins by explaining what the sales process means. Then we discuss methods of prospecting that may help Larry Long, John Alexander, and Kathryn Reece plan their sales program. First let's see how the Tree of Business Life relates to prospecting.

THE TREE OF BUSINESS LIFE: PROSPECTING

Many types of selling require prospecting. Without previous knowledge of who might purchase a product, the salesperson locates individuals and/or organizations that have the money, authority, and the desire to buy. Because people tend to do business with the people they know, plus feel salespeople are not honest or ethical, prospecting is not easy. Buying from a stranger is getting harder and harder. People want to trust the person they buy from and they buy from people they know.

All salespeople who begin their sales careers prospecting look forward to the day when most of their sales come from present customers. Frequently, these salespeople gain new customers through referrals from customers. Referrals are earned by demonstrating your integrity, trustfulness, and character to the customer who eventually provides you the referral. Ethical service builds relationships and is based upon the truth.

EXHIBIT 7.1

The selling process has
10 important steps.

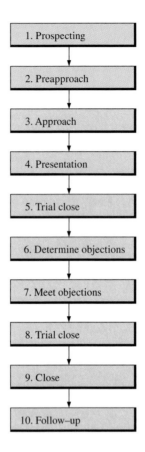

EXHIBIT 7.1

The selling process has
10 important steps.

1. Prospecting

2. Preapproach

3. Approach

4. Presentation

5. Trial close

6. Determine objections

7. Meet objections

8. Trial close

9. Close

10. Follow–up

THE SALES PROCESS HAS 10 STEPS

As discussed in Chapter 1, the **sales process** refers to a sequential series of actions by the salesperson that leads toward the customer taking a desired action and ends with a follow-up to ensure purchase satisfaction. Although many factors may influence how a salesperson makes a presentation in any one situation, a logical, sequential series of actions exists that, if followed, can greatly increase the chances of making a sale. This selling process involves 10 basic steps, as listed in Exhibit 7.1. Steps one and two are discussed in this chapter, and all steps are discussed in greater detail in the following chapters. Steps three through nine comprise the sales presentation itself. Before a sales presentation can be attempted, several important preparatory activities should be carried out.

STEPS BEFORE THE SALES PRESENTATION

As indicated in Exhibit 7.2, a successful salesperson begins with prospecting—obtaining an appointment with the prospect and planning the sales interview prior to ever actually meeting with the prospect. Like a successful lawyer, the salesperson does a great amount of background work before meeting the judge—the prospect. One rule of thumb states that a good sales process involves 20 percent presentation, 40 percent preparation, and 40 percent follow-up, especially when selling large accounts. However, even that varies from account to account. At Xerox, the national account manager will spend up to 18 months preparing a detailed description of a

EXHIBIT 7.2

Before the sales presentation.

potential national account. This report, which can easily end up being 50 pages long, is basically a business plan for selling the prospect. Thus preparation time for this sales call would be greater than the 40 percent rule of thumb.[1] As in most professions, success in selling often requires as much or more preparation before and between calls than is involved in actually making the calls themselves.

In Chapter 1, we said, "Nothing happens until someone sells something." However, even selling requires a preceding step: Nothing happens until someone does some prospecting.

PROSPECTING— THE LIFEBLOOD OF SELLING

Prospecting is the first step in the selling process. A **prospect** is a qualified person or organization that has the potential to buy your good or service. **Prospecting** is the lifeblood of sales because it identifies potential customers. A salesperson must look constantly for new prospects for two reasons:

1. To increase sales.
2. To replace customers that will be lost over time.

A prospect should not be confused with a lead. The name of a person or organization that might be a prospect is referred to as a **lead.** A lead can also be referred to as a suspect, indicating that the person or organization is suspected of being a prospect. Once the lead has been qualified, it becomes a prospect.[2] As a salesperson, you can ask yourself three questions to determine if an individual or organization is a **qualified prospect:**

You find people that are MAD.

1. Does the prospect have the *m*oney to buy?
2. Does the prospect have the *a*uthority to buy?
3. Does the prospect have the *d*esire to buy?

A simple way to remember this qualifying process is to think of the word *mad*. A true prospect must have the financial resources, money or credit, to pay and the authority to make the buying decision. The prospect also should desire your product. Sometimes an individual or organization may not recognize a need for your product. As later chapters show, your challenge is to create a desire for the product.

Locating leads and qualifying prospects are important activities for salespeople. Take, for example, computer salesperson Matt Suffoletto's comments on prospecting:

> Prospecting is the process of acquiring basic demographic knowledge of potential customers for your product. Lists that are available from many vendors break down businesses in a given geography by industry, revenue, and number of employees. These lists can provide an approach to mass marketing, via either mailings or telephone canvassing. That canvassing is either done by the salesperson or through an administrative sales support person. No matter who performs the canvas or how it is done, it is an important element in increasing sales productivity. The next step of qualifying the potential customer is often included in the prospecting process. Qualification is a means of quickly determining two facts. First, is there a potential need for your product? Second, is the prospect capable of making a purchase decision? Specifically, does he or she have the decision authority and the financial ability to acquire your product?

WHERE TO FIND PROSPECTS

Sources of prospects can be many and varied or few and similar, depending on the service or good the salesperson sells. Naturally, persons selling different services and goods might not use the same sources for prospects. A salesperson of oil-field pipe supplies would make extensive use of various industry directories in a search for names of drilling companies. A life insurance salesperson would use personal acquaintances and current customers as sources of prospects. A pharmaceutical salesperson would scan the local newspaper looking for announcements of new physicians and hospital, medical office, and clinical laboratory openings, whereas a sales representative for a company such as General Mills or Quaker Oats would watch for announcements of construction of new grocery stores and shopping centers.

Top real estate salesperson Vikki Morrison feels that prospecting, which for her means knowing people in her neighborhood, has greatly aided her in becoming a successful salesperson. She strives to become her prospect's friend.

"In my area, most of the people I see are wives—and any woman who tried to farm in this tract in high heels and a dress, dripping with jewelry, would never make it," she believes. "I'm not trying to impress anybody. These people either know me or they know about me from the neighbors. I'm no threat—especially in my tennies, pants, and T-shirt!

"Usually, I never meet the husband until the actual listing—then he wants to meet me to find out if I really know what I'm doing in real estate. As far as he's concerned, I'm just a friend of his wife's. These are the people I care about," she explains. "If someone needs a plumber or babysitter or a dentist, they call me. If I need a closing gift and someone on the block does creative things, I call them. We're all in this together!"

PLANNING A PROSPECTING STRATEGY

Frequently salespeople, especially new ones, have difficulty prospecting. Meeting strangers and asking them to buy something can be uncomfortable for people. As Exhibit 7.3 illustrates, many salespeople prefer to see others who have similar characteristics to themselves—although in most cases, the similarity need not go this far!

To be successful, prospecting requires a strategy. Prospecting, like other activities, is a skill that can be constantly improved by a dedicated salesperson. Some salespeople charge themselves with finding X number of prospects per week.

EXHIBIT 7.3

Many salespeople prefer to contact prospects having similar characteristics as themselves.

Indeed, Xerox (a large manufacturer of copiers and other types of business equipment) asks its sales force to allocate a portion of each working day to finding and contacting several new prospects. A successful salesperson continually evaluates prospecting methods, comparing results and records with the mode of prospecting used in pursuit of a prospecting strategy that will result in the most effective contact rate.[3]

PROSPECTING METHODS

The actual method by which a salesperson obtains prospects may vary. Exhibit 7.4 shows several of the more popular prospecting methods.

E-Prospecting on the Web

The most recent advancement in prospecting is the use of the Internet to find potential buyers. This is called e-prospecting, and it is a fast and easy way to find information about individuals or businesses by using technology.

Individuals

Finding information on the Internet about individuals can be very helpful to a salesperson. For example, Yahoo offers a people search on their site, yahoo.com, and it is free. The site can even give you a list of an individual's neighbors and their phone numbers. Some sites, such as peoplesearch.com, can provide you with extensive information about someone for a fee. Peoplefinder.com offers a list of over 200 different links to sites that search for information about people. Some of the links are free, and others are not, depending on the amount of information they give. A search engine could also be used to find information on a person.

Organizations

It may be important for a salesperson to find information about a company. In today's e-driven world, most businesses have their own Web sites. On these sites, a salesperson can find useful information that can help them decide if the company is a potential buyer. Many businesses may be found by simply entering the company's name followed by ".com." For example, if you are looking for information on Dell, you can type in www.dell.com as the universal resource locator (URL), and it will take you to the company's Web site. Bigyellow.com, Bigbook.com, and Switchboard.com are all Web sites that offer a search for businesses. Search engines,

EXHIBIT 7.4

Prospecting methods that work!

Prospecting is the lifeblood of selling. While some salespeople don't have to prospect, most rely on prospecting to increase sales and make money. Here are 12 popular methods:

- E-prospecting
- Cold canvassing
- Endless chain—customer referral
- Orphaned customers
- Sales lead clubs
- Prospect lists
- Get published
- Public exhibitions and demonstrations
- Center of influence
- Direct mail
- Telephone and telemarketing
- Observation
- Networking

Which methods use referrals from customers and other people?

such as www.yahoo.com, www.altavista.com, and www.lycos.com can also be very helpful in finding a business's Web address. Many cities also have their own Web sites now, and they often list information on companies in the area and links to their Web sites.

Cold Canvassing

The **cold canvass prospecting method** is based on the law of averages. For example, if past experience reveals that 1 person out of 10 will buy a product, then 50 sales calls could result in five sales. Thus, the salesperson contacts in person, by phone, and/or by mail as many leads as possible, recognizing that a certain percentage of people approached will buy. There is generally no knowledge about the individual or business the salesperson calls on. This form of prospecting relies solely on the volume of cold calls made.

The door-to-door and the telephone salesperson both employ cold canvas prospecting. For example, each summer The Southwestern Company hires college students to sell its books and other educational publications. These salespeople go into a town and knock on the door of every person living on each block they work, often contacting up to 75 people each day. They frequently ask people if they know of others who might like to purchase their products. Many office supply salespeople do the same thing, going from one business to another. Real estate, insurance, and stock brokerage firms are other businesses that use cold calls.

Endless Chain Customer Referral

Cold calling is tough! Contacting strangers day after day is challenging even for the most motivated individuals. Yet many new salespeople have to begin their sales careers cold calling to get customers. Once someone is sold, the salesperson has two possibilities for future sales.

First, satisfied customers are likely to buy again from the salesperson. That is why I stress the importance of building a relationship with the customer. It is critical to your success. Second, the customer often refers the salesperson to someone she knows. This is known as the **endless chain referral method** of prospecting. This is a very effective method for finding customers. *Customers* and *customer referrals* are the two best sources of future sales, with repeat sales from customers being better. A **referral** is a person or organization recommended to you by someone who feels that this person or organization could benefit from you or your product.

Customers and customer referrals are your future.

Don't ask current customers, "Do you know anyone else who could use my product?" Rarely are clients eager to judge whether colleagues are prepared to make a purchase. Instead, ask whether your customer knows any other individuals or organizations who might be interested in finding out about your product.

If you sense hesitation from customers to give out referrals, it's probably because they are afraid that their associates may not want to be pestered. Say, "Let me tell you what I'm going to do with any names you give me. I will make one phone call to each party, indicate that you were nice enough to give me their names and give them a brief outline of what we do.

"If they express an interest, we will get together and I will give them the same professional service I've given you. If, on the other hand, they express no interest, I will thank them for their time and never call them again." This approach puts your customers at ease and moves solid, new prospects onto your lead list.

Don't forget that your prospects are friends, neighbors, relatives—anyone and everyone you know or come into contact with. They may know people who are looking for your product and the great service you provide your customers. Everyone is a prospect!

Orphaned Customers

Orphaned Customers: Customer's whose salesperson has left the company. Salespeople often leave their employers to take other jobs; when they do, their customers are orphaned. These orphans are great prospects. A salesperson should quickly contact such customers to begin developing relationships. You can turn orphans into a lead-generating gold mine.

In addition, if you've been selling for a while you've surely built up a backlog of inactive accounts. Weed out the names who for whatever reason will never buy. The rest are solid prospects. Call them again and find out why they're not buying from you anymore. What would it take to change that? They may have stopped ordering your type of product altogether, or they may have gone with a competitor because of a special one-time offer, or there may have been a management change and therefore a change in buying patterns. You have to determine why the customer stopped buying from you. After you do that, reestablishing contact and turning that prospect into a customer again is standard sales procedure (SSP).

Sales Lead Clubs

Organize a group of salespeople in related but noncompetitive fields to meet twice a month to share leads and prospecting tips. To get started, write a formal mission statement, charge dues to ensure commitment, and grant membership to only one salesperson from each specific field. Next, set up administrative procedures and duties to keep the club on track and committed to its stated mission.

Finally, establish guidelines for what constitutes a good lead and track prospect information and effectiveness. Group the leads by effectiveness so members can better understand which leads can help the rest. You may even have every member who closes a lead contribute to a kitty. Each month the winner can be the member who provided the most closed leads.

Get Lists of Prospects

Make a list of what your ideal prospect looks like. Ask yourself the following questions:

- Who are my ideal prospects?
- Which economic bracket do they usually fall into?
- What kinds of organizations do they belong to?
- What characteristics do most of my existing customers share?
- Are they married, single, widowed, or divorced?
- Do they have children?
- Do they have particular political leanings?
- Do they have similar occupations, educations, hobbies, illnesses, transportation needs, or family concerns?

And the key question:

- Where am I most likely to find the greatest conglomeration of people who fit my prospect's profile?

List Number One. Take the information you have accumulated and apply it. Go to the library and look up the Standard Industrial Classification (SIC) code number for your ideal prospects' businesses. Ask a librarian for help if you need it. Every type of business has a specific SIC code. Related industries have similar numbers; scan the directory to locate the numbers that fit the profile. This should provide you with an excellent prospect list. In addition, literally hundreds of other business directories can help you generate lists based on corporate profiles.

List Number Two. What kinds of publications do your ideal prospects likely read? Find out whether these publications sell lists of subscribers. If a publication's readership matches your prospect profile well enough, this list should be well worth the cost.

List Number Three. Go to the Standard Rate and Data Service's directory of firms that sell lists. These companies offer a variety of criteria that you can use to generate a quality prospect list. Dun & Bradstreet is an example of such a company. For your convenience, the information may even be available on computer disk.

Become an Expert—Get Published

Although you may give your services as a writer away for free, the residual benefits make your efforts well worth the time. Submit articles about your field or industry to journals, trade magazines, and newspapers. Your submissions don't have to be glossy and expensive; just fill them with information that people can genuinely use, then make sure you have no spelling or grammatical mistakes. Instead of getting paid, ask the publication to include your address and telephone number at the end of the article and to write a little blurb about your expertise.

By convincing an editor that you're an expert in your field, you become one. Once prospects think of you as an expert you'll be the one they contact when they're ready to buy. In addition, prospects who call you for advice can come to depend on you and your product. Thus, you attract prospects without having to go out prospecting.

Public Exhibitions and Demonstrations

Exhibitions and demonstrations frequently take place at trade shows and other types of special interest gatherings. Many times, related firms sponsor a booth at such shows and staff it with one or more salespeople.[4] As people walk up to the booth to examine the products, a salesperson has only a few minutes to qualify leads and get names and addresses in order to contact them later at their homes or offices for demonstrations. Although salesperson–buyer contact is usually brief, this type of gathering gives a salesperson extensive contact with a large number of potential buyers over a brief time. Remember, however, that success at trade shows stems from preparation. Here are several things to do:

- Set up an interesting display to get people's attention. A popcorn machine, juggler, or inexpensive giveaway are good ideas.
- Write down your message so that it fits on the back of a business card.
- Practice communicating two or three key points that get your message across succinctly. Get it down pat but don't memorize your sales pitch to make it sound overly canned.
- Make a list of the major buyers at the show you want to pursue for contacts.
- Set up to maximize your display's visibility based on the flow of traffic.
- Be assertive in approaching passersby. Instead of the common "Hello" or "How are you?" try "Do you use [product or service] in your operations?" or "Have you seen [product or service]? If I can show you how to be more profitable, would you be interested?" Next offer them a sample to handle, but not to keep. Don't let them take the item and move on without talking to you.
- Use lead cards to write down prospect information for efficient and effective postshow follow-up.
- Be prepared for rejection. Some buyers will ignore you. Don't take it personally. Be brief but professional. Your time is too valuable to waste on nonprospects.

MAKING THE SALE

Successful Selling Secrets: Vikki Morrison

"There are no secrets to successful selling. There is only hard work from 7:00 in the morning to 10:00 at night. The biggest secret is total honesty at all times with all parties. You should act with integrity and treat clients with the same respect you want from them.

"Never call clients with anything but calm assurance in your voice, because if they feel you are panicked, they will become panicked. Your walk, speech, mannerisms, and eye-to-eye contact say more about you than you'll ever know, so practice all forms of your presentation every day in every way. I suppose a secret is to save the best house for last. I just try to do the best job for the client, even when it means turning them over to another agent who would have a more suitable property in a different area."

Morrison does not work alone; she uses her available resources in selling. A computer terminal in her office gives her up-to-date information on listings and an analysis of proposed transactions. She personally employs three assistants to help her keep up with the listings and shoppers. Vikki Morrison knows the value of the real estate in her area and

can give free market analysis with less than one hour's notice.

"An important part of my job is providing customers personal service via constant follow-up, before the appointment, during, and after the sale. I have periodic follow-ups to see how they like their new home or investments. Anniversary flowers and cards on their birthday are a specialty of mine. I try to eliminate any and all of their buying fears when I can, and be available to reassure them.

"I sell on emotional appeal. No matter what the facts, most people still buy based on emotion. The triggers for someone's emotional side can be quite varied. For example, for some men, their families are their hot button; for others, the greed appeal of a good deal is more important. Every person is different and should be handled as the very important individual that they are.

"Another factor in my selling is that I care about my clients. They know it, I know it, and they feel it when I'm working with them and long after the escrow is closed. These people are my good friends and we have fun together."

Center of Influence

Prospecting via the **center of influence method** involves finding and cultivating people in a community or territory who are willing to cooperate in helping to find prospects. They typically have a particular position that includes some form of influence over other people, as well as information that allows the salesperson to identify good prospects. For example, a person who graduates from college and begins work for a local real estate firm might contact professors and administrators at his alma mater to obtain the names of teachers who have taken a job at another university and are moving out of town. He wants to help them sell their homes.

Clergy, salespeople who are selling noncompeting products, officers of community organizations like the chamber of commerce, and members of organizations such as the Lions Club or a country club are other individuals who may function as a center of influence. Be sure to show your appreciation for this person's assistance. Keeping such influential persons informed on the outcome of your contact with the prospect helps to secure future aid.

Direct Mail

In cases where there are a large number of prospects for a product, **direct-mail prospecting** is sometimes an effective way to contact individuals and businesses. Direct-mail advertisements have the advantage of contacting large numbers of people, who may be spread across an extended geographical area, at a relatively low cost when compared to the cost of using salespeople. People who request more information from the company subsequently are contacted by a salesperson.

Telephone and Telemarketing

Like direct marketing, use of **telephone prospecting** to contact a large number of prospects across a vast area is far less costly than use of a canvassing sales force, though usually more costly than mailouts.[5]

This person-to-person contact afforded by the telephone allows for interaction between the lead and the caller—enabling a lead to be quickly qualified or rejected. Salespeople can even contact their local telephone company for help in incorporating the telephone into the sales program.

One example of telephone prospecting is the aluminum siding salesperson who telephones a lead and asks two questions that quickly determine if that person is a prospect. The questions are

Telephone Salesperson: Sir, how old is your home?

Lead: One year old.

Telephone Salesperson: Is your home brick or wood?

Lead: Brick!

Telephone Salesperson: Since you do not need siding, would you recommend we contact any of your neighbors or friends who can use a high-quality siding at a competitive price? [Endless chain technique]

A big sales buzzword today is **telemarketing.** Telemarketing is a marketing communication system using telecommunication technology and trained personnel to conduct planned, measurable marketing activities directed at targeted groups of consumers.

The internal process of a telemarketing center is shown in Exhibit 7.5. Many firms initiate telemarketing ventures by featuring an 800 phone number in an advertisement. Print ads may make a coupon available for the reader. When the coupon response or a telephone call comes into the center, a trained specialist handles it. This person may take an order (in the case of a telephone call) or transfer the person to a telephone selling or *teleselling unit.* The specialist may provide information or service. The specialist also can determine whether the customer has sufficient potential to warrant a face-to-face sales call. The duties of a telemarketing specialist are based on the type of product being sold and to whom it is sold.

EXHIBIT 7.5

The processing system within a telemarketing center.

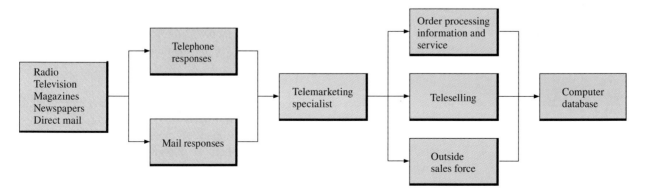

EXHIBIT 7.6

Reports from a telemarketing center to other marketing groups within the firm.

Advertising
- Inquiries per advertisement
- Profiles of respondents
- Sales-conversion rates per advertisement

Physical Distribution
- Consumers' orders
- Distributors' orders
- Tracing and dispatching
- Shipment requirements
- Inventory requirements
- Product return needs
- Customer-service needs

Market Management
- Segment analyses
- Marginal-account identification

Product Management
- Sales per product
- Questions and complaints
- Consumer profiles

Marketing Research
- Demographic data
- Image and attitude
- Forecasting data

Sales Management
- Lead qualification
- Marginal-account status

From thousands of such contacts with the public, a firm can develop a valuable database that produces various informational reports. Many companies use telemarketing centers in this way. Exhibit 7.6 describes some of their informational reports.

As an example, the Westinghouse Credit Corporation uses telemarketing to qualify leads and develop live prospects for its field sales force. Specialists at the Westinghouse telemarketing center call prospects to determine interest level and to verify addresses. Having qualified a number of prospects, they transfer the leads to the various sales branch offices.

Observation

A salesperson often can find prospects by constantly watching what is happening in the sales area—the **observation method.** Office furniture, computer, and copier salespeople look for new business construction in their territories. New families moving into town are excellent leads for real estate and insurance salespeople. No matter what prospecting method you use, you must always keep your eyes and ears open for information on who needs your product.

Networking

For many salespeople, prospecting never ends. They are always on the lookout for customers. Everyone they meet may be a prospect, or that person may provide a name that could lead to a sale. The term given to making and using contacts is **networking.**

Of the many ways to find new prospects, networking can be the most reliable and effective. People want to do business with, and refer business to, people they know, like, and trust. The days of the one-shot salesperson are over; the name of the game today is relationship building.

Building a network is important, but cultivating that network brings sales. The key is positioning, not exposure. The goal of cultivating your network is to fill a niche in the mind of each of your contacts so when one of those contacts, or someone he or she knows, needs your type of product or service, you are the *only* possible resource that would come to mind.

Here are several tips for cultivating your network to dramatically increase your referral business:

1. Focus on meeting *center-of-influence* people. These people have established a good reputation and have many valuable contacts. A few places to find the key people in your industry are trade association meetings, trade shows, or any business-related social event.
2. Ninety-nine percent of your first conversation with a networking prospect should be about his or her business. People want to talk about *their* business, not yours.
3. Ask open-ended, feel-good questions like, "What do you enjoy most about your industry?"
4. Be sure to ask, "How would I know if someone I'm speaking with would be a good prospect for you?" If you're on the lookout to find this person new business, he will be more inclined to do the same for you.
5. Get a networking prospect's business card. It's the easiest way to follow up with your new contact.
6. Send a handwritten thank-you note that day: "It was nice meeting you this morning. If I can ever refer business your way, I certainly will."
7. When you read newspapers and magazines, keep the people in your network in mind. If you find an article one of your contacts could use or would enjoy, send it.
8. Stay on your contacts' minds by sending them something every month; notepads with your name and picture are perfect. They will keep these pads on their desks and be constantly reminded of you and your product or service.
9. Send leads. The best way to get business and referrals is to give business and referrals.
10. Send a handwritten thank-you note whenever you receive a lead, regardless of whether it results in a sale.

When meeting someone, tell them what you sell. Ask what they do. Exchange business cards and periodically contact the person. Eventually, you may build a network of people talking to each other, sharing ideas, and exchanging information. Also, you can use several of the previously discussed methods of prospecting, such as the endless chain or center of influence methods, to build your network.

Don't wait for your ship to come in . . . swim out to it.

PROSPECTING GUIDELINES

Like many other components of the selling process, prospecting methods should be chosen in light of the major factors defining a particular selling situation. As in most other optional situations discussed in this book, there is no one optimal mode of prospecting to fit all situations. Generalizations can be made, however, regarding the criteria used in choosing an optimal prospecting method for a particular selling situation. Three criteria you should use in developing the best prospecting method require you to take these actions:

1. *Customize* or choose a prospecting method that fits the specific needs of your individual firm. Do not copy another company's method; however, it's all right to adapt someone's method.
2. Concentrate on *high potential* customers first, leaving for later prospects of lower potential.
3. Always *call back* on prospects who did not buy. With new products, do not restrict yourself to present customers only. A business may not have purchased

your present products because they did not fit their present needs; however, your new product may be exactly what they need.

Always keep knocking on your prospect's and customer's door to help them solve problems through the purchase of your product. Only in this way can you maximize your long-term sales and income.

Referrals Used in Most Prospecting Methods

Referrals can be directly used in (1) cold canvassing, (2) endless chain customer referrals, (3) orphaned customers, (4) sales lead clubs, (5) public exhibitions and demonstrations, (6) center of influence, (7) telephone, and (8) networking. Eight of the twelve popular prospecting methods directly ask someone if they know others who might be interested in their product.

Many salespeople using these methods are reluctant to ask for referrals. Yet if they would, sales would increase. Try it! If done correctly, people will give referrals. Here are some ideas on getting referrals to increase your prospect pool.

The Prospect Pool

Referrals come from prospects. Different sources of prospects form the prospect pool. The **prospect pool** is a group of names gathered from various sources. Your source, for example, may be a mailing list, telephone book, referrals, orphans, or existing customers. As Exhibit 7.7 shows, a prospect pool is usually created from four main sources.[6]

1. **Leads**—people and organizations you know nothing, or very little, about.
2. **Referrals**—people or organizations you frequently know very little about other than what you learned from the referral.
3. **Orphans**—company records provide your only information about these past customers.
4. **Your customers**—the most important prospects for future sales.

Most salespeople required to create customers through prospecting do not like to cold call. They have the goal of a prospect pool composed of customers, referrals, and, when available, orphans. The secret to reaching this goal is the referral cycle.

EXHIBIT 7.7

Components of the prospect pool.

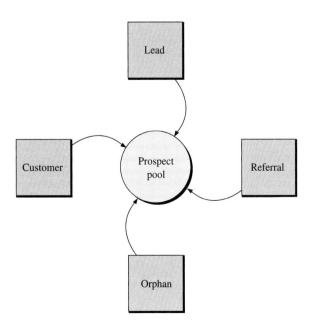

THE REFERRAL CYCLE

Obtaining referrals is a continuous process without beginning or end. The salesperson is always looking for the right opportunity to find a referral. The **referral cycle** provides guidelines for a salesperson to ask for referrals in four commonly faced situations, as shown in Exhibit 7.8.

If you have a sales presentation at 10 A.M., you can begin the referral cycle in the presentation phase. If you are delivering a product to a client, you can start the cycle in the product delivery phase. If you are planning to make telephone calls to leads, referrals, orphans, or customers tonight, you can begin in the preapproach phase.

Regardless of where you are in the referral cycle, you can begin at that point. Perfect your techniques so that you will be working on every phase of the cycle simultaneously. Direct any contact with the prospect toward presenting yourself and your product in such a way as to overcome any objections you could face later when asking for referrals and, of course, when making a sale.

The Parallel Referral Sale

Salespeople must sell the product, plus sell the prospect on providing referrals. This is known as the **parallel referral sale.** Equal emphasis must be given to both the product sale and the referral sale. You must nurture a parallel referral sale from the time of the initial contact, such as when making an appointment. The referral sale should receive equal importance, effort, and emphasis as the product sale. This is the key to the referral cycle.

The Secret Is to Ask Correctly

Many salespeople do not ask for referrals. If they do ask, they often do so infrequently and incorrectly. Understand that if others—even customers—never had objections to giving referrals there would be no problem in getting them. A salesperson could simply ask for referrals and live happily ever after. Unfortunately, this is not the case. Here are examples of why some clients may not wish to give referrals:

- Clients are afraid of upsetting friends and relatives.
- Clients do not want friends to think they're talking about them.

EXHIBIT 7.8

The referral cycle: When to ask for referrals.

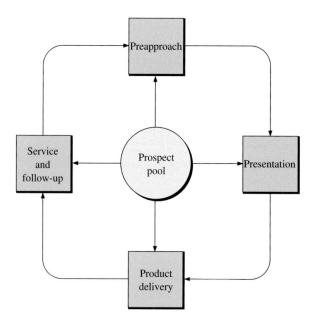

- Clients may believe in the product but not in the salesperson.
- Clients fear the salesperson may not be around years down the road.
- Clients do not feel they can benefit from giving the salesperson referrals.

It is absolutely essential that you consider these objections when asking for referrals. By doing so, you will obtain more referrals, get more appointments, and make more sales.

When to Ask

Properly asking for referrals can greatly improve a person's sales. Sounds simple doesn't it? All one needs to do is ask others for referrals. It's simple, but not as simple as it first sounds. It is important to ask professionally at each phase of the referral cycle.

The Preapproach

The harvest can be bountiful, but people who will ask are few.

Great care must be taken during the preapproach contact phase of the referral cycle. Whether the initial contact is face to face or via telephone, the effectiveness of your approach will be the deciding factor in determining whether you are given the opportunity to make a sales presentation.

Many prospects will hang up the phone as soon as they suspect an attempt is being made to sell them something. If, in the first several seconds, you fail to overcome their initial feelings of discomfort and intrusion, your chances of developing a relationship are slim.

Mentioning that a firm or business acquaintance of theirs recommended that you call helps alleviate some of the initial anxiety in dealing with quick objections. This is one of the reasons why working on referrals is so effective. Certainly, people are willing to listen a bit longer if they know a person they trust is the reason for this personal contact. Here's an example:

> Hello, is this John? . . . Hi, John, my names is Charles Futrell from Merrill Lynch. George and Barbara Smith are clients of mine. I met with them last week and helped them set up their retirement program. They were really pleased with both my products and service. *And since I work primarily through referrals*, they were kind enough to mention that you might be interested in learning about the value I have to offer.
>
> I'd like to set up a time to stop by your home or office and share some ideas that you may find of great benefit. *It's not really important to me that we do business*; all I ask is if you appreciate the time we share together, if you feel that you benefit from the time we spend together, and, most important, if you respect my integrity, *You would be willing to pass my name on to a friend or business associate who may also benefit from my services*, just as George and Barbara did. Is that fair enough?

We have begun the process of selling the prospect—and hopefully customer—on giving us one or more referrals. We are telling John that it is not important for me to make a sale. We are asking if he feels it is reasonable, if and only if he is happy with me, that he pass my name on just as his friends did. It is easy for John to answer yes. I have presented my offer in a nonthreatening manner that was endorsed by his friends George and Barbara.

To say "it's not really important to me that we do business" is very unusual. People are not accustomed to hearing a salesperson say that it is not important to make a sale.

The Presentation

Depending on the particular industry you represent, the situation in which you present your product for sale may be called by a variety of names. It could be a meeting, appointment, interview, or presentation. Hereafter, we refer to it as the presentation.

During the presentation you have the greatest opportunity to influence your prospect. It is important to understand that your prospect will scrutinize everything you say and do, whether it be through words, expressions, or body language. During this presentation you also must be conscious of presenting your desire to get referrals.

The presentation phase of the referral cycle actually begins when you sit down with your prospects for the purpose of making a sales presentation. As comfortably as possible, you should make a conscious effort to mention the referring person. This may be a remark as simple as, "George told me that you like to golf. Did you get a chance to get out this week?" or "Barbara mentioned that you like to garden. Did the last frost we had affect your plants at all?"

This initial contact plants the seed for the beginning of the parallel referral sale. During the next 10 or 15 minutes there should be no discussion about the product or service being offered. This time is best used to build rapport and help break down any barriers between the prospects and their perception of you as a salesperson. To accelerate this process you should mention the referring person as often as possible. It is easy to tell when the barriers begin to come down. The walls of resistance have fallen when you begin to feel comfortable with your prospects. If you do not feel comfortable with your prospects, they certainly will not feel comfortable with you.

Once you establish rapport, you should take a moment to explain to your prospects what will occur during the time you will be together. It doesn't matter what good or service you are selling; this approach should be used regardless. Then when appropriate, mention the referrals. Here are two examples:

> John and Nonnie, if you're happy with my service, I hope you will be willing to pass my name on to other people who would appreciate the same honesty and integrity I have extended to you. I don't do this because I'm a good guy, or because I'm a good Christian; I do it because it makes good business sense. If I take care of you, you'll take care of me. And my livelihood depends on getting referrals. My success and the success of my business is totally dependent on getting quality referrals from my client. I realize that you will introduce me to your friends, family, and business associates only if the quality and integrity of the service I provide surpasses that to which you've grown accustomed. This I pledge.

Product Delivery

Almost every selling profession has some type of product delivery phase. The delivery phase is more obvious with some products than others. For example, in the life insurance industry it involves the agent physically handing the policy to the client. In real estate, it would be the day the sale closes on the home or property. With computers, it would be the day that the system is installed and useable. In advertising, it would be the day that the ad runs in the publication. Automobile buyers go to the dealership or have the salesperson deliver the vehicle to them. Whatever your profession, you should identify the precise moment that your product becomes of value to your customer, and at this point the product delivery phase begins. Here's an example of how to make the referral sale:

> I'm sure by now, John, you realize that I work strictly through referrals. I am constantly striving to bring my clients even greater service by improving my business. I have a very important question for you and would appreciate your giving this some thought. Is

there any one thing that you would like to see me change or improve that would increase the likelihood of my getting referrals from you in the future?

This is only an example to get you thinking about how to properly ask for the referral. And you do need to always ask!

Service and Follow-Up

Customer service is the performance of any helpful or professional work or activity for a person, family, or organization. The service and follow-up phase of the referral cycle provides you with ongoing opportunities to maintain contact with your clients. Anytime that you have contact with your clients you encounter the possibility of getting more referrals. The quality and quantity of service will help enhance the quality and quantity of the referrals you receive. High-quality service helps create a very professional and caring image that clients are not afraid of sharing with their friends, family, and business associates; a high quantity of service helps keep you and your product fresh in the clients' mind. Service is one of the key components of the Golden Rule. Service shows you have a servant heart and care about the customer rather than solely the money you make from the sale.

For many salespeople, the product delivery phase represents the end of the relationship with their clients. There are three reasons why this happens. First, the nature of the business may not require any additional service. Second, although there may be a need for continued service, salespeople are so preoccupied with prospecting or selling that they cannot devote adequate time to providing adequate service. Third, salespeople may not realize that providing their clients with quality service can benefit them in expanding the quality and quantity of their business. What it comes down to is no need, no time, or no benefit. Here is an example of what might be said during a typical annual follow-up:

> Hello, John. This is Charles Futrell. As I promised when we first did business, this is my "official" once-a-year call to let you know that I am thinking about you. Do you have any questions? Is there anything I can do for you? . . . I also want to make sure you and Nonnie have received your birthday cards and quarterly newsletters. What do you think of my newsletters? . . . Terrific. I'll let you go now. Don't forget, you've got my number if you need any help. Please keep me in mind when talking to your friends and business associates. As you know, John, I depend on quality clients like you and Nonnie to keep me in business. One of the reasons I work so hard to help my customers is because of the people you refer to me. Your referrals are really appreciated. (Pause) John, is there anyone you or Nonnie feel I should help? (Pause) Thank you very much! I look forward to seeing you soon. Goodbye.

One season when I coached little league baseball, a six-year-old player said, "Coach, I've never hit the ball." I replied, "Well Steve, you never swing at the ball." Steve was afraid the pitcher would hit him with the ball. Like Steve, salespeople are afraid to swing or rather ask someone for a referral. People are not going to hit you if you ask with a smile on your face. Have you ever had a salesperson ask you for a referral? I never have! What a shame it is not to ask someone if they know who could use your help. The secret of obtaining referrals is to always professionally ask people. The main times to ask for referrals are shown in Exhibit 7.8.

Don't Mistreat the Referral

One final thought on referrals—don't mistreat them! The salesperson who mistreats a referral can lose the referring customer and the prospect. Like dropping a rock into a pool of water, it can have a ripple effect. Be sure to treat the referral in a professional manner. Always follow through on what you have told the referral.

Once you have sold the referral, and gotten more referrals, ask the *new* customer to contact the *referring* customer on her experience with the salesperson. Now you have two customers giving you referrals. This can create an *endless chain* of referrals, helping to quickly fill your prospect pool with only customers and referrals.

Tracking Referrals

Keeping track of referrals is just as important as staying in contact with customers. Whether you use index cards or a computerized contact system, it's important to keep detailed records on all information you collect on the prospect/customer. (See Chapter 8's discussion of the customer profile and Chapter 6's review of computerized customer contact programs.)

CALL RELUCTANCE COSTS YOU MONEY!

What good is knowing how to prospect if you won't prospect? All salespeople seem to have call reluctance from time to time. An estimated 40 percent of all salespeople suffer a career-threatening bout of call reluctance at some point. In its milder forms, call reluctance keeps countless salespeople from achieving their potential. Research indicates that 80 percent of all first-year salespeople who don't make the grade fail because of insufficient prospecting.

Call reluctance refers to not wanting to contact a prospect or customer. This tricky demon assumes a dozen faces and comes disguised as a salesperson's natural tendencies.

Countermeasures for call reluctance are numerous and depend on the type of reluctance experienced by the person. But the initial step is always the same: "You must admit you have call reluctance and that your call reluctance is keeping you from helping others and earning what you're worth." For many salespeople, owning up to call reluctance is the most difficult part of combating it.[7]

Salespeople must seek out prospects to find them. In basketball, as in sales, you'll always miss 100 percent of the shots you don't take. If you do not call on people you cannot make a sale. So in sales you must knock, so the door will be opened for you. Before you knock you often need an appointment.

In basketball you'll always miss 100 percent of the shots you don't take.

OBTAINING THE SALES INTERVIEW

Given a satisfactory method of sales prospecting and an understanding of the psychology of buying, a key factor in the selling process that has yet to be addressed is obtaining a sales interview. Although cold calling (approaching a prospect without prior notice) is suitable in a number of selling situations, industrial buyers and some other types of individuals may have neither the time nor the desire to consult with a sales representative who has not first secured an appointment.

The Benefits of Appointment Making

The practice of making an appointment before calling on a prospect can save a salesperson hours in time wasted traveling and waiting to see someone who is busy or even absent. When the salesperson makes an appointment, a buyer knows someone is coming. People are generally more receptive when they expect someone than when an unfamiliar salesperson pops in. Appointment making is often associated with a serious, professional image and is sometimes taken as an outward gesture of respect toward a prospect.

MAKING THE SALE

Getting an Appointment Is Not Always Easy

The owner of an oil field supply house in Kansas City was Jack Cooper's toughest customer. He was always on the run, and Jack had trouble just getting to see him, much less getting him to listen to a sales presentation. Jack would have liked to take him to lunch so he could talk to him, but the owner never had time. Every day he called a local hamburger stand and had a hamburger sent to his office so he wouldn't have to waste time sitting down to eat.

Jack wanted to get the owner interested in a power crimp machine that would enable him to make his own hose assemblies. By making them himself, the owner could save about 45 percent of his assembly costs—and Jack would make a nice commission.

The morning Jack was going to make his next call, his wife was making sandwiches for their children to take to school. Jack had a sudden inspiration. He asked his wife to make two deluxe bag lunches for him to take with him.

Jack arrived at the supply house just before lunchtime. "I know you're too busy to go out for lunch," he told the owner, "so I brought it with me. I thought you might like something different for a change."

The owner was delighted. He even took time to sit down and talk while they ate. After lunch, Jack left with an order for the crimper—plus a standing order for hose and fittings to go with it!

From the salesperson's point of view, an appointment provides a time set aside for the buyer to listen to a sales presentation. This is important because adequate time to explain a proposition improves the chance of making the sale. In addition, a list of appointments aids a salesperson in optimally allocating each day's selling time. Appointments can be arranged by telephone or by contacting the prospect's office in person.

Telephone Appointment

For obvious time and cost benefits, salespeople usually phone to make sales appointments. Though seemingly a simple task, obtaining an appointment over the telephone is frequently difficult. Business executives generally are busy and their time is scarce. However, these practices can aid in successfully making an appointment over the telephone:

- Plan and write down what you will say. This helps you organize and concisely present your message.
- Clearly identify yourself and your company.
- State the purpose of your call and briefly outline how the prospect may benefit from the interview.
- Prepare a brief sales message, stressing product benefits over features. Present only enough information to stimulate interest.
- Do not take no for an answer. Be persistent even if there is a negative reaction to the call.
- Ask for an interview so that you can further explain product benefits.
- Phrase your appointment request as a question. Your prospect should be given a choice, such as: "Would nine or one o'clock Tuesday be better for you?"

Successful use of the telephone in appointment scheduling requires an organized, clear message that captures interest quickly. Before you dial a prospect's number, mentally or physically sketch out exactly what you plan to say. While on the

MAKING THE SALE

Does Your Mental Attitude Influence Your Life?

Yogi Berra has been quoted as saying, "Whatever you do in life, 90 percent of it is half mental." What does that mean to you? What do the following statements from famous motivational writers over the last 70 years mean to you? Have you ever been reluctant to do something? How does this relate to prospecting?

■ "Positive mental attitude governs your life and mind and it is the starting point of all riches." Napoleon Hill.

■ "I will greet this day with love in my heart." Og Mandino.

■ "Let's fill our minds with thoughts of peace, courage, health, and hope for our life is what our thoughts make it." Dale Carnegie.

■ "Count your blessings—not your troubles." Dale Carnegie.

■ "When fate hands us a lemon, let's try to make lemonade." Dale Carnegie.

■ "I will persist until I succeed." Og Mandino.

■ "Sharpen the saw—renew the physical, spiritual, mental, and social/emotional dimensions of your nature." Stephen Covey.

telephone get to the point quickly (as you may have only a minute), disclosing just enough information to stimulate the prospect's interest. For example:

> Mr. West, this is Sally Irwin of On-Line Computer Company calling you from Birmingham, Alabama. Businessmen such as yourself are saving the costs of rental or purchase of computer systems, while receiving the same benefits they get from the computer they presently have. May I explain how they are doing this on Tuesday at nine o'clock in the morning or would one o'clock in the afternoon be preferable?

One method for obtaining an appointment with anyone in the world is for you to have someone else make it for you. Now, that sounds simple enough, doesn't it? However, do not just have anyone make the appointment. It should be a satisfied customer. Say, "Listen, you must know a couple of people who could use my product. Would you mind telling me who they are? I'd like you to call them up and say I'm on my way over." Or, "Would you just call them up and ask them if they would meet with me?" This simple technique frequently works. In some situations, an opportunity to make an appointment personally arises or is necessitated by circumstances.

Personally Making the Appointment

Many business executives are constantly bombarded with an unending procession of interorganizational memos, correspondence, reports, forms, and *salespeople.* To use their time optimally, many executives establish policies to aid in determining whom to see, what to read, and so on. They maintain gatekeepers (secretaries or receptionists) who execute established time-use policies by acting as filters for all correspondence, telephone messages, and people seeking entry to the executive suite. Successful navigation of this filtration system requires a professional salesperson who (1) is determined to see the executive and believes it can be done; (2) develops friends within the firm (many times including the gatekeepers); and (3) optimizes time by calling only on individuals who make or participate in the purchase decision.

Believe in Yourself. As a salesperson, believe that you can obtain interviews because you have a good offer for prospects. Develop confidence by knowing your

MAKING THE SALE

Customer Call Reluctance—Your Own Worst Enemy

According to a study by Behavioral Sciences Research Press, the problem of call reluctance in sales is widespread and costly.[8] Among the findings of the Dallas research and sales training firm:

- Some 80 percent of all new salespeople who fail within their first year do so because of insufficient prospecting activity.
- Forty percent of all sales veterans experience one or more episodes of call reluctance severe enough to threaten their continuation in sales. It can strike at any time.

- The call-reluctant salesperson loses more than 15 new accounts per month to competitors.
- Call-reluctant stockbrokers acquire 48 fewer new accounts per year than brokers who have learned to manage their fear.
- In some cases, the call-reluctant salesperson loses $10,800 per month in gross sales.
- In others, call reluctance costs the salesperson $10,000 in lost commissions per year.

products and by knowing prospects—their business and needs. Speak and carry yourself as though you expect to get in to see the prospect. Instead of saying, "May I see Ms. Vickery," you say, while handing the secretary your card, "Could you please tell Ms. Vickery that Ray Baker from XYZ Corporation is here?"

Develop Friends in the Prospect's Firm. Successful salespeople know that people within the prospect's firm often indirectly help in arranging an interview and influence buyers to purchase a product. A successful Cadillac salesperson states:

> To do business with the boss, you must sell yourself to everyone on his staff.
> I sincerely like people—so it came naturally to me. I treat secretaries and chauffeurs as equals and friends. Ditto for switchboard operators and maids. I regularly sent small gifts to them all. An outstanding investment.
> The little people are great allies. They can't buy the product. But they can kill the sale. Who needs influential enemies? The champ doesn't want anyone standing behind him throwing rocks. In many cases, all you do is treat people decently—an act that sets you apart from 70 percent of your competitors.

Matt Suffoletto, the computer salesperson mentioned earlier, says it another way:

> I have observed one common distinction of successful salespeople. They not only call on the normal chain of people within the customer's organization, but they have periodic contact with higher level decision makers to communicate the added value which their products and services have provided. This concept, when exercised judiciously, can have a tremendous impact on your effectiveness.

Respect, trust, and friendship are three key elements in any salesperson's success. Timing is also important.

Call at the Right Time on the Right Person. Both gatekeepers and busy executives appreciate salespeople who do not waste their time. By using past sales call records or calling the prospect's receptionist, a salesperson can determine when the prospect prefers to receive visitors. Direct questions, such as asking the receptionist, "Does Mr. Smith purchase your firm's office supplies?" or "Whom should I see concerning the purchase of office supplies?" can be used in determining whom to see.

Do Not Waste Time Waiting. Once you have asked the receptionist if the prospect can see you today, you should (1) determine how long you will have to wait, and whether you can afford to wait that length of time; (2) be productive while waiting by reviewing how you will make the sales presentation to the prospect; and (3) once an acceptable amount of waiting time has passed, tell the receptionist, "I have another appointment and must leave in a moment." When politely approached, the receptionist will usually attempt to get you in. If still unable to enter the office, you can ask for an appointment as follows: "Will you please see if I can get an appointment for 10 on Tuesday?" If this request does not result in an immediate interview, it implies the establishment of another interview time. If you establish a positive relationship with a prospect and with gatekeepers, waiting time normally decreases while productivity increases.

WIRELESS E-MAIL HELPS YOU KEEP IN CONTACT AND PROSPECT

No one needs constant contact with the home office, customers, and prospects more desperately than a sales representative. Although e-mail is one of the best ways to accomplish that, adapting e-mail to meet the requirements of the itinerant sales rep has never been simple.

This is the problem that Jeff Pruss, a sales rep for Hewlett-Packard's Computer Products Organization in Pleasanton, California, faces every day. His sales team's solution is to use WyndMail for Windows to keep in touch with co-workers, customers, and prospects. "We're not very often at our desks, nor do we necessarily have a phone jack," Pruss says. "Wireless e-mail helps keep us mobile."

Pruss explains that his team chose WyndMail for several reasons. One reason was very simple: It was the only wireless e-mail program for Windows on the market at the time. A more important reason, he adds, was that Wynd Communications "was very responsive to our particular needs." For example, the first version of the address book didn't operate the way the team wanted it to—it always sorted by last name. Wynd very quickly addressed that issue, he says. "In the new version, WyndMail enables each of us to open our address books in our own preferred sort order. It feels the way we like it to feel," says Pruss.

To connect to the outside world, WyndMail uses the RAM Mobile Data network and the Internet. Some of his peers questioned WyndMail's apparently high costs, but Pruss says his co-workers "don't know what they're missing. It's worth the money."

The only "problem" with WyndMail's service, according to Pruss, is that there is only one place where the coverage hasn't been good: Lake Tahoe. "This is a good thing," he commented wryly, "because when I'm skiing, I want to relax."

SUMMARY OF MAJOR SELLING ISSUES

The sales process involves a series of actions beginning with prospecting for customers. The sales presentation is the major element of this process. Before making the presentation, the salesperson must find prospects to contact, obtain appointments, and plan the entire sales presentation.

Prospecting involves locating and qualifying the individuals or businesses that have the potential to buy a product. A person or business that might be a prospect is a *lead*. These questions can determine if someone is qualified: Is there a real need? Is the prospect aware of that need? Is there a desire to fulfill the need? Does the

ETHICAL DILEMMA

What an Offer! Or Is It?

You are a new life insurance agent and have just made a sale to an old family friend who is the personnel manager for a large manufacturing company in your town. To help you in your prospecting, he offers you a large file of personnel data on the employees of the company, including income, family size, phone numbers, and addresses.

This information would be very valuable. You are sure to make 5 to 10 sales from this excellent prospect list. As he hands you the material, you notice it is stamped, "Not for Publication, Company Use Only!"

What would be the most ethical action to take?

1. Take the information. It could really help you get started.
2. Thank your friend for the offer but refuse the information. It would not be right to accept something that is marked confidential.
3. Refuse the information and tell your friend that it was not in good practice for him to offer it. Let him know that if anything like this were to happen again, you would have to report him to the proper people in his company

prospect believe a certain product can be beneficial? Does the prospect have the finances and authority to buy? and Are potential sales large enough to be profitable to me?

Several of the more popular prospecting methods are cold canvass and endless chain methods, public exhibitions and demonstrations, locating centers of influence, direct mailouts, and telephone and observation prospecting. To obtain a continual supply of prospects, the salesperson should develop a prospecting method suitable for each situation.

Once a lead has been located and qualified as a prospect, the salesperson can make an appointment with that prospect by telephone or in person. At times, it is difficult to arrange an appointment, so the salesperson must develop ways of getting to see the prospect. Believing in yourself and feeling that you have a product the prospect needs are important.

MEETING A SALES CHALLENGE

Larry Long, John Alexander, and Kathryn Reece analyzed the proposed prospecting systems fairly well. Old customers are easy to see and know the company. However, some people will quickly point out that just because a firm buys one thing from a company does not mean that it will buy another. Xerox learned that lesson in marketing its line of word processors. Companies often are fooled by their corporate egos into thinking that their existing customers will buy just about anything they make.

Going after IBM seems to scare John for some reason. However, think a minute. Exactly what will IBM do that they won't do competitively anyway? They have some competition from all sides by many firms. If the company has a good cost story to tell, then go after the big users to whom the cost savings will be significant.

In short, all the systems have virtues and none should be excluded from consideration. New blood is needed. You can't stay in business by just relying on one set of customers. So much depends, however, on the particular territory. Some territories may have few old customers or few IBM users. The salesperson must adapt to the characteristics of the territory.

KEY TERMS FOR SELLING

SALES APPLICATION QUESTIONS

1. What is the difference between a lead and a prospect? What should you, as a salesperson, do to qualify a potential customer?
2. This chapter termed prospecting the *lifeblood of selling*.
   a. Where do salespeople find prospects?
   b. List and briefly explain seven prospecting methods discussed in this chapter. Can you think of other ways to find prospects?
3. Assume that you have started a business to manufacture and market a product line selling for between $5,000 and $10,000. your primary customers are small retailers. How would you uncover leads and convert them into prospects without personally contacting them?
4. Assume you had determined that John Firestone, vice president of Pierce Chemicals, was a prospect for your paper and metal containers. you call Mr. Firestone to see if he can see you this week. When his secretary answers the telephone, you say, "May I speak to Mr. Firestone, please?" and she says, "What is it you wish to talk to him about?" How would you answer her question? What would you say if you were told, "I'm sorry, but Mr. Firestone is too busy to talk with you?"
5. You are a new salesperson. Next week, your regional sales manager will be in town to check your progress in searching for new clients for your line of industrial chemicals. You have learned that Big Industries, Inc., a high-technology company, needs a supplier of your product. Also, a friend has told you about 12 local manufacturing firms that could use your product. The sales potential of each of these firms is about one-tenth of Big Industries. Knowing that your sales manager expects results, explain how you will qualify each lead (assuming the 12 smaller firms are similar).

FURTHER EXPLORING THE SALES WORLD

Contact several salespeople in your community and ask them to discuss their prospecting system and the steps they use in planning their sales calls. Write a short paper on your results and be prepared to discuss it in class.

SELLING EXPERIENTIAL EXERCISE

To measure your attitude toward selling, complete this exercise. On another sheet of paper write a 5 to indicate that your attitude could not be better in this area; write a 1 to indicate that you definitely do not agree. Write a 2, 3, or 4 if you are saying something in between disagree and agree.

Your Attitude toward Selling

	Disagree				Agree
1. There is nothing demeaning about selling a good or service to a prospect.	1	2	3	4	5
2. I would be proud to tell friends selling is my career.	1	2	3	4	5
3. I can approach customers, regardless of age, appearance, or behavior, with a positive attitude.	1	2	3	4	5
4. On bad days—when nothing goes right—I can still be positive.	1	2	3	4	5
5. I am enthusiastic about selling.	1	2	3	4	5
6. Having customers turn me down does not cause me to be negative.	1	2	3	4	5
7. The idea of selling challenges me.	1	2	3	4	5
8. I consider selling to be a profession.	1	2	3	4	5
9. Approaching strangers (customers) is interesting and usually enjoyable.	1	2	3	4	5
10. I can always find something good in a customer.	1	2	3	4	5

Total Score _____

Add up your score. If you scored more than 40, you have an excellent attitude toward selling as a profession. If you rated yourself between 25 and 40, you appear to have serious reservations. A rating under 25 indicates that another type of job is probably best for you.[9]

CHAPTER 7

Prospecting—The Lifeblood of Selling

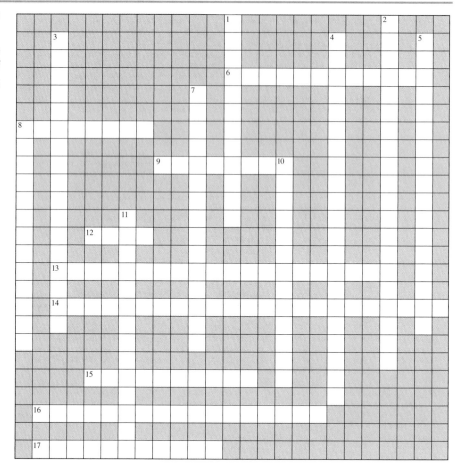

Across

6. A sequential series of actions by the salesperson that leads toward the prospect taking a desired action and ends with follow-up to ensure purchase satisfaction.

8. A prospect who has been referred to a salesperson by another person.

9. A qualified person or organization that has the potential to buy a salesperson's good or service.

12. A person or organization that might be a prospect.

13. Not only selling a product but also selling the idea of giving prospects names as well.

14. A method by which the salesperson finds and cultivates people who are willing to cooperate in helping to find prospects.

15. The continuous prospecting method of making and utilizing contacts.

16. Customers whose salesperson has left the company.

17. The process of identifying potential customers.

Down

1. A group of names, gathered from various sources, that are prospective buyers.

2. The process of reaching potential customers over the phone.

3. A prospect who has the financial resources to pay, the authority to

make the buying decision, and a desire for the product.

4. The process of mailing advertisements to a large number of people over an extended geographic area.

5. The process of finding prospects by a salesperson constantly watching what is happening in the sales area.

7. Activities and programs provided by the seller to make the relationship satisfying for the customer.

8. Provides guidelines for a salesperson to ask for referrals in four commonly faced situations experienced by salespeople.

10. A marketing communication system using telecommunication technology and trained personnel to conduct planned, measurable marketing activities directed at targeted groups of consumers.

11. Not wanting to contact a prospect or customer.

CASE 7-1
Canadian Equipment Corporation

You work for the Canadian Equipment Corporation selling office equipment. Imagine entering the lobby and reception room of a small manufacturing company. You hand the receptionist your business card and ask to see the purchasing agent. "What is this in reference to?" the secretary asks, as two other salespeople approach.

Question

Which of the following alternatives would you use and why?
a. Give a quick explanation of your equipment, ask whether the secretary has heard of your company or used your equipment, and again ask to see the purchasing agent.
b. Say, "I would like to discuss our office equipment."
c. Say, "I sell office equipment designed to save your company money and provide greater efficiency. Companies like yours really like our products. Could you help me get in to see your purchasing agent?"
d. Give a complete presentation and demonstration.

CASE 7-2
Montreal Satellites

As a salesperson for Montreal Satellites, you sell television satellite dishes for homes, apartments, and businesses. After installing a satellite in Jeff Sager's home, you ask him for a referral. Jeff suggests you contact Tom Butler, his brother-in-law.

Mr. Butler is a well-known architect who designs and constructs unique residential homes. Your objective is to sell Mr. Butler a satellite for his office and home in hopes that he will install them in the homes he builds. Certainly he is a center of influence and a good word from him to his customers could result in numerous sales. Thus, another objective is to obtain referrals from Mr. Butler.

Questions

1. After eight attempts, you now have Mr. Butler on the telephone. What would you say in order to get an appointment and set the stage for getting referrals?
2. You get the appointment and are now in Mr. Butler's office trying to get him to buy a satellite for his home and office. Sometime during the presentation you are going to ask for a referral. What would you say?

3. Mr. Butler buys a satellite for his home but not his office. You install the satellite yourself and then spend 15 minutes showing Mr. and Mrs. Butler and their two teenagers how to use it. Before you leave, how would you ask for a referral?

4. Three months after the installation you are talking to Mr. Butler. How would you ask for a referral?

8 CHAPTER

Planning the Sales Call Is a Must!

LEARNING OBJECTIVES

Planning the sales call is the second step in the selling process. It is extremely important to spend time planning all aspects of your sales presentation. After studying this chapter, you should be able to

- Explain the importance of sales call planning.

- List the four planning steps in order and understand them.

- Develop a customer benefit plan.

- Describe the prospect's five mental steps in buying.

After being hired, trained, and given a sales territory, you have been assigned by your boss to work with three of your company's salespeople. You immediately notice they are not doing what you've been trained to do. They walk into an office, introduce themselves, and ask if the customer needs anything today. Prospects rarely buy, and customers tell them what they need. This doesn't seem like selling to you. It's order taking, and that type of job is not for you.

The problem is, how do you get someone to listen to you? How do you know what they think of your product? How do you know when they're ready to buy? Next Monday, you call on your first customer. What are you going to do?

THE TREE OF BUSINESS LIFE: PLANNING

A sales manager was working with his new salesperson one day. The boss asked, "What is your purpose for calling on this prospect today?" The salesperson replied, "To sell them something?" The sales manager said "That's great, but what is your purpose?"

Begin Your Plan With Purpose!

The sales manager's question is forcing the new salesperson to create a broad philosophical statement toward a business meeting with a customer or prospect. Purpose is broad in scope. Purpose is not a list of plans, goals, or objectives that differ from one sales call to another. Purpose is a constant truth that guides your business life. Purpose directs how you approach each sales call. It defines success for you. Purpose classifies your relationships. It helps define who you are as a sales professional.

Knowing your purpose focuses your sales efforts to serve others. It concentrates your effort and energy on what is important. Knowing your purpose motivates your life and your reason to get out of bed in the morning. Purpose produces passion. Nothing energizes like a clear purpose. Conversely, passion evaporates like smoke in the wind without purpose.

Hopefully your **purpose** for making any sales call is to make a contribution to the welfare of the person or organization. You want to help someone. Could you be enthusiastic and passionate about asking someone to buy something that would help them? You want to make a contribution to the welfare of others—don't you? So how do you help someone? You need a plan that is related to your purpose.

What's a Plan?

A **plan** is a method of achieving an end. A plan involves what you want to accomplish and how you will do it. The foundation of your plan must be based upon the truth.

You see "The Tree of Business Life" from time to time as a reminder of the importance of truth. For from your honesty (integrity), people realize you can be trusted. Your honesty and trustworthiness form your character or who you are to others. Your use of facts (truth) without distortion by personal feelings or prejudices makes you like a superhero, a super salesperson. How?

You want to help someone in need! How? Sell them something? Why? It will help them meet their need. You can do that!

What Is Success?

Purpose
↓
Plan
↓
Success

With purpose comes a plan; with a plan comes success. What will be a successful sales call? How do you define success? For example:

- A baseball coach might define success as winning more games than losing. Her or his boss might define success as winning the national championship or the World Series.
- You might define success as making an "A" or just passing this course.
- A salesperson might define success as making sales quota this year or being the top salesperson in the company.

But what about calling on the individual customer? What is a success for you? It goes back to purpose. **Success** is setting a goal and accomplishing it. You are meeting with someone with the purpose of helping him or her. Your purpose, plan, and goal do not center on selling but helping. Can you fail?

Successful but No Sale

How could you "not" make a sale and still have a successful sales call? What if your customer did not have a need? You did not fail. What if your product would not help meet the needs of the person? How could you say you were not successful?

Now consider this. There are reasons you may not make a sale. Agreed? But there should never be a reason that you do not meet the "purpose" of your business meeting. Why? What is your purpose? To help someone!

Review Until You Understand

This section of your book is so important to your understanding that I hope you will take time to review it several times during the next few days. The fundamentals taught in this book will benefit you only when you believe in them. You must learn these words of truth. They must guide your actions. They must come from your heart. When you truly are a person of integrity, truthfulness, and good character, people's needs will become more important than your self-centered needs.

The Gap

Many people do not trust salespeople. Often salespeople are self-centered, only wanting to make a sale for their own benefit. How can the gap between seller and buyer be crossed? The seller has to build a bridge!

Exhibit 8.1 illustrates the gap often found between buyer and seller. Imagine the buyer on the right wondering if he can trust the seller. Only through truth can trust be supported to bridge the gap between people—seller and buyer. Truth that is without distortion due to personal feelings or prejudices is the center pole supporting trust.

Remove truth and the bridge collapses. There can be no long-term relationships between two parties without trust based upon truth. One lie, one misrepresentation, can lead to separation, even divorce between seller and buyer. Has that ever happened to you in your life?

Before ever making the sales call, the salesperson reviews the purpose for the meeting. Now the salesperson plans how to help solve problems and fulfill the needs of the person or organization. Careful planning of every aspect of the sales call helps the salesperson be organized and prepared to interact with the customer. For each prospect or customer a salesperson is often faced with a specific, unique

EXHIBIT 8.1

Only through truth can trust be supported to bridge the gap between people.

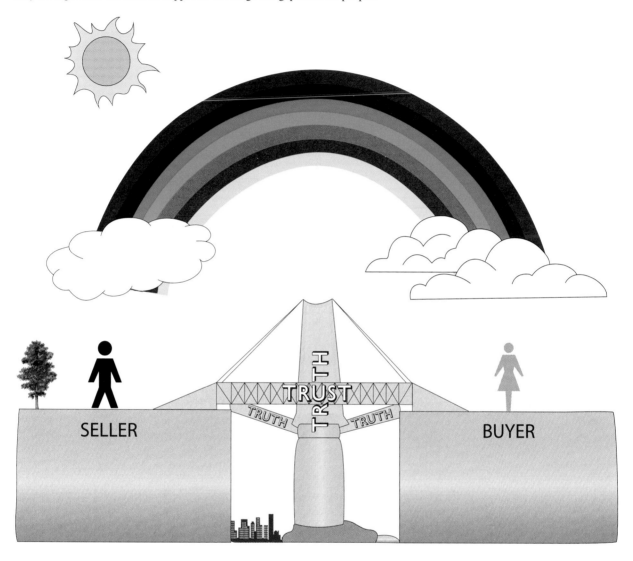

set of problems to solve or needs to fulfill. As a result, each sales call requires a specific solution from the salesperson. You plan in order to help. Planning is part of ethical service which leads to building relationships with the customer.

STRATEGIC CUSTOMER SALES PLANNING—THE PREAPPROACH

Once the prospect has been located, or the salesperson determines which customer to call on, the salesperson is ready to plan the sales call. Planning is often referred to as the preapproach (see Exhibit 8.2). This chapter discusses the many aspects of planning a sales call. Let's begin by learning why salespeople should consider the customer's needs in order to recommend a creative solution that will benefit both the buyer and seller.

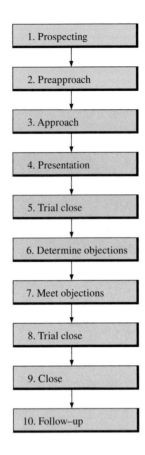

EXHIBIT 8.2

The preapproach involves
planning the sales presentation.

1. Prospecting

2. Preapproach

3. Approach

4. Presentation

5. Trial close

6. Determine objections

7. Meet objections

8. Trial close

9. Close

10. Follow–up

High-performing salespeople tend to be strategic problem solvers for their customers (refer back to Exhibit 1.8). **Strategic** refers to programs, goals, and problems of great importance to customers. The top salespeople who are effective strategic problem solvers have the skills and knowledge to be able to

- Uncover and understand the customer's strategic needs by gaining in-depth knowledge of the customer's organization.
- Develop solutions that demonstrate a creative approach to addressing the customer's strategic needs in the most efficient and effective manner possible.
- Arrive at a mutually beneficial agreement.

These key terms—strategic needs, creative solutions, and mutually beneficial agreements—are critical to strategic problem solving. When properly excuted by the salesperson, they create a **strategic customer relationship** or a formal relationship with the customer, the purpose of which is joint pursuit of mutual goals. Strategic goals for a customer typically include reducing costs and/or increasing productivity, sales, and profits. The sales organization has goals of increasing sales and profits.

Strategic Needs   The salesperson who understands the full range of the customer's needs is in a much better position to provide a product solution that helps the customer progress more efficiently and effectively toward achieving his or her organization's strategic goal. "The top salespeople have an in-depth understanding of our needs," said one business purchasing agent. "They can match up their products with these needs to help us reach our goals."

Creative Solutions

The difference between the ordinary and the extraordinary is the little extra effort.

For each customer, a salesperson is often faced with a specific, unique set of problems to solve. As a result, each customer requires a specific solution from the sales organization. The ability of a salesperson to tailor a "custom" solution for each customer is critical today. The salesperson needs to use creative problem solving to identify the specific solution that meets each customer's needs. Instead of one product, the salesperson often must create the solution from a mix of goods and services. Usually, the solution represents one of two options:

1. A customized version or application of a product and/or service that efficiently addresses the customer's specific strategic needs.
2. A mix of goods and services—including, if appropriate, competitors' products and services—that offers the best possible solution in light of the customer's strategic needs.

The better a salesperson is at creatively marshaling all available resources to address a customer's strategic needs, the stronger the customer relationship becomes. Today's salespeople need to be **creative problem solvers** who have the ability to develop and combine nontraditional alternatives to meet the specific needs of the customer.

Mutually Beneficial Agreements

Salespeople and customers say that a significant shift has occurred in their expectations of the outcome of sales agreements—from the adversarial "win–lose" to the more collaborative "win–win" arrangement. To achieve a mutually beneficial agreement, salespeople and customers must work together to develop a common understanding of the issues and challenges at hand.

Information about an organization's business strategies and needs is often highly confidential. But more and more customers, in the interest of developing solutions that will help achieve their strategic goals, are willing to let salespeople cross the threshold of confidentiality.

The Customer Relationship Model

The customer relationship model shown in Exhibit 8.3 brings together the main elements of consultative selling. It shows that customers have strategic needs that salespeople must meet through creative solutions. In doing so, both buyer and seller

---

EXHIBIT 8.3

Consultative selling—customer relationship model.

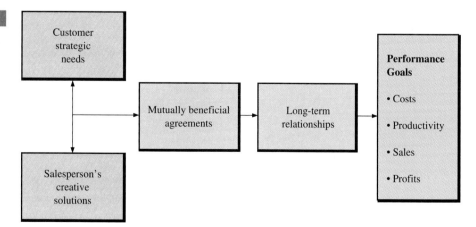

benefit. The customer reaches his/her goal, as does the seller. This results in the seller being able to sell the customer again and again and again—building a long-term relationship. Strategic customer sales planning is extremely important to the success of today's salespeople. Let's examine the important aspects of the second step in our customer relationship process, called the preapproach. The **preapproach** refers to planning the sales call on a customer or prospect.

Reasons for Planning the Sales Call

In the fairy tale *Alice in Wonderland* Alice said to the Cheshire Cat, "Would you tell me, please, which way I ought to go from here?" "That depends a good deal on where you want to get to," said the Cat. "I don't much care where . . . ," said Alice. "Then it doesn't matter which way you go," said the Cat.[1] Top salespeople realize they cannot be like Alice. They live in the real world, not wonderland.

Planning the sales call is the key to success (see Exhibit 8.4). Salespeople say there are numerous reasons for planning the sales call, and four of the most frequently mentioned reasons are (1) planning aids in building confidence; (2) it develops an atmosphere of goodwill between the buyer and seller; (3) it reflects professionalism; and (4) it generally increases sales because the salesperson understands the buyer's needs.

Builds Self-Confidence

In giving a speech before a large group, most people are nervous. You can greatly reduce this nervousness and increase self-confidence by planning what to say and practicing your talk. The same is true in making a sales presentation. By carefully planning your presentation, you increase confidence in yourself and your ability as a salesperson. This is why planning the sales call is especially important.

Develops an Atmosphere of Goodwill

The salesperson who understands a customer's needs and is prepared to discuss how a product will benefit the prospect is appreciated and respected by the buyer. Knowledge of a prospect and concern for the prospect's needs demonstrate a sincere interest in a prospect that generally is rewarded with an attitude of goodwill from the prospect. This goodwill gradually builds the buyer's confidence and results in a belief that the salesperson can be trusted to fulfill obligations.

EXHIBIT 8.4

Planning is the key to success.

The sales team rehearses an upcoming sales call.

Creates Professionalism

> *"You don't have to be great to start, but you have to start to be great. Start by planning."*
>
> JOE SABAH

Good business relationships are built on your knowledge of your company, industry, and customer's needs. Show prospects that you are calling on them to help solve their problems or satisfy their needs. These factors are the mark of a professional salesperson, who uses specialized knowledge in an ethical manner to aid customers.

Increases Sales

A confident salesperson who is well prepared to discuss how products address particular needs always will be more successful than the unprepared salesperson. Careful planning ensures that you have diagnosed a situation and have a remedy for a customer's problem. Planning ensures that a sales presentation is well thought out and appropriately presented.

Like other beneficial presales call activities, planning is most effective (and time efficient) when done logically and methodically. Some salespeople try what they consider planning, later discarding the process because it took too much time. In many cases, these individuals were not aware of the basic elements of sales planning.

Elements of Sales Call Planning

Exhibit 8.5 depicts the four components of **sales call planning:** (1) determining the sales call objective; (2) developing or reviewing the customer profile; (3) developing a customer benefit plan; and (4) developing the individual sales presentation based on the sales call objective, customer profile, and customer benefit plan.

Always Have a Sales Call Objective

The **sales call objective** is the main purpose of a salesperson's contact with a prospect or customer.

Is it possible to make a sales call without having a sales call objective in mind? Why can't salespeople just go in and see what develops? They can: in fact, a survey call is a legitimate sales technique. However, when all the calls that salespeople make are survey calls, they should be working exclusively for the market research department.

The Precall Objective

Selling is not a very complex process. It's just difficult to do on a consistent basis. That's why, whether you regard it as an art or a science, the discipline of selling starts with setting a precall objective.

If anyone doubts this, remember that, by definition, a sales call must move systematically toward a sale. Often, we're not talking about elaborate planning. Sometimes it only takes a few seconds before a call. But on every occasion, it's vital for the sales representative to answer one simple question: "If this call is successful, what will result?"

Taking the time to do this starts the selling process in motion. Before every sales call, ask yourself, "What am I going in here for? What is the result I'm trying to make happen? If they give me the opportunity, what am I going to recommend?"

EXHIBIT 8.5

Steps in the preapproach: planning the sale.

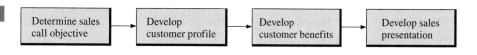

Determine sales call objective → Develop customer profile → Develop customer benefits → Develop sales presentation

Focus and Flexibility

Writing down your precall objective increases the focus of your efforts. Given today's rising costs, this focus is essential. If salespeople are just going around visiting customers to see what develops, they are merely well-paid tourists. If they are professional sales representatives, they should be moving their customers toward a predetermined goal.

Knowing where you are going definitely increases the likelihood of getting there. Obviously, if the precall objective turns out to be inappropriate as the sales call develops, it's easy to switch tactics. Often, such changes involve a simple redirection.

Making the Goal Specific

When asked the purpose of a call, some salespeople say enthusiastically, "It's to get an order. Let's go!" Of course, everyone's in favor of getting orders, but that's more likely to happen if salespeople stop and ask themselves questions such as these: What need of this prospect can I serve? Which good or service is best for this account? How large an order should I suggest? The more specific the objective, the better.

Moving toward Your Objective

Just because a salesperson isn't making a formal presentation doesn't mean that the call shouldn't be planned. Sometimes the sales call has a limited objective. Guiding the customer in the direction of that preplanned outcome is what I see experienced salespeople doing on most sales calls. They do it with such simple questions as these:

- If we can meet the spec, can you set up a trial?
- How soon will the vice president be available to make a decision?
- Can you schedule a demonstration before the end of the month?

Set an Objective for Every Call

Don't let anyone tell you that selling is so repetitive that the next step becomes a matter of rote. Knowing where you are going may be rote, but getting there requires thinking and skill. Set a **SMART** call objective that is

Be SMART about planning.

Specific—to get an order is *not* specific.

Measurable—quantifiable (number, size, etc.).

Achievable—not too difficult to fulfill.

Realistic—not too easy to fulfill.

Timed—at this call or before the end of the financial year.

It's amazing how often even veteran salespeople skip the precall objective step in favor of just seizing whatever opportunities present themselves. As a professional, it's your responsibility to avoid this kind of behavior. Commit to having an objective for every call, and after a call check your results against that objective. This is a simple truth that the best sales professionals have known all along. Often the most important step in a sale takes place without the customer even being there.

In addition, the sales call objective should be directly beneficial to the customer. For example, the Colgate salesperson might have the objectives of checking all merchandise, having the customer make a routine reorder on merchandise, and selling promotional quantities of Colgate toothpaste.

The Colgate salesperson might call on a chain store manager with the multiple objectives of making sure that Colgate products are placed where they sell most rapidly; replenishing the store's stock of Colgate products so that customers will not leave the store disgruntled due to stockouts, and aiding the manager in deciding how much promotional Colgate toothpaste and Rapid Shave shaving cream should be displayed.

Industrial salespeople develop similar objectives to determine if customers need to reorder or to sell new products.

Customer Profile Provides Insight

A customer profile sheet, as shown in Exhibit 8.6, can be a guide for determining the appropriate strategy to use in contacting each customer. The salesperson should review as much relevant information as possible regarding the firm, the buyer, and the individuals who influence the buying decision—before making a sales call—to

EXHIBIT 8.6

Information used in a profile and for planning.

Customer Profile and Planning Sheet

1. Name: _____
   Address: _____
2. Type of business: _____
   Name of buyer: _____
3. People who influence buying decisions or aid in
   using or selling our product: _____
4. Buying hours and best time to see buyer: _____
5. Receptionist's name: _____
6. Buyer's profile: _____
7. Buyer's personality style: _____
8. Sales call objectives: _____
9. What are customer's important buying needs: _____
10. Sales presentation: _____
    a. Sales approach: _____
    b. Features, advantages, benefits: _____
    c. Method of demonstrating FAB: _____
    d. How to relate benefits to customer's needs: _____
    e. Trial close to use: _____
    f. Anticipated objections: _____
    g. Trial close to use: _____
    h. How to close this customer: _____
    i. Hard or soft close: _____
11. Sales made—product use/promotional plan agreed on:
    _____
12. Post–sales call comments (reason did/did not buy, what to do on next call; follow-up
    promised): _____

properly develop a customized presentation. The salesperson also must consider the material discussed in Chapter 4 concerning why the buyer buys at this time. A **customer profile** should tell you such things as these:

- Who makes the buying decisions in the organization—an individual or committee?
- What is the buyer's background? The background of the buyer's company? The buyer's expectations of you?
- What are the desired business terms and requirements of the account, such as delivery, credit, technical service?
- What competitors successfully do business with the account? Why?
- What are the purchasing policies and practices of the account? For example, does the customer buy special price offer promotions, or only see salespeople on Tuesdays and Thursdays?
- What is the history of the account? For example, past purchases of our products, inventory turnover, profit per shelf foot, our brand's volume sales growth, payment practices, and attitude toward resale prices.

Determine this information from a review of records on the company or through personal contact with the company.

Customer Benefit Plan: What It's All About!

Beginning with your sales call objectives and what you know about your prospect, you are ready to develop a **customer benefit plan.** The customer benefit plan contains the nucleus of the information used in your sales presentation; thus it should be developed to the best of your ability. Remember to consider the Golden Rule in your customer benefit plan by incorporating this four-step process:

Step 1. Select the features, advantages, and benefits of your product to present to your prospect. (See Chapter 4.) This addresses the issue of why the buyer should purchase your product. The main reason the prospect should purchase your product is that its benefits fulfill certain needs or solve certain problems. Carefully determine the benefits you wish to present.

Step 2. Develop your marketing plan. If selling to wholesalers or retailers, your marketing plan should include how, once they buy, they will sell your product to their customers. An effective marketing plan includes suggestions on how a retailer, for example, should promote the product through displays, advertising, proper shelf space and positioning, and pricing.

Did you hear the story of the guy who went into a small grocery store and asked the owner if he had any salt? "Do I have salt!?" shouted the grocer. He showed the shopper shelves full of salt and then took him to the storeroom and showed him boxes of salt saying, "Do I have salt!?" Next they went to the basement to see more boxes where the grocer again exclaimed, "Do I have salt!?"

Do you think the grocer will buy more salt when the salesperson returns? Chances are he will want to return salt, not buy it. To help this grocer generate revenue to pay his rent and employees, the salt salesperson must help him sell salt. How? Well, maybe give away a box of 39-cent salt with each purchase over $5. This might draw more customers into the store. In consumer sales with national companies it is often easy to sell the customer. If the customer cannot sell what you sold, then, you

EXHIBIT 8.7

Examples of topics contained in the marketing plan segment of your sales presentation.

Resellers	End-Users
1. Advertising	1. Availability
■ Geographic	2. Delivery
–National	3. Guarantee
–Regional	4. Installation
–Local	■ Who does it?
–Co-op	■ When?
■ Type	■ How?
–Television	5. Maintenance/service
–Radio	6. Training on use
–Direct-mail	7. Warranty
–Internet	
2. Sales Promotion	
■ Contests	
■ Coupons	
■ Demonstrations	
■ Samples	
■ Sweepstakes	
■ POP displays	
3. Sales Force	
■ Working with their salespeople	
4. Trade Shows	

will not sell anything. So follow the Golden Rule providing strategies on selling through to the reseller's customers.

For an end-user of the product, such as the company that buys your manufacturing equipment, computer, or photocopier, develop a program showing how your product is most effectively used or coordinated with existing equipment.

Exhibit 8.7 has other examples of topics often discussed in the marketing plan segment of your sales presentation. Many of these topics were discussed in Chapter 6.

Step 3. Develop your business proposition, which includes items such as price, percent markup, forecasted profit per square foot of shelf space, return on investment, and payment plan. Value analysis is an example of a business proposition for an industrial product. Other examples of topics discussed in the business proposition segment of your sales presentation are shown in Exhibit 8.8.

Step 4. Develop a suggested purchase order based on a customer benefit plan. A proper presentation of your customer needs analysis and your product's ability to fulfill these needs, along with a satisfactory business proposition and marketing plan, allows you to justify to the prospect what product and/or how much to purchase. This suggestion may include, depending on your product, such things as what to buy, how much to buy, what assortment to buy, and when to ship the product to the customer.

You should also develop visual aids to effectively communicate the information developed in these four steps. The visuals should be organized in the order you discuss them. Your next step is to plan all aspects of the sales presentation.

EXHIBIT 8.8

Examples of topics contained in the business proposition segment of your sales presentation.

Resellers	End-Users
1. List price	1. List price
2. Shipping costs	2. Shipping costs
3. Discounts	3. Discounts
■ Cash	■ Cash
■ Consumer	■ Quantity
■ Quantity	4. Financing
■ Trade	■ Payment plans
■ Financing	■ Interest rates
–Payment plans	5. ROI
–Interest rate	6. Value analysis
4. Markup	
5. Profit	

The Sales Presentation Is Where It All Comes Together

It is now time to plan your **sales presentation** from beginning to end. This process involves developing steps 3 to 9 of the sales presentation described in Exhibit 8.2: the approach, presentation, and trial close method to uncover objections; ways to overcome objections; additional trial closes; and the close of the sales presentation. Each step is discussed in the following chapters.

New salespeople often ask their sales trainers to be more specific on how to construct the sales presentation. In addition to the 10 steps in the selling process shown in Exhibit 8.2, they ask, "What's involved in the presentation itself?" Exhibit 8.9 summarizes the major phases within the sales presentation. Before briefly discussing them, let's review a few things.

Before developing your presentation, you need to determine the prospect or customer to call on; make an appointment; and then plan the sales call. This process is shown in Exhibit 7.2. The steps in planning the call are shown in Exhibit 8.5. Now that we know whom we will call on and what our objective will be, it's time to plan out and prepare the sales presentation itself.

The major phases within the presentation are shown in Exhibit 8.9. Please understand that Exhibit 8.9 is more specific than Exhibit 8.2 in showing the selling process steps. You should plan out everything that is included in Exhibit 8.9. You should also do each phase in the exact order shown in Exhibit 8.9 in order to create a well-organized presentation.

Here's how you create the presentation. Based on the homework you have done on the prospect or customer, create the opening (approach) of the presentation. This is discussed in Chapter 10. Then prepare your FABs, marketing plan, and business proposition. They were discussed earlier in this chapter and in previous chapters. Based on what you feel the customer should buy, prepare a suggested purchase order and choose a closing method that feels natural for you to use when asking for the business. Should you make the sale or not make the sale, it is important to know how to exit the buyer's office. Closing the sale and the exit are discussed in Chapter 13.

Visual aids and demonstrations should be used to help create an informative and persuasive sales presentation. As mentioned earlier, the *last step* in planning your sales call is the development and rehearsal of the sales presentation.

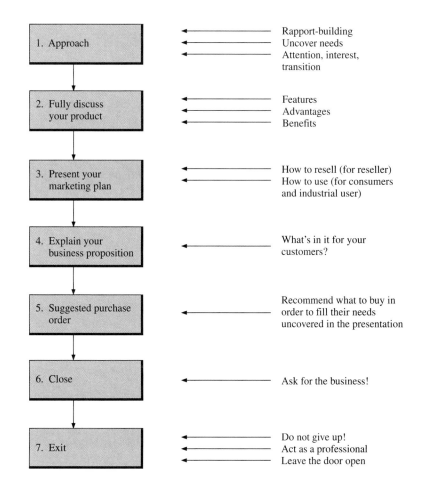

EXHIBIT 8.9

Major phases in your presentation: a sequence of events to complete in developing a sale presentation.

In developing the sales presentation, think of leading the prospect through the five steps or phases that salespeople believe constitute a purchase decision. These phases are referred to as the prospect's mental steps.

THE PROSPECT'S MENTAL STEPS

In making a sales presentation, consider the **prospect's mental steps:** quickly obtain the prospect's full attention, develop interest in your product, create a desire to fulfill a need, establish the prospect's conviction that the product fills a need, and finally, promote action by having the prospect purchase the product. As shown in Exhibit 8.10, these steps occur in the following order.

Attention

From the moment you begin to talk, quickly capture and maintain the prospect's **attention.** This may be difficult at times because of distractions, pressing demands on the prospect's time, or lack of interest. Carefully plan what to say and how to say it. Since attention-getters have only a temporary effect, be ready to quickly move to Step 2, sustaining the prospect's interest.

Interest

Before meeting with prospects, determine their important buying motives. These can be used in capturing **interest.** If you don't do this ahead of time you may have to determine them at the beginning of your presentation by asking questions. Prospects

EXHIBIT 8.10

The prospect's five mental steps in buying.

Attention → Interest → Desire → Conviction → Purchase

enter the interest stage if they listen to and enter into a discussion with you. Quickly strive to link your product's benefits to prospects' needs. If this link is completed, prospects usually express a desire for the product.

Desire

"Friendship is one heart in two bodies. Strive to make the other person's desires come true."

JOESPH ZABARA

Using the FAB formula (Chapter 4), strive to bring prospects from lukewarm interest to a boiling **desire** for your product. Desire is created when prospects express a wish or wanting for a product like yours.

To better determine if they should purchase the product, prospects may have questions for you and may present objections to your product. Anticipate prospects' objections and provide information to maintain their desire.

Conviction

While prospects may desire a product, they still have to be convinced that your product is best for their needs and that you are the best supplier of the product. In the **conviction** step, strive to develop a strong *belief* that the product is best suited to prospects' specific needs. Conviction is established when no doubts remain about purchasing the product from you.

Purchase or Action

Once the prospect is convinced, plan the most appropriate method of asking the prospect to make a **purchase** or take some **action.** If each of the preceding steps has been implemented correctly, closing the sale is the easiest step in the sales presentation.

OVERVIEW OF THE SELLING PROCESS

We have briefly discussed the various steps in the selling process, reviewed the sales presentation, and examined the five mental steps a prospect moves through while purchasing a product. Each step will be examined in more depth later, along with methods and techniques that successful salespeople use to lead the prospect to make the correct purchase decision. Exhibit 8.11 presents an overview of the selling process and gives corresponding examples of the prospect's mental stages and questions that may be posed at various points during the presentation.

The presentation's approach gets the prospect's attention and interest by having the prospect recognize a need or problem and state a wish to fulfill the need or solve the problem. The presentation constantly maintains interest in the information you present and generates desire for the product.

Uncovering and answering the prospect's questions and revealing and meeting or overcoming objections results in more intense desire. This desire is transformed into the conviction that your product can fulfill the prospect's needs or solve problems. Once you have determined that the prospect is in the conviction stage, you are ready for the close.

ETHICAL DILEMMA

To Check, or Not to Check . . .

You have been working part-time for a large national department store chain for the past year. Your store, like others in the mall, has been experiencing a higher than normal amount of shoplifting. Store management has hired off-duty police wearing street clothes to walk around the store as if shopping and arrest thieves. The store manager strongly enforces the store policy that all people caught will be arrested.

For several months, you have suspected a fellow salesperson of taking office supplies home on a frequent basis. You have overlooked these discrepancies because she helped you learn the ropes when you started, and you believe that everyone takes a supply or two on occasion. Today, you saw the person take a damaged jogging suit, give the customer credit, and then put it in a store bag and place it under the counter. That night, as you were both leaving, the person had the bag with something in it. It could be the jogging suit

or just something that your co-worker purchased earlier. You want to know if the jogging suit is in the bag, but you also know that if it is the jogging suit, the store manager will prosecute her.

What would be the most ethical action to take?

1. Take your manager aside and tell him/her what you witnessed. Let your manager handle the situation from there since it is potentially dangerous.
2. Do nothing. It is not your responsibility to investigate the situation. Let your manager find out him/herself.
3. Pull the person aside and explain that you thought you saw him/her put something in the bag. Let your coworker know that you aren't going to tell anyone if it is true, but that the person should really stop to avoid jeopardizing her or his job.

EXHIBIT 8.11

The selling process and examples of prospect's mental thoughts and questions.

Steps in the Selling Process	Prospect's Mental Steps	Prospect's Potential Verbal and Mental Questions
1. Prospecting Salesperson locates and qualifies prospects.		
2. Preapproach Salesperson determines sales call objective and develops customer profile, customer benefit program, and selling strategies. Customer's needs are determined.		
3. Approach Salesperson obtains interview, meets prospect, and begins individualized sales presentation. Needs are further uncovered.	*Attention* due to arousal of potential need or problem. *Interest* due to recognized need or problem and the desire to fulfill the need or solve the problem.	Should I see salesperson? Should I continue to listen, interact, devote much time to a salesperson? What's in it for me?
4. Presentation Salesperson relates product benefits to needs, using demonstration, dramatizations, visuals, and proof statements.	*Interest* in information that provides knowledge and influences perceptions and attitude. *Desire* begins to develop based on information evaluation of product features,	Is the salesperson prepared? Are my needs understood? Is the seller interested in my needs? Should I continue to listen and interact? So what? (to statements about features)

(continued)

EXHIBIT 8.11   *(concluded)*

Steps in the Selling Process	Prospect's Mental Steps	Prospect's Potential Verbal and Mental Questions
	advantages, and benefits. This is due to forming positive attitudes that product may fulfill need or solve problem. Positive attitudes brought about by knowledge obtained from presentation.	Prove it! (to statements about advantages) Are the benefits of this product the best to fulfill my needs?
5. Trial Close Salesperson asks prospect's opinion on benefits during and after presentation.	*Desire* continues based on information evaluation.	
6. Objections Salesperson uncovers objections	*Desire* continues based on information evaluation.	Do I understand the salesperson's marketing plan and business proposition? I need more information to make a decision. Can you meet my conditions?
7. Meet Objections Salesperson satisfactorily answers objections.	*Desire* begins to be transformed into belief. *Conviction* established due to belief the product and salesperson can solve needs or problems better than competitive products. Appears ready to buy.	Let me see the reaction when I give the salesperson a hard time. I have a minor/major objection to what you are saying. Is something nonverbal being communicated? Did I get a reasonable answer to my objection?
8. Trial Close Salesperson uses another trial close to see if objections have been overcome or, if presentation went smoothly before the close, to determine if the prospect is ready to buy.	*Conviction* becomes stronger.	Can I believe and trust this person? Should I reveal my real concerns?
9. Close Salesperson has determined prospect is ready to buy and now asks for the order.	*Action* (purchase) occurs based on positive beliefs that the product will fulfill needs or solve problems.	I am asked to make a buying decision now. If I buy and I am dissatisfied, what can I do? Will I receive after-the-sale service as promised? What are my expectations toward this purchase? Why don't you ask me to buy? Ask one more time and I'll buy.
10. Follow-up Salesperson provides customer service after the sale.	*Satisfaction–Dissatisfaction*	Did the product meet my expectations? Am I experiencing dissonance? How is the service associated with this product? Should I buy again from this salesperson?

SUMMARY OF MAJOR SELLING ISSUES

Most salespeople agree that careful planning of the sales call is essential to success in selling. Among many reasons why planning is so important, four of the most frequently mentioned are that planning builds self-confidence, develops an atmosphere of goodwill, creates professionalism, and increases sales. By having a logical and methodical plan, you can decide what to accomplish and then later measure your accomplishments with your plan.

There are four basic elements of sales call planning. First, you must always have a sales call objective—one that is specific, measurable, and beneficial to the customer. Second, as a salesperson, you must also develop or review the customer profile. By having relevant information about your customer, you can properly develop a customized presentation. You can find information on the background, needs, and competitors of your potential buyer by reviewing your company's records or by personally contacting the buyer and the company.

The third step in planning your sales call involves developing your customer benefit plan. To do this, look at why the prospect should purchase your product and develop a marketing plan to convey those reasons and the benefits to your prospect. Then, develop a *business proposition* by listing your price, percent markup, return on investment, and other quantitative data about your product in relation to your prospect. Lastly, develop a *suggested purchase order* and present your analysis, which might include suggestions on what to buy, how much to buy, what assortment to buy, and when to ship the product.

Finally, plan your whole sales presentation. Visual aids can help make your presentation informative and creative. In making your call, think in terms of the phases that make up a purchase decision—the mental steps: capturing the prospect's attention, determining buying motives, creating desire, convincing the person that your product is best suited to her or his needs, and then closing the sale.

By adhering to these guidelines for planning your sales presentation, you may spend more time planning than on the actual sales call. However, it will be well worth it.

MEETING A SALES CHALLENGE

The purpose of your sales presentation is to provide information so the prospect can make a rational, informed buying decision. You provide this information using your FABs, marketing plan, and business approval.

The information you provide allows the buyer to develop positive personal *beliefs* toward your product. The beliefs result in *desire* (or *need*) for the type of product you sell. Your job, as a salesperson, is to convert that need into a want and into the *attitude* that your product is the best product to fulfill a certain need. Furthermore, you must convince the buyer not only that your product is the best, but that you are the best source to buy from. When this occurs, your prospect has moved into the *conviction* stage of the mental buying process. Listen and watch for it.

When a real need is established, the buyer will want to fulfill that need, and there is a high probability that he or she will choose your product. Whether to buy or not is a "choice decision," and you provide the necessary information so that the customer chooses to buy from you.

When you are prepared, the prospect or customers recognize it. This gives you a better chance of giving your presentation and thus increases your sales, because the more presentations given, the more people sold. Veteran salespeople have a tendency to not prepare. Many get lazy and fall into a bad habit of "winging it." Top sales professionals rarely are unprepared. Do you want to be an order taker or an order getter? Your success is entirely up to you!

KEY TERMS FOR SELLING

purpose   255
plan   255
success   256
strategic   258
strategic customer relationship   258
creative problem solvers   259
preapproach   260
sales call planning   261
sales call objective   261

customer profile   264
customer benefit plan   264
sales presentation   266
prospect's mental steps   267
attention   267
interest   267
desire   268
conviction   268
purchase or action   268

SALES APPLICATION QUESTIONS

1. What are the elements to consider when planning a sales call? Explain each one.

2. An important part of planning a sales call is the development of a customer benefit plan. What are the major components of the customer benefit plan? What is the difference in developing a customer benefit plan for a General Foods salesperson selling consumer products versus an industrial salesperson selling products for a company such as IBM?

3. Many salespeople feel a prospect goes through several mental steps in making a decision to purchase a product. Discuss each one of these steps.

4. Outline and discuss the sequence of events in developing a sales presentation.

5. Some salespeople feel a person should not be asked to buy a product until the prospect's mind has entered the conviction step of the mental process. Why?

6. What is the difference, if any, between the selling process and the sales presentation?

7. Define the term *selling process*. Second, list the major steps in the selling process on the left side of a piece of paper. Third, beside each step of the selling process, write the corresponding mental step that a prospect should experience.

8. Below are 13 situations salespeople commonly face. For each situation, determine the mental buying stage that your prospect is experiencing. Give a reason why the prospect is at that stage.

   a. "Come on in; I can only visit with you for about five minutes."
   b. "That sounds good, but how can I be sure it will do what you say it will?"
   c. "Yes, I see your copier can make 20 copies a minute and copy on both sides of the page. Big deal!"
   d. The buyer thinks, "Will the purchase of this equipment help my standing with my boss?"
   e. "I didn't know there were products like this on the market."
   f. The buyer thinks, "I'm not sure if I should listen or not."
   g. "I wish my equipment could do what yours does."
   h. "Well, that sounds good, but I'm not sure."
   i. "What kind of great deal do you have for me today?"
   j. "When can you ship it?"
   k. You discuss your business proposition with your buyer, and you receive a favorable nonverbal response.
   l. "I like what you have to say. Your deal sounds good. But I'd better check with my other suppliers first."

m. You have completed your presentation. The buyer has said almost nothing to you, asking no questions and giving no objections. You wonder if you should close.

9. Think of a product sold through one of your local supermarkets. Assume you were recently hired by the product's manufacturer to contact the store's buyer to purchase a promotional quantity of your product and to arrange for display and advertising. What information do you need for planning the sales call, and what features, advantages, and benefits would be appropriate in your sales presentation?

FURTHER EXPLORING THE SALES WORLD

Ask a buyer for a business in your community what salespeople should do when calling on a buyer. Find out if the salespeople that this buyer sees are prepared for each sales call. Ask why or why not the buyer purchases something. Do salespeople use the FAB method as discussed in this chapter? Does the buyer think privately, "So what?" "Prove it!" and "What's in it for me?" Finally, ask what superiors expect of a buyer in the buyer's dealing with salespeople.

SELLING EXPERIENTIAL EXERCISE

SMART Course Objective Setting

Do you set objectives for each of your classes? Are your course objectives SMART—specific, measurable, achievable, realistic, and timed? Salespeople set objectives for each customer. Would you consider setting objectives for each class, constantly measuring your performance, and reevaluating your progress toward the objective? You can do this by answering the questions in Exhibit 8.12.

Enough time has passed in your selling course that you have one or more grades. Let's assume you want to make an "A" in the class. Ask your instructor or see your class syllabus for the total points you can earn in your sales course. Assuming no curve, multiply the maximum points by 0.9. If you can earn a maximum of 1,000 points, then you only need 900 points for an 'A.' Your goal now becomes a total score of 900 points on all graded activities.

Subtract the total points you have earned so far from the number of points needed to reach your objective—900 points. How many remaining test(s) and assignment(s) are ahead? Determine if you can reach your course grade objective by making an 80, 90, or 95 percent average on all remaining test(s) and assignment(s). Each time

---

EXHIBIT 8.12

SMART course objective setting.

- What grade do you want to make in this course? Write on this line _____.
- How many points do you have to earn in this class to reach your objective? _____.
  (Total points multiplied by 0.9. See your syllabus for total course points.)
- How many points do you now have in the course? _____.
- How many points do you need to earn to reach your objective? _____.
- Can you reach your objective? _____Yes; _____No.
- On a scale of 1 to 10—with 10 being the maximum effort—how hard are you willing to work in this course to reach your objective? Be honest with yourself. My "effort score" will be _____.
- In your class notes, write a statement explaining how you will reach your grade objective.

you receive a grade for a major assignment, recalculate your progress toward scoring 900 points and making your "A."

As in sales, usually a person's class performance is a function of their ability and motivation. This is why class performance is a function (f) of an individual's ability times motivation, or

Class performance = f(Ability $\times$ Motivation)

Now for the most important question of all. The answer to this question will determine your future grade in this or any class. "How hard are you willing to work in reaching your course grade objective?" On a scale of 1 to 10—with 10 being the maximum effort—how hard are you willing to work in this course to reach your objective.

Be honest with yourself! Write it down! This is important, write it down, please.

My effort score is _____ (1 to 10).

Each time you recalculate your progress toward your goal of making an "A" in this class, reconsider your "effort score." Write down all future "effort scores." See if over time your "effort score" begins to decline, increase, or stay the same.

STUDENT APPLICATION LEARNING EXERCISES (SALES)

At the end of appropriate chapters beginning with Chapter 4, you will find Student Application Learning Exercises (SALES). SALES are meant to help you construct the various segments of your sales presentation. SALES build upon one another so that after you complete them, you will have constructed the majority of your sales presentation.

(Sale 3 of 7)

In planning the sales presentation, it is necessary to create a marketing plan. Review the section beginning on page 264 entitled "Customer Benefit Plan: What It's All About." The marketing plan is described in Step 2 on page 264. Stop your study on page 265. Carefully study: Exhibits 8.6, 8.7, and 8.8. Review the advertising and sales promotion sections contained in pages 185–189. To make **SALE 3:**

1. List three **FABs** you could discuss in your marketing plan.

Feature	Advantage	Benefit
a.		
b.		
c.		

2. Write out one **SELL Sequence** using the **FABs.** Label each of the components of the **SELL Sequence** using parentheses as shown on page 119.

CHAPTER 8

Planning the Sales Call Is a Must!

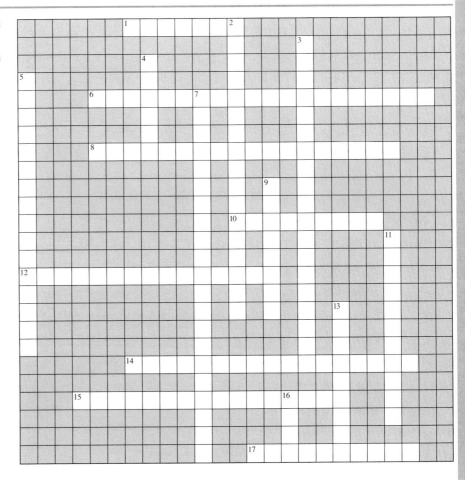

Across

1. Setting a goal and accomplishing it.

6. In making a sales presentation, quickly obtain the prospect's full attention, develop interest in your product, create desire to fulfill a need, establish the prospect's conviction that the product fills a needs, and finally, promote action by having the prospect purchase the product.

8. The main purpose of a salesperson's call to a prospect or customer.

10. The first step in the prospect's mental steps. From the moment a salesperson begins to talk, he or she should try to quickly capture and maintain this.

12. Relevant information regarding the firm, the buyer, and individuals who influence the buying decision.

14. The actual presentation of the sales message to the prospect.

15. Sales call purpose is to make a contribution to the welfare of a person or organization.

17. In this step of the prospect's mental steps, the salesperson should strive to develop a strong belief that the product is best suited to the prospects' specific needs. It is established when no doubts remain about purchasing the product.

Down

2. The process of preparing to approach a prospect attempting to make a sale.

3. A plan that contains the nucleus of information used in the sales presentation.

4. The third step in the prospect's mental steps. It is created when prospects express a wish or want for a product.

5. The final step in the prospect's mental steps. Once the prospect is convinced, the salesperson should plan the most appropriate method of asking the prospect to buy or act.

7. A person with the ability to develop and combine nontraditional alternatives in order to meet specific needs of the customer.

9. The second step in the prospect's mental steps. It is important for the salesperson to capture the prospect's interest in the product. If this link is completed, prospects usually express a desire for the product.

11. Planning the sales call on a customer or prospect.

13. Programs, goals, and projects of great importance.

16. A method of achieving and end.

CASE 8-1
Ms. Hansen's Mental Steps in Buying Your Product

Picture yourself as a Procter & Gamble salesperson who plans to call on Ms. Hansen, a buyer for your largest independent grocery store. Your sales call objective is to convince Ms. Hansen that she should buy the family-size Tide detergent. The store now carries the three smaller sizes. You believe your marketing plan will help convince her that she is losing sales and profits by not stocking Tide's family size.

You enter the grocery store, check your present merchandise, and quickly develop a suggested order. As Ms. Hansen walks down the aisle toward you, she appears to be in her normal grumpy mood. After your initial greeting and handshake, your conversation continues:

Salesperson: Your sales are really up! I've checked your stock in the warehouse and on the shelf. This is what it looks like you need. [You discuss sales of each of your products and their various sizes, suggesting a quantity she should purchase based on her past sales and present inventory.]

Buyer: OK, that looks good. Go ahead and ship it.

Salesperson: Thank you. Say, Ms. Hansen, you've said before that the shortage of shelf space prevents you from stocking our family-size Tide—though you admit you may be losing some sales as a result. If we could determine how much volume you're missing, I think you'd be willing to make space for it, wouldn't you?

Buyer: Yes, but I don't see how that can be done.

Salesperson: Well, I'd like to suggest a test—a weekend display of all four sizes of Tide.

Buyer: What do you mean?

Salesperson: My thought was to run all sizes at regular shelf price without any ad support. This would give us a pure test. Six cases of each size should let us compare sales of the various sizes and see what you're missing by regularly stocking only the smaller sizes. I think the additional sales and profits you'll get on the family size will convince you to start stocking it regularly. What do you think?

Buyer: Well, maybe.

Questions

1. Examine each item you mentioned to Ms. Hansen, stating what part of the customer benefit plan each of your comments is concerned with.
2. What are the features, advantages, and benefits in your sales presentation?
3. Examine each of Ms. Hansen's replies stating the mental buying step she is in at that particular time during your sales presentation.
4. At the end of the conversation, Ms. Hansen said, "Well, maybe." Which of the following should you do now?
   a. Continue to explain your features, advantages, and benefits.
   b. Ask a trial close question.
   c. Ask for the order.
   d. Back off and try again on the next sales call.
   e. Wait for Ms. Hansen to say, "OK, ship it."

CASE 8-2

Machinery Lubricants, Inc.

Ralph Jackson sells industrial lubricants to manufacturing plants. The lubricants are used to lubricate the plant's machinery. Tomorrow, Ralph plans to call on the purchasing agent for Acme Manufacturing Company.

For the past two years, Ralph has been selling Hydraulic Oil 65 in drums to Acme. Ralph's sales call objective is to persuade Acme to switch from purchasing oil in drums to a bulk oil system. Last year, Acme bought approximately 364 drums or 20,000 gallons at a cost of $1.39 a gallon or $27,800, with a deposit of $20 for each drum. Traditionally, many drums are lost, and one to two gallons of oil may be left in each drum when returned by customers. This is a loss to the company.

Ralph wants to sell Acme two 3,000-gallon storage tanks at a cost of $1,700. He has arranged with Pump Supply Company to install the tanks for $1,095. Thus, the total cost of the system will be $2,795. This system reduces the cost of the oil from $1.39 to $1.25 per gallon, which will allow it to pay for itself over time. Other advantages include having fewer orders to process each year, a reduction in storage space, and less handling of the oil by workers.

Question

If you were Ralph, how would you plan the sales call?

CASE 8-3

Telemax, Inc.

Ellen St. James, a marketing director for Telemax, is walking through an antique store with Monica, a customer and friend. Ellen is in charge of a project called Stardust, a new telecommunication product in which her company has invested heavily. Monica informs Ellen that she has learned from a marketer at PCI, one of Telemax's major competitors and the industry leader, that they are planning to introduce a product similar to Stardust. Ellen is immediately upset, but tries to hide this fact

Video

Case

from Monica. Ellen states that she has heard about this product and asks Monica if she was able to find out when the product will be introduced. Monica states that she had asked the marketer this question, but he did not give her a straight answer.

Ellen is having lunch with Carl, her former subordinate at Telemax. Ellen and Carl start talking about work and Ellen confides to Carl that Stardust will be available in 90 days. Ellen explains that she needs to know when PCI is introducing its product because, if Stardust is introduced after or at the same time as PCI's product, Telemax probably will not be able to gain the needed market share. Ellen asks Carl for advice on how to get this information and he gives her several suggestions, including: putting someone on PCI's payroll, asking her customers for information, hiring a private investigator, and pushing Stardust through Telemax's quality assurance department. Ellen, however, does not feel comfortable using any of these tactics. Carl recalls that Ellen hired an ex-PCI employee, Frank Cilento, and recommends that she finds out what he knows or can find out. Ellen remarks that Frank is up for a promotion. As the vignette closes, Ellen is left to consider whether to use the possibility of promotion as leverage with Frank.[2]

Questions

1. What are the main ethical issues, if any, in the Telemax, Inc. case? Describe each ethical issue.
2. What are Ellen's options?
3. How do the three levels of moral development relate to Ellen's situation?
4. What would you do?

Carefully Select Which Sales Presentation Method to Use

MAIN TOPICS

The Tree of Business Life: Presentation

Sales Presentation Strategy

Sales Presentation Methods—Select One Carefully

The Group Presentation

Negotiating So Everyone Wins

Sales Presentations Go High-Tech

Select the Presentation Method, Then the Approach

Let's Review before Moving On!

LEARNING OBJECTIVES

To know the best way to begin the sales presentation, first determine the type of sales presentation to use for each prospect or customer. After studying this chapter, you should be able to

- State why you first select a sales presentation method and then select the approach.

- Describe the different sales presentation methods; know their differences; and know the appropriate situation for using a particular method.

- Better understand how to give a presentation to a group of prospects.

- Understand why negotiations can be an important part of the presentation.

It took you four hours to plan, prepare, and practice your sales presentation to the largest manufacturer in your sales territory. Although they have never purchased before, you feel your product will benefit them. You arrive on time for your appointment with Juan Gomez.

Mr. Gomez's secretary takes you into a large conference room, saying, "They'll be with you in a few minutes." "They," you think. "Who is coming?" you ask. "The head of accounting, production, and two engineers—and the president wants us to call her once the meeting gets under way." As she leaves, you become dizzy, your stomach gets upset, and you feel weak in the knees. "I've never given a presentation to a group—let alone experts. And the president of the company. Oh, my—what am I going to do?" What would you do?

Salespeople, sales trainers, and sales managers agree that the most challenging, rewarding, and enjoyable aspect of the buyer–seller interaction is the **sales presentation.** An effective sales presentation completely and clearly explains all aspects of a salesperson's proposition as it relates to a buyer's needs. Surprisingly, attaining this objective is not as easy as you might think. Few successful salespeople will claim that they had little trouble developing a good presentation or mastering the art of giving the sales presentation. How then can you, as a novice, develop a sales presentation that will improve your chances of making the sale?

You must first select a sales presentation method according to your prior knowledge of the customer, your sales call objective, and your customer benefit plan. Once you have made the selection, you are ready to develop your sales presentation. The particular sales presentation method that you select will make an excellent framework on which to build your specific presentation.

Once you select the presentation method for a specific prospect or customer, it is time to determine how to open or begin the sales presentation. Steps 3 through 9 of the sales process compose the seven steps within the sales presentation itself. The sales opener, or approach, as shown in Exhibit 9.1, is the first major step in the sales presentation. The approach is discussed in Chapter 10.

This chapter discusses the four different sales presentation methods, including how to conduct a group presentation. Negotiations are also introduced in this chapter, since they are often necessary regardless of the presentation method used.

THE TREE OF BUSINESS LIFE: PRESENTATION

Salespeople face various types of prospects, customers, and organizations each day requiring the skill to use different presentation methods based upon the situation. What is not different from one sales call to another is the purpose of meeting with someone. You want to help the person or organization. From your honesty within the presentation, people will realize your can be trusted.

The heart of the sales presentation is the discussion of the product, marketing plan, and business proposition. The question is, "To whom is the presentation being given?" Once this question is answered, the salesperson can choose the type of sales presentation method best suited to the prospect or customer. That is what this chapter is about. Your selection of the best presentation method for the situation will allow you to improve the chances of helping the customer. Thus, you must master the art of delivering a good sales presentation. This will lead to solving the customer's problems. With great presentations you can ethically serve others, building

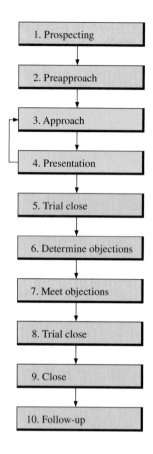

long-term relationships, based upon the truth. As you travel from place to place, helping others you touch, you improve their lives. What a wonderful calling this will be if you truly love to sell and help your business neighbors in the community.

SALES PRESENTATION STRATEGY

Salespeople work with customers in different ways. As discussed in Chapter 2, salespeople may be involved in transactional, relationship, or partnering selling. Thus, salespeople face numerous situations, including these:

- **Salesperson to buyer:** A salesperson discusses issues with a prospect or customer in person or over the phone.
- **Salesperson to buyer group:** A salesperson gets to know as many members of the buyer group as possible.
- **Sales team to buyer group:** A company sales team works closely with the members of the customer's buying group.
- **Conference selling:** The salesperson brings company resource people to discuss a major problem or opportunity.
- **Seminar selling:** A company team conducts an educational seminar for the customer company about state-of-the-art developments.

Each customer contact represents a unique challenge for the salespeople. Thus, the salesperson needs to understand the various sales presentation methods.

SALES PRESENTATION METHODS— SELECT ONE CAREFULLY

The sales presentation involves a persuasive vocal and visual explanation of a business proposition. Of the many ways of making a presentation, four methods are presented here to highlight the alternatives available to help sell your products.

As shown on the continuum in Exhibit 9.2, the four sales presentation methods are (1) memorized, (2) formula, (3) need-satisfaction, and (4) problem-solution selling methods.[1] The basic difference in the four methods is the percentage of the conversation controlled by the salesperson. In the more structured memorized and formula selling techniques, the salesperson normally has a monopoly on the conversation, whereas the less structured methods allow for greater buyer–seller interaction; both parties participate equally in the conversation. Transactional selling generally is more structured, whereas partnering requires a more customized presentation, with relationship selling typically somewhere in between (see Exhibit 9.2).

The Memorized Sales Presentation

The **memorized presentation** is based on either of two assumptions: that a prospect's needs can be stimulated by direct exposure to the product, via the sales presentation, or that these needs have already been stimulated because the prospect has made the effort to seek out the product. In either case, the salesperson's role is to develop this initial stimulus into an affirmative response to an eventual purchase request.

The salesperson does 80 to 90 percent of the talking during a memorized sales presentation, only occasionally allowing the prospect to respond to predetermined questions, as shown in Exhibit 9.3. Notably, the salesperson does not attempt to

EXHIBIT 9.2

The structure of sales presentations.

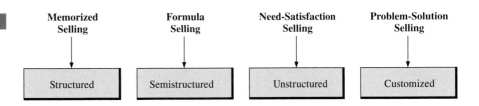

EXHIBIT 9.3

Participation time by customer and salesperson during a memorized sales presentation.

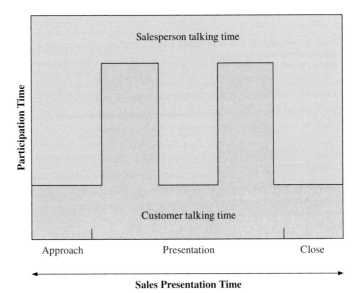

The difference between a successful person and others is not a lack of strength, not a lack of knowledge, but rather in a lack of will.

determine the prospect's needs during the interview, but gives the same canned sales talk to all prospects. Since no attempt is made at this point to learn what goes on in the consumer's mind, the salesperson concentrates on discussing the product and its benefits, concluding the pitch with a purchase request. The seller hopes that a convincing presentation of product benefits will cause the prospect to buy.

National Cash Register Co. pioneered the use of canned sales presentations. During the 1920s, an analysis of the sales approaches of some of its top salespeople revealed to NCR that they were saying the same things. The firm prepared a series of standardized sales presentations based on the findings of their sales approach analysis, ultimately requiring its sales force to memorize these approaches to use during sales calls. The method worked quite well for NCR and was later adopted by other firms. Canned sales presentations are still used today, mainly in telephone and door-to-door selling.

Actually, parts of any presentation may be canned, yet linked with free-form conversation. Over time, most salespeople develop proven selling sentences, phrases, and sequences in which to discuss information. They tend to use these in all presentations.

Despite its impersonal aura, the canned or memorized sales presentation has distinct advantages, as seen in Exhibit 9.4.[2]

- It ensures that the salesperson gives a well-planned presentation and that all of the company's salespeople discuss the same information.
- It both aids and lends confidence to the inexperienced salesperson.
- It is effective when selling time is short, as in door-to-door or telephone selling.
- It is effective when the product is nontechnical—such as books, cooking utensils, and cosmetics.

As may be apparent, the memorized method has several major drawbacks:

- It presents features, advantages, and benefits that may not be important to the buyer.
- It allows for little prospect participation.
- It is impractical to use when selling technical products that require prospect input and discussion.
- It proceeds quickly through the sales presentation to the close, requiring the salesperson to close or ask for the order several times, which may be interpreted by the prospect as high-pressure selling.

The story is told of the new salesperson who was halfway through a canned presentation when the prospect had to answer the telephone. When the prospect finished the telephone conversation, the salesperson had forgotten the stopping point and started over again. The prospect naturally became angry.

In telling of his early selling experiences, salesperson John Anderson remembers that he was once so intent on presenting his memorized presentation that halfway through it the prospect yelled, "Enough, John, I've been waiting for you to see me. I'm ready to buy. I know all about your products." Anderson was so intent on giving his canned presentation, and listening to himself talk, that he did not recognize the prospect's buying signals.

For some selling situations, a highly structured presentation can be used successfully. Examine its advantages and disadvantages to determine if this presentation is appropriate for your prospects and products.

Some situations may seem partially appropriate for the memorized approach but require a more personal touch. Such circumstances warrant the examination of formula selling.

EXHIBIT 9.4

Dyno Electric Cart memorized presentation.

Situation: You call on a purchasing manager to elicit an order for some electric cars (like a golf cart) to be used at a plant for transportation around the buildings and grounds. The major benefit to emphasize in your presentation is that the carts save time; you incorporate this concept in your approach. For this product, you use the memorized stimulus–response presentation.

Salesperson: Hello, Mr. Pride, my name is Karen Nordstrom, and I'd like to talk with you about how to save your company executives' time. By the way, thanks for taking the time to talk with me.

Buyer: What's on your mind?

Salesperson: As a busy executive, you know time is a valuable commodity. Nearly everyone would like to have a few extra minutes each day and that is the business I'm in, selling time. While I can't actually sell you time, I do have a product that is the next best thing . . . a Dyno Electric Cart—a real time-saver for your executives.

Buyer: Yeah, well, everyone would like to have extra time. However, I don't think we need any golf carts. [First objection.]

Salesperson: Dyno Electric Cart is more than a golf cart. It is an electric car designed for use in industrial plants. It has been engineered to give comfortable, rapid transportation in warehouses, plants, and across open areas.

Buyer: They probably cost too much for us to use. [Positive buying signal phrased as an objection.]

Salesperson: First of all, they only cost $2,200 each. With a five-year normal life, that is only $400 per year plus a few cents for electricity and a few dollars for maintenance. Under normal use and care, these carts only require about $100 of service in their five-year life. Thus, for about $50 a month, you can save key people a lot of time. [Creative pricing—show photographs of carts in use.]

Buyer: It would be nice to save time, but I don't think management would go for the idea. [Third objection, but still showing interest.]

Salesperson: This is exactly why I am here. Your executives will appreciate what you have done for them. You will look good in their eyes if you give them an opportunity to look at a product that will save time and energy. Saving time is only part of our story. Dyno carts also save energy and thus keep you sharper toward the end of the day. Would you want a demonstration today or Tuesday? [Alternative close.]

Buyer: How long would your demonstration take? [Positive buying signal.]

Salesperson: I only need one hour. When would it be convenient for me to bring the cart in for your executives to try out?

Buyer: There really isn't any good time. [Objection.]

Salesperson: That's true. Therefore, the sooner we get to show you a Dyno cart, the sooner your management group can see its benefits. How about next Tuesday? I could be here at 8:00 and we could go over this item just before your weekly management group meeting. I know you usually have a meeting Tuesdays at 9:00 because I tried to call on you a few weeks ago and your secretary told me you were in the weekly management meeting. [Close of the sale.]

Buyer: Well, we could do it then.

Salesperson: Fine, I'll be here. Your executives will really be happy! [Positive reinforcement.]

The Formula Presentation

The **formula presentation,** often referred to as the *persuasive selling presentation,* is akin to the memorized method: It is based on the assumption that similar prospects in similar situations can be approached with similar presentations. However, for the formula method to apply, the salesperson must first know something about the prospective buyer. The salesperson follows a less structured, general outline in making a presentation, allowing more flexibility and less direction.

The salesperson generally controls the conversation during the sales talk, especially at the beginning. Exhibit 9.5 illustrates how a salesperson should take charge during a formula selling situation.[3] For example, the salesperson might make a sales

Participation time by a customer and salesperson during a formula sales presentation.

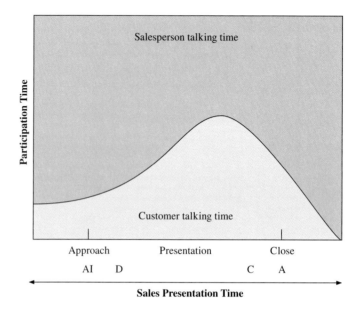

opener (approach), discuss the product's features, advantages, and benefits, and then start to solicit comments from the buyer using trial closes, answering questions, and handling objections. At the end of the participation curve, the salesperson regains control over the discussion and moves in to close the sale.

The formula selling approach obtains its name from the salesperson using the attention, interest, desire, and action (AIDA) procedure of developing and giving the sales presentation. We earlier added conviction (C) to the procedure because the prospect may want or desire the product, yet not be convinced this is the best product or the best salesperson from whom to buy.

Straight rebuy situations, especially with consumer goods, lend themselves to this method. Many prospects or customers buy because they are familiar with the salesperson's company. The question is, how can a salesperson for Quaker Oats, Revlon, Gillette, Procter & Gamble, or any other well-known manufacturer develop a presentation that convinces a customer to purchase promotional quantities of a product, participate in a local advertising campaign, or stock a new, untried product?

SmithKline Beecham Products, a consumer goods manufacturer, has developed a sequence, or formula, for its salespeople to follow. They refer to it as the *10-step productive retail sales call*. The SmithKline Beecham salesperson sells products such as Cling Free Sheets, Aquafresh toothpaste, Aqua-Velva, and Sucrets. The 10 steps and their major components are shown in Exhibit 9.6.

Formula selling is effective for calling on customers who currently buy and for prospects about whose operations the salesperson has learned a great deal. In such situations, formula selling offers significant advantages:

- It ensures that all information is presented logically.
- It allows for a reasonable amount of buyer–seller interaction.
- It allows for smooth handling of *anticipated* questions and objections.

When executed in a smooth, conversational manner, the formula method of selling has no major flaws, as long as the salesperson has correctly identified the prospect's needs and wants. The Procter & Gamble formula sales presentation given as an

EXHIBIT 9.6

The 10-step productive retail sales call.

Step Number	Action
1. Plan the cell.	■ Review the situation. ■ Analyze problems and appointments. ■ Set objectives. ■ Plan the presentation. ■ Check your sales materials.
2. Review plans.	■ Before you leave your car to enter the store, review your plans, sales call objectives, suggested order forms, and so on.
3. Greet personnel.	■ Give a friendly greeting to store personnel. ■ Alert the store manager for sales action.

4. Check store conditions.	■ Note appearance of stock on shelf.
	■ Check distribution and pricing.
	■ Note out-of-stocks.
	■ Perform a quick fix by straightening shelf stock.
	■ Report competitive activity.
	■ Check back room (storeroom):
	    Locate product to correct out-of-stocks.
	    Use reserve stock for special display.
	■ Update sales plan if needed.

5. Approach.	■ Keep it short.
6. Presentation.	■ Make it logical, clear, interesting. ■ Tailor it to dealer's style. ■ Present it from dealer's point of view. ■ Use sales tools.
7. Close.	■ Present a suggested order (ask for the order). ■ Offer a choice. ■ Answer questions and handle objections. ■ Get a real order.
8. Merchandising	■ Build displays. ■ Dress up the shelves.
9. Records and reports.	■ Complete them immediately after the call.
10. Analyze the call.	■ Review the call to spot strong and weak points. How could the sales call have been improved? How can the next call be improved?

example in Exhibit 9.7 can be given to any retailer who is not selling all available sizes of Tide (or of any other product). In this situation, a formula approach is used in calling on a customer the salesperson has sold to previously. If, on the other hand, the salesperson did not know a customer's needs and used this Tide presentation, chances are customer objections would arise early in the presentation—as they sometimes do with the memorized sales presentation method. The formula technique is not adaptable to all complex selling situations; a number of them require other sales presentations.

The Need-Satisfaction Presentation

The **need-satisfaction presentation** is different from the memorized and the formalized approach; it is designed as a flexible, interactive sales presentation. It is the most challenging and creative form of selling.

EXHIBIT 9.7

A formula approach sales presentation.

Formula Steps	Buyer–Seller Roles	Sales Presentation
Summarize the situation for *attention* and *interest*.	**Salesperson:**	Ms. Hansen, you've said before that the shortage of shelf space prevents you from stocking our family-size Tide—though you admit you may be losing some sales as a result. If we could determine *how much* volume you're missing, I think you'd be willing to *make* space for it, wouldn't you? [Trial close.]
State your marketing plan for *interest*.	**Buyer:**	Yes, but I don't see how that can be done.
	Salesperson:	Well, I'd like to suggest a test—a weekend display of all four sizes of Tide.
	Buyer:	What do you mean?
Explain your marketing plan for *interest* and *desire*.	**Salesperson:**	My thought was to run all sizes at regular shelf price *without* any ad support. This would give us a pure test. Six cases of each size should let us compare sales of the various sizes and see what you're missing by regularly stocking only the smaller sizes. I think the additional sales and profits you'll get on the family size will convince you to start stocking regularly. [Reinforce key benefits.] What do you think? [Trial close.]
Buyer appears to be in *conviction* stage.	**Buyer:**	Well, maybe. [Positive reaction to trial close.]
Suggest an easy next step or *action*.	**Salesperson:**	May I enter the six cases of family-size Tide in the order book now? [Close.]

Winners don't set limits, they set goals.

The salesperson typically starts the presentation with a probing question such as, "What are you looking for in investment property?" or "What type of computer needs does your company have?" This opening starts a discussion of the prospect's needs and also gives the salesperson an opportunity to determine whether any of the products being offered might be beneficial. When something the prospect has said is not understood by the salesperson, it can be clarified by a question or by restating what the buyer has said. The need-satisfaction format is especially suited to the sale of industrial and technical goods with stringent specifications and high price tags.

Often, as shown in Exhibit 9.8, the first 50 to 60 percent of conversation time (referred to as the **need-development** phase) is devoted to a discussion of the buyer's needs.[4] Once aware of the prospect's needs (the **need-awareness** phase), the salesperson begins to take control of the conversation by restating the prospect's needs to clarify the situation. During the last stage of the presentation, the **need-fulfillment** (or need-satisfaction) phase, the salesperson shows how the product will satisfy mutual needs. As seen in Exhibit 9.9, the salesperson selling the Dyno Electric Cart begins the interview with the prospect by using the planned series of questions to uncover problems and to determine whether the prospect is interested in solving them.[5]

Should you have to come back a second time to see the prospect, as is often the case in selling industrial products, you would use the formula sales presentation method in calling on the same prospect. You might begin with a benefit statement such as this:

EXHIBIT 9.8

Participation time by customer and salesperson during need-satisfaction and problem–solution sales presentations.

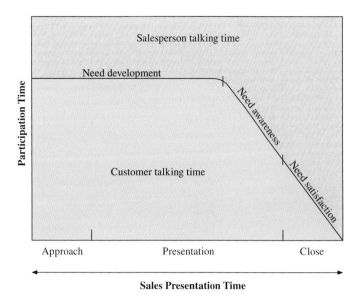

Mr. Pride, when we talked last week, you were interested in saving your executives time and energy in getting to and from your plant, and you felt the Dyno Electric Cart could do this for you. (You could pause to let him answer or say, "Is that correct?")

From the buyer's response to your question, you can quickly determine what to do. If the buyer raises an objection, you can respond to it. If the buyer requests more information, you can provide it. If what you have said about your product has pleased the buyer, you simply ask for the order.

Be cautious when uncovering a prospect's needs. Too many questions can alienate the prospect. Remember, initially many prospects do not want to open up to salespeople. Actually, some salespeople are uncomfortable with the need-satisfaction approach because they feel less in control of the selling situation than with a canned or formula presentation. A good point to remember is that you are not a performer on a stage, but rather, your job is to meet your prospect's needs—not your own. Eventually, you can learn to anticipate customer reactions to this presentation and learn to welcome the challenge of the interaction between you and the buyer.

The Problem–Solution Presentation

In selling highly complex or technical products such as insurance, industrial equipment, accounting systems, office equipment, and computers, salespeople often are required to make several sales calls to develop a detailed analysis of a prospect's needs. After completing this analysis, the salesperson arrives at a solution to the prospect's problems and usually uses both a written analysis and an oral presentation. The **problem–solution presentation** usually consists of six steps:

1. Convincing the prospect to allow the salesperson to conduct the analysis.
2. Making the actual analysis.
3. Agreeing on the problems and determining that the buyer wants to solve them.
4. Preparing the proposal for a solution to the prospect's needs.
5. Preparing the sales presentation based on the analysis and proposal.
6. Making the sales presentation.

The problem–solution presentation is a flexible, customized approach involving an in-depth study of a prospect's needs, and it requires a well-planned presentation.

A need-satisfaction presentation.

Salesperson: Mr. Pride, you really have a large manufacturing facility. How large is it?

Buyer: We have approximately 50 acres under roof, with our main production building almost 25 acres under one roof. We use six buildings for production.

Salesperson: How far is it from your executives' offices to your plant area? It looks like it must be two miles over to there.

Buyer: Well, it does, but it's only one mile.

Salesperson: How do your executives get to the plant area?

Buyer: They walk through our underground tunnel. Some walk on the road when we have good weather.

Salesperson: When they get to the plant area, how do they get around in the plant?

Buyer: Well, they walk or catch a ride on one of the small tractors the workers use in the plant.

Salesperson: Have your executives ever complained about having to do all that walking?

Buyer: All the time!

Salesperson: What don't they like about the long walk?

Buyer: Well, I hear everything from "It wears out my shoe leather" to "It's hard on my pacemaker." The main complaints are the time it takes them and that some older executives are exhausted by the time they get back to their offices. Many people need to go to the plant but don't.

Salesperson: It sounds as if your executives are interested in reducing their travel time and not having to exert so much energy. By doing so, doesn't it seem they would get to the plant as they need to, saving them time and energy and saving the company money?

Buyer: I guess so.

Salesperson: Mr. Pride, on the average, how much money do your executives make an hour?

Buyer: Maybe $30 an hour.

Salesperson: If I could show you how to save your executives time in getting to and from the plant, would you be interested?

Buyer: Yes, I would. [Now the salesperson moves into the presentation.]

Often, the need-satisfaction and problem–solution presentations are used when it is necessary to present the proposal to a group of individuals.

Comparison of Presentation Methods

Exhibit 9.10 illustrates differences in the four sales presentation methods. It also shows the wide variety of sales jobs available for you to choose from by people seeking a career. Hopefully you will see that selling different products in different industries has similarities but many differences in salespeople's job activities.[6]

Some of the students in my personal selling classes say, "I do not want to have a sales career." I ask "Why?" "I do not want to do any cold-call type of prospecting and no straight commission" they might reply. I describe sales jobs with straight salaries and bonuses with no cold-calling and then ask "What about working for these companies?" "That sounds fine," they may say.

Different strokes for difference folks

What are the main things you are looking for in a job? Well, there is a sales job that has what you are looking for somewhere. Remember the chapter's introductory sales challenge of the salesperson faced with meeting with a group?

What Is the Best Presentation Method?

Each of these sales presentation methods is the best one when the method is properly matched with the *situation*. For example, the stimulus–response method can be used when time is short and the product is simple. Formula selling is effective in repeat purchases or when you know or have already determined the needs of the prospect.

EXHIBIT 9.10

Important characteristics of types of sales calls.

Characteristics	Memorized (Structured)	Formula (Semistructured)	Need-Satisfaction (Unstructured)	Problem Solution (Customized)
Relationship	Transactional	Relationship	Partnering	Partnering
When Used	New customer door-to-door; telesales	Repeat customer	New customer; new opportunity	New customer; new opportunity
Opening	Canned	Reminder of past status	Questions	Request for study
Presentation Time	Minutes	Half hour(s)	Day(s)	Week(s)
Multiple Calls?	No	Sometimes	Frequently	Always
Type of Negotiations	None	Several variables	Multiple variables	Complex
Script Flexibility	None	Modest	No script	No script
Assumed Interest Level	Already established, or can be generated	Already established	Not established, or not kinown	Not known
Prior Contact with Buyer?	Not usually	Usually	Not necessarily	Not necessarily
Type Product	Trivial; simple	Simple; previously sold	Industrial/technical	Complex
Sample Product	Vegetable dicer, vacuum cleaner cosmetics	Premium cable channel Consumer goods cars	Home entertainment center Computer Real estate	Internet network; Warehouse system Company insurance
Salary ($)	30–50K	40–70K	50–90K	80–200K1

The need-satisfaction method is most appropriate when you must gather information from the prospect, as in often the case in selling industrial products. Finally, the problem-solving presentation is excellent for selling high-cost technical products or services, and especially for system selling involving several sales calls and a business proposition. To help improve sales, the salesperson should understand and be able to use each method based on each situation. Remember the chapter's introductory sales challenge of the salesperson faced with meeting with a group?

THE GROUP PRESENTATION

At times you will meet with more than one decision maker for a group presentation.[7] Many group presentation elements are similar to other types of presentations. The primary difference is that either you or your team present the proposal to a group of decision makers.

The group presentation, depending on size, may be less flexible than a one-on-one meeting. The larger the group, the more structured your presentation. It would not work if everyone jumped in with feedback and ideas simultaneously, so a semblance of order has to be arranged. As the salesperson in charge, you can structure the presentation and provide a question-and-answer period at the end of or during the presentation.

The ideal situation is to talk with most or all of the decision makers involved during the analysis phase. That way, they will have contributed to determining what is needed. The points you discuss will hit on thoughts they have expressed regarding the problems at hand. In the initial part of the presentation, you should accomplish the following steps:

Give a Proper Introduction

State your name, company, and explain in a clear, concise sentence the premise of your proposal. For example, your statement might sound like this: "Good morning. I'm Jeff Baxter from International Hospitality Consultants. I'm here to share my findings, based on research of your company and discussions with Mary Farley, that suggest my company can help increase your convention bookings by 15 to 30 percent."

Establish Credibility

Give a brief history of your company that includes the reason the business was started, the company philosophy, its development, and its success rate. Mention a few companies that you have worked with in the past, especially if they are big names. This reassures the client by letting the group know who you are and the extent of your experience and credibility.

Provide an Account List

Have copies of an account list available for everyone in attendance. It would be monotonous to say each company that you've worked with. Instead, hand out copies either in advance or while you talk. This list shows the various sizes, locations, and types of companies you've helped in the past.

State Your Competitive Advantages

Right up front you can succinctly tell the group where your company stands relative to the competition. Don't get into a detailed analysis of comparative strengths and weaknesses; just make it clear that you can do better than the competition.

Give Quality Assurances and Qualifications

Get the group on your side by stating guarantees in the beginning. This shows pride in your product and that you don't skirt the issue of guarantees. Also, give your company's qualifications and credentials. For example, "We are certified by the United States government and licensed in 48 states to treat or move toxic waste," or "I have copies of the test reports from an independent lab." If your company has an impressive money-back guarantee or an extended warranty, mention it.

Cater to the Group's Behavioral Style

Every group comprises individuals with personal styles. However, a group also exhibits an overall or dominant style; that is, it has a decision-making mode that characterizes one of the four behavioral styles (see Chapter 4). If you can quickly determine the group style, you will hold their attention and give them what they want more effectively. Some people are more impatient than others. If you don't address their needs, you will lose their attention.

Get People Involved

"The only place where success comes before work is in a dictionary."

VIDAL SASSOON

After establishing the credibility of your company, involve the group in the presentation. The first thing to do is go around the room asking for everyone's input into the decision-making criteria for making the purchase. Preface this with, "I spoke to Fred, Sally, and Sue and learned their views on what your company would like to see changed in this area. In my research, I discovered it would also benefit you to have X, Y, and Z improved. I'd like to hear all of your thoughts on this matter." Ask each person to add to the list of benefits and the decision-making criteria. Take notes, perhaps on a flip chart, of what everyone says to help shape your presentation.

After everyone has had a chance to speak, go through your presentation exactly as in a one-on-one presentation. The primary difference is that you want to answer all the questions, fears, and concerns in the group. Meet each person's specific needs with a specific proposal.

When using this method, it is essential during your preparation to brainstorm all possible concerns and questions the decision makers may have. This information comes from talking to people within the company, other salespeople, and people in the industry. Be so well prepared that there is nothing they could come up with as decision-making criteria that you haven't already thought of and answered.

The Proposal

When you prepare for a group, write a proposal document that ranges from one page to an entire notebook with data, specifications, reports, and solutions to specific problems. The proposal document is a reference source that tells your customer what she bought if she said yes and what she didn't buy if the answer was no. This document addresses everything you and your prospect discussed in the analysis phase: problems, success criteria, decision-making criteria, and how your product or service answers each. At the end, include relevant documents and copies of testimonial letters from satisfied customers.

During your presentation, do not read from the document. It is not the presentation; it is strictly a resource of facts to give your prospect after a decision is made. In addition, when making your presentation, do not expect to cover every point in the proposal unless you are brief. Your presentation will focus on the issues that relate to the customer's specific need gap; tangential information should be left in the document. Remember that proposal documents don't sell products; people sell products. The document is no substitute for a first-rate presentation.

No Prices

The best way to present a proposal document is without prices. There are several reasons for this. First, some people will go directly to the prices without reading through the document. Second, prices tend to prejudice non–decision makers—who should not be concerned with prices. If the decision maker asks why the prices are missing, tell him, "I thought you would prefer the flexibility of showing the document to other people without their knowing prices. It's a matter of confidentiality." The third reason is politics. Imagine a board of directors that has not had a raise in two years looking at a document that proposes a $2 million computer for the company. This may stir up problems.

Make it clear that you are not trying to hide the prices and that you would be more than happy to talk about them with the appropriate people, the decision makers. It is important to present prices in the proper perspective and context.

When you share the proposal, address each problem and give specific information about your solutions. Make sure you discuss features, advantages, and benefits—and get feedback from the group. Ask trial closes like these:

- "Can you see any other advantages to this?"
- "How do you feel about that? Do you think that would solve the problem?"

Summarize Benefits

At the end, summarize your proposal by giving a benefits summary: "Here is what you will get if you accept my proposal." Talk about how the benefits will address their specific problems.

Before your presentation, find out from your primary contact in the company if the group will make a decision while you are there or if they will discuss it and

Negotiating

- When you give something up, try to gain something in return. When you give something for nothing, there is a tendency for people to want more. In all fairness to you and your prospect, balance what you give and receive. For example, "I'll lower the price if you pay in full within 30 days" or "I'll give you 10 percent off, but you will be charged for additional services such as training."
- Look for items other than price to negotiate. For example, gain some flexibility by offering better terms, payment plans, return policies, and delivery schedules; lower deposits or cancellation fees; or implementation and

training programs. Often these items are provided for less than your company would lose if you lowered the price.
- Do not attack your prospect's demand; look for the motive behind it. Never tell a prospect his demand is ridiculous or unreasonable. Remain calm and ask for the reason behind the desire.
- Do not defend your position; ask for feedback and advice from the prospect. If you meet resistance to an offer, don't be defensive. Say something like, "This is my thinking. What would you do if you were in my position?"

inform you later. You also should know if they are responsible for dealing with the financial aspects of the purchase. If so, you will have to talk about the costs and the benefits they will receive in relation to the costs. If they will not be concerned with prices, don't discuss them.

When you have completed the benefits summary, solicit impressions from the group. Ask if they agree that the solution you proposed would solve their problem or meet their needs. Without asking for it, get a feeling for the disposition of the group. If you are working with one person, it is easier to ask for an impression.

At the end of your summary, ask if there are any questions. At this point, you are close to the end of your allotted time. When someone asks a question that is answered in your proposal document, refer him to the appropriate section of the document and assure him that a complete answer is provided.

NEGOTIATING SO EVERYONE WINS

No matter what type of presentation method you use, or whether you talk to one person or a group of people, be prepared to negotiate. Many salespeople negotiate during the confirming phase of the sale. Their products or services are big-ticket items with many negotiable details. The negotiating process during the sale confirmation becomes a critical point that can affect the business relationship.

There are many negotiating styles with various names. For example, there are cooperative, competitive, attitudinal, organizational, and personal modes of negotiating. Most inexperienced negotiators operate in the competitive mode because they mistakenly think the shrewd businessperson is one who wins at the other's expense. With a win–lose attitude in mind, they "don't show all their cards" and use other strategies to gain the upper hand. Often this is done at the expense of the business relationship.

If you see prospects as adversaries rather than business partners, you will have short-term, adversarial relationships. The tension, mistrust, and buyer's remorse created are not worth the small gains you may win using this negotiating style. There is a better way.

Professional salespeople negotiate in a way that achieves satisfaction for both parties. They rely on trust, openness, credibility, integrity, and fairness. Their attitude

MAKING THE SALE

Matt Suffoletto of IBM Uses the Problem–Solution Presentation Method

"A successful salesperson has expertise in the products he or she sells, as well as an in-depth knowledge of the customer's business. The salesperson often makes recommendations which alter the mainstream of the customer's business process. Recognizing the requirement of business skills, IBM provides training in both the technical aspects of our products, as well as their industrial application.

"My territory consists of manufacturing customers; hence, I pride myself in understanding concepts such as inventory control, time phased requirements planning, and shop floor control. Typically, I work with customer user department and data processing people to do application surveys and detailed justification analysis. After the background work is completed, I make proposals and presentations to educate the chain of decision makers on the IBM recommendations.

"Selling involves the transformation of the features of your product into benefits to the customer. The principal vehicles for that communication are the sales call, formal presentations, and proposal. The larger the magnitude of the sale, the more time and effort is spent on presentations and proposals. A proposal may range from a simple one-page letter and attachment with prices, terms, and conditions, to multivolume binders with detailed information on the product, including its use, detailed justification, implementation schedules, and contracts. The wide range of comprehensiveness implies an equal range in time commitment of the salesperson.

"Very few sales are made in a single call. At the first sales call, the salesperson generally searches for additional information that needs to be brought back, analysis that needs to be done, or questions to be answered. These are opportunities to demonstrate responsiveness to the customer. Getting back to the customer in a very timely and professional manner is a way to build trust and confidence into a business relationship."

is not, "How can I get what I want out of this person?" It's "There are many options to explore that will make both of us happy. If two people want to do business, the details will not stand in the way." It is important *not* to negotiate the details before your customer has made a commitment to your solution.

Phases of Negotiation

If your product or service requires negotiating on a regular basis, set the stage for negotiation early in the sales process. There are things you can do to prepare for negotiation from the beginning.

Planning

The number one asset of a strong negotiator is preparation. During the planning phase, after completing a competition analysis, you know how your company compares with the competition for price, service, quality, reputation, and so on. This knowledge is important at negotiation time. You may be able to offer things the competition cannot. It is advantageous to point out these advantages to your prospect when the time is right.

Before you make a proposal to a client, search your company's sales records to find any reports of previous sales to your prospect or similar businesses. If these records documented the successes and failures of negotiating, you will learn from other salespeople's experience. For this reason, your call reports should include details of what transpired during any negotiation. The knowledge gained from these records is not a strategy per se, but insight into the priorities of this market segment. For example, businesses in a certain industry segment may value service more than price, or they may care more about help in training and implementation than a discount.

ETHICAL DILEMMA

To Fix the Mistake . . . or Not

A favorite customer of yours, Dick Sargent, has been having trouble lately paying his bills. Dick owns a small manufacturing plant. He employs six people. Bad economic conditions in his area severely hurt Dick's small business. Thus, sales for this account have dropped 60 percent.

Last week, you arranged for him to buy a six-month supply of plastic pipe he uses to manufacture his best-selling product. Due to the quantity purchased, your company's credit manager said he could pay for it in equal payments over the next four months,

Today, Dick calls you to thank you for the extended credit and for the extra $100 discount. You realize there has been a billing error on his $15,000 order.

What would be the most ethical action to take?

1. Apologize to Dick and tell him that there has been an error. Offer to go and talk to your boss to see if there is a way to get him some type of discount.
2. Nothing. It's only $100—chances are that nobody will notice and you like helping out your favorite customer.
3. Tell Dick that there has been an error but that you will keep it quiet if he does. Let Dick decide if he is comfortable with that.

During your preparation, review the various bargaining chips available to you. Some of the questions to answer include these:

- What extra services can you offer?
- How flexible is the price or the payment plan?
- Are deposits and cancellation fees negotiable?
- Is there optional equipment you can throw in for free?
- Can you provide free training?
- What items in the negotiation will be inflexible for you?
- How can you compensate for these items?

Meeting

When you meet a prospect, you start building the relationship by proving you are someone who is credible, trustworthy, and, it is hoped, the type of person your prospect likes to do business with. If you are all these things, you will eliminate tension from the relationship and thereby ease the negotiation process.

As proof of this concept, imagine selling your car to a friend. Now imagine selling it to a stranger. Who would be easier to negotiate with? The friend, of course. For both of you, the top priority is the relationship; the secondary priority is the car deal.

Studying

When you study a prospect's business, look at the big picture. As mentioned earlier in the book, don't focus on features; look for benefits you can provide. Look behind a prospect's demands for reasons. You can ask, "What are you trying to accomplish by asking for this?" After the prospect answers, you may be able to say, "We can accomplish that another way. Consider this alternative . . . ." The more options for providing benefits, the more flexible the negotiation.

During this phase, you must find out what other competitors' products or services your prospect is considering. This gives insight into what they are looking for and willing to pay. If you are selling a half-million-dollar CAT scanner and your prospect is also considering a three-quarter-million-dollar CAT scanner, you know your product is not priced too high. If, however, your prospect is looking at a lot of lower-priced units, it may be an uphill struggle to get the prospect to spend what you're asking. Knowing who your competitors are will help you assess bargaining strengths and weaknesses.

Every purchase is made with decision-making criteria in mind, either consciously or subconsciously. Find out what they are for your prospect and the prospect's company. Within those criteria, there are usually three levels of desire: must have, should have, and would be nice to have. Be clear about these levels and how they create limits for negotiations. Obviously, "must haves" are much less flexible than "would be nice to haves."

Proposing

Proposing is another phase that indirectly affects subsequent negotiations. What you do in the presentation sets the stage for what may come later. During your presentation, tie features and advantages to benefits and emphasize unique benefits. In this way, your product or service and company are positioned above the competition. It is important to position yourself as well. Don't be afraid to let your prospect know she is getting you and everything you have promised to do after the sale.

The successful resolution of a negotiation starts with a commitment to do business together. It is then necessary for both parties to maintain common interests and resolve any conflicts cooperatively. The key to selling and negotiating is to always seek a win–win solution in which both buyer and seller are happy.

SALES PRESENTATIONS GO HIGH-TECH

Videos, CD-ROMs, satellite conferencing, and computer hardware and software are increasingly being used in sales presentations. Whether in transactional, relationship, or partnering situations, salespeople are finding high-tech sales presentations effective in providing customers with the necessary information to make informed decisions. Chapter 11 discusses these important selling tools further.

SELECT THE PRESENTATION METHOD, THEN THE APPROACH

Before developing the presentation, you must know which presentation method you will use. Once you determine which presentation method is best for your situation, plan what you will do when talking with your prospect. Your initial consideration should be how to begin your sales presentation.

LET'S REVIEW BEFORE MOVING ON!

So what have you learned from your textbook? You have come a long way, in a short time, in understanding the many challenges facing today's salesperson. It is a big job—one full of personal and financial rewards.

Before moving on to learning specific sales communications techniques used in the selling process, take a look at Exhibit 9.11.[8] You have learned about the discussion sequence, buyer's mental steps, and a little about the selling process.

EXHIBIT 9.11

The parallel dimensions of selling. When you understand their sequences and interactions you are ready to go sell something!

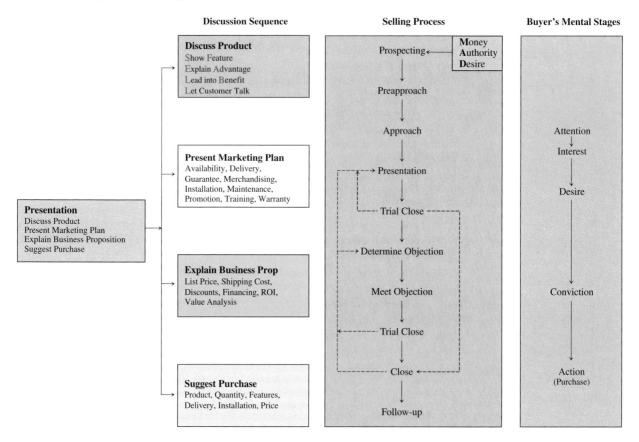

What's Important to Know?

Top-performing salespeople use the parallel dimensions of selling to plan, create, and execute their presentation. One of the main reasons to study and understand Exhibit 9.11 is to learn how the three dimensions of selling—discussion sequence, selling process, buyer's mental steps—interact, often at the same time, to form a specific sales presentation.

After finding a prospect, for example, the salesperson plans the sales call. The opening of the presentation, referred to as the approach, is created to quickly capture the buyer's attention, stimulate interest in listening to the presentation, and provide a smooth transition into the presentation.

What do you talk about in the presentation? The discussion sequence column in Exhibit 9.12 outlines this for you. First you discuss the product, then the marketing plan, followed by the business proposition, and finally the suggested purchase. Each of the four discussion sequence elements presents examples of information to provide the buyer. For example, the marketing plan should include a discussion of product availability, delivery, guarantee, and the like. The business proposition, on the other hand, talks about things such as price, shipping cost, and discounts.

The salesperson wants to ask for the order—close—when the buyer is in the conviction stage. If the salesperson senses the buyer feels a need for the product, it is time to close by recommending a suggested purchase, which may include a discussion of the specific product, quantity, features, and so forth. The discussion sequence is designed to help move the buyer through the five mental steps in the buying process.

As you study Exhibit 9.11, look back through your textbook and your class notes to refresh your memory on the relationships shown there. When reading future chapters, especially Chapters 10, 11, 12, 13, and 14, refer back to Exhibit 9.11 to determine how that particular chapter fits into the three parallel dimensions of selling. Once you master these dimensions you will be able to accomplish the following:

- Make a professional sales presentation in any situation.
- Show a recruiter, or your sales manager, that you understand the sales process.
- Train other people to become sales professionals.
- Know that in a role as a consultant, you can quickly understand any organization's current selling process and sales program, what their sales force will like, and what will help increase sales.

In the next chapter you will learn of the various considerations involved in making a great first impression when you meet the buyer or prospect. Please remember, you only have one chance to make a great first impression!

The Golden Rule Makes Sense

Using the parallel dimensions of selling allows you to follow the Golden Rule. How? If you were a purchasing agent for a business, wouldn't you want to have salespeople who have a plan presentation containing all of the information about the product, marketing plan, and business proposition based upon your needs? You bet you would! And wouldn't you want the salesperson to meet your objections or answer all of your questions truthfully? Yes! And most important, wouldn't you want the salesperson to place your needs first, over making a sale. Absolutely!

The Golden Rule of Personal Selling makes sense in today's competitive business world. Its use sets you apart from all of the other salespeople who only want to make a sale and fast dollar, often by using lies and high-pressure tactics. Treat your prospects and customers as your business neighbors. If you care, they will care!

Dale Carnegie Gives a Word of Warning!

Winning friends and influencing people may require a change of heart.

One of the most famous business books of the last century was *How to Win Friends and Influence People* written by Dale Carnegie.[9] Mr. Carnegie gave a word of warning to people who would use advice given in his wonderful book as techniques just to win friends and influence people for their own self-centered purposes. On page 208 he said, "the principles taught in this book will work only when they are from the heart. I am not advocating a bag of tricks. I am talking about a new way of life." Mr. Carnegie wrote this powerful "truth" in 1936.

Your author is saying the same thing in the 21st century. The contents of this book can be used for good or evil. For good, by placing others first and treating people as you would like to be treated. Practicing the Golden Rule from your heart will allow you to win friends and influence people. For evil, by placing you first and taking advantage of others' good nature. It is up to you. But please remember, you can mislead some of the people some of the time, but not all of the people all of the time. You can get away with putting your self-interest first only for so long. That is why so many people are not successful in sales.

To be successful in sales over time, you must truly believe in treating others ethically, caring for them as a person and business. If you feel this in your heart, you will never work another day in your life. You have found your calling, so keep contacting others to satisfy their needs! You are a true salesperson if you care.

SUMMARY OF MAJOR SELLING ISSUES

To improve your chances of making a sale, you must master the art of delivering a good sales presentation. An effective presentation will work toward specifically solving the customer's problems. The sales presentation method you select should be based on prior knowledge of the customer, your sales call objective, and your customer benefit plan.

Because prospects want to know how you and your product will benefit them and the companies they represent, you must show that you have a right to present your product because it has key benefits for them. Many different sales presentation methods are available. They differ from one another depending on what percentage of the conversation is controlled by the salesperson. The salesperson usually does most of the talking in the more structured memorized and formula selling techniques, while more buyer–seller interaction occurs in the less structured methods.

In the memorized presentation, or stimulus–response method, the salesperson does 80 to 90 percent of the talking, with each customer receiving the same sales pitch. Although this method ensures a well-planned presentation and is good for certain nontechnical products, it is also somewhat inflexible, allowing little prospect participation. The formula presentation, a persuasive selling presentation, is similar to the first method, but it takes the prospect into account by answering questions and handling objections.

The most challenging and creative form of selling uses the need-satisfaction presentation. This flexible method begins by raising questions about what the customer specifically needs. After you are aware of the customer's needs, you can then show how your products fit these needs. You must be cautious because many people don't want to open up to the salesperson.

When selling highly complex or technical products like computers or insurance, a problem–solution presentation consisting of six steps is a good sales method. This method involves developing a detailed analysis of the buyer's specific needs and problems and designing a proposal and presentation to fit these needs. This customized method often uses a selling team to present the specialized information to the buyer.

In comparing the four presentation methods, there is no one best method. Each one must be tailored to meet the particular characteristics of a specific selling situation or environment.

MEETING A SALES CHALLENGE

Don't panic! You've done everything you could have done. You have worked hard on this presentation, and you are prepared. This will be a challenge you can handle. As all pros know, on any sales call you have to be prepared to adapt to the situation. They must be very interested, or they would not have these executives attend the meeting.

This presentation is similar to the one-on-one you practiced but less flexible. Once the group has assembled, they will ask you to begin—so first introduce yourself and explain in a clear, concise sentence the premise of your proposal. Follow the remaining five group-presentation suggestions in this chapter. Invite everyone to ask questions throughout your talk.

KEY TERMS FOR SELLING

sales presentation   281
memorized presentation   283
formula presentation   285
need-satisfaction presentation   287

need development   288
need awareness   288
need fulfillment   288
problem–solution presentation   289

SALES APPLICATION QUESTIONS

1. What are the four sales presentation methods discussed in this chapter? Briefly explain each method; include any similarities and differences in your answer.
2. One salesperson profiled in this book stated that he concentrates on the need-fulfillment phase of the sales presentation. Is he correct in his approach? Why or why not?
3. Assume that a salesperson already knows the customer's needs. Instead of developing the customer's needs as a part of the sales presentation, he goes directly to the close. What are your feelings on this type of sales presentation?
4. To properly use the formula sales presentation, what information does the seller need?
5. What steps are required to develop and use the need-satisfaction presentation?
6. Assume you are selling a product requiring you to typically use the problem-solving sales presentation method. You have completed your study of a prospect's business and are ready to present your recommendation to her. What is your selling strategy?
7. According to Exhibit 9.11, what should be occurring in the buyer's mental state during the "Approach" step of the selling process?
8. Assume that you are a salesperson for a cable company. You have a repeat customer that has already established their interest level in your product. What type of sales call should you use?

FURTHER EXPLORING THE SALES WORLD

Assume that you are a salesperson selling a consumer item such as a wristwatch. Without any preparation, make a sales presentation to a friend. If possible, record your sales presentation on a tape recorder. Analyze the recording and determine the approximate conversation time with your prospect. On the basis of your analysis, which of the four sales presentation methods discussed in Chapter 9 did you use? How early in the sales presentation did your prospect begin to give you objections?

SELLING EXPERIENTIAL EXERCISE

What Are Your Negotiation Skills?

The following 10 personal characteristics necessary to successful negotiation can help you determine the potential you already possess and also identify areas where improvement is needed. On a separate piece of paper, write the number that best reflects where you fall on the scale. The higher the number, the more the characteristic describes you. When you have finished, total the numbers.

1.	I am sensitive to the needs of others.	1	2	3	4	5	6	7	8	9	10
2.	I will compromise to solve problems when necessary.	1	2	3	4	5	6	7	8	9	10
3.	I am committed to a win-win philosophy.	1	2	3	4	5	6	7	8	9	10
4.	I have a high tolerance for conflict.	1	2	3	4	5	6	7	8	9	10
5.	I am willing to research and analyze issues fully.	1	2	3	4	5	6	7	8	9	10
6.	Patience is one of my strong points.	1	2	3	4	5	6	7	8	9	10
7.	My tolerance for stress is high.	1	2	3	4	5	6	7	8	9	10
8.	I am a good listener.	1	2	3	4	5	6	7	8	9	10
9.	Personal attack and ridicule do not unduly bother me.	1	2	3	4	5	6	7	8	9	10
10.	I can identify bottom line issues quickly.	1	2	3	4	5	6	7	8	9	10

If you scored 80 or more, you have characteristics of a good negotiator. You recognize what negotiating requires and seen willing to apply yourself accordingly. If you scored between 60 and 79, you should do well as a negotiator but have some characteristics that need further development. If your evaluation is less than 60, you should go over the items again carefully. You may have been hard on yourself, or you may have identified some key areas on which to concentrate as you negotiate. Repeat this evaluation again after you have had practice negotiating.[10]

CHAPTER 9

Carefully Select Which Sales Presentation Method to Use

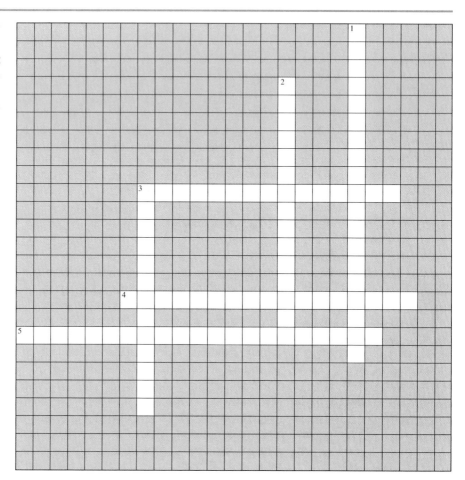

Across

3. In a need-satisfaction sales presentation, the stage at which the discussion is devoted to the buyer's needs.

4. The actual presentation of the sales message to the prospect.

5. A type of presentation in which the salesperson does 80 to 90 percent of the talking, focusing on the product and its benefits rather than attempting to determine the prospect's needs.

Down

1. A presentation by which the salesperson follows a general outline that allows more flexibility and tries to determine prospect needs.

2. The last phase of need-satisfaction sales presentation. Here, the salesperson shows how the product will satisfy mutual needs.

3. The stage at which the salesperson is aware of the buyer's needs and takes control of the situation by restating those needs to clarify the situation.

CASE 9-1
Cascade Soap Company

Mike Bowers sells soap products to grocery wholesalers and large retail grocery chains. The following presentation occurred during a call he made on Bill Reese, the soap buyer for a grocery store.

Salesperson: Bill, you have stated several times that the types of promotions or brands that really turn you on are ones that carry the best profit. Is that right?

Customer: Yes, it is. I'm under pressure to increase my profit-per-square-foot in my department.

Salesperson: Bill, I recommend that you begin carrying the king size of Cascade. Let's review the benefits and economics of this proposal. King-size Cascade would cost you 86.8¢ a box. The average resale in this market is 99¢. That means that you would make 12.2¢ every time you sell a box of king-size Cascade. Based on my estimated volume for your store of $40,000 per week, you would sell approximately two cases of king-size Cascade per week. That is $19.80 in new sales and $2.44 in new profits per week for your store. As you can see, the addition of Cascade 10 to your automatic dishwashing detergent department will increase your sales and, even more importantly, increase your profits—and this is what you said you wanted to do, right?

Customer: Yes, I am interested in increasing profits.

Salesperson: Do you want me to give this information to the head stock clerk so that she can make arrangements to put Cascade 10s on the shelf? Or would you like me to put it on the shelf on my next call?

Questions

1. What sales presentation method was Mike using?
2. Evaluate Mike's handling of this situation

CASE 9-2
A Retail Sales Presentation

A customer is looking at a display of Cross gold pens and pencils.

Customer: I'm looking for a graduation gift for my brother, but I'm not necessarily looking for a pen and pencil set.

Salesperson: Is your brother graduating from college or high school?

Customer: He is graduating from college this spring.

Salesperson: I can show you quite a few items that would be appropriate gifts. Let's start by taking a look at this elegant Cross pen and pencil set. Don't they look impressive?

Customer: They look too expensive. Besides, a pen and pencil set doesn't seem like an appropriate gift for a college graduate.

Salesperson: You're right, a Cross pen and pencil set *does* look expensive. Just imagine how impressed your brother will be when he opens your gift package and finds these beautiful writing instruments. Even though Cross pen and pencil sets look expensive, they are actually quite reasonably priced, considering the total value you are getting.

Customer: How much does this set cost?

Salesperson: You can buy a Cross pen and pencil set for anywhere from $15 to $300. The one I am showing you is gold-plated and costs only $28. For this modest amount you can purchase a gift for your brother that will be attractive, useful, last a lifetime, and will show him that you truly think he is deserving of the very best. Don't you think that is what a graduation gift should be?

Customer: You make it sound pretty good, but frankly I hadn't intended to spend that much money.

Salesperson: Naturally, I can show you something else. However, before I do that, pick up this Cross pen and write your name on this pad of paper. Notice that in addition to good looks, Cross pens offer good writing. Cross is widely acclaimed as one of the best ball-point pens on the market. It is nicely balanced, has a point that allows the ink to flow on the paper smoothly, and rides over the paper with ease.

Customer: You're right, the pen writes really well.

Salesperson: Each time your brother writes with this pen, he will remember that you gave him this fine writing instrument for graduation. In addition, Cross offers prestige. Many customers tell us that Cross is one of the few pens they have used that is so outstanding that people often comment on it by brand name. Your brother will enjoy having others notice the pen he uses is high in quality.

Customer: You're right. I do tend to notice when someone is using a Cross pen.

Salesperson: You can't go wrong with a Cross pen and pencil set for a gift. Shall I wrap it for you?

Customer: It's a hard decision.

Salesperson: Your brother will be very happy with this gift.

Customer: Okay. Go ahead and wrap it for me.

Salesperson: Fine. Would you like me to wrap up another set for you to give yourself?

Customer: No, one is enough. Maybe someone will buy one for me someday.[11]

Questions

1. Describe the selling techniques being used by the retail salesperson.
2. Evaluate the salesperson's handling of this situation.

CASE 9-3
Negotiating with a Friend

Barney wants to buy a car. He spotted a high-quality used car on a dealer's lot over the weekend. He would buy it immediately if he had more cash. The dealer will give him only $1,200 on a trade for his current automobile. The car Barney wants is really great, and chances are good it will be sold in short order. Barney has planned carefully and decided he can swing the deal if he can sell his present vehicle to a private party for around $2,000. This would give him $1,500 for a down payment and $500 for accessories he wishes to add. The car is in good condition except for a couple of minor dents in the fender. The snow tires for his current car won't fit the new one but can probably be sold; that will help. Barney can remove the new stereo system he installed last month and place it in the new car.

Billie, one of Barney's co-workers, heard that Barney wants to sell his car and plans to talk to him about it. Her daughter is graduating from college in three months and will need a car to drive to work. Billie can only afford about $1,800 including any repairs that might be required, and she needs to reserve enough money for snow tires. Her daughter has seen the car and thinks it's sporty, especially with the stereo. Billie checked the blue book price for the model of Barney's car, and she knows the average wholesale price is $1,200 and the average retail price is $1,950.[12]

Questions

1. What are Barney's objectives?
2. What are Billie's objectives?
3. What are likely to be the points of conflict?
4. What power does Barney have?
5. What power does Billie have?
6. How important is time to Barney?
7. How important is time to Billie?
8. What are some possible points of compromise?

Begin Your Presentation Strategically

LEARNING OBJECTIVES

You have selected your prospect, planned the sales call, and determined the appropriate presentation method. Now, you must determine how to begin the sales presentation. This step in the selling process is called the *approach*. After studying this chapter, you should be able to

- Explain the importance of using an approach and provide examples of approaches.

- Illustrate why the approach should have a theme that is related to the presentation and the prospect's important buying motives. What is an example?

- Present four types of questioning techniques for use throughout the presentation and give an example of each technique.

- Understand the importance of being flexible in your approach.

You are making a cold call on the office manager of a local bank—Citizen's National. You assume one of the manager's responsibilities consists of ordering office supplies. Based on your experience with other banks, you suspect the volume of orders would be small but steady throughout the year.

As a salesperson for University Office Supplies, you especially want to sell your new equipment for mailing out bank statements, along with the paper and other products associated with this job. Since this is a small bank, you decide to go in cold, relying on your questioning ability to uncover potential problems and make the prospect aware of them.

You are now face-to-face with the manager. You have introduced yourself, and after some small talk you feel it is time to begin your presentation. Many salespeople face this situation several times each day. What would you do? What type of presentation would you use? How would you begin the presentation?

Have you ever been told, "You get only one opportunity to make a good first impression"? If the first minute of talking with a prospect creates a bad impression, it can take hours to overcome it—if you ever do. Many times, salespeople get only one chance to sell a prospect.

The approach—or beginning—of your presentation is essential to the prospect's allowing you to discuss your product. If done incorrectly the prospect may stop you from telling your sales story. You need to have a good beginning in order to have a good ending to your sales presentation.

This chapter introduces you to the *dos* and *don'ts* of beginning your sales presentation. Many salespeople are nervous about contacting prospects. Let's begin our discussion of the approach by first relating it to the Tree of Business Life.

THE TREE OF BUSINESS LIFE: THE BEGINNING

Beginning with an end in mind, says Stephen Covey, is a habit of successful people. Salespeople should begin their sales presentation knowing the key benefits to be discussed and having a reasonable idea of what to suggest that the prospect or customer buy to solve his or her needs. Covey also believes that to be successful you should seek first to understand, then to be understood. This is great advice for salespeople. Salespeople should understand the customer's needs in order to suggest solutions.

Knowing you can help solve their problem(s) provides great caring, confidence, and excitement in your mind, body movements, and speech. You are there to help the person. Wow, what a wonderful feeling you may experience in your mind, body, and soul. With enthusiasm outwardly radiating your inward glow, your words are like a lamp burning and shining in the dark. You are the light speaking the truth. The seed for the business relationship is planted in fertile ground. It is clear you are there for the other person—not yourself.

The care shown at the beginning of your conversation allows you to give your presentation. This often results in a sale.

Ethical service after the sale builds true long-term relationships and nourishes the Tree of Business Life so it can grow as a giant oak tree. The beginning of the sales presentations is called the approach.

WHAT IS THE APPROACH?

A golf shot from the fairway toward the green is referred to as the approach, as are the steps a bowler takes before delivering the bowling ball. Both the golfer and bowler take preliminary steps before attempting to score.

The salesperson is similar to the golfer and bowler in this respect. Imagine this: The salesperson locates a prospect or identifies a customer to contact, gets an appointment, plans the presentation, and arrives at the prospect/customer's business. The salesperson is called into the office. The approach phase of the selling process begins. The salesperson begins the preliminary steps toward getting the buyer to listen to the sales presentation.

Every sale begins with an approach.

For salespeople, the **approach** refers to the time from when they first see the buyer to when they begin to discuss the product. The approach could last seconds or minutes depending upon the time it takes to meet, greet, build rapport, and go through one of the approach communication techniques discussed later in this chapter.

As you see in Exhibit 10.1, the approach, the third step in the selling process, is the first step in the actual sales presentation. I caution you not to take the approach step in the selling process lightly—it is very serious. Many sales trainers feel that it can be the most important step toward helping customers solve their

EXHIBIT 10.1

The approach begins the sales presentation.

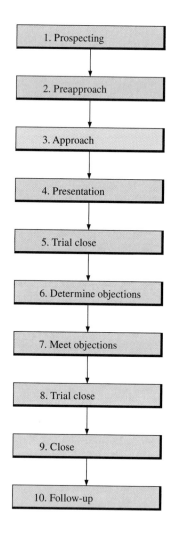

1. Prospecting

2. Preapproach

3. Approach

4. Presentation

5. Trial close

6. Determine objections

7. Meet objections

8. Trial close

9. Close

10. Follow-up

needs through buying your products. If the approach is unsuccessful, you may never get the opportunity to give your product presentation.

Take a minute now to consider the similarities and differences between the approach for the golfer, bowler, and salesperson. At the same time, study Exhibit 10.1 and the actions taken by the salesperson in the approach. It may help you see the importance of the approach in the sales presentation. Certainly it will help you understand this and the next chapter better.

THE RIGHT TO APPROACH

You have the right (or duty) to present your product if you can show that it will definitely benefit the prospect. In essence, you have to prove *you* are worthy of the prospect's time and serious attention. You may earn the right to this attention in a number of ways:

- By exhibiting specific product or business knowledge.
- By expressing a sincere desire to solve a buyer's problem and satisfy a need.
- By stating or implying that your product will save money or increase the firm's profit margin.
- By displaying a service attitude.

Basically, prospects want to know how you and your product will benefit *them* and *the companies* they represent. Your sales approach should initially establish, and thereafter concentrate on, your product's key benefits for each prospect.

This strategy is especially important during the approach stage of a presentation because it aids in securing the prospect's interest in you and your product. At this point, you want this unspoken reaction from the prospect: "Well, I'd better hear this salesperson out. I may hear something that will be of use to me." Now that you have justified your right to sell to a prospect, determine how to present your product.

THE APPROACH— OPENING THE SALES PRESENTATION

Raleigh Johnson spent days qualifying the prospect, arranging for an appointment, and planning every aspect of the sales presentation; and in the first 60 seconds of the sales presentation, he realized his chance of selling was excellent. He quickly determined the prospect's needs and evoked attention and interest in his product because of the technique he used to begin the sales interview.

A buyer's reactions to the salesperson in the early minutes of the sales presentation are critical to a successful sale. This short period is so important that it is treated as an individual step in selling, referred to as the approach. Part of any approach is the prospect's first impression of you.

Your Attitude during the Approach

As Exhibit 10.2 shows, it is common for a salesperson to experience tension in various forms when contacting a prospect. Often this is brought on when the salesperson has preconceived ideas that things may go wrong during the sale. Prospects may be viewed as having negative characteristics that make the sales call difficult.

All salespeople experience some degree of stress at times. Yet successful salespeople have learned a relaxation and concentration technique called **creative imagery** that allows them to cope with stress. The salesperson envisions the worst that can happen. Then preparation is made to react to it and even accept it if need be. The best that can happen is also envisioned, as seen in Exhibit 10.3. Furthermore,

EXHIBIT 10.2

Making sure your attitude is positive.

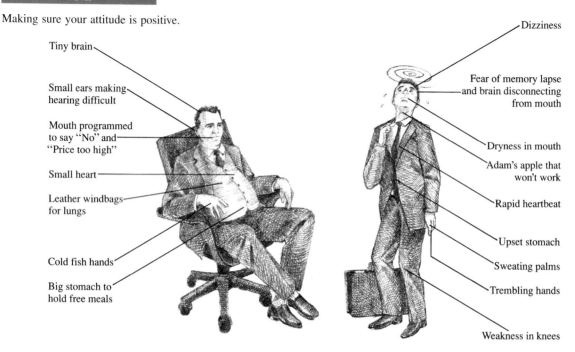

Tiny brain

Small ears making
hearing difficult

Mouth programmed
to say "No" and
"Price too high"

Small heart

Leather windbags
for lungs

Cold fish hands

Big stomach to
hold free meals

Dizziness

Fear of memory lapse
and brain disconnecting
from mouth

Dryness in mouth

Adam's apple that
won't work

Rapid heartbeat

Upset stomach

Sweating palms

Trembling hands

Weakness in knees

EXHIBIT 10.3

Creative imagery is a great way
to relax while psyching yourself
up before seeing your prospect.

Picture worst and best that can
happen, plus success.

contingency plans are mentally prepared should the planned sales presentation need to be abandoned.

The last question the salesperson should ask herself is, "What are the chances that things will go wrong?" Chances are the answer involves a low probability. Usually, there is less than a 1 percent chance that things will go wrong, especially when careful planning has taken place before the sales call. A greater than 99 percent probability that things will go as planned should dim fears of the most worrisome salespeople.

The First Impression You Make Is Critical to Success

You only have one chance to make a good first impression.

When you meet your prospect, the initial impression you make is based on appearances. If this impression is favorable, your prospect is more likely to listen to you; if it is not favorable, your prospect may erect communication barriers that are difficult to overcome.

The first impression is centered on the image projected by your (1) appearance and (2) attitude. Here are some suggestions for making a favorable first impression:

- Wear business clothes that are suitable and fairly conservative.
- Be neat in dress and grooming.
- Refrain from smoking, chewing gum, or drinking when in your prospect's office.
- Keep an erect posture to project confidence.
- Leave all unnecessary materials outside the office (overcoat, umbrella, or newspaper).
- If possible, sit down. Should the prospect not offer a chair, ask, "May I sit here?"
- Be enthusiastic and positive throughout the interview.
- Smile, always smile! (Try to be sincere with your smile; it will aid you in being enthusiastic and positive toward your prospect.)
- Do not apologize for taking the prospect's time.
- Do not imply that you were just passing by and that the sales call was not planned.
- Maintain eye contact with the prospect.
- If the prospect offers to shake hands, do so with a firm, positive grip while maintaining eye contact.

A person's name is music to their ears.

- If possible, before the interview, learn how to pronounce your prospect's name correctly and use it throughout the interview. Should the prospect introduce you to other people, remember their names by using the five ways to remember names shown in Exhibit 10.4.

Like an actor, the salesperson must learn how to project and maintain a positive, confident, and enthusiastic first impression no matter what mood the prospect is in when the salesperson arrives.

EXHIBIT 10.4

Five ways to remember prospect's name.

1. Be sure to hear the person's name and use it: "It's good to meet you, Mr. Firestone."
2. Spell it out in your mind, or if it is an unusual name, ask the person to spell the name.
3. Relate the name to something you are familiar with, such as relating the name Firestone to Firestone automobile tires.
4. Use the name in the conversation.
5. Repeat the name at the end of the conversation, such as "Goodbye, Mr. Firestone."

EXHIBIT 10.5		Approach Techniques		
The approach techniques for each of the four sales presentation methods.	**Sales Presentation Methods**	**Statement**	**Demonstration**	**Questions**
	Memorized (canned)	✔	✔	✔
	Formula (persuasive selling)	✔	✔	✔
	Need-satisfaction			✔
	Problem-solving			✔

Examine and assign a degree of importance to these factors before entering your customer's office:

- Your sales call *objective.*
- The *type of approach* that will be well received.
- Your *customer benefit plan.*

This approach selection process can greatly aid in making a positive first impression.

Approach Techniques and Objectives

Approach techniques are grouped into three general categories: (1) opening with a statement; (2) opening with a demonstration; and (3) opening with one or more questions.

Your choice of approach technique depends on which of the four sales presentation methods you have selected based on your situation and sales presentation plan. Exhibit 10.5 presents one way of determining the approach technique to use. Using questions in a sales approach is feasible with any of the four presentation methods, whereas statements and demonstrations typically are reserved for either the memorized or formula sales presentation methods. Because of their customer-oriented nature, the need-satisfaction and problem–solution sales presentation methods always employ questions at the outset. This chapter reviews each of the approach techniques with examples of their uses and benefits.

Both the statement and demonstration approach techniques have three basic objectives:

1. To capture the prospect's *attention.*
2. To stimulate the prospect's *interest.*
3. To provide a *transition* into the sales presentation.

Imagine the prospect silently asking three questions: (1) "Shall I see this person?" (2) "Shall I listen, talk with, and devote more time to this person?" and (3) "What's in it for me?" The answers to these questions help determine the outcome of the sale. If you choose to use either of these two approaches, create a statement or demonstration approach that causes the prospect to say yes to each of these three questions.

Small Talk Warms 'em Up

In most, if not all, sales calls the approach consists of two parts. First is usually a "small talk" or rapport-building phase. You might talk about the weather, sports, or anything. This is especially true when calling on a prospect who has a feeler, intuitor, or thinker personality style.* The senser, however, may want to get directly to business.

* Refer back to Chapter 4 for the discussion on personality styles.

The second part of the approach is the planned, formal selling technique used as a lead-in to the upcoming discussion of the product. It consists of using either a statement, demonstration, or one or more questions. Which of these three to use is based on the situation.

The Situational Approach

The situation you face determines which approach technique you use to begin your sales presentation. The situation is dictated by a number of variables that only you can identify. Some of the more common situational variables are

- The type of *product* you are selling.
- Whether this is a *repeat call* on the same person.
- Your degree of knowledge about the *customer's needs*.
- The *time* you have for making the sales presentation.
- Whether the customer is *aware of a problem*.

The sales approach can be a frightening, lonely, heart-stopping experience. It can easily lead to ego-bruising rejection. Your challenge is to move the prospect from an often cold, indifferent, or sometimes even hostile frame of mind to an aroused excitement about the product. By quickly gaining the prospect's attention and interest, the conversation can make a smooth transition into the sales presentation, which greatly improves the probability of making the sale.

In addition to creating attention, stimulating interest, and providing for transition, using questions in your approach includes the following objectives:

1. To *uncover* the needs or problems *important* to the prospect.
2. To determine if the prospect wishes to *fulfill* those needs or *solve* these problems.
3. To have the prospect *tell you* about these needs or problems, and the intention to do something about them.

Because people buy to fulfill needs or solve problems, the use of questions in your approach is preferable to statements or demonstrations. Questions allow you to uncover needs, whereas statements and demonstrations are appropriate when you assume knowledge of the prospect's needs. However, the salesperson can use all three approach techniques in the proper situation. Exhibit 10.6 shows the three basic approach techniques and examples of each technique you will study, beginning with opening statements. Be sure and remember the Golden Rule when creating your approach.

The Golden Rule. Many salespeople are tempted to exaggerate their product's benefits in the approach. Why? Because of what you just read. Should the salesperson not get a person's attention and interest quickly, that person may not allow the presentation. This is well known by top salespeople. So there can be temptation in one's own interest to exaggerate a product's benefits. People do not want to be taken

EXHIBIT 10.6

Approach techniques for opening the presentation.

Statements	Demonstrations	Questions
Introductory	Product	Customer Benefit
Complimentary	Showmanship	Curiosity
Referral		Opinion
Premium		Shock
		Multiple Question (SPIN)

advantage of by salespeople. Promising too much can lose the sale and destroy the relationship, so follow the Golden Rule by placing the other person's interest before your self-interest. Let's see how to open the presentation with attention-getting statements.

Opening with Statements

Opening statements are effective if properly planned, especially if the salesperson has uncovered the prospect's needs before entering the office. Four statement approaches frequently used are (1) the introductory approach; (2) the complimentary approach; (3) the referral approach; and (4) the premium approach.

The **introductory approach** is the most common and the least powerful because it does little to capture the prospect's attention and interest. It opens with the salesperson's name and business: "Hello, Ms. Crompton, my name is John Gladstone, representing the Pierce Chemical Company."

The introductory approach is needed when meeting a prospect for the first time. In most cases, though, the introductory approach should be used in conjunction with another approach. This additional approach could be the complimentary approach.

Everyone likes a compliment. If the **complimentary approach** is sincere, it is an effective beginning to a sales interview:

- Ms. Rosenburg, you certainly have a thriving restaurant business. I have enjoyed many lunches here. While doing so, I have thought of several products that could make your business even better and make things easier for you and your employees.
- Mr. Davidson, I was just visiting with your boss who commented that you were doing a good job in keeping your company's printing costs down. I have a couple of ideas that may help you further reduce your costs!

Sometimes a suitable compliment is not in order or cannot be generated. Another way to get the buyer's attention is to mention a mutual acquaintance as a reference (see Exhibit 10.7).

The use of another person's name, the **referral approach**, is effective if the prospect respects that person; it is important to remember, however, that the referral

---

EXHIBIT 10.7

The referral approach.

Angie was creative in using the referral approach. A friend of the buyer allowed her to tape a brief introductory message. She put the tape recorder on his desk and let the buyer listen. It was a great way to open her presentation.

approach can have a negative effect if the prospect does not like the person you refer to:

- Ms. Rosenburg, my name is Carlos Ramirez, with the Restaurant Supply Corporation. When I talked to your brother last week, he wanted me to give you the opportunity to see Restaurant Supply's line of paper products for your restaurant.
- Hello, Mr. Gillespie—Linda Crawford with the Ramada Inn suggested that I contact you concerning our new Xerox table copier.

One salesperson tells of having a customer tape-record a brief introduction to a friend. When calling on the friend, the salesperson placed the recorder on the desk and said, "Amos McDonald has a message for you, Ms. James . . . let's listen."

Few people can obtain a reference for every prospect they intend to contact (this may be especially true for a beginning salesperson). Even if you don't know all the right people, you can still get on track by offering the buyer something for nothing—a premium.

A **premium approach** is effective because everyone likes to receive something free. When appropriate, use free samples and novelty items in a premium approach.

- Early in the morning of her first day on a new campus, one textbook salesperson makes a practice of leaving a dozen doughnuts in the faculty lounge with her card stapled to the box. She claims that prospects actually come looking for her!
- Mr. Jones, here is a beautiful desk calendar with your name engraved on it. Each month I will place a new calendar in the holder which, by the way, will feature one of our products. This month's calendar, for example, features our lubricating oil.
- Ms. Rogers, this high-quality Fuller hair brush is yours, free, for just giving me five minutes of your time.
- Ms. McCall [handing her the product to examine], I want to leave samples for you, your cosmetic representative, and your best customers of Revlon's newest addition to our perfume line.

Creative use of premiums is an effective sales approach. Demonstrations also leave a favorable impression with a prospect.

> *"Begin in terms of the other man's interest."*
>
> DALE CARNEGIE

Demonstration Openings

Openings that use demonstrations and drama are especially effective because of their ability to force the prospect into participating in the interview. Of the two methods discussed here, the product approach is more frequently used alone or in combination with statements and questions.

In the **product approach,** the salesperson places the product on the counter or hands it to the customer, saying nothing. The salesperson waits for the prospect to begin the conversation. The product approach is useful if the product is new, unique, colorful, or if it is an existing product that has changed noticeably.

If, for example, Pepsi-Cola completely changed the shape of its bottle and label, the salesperson would simply hand the new product to the retail buyer and wait for a reaction. In marketing a new pocket calculator for college students, the Texas Instruments salesperson might simply lay the product on the buyer's desk and wait. It is possible to effectively combine the product approach with the showmanship approach.

The **showmanship approach** involves doing something unusual to catch the prospect's attention and interest; this should be done carefully so that the approach

A Precall Approach Worked!

At a toastmasters meeting, Phil Proctor of Associated Printing in Ft. Lauderdale, Florida, was approached by another club member about a printing job for her direct-mail company. As VP of sales and marketing, he was interested in the sample she showed him. "Is it something you can handle?" she asked. When she told Phil that her company produced 30 million direct-mail pieces per month "at a total printing cost of more than $1 million each month," he said, "Of course." However, he still had to convince the COO of her company that they were the best choice for the job.

To create meeting interest, he routinely uses a corny but effective prop: a simple bag of bread with a note that reads, "Our clients say we're the greatest thing since . . . sliced bread." It's a little out of the box, but it works as an immediate door opener.

This time, with so much at stake, he decided to do a little extra research. With a quick call to his secretary, he learned that the COO was Jewish. Instead of sending normal bakery bread, Phil sent a fresh loaf of Challah bread. The results were incredible. The COO's secretary called him soon after his package arrived with an invitation to come to the office that afternoon. The COO was absolutely ecstatic. He thought it was the boldest, most creative introduction he'd ever seen. Even though he was about to commit to another company, he changed his mind at the last minute and insisted on splitting all the work between the two companies.

With the good recommendation from his fellow club member, and the initiative he showed in the sales process, Phil closed the sale before he even made the call.[1]

does not backfire, which can happen if the demonstration does not work or is so flamboyant that it is inappropriate for the situation.

- "Ms. Rosenburg, our paper plates are the strongest on the market, making them drip-free, a quality your customers will appreciate." [The salesperson places a paper plate on her lap and pours cooking grease or motor oil onto it while speaking to the prospect.]
- As she hands the buyer a plate from a new line of china, she lets it drop to the floor. It does not break. While picking it up, she says, "Our new breakthrough in treating quality china will revolutionize the industry. Your customers, especially newlyweds, will love this feature. Don't you think so?"
- The salesperson selling Super Glue would repeat the television advertisement for the prospect. In the prospect's office, the salesperson glues two objects together, such as a broken handle onto a coffee cup, waits one minute, hands the cup to the buyer for a test, and then begins the sales presentation. The mended cup can be left with the buyer as a gift and a reminder.
- The life insurance salesperson hands the prospect a bunch of daisies, saying, "Steve, when you're pushing daisies, what will your family be doing?" [This is probably too tactless to use on anyone except a close friend, but you get the picture.]

Opening with Questions

Questions are the most common openers because they allow the salesperson to better determine the prospect's needs and force the prospect to participate in the sales interview. The salesperson should use only questions that experience and pre-planning have proven receive a positive reaction from the buyer, since a negative reaction is hard to overcome.

Like opening statements, opening questions can be synthesized to suit a number of selling situations. The following sections introduce several basic questioning approaches. This listing is by no means exclusive, but it introduces you to a smattering of questioning frameworks. With experience, a salesperson develops a knack for determining what question to ask what prospect.

Customer Benefit Approach

Using this approach, the salesperson asks a question that implies the product will benefit the prospect; if it is their initial meeting, the salesperson can include both his (her) and the company's name:

- Hi. I'm Charles Foster of ABC Shipping and Storage Company! Mr. McDaniel, would you be interested in a new storage and shipping container that will reduce your transfer costs by 10 to 20 percent?
- Would you be interested in saving 20 percent on the purchase of our IBM computers?
- Ms. Johnson, did you know that several thousand companies—like yours—have saved 10 to 20 percent of their manufacturing cost as described in the *Newsweek* article? [Continue, not waiting for a response.] They did it by installing our computerized assembly system! Is that of interest to you?

Be excited, enthusiastic about benefits!

Your **customer benefit approach** statement should carefully be constructed to anticipate the buyer's response. However, always be prepared for the unexpected, as when the salesperson said, "This office machine will pay for itself in no time at all." "Fine," the buyer said; "As soon as it does, send it to us."

A customer benefit approach can also be implemented through the use of a direct statement of product benefits. Although the customer benefit approach begins with a question, it can be used with a statement showing how the product can benefit the prospect. The three customer benefit questions shown earlier can be converted into benefit statements:

- Mr. McDaniel, I want to talk with you about our new storage and shipping container, which will reduce your costs by 10 to 20 percent.
- I'm here to show you how to save 20 percent on the purchase of our IBM computers.
- Ms. Johnson, several thousand companies—like yours—have saved 10 to 20 percent on their manufacturing cost by installing our computerized assembly system! I'd like 15 minutes of your time to show how we can reduce your manufacturing costs.

Benefit statements are useful in situations in which you know the prospect's or customer's critical needs and have a short time to make your presentation. However, to ensure a positive atmosphere, you can follow statements with a short question—"Is that of interest to you?"—to help ensure that the benefits are important to the buyer. Even if you know of the buyer's interest, a positive response—"Yes"—to your question is a commitment: The buyer will listen to your presentation because of the possible benefits your product offers.

Furthermore, you can use the buyer's response to this question as a reference point throughout your presentation. A continuation of an earlier example illustrates the use of a reference point:

- Mr. McDaniel, earlier you mentioned interest in reducing your shipping costs. The [now mention your product's feature] enables you to [now discuss your product's advantages]. And the benefit to you is reduced manufacturing costs.

EXHIBIT 10.8

The curiosity approach.

"Mr. Chan, do you know why 300 banks use our customer information system?"

Sometimes, salespeople have to prepare an approach that temporarily baffles a prospect. One common method of baffling entails the exploration of human curiosity.

Curiosity Approach

The salesperson asks a question or does something to make the prospect curious about the product or service (see Exhibit 10.8). For example, a salesperson for McGraw-Hill, the company that publishes this book, might use the **curiosity approach** by saying:

- Do you know why college professors such as yourself have made this [as she hands the book to the prospect] the best-selling book about how to sell on the market?
- Do you know why a recent *Newsweek* article described our new computerized assembly system as revolutionary? [The salesperson briefly displays the *Newsweek* issue, then puts it away before the customer can request to look at the article. Interrupting a sales presentation by urging a prospect to review an article would distract the prospect's attention for the remainder of the interview.]

One manufacturer's salesperson sent a fax to a customer saying, "Tomorrow is the big day for you and your company." When the salesperson arrived for the interview, the prospect could not wait to find out what the salesperson's message meant.

In calling on a male buyer who liked chocolate candy, a saleswoman set a candy box on the buyer's desk. After some chatting, the buyer said, "What's in the box?" The salesperson handed the box to the buyer and said, "Open it." Inside was a product she wanted to sell instead of the chocolate it originally contained. After he bought, she gave him the chocolate to go with his coffee. Selling can be fun, especially if the salesperson enjoys being creative.

Opinion Approach

People are usually flattered when asked their opinion on a subject. Most prospects are happy to discuss their needs if asked correctly. Here are some examples:

- I'm new at this business, so I wonder if you could help me? My company says our Model 100 copier is the best on the market for the money. What do you think?
- Mr. Jackson, I've been trying to sell you for months on using our products. What is your honest opinion about our line of electric motors?

The **opinion approach** is especially good for the new salesperson because it shows that you value the buyer's opinion. Opinion questioning also shows that you will not challenge a potential buyer's expertise by spouting a memorized pitch. Additionally, opinion questions may reveal previously unexplored opportunities for your product to meet even more of the prospect's needs.

Shock Approach

As its title implies, the **shock approach** uses a question designed to make the prospect think seriously about a subject related to the salesperson's product. For example:

- Did you know that you have a 20 percent chance of having a heart attack this year? (Life insurance)
- Did you know that home burglary, according to the FBI, has increased this year by 15 percent over last year? (Alarm system)
- Shoplifting costs store owners millions of dollars each year! Did you know that there is a good chance you have a shoplifter in your store right now? (Store cameras and mirrors)

This type of question must be used carefully, as some prospects may feel you are merely trying to pressure them into a purchase by making alarming remarks.

Multiple-Question Approach (SPIN)

In many selling situations, it is wise to use questions to determine the prospect's needs. A series of questions is an effective sales interview opener. Multiple questions force the prospect to immediately participate in the sales interview and quickly develop two-way communication. Carefully listening to the prospect's needs aids in determining what features, advantages, and benefits to use in the sales presentation (see Exhibit 10.9).

Questions encourage others to talk. Be a good listener.

A relatively new method of using multiple questions is the **multiple-question approach (SPIN)**, which involves using a series of four types of questions in a specific sequence.[2] SPIN stands for (1) **S**ituation, (2) **P**roblem, (3) **I**mplication, and (4) **N**eed-payoff questions. Since SPIN requires questions asked in their proper sequence, its parts are carefully described in the following four steps.

Step 1

Situation questions. Ask about the prospect's general situation as it relates to your product.

In the SPIN approach, the sales rep uses a specific sequence of questions to effectively open
a sales interview.

Industrial Examples

- Dyno Electric Cart salesperson to purchasing agent: "How large are your manufacturing plant facilities?"
- IBM computer salesperson to purchasing agent: "How many secretaries do
  you have in your company?"

Consumer Examples

- Real estate salesperson to prospect: "How many people do you have in your
  family?"
- Appliance salesperson selling a microwave oven to prospect: "Do you like to
  cook?" "Do you and your family eat out much?"

As the name of this question implies, the salesperson first asks a situation question that helps provide a general understanding of the buyer's needs. Situation questioning allows the salesperson to move smoothly into questions on specific problem
areas. Also, beginning an approach using specific questions may make the prospect
uncomfortable and unwilling to talk to you about problems—the prospect may even
deny them. These are warm-up questions that enable you to gain a better understanding of the prospect's business.

*"Become genuinely
interested in other
people—ask questions."*

DALE CARNEGIE

Step 2

Problem questions. Ask about specific problems, dissatisfactions, or difficulties the
prospect perceives relative to your situation question.

Industrial Examples

- Dyno Electric Cart salesperson to purchasing agent: "Have your executives
  ever complained about having to do so much walking in and around the plant?"

- IBM computer salesperson to purchasing agent: "Do your Canon word processors do all that your secretaries want them to do?" (You may have previously asked the secretaries this question and know that they are dissatisfied.)

Consumer Examples

- Real estate salesperson to prospect: "Has your family grown so that you need more space?"
- Appliance salesperson selling microwave oven to prospect: "Are you happy with your present oven?" "Are there times when you must quickly prepare meals?"

Problem questions are asked early in the presentation to bring out the needs or problems of the prospect. Your goal is to have the prospect admit, "Yes, I do have a problem."

To maximize your chance of making the sale, determine which of the prospect's needs or problems are important (explicit needs) and which are unimportant. The more explicit needs you can discover, the more vividly you can relate your products' benefits to areas the prospect is actually interested in, and thus, the higher your probability of making the sale.

In this step, the prospect recognizes an important or explicit need or problem, along with a desire to fulfill the need or solve the problem. Problem questions are useful in developing explicit needs.

If the prospect should state a specific need after your situation or problem questions, do not move directly into your sales presentation. Continue with the next two steps to increase your chances of making the sale. A prospect may sometimes not appreciate all the ramifications of a problem.

Step 3

Implication questions. Ask about the implications of the prospect's problems or how a problem affects various related operational aspects of a home, life, or business (see Exhibit 10.10).

Industrial Examples

- Dyno Electric Cart salesperson to purchasing agent: "It sounds as if your executives would have an interest in reducing their travel time and not having to exert so much energy in transit. Doesn't it seem that if they could do so, they would get to the plant as quickly as they need to, saving themselves time and energy, and saving the company money?"

EXHIBIT 10.10

A popular multiple-question approach is the SPIN.

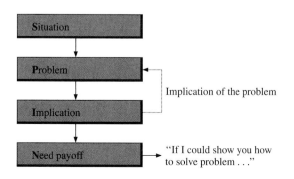

- IBM computer salesperson to purchasing agent: "Does this problem mean your secretaries are not as efficient as they should be, thus increasing your costs per page typed?"

Consumer Examples

- Real estate salesperson to prospect: "So with the new baby and your needing a room as an office in your home, what problems does your current residence create for you?"
- Appliance salesperson to prospect: "With both of you working, does your present kitchen oven mean . . . inconvenience for you? . . . that you have to eat out more than you want to? . . . that you have to eat junk foods instead of well-balanced meals?"

Implication questions seek to help the prospect realize the true dimensions of a problem. The phrasing of the question is important in getting the prospect to discuss problems or areas for improvement, and it fixes them in the prospect's mind. In this situation, the prospect is motivated to fulfill this need or solve this problem.

If possible, attach a bottom-line figure to the implication question. You want the prospect to state, or agree with you, that the implications of the problem are causing such things as production slowdowns of 1 percent, resulting in increased cost of 25 cents per unit; increased reproduction costs of 1 cent per copy; loss of customers; or the need to hire added personnel to make service calls costing an extra $500 per week.

Use these hard data later in your discussion of the business proposition. Using the prospect's data, you can show how your product can influence the prospect's costs, productivity, or customers.

S-P-I questions do not have to be asked in order, and you can ask more than one of each type. You will generally begin with a situation question and follow with a problem question. However, you could ask a situation question, a problem question, and another situation question, for example. The need-payoff question, however, is always last.

Step 4

Need-payoff question. Ask if the prospect has an important, explicit need.

Industrial Examples

- Dyno Electric Cart salesperson to purchasing agent: "If I could show you how you can solve your executives' problems in getting to and from your plant, and at the same time save your company money, would you have an interest?"
- IBM computer salesperson to purchasing agent: "Would you be interested in a method to improve your secretaries' efficiency at a lower cost than you now incur?"

Consumer Examples

- Real estate salesperson to prospect: "If I could show you how to cover your space problems at the same cost per square foot, would you be interested?"
- Appliance salesperson to prospect: "Do you need a convenient way to prepare well-balanced, nutritious meals at home?"

Phrasing the need-payoff question is the same as opening with a benefit state-ment. However, in using the SPIN approach, the prospect defines the need. If the prospect responds positively to the need-payoff questions, you know this is an im-portant (explicit) need. You may have to repeat the P-I-N questions to fully develop all of the prospect's important needs.

The Procter & Gamble and Tide sales presentation in Exhibit 9.7 is an example of using the P-I-N approach for a customer with whom you are familiar. Let's say your customer says yes to the need-payoff question: "If we could determine how much volume you're missing, I think you'd be willing to make space for the larger size, wouldn't you?" Then, you move directly into a brief sales presentation.

If the answer is no, this is not an important need. Start over again by asking Prob-lem, Implication, and Need-payoff questions to determine important needs.

Product Not Mentioned in SPIN Approach

As you see from SPIN examples, the product is not mentioned in the approach. This allows you to develop the prospect's need without revealing exactly what you are selling.

When a salesperson first walks into the buyer's office and says, "I want to talk about Product X," the chances of a negative response greatly increase because the buyer does not perceive a need for the product. SPIN questions allow you to better determine the buyer's needs before starting the presentation.

TECHNOLOGY IN THE APPROACH

How can a salesperson quickly capture a prospect's attention and interest? If tech-nology can be incorporated into the approach, it can be a powerful attention-grabber!

Imagine a salesperson asking an organization's purchasing agent to follow her to the parking lot to "see something." She doesn't discuss the product until after the prospect has entered her mobile office, as discussed in Chapter 6.

A salesperson could hand the buyer a new pager or place a new laptop computer on his desk without saying anything. Or using a palm-top computer, a salesperson could open with a demonstration of her new presentation software and hardware.

Technology can be a wonderful way to creatively and professionally begin a sales presentation. Sounds, visuals, and touch cause the prospect's mind to instantly focus on the salesperson's words and actions.

IS THE APPROACH IMPORTANT?

You have to show up at the customer's business to make your approach. Comedian Woody Allen is famous for his quote "Eighty percent of success is showing up." Before a Baltimore Orioles baseball game Cal Ripken received a standing ovation from 46,272 people. The game against the California Angels had not started. He just showed up to play in the game. This was, however, Ripken's 2,131st consecutive game to play breaking Lou Gehrig's record. On September 6, 1995, Cal Ripken became a baseball legend just for showing up. So is the approach important? Yes it is!

Just as the golfer has several different golf clubs to choose from in order to make the approach shot, so the salesperson needs numerous communication techniques to open the sales conversation. Typically the golfer has a few clubs (irons) to hit the

EXHIBIT 10.11

Golf, as in sales, has an approach. If you blow your approach you may blow the sale!

golf ball onto the green (see Exhibit 10.11). The salesperson also has several approach techniques that have worked in the past, and thus are used each day.

USING QUESTIONS RESULTS IN SALES SUCCESS

Because this chapter introduces questioning techniques, and because properly questioning a prospect or customer is important to sales success, you are ready for the many uses and types of questions.

Asking questions, sometimes called *probes*, is an excellent technique for (1) obtaining information from the prospect, (2) developing two-way communication, and (3) increasing prospect participation.

Questions show you care!

When using questions in selling, you need to know or anticipate the answer you want for a question. Once you know the desired answer, you can develop the question. This procedure can be used to request information you do not have, and to confirm information you already know.

An ideal question is one a prospect is willing and able to answer. You should ask only questions that help make the sale, so use questions sparingly and wisely.

Why would asking a question get the prospect's attention? To give an answer, a prospect must think about the topic. You can use four basic categories of questions at any point during the presentation. These categories are (1) direct, (2) nondirective, (3) rephrasing, and (4) redirect questions.

The Direct Question

The **direct question**, or closed-ended question, can be answered with very few words. A simple yes or no answers most direct questions. They are especially useful in moving a customer toward a specific topic. Examples the salesperson might use include questions such as these: "Mr. Berger, are you interested in saving 20 percent on your manufacturing costs?" or, "Reducing manufacturing costs is important, isn't it?" You can anticipate a yes response to these questions.

Never phrase the direct question as a direct negative–no question. A *direct negative–no question* is any question that can be answered in a manner that cuts you off completely. The retail salesperson says, "May I help you?" and the reply usually is, "No, I'm just looking." It's like hanging up the telephone on you. You are completely cut off.

Other types of direct questions ask "What kind?" or "How many?" The questions also ask for a limited, short answer from the prospect. The implication and need-payoff questions used in SPIN are examples of direct questions used for the approach.

However, the answer to a direct question does not really tell you much, because there is little feedback involved. You may need more information to determine the buyer's needs and problems, especially if you could not determine them before the sales call. Nondirective questioning aids you in the quest for information.

The Nondirective Question

To open up two-way communication, the salesperson can use an open-ended or **nondirective question** by beginning the question with one of six words: Who, what, where, when, how, or why. Examples include the following:

- Who will use this product?
- What features are you looking for in a product like this?
- Where will you use this product?
- When will you need the product?
- How often will you use the product?
- Why do you need or want to buy this type of product?

One-word questions such as Oh? or Really? also can be useful in some situations. One-word questions should be said with emphasis: Oh?! This prompts the customer to continue talking. Try it—it works.

To practice using the open-ended questioning technique, ask a friend a question—any question—beginning with one of these six words, or use a one-word question, and see what answer you get. Chances are, the response will consist of several sentences. In a selling situation, this type of response allows the salesperson to better determine the prospect's needs.

The purpose of using a nondirective question is to obtain unknown or additional information, to draw out clues to hidden or future needs and problems, and to leave the situation open for free discussion of what is on the customer's mind. Situation and implication questions are examples of the nondirective question.

The Rephrasing Question

The third type of question is called the **rephrasing question**. At times, the prospect's meaning is not clearly stated. In this situation, if appropriate, the salesperson might say:

- Are you saying that price is the most important thing you are interested in? [sincerely, not too aggressively]
- Then what you are saying is, if I can improve the delivery time, you would be interested in buying?

This form of restatement allows you to clarify meaning and determine the prospect's needs. If the prospect answers yes to the second question, you would find a way to improve delivery. If no is the answer to the delivery question, you know delivery time is not an important buying motive; continue to probe for the true problem.

The Redirect Question

The fourth type of question is the **redirect question**. This is used to redirect the prospect to selling points that both parties agree on. There are always areas of agreement between buyer and seller even if the prospect is opposed to purchasing the

Keep Quiet and Get the Order

Dennis DeMaria, a branch manager for Westvaco from Folcroft, Pennsylvania, says, "One of the biggest single weapons you as a salesperson can use in getting an order from a customer or prospect is keeping quiet and patiently waiting for the buyer to answer your questions. A general rule in the selling profession is that the person who asks the questions is the person who has control of the interview. The information obtained from asking questions is the necessary ammunition you use to find the buyer's likes, dislikes, hot buttons, and areas to avoid. This valuable information also informs the salesperson whether the customer is ready to buy or whether he or she could continue selling.

"Experience has shown that salespeople *do* ask questions but they forget the most important part of this sales principle: *After you ask a question, you must be patient, don't talk, and let the buyer answer.* It does not matter how long it takes for the buyer to respond; keep quiet and wait for the answer. Remember, the first person to speak after a question has been asked, loses."[3]

product. The redirect question is an excellent alternative or backup opener. This example clarifies the concept of redirective questioning:

Imagine you walk into a prospect's office, introduce yourself, and get this response, "I'm sorry, but there is no use in talking. We are satisfied with our present suppliers. Thanks for coming by." Respond by replacing your planned opener with a redirecting question. You might say:

- Do we agree that having a supplier who can reduce your costs is important?
- You would agree that manufacturers must use the most cost efficient equipment to stay competitive these days, wouldn't you?
- Wouldn't you agree that you continually need to find new ways to increase your company's sales?

Using a redirect question moves the conversation from a negative position to a positive or neutral one while reestablishing communication between two people. The ability to redirect a seemingly terminated conversation through a well-placed question may impress the prospect simply by showing that you are not a run-of-the-mill order-taker, but a professional salesperson who sincerely believes in the beneficial qualities of your product.

Three Rules for Using Questions

The first rule is to use only questions that you can anticipate the answer to or that will not lead you into a situation from which you cannot escape. Although questions are a powerful selling technique, they can easily backfire.

The second rule in using a question is to pause or wait after submitting a question to allow the prospect time to respond to it. Waiting for an answer to a well-planned question is sometimes an excruciating process—seconds may seem like minutes. A salesperson must allow the prospect time to consider the question, and hope for a response. Failing to allow a prospect enough time defeats the major purpose of questioning, which is to establish two-way communication between the prospect and the salesperson.

The third rule is to listen. Many salespeople are so intent on talking that they forget to listen to what the prospect says (or they disregard nonverbal signals). Salespeople need to listen consciously to prospects so that they can ask intelligent, meaningful questions that aid both themselves and their prospects in determining what

ETHICAL DILEMMA

Oh, How You'd Love to Know!

Selling has always been fun for you, maybe because of your success in selling high-priced merchandise to the automotive industry. The only thing you do not like is the length of time it takes to sell someone. Your average sale takes about eight sales calls, 30 to 40 hours analyzing the prospect's operation, and submitting a bid in competition with six to eight other suppliers. Your average sale last year was $425,000.

During prolonged negotiation with a large customer, it becomes apparent that the purchasing agent wants to do business with you. For example, he has indicated in subtle ways that he wants to work with your firm and has offered to share prices from your competitors with you. If you accept the list of your competitors' bid prices, you will not have to spend so much time compiling the bid, plus you will be guaranteed business that will produce 20 percent more sales than expected. You also realize that this explicitly breaks the confidentiality of your competitors and your business could suffer if word got out about your transaction.

What would you do?

1. Take the competitors' bid prices your prospective customer offers. It will save you time and earn you and your company more money in the long run.
2. Do not take the offered competitors' bid prices. Not only could it affect your business, but it is also not fair to your competition. You need to work for each sale you get.
3. Don't take the competitors' bid prices because it would break your competitors' confidentiality. However, tell your customer that were he to tell you a "good" number to bid (based on what he knows about the competitors' bids), you could submit an appropriate bid.

needs and problems exist and how to solve them. Prospects appreciate a good listener and view a willingness to listen as an indication that the salesperson is truly interested in their situation.

IS THE PROSPECT STILL NOT LISTENING?

What happens when, using your best opening approach, you realize that the prospect is not listening? What about prospects who open mail, who fold their arms while looking at the wall or beyond you into the hallway, who make telephone calls in your presence, or who may even doze off?

This is the time to use one of your alternative openers that tunes the prospect in to your message. The prospect must be forced to participate in the talk by using either the question or demonstration approach. By handing the person something, showing something, or asking a question, you can briefly recapture attention, no matter how indifferent a prospect is to your presence.

If you can overcome such preoccupation or indifference in the early minutes of your interview by quickly capturing the prospect's attention and interest, the probability of your making a sale will greatly improve. This is why the approach is so important to the success of a sales call.

It is crucial to never become flustered or confused when a communication problem arises during your approach. As mentioned earlier, the salesperson who can deftly capture another person's imagination earns the right to a prospect's full attention and interest. Your prospect should not be handled as an adversary, for in that type of situation you seldom gain the sale.

BE FLEXIBLE IN YOUR APPROACH

Picture yourself as a salesperson getting ready for coming face-to-face with an important prospect, Ellen Myerson. You have planned exactly what you are to say in the sales presentation, but how can you be sure Myerson will listen to your sales presentation? You realize she is busy and may be indifferent to your presence in the office; she probably is preoccupied with her own business-related situation and several of your competitors already may have seen her today.

You have planned to open your presentation with a statement on how successful your word-processor software has been in helping secretaries save time and eliminate errors in their typing. When you enter the office, Myerson comments on how efficient her secretaries are and how they produce error-free work. From her remarks, you quickly determine that your planned statement approach is inappropriate. What do you do now?

You might begin by remarking how lucky she is to have such conscientious secretaries, and then proceed into the SPIN question approach, first asking questions to determine general problems that she may have, and second using further questions to uncover specific problem areas she might like to solve. Once you have determined specific problems, you could ascertain whether they are important enough for her to want to solve them in the near future. If so, you can make a statement that summarizes how your product's benefits will solve her critical needs, and test for a positive response. A positive response allows you to conditionally move into the sales presentation.

No matter what, always smile! Show you care.

SUMMARY OF MAJOR SELLING ISSUES

As the first step in your sales presentation, the approach is a critical factor. To ensure your prospects' attention and interest during a memorized or formula mode of presentation, you may want to use a statement or demonstration approach. In more technically oriented situations in which you and the prospects must agree on needs and problems, a questioning approach (SPIN, for instance) is in order. Generally, in developing your approach, imagine your prospects asking themselves, "Do I have time to listen to, talk with, or devote to this person? What's in it for me?"

Words alone will not ensure that you are heard. The first impression that you make on a prospect can negate your otherwise positive and sincere opening. To ensure a favorable impression in most selling situations, dress conservatively, be well groomed, and act as though you are truly glad to meet the prospect.

Your approach statement should be especially designed for each prospect. You can choose to open with a statement, question, or demonstration by using any one of the techniques. You should have several alternative approaches ready in case you need to alter your plans for a specific situation.

Carefully phrased questions are useful at any point in a sales presentation. Questions should display a sincere interest in prospects and their situations. Skillfully handled questions employed in a sales approach can wrest a prospect's attention from distractions and center it on you and your presentation. Questions are generally used to determine prospect wants and needs, thereby increasing prospect participation in the sales presentation. Four basic types of questions discussed in this chapter are direct, nondirective, rephrasing, and redirect questions.

In using questions, ask the type of questions that you can anticipate the answer to. Also, remember to allow prospects time to completely answer the question. Listen carefully to their answers for a guide as to how well you are progressing toward selling to them. Should you determine that your prospect is not listening, do something to regain attention. Techniques such as offering something or asking questions can refocus the prospect's attention long enough for your return to the presentation.

MEETING A SALES CHALLENGE

Questions are important tools for salespeople. They help uncover needs and problems, obtain valuable selling information, and qualify the prospect's interest and buying authority. So it pays to ask good ones.

Because you may need to first develop an analysis of the bank's operation, the need-satisfaction or problem-solving presentation methods would work well for this situation. Begin with questions that are direct, well aimed, and most importantly, force the prospect to talk about a specific problem. Questions that cannot be answered *yes* or *no* provide the most information. A multiple-question approach, such as SPIN, would be appropriate for this situation.

KEY TERMS FOR SELLING

approach   308
creative imagery   309
introductory approach   314
complimentary approach   314
referral approach   314
premium approach   315
product approach   315
showmanship approach   315
customer benefit approach   317

curiosity approach   318
opinion approach   319
shock approach   319
multiple-question approach (SPIN)   319
direct question   324
nondirective question   325
rephrasing question   325
redirect question   325

SALES APPLICATION QUESTIONS

1. Explain the reasons for using questions when making a sales presentation. Discuss the rules for questioning that the salesperson should follow.
2. What are three general categories of the approach? Give an example of each.
3. What is SPIN? Give an example of a salesperson using SPIN.
4. Discuss each of the four types of questions. In each of the following instances, determine if a direct, nondirective, rephrasing, or redirect question is being used.
   a. "Now let's see if I have this right; you are looking for a high-quality product and price is no object?"
   b. "What type of clothes are you looking for?"
   c. "Are you interested in Model 101 or Model 921?"
   d. "Well, I can appreciate your beliefs, but you would agree that price is not the only thing to consider when buying a copier, wouldn't you?"
   e. "When would you like to have your new Xerox 9000 installed?"
   f. "Are you saying that *where* you go for vacation is more important than the cost of getting there?"
   g. "You would agree that saving time is important to a busy executive like yourself, wouldn't you?"
5. Which of the following approaches do you think is the best? Why?
   a. "Ms. Jones, in the past, you've made it a practice to reduce the facings on heavy-duty household detergents in the winter months because of slower movement."
   b. "Mr. Brown, you'll recall that last time I was in, you expressed concern over the fact that your store labor was running higher than the industry average of 8 percent of sales."
   c. "Hi! I'm Jeanette Smith of Procter & Gamble, and I'd like to talk to you about Cheer. How's it selling?"

6. Assume you are a salesperson for NCR (National Cash Register Corporation) and you want to sell Mr. Johnson, the owner/manager of a large independent supermarket, your computerized customer checkout system. You have just met Mr. Johnson inside the front door of the supermarket, and after your initial introduction, the conversation continues:

Salesperson: Mr. Johnson, your customers are really backed up at your cash registers, aren't they?

Buyer: Yeah, it's a real problem.

Salesperson: Do your checkers ever make mistakes when they are in a rush?

Buyer: They sure do!

Salesperson: Have you ever thought about shortening checkout time while reducing checker errors?

Buyer: Yes, but those methods are too expensive!

Salesperson: Does your supermarket generate over $1 million in sales each month?

Buyer: Oh, yes—why?

Salesperson: Would you be interested in discussing a method of decreasing customer checkout time by 100 percent and greatly reducing the number of errors made by your checkers, if I can show you that the costs of solving your problems will be more than offset by your savings?

   a. Using the framework of the SPIN approach technique, determine whether each of the above questions asked by the salesperson is a **S**ituation, **P**roblem, **I**mplication, or **N**eed-payoff question.
   b. If Mr. Johnson says yes to your last question, what should you do next?
   c. If Mr. Johnson says no to your last question, what should you do next?

7. As a salesperson for Gatti's Electric Company, Cliff Defee is interested in selling John Bonham more of his portable electric generators. John is a construction supervisor for a firm specializing in constructing large buildings such as shopping centers, office buildings, and manufacturing plants. He currently uses three of Cliff's newest models. Cliff just learned that John will be building a new manufacturing plant. As Cliff examines the specifications for the new plant, he feels John will require several additional generators. Two types of approaches Cliff might make are depicted in the following situations:

Situation A:

Salesperson: I see you got the Jonesville job.

Buyer: Sure did.

Salesperson: Are the specs OK?

Buyer: Yes.

Salesperson: Will you need more machines?

Buyer: Yes, but not yours!

Situation B:

Salesperson: I understand you have three of our electric sets.

Buyer: Yes, I do.

Salesperson: I'm sure you'll need additional units on your next job.

Buyer: You're right, I will.

Salesperson: Well, I've gone over your plant specifications and put together products just like you need.

Buyer: What I don't *need* are any of your lousy generators.

Salesperson: Well, that's impossible. It's a brand new design.

Buyer: Sorry, I've got to go.

    a. Briefly describe the approaches in situations A and B. In both situations, Cliff is in a tough spot. What should he do now?
    b. What type of approach could Cliff have made that would have allowed him to uncover John's dissatisfaction? Would the approach you are suggesting also be appropriate if John were satisfied with the generators?

8. This is a cold call on the warehouse manager for Coats Western Wear, a retailer with four stores. You know most of the manager's work consists of deliveries from the warehouse to the four stores. Based on your experience, you suspect that the volume of shipments to the warehouse fluctuates; certain seasons of the year are extremely busy.

    As a salesperson for Hercules Shelving, you want to sell the manager your heavy-duty-gauge steel shelving for use in the warehouse. Since this is a relatively small sale, you decide to go in cold, relying only on your questioning ability to uncover potential problems and make the prospect aware of them.

    You are now face-to-face with the warehouse manager. You have introduced yourself and after some small talk it is time to begin your approach. Which of the following questions would be best?
    a. "Have you had any recent storage problems?"
    b. "How do you take care of your extra storage needs during busy seasons such as Christmas?"
    c. "Can you tell me a little about your storage problems?"

FURTHER EXPLORING THE SALES WORLD

1. Television advertisements are constructed to capture the viewer's attention and interest to sell a product or service quickly. Examine at least five commercials and report on the method each one used to get your attention, stimulate your interest, and move you from this attention–interest phase into discussing the product. Determine whether the first few seconds of the commercial related to the product's features, advantages, or benefits, and if so, how? Using a tape recorder may help you.
2. Assume that you have a 30-minute job interview next week with a representative of a company you are really interested in. How would you prepare for the interview, and what could you do during the first few minutes of

the interview to get the recruiter interested in hiring you? Can you see any differences between this interview situation and the environment of a salesperson making a sales call?

SELLING EXPERIENTIAL EXERCISE

The most successful people in customer contact jobs claim that being sharp mentally means communicating a positive self-image. Like an actor or actress, interacting with others requires you to be on stage at all times. Creating a good first impression is essential. Also important is understanding the direct connection between your attitude and how you look to yourself. The better your self-image when you encounter customers, clients, or guests, the more positive you are.

Plan Your Appearance—It Projects Your Image!

On a separate sheet of paper, rate yourself on each of the following grooming areas. If you write 5, you are saying that improvement is not required. If you write a 1, or 2, you need considerable improvement. Be honest.[4]

	Excellent	Good	Fair	Weak	Poor
■ Hairstyle, hair grooming (appropriate length and cleanliness)	5	4	3	2	1
■ Personal cleanliness habits (body)	5	4	3	2	1
■ Clothing, piercings and jewelry (appropriate to the situation)	5	4	3	2	1
■ Neatness (shoes shined, clothes clean, well-pressed, etc.)	5	4	3	2	1
■ Fragrances, tattoos, and makeup	5	4	3	2	1
■ General grooming: Does your appearance reflect professionalism on the job?	5	4	3	2	1

When it comes to appearance on the job. I would rate myself:

❑ Excellent   ❑ Good   ❑ Need improvement

CHAPTER 10

Begin Your Presentation Strategically

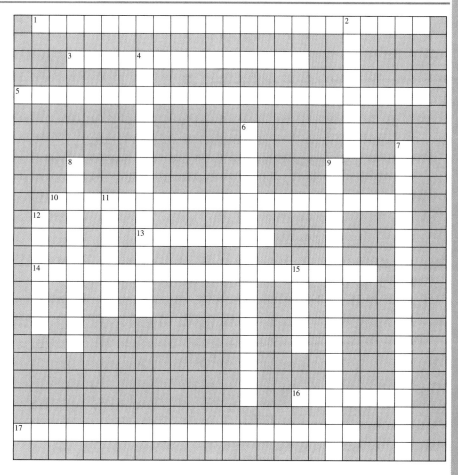

Across

1. An approach by which the salesperson asks a question(s) that implies that the product will benefit the prospect.

3. A question that by and large can be answered with a yes or no response or at most by a very short response consisting of a few words.

5. An approach in which the salesperson uses three types of questions—situation, problem implication, and need–payoff—to get a better understanding of the prospect's business.

10. An approach that opens with a compliment that is sincere and therefore effective.

13. Opening of the presentation from first talk with person to discussion of the product.

14. A question that opens up two-way communication by beginning the question with who, what, where, when, how, or why.

16. For a ____ approach the salesperson places the product on the counter or hands it to the customer, saying nothing.

17. The most common but least powerful approach; it does little to capture the prospect's attention.

Down

2. A ____ approach uses a third person's name as a reference to approach the buyer.

4. A relaxation and concentration technique that aids in stress management, in which a salesperson envisions successful coping in various sales situations.

6. A question that guides the prospect back to selling points that both parties agree on.

7. A question in which the salesperson rephrases what the prospect has said in order to clarify meaning and determine the prospect's needs.

8. A _____ approach involves doing something unusual to catch the prospect's attention and interest.

9. An approach by which the salesperson asks a question or does something to make the prospect curious about the product.

11. An approach in which the salesperson offers a prospect something as an inducement to buy, is known as a _____ approach.

12. _____ approach is an approach by which a salesperson shows that the buyer's opinion is valued.

15. An approach that uses a question designed to make the prospect think seriously about a subject related to the salesperson's product is called a _____ approach.

STUDENT APPLICATION LEARNING EXERCISES (SALES)

To make **SALE 4** first select the method you will use for your presentation. See pages 283–294. Next, write down the name of the approach technique you will use for this presentation method. See pages 313–323.

Presentation method: _____

Approach technique: _____

(SALE 4 of 7)

Now write out what you will actually say in your approach, including what the buyer should say. Relate your approach to your **FABs** developed in **SALE 1** so you have a smooth transition into discussing your product.

Seller:

Buyer:

Imagine you have now finished the approach. Write out the buyer–seller dialogue for the first two **SELL Sequences.** Refer back to **SALE 1.** Create an imaginary response by the buyer to each of your trial closes.

SELL 1

Seller:

Buyer:

SELL 2

Seller:

Buyer:

Role-play your approach and **SELL Sequences** with someone to see if you are satisfied. If available, use a tape recorder to listen to your speed, voice inflections, phrases and any unwanted mannerisms, such as frequently repeating "uh" or "I see."

CASE 10-1
The Thompson Company

Before making a cold call on the Thompson Company, you did some research on the account. Barbara Thompson is both president and chief purchasing officer. In this dual capacity, she often is so rushed that she is impatient with salespeople. She is known for her habit of quickly turning down the salesperson and shutting off the discussion by turning and walking away. In looking over Thompson's operation, you notice that the inefficient metal shelving she uses in her warehouse is starting to collapse. Warehouse employees have attempted to remedy the situation by building wooden shelves and reinforcing the weakened metal shelves with lumber. They also have begun stacking boxes on the floor, requiring much more space.

You recognize the importance of getting off to a fast start with Thompson. You must capture her attention and interest quickly or she may not talk with you.

Questions

Which of the following attention-getters would you choose?

1. Ms. Thompson, I'd like to show you how Hercules shelving can save you both time and money.
2. Ms. Thompson, can you spare a few minutes of your time to talk about new shelving for your warehouse?
3. Ms. Thompson, how would you like to double your storage space?

CASE 10-2
The Copy Corporation

Assume you are contacting the purchasing agent for office supplies of a large chain of retail department stores. After hearing that the company is opening 10 new stores, you determine that they will need a copier for each store. Three months earlier, you had sold this purchasing agent a lease agreement on two large machines. The buyer wanted to try your machines in the company's new stores. If they liked them, you would get the account. Unknown to you, one of the machines was broken, which caused the purchasing agent to be pressured by a store manager to replace it immediately. As you walk into the purchasing agent's office, you say:

Salesperson: I understand you are opening 10 new stores in the next six months.

Buyer: I don't know who told you, but you seem to know!

Salesperson: If you'll let me know when you want a copier at each store, I'll arrange for it to be there.

Buyer: Look, I don't want any more of your lousy copiers! When the leases expire, I want you here to pick them up, or I'll throw them out in the street! I've got a meeting now. I want to see you in three months.

Questions

1. Describe this situation, commenting on what the salesperson did correctly and incorrectly.
2. Develop another approach the salesperson could use to uncover the problems experienced by the purchasing agent.

CASE 10-3
Electronic Office Security Corporation

Ann Saroyan is a salesperson for the Electronic Office Security Corporation. She sells industrial security systems that detect intruders and activate an alarm. When Ann first began selling, she used to make brief opening remarks to her prospects and then move quickly into her presentation. Although this resulted in selling many of her security systems, she felt there must be a better method.

Ann began to analyze the reasons prospects would not buy. Her conclusion was that even after her presentation, prospects still did not believe they needed a security alarm system. She decided to develop a multiple-question approach that would allow her to determine the prospect's attitude toward a need for a security system. If the prospect does not initially feel a need for her product, she wants her approach to help convince the prospect of a need for a security system.

Ann developed and carefully rehearsed her new sales presentation. Her first sales call using her multiple-question approach was with a large accounting firm. She asked the receptionist whom she should see and was referred to Joe Bell. After she waited 20 minutes, Bell asked her to come into his office. The conversation went like this:

1. **Salesperson:** This is a beautiful old building, Mr. Bell. Have you been here long?

   Buyer: About 10 years. Before we moved here, we were in one of those ugly glass and concrete towers. Now, you wanted to talk to me about office security.

2. **Salesperson:** Yes, Mr. Bell. Tell me, do you have a burglar alarm system at present?

   Buyer: No, we don't. We've never had a break-in here.

3. **Salesperson:** I see. Could you tell me what's the most valuable item in your building?

   Buyer: Probably the computer.

4. **Salesperson:** And is it fairly small?

   Buyer: Yes, amazingly, it's not much bigger than a typewriter.

5. **Salesperson:** Would it be difficult to run your business without it—if it were stolen for example?

   Buyer: Oh, yes, that would be quite awkward.

6. **Salesperson:** Could you tell me a bit more about the problem you would face without your computer?

   Buyer: It would be inconvenient in the short term for our accounts and records people, but I suppose we could manage until our insurance gave us a replacement.

7. **Salesperson:** But without a computer, wouldn't your billing to customers suffer?

   Buyer: Not if we got the replacement quickly.

8. **Salesperson:** You said the computer itself is insured. Do you happen to know if the software—the programs, your customer files—are also insured?

   Buyer: I don't believe so; our insurance covers the equipment only.

9. **Salesperson:** And do you keep backup records somewhere else—in the bank, for example?

   Buyer: No, we don't.

10. **Salesperson:** Mr. Bell, in my experience, software isn't left behind after a theft. Wouldn't it be a serious problem to you if that software were taken?

    Buyer: Yes, you're right, I suppose. Redevelopment would certainly cost a lot. The original programs were expensive.

11. **Salesperson:** And even worse, because software development can take a long time, wouldn't that hold up your billings to customers?

    Buyer: We could always do that manually.

12. **Salesperson:** What effect would that have on your processing costs?

    Buyer: I see your point. It would certainly be expensive to run a manual system, as well as being inconvenient.

13. **Salesperson:** And if you lost your software, wouldn't it also make it harder to process customer orders?

    Buyer: Yes. I don't have much contact with that part of the business, but without order processing and stock control I'm sure we would grind to a halt in a matter of days.

14. **Salesperson:** Are there any other items in the building that would be hard to replace if stolen?

    Buyer: Some of the furnishings. I would hate to lose this antique clock, for example. In fact, most of our furnishings would be very hard to replace in the same style.

15. **Salesperson:** So, if you lost them, wouldn't it hurt the character of your office?

    Buyer: Yes, it would be damaging. We've built a gracious, civilized image here, and without it we would be like dozens of other people in our business—the glass and concrete image.

16. **Salesperson:** This may sound like an odd question, but how many doors do you have at ground level?

    Buyer: Let me see . . . uh . . . six.

17. **Salesperson:** And ground-level windows?

    Buyer: About 10 or a dozen.

18. **Salesperson:** So there are 16 or 18 points where a thief could break in, compared with 1 or 2 points in the average glass and concrete office. Doesn't that concern you?

Buyer: Put that way, it does. I suppose we're not very secure.

Questions

1. Did the dialogue between buyer and seller seem natural to you?
2. Did the salesperson use too many questions in her approach?
3. Analyze each of the salesperson's questions and state whether it is a situation, problem, implication, or need-payoff type of question.
4. Analyze each of the buyer's responses to the salesperson's questions and state what type of need the salesperson's question uncovered. Was it an implied or minor need response or was it an explicit or important need response? Why?
5. How would you improve on this salesperson's approach?
6. After the buyer's last statement, which of the following would you do?
   a. Move into the presentation.
   b. Ask a problem question.
   c. Ask a need-payoff question.
   d. Ask for an appointment to fully discuss your system.

CHAPTER 11

Elements of a Great Sales Presentation

LEARNING OBJECTIVES

The fourth step in the sales process is the presentation. Here, you discuss with the buyer the product's features, advantages, and benefits, your marketing plan, and the business proposition. After studying this chapter, you should be able to

■ Discuss the purpose and essential steps of the sales presentation.

■ Give examples of the six sales presentation mix elements.

■ Describe difficulties that may arise during the sales presentation and explain how to handle them.

■ State how to handle discussion of the competition.

■ Explain the need to properly diagnose the prospect's personality to determine the design of the sales presentation.

You are a mill salesperson for Superior Carpets. You have been talking about several of your new carpet's features, advantages, and benefits to a retailer. You have just told your customer that because of Superior's new technology, the synthetic fibers in your new product will not fade even if exposed to direct sunlight. Your customer then says, "That sounds great, but I don't know. I've had too many customers complain about fading."

What do you do in this situation? As you see, the customer doubts whether your carpet will resist fading. How do you prove the carpet will not fade? What if the customer will not take your word?

The presentation part of the selling process is a persuasive vocal and visual explanation of a proposition. In developing your presentation, consider the elements you will use to provide the information a buyer needs to make a buying decision. At any time a customer may mention a concern, as in "Facing a Sales Challenge" above. A proper response is needed to make the sale.

This chapter discusses the elements of the presentation—the fourth step in the sales process (see Exhibit 11.1). We examine the purpose and essential steps in the presentation. Next, we review and expand on the presentation techniques salespeople use and how to handle the customer in the sales challenge. The chapter ends by discussing the importance of the proper use of trial closes and difficulties that may arise in the presentation, along with the need to design your presentation around an individual situation and buyer. Let's first see what business life is about.

THE TREE OF BUSINESS LIFE: PRESENTATION

Visualize you are in front of a purchasing agent for a company. Across the desk from you is a 50-year-old person who has been a buyer for this company 20 years. Do you think this person would know his or her organization and its needs? Would this person have experience in dealing with salespeople? If the buyer sees 5 to 10 salespeople a day, over 40,000 salespeople may be sitting where you are in this imaginary business meeting.

Purchasing agents are busy people. You may have a 30-minute appointment. This is why preparation may take hours for a few-minute presentation. You are expected to know your products, something about his or her organization, and how your product can help the company before ever walking in the buyer's office. You are expected to present your product, marketing plan, and business proposition in a clear, concise, organized manner so that it is easy to determine if the product is of value to the buyer.

Truthfully showing and telling about your product shows you are a person with integrity and character, who is focused on unselfishly helping this person. Should there be a hint of exaggeration, the buyer may not buy. Yet after several business meetings over time with Superior Carpets, mentioned in "Facing a Sales Challenge," the buyer may believe you about the product not fading, especially if you have been truthful in the past and you use a proof statement as discussed in this chapter. Ethical service will build true relationships between buyer and seller.

The presentation is the heart of the sale. An effective approach allows a smooth transition into discussing your product's features, advantages, and benefits.

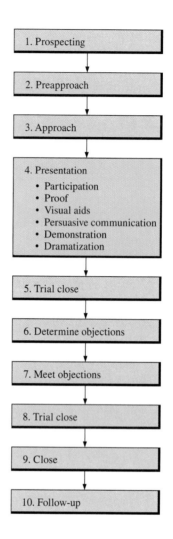

1. Prospecting

2. Preapproach

3. Approach

4. Presentation
   • Participation
   • Proof
   • Visual aids
   • Persuasive communication
   • Demonstration
   • Dramatization

5. Trial close

6. Determine objections

7. Meet objections

8. Trial close

9. Close

10. Follow-up

THE PURPOSE OF THE PRESENTATION

The main goal of your presentation is to provide information to the prospect/customer. This information includes the discussion of your product, marketing plan, and business proposition. Once you have given your presentation, the person is in a much better position to know if your product should be purchased. However, we know that a prospective buyer considers many things before making a decision about what product to buy. As we have seen, the approach or first few minutes of the interview should be constructed to determine the prospect's need, capture attention and interest, and allow for a smooth transition into the presentation.

The presentation is a continuation of the approach. What is the purpose of the presentation? It provides *knowledge* via the features, advantages, and benefits of your product, marketing plan, and business proposal. This allows the buyer to develop positive personal *beliefs* toward your product. These beliefs result in *desire* (or *need*) for the type of product you sell. Your job, as a salesperson, is to convert that need into a want and into the *attitude* that your product is the best product to fulfill a certain need. Furthermore, you must convince the buyer that not only is your product the best but also that you are the best source to buy from. When this occurs, your prospect has moved into the *conviction* stage of the mental buying process.

EXHIBIT 11.2

The five purposes of the presentation.

```
┌──────────────┐
│ 1. Knowledge │──────┐
└──────────────┘      │
       │              │
       ▼              │
┌──────────────┐      │
│ 2. Beliefs   │──────┤
└──────────────┘      │
       │              │
       ▼              │
┌──────────────┐      │      ┌────────────────┐
│ 3. Desire    │──────┼─────▶│ Sales success  │
└──────────────┘      │      └────────────────┘
       │              │
       ▼              │
┌──────────────┐      │
│ 4. Attitude  │──────┤
└──────────────┘      │
       │              │
       ▼              │
┌──────────────┐      │
│ 5. Conviction│──────┘
└──────────────┘
```

A real need is established, the buyer wants to fulfill that need, and there is a high probability that your product is best. This results in you making a sale, as shown in Exhibit 11.2. Whether or not to buy is a choice decision, and you have provided the necessary information so that the customer chooses to buy from you.

Assume, for example, that you are a salesperson for IBM and you wish to sell 10 of your new personal computers, costing $5,000 each, to a company. The prospect's company uses your competitor's products, which cost $3,000 each. How should you conceptualize the prospect's thought processes regarding whether or not to buy from you (as shown in Exhibit 11.1) to develop your presentation?

Begin by realizing that the prospect has certain attitudes toward her current personal computers. The prospect's job performance is judged by her management of certain responsibilities. Thus, improving the performance of company employees is important. However, the prospect knows nothing about you, your product, or your product's benefits. The prospect may feel that IBM products are good, high-quality, expensive products. However, you cannot be sure about the buyer's current attitudes.

Dale Carnegie stressed that an easy way to become a good conversationalist is to be a good listener and encourage others to talk about themselves. You might develop a SPIN approach to determine the buyer's attitudes toward personal computers in general and your personal computer specifically. Once you have addressed each of the four SPIN questions, and you feel more information about your product is needed, begin the presentation.

Present the product information that allows the buyer to develop a positive attitude toward your product. Next, possibly using a value-analysis proposal, show how your product can increase efficiency, reduce costs, and pay for itself in one year, using a return-on-investment (ROI) technique. A positive reaction from your prospect indicates that she has reached the desire stage of the mental buying process. There is a need for some brand of personal computer.

Now, show why your IBM personal computer is the best solution to the buyer's need and show that you will provide service after the sale. A positive response on these two items indicates that the prospect believes your product is best and that the conviction stage has been reached. The prospect wants to buy the IBM personal computer.

Up to this point, you have discussed your product's features, advantages, and benefits, your marketing plan, and your business proposition. You have *not* asked the prospect to buy. Rather, you have developed a presentation to lead the prospect

"An easy way to become a good conversationalist is to be a good listener and encourage others to talk about themselves."

DALE CARNEGIE

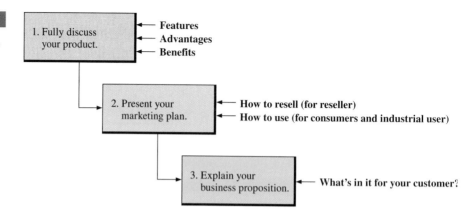

EXHIBIT 11.3

Three essential steps within the presentation.

through four of the five mental buying steps: the attention, interest, desire, and conviction steps. It may take you five minutes, two hours, or several weeks of repeat calls to move the prospect into the conviction stage.

You must move the prospect into the conviction stage before a sale is made. So hold off asking the prospect to buy until the conviction stage. Otherwise, this usually results in objections, failure to listen to your whole story, and fewer sales. The sales presentation has seven major steps. Each step is taken in order to logically and sequentially move the prospect into the conviction stage of the buying process.

When a person buys something, did you ever stop to think about what is actually purchased? Is the customer really buying your product? No. What the customer is actually buying is a mental picture of the future in which your product helps to fulfill some expectation. The buyer has mentally conceived certain needs. Your presentation must create mental images that move your prospect into the conviction stage.

THREE ESSENTIAL STEPS WITHIN THE PRESENTATION

No matter which of the four sales presentation methods is used, your presentation must follow these three essential steps, also shown in Exhibit 11.3.*

Step 1

Fully discuss the *features, advantages, and benefits* of your product. Tell the whole story.

Step 2

Present your marketing plan. For wholesalers and retailers, this is your suggestion on how they should *resell* the product. For end users, it is your suggestion on how they can *use* the product.

Step 3

Explain your business proposition. This step relates the *value* of your product to its *cost*. It should be discussed last, since you always want to present your product's benefits and marketing plan relative to your product's price.

* The three steps are discussed in Chapter 8 under "Customer Benefit Plan."

Salespeople use these FABs in their presentations.

Features, Advantages, and Benefits of Bix Buckwheat Pancake Mix

Features	Advantages	Benefits
Product		
1. Traditional "farmhouse" recipe, with freshest ingredients; fortified with vitamins A, B, C, and D; no preservatives	1. Great tasting, fluffy and light; highly nutritious	1. Provides an appealing item; expands breakfast menu; increases breakfast business
2. User needs only to add water, stir, and cook	2. Quick and easy to prepare	2. Requires minimal kitchen time and labor
Marketing Plan		
3. Just-in-time delivery: weekly or as needed	3. No need to store large quantities	3. Requires minimal inventory space; keeps inventory costs low
4. Local distribution center	4. Additional orders can be filled quickly	4. Prevents out-of-stock situations
5. An experienced sales representative to serve account	5. Knowledge and background in food-service industry	5. Provides assistance for meeting changing needs and solving business problems
Business Proposition		
6. Quantity discounts	6. Reduces costs	6. Increases your profits
7. Extended payment plans	7. Reduces interest costs	7. Increases your profits

Remember Your FABs!

It is extremely important to emphasize benefits throughout the presentation. Using the SELL Sequence communication technique when discussing the product, marketing plan, and business proposition greatly improves your chances of making the sale.

Assume you sell food products to hotels and food retail chains and one of your products is a pancake mix. Notice in Exhibit 11.4 the FABs for each of the three essential steps within the presentation. Even for a product like pancake mix, salespeople should use benefits to paint a visual picture in the minds of the buyers of how this product will fulfill their needs. This is what Golden Rule selling is all about—relating your product's benefits to a customer's needs in a truthful and ethical manner.

Ideally, the salesperson should present information in each of the steps shown in Exhibit 11.3 to create a visual picture in the prospect's mind of the benefits of the purchase. To do this, use persuasive communication and participation techniques, proof statements, visual aids, dramatization, and demonstrations as you move through each of the three steps during the presentation.

THE SALES PRESENTATION MIX

Salespeople sell different products in different ways, but all salespeople use six classes of presentation elements to some degree in their presentations to provide meaningful information to the customer. These elements are called the *presentation mix*.

The **sales presentation mix** refers to the elements the salesperson assembles to sell to prospects and customers. While all elements should be part of the presentation, it is up to the individual to determine how much each element is emphasized. This determination is primarily based on the sales call objective, customer profile, and customer benefit plan. Let's examine each of the six elements, as shown in Exhibit 11.5.

The salesperson's presentation mix. Choose some or all of these ingredients for a great presentation.

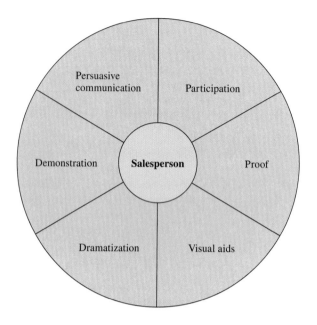

Persuasive Communication

To be a successful salesperson, do you need to be a smooth talker? No, but you do need to consider and use factors that promote clear communication of your messages. In Chapter 4, we discussed seven factors that help you be a better communicator:

1. Using questions.
2. Being empathic.
3. Keeping the message simple.
4. Creating mutual trust.
5. Listening.[1]
6. Having a positive attitude and enthusiasm.
7. Being believable.

The SELL Sequence and Trial Close

The use of a question to induce feedback is an excellent persuasive communication technique. As illustrated in Exhibit 11.1, the trial close should be used after making a strong selling point in the presentation, after the presentation itself, after answering an objection, and immediately before you move to close the sale.

When a question is coupled with discussing a product's feature, advantage, and benefit, it forms the SELL Sequence. The SELL Sequence is a great method of determining if the FAB is of interest to the buyer. Thus, the SELL Sequence is an effective form of persuasive communication.

Additional persuasive factors to consider in the presentation are logical reasoning, persuasive suggestions, a sense of fun, personalized relationships, trust, body language, a controlled presentation, diplomacy, the Paul Harvey dialogue or conversation style, and using words as selling tools.

Logical Reasoning

The application of logic through reasoning is an effective persuasive technique that appeals to prospects' common sense by requiring them to think about the proposition and to compare alternative solutions to problems. It can create excellent results when applied to selling computers, heavy equipment, and communication systems. This is especially true when selling complicated proposals involving comparative cost data, when price versus benefits must be judged, and when the product is a radically new concept.

Logical reasoning involves a presentation constructed around three parts: a major premise, a minor premise, and a conclusion. Here is an example:

1. *Major premise:* All manufacturers wish to reduce costs and increase efficiency.
2. *Minor premise:* My equipment will reduce your costs and increase your efficiency.
3. *Conclusion:* Therefore, you should buy my equipment.

If presented exactly in this straightforward manner, the logical formula may be too blunt; the prospect may raise defenses. However, you can develop the framework or presentation outline to determine if the prospect is interested in reducing costs and increasing manufacturing efficiency. If so, then present a value analysis that shows the benefits of your product over alternatives. Information such as performance data, costs, service, and delivery information can be presented in a persuasive manner using various elements of the presentation mix.

Persuasion through Suggestion

Suggestion, like logical reasoning, is used effectively to persuade prospects. The skilled use of suggestions can arouse attention, interest, desire, conviction, and action. Types of suggestions that may be considered for the presentation are listed below.

1. **Suggestive propositions** imply that the prospect should act now, such as, "Shouldn't you go ahead and buy now before the price goes up next month?" Prospects often like to postpone their buying decisions, so the suggestive approach can help overcome this problem.
2. **Prestige suggestions** ask the prospect to visualize using products that famous people, companies, or persons the prospect trusts use, such as, "The National Professional Engineers Association has endorsed our equipment. That's the reason several hundred *fortune* 500 manufacturers are using our products. This elite group of manufacturers finds that the equipment helps increase their profits, sales, and market share. Is this of interest to you?"
3. **Autosuggestion** attempts to have prospects imagine themselves using the product. Television advertisements frequently use this form of suggestion. The salesperson visualizes the product, saying, "Just imagine how this equipment will look and operate in your store. Your employees will perform much better and they will thank you."

4. The **direct suggestion** is used widely by professional salespeople in all industries because it does not "tell" but suggests buying, which does not offend the buyer. Such a suggestion might state: "Based on our survey of your needs, I suggest you purchase. . . ." or "Let's consider this: We ship you three train carloads of Whirlpool washers and dryers in the following colors and models. . . ."
5. The **indirect suggestion** is used at times for some prospects when it is best to be indirect in suggesting a recommended course of action. Indirect suggestions help instill in prospects' minds factors such as doubt about a competitor's products or desire for your product, which makes it seem as if it is their idea: "Should you buy 50 or 75 dozen 12-oz. cans of Revlon hairspray for your promotion?" or "Have you talked with anyone who has used that product?"

6. The **countersuggestion** evokes an opposite response from the prospect: "Do you really want such a high-quality product?" Often, the buyer will begin expanding on why a high-quality product is needed. This is an especially effective technique to include in the presentation if you have already determined that the prospect wants a high-quality product.

Make the Presentation Fun

Selling is fun, not a battle between the prospect and salesperson, so loosen up and enjoy the presentation. This is easy to do once you believe in yourself and what you are selling—so sound like it! Have the *right mental attitude* and you will be successful.

Personalize Your Relationship

When I worked for a large national industrial manufacturer, my sales manager taught me to personalize the presentation. He would say, "Charles, you are enthusiastic; you believe in yourself, your products, your company; and you give a very good presentation. To improve, however, you need to personalize your relationship with each of your customers. In some manner, let them know during your presentation that you have their best interests at heart." He would always say, "Show 'em that you love 'em."

I came up with the short phrase, "You have me." Once I incorporated this into my presentation at the appropriate time, I saw a significant increase in my total sales and sales-to-customer call ratio by saying something like: "You are not only buying my products but me as well. You have me on call 24 hours a day to help you in any way I can."

Yes, it sounds corny, but it helped show customers that I cared for them and that they could believe in me. This helped build trust between us. You might choose a different way, yet be sure to demonstrate that you look out for their interests.

Build Trust

Two of the best and easiest ways to build your persuasive powers with prospects are *being honest* and *doing what you say you will do.* This builds trust, which increases sales. Most professional buyers have elephantlike memories that can be used to your advantage if you follow through after the sale as you said you would when presenting the proposal.

> *I shall not pass this way again, so I should do good as I go.*
>
> MAHATMA GANDHI

Honesty is always the best policy, and it is an effective way to build trust. The salesperson should never claim more than the product can accomplish. If the product does not live up to expectations, apologize, return the product for credit, or trade for another product. This action is important in obtaining repeat sales. It builds trust; the next time the prospect is reluctant to buy, you say, "Haven't I always taken care of you? Trust me, this product is what you need. I guarantee it!"[2]

Remember that you do business with the one you trust and you trust the one you know. Trust develops over time. This would be a good time to review Chapter 1's discussion of the characteristics needed for the sales job shown in Exhibit 1.11. They are:

- Caring for customers.
- Joy in your work.
- Harmony in relationships.
- Patience in closing the sale.
- Kindness to all you contact.
- Morally ethical.
- Faithful to your word.
- Fairness.
- Self-control.

People having these personal traits easily build trust with others. So can you!

Use Body Language—Send Green Signals

The eyes are the lamps of your body.

Just as you watch for buying signals from a prospect, the prospect watches your facial expressions and body movements. The salesperson's nonverbal communication must project a positive image to the prospect, one that shows you know what you are talking about and understand the buyer's needs. Your customer will think, "I can trust this person."

The best nonverbal selling technique is the smile. As a sales manager once said, "It's often not what you say but how you say it, and you can say almost anything to anyone if you do it with a smile. So, practice your facial expressions and smile—always smile."

As discussed in Chapter 5, project "green" signals. If you are excited about helping the other person, it will show nonverbally. Your whole body will radiate a form of light through your eyes showing that you care. Your eyes are the lamps of your thoughts. People can tell you care.

Control the Presentation

In making the presentation, direct the conversation to lead the prospect through the presentation and proposal. The salesperson often faces difficulties on how to maintain control and what to do if the prospect takes control of the conversation. For example, what do you do if the prospect likes to talk about hobbies, attacks your company or products for poor service or credit mix-ups, or is a kidder and likes to poke fun at your products?

When this happens, the salesperson should stay with a planned presentation if possible. If there is some complaint, this should be addressed first. If the prospect likes to talk about other things, do so briefly. When the prospect's attention and interest are hard to maintain, questions or some manner of eliciting participation in the presentation are the two best methods to rechannel the conversation.

Be sure to control the visual aids and any materials you use in the presentation. New salespeople often make the mistake of handing prospects their catalog, price list, or brochures showing several products. When buyers are looking through these items, chances are that they are not listening. Too much information can cause frustration and they will not buy. So, keep your product materials and discuss the information you wish to present while prospects look at and listen to you.

Be a Diplomat

"Never tell a person they are wrong."
DALE CARNEGIE

All salespeople face the situation in which prospects feel they are right or know it all, and the salesperson has different opinions. For example, the salesperson previously may have sold the prospect's company a machine that always breaks down because of its operator, not the equipment, yet the salesperson's company is blamed. What to do?

The salesperson has to be a diplomat in cases in which tempers rise and prospects are wrong but feel they are correct and will not change their opinions. Retreat may be the best option; otherwise, you risk destroying the relationship. If you challenge the prospect, you could win the battle only to lose the war. This is a decision that the salesperson must make based on individual situations.

Dale Carnegie once said that a sure way of not making an enemy is to show respect for the other person's opinions, Never tell a person he or she is wrong. Would this apply to both your customers and others in your life?

Use the Paul Harvey Dialogue

Pleasant words are a honeycomb, sweet to the soul and healing to the bones. To hear someone with the gift of speaking listen to Paul Harvey. Paul Harvey has the most listened-to radio news broadcast in America because of what he says and how he says it. Listen to his unique conversation style yourself. (His broadcast is syndicated; you may have to search to find it.) Then use the **Paul Harvey dialogue.** Construct your presentation to incorporate his excellent methods of speech, delivery, and particularly how he builds suspense into his stories. With these techniques, your talk comes alive rather than sounding like a dull, memorized presentation spoken in a monotone voice.

Simile, Metaphor, and Analogy

Words are communication tools. Similes, metaphors, analogies, pauses, silence, and changes in the rate of speaking, tone, and pitch are effective methods of gaining prospects' attention and capturing their interest in a proposal.

A **simile** is a direct comparison statement using the word *like* or *as:* A poorly manicured lawn is *like* a bad haircut. Our Sylvania Safeline bulbs are *like* a car's shatterproof windshield. Shaklee diet drinks are *like* a chocolate milkshake. The carton folds *as flat as* a pancake for storage.

A **metaphor** is an *implied* comparison that uses a contrasting word or phrase to evoke a vivid image: Our power mowers *sculpt* your lawn. Our cabin cruiser *plows* through the waves smoothly. The computer's *memory* stores your data. The components *telescope* into a two-inch-thick disk.

The **analogy** compares two different situations that have something in common such as, "Our sun screen for your home will stop the sun's heat and glare before it hits your window. It's like having a shade tree in front of your window without blocking the view." Remember to talk the prospect's language by using familiar terminology and buzzwords in a conversational tone.

Participation Is Essential to Success

The second major part of the presentation involves techniques for motivating the prospect to participate in the presentation. Four ways to induce participation are

1. Questions.
2. Product use.
3. Visuals.
4. Demonstrations.

We have already discussed the use of questions and will discuss the use of visuals and demonstrations later, so let's briefly consider having prospects use the product:

- If you sell stereos, let them see, hear, and touch them!
- If you sell food, let them see, smell, and taste it!
- If you sell clothes, let them touch and wear them!

By letting prospects use the product, you can appeal to their senses: sight, sound, touch, smell, and taste. The presentation should be developed with appeals to the senses, since people often buy because of emotional needs and the senses are keys to developing emotional appeals.

Proof Statements Build Believability

Prospects often say to themselves, before I buy, you must *prove it.* "Prove it" is a thought everyone has at times. Salespeople must prove that they will do what they promise, such as helping to make product displays when the merchandise arrives.

Usually, prove it means proving to a prospect during a presentation that the product's benefits and salesperson's proposal are legitimate.

Because salespeople often have a reputation for exaggeration, at times prospects are skeptical of the salesperson's claims. By incorporating **proof statements** into the presentation, the salesperson can increase the prospect's confidence and trust that product claims are accurate. Several useful proof techniques are the customer's past sales figures, the guarantee, testimonials, company proof results, and independent research results.

Past Sales Help Predict the Future

Salespersons frequently use customers' past sales proof statements when contacting present customers. Customers keep records of their past purchases from each of their suppliers; the salesperson can use these to suggest what quantities of each product to purchase. For example, the Colgate salesperson checks a customer's present inventory of all products carried, determines the number of products sold in a month, subtracts inventory from forecasted sales, and suggests the customer purchase that amount. It is difficult for buyers to refuse when presentations are based on their own sales records. If they are offered a price discount and promotional allowances, they might purchase 3 to 10 times the normal amount (a promotional purchase).

Assume, for example, that a food store normally carries 10 dozen of the king-size tubes of Colgate toothpaste in inventory with 3 dozen on the shelf, and sells approximately 20 dozen a month. The salesperson produces the buyer's past sales record and says, "You should buy 7 to 10 dozen king-size Colgate toothpaste." If offering promotional allowances, the salesperson might say:

> The Colgate king-size is your most profitable and best-selling item. You normally sell 20 dozen Colgate king-size each month with a 30 percent gross profit. With our 15 percent price reduction this month only, and our advertising allowances, I suggest, based on your normal sales, that you buy 80 to 100 dozen, reduce the price 15 percent, display it, and advertise the discount in your newspaper specials. This will attract people to your store, increase store sales, and make your normal profit.

The salesperson stops talking to see the buyer's reaction. A suggested order plus an alternative on the quantity to purchase have been proposed. Does the quantity seem high? It may be high, just right, or low, but it is the buyer's decision. The salesperson is saying that, given past sales and the customer benefit plan, the customer can sell X amount.

Be realistic about your suggested increase in order size. Some salespeople double the size of the order, expecting the prospect to cut it in half. Your honesty builds credibility with the buyer.

The Colgate salesperson might suggest purchases not only of toothpaste but of all Colgate products. That same sales call could involve multiple presentations of several products that have promotional allowances plus the recommended purchase of 10 or more items based on present inventories and the previous month's sales.

The Guarantee

The guarantee is a powerful proof technique. It assures prospects that if they are dissatisfied with their purchase, the salesperson or the company will stand behind a product. The manufacturer has certain product warranties that the retail salesperson can use in a presentation.

Furthermore, the consumer goods salesperson selling to retailers might say, "I'll guarantee this product will sell for you. If not, we can return what you do not sell." The industrial salesperson may explain the equipment's warranties and service policies and state, "This is the best equipment that you can buy for your situation. If you are not 100-percent satisfied after you have used it for three months, I will return it for you."

Testimonials

A key to your happiness is making others' dreams come true.

Testimonials in the presentation as proof of the product's features, advantages, and benefits are an excellent method to build trust and confidence. Today, manufacturers effectively advertise their consumer products using testimonials. Professional buyers are impressed by testimonials from prominent people, experts, and satisfied customers about a product's features, advantages, and benefits.

Company Proof Results

Companies routinely furnish data concerning their products. Consumer goods salespeople can use sales data such as test market information and current sales data. Industrial salespeople use performance data and facts based on company research as proof of their product's performance.

A consumer goods manufacturer gave its salespeople test market sales information to use in their presentations on a new product being introduced nationally. Using this information, a salesperson might say:

> Our new product will sell as soon as you put it on your shelf. The product was a success in our Eastern test market. It had 9.8 percent market share only nine months after the start of advertising. Laboratory tests proved our formula superior to that of the leading competition in our consumer product tests. It had a high repurchase rate of 50 percent after sampling. This means increased sales and profits for you.

Independent Research Results

Proof furnished by reputable sources outside the company usually has more credibility than company-generated data. Pharmaceutical salespeople frequently tell physicians about medical research findings on their products published in leading medical journals by medical research authorities.

"On a typical day selling pharmaceuticals," says Sandra Snow of The Upjohn Company,

> I see as many physicians as possible and initiate a discussion with them about one of our products that will have importance to them in medicine. I attempt to point out advantages that our drugs have in various states by using third-party documentation published in current medical journals and texts. The information has much more meaning to a physician who knows that it is not me or The Upjohn Company that has shown our drug to have an advantage, but rather a group of researchers who have conducted a scientific study. All of the material that we give to the physicians has been approved for our use by the Food and Drug Administration.

Publications such as *Road Test Magazine* and *Consumer Reports,* newspaper stories, and government reports such as Environmental Protection Agency publications may contain information the salesperson can use in the presentation. For a proof statement referring to independent research results to be most effective, it should

EXHIBIT 11.6

Proof statements help prove what you say.

Feature	Advantage	Benefit	Proof
■ New consumer product	Will be big seller	Excellent profits	Test-market results
■ High energy-efficiency rating	Uses less electricity	Saves 10% on energy costs	*Consumer Reports* magazine
■ Electronic mail software	Gets information to sales force instantly	Reduces mailing and telephone costs	Testimonials
■ Buy 100 cases	Reduces out-of- stocks	Increases sales, profits, customer satisfaction	Customer's past sales or personal guarantee

contain (1) a restatement of the benefit before proving it, (2) the proof source and relevant facts or figures about the product, and (3) expansion of the benefit. Consider the following example of a salesperson's proof statement:

I'm sure that you want a radio that's going to sell and be profitable for you (**benefit restatement**). Figures in *Consumer Guide* and *Consumer Sales* magazines indicate that the Sony XL-l00 radios, although the newest on the market, are the third largest in sales (**source and facts**). Therefore, when you handle the Sony XL line, you'll find that radio sales and profits will increase, and more customers will come into your store (**benefit expansion**).

Proof statements must be incorporated into the presentation. They provide a logical answer to the buyer's challenge of "prove it!"

Exhibit 11.6 shows four examples of using proof to support what is said about FABs—features, advantages, benefits. Proof statements are a great way to substantiate your sales claims. Often, proof statements are presented through visual aids.

The Visual Presentation— Show and Tell

In giving a sales presentation, as a salesperson you do two things: You *show* and *tell* the prospect about a proposal. You *tell* using persuasive communications, participation techniques, and proof statements. You *show* by using visual aids.

People retain approximately 10 percent of what they hear but 50 percent of what they see. Consequently, you have five times the chance of making a lasting impression with an illustrated sales presentation rather than with words alone.

Visuals are most effective when you believe in them and have woven them into your sales presentation message. Use them to

- ■ Increase retention.
- ■ Reinforce the message.
- ■ Reduce misunderstanding.
- ■ Create a unique and lasting impression.
- ■ Show the buyer that you are a professional.

The visual presentation (showing) incorporates the three remaining elements of the presentation mix: visual aids, dramatization, and demonstration. There is some overlap among the three; for example, a demonstration uses visuals and has some drama. Let's examine each of the elements and consider how they can be used in a sales presentation.

VISUAL AIDS HELP TELL THE STORY

Visuals, or visual aids, are devices that chiefly appeal to the prospect's vision, with the intent of producing mental images of the product's features, advantages, and benefits. Many companies routinely supply salespeople with visuals for their products. Some common visuals are

- The product.
- Charts and graphics illustrating product features and advantages such as performance and sales data.
- Photographs and videos of the product and its uses.
- Models or mock-ups of products, especially for large, bulky products.
- Equipment such as videos, slides, audiocassettes, and computers.
- Sales manuals and product catalogs.
- Order forms.
- Letters of testimony.
- A copy of the guarantee.
- Flip boards and posters.
- Sample advertisements.

Most visual aids are carried in the salesperson's bag (see Exhibit 11.7). The sales bag should be checked before each sales call to ensure that all visuals necessary for the presentation are organized in a manner that allows the salesperson to easily

EXHIBIT 11.7

Visual aids are an important part of this salesperson's presentation.

1. She reviews the call plan before seeing buyer.

2. She places products and visual aids in her sales bag.

3. Some visual aids are furnished by her company.

4. She uses personally developed sales aids customized to her buyer.

access needed visuals. Only new, top-quality, professionally developed visuals should be used. Tattered, torn, or smudged visuals should be routinely discarded. The best visual aid is the actual product.

DRAMATIZATION IMPROVES YOUR CHANCES

Dramatics refers to talking or presenting the product in a striking, showy, or extravagant manner. Thus, sales expertise can involve **dramatization** or a theatrical presentation of products. However, dramatics should be incorporated into the presentation only when you are 100 percent sure that the dramatics will work effectively. This was not considered by the salesperson who set the buyer's trash can on fire. When the salesperson had difficulty extinguishing the fire with a new fire extinguisher, the buyer ran out of the room because of the extensive smoke. However, if implemented correctly, dramatics are effective. One of the best methods of developing ideas for the dramatization of a product is to watch television commercials. Products are presented using visuals, many products are demonstrated, and most products are dramatized. Take, for example, the following television advertisements:

■ "We challenged the competition . . . and they ran!" says the Heinz tomato ketchup advertisement. Two national brands of ketchup and Heinz ketchup are poured into paper coffee filters held up by tea strainers. The competition's ketchup begins to drip and then runs through the filter. The Heinz ketchup does not drip or run, which indicates the high quality of Heinz ketchup relative to the competition.
■ Bounty paper towel advertisements show coffee spilled and how quickly the product absorbs the coffee relative to the competitive paper towel.
■ The STP motor-oil additive advertisement shows a person dipping one screwdriver into STP motor-oil additive and another screwdriver into a plain motor oil. The person can hold with two fingers the end of the screwdriver covered with plain motor oil. The screwdriver covered with STP motor-oil additive slips out of the fingers—indicating STP provides better lubrication for an automobile engine.

Use a dramatic demonstration to set yourself apart from the many salespeople that buyers see each day. Buyers, such as industrial purchasing agents, like to see you, as they know you will have an informative and often entertaining sales presentation. One salesperson known for his effective presentation was George Wynn. George was an industrial salesperson for Exxon, and he was responsible for sales of machine lubricating oils and greases in Dayton, Cincinnati, and Columbus, Ohio.

One group of products Wynn sold were oils and greases for the food-processing industry. These lubricants had to be approved by the federal Food and Drug Administration for incidental food contact. One of the products was a lubricating grease, Carum 280. Wynn ordered a number of one-pound cans for customer samples. As Wynn started his sales presentation of these Food and Drug Administration (FDA) approved products, he would take one of the cans from his sample case, open it, and spread this grease on a slice of bread. After taking a bite of bread spread with the grease, he then offered a bite to the buyer. The buyer generally refused the offer. However, in the mind of the buyer, this dramatic demonstration set Wynn's presentation apart from others. It helped prove to the buyer the product was safe to use in a food-processing plant.

Another of Wynn's dramatic demonstrations involved lubricating greases used by the steel industry. Greases that resist high temperatures are desirable for most applications in the steel industry. Exxon developed a line of temperature-resistant greases that used a new thickener that held the oil in suspension better than competitive products. To demonstrate this product attribute, Wynn used a pie tin held at a 45-degree angle centered over a small lighted alcohol lamp. A small glob of the Exxon grease and globs of several better-known competitors were placed on the pie tin. As the pie tin was heated, the oil separated from each of the competitive greases and ran down the pie tin. The oil did not separate from the Exxon product, dramatically demonstrating the high temperature resistance of this steel-mill grease as compared with leading competitive products.

DEMONSTRATIONS PROVE IT

One of the best ways to convince a prospect that a product is needed is to show the merits of the product through a **demonstration** as George Wynn did. If a picture is worth a thousand words, then a demonstration is worth a thousand pictures. Therefore, it is best to show the product, if possible, and have the prospect use it. If this is not feasible, then pictures, models, videotapes, films, or slides are the best alternatives. Whatever the salesperson is attempting to sell, the prospect should be able to see it.

Let the prospect feel, see, hear, smell, use the product.

Psychological studies have shown that people receive 87 percent of their information on the outside world through their eyes and only 13 percent through the other four senses. What this says to the salesperson is to make a product visible. Also, let the prospect feel, see, hear, smell, and use the product. The dynamic demonstration appeals to human senses by telling, showing, and creating buyer–seller interaction (see Exhibit 11.8).

Demonstrations are part of the dramatization and fun of your presentation. Do not underestimate their ability to make sales for you, no matter how simple they may appear. For example, a glass company once designed shatterproof glass. This was not standard equipment in automobiles at the time, as it is now. The company

EXHIBIT 11.8

Virtual reality demonstration.

This prospect experiences what virtual reality is all about. A demonstration is worth a thousand pictures in helping make a sale.

had its salespeople going around the country trying to sell shatterproof glass. One of the salespeople completely outsold the rest of the sales force. When they had their convention, they said, "Joe, how come you sell so much glass?" He replied, "Well, what I've been doing is taking little chunks of glass and a ball-peen hammer along with me on sales calls. I take a little chunk of glass, and I hit it with the hammer. This shows that it's shatterproof. It splinters, but doesn't shatter and fall all over the ground. This has helped me sell a lot of glass."

So, the next year they equipped every salesperson with a ball-peen hammer and little chunks of glass. But an interesting thing happened. Joe still far outsold the rest of the sales force. So when the convention occurred the next year, they asked, "Joe, how is it you're selling so much? You told us what you did last year. What are you doing differently?" He replied, "Well, this year, I gave the glass *and* the hammer to the customer to let *them* hit it." You see, the first year Joe had dramatization in his demonstration; the second year he had dramatization and participation. Again, it's often not what you say but how you say it that makes the sale.

A Demonstration Checklist

There are seven points to remember as you prepare your demonstration. These points are shown in Exhibit 11.9. Ask yourself if the demonstration is really beneficial and appropriate for your prospects. Every sale does not need a demonstration nor will all products lend themselves to a demonstration.

If the demonstration is appropriate, what is its objective? What should the demonstration accomplish? Next, be sure you have properly planned and organized the demonstration; rehearse it so the demonstration flows smoothly and appears natural. Take your time in talking and going through your demonstration; make it look easy. Remember, if you, the expert, cannot operate a machine, for example, imagine how difficult it will be for the prospect.

The only way to ensure a smooth demonstration is to practice. Yet, there is always the possibility that the demonstration will not go as planned or will backfire no matter how simple. Be prepared. Remember the example of a former student who was demonstrating his new Kodak slide projector. Two bulbs in a row burned out as he demonstrated the product to a buyer for a large discount chain. He anticipated what could go wrong and always carried extra parts in his sales bag. When the first bulb went out, he talked of how easy it was to change bulbs, and when the second one blew, he said, "I want to show you that again," with a smile. He always carried two spare bulbs, now he carries three.

Finally, make sure your demonstration presents the product in an ethical and professional manner. You do not want to misrepresent the product or proposal. A complex product, such as a large computer system, can be presented as simple to install with few start-up problems, yet the buyer may find the computer system difficult to operate.

EXHIBIT 11.9

Seven points to remember about demonstrations.

- ☑ Is the demonstration *needed* and *appropriate?*
- ☑ Have I developed a specific demonstration *objective?*
- ☑ Have I properly *planned* and *organized* the demonstration?
- ☑ Have I rehearsed to the point that the demonstration *flows smoothly* and appears to be *natural?*
- ☑ What is the probability that the demonstration will go as *planned?*
- ☑ What is the probability that the demonstration will *backfire?*
- ☑ Does my demonstration present my product in an *ethical* and *professional* manner?

Use Participation in Your Demonstration

Confucius, the famous Chinese philosopher (551–479 B.C.), is often credited with saying, "Tell me and I'll forget. Show me and I'll remember. Involve me and I'll understand." By having the prospect participate in the demonstration, you obtain a buyer's attention and direct it where you want it. It also helps the prospect visualize owning and operating the product. The successful demonstration aids in reducing buying uncertainties and resistance to purchase. A successful demonstration involves the prospect in four ways; it

1. Lets the prospect do something simple.
2. Lets the prospect work an important feature.
3. Lets the prospect do something routine or frequently repeated.
4. Has the prospect answer questions throughout the demonstration.

First, ask the prospect to do something simple with a low probability of foul-ups. Second, in planning the demonstration, select the main features that you will stress in the interview and allow the prospect to participate on the feature that relates most to an important buying motive. Again, keep it simple.

A third way to have a successful demonstration is by having the prospect do something with the product that is done frequently. Finally, receive feedback from the prospect throughout the demonstration by asking questions or pausing in your conversation. This is extremely important, as it will

- Determine the prospect's attitude toward the product.
- Allow you to progress in the demonstration or wait and answer any questions or address any objections.
- Aid in moving the prospect into the positive yes mood.
- Set the stage for closing the sale.

Little agreements lead to the big agreement and saying yes. Phrase questions in a positive manner such as "That is really easy to operate, isn't it?" instead of, "This isn't hard to operate, is it?" They ask the same thing, yet the response to the first question is positive instead of negative. The best questions force the prospect to place the product in use mentally, such as the question phrased, Do you feel this feature could increase your employees' productivity? This yes answer commits the buyer to the idea that the feature will increase employee productivity. Remember, it is often not what you say but how you say it.

Reasons for Using Visual Aids, Dramatics, and Demonstrations

As we have seen, visual aids, dramatics, and demonstrations are important to the salesperson's success in selling a prospect. The reasons to use them include wanting to

- Capture attention and interest.
- Create two-way communication.
- Involve the prospect through participation.
- Afford a more complete, clear explanation of products.
- Increase a salesperson's persuasive powers by obtaining positive commitments on a product's single feature, advantage, or benefit.

Guidelines for Using Visual Aids, Dramatics, and Demonstrations

Although visual aids, dramatics, and demonstrations are important, their proper use is critical to their effectiveness. When using them, consider

- Rehearsing by practicing in front of a mirror, on a tape recorder, and/or on videotape. Once you are ready to make the presentation, begin using it with less important prospects. This allows you time to refine the presentation before contacting more important accounts.

EXHIBIT 11.10

Which buyer senses are being appealed to by the seller?

- Customizing them to the sales call objective—the prospect's customer profile and the customer benefit plan—and concentrating on the prospect's important buying motives, using appropriate multiple appeals to sight, touch, hearing, smell, and taste (see Exhibit 11.10).
- Making them *simple, clear,* and *straightforward.*
- Being sure you control the demonstration by not letting the prospect divert you from selling. It can be disastrous to have the prospect not listen or pass up major selling points you wished to present.
- Making them *true to life.*
- Encouraging *prospect participation.*
- Incorporating *trial closes* (questions) after showing or demonstrating a major feature, advantage, or benefit to determine if the prospect believes the presentation and considers it important.

TECHNOLOGY CAN HELP!

Technology provides excellent methods of presenting information to the buyer in a visually attractive and dramatic manner. Using a computer in front of the buyer can be impressive. Today, multimedia computers present video clips, play sound bites, show beautifully illustrated graphics, and can be connected to projection equipment for great presentations. Computer software can quickly crunch data—providing instant solutions to buyers' questions. Salespeople selling products such as service, real estate, and industrial equipment can quickly show buyers a product's cost when considering different installment payment schedules at various interest rates.

Overhead transparencies, 35-mm slides, and black-and-white handouts are being replaced by dynamic software packages, interactive multimedia programs, active-matrix color screens, and multimedia projectors that bring computer images to life. Remember, it's often not what you say but how you say it that makes the sale.

THE SALES PRESENTATION GOAL MODEL

"Wow!" you say. There are many things to consider when creating a sales presentation. Persuasive communication, participation, proof statements, visual aids, dramatization, demonstration that may or may not include technology. How do I decide what elements of the sales presentation mix to use in a sales presentation? It depends on the goal of your presentation and the answers to six questions.

The sales presentation goal model.

The Presentation Goal Model

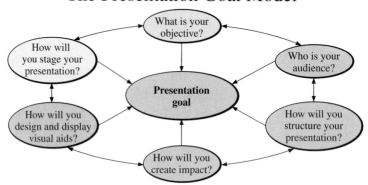

Exhibit 11.11 will help you decide whether to use some or all of the sales presentation mix ingredients. You need to answer these six questions:

1. What is your objective?
2. Who is your audience?
3. How will you structure your presentation?
4. How will you create impact?
5. How will you design and display visual aids?
6. How will you stage your presentation?

Your sales presentation goal(s) and the answers to these six questions will be your guide to skillfully show and tell your customers how your product will fulfill their needs.

THE IDEAL PRESENTATION

In the ideal presentation, your approach technique quickly captures your prospect's interest and immediately identifies signals that the prospect has a need for your product and is ready to listen. The ideal prospect is friendly, polite, and relaxed; will not allow anyone to interrupt you; asks questions; and participates in your demonstration as planned. This allows you to move through the presentation skillfully.

The ideal customer cheerfully and positively answers each of your questions, allowing you to anticipate the correct moment to ask for the order. You are completely relaxed and sure of yourself when you come to the close. The customer says yes, and enthusiastically thanks you for your valuable time. Several weeks later, you receive a copy of the letter your customer wrote to your company's president glowing with praise for your professionalism and sincere concern for the customer.

BE PREPARED FOR PRESENTATION DIFFICULTIES

Yes, a few sales presentations are like the previous example; but most presentations have one or more hurdles you should prepare for. While all of the difficulties you might face cannot be discussed here, three main problems that are encountered during sales presentations are handling an interruption, discussing your competition, and making the presentation in a less-than-ideal situation.

How to Handle Interruptions

It is common for interruptions to occur during the presentation. The secretary comes into the office or the telephone rings, distracting the prospect. What should you do?

First, determine if the discussion that interrupted your presentation is personal or confidential. If so, by gesture or voice you can offer to leave the room—this is always appreciated by the prospect. Second, while waiting, regroup your thoughts and mentally review how to return to the presentation. Once the discussion is over, you can

1. Wait quietly and patiently until you have regained the prospect's attention completely.
2. Briefly restate the selling points that had interested the prospect, for example: "We were discussing your needs for a product such as ours and you seemed especially interested in knowing about our service, delivery, and installation. Is that right?"
3. Do something to increase the prospect's participation, such as showing the product, using other visuals, or asking questions. Closely watch to determine if you have regained the prospect's interest.
4. If interest is regained, move deeper into the presentation.

Should You Discuss the Competition?

Competition is something all salespeople must contend with every day. If you sell a product, you must compete with others selling comparable products. How should you handle competition? Basically, remember three considerations: (1) do not refer to a competitior unless absolutely necessary; (2) acknowledge your competitor only briefly; and (3) make a detailed comparison of your product and the competition's product.

Do Not Refer to Competition

First of all, lessen any surprises the buyer may present by properly planning for the sales call. In developing your customer profile, chances are that you will learn what competing products are used and your prospect's attitude toward your products and competitors' products. Based on your findings, you can develop the presentation without specifically referring to competition.

Acknowledge Competition and Drop It

Did you think there was so much to know about personal selling?

Many salespeople feel their competition should not be discussed unless the prospect discusses it. Then, acknowledge competition briefly and return to your product. "Yes, I am familiar with that product's features. In fact, the last three of my customers were using that product and have switched over to ours. May I tell you why?"

Here, you do not knock competition, but acknowledge it and in a positive manner move the prospect's attention back to your products. If the prospect continues to discuss a competing product, you should determine the prospect's attitude toward it. You might ask, "What do you think about the IBM 6000 computer system?" The answer will help you mentally determine how you can prove that your product offers the prospect more benefits than your competitor's product.

Make a Detailed Comparison

At times, it is appropriate to make a detailed comparison of your product to a competing one, especially for industrial products. If products are similar, emphasize your company's service, guarantees, and what you do personally for customers.

If your product has features that are lacking in a competitor's product, refer to these advantages. "Our product is the only one on the market with this feature! Is this

Lying Like a Dog

You are in the competitive business of selling office machines. You have an appointment with the senior partner of a large medical center. She has already studied several competitive products. Her hot buttons are low operating costs and low maintenance. You know that four competitors have demonstrated their products to your prospect.

After you have shown her the benefits of your product, she asks you, "Tell me, what makes your machine better than Brand X?" You restate some of your obvious product benefits and she comes back with, "The salesperson with company X told me that they use a special kind of toner that is superior to what you use for your machine by 20 percent." You know that this is an obvious lie, so you ask, "What evidence did this salesperson give you to prove the claim?" She shows you a customer testimonial letter that talks about satisfaction with the machine, but it says nothing about a longer lifetime. You reply carefully, "That's the first time I have ever seen a letter praising a brand X machine."

Next, she shows you another piece of paper, a chart that graphically illustrates the operating costs of five different brands. The chart says on the bottom, "Marketing Research Brand X, 2002." It shows your machine with the highest operating costs over a five-year period, and it shows brand X in the leading position with 50 percent lower operating costs. You are stunned by this unfair comparison. You try to control your temper.

What would be the most ethical action to take?

1. Tell your customer that you have never heard or seen the information she is showing you. Offer to do some additional research into the matter so that she can make her decision based on the most accurate information possible.
2. Do your best to refute the information on the chart. It is not your job to tell the customer that your competitor is being untruthful. It is only your job to sell your product.
3. Tell your customer that you believe that the brand X research is misleading. Based on everything you have seen or heard, brand X does not meet the standards it states.

important to you?" Ask the question and wait for the response. A yes answer takes you one step closer to the sale.

Often the prospect can use both your product and a competitor's product. For example, a pharmaceutical salesperson is selling an antibiotic that functions like penicillin and kills bacteria resistant to penicillin. However, it costs 20 times more than penicillin. This salesperson would say, "Yes, Dr. Jones, penicillin is the drug of choice for . . . disease. But do you have patients for whom penicillin is ineffective?" "Yes, I do," says the doctor." "Then, for those patients, I want you to consider my product because. . . ."

Competition Discussion Based on the Situation. Whether or not you discuss competition depends on the prospect. Based on your selling philosophy and your knowledge of the prospect, you can choose how to deal with competition. If you are in doubt due to insufficient prospect knowledge, it is best not to discuss competition.

Be Professional   No matter how you discuss competition with your prospect, always act professionally. If you discuss competition, talk only about information that you know is accurate, and be straightforward and honest—not belittling and discourteous.

Your prospect may like both your products and the competitor's products. A loyalty to the competitor may have been built over the years; by insulting competition, you may insult and alienate your prospect. However, the advantages and disadvantages of a competitive product can be demonstrated acceptably if done professionally. One salesperson relates this story:

Several customers I called on were loyal to my competitors; however, just as many were loyal to my company. I will always remember the president of a chain of retail stores who flew 500 miles to be at one of our salesperson's retirement dinners. In his talk, he noted how 30 years ago, when he opened his first store, this salesperson extended him company credit and made him a personal loan that helped him get started.

It would be difficult for a competing salesperson to sell to this loyal customer. When contacting customers, especially ones buying competitive products, it is important to uncover why they use competitive products before discussing competition in the presentation.

The Golden Rule. Everything you do and say should be based upon the Golden Rule, especially as it relates to competitors. Take a minute to review the section entitled "Others Includes Competitors" in the appendix to Chapter 1, "The Golden Rule of Personal Selling as Told by a Salesperson."

In everything, you want to do to others what you would have them do to you. Remember the George Wynn story discussed earlier in this chapter. Assume you, for example, are a purchasing agent for a food-processing plant and this week the FDA passed a new law on the type of lubricating oils and greases that you can use for manufacturing ice cream. You do not have this type of lubricant. A salesperson calls on you and says his lubricants are not FDA approved. Wouldn't you want the salesperson to tell you where you could quickly buy the product you need? Sure you would! George Wynn would be happy to help his customer. What would you do?

Where the Presentation Takes Place

The ideal presentation happens in a quiet room with only the salesperson, the prospect, and no interruptions. However, at times the salesperson may meet the prospect somewhere other than a private office and need to make the presentation under less than ideal conditions.

For short presentations, a stand-up situation may be adequate; however, when making a longer presentation, you may want to ask the prospect, "Could we go back to your office?" or make another appointment.

Diagnose the Prospect to Determine Your Sales Presentation

You have seen that in contacting prospects you must prepare for various situations. That is why selling is so challenging and why companies reward their salespeople so well. A major challenge is adapting your sales presentation to each potential buyer. In Chapter 4, you read about selling based on personality. Reexamine that discussion to better understand how and why you should be prepared to adapt your presentation.

SUMMARY OF MAJOR SELLING ISSUES

The sales presentation is a persuasive vocal and visual explanation of a proposition. While there are numerous methods for making a sales presentation, the four common ones are the memorized, formula, need-satisfaction, and problem-solution selling methods. Each method is effective if used for the proper situation.

In developing your presentation, consider the elements of the sales presentation mix that you will use for each prospect. The proper use of persuasive communication techniques, methods to develop prospect participation, proof statements, visual aids, dramatization, and demonstrations increases your chance of illustrating how your products will satisfy your prospect's needs.

It is often not what we say but how we say it that results in the sale. Persuasive communication techniques (questioning, listening, logical reasoning, suggestion, and the use of trial closes) help to uncover needs, to communicate effectively, and to pull the prospect into the conversation.

Proof statements are especially useful in showing your prospect that what you say is true and that you can be trusted. When challenged, prove it by incorporating facts in your presentation on a customer's past sales—guaranteeing the product will work or sell, testimonials, and company and independent research results.

To both show and tell, visuals must be properly designed to illustrate features, advantages, and benefits of your products through graphics, dramatization, and demonstration. This allows you to capture the prospect's attention and interest; to create two-way communication and participation; to express your proposition in a clearer, more complete manner; and to make more sales. Careful attention to development and rehearsal of the presentation is needed to ensure it occurs smoothly and naturally.

Always prepare for the unexpected, such as a demonstration that falls apart, interruptions, the prospect's questions about the competition, or the necessity to make your presentation in a less than ideal place, such as in the aisle of a retail store or in the warehouse.

The presentation part of the overall sales presentation is the heart of the sale. It is where you develop the desire, conviction, and action. By giving an effective presentation, you have fewer objections to your proposition, which makes for an easier sale close.

If you want to be a real professional in selling, acquire or create materials that convey your message and convince others to believe it. If you try to sell without using the components of the sales presentation mix, you are losing sales not because of what you say but how you say it. Exhibits, facts, statistics, examples, analogies, testimonials, and samples should be part of your repertoire. Without them, you are not equipped to do a professional job of selling.

MEETING A SALES CHALLENGE

The carpet's ability to resist fading is important to the customer who needs proof your carpet will not fade. In this situation, the proof statement should be authoritative, using independent research results, if possible. Here is an example of an effective proof statement:

"Mr. Jones, a carpet made of our new XT-15 synthetic fibers will not fade." (**Restatement of the benefit.**) "A recent study conducted by the Home Research Institute and reported in the *Home Digest* proves that our fibers hold their colors much better than natural fibers." (**A proof of the benefit.**) "And since Superior's carpets are made with synthetic fibers, you'll never hear any complaints about these carpets fading." (**An expansion of the benefit.**) "What do you think?" (**Trial close.**)

KEY TERMS FOR SELLING

sales presentation mix 345	Paul Harvey dialogue 350
logical reasoning 347	simile 350
suggestive propositions 347	metaphor 350
prestige suggestions 347	analogy 350
autosuggestion 347	proof statements 351
direct suggestion 347	visuals 353
indirect suggestion 347	dramatization 355
countersuggestion 348	demonstration 356

SALES APPLICATION QUESTIONS

1. You plan to give a demonstration of the Dyno Electric Cart to the purchasing agent of a company having a manufacturing plant that covers 200 acres. Which of the following is the best technique for your demonstration? Why?

   a. Let your prospect drive the cart.

  b. You drive the cart and ask the prospect to ride so that you can discuss the cart's benefits.

  c. Leave a demonstrator and return a week later to see how many the prospect will buy.

2. When contracting a purchasing agent for your Dyno Electric Carts, you plan to use your 10-page visual presenter to guide the prospect through your benefit story. This selling aid is a binder containing photographs of your cart in action along with its various color options, a guarantee, and a testimonial. Should you

  a. Hand over the binder? Why?

  b. Hold on to it? Why?

3. Assume you were halfway through your presentation when your prospect had to answer the telephone. The call lasted five minutes. What would you do?

4. Discuss the various elements of the sales presentation mix and indicate why you need to use visuals during your presentation.

5. In your proof statement of the benefit, cite your proof source, in addition to relevant facts or figures about your product. Which of the following is a correct proof of a benefit?

  a. Well, an article in last month's *Appliance Report* stated that the Williams blender is more durable than the other top 10 brands.

  b. You'll get 10 percent more use from the Hanig razor.

  c. *Marathon* is the most widely read magazine among persons with incomes over $25,000 per year.

  d. Figures in *Marathon* magazine indicate that your sales will increase if you stock Majestic housewares in your store.

6. Examine the following conversation:

Customer: What you say is important, all right, but how do I know that these chairs will take wear and tear the way you say they will?

Salesperson: The durability of a chair is an important factor to consider. That's why all Crest chairs have reinforced plastic webbing seats. *Furniture Dealer's Weekly* states that the plastic webbing used in Crest chairs is 32 percent more effective in preventing sagging chair seats than fabric webbing. This means that your chairs will last longer and will take the wear and tear that your customers are concerned about.

 Look at each sentence in this conversation and state if it is

  a. An expansion of the benefit.

  b. A restatement of the benefit.

  c. A proof of the benefit.

7. After a two-hour drive to see an important new prospect, you stop at a local coffee shop for a bite to eat. As you look over your presentation charts, you spill coffee on half a dozen of them. You don't have substitute presentation charts with you. What should you do?

  a. Phone the prospect and say that you'd like to make another appointment. Say that something came up.

  b. Keep the appointment. At the start of your presentation, tell the prospect about the coffee spill and apologize for it.

  c. Go ahead with your presentation, but don't make excuses. The coffee stains are barely noticeable if you're not on the lookout for them.

FURTHER EXPLORING THE SALES WORLD

1. What is one thing in this world on which you are an expert? Yourself! Develop a presentation on yourself for a sales job with a company of your choice. Relate this assignment to each of the 10 steps of the selling process.
2. Visit several retail stores in your community such as an appliance, bicycle, or sporting goods store and report on the demonstration techniques, if any, that were used in selling a product. Suggest ways that you would have presented the product.
3. Report on one television advertisement that used each of the following: a proof statement, a demonstration, unusual visual aids, and a dramatization.
4. In your library are magazines in which companies advertise their products to retail and wholesaler customers, along with information about current price discounts. Find at least three advertisements containing current price discounts manufacturers offer to wholesalers and/or retailers. How might you use this information in a sales presentation?

STUDENT APPLICATION LEARNING EXERCISE (SALES)

An important part of consultative selling is the use of questions to uncover the customer's needs. You have planned some of your questions in constructing your **SELL** Sequences. **SELL Sequences** should be contained in your discussion of the product, marketing plan, and business proposition.

(Sale 5 of 7)

Every important sales presentation should contain most—if not all—of the presentation mix ingredients shown in Exhibit 11.5 on page 346. To make **SALE 5**:

1. Construct and write out one SELL Sequence. After your trial close, the buyer questions what you have just said. The buyer sounds as if unsure what you are saying is true. Create a proof statement that shows your claim is true. See pages 352–353.

   SELL SEQUENCE:
   Buyer's skeptical remark:
   Proof statement:

2. Create one analogy, simile, and metaphor to use in your role-play. See page 350.

   Analogy:
   Simile:
   Metaphor:

3. Describe a demonstration you could do of one of your product's benefits. If possible, add dramatization. Remember, simply showing the product is not a demonstration.

4. Describe three visual aids you could use in your presentation. Flip charts and notebooks are easy to develop, or you can place your visuals in a folder and pull out one at a time as you discuss it.

   Visual 1:
   Visual 2:
   Visual 3:

CHAPTER 11

**Elements of a
Great Sales
Presentation**

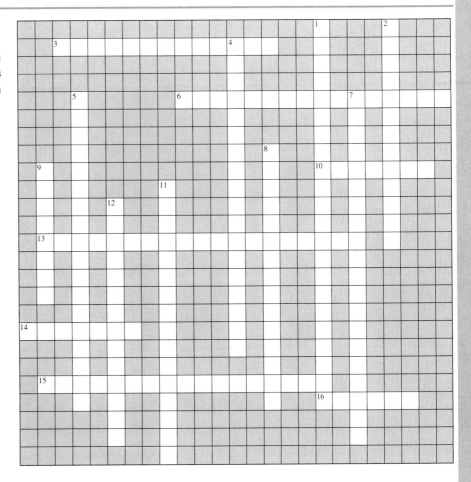

Across

3. The theatrical presentation of products.
6. Persuasive techniques that appeal to the prospect's common sense by applying logic through reason.
10. Illustrative material that aids a prospect in increasing memory retention of a presentation.
13. A technique in which the salesperson has the prospect visualize using products that people whom the prospect trusts use.
14. A comparison between two different situations that have something in common.
15. A suggestion that evokes an opposite response from the prospect.
16. A direct comparison statement using the word *like* or *as*.

Down

1. A proposition that implies that the prospect should act now.
2. The process of showing a product to a prospect and letting him or her use it, if possible.
4. A statement by the salesperson recommending that the prospect undertake some action while making it seem that the idea to do so is the prospect's.
5. The process of incorporating methods of speech and delivery to make talk come alive rather than sounding dull and memorized.

7. The key communication elements used by the salesperson in the presentation.

8. Statements that substantiate claims made by the salesperson.

9. An implied comparison that uses a contrasting word or phrase to evoke a vivid image.

11. An approach that suggests that prospects should buy rather than telling them to buy.

12. A kind of suggestion that attempts to have prospects imagine themselves using the product.

CASE 11-1
Dyno Electric Cart Company

You plan a call-back on Conway Pride and the president of his company to sell them several of your electric carts. (See Exhibit 9.4 in Chapter 9.) The company's manufacturing plant covers some 200 acres and you have sold up to 10 carts to many companies smaller than this one. Since Pride allows you to meet with his company's president and maybe other executives, you know he is interested in your carts.

You are determined to make a spellbinding presentation of your product's benefits using visual aids and a cart demonstration. Mr. Pride raised several objections on your last presentation that may be restated by other executives. Your challenge is to develop a dramatic, convincing presentation.

Questions

1. You plan to give a cart demonstration to show how effective it is in traveling around the plant. Which of the following is the best technique for the demonstration?
   a. Get Pride and the president involved by letting them drive the cart.
   b. You drive, letting them ride so they will listen more carefully to you.
   c. Leave a demonstrator and check back the next week to see how many they will buy.

2. You also plan to use a 10-page visual presenter to guide them through your benefit story. This selling aid is in a binder and contains photographs of your cart in action, along with its various color options, guarantee, and testimonials. Should you:
   a Get Pride to participate by letting him hold it?
   b. Handle it yourself, allowing him to watch and listen while you turn the pages and tell your story?

CASE 11-2
Major Oil, Inc.*

Tim Christensen sells industrial lubricants to manufacturing plants. The lubricants are used for the plants' machinery. He is calling on Ben Campbell, a purchasing agent for Acme Manufacturing Company. Ben currently buys Tim's Hydraulic Oil 65 in drums. Tim's sales call objective is to persuade Ben to switch from purchasing his oil in drums to a bulk oil system. The secretary has just admitted him to Ben's office.

Salesperson: Hello, Ben.

Customer: Well, if it isn't Tim Christensen, my lube oil salesperson! How is everything over at Major Oil these days?

* Case developed by George Wynn, Professor of Marketing, James Madison University, © 2004.

Salesperson: Fine! We're adding to our warehouse, so we won't be quite as crowded. Say, I know you like to fly. I was just reading in a magazine about the old Piper Tri-Pacer.

Customer: Yeah! I do enjoy flying and fooling with old airplanes. I just got back this weekend from a fly-in over at Houston.

Salesperson: You don't say! What type of planes did they have?

Customer: They had a bunch of homebuilts. You know, many pilots spend from 5 to 15 years just building their own planes.

Salesperson: Would you like to build your own plane someday?

Customer: Yes, I would. But you know, this job takes so much time—and with my schedule here and some travel, I don't know if I'll ever get time to start on a plane, much less finish one.

Salesperson: Well, I don't know that I can save you that much time, but I can save the people in the plant time and reduce your cost of Hydraulic Oil 65. Also, I may even save your office some time and expense by not having to place so many orders.

You know, we talked a couple of weeks ago about the possibility of Acme buying Hydraulic Oil 65 in bulk and thus reducing the cost per gallon by buying larger quantities each time you order. In addition, you will save tying your money up in the $20 drum deposit or even losing the deposit by losing or damaging the empty drum.

Customer: Sounds like this is fixing to cost us some money.

Salesperson: Well, we might have to spend a little money to save a larger amount, plus make it easier and quicker in the plant. Do you know exactly what you are paying for Hydraulic Oil 65 now?

Customer: I think it's about $1.40 a gallon.

Salesperson: That's close. Your delivery cost is $1.39 per gallon, not counting drum deposit. You used approximately 20,000 gallons of Hydraulic Oil 65 last year at a total cost of $27,800.

Customer: Between what I pay at the gas station and what we pay here, I see why Major Oil is getting bigger and richer all the time. How much money can you save us?

Salesperson: Well, we try to get by and make ends meet. However, I can save your company more than $2,800 per year on oil costs alone.

Customer: That sounds awful big. How are you going to do that?

Salesperson: I am going to show you how you can purchase oil in bulk, save 14¢ per gallon on each gallon you buy (14¢ times 20,000 gallons equals $2,800), and eliminate handling those drums and having your money tied up in deposits. Last year, you purchased about 364 drums—and I'll bet you did not return all the drums to us.

Customer: I know we damaged some drums, and I imagine we furnished some trash barrels for our employees. I wonder how much of a total deposit we pay?

Salesperson: The total deposit on those drums was $7,280. Are you and your company totally satisfied with the performance of Hydraulic Oil 65?

Customer: It seems so. I have heard nothing to the contrary, and our bearing supplier, Timken, says that the oil is doing a first-class job. You know, this savings sounds good in theory, but will it really work? Besides, where will we put a big bulk system?

Salesperson: Ben, I've already thoroughly checked into what the total equipment and installation will cost. Here's a picture of the installation we made over at the Foundry and Machine Shop. We put the installation above ground to save the expense of digging holes for the tanks. The cover shown here in the picture protects the pump and motor from the weather, and the pipe into the shop goes underground. There's a control switch for the pump motor mounted inside the building next to the nozzle outlet. It looks good, doesn't it?

Customer: It certainly does, Tim, but what about the cost?

Salesperson: We can get two new 3,000-gallon tanks delivered here for a cost of $1,700 from our tank supplier. This is about $120 less than what you could buy them for. Our quantity purchases of tanks give us a little better price—and we'll be glad to pass those savings on to you. I have checked with Pump Supply Company, and they have in stock the pump and motor with flexible coupling and built-in pump relief valve, just what we need for handling this oil. The cost is $475. The control switch, pipe, pipe fittings, inside hose, and nozzle come to $120, and the person who does our installation work has given me a commitment to do all the installation work for $500, including furnishing the blocks to make the tank supports.

This totals $2,795, so let's round off to $2,800. And at a savings of 14¢ per gallon, based on your present usage of 20,000 gallons per year, this would be paid off in about 12 months, during which time you'd pay $1.25 per gallon for your oil rather than the $1.39 you now pay. How does that sound to you, Ben?

Customer: That sounds pretty good to me, Tim. Didn't you have an article about this in a recent issue of your company magazine?

Salesperson: We sure did. It was in the March issue. Here it is, right here. The situation was a little different, but the basic idea is the same. Our company has used this idea to considerable advantage; and over the past three years, I have set up six installations of this type. Do you have any questions regarding the plan I've outlined?

Customer: Just one thing—you know we're short on space behind the warehouse. Have you thought about where we might locate an installation of this type?

Salesperson: Yes, I have, Ben. Recall one of our earlier conversations where you told me about your plans to clean up that old scrap pile near the corner of the warehouse. That would be an ideal location. We could then locate the control switch, filling hose, and nozzle right on the inside at the end of the assembly line so the units could have their initial oil fill just before they come off the assembly line. How would that fit into your plans?

Customer: That's a good idea, Tim. That way we can get that junk pile cleaned up, replace it with a decent looking installation, and then make our initial oil fill the last step in our assembly procedure.

Salesperson: Do you have any other questions, Ben?

Customer: No, I believe I've got the whole picture now.

Salesperson: Good. Now, to sum up our thinking, Ben, the total cost of installation will be about $3,000. Immediately on completion of the installation, and when you receive your first transport truckload shipment of Hydraulic Oil 65, instead of being billed at $1.39 per gallon, as you are now paying for barrel deliveries, you will be billed $1.25 per gallon. I'll work with Bill Smith, the plant superintendent, and I'll handle all the outside contacts so that we can make the installation with little turmoil.

Customer: That sounds good to me. When can we start the installation?

Salesperson: Tomorrow. I'll bring a contract for you to have your people sign. It should take about three to four weeks after the contract is signed.

Customer: Good. What do I need to do right now?

Salesperson: If you'll arrange to clean the junk out of the corner, then we'll be ready. I'll order the equipment and have it moving so that we can be ready in about four weeks. What would be the best time to see you tomorrow?

Customer: Anytime will be OK with me, Tim.

Salesperson: Swell, Ben. Thanks for your help. I know you will be pleased with this new installation and also save money. See you tomorrow.

Questions

1. Evaluate Tim's sales presentation. Include in your answer comments on his approach, presentation, use of trial closes, handling of objections, and his close.
2. How would you develop visual materials to illustrate Tim's sales presentation, including the arithmetic?
3. Now that Tim has sold to Ben, what should Tim do next?

CASE 11-3

Dumping Inventory: Should This Be Part of Your Presentation?

Ron Kapra is sales manager at Electra Toy Company, a retail toy store specializing in electronic games. Ron's brother-in-law Jerry works for the company that manufactures the Lasertron electronic game. Jerry mentioned to Ron that the company is coming out with the Lasertron II in three months. However, it will not be announced to retailers for another two months.

Lasertron II will have advanced technology over the present model. The new game cartridges will not be compatible with Lasertron I. Once Lasertron II comes on the market, consumers will want it and not the present model. Jerry explains that for any of the present models the retailer returns after the introduction of Lasertron II, the manufacturer will refund to the retailer the retailer's original cost of Lasertron I.

Video

Case

The Way to Make Extra Sales

Kapra has decided to run a special sale offering 20 percent off the regular price of Lasertron I. With 1,000 cases in stock, Ron wants to sell as many of the present model as possible to his customers. Then when the new model comes out, the same customers will come in and purchase Lasertron II. This will greatly increase sales, Ron feels.

Salesperson Is Unsure

Bill Corrington has been a top salesperson with Electra Toy for about two years. Although excited about the new model, Bill questions Ron's idea. Bill feels his customers trust him. If he sold them Lasertron now and the new model came out in a few months, customers would be upset with him. Bill feels this is no way to treat customers. However, Ron sees nothing wrong. "The loss of a few customers will be offset by the increase in sales," says Ron.

Questions

1. What are the ethical considerations, if any, in this case?
2. At what level of moral development are Ron and Bill operating in this business situation? Explain your answers.
3. What would you do if your were Ron?
4. What would you do if you were Bill?

12

Welcome Your Prospect's Objections

LEARNING OBJECTIVES

When you learn how to skillfully handle your prospect's questions, resistance, and objections, you are a professional. After studying this chapter, you should be able to

- Explain why you should welcome a prospect's objections.

- Describe what to do when objections arise.

- Discuss seven basic points to consider in meeting a prospect's objections.

- Explain six major categories of prospect objections and give an example of how to handle each of them.

- Present, illustrate, and use in your presentation several techniques for meeting prospect objections.

- Describe what to do after meeting an objection.

As you drive into the parking lot of a top distributor of your home building supplies, you recall how only two years ago they purchased the largest opening order you ever sold. Last year, their sales doubled and this year you hope to sell them over $100,000 of supplies.

As you wait, the receptionist informs you that since your last visit, your buyer, Mary Smalley, was fired and another buyer, Nonnie Young, was transferred to her place. Mary and you had become good friends over the past two years and you hated to see her go.

As you enter the new buyer's office, Young asks you to have a seat and then says: "I've got some bad news for you. I'm considering switching suppliers. Your prices are too high."

What would you do in this situation? What would you say to the buyer? Salespeople commonly face challenges; in most presentations, they experience objections. How does a professional salesperson handle a potentially difficult situation?

Be prepared! No two sales calls are exactly alike. You never know when the customer will say something making you wonder if you will be allowed to give the presentation you have worked on for hours.

This chapter examines resistance a saleperson may receive during a sales call. It discusses how to meet objections, communication techniques to use in overcoming objections, and how to proceed after addressing an objection. Many of these same communication methods can be used with your friends, family, and people you meet every day. Try them out this week. See if they help you better understand why someone gives you an objection and if the communication technique provides a smooth transition into telling your side of the story.

Welcome objections! Think of them in positive terms. In sales, always reflect on why you are calling on this prospect or customer. As discussed in Chapter 8, focus on your purpose and plan for the sales call.

Listen first, speak last.

PETER F. DRUCKER

THE TREE OF BUSINESS LIFE: OBJECTIONS

A customer gives you an objection saying your product is not what is needed. What do you do if you are following the Golden Rule of Selling? Say, "OK, thanks for your time," and leave? Maybe, maybe not. It depends upon whether the other person is correct. If correct, you politely leave. If not correct, you politely, professionally, and ethically strive to show the person how your product will help her or him. Is this being pushy?

It depends on your purpose. Is your purpose to help or make the sale? Both you say! What is your main purpose for the sales call? If it is to make the sale, you are being self-centered. Only thinking of you. Probably over time you will lose interest in your sales career even if you are earning a high income. If your purpose is to help others, rewards may come but you are in business to help make the company successful so that the business, in turn, can help others. Chances are you will love selling. Thus, when objections arise, view them as challenges to help. Helping through providing ethical service builds long-term relationships. Remember, professionals welcome objections!

WELCOME OBJECTIONS!

When a prospect first gives an objection, *smile*, because that's when you start earning your salary. You want to receive personal satisfaction from your job and at the same time increase your salary—right? Well, both occur when you accept objections as a challenge that, handled correctly, benefit both your prospect and you. The more effectively you meet customers' needs and solve their problems, the more successful you will be in sales. If you *fear* objections, you will *fumble* your response, which often causes *failure*.

Remember, although people want to buy, they do not want to be taken advantage of. Buyers who cannot see how your offering will fulfill their needs ask questions and raise objections. If you cannot effectively answer the questions or meet the objections, you will not make the sale. It is *your* fault, not the buyer's, that the sale was not made if you sincerely believe your offering fulfills a need but the prospect still will not buy. The salesperson who can overcome objections when they are raised and smoothly return to a presentation will succeed.

WHAT ARE OBJECTIONS?

Interestingly, prospects who present objections often are easily sold on your product. They are interested enough to object; they want to know what you have to offer.

Opposition or resistance to information or to the salesperson's request is labeled a **sales objection.** Welcome sales objections because they indicate prospect interest and help determine what stage the prospect has reached in the buying cycle—attention, interest, desire, conviction, or readiness to close.

WHEN DO PROSPECTS OBJECT?

The prospect may object at any time during your sales call—from introduction to close. Imagine walking into a retail store, carrying a sales bag, and the buyer yells out, "Oh no, not another salesman. I don't even want to see you, let alone buy from you!" What do you say?

I said, "I understand. I'm not here to sell you anything, only to check your stock, help stock your shelves, and return any old or damaged merchandise for a refund." As I turned to walk away, the buyer said, "Come on back here; I want to talk to you."

If I had simply said OK, I would not have made that sale. I knew that I could benefit that customer, and my response and attitude showed it. The point is always to be ready to handle a prospect's objections, whether at the approach, during the presentation, after a trial close, after you have already met a previous objection, or during the close of the sale.

OBJECTIONS AND THE SALES PROCESS

Objections can occur at any time. Often times, however, the prospect allows you to make a presentation, often asking questions along the way. Inexperienced salespeople traditionally finish their presentation and wait for the prospect's response.

Experienced, successful salespeople have learned to use the system shown in Exhibit 12.1. After the presentation, they use a trial close to determine the prospect's attitude toward the product and if it is time to close.

Remember, the *trial close* asks for the prospect's opinion, not a decision to buy. The trial close asks about what was said in the presentation. Since you may not know the prospect's opinion, it is too early to close. Typically, the trial close causes the prospect to ask questions and/or state objections. The salespeople should be prepared to respond in one of four ways:

1. If there is a positive response to the trial close immediately after the presentation, move to the close as shown on the right side of Exhibit 12.1, moving from Step 5 to Step 9.
2. If the prospect raises an objection, understand or clarify it, respond to it, and ask another trial close to see if you have met the objection. If you have, then move to the close.
3. After meeting one objection, be prepared to determine if there are other objections. You may have to move from Step 8 back to Step 6.
4. If, after responding to the objection and asking a trial close, you have not overcome the objection, return to your presentation (Step 4) and further discuss the product relative to the objection.

Thus, there are several strategies that a salesperson needs to handle objections. It is important to adapt to the situation. A big help to successfully handling objections is to thoroughly understand several points.

EXHIBIT 12.1

When objections occur, quickly determine what to do.

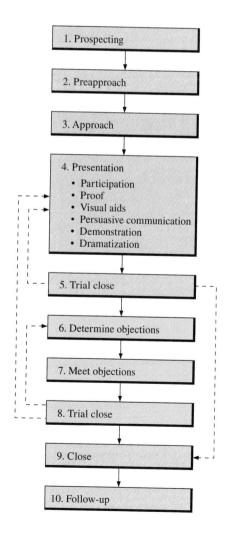

BASIC POINTS TO CONSIDER IN MEETING OBJECTIONS

No matter what type of objections the prospect raises, there are certain basic points to consider in meeting objections. They are to

- Plan for objections.
- Anticipate and forestall.
- Handle objections as they arise.
- Be positive.
- Listen—hear them out.
- Understand objections.
- Meet the objection.

The salesperson can plan for each of these basic points for meeting objections.

Plan for Objections

Plan for objections that your presentation might raise. Consider not only the reasons that prospects should buy but why they should *not* buy. Structure your presentation to minimize the disadvantages of your product. Do not discuss disadvantages unless prospects raise them in the conversation.

After each sales call, review the prospect's objections. Divide them into major and minor objections. Then develop ways to overcome them. Your planning for and rehearsal of overcoming objections allows you to respond in a natural and positive manner. Planning for and review of the sales call allows you to anticipate and forestall objections.

Only through hardship can one truly learn.

Anticipate and Forestall

Forestalling the objection has the salesperson discussing an objection before the prospect raises it. It often is better to forestall or discuss objections before they arise. The sales presentation can be developed to address anticipated objections directly.

For example, take an exterior house paint manufacturer's salesperson who learns that an unethical competitor is telling retail dealers that his paint starts to chip and peel after six months. Realizing the predicament, this salesperson develops a presentation that states, "Three independent testing laboratories have shown that this paint will not chip or peel for eight years after application." The salesperson has forestalled or answered the objection before it is raised by using a proof statement. This technique also can prevent a negative mood from entering the buyer–seller dialogue.

Another way to anticipate objections is to discuss disadvantages before the prospect does. Many products have flaws, and they sometimes surface as you try to make a sale. If you know of an objection that arises consistently, discuss it. If you acknowledge it first, you don't have to defend it.

On the other hand, a customer who has an objection feels compelled to defend that objection. For example, you might be showing real estate property. En route to the location you say, "You know, before we get out there, I just want to mention a couple of things. You're going to notice that it needs a little paint in a few places, and I noticed a couple of shingles on the roof the other day that you may have to replace." When you arrive, your customer may take a look and say, "Well, those shingles aren't so bad and we're going to paint it anyway." Yet, if you reached the house without a little prior warning of small defects, those items are often what a customer first notices.

A third way of using an anticipated objection is to brag about it and turn it into a sales benefit. A salesperson might say, "I want to mention something important before we go any further. Our price is a high one because our new computerized electronics provide technology found in no other equipment. It will improve your operation and eliminate the costly repairs you are now experiencing. In just a minute, I want to fully discuss your investment. Let's first discuss the improvements we can provide. Take a look at this."

This takes the sting out of the price objection because you have discussed it. It is difficult for a buyer to come back and say, "It's too high," because you have mentioned that already. So, there are times when you can anticipate objections and use them advantageously.

Handle Objections as They Arise

At times, situations arise in which it is best to postpone your answer to an objection. When the objection raised will be covered later in your presentation, or when you build to that point, pass over it for a while. However, it is best to meet objections as they arise; postponement may cause a negative mental picture or reaction such as these:

- The prospect may stop listening until you address the objection.
- The prospect may feel you are trying to hide something.
- You also feel it's a problem.
- You cannot answer because you do not know the answer or how to deal with this objection.
- It may appear that you are not interested in the prospect's opinion.

The objection could be the only item left before closing the sale. So, meet the objection, determine if you have satisfied the prospect, use another trial close to uncover other objections, and if there are no more objections, move toward closing the sale.

Be Positive

"Positive mental attitude governs your life and mind and is the starting point of all riches."

NAPOLEON HILL

When responding to an objection, use positive body language such as a smile. Strive to respond in a manner that keeps your prospect friendly and in a positive mood. Do not take the objection personally. Never treat the objection with hostility. Take the objection in stride by responding respectfully and showing sincere interest in your prospect's opinion.

At times, the prospect may raise objections based on incorrect information. Politely deny false objections. Be realistic; all products have drawbacks, even yours. If a competitor's product has a feature your product lacks, demonstrate the overriding benefits of your product.

Listen—Hear Them Out

"Listen with the intent to understand the other person."

STEPHEN COVEY

Many salespeople leap on an objection before the other person has a chance to finish. The prospect barely says five words—and already the salesperson is hammering away as though the evil thing will multiply unless it's stomped out. "I have to prove he is mistaken, or he won't take the product," is a panicky reaction to the first hint of any objection.

Not only does the prospect feel irritated at being interrupted, but the prospect also feels pushed and uneasy. Your prospect will ask, "Why's he jumping on that so fast and so hard? I smell a rat." Suppose you run south when the prospect heads north, and you answer the wrong objection or even raise one that the prospect hadn't thought of?[1] Review the listening guidelines discussed in Chapter 5; they apply.

Understand Objections

When customers object, they do one of several things, as shown in Exhibit 12.2. They are either requesting more information, setting a condition, or giving a genuine objection. The objection can be hopeless or true.

What does a prospect mean by
an objection?

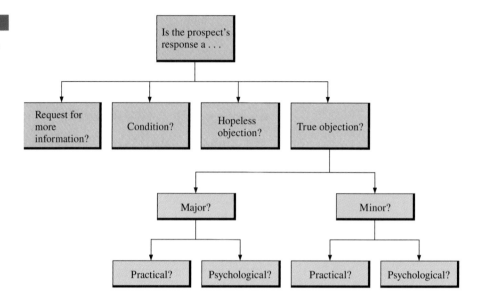

Request for Information

Many times, prospects appear to make objections when they are requesting more
information. That is why it is important to listen. If prospects request more information, chances are that they are in the conviction stage. You have created a desire;
they want the product, but they are not convinced that you have the best product or
you are the best supplier. If you feel this may be the case, supply the requested information indirectly.

A Condition

At times, prospects may raise an objection that turns into a **condition of the sale.**
They are saying, "If you can meet my request, I'll buy," or "Under certain conditions, I will buy from you."

   If you sense that the objection is a condition, quickly determine if you can help
the prospect meet it. If you cannot, close the interview politely. Take the following
real estate example:

Prospect: It's a nice house, but the price is too high. I can't afford a $1,000 a
month house payment. [You do not know if this is an objection or a condition.]

Salesperson: I know what you mean [acknowledging the prospect's viewpoint].
If you don't mind my asking, what is your monthly salary?

Prospect: My take-home pay is $1,400 a month.

   In this case, the prospect has set a condition on the purchase that cannot be met
by the salesperson realistically; it is not an objection. Continuing the exchange by
bargaining would waste time and possibly anger the prospect. Now that the prospect's
income is known, the salesperson can show a house in the prospect's price range.

Negotiation Can Overcome a Condition. Often, conditions stated by the prospect
are overcome through negotiation between buyer and seller. **Negotiation** refers to
reaching an agreement mutually satisfactory to both buyer and seller. Prospects may

say things like, "I'll buy your equipment if you can deliver it in one month instead of three," or "If you'll reduce your price by 10 percent, I'll buy."

If you determine that this type of statement is a condition rather than an objection, through negotiation you may make the sale with further discussion and an eventual compromise between you and the buyer. In the example above, you might ask the manufacturing plant if equipment can be shipped to the prospect in two months instead of three. This arrangement may be acceptable to the prospect. You may have a current customer who has that piece of equipment but is not using it. You might arrange for the prospect to lease it from your customer for three months.

If the prospect sets a price condition saying, "I will buy your product only if you reduce your price by 10 percent," determine if your company will reduce the price if the buyer will purchase a larger quantity. Consider this example. As a state agency, Texas A&M University purchased much of its office equipment on a bid system. The IBM salesperson could not sell the Texas A&M Marketing Department a word processor because the cost of a single machine was too high for the department's budget. The department wanted the machine; however, they could not afford it. Instead of giving up, the salesperson went to other departments in the university and found a need for a total of 16 machines (at a lower price of $4,000 per word processor, less than the price of one machine). IBM could lower the price substantially because of the large number of machines purchased. The salesperson determined that price was a condition, found a way to overcome the condition, and made the sale. Through initiation and inquiry, a potentially lost sale became a multiple victory beneficial to all parties.

There are two broad categories of objections. One of them is called *hopeless*. A hopeless objection is one that cannot be solved or answered. Examples of hopeless objections are I already have one, I'm bankrupt, and I'd like to buy your life insurance, but the doctor only gives me 30 days to live. Hopeless objections cannot be overcome.

If your prospect does not buy, and no condition exists or the objection is not hopeless, it is your fault if you did not make the sale because you could not provide information to show how your offering would suit the buyer's needs.

The second category is the objection that can be answered. Called a true objection, it has two types: major and minor.

Major or Minor Objections

Once you determine that the prospect has raised a true objection, determine its importance. If it is of little or no importance, quickly address it and return to selling. Do not provide a long response or turn a minor objection into a major discussion item. The minor objection is often a defense mechanism of little importance to the prospect. Concentrate on objections directly related to the prospect's important buying motives.

Practical or Psychological Objection

Objections, minor or major, can be **practical** (overt) or **psychological** (hidden) in nature. Exhibit 12.3 gives some examples. A real objection is tangible, such as a high price. If this is a real objection, and the prospect says so, you can show that your product is of high quality and worth the price, or you might suggest removing some optional features and reducing the price. As long as the prospect states the real objection to purchasing the product clearly, you should be able to answer the objection.

EXHIBIT 12.3

Examples of objections.

Practical	Psychological
■ Price	■ Resistance to spending money
■ Product is not needed	■ Resistance to domination
■ Prospect has an overstock of your or your competitor's products	■ Predetermined beliefs
	■ Negative image of salespeople
■ Delivery schedules	■ Dislikes making a buying decision

EXHIBIT 12.4

Six major categories of objections.

1. Hidden objections	2. Stalling objections	3. No-need objections	4. Money objections	5. Product objections	6. Source objections

However, prospects do not always clearly state their objections. Rather, they often give some excuse why they are not ready to make a purchase, which conceals real objections. Usually, the prospect cannot purchase the product until hidden objections are rectified. You must uncover a prospect's hidden objections and eliminate them.

Meet the Objection

Once you fully understand the objection, you are ready to respond to the prospect. How to respond depends on the objection. During the year, a salesperson will hear hundreds of objections. Prospects object to various items in different ways.

Generally, objections fall into six categories. By grouping objections, you can better plan how to respond. Let's examine these six categories and discuss specific techniques for meeting objections.

SIX MAJOR CATEGORIES OF OBJECTIONS

Most objections that salespeople encounter can be placed into the six categories shown in Exhibit 12.4. Know how you will handle each situation before it occurs. An advance idea about how you handle these objections will help you become a better salesperson by improving your image as a problem solver.

The Hidden Objection

Prospects who ask trivial, unimportant questions or conceal their feelings beneath a veil of silence have **hidden objections.** They do not discuss their true objections to a product because they may feel they are not your business, they are afraid objections will offend you, or they may not feel your sales call is worthy of their full attention.

Such prospects may have a good conversation with you without revealing their true feelings. You have to ask questions and carefully listen to know which questions to ask in order to reveal their true objections to your product. Learning how to determine what questions to ask a prospect and how to ask them are skills developed by conscious effort over time. Your ability to ask probing questions improves with each sales call if you try to develop this ability.

Smoke Out Hidden Objections

With prospects who are unwilling to discuss their objections or who may not know why they are reluctant to buy, be prepared to smoke out objections by asking questions. Do what you can to reveal the objections. Consider the following questions:

- What would it take to convince you?
- What causes you to say that?
- Let's consider this, suppose my product would [do what prospect wants] . . . then you would want to consider it, wouldn't you?
- Tell me, what's really on your mind?

Uncovering hidden objections is not always easy. Observe the prospect's tone of voice, facial expressions, and physical movements. Pay close attention to what the prospect is saying. You may have to read between the lines occasionally to find the buyer's true objections. All these factors will help you discover whether objections are real or simply an excuse to cover a hidden objection.

Prospects may not know consciously what their real objections are. Sometimes they claim that the price of a product is too high. In reality, they may be reluctant to spend money on anything. If you attempt to show that your price is competitive, the real objection remains unanswered and no sale results. Remember, you cannot convince anyone to buy until you understand what a prospect needs to be convinced of.

If, after answering all apparent questions, the prospect is still not sold, you might subtly attempt to uncover the hidden objection. You might ask the prospect what the real objection is. Direct inquiry should be used as a last resort because it indirectly may amount to calling the prospect a liar, but if it is used carefully, it may enable the salesperson to reveal the prospect's true objection. Smoking out hidden objections is an art form skillful salespeople develop over time. Its successful use can greatly increase sales. This approach should be used carefully, but if it enables the salesperson to uncover a hidden objection, then it has served its purpose.

"Every adversity carries with it the seed of an equivalent or greater benefit."

NAPOLEON HILL

The Stalling Objection

When your prospect says, "I'll think it over," or "I'll be ready to buy on your next visit," you must determine if the statement is the truth or if it is a smoke screen designed to get rid of you. The **stalling objection** is a common tactic.

What you discovered in developing your customer profile and customer benefit plan can aid you in determining how to handle this type of objection. Suppose that before seeing a certain retail customer, you checked the supply of your merchandise in both the store's stockroom and on the retail shelf and this occurs:

Buyer: I have enough merchandise for now. Thanks for coming by.

Salesperson: Ms. Marcher, you have 50 cases in the warehouse and on display. You sell 50 cases each month, right?

You have forced her hand. This buyer either has to order more merchandise from you or tell you why she is allowing her product supply to dwindle. An easily handled stall is illustrated in Exhibit 12.5. When the prospect says, "I'm too busy to see you now," you might ask, "When would be a good time to come back today?"

One of the toughest stalls to overcome arises in selling a new consumer product. Retail buyers are reluctant to stock consumer goods that customers have not yet asked for, even new goods produced by large, established consumer product manufacturers. The following excerpt is from a sales call made by an experienced consumer goods salesperson on a reluctant retail buyer. This excerpt begins with an interruption the buyer makes during a presentation of a new brand of toothpaste:

"Honest differences are often a healthy sign of progress."

MAHATMA GANDHI

Buyer: Well, it sounds good, but I have seven brands and 21 different sizes of toothpaste now. There is no place to put it. [A false objection—smoke screen.]

EXHIBIT 12.5

Imagine walking in to your prospect's office, who says, "I'm too busy to see you now." What would you say?

"Always do right. It will gratify some and astonish the rest."

MARK TWAIN

Salesperson: Suppose you had 100 customers walk down the aisle and ask for Colgate 100 Toothpaste. Could you find room then?

Buyer: Well, maybe. But I'll wait until then. [The real objection.]

Salesperson: If this were a barbershop and you did not have your barber pole outside, people wouldn't come in because they wouldn't know it was a barbershop, would they?

Buyer: Probably not.

Salesperson: The same logic applies to Colgate 100. When people see it, they will buy it. You would agree that our other heavily advertised products sell for you, right? [Trial close.]

Buyer: Yeah, they do. [Positive response; now reenter your selling sequence.]

The salesperson eliminated the stall in this case through a logical analogy.

A third common stall is the alibi that your prospect must have approval from someone else, such as a boss, buying committee, purchasing agent, or home office. Because the buyer's attitude toward purchasing your product influences the firm's buying decision, it is important that you determine the buyer's attitude toward your product.

When the buyer stalls by saying, "I will have to get approval from my boss," you can counter by saying, "If you had the authority, you would go ahead with the purchase, wouldn't you?" If the answer is yes, chances are that the buyer will positively influence the firm's buying decision. If not, you must uncover the real objections. Otherwise, you will not make the sale.

An additional response to the "I've got to think it over" stall is, "What are some of the issues you have to think about?" Or you may focus directly on the prospect's stall by saying, "Would you share with me some things that hold you back?"

SELLING TIPS

Stalling Objections

A. I have to think this over.

1. Let's think about it now while it is fresh in your mind. What are some of the items you need to know more about?

2. I understand that you want more time to think. I would be interested in hearing your thoughts about the reasons for and the reasons against buying now.

3. You and I have been thinking this over since the time we first met. You know that this is a terrific opportunity, you like the product, and you know it will save you money. Right? [If prospect says yes:] Let's go ahead now!

B. I'm too busy.

1. I appreciate how busy you are. When could we visit for just a few minutes? [Stop or add a benefit for seeing you.]

C. I'm too busy. Talk to _____ first.

1. Does he/she have the authority to approve the purchase? [If prospect says yes:] Thank you. I'll tell him/her you sent me. [If prospect says no:] Well, then why should I talk with him/her?

2. We almost never deal with purchasing managers. This is an executive-level decision. I need to talk with you.

D. I plan to wait until next fall.

1. Why?

2. Some of my best customers said that. Once they bought, they were sorry they waited.

3. You promise me you will buy this fall? [If prospect says yes, then:]

    a. OK, let's finalize the order today and I'll have it ready to arrive October 1.

    b. Great! Should I call you in September or October so we can set it up?

4. What if I could arrange for it to be shipped to you now but you didn't have to pay for it until the fall?

Another effective response to "I've got to talk to my boss" is, "Of course you do. What are some things that you would talk about?" This allows you to agree with the reluctant prospect. You are now on the buyer's side. It helps encourage the buyer to talk and to trust you. This empathic response ("Of course you do.") puts you in the other person's position.

Sometimes, the prospect will not answer the question. Instead, the response is, "Oh, I just need to get an opinion." You can follow up with a multiple-choice question such as, "Would you explore whether this is a good purchase in comparison with a competitor's product or would you wonder about the financing?" This helps display an attitude of genuine caring.

As with any response to an objection, communicate a positive attitude. Do not get demanding, defensive, or hostile. Otherwise, your nonverbal expressions may signal a defensive attitude—reinforcing the prospect's defenses.

Your goal in dealing with a stall is to help prospects realistically examine reasons for and against buying now. If you are absolutely sure it is not in their best interest to buy now, tell them so. They will respect you for it. You will feel good about yourself. The next time you see these customers, they will be more trusting and open with you.

However, the main thing to remember is to not be satisfied with a false objection or a stall; see the box, "Selling Tips, Stalling Objections." Tactfully pursue the issue until you have unearthed the buyer's true feelings about your product. If this does not work (1) present the benefits of using your product now; (2) if there is a special price deal, mention it; and (3) if there is a penalty for delay, mention it. Bring out any or all of your main selling benefits and keep on selling!

SELLING TIPS

No-Need Objections

A. I'm not interested.

1. May I ask why?
2. You are not interested now or forever?
3. I wouldn't be interested if I were you, either. However, I know you'll be interested when you hear about. . . . It is very exciting! [If prospect still says no.] What would be a better time to talk?
4. Some of my best customers first said that until they discovered . . . [state benefits].
5. You are not interested? Then who should I talk to who would be interested in . . . [state benefits].

B. The . . . we have is still good.

1. Good compared to what?
2. I understand how you feel. Many of my customers said that before they switched over. However, they saw that this product would . . . [discuss benefits of present product or service versus what you are selling].

3. That's exactly why you should buy—to get a good trade now.
4. What stops you from buying?

C. We are satisfied with what we have now.

1. Satisfied in what way?
2. What do you like most about what you have right now? [then compare to your product].
3. I know how you feel. Often we're satisfied with something because we have no chance [or don't have the time] to compare it with something better. I've studied what you are using and would like a few minutes to compare products and show you how to . . . [state benefits].
4. Many of our customers were happy with what they had before they saw our product. There are three reasons they switched . . . [state three product benefits].

The No-Need Objection

The prospect says, "Sounds good. I really like what you had to say, and I know you have a good product, but I'm not interested now. Our present product [or supply or merchandise] works well. We will stay with it." Standing up to conclude the interview, the prospect says, "Thanks very much for coming by." This type of objection can disarm an unwary salesperson.

The **no-need objection** is used widely because it politely gets rid of the salesperson. Some salespeople actually encourage it by making a poor sales presentation. They allow prospects to sit and listen to a sales pitch without motivating them to participate by showing true concern and asking questions. Therefore, when the presentation is over, prospects can say quickly, "Sounds good, but. . . ." In essence, they say no, making it difficult for the salesperson to continue the call. While not always a valid objection, the no-need response strongly implies the end of a sales call.

The no-need objection is especially tricky because it also may include a hidden objection and/or a stall. If your presentation was a solo performance or a monologue, your prospect might be indifferent to you and your product, having tuned out halfway through the second act. Aside from departing with a "Thanks for your time," you might resurrect your presentation by asking questions. See the box, "Selling Tips, No-Need Objections" for ways to respond to the no-need objections.

The Money Objection

The **money objection** encompasses several forms of economic excuses: I have no money, I don't have that much money, It costs too much, or Your price is too high. These objections are simple for the buyer to say, especially in a recessionary economy.

Often, prospects want to know the product's price before the presentation, and they will not want you to explain how the product's benefits outweigh its costs. Price is a real consideration and must be discussed, but it is risky to discuss product price

SELLING TIPS

Money Objections

A. Your price is too high.

1. Compared to what?
2. How much did you think it would cost?
3. We can lower the price right now, but we need to decide what options to cut from our proposal. Is that what you really want to do?
4. Our price is higher than the competition. However, we have the best value (now explain).
5. How high is too high?
6. If it were cheaper, would you want it?

B. I can't afford it.

1. Why?
2. If I could show you a way to afford this purchase, would you be interested?
3. I sincerely believe that you cannot afford *not* to buy this. The benefits of . . . far outweigh the price. Right?
4. You cannot afford to be without it! The cost of not having it is greater than the cost of having it. Think of all the business you can lose, the productivity you can lose, that lost income from not having the latest, best, and most reliable technology. You'll love it! You'll wonder how you've done without it! Let's discuss how you can afford it—OK?
5. Do you mean you can't afford it now or forever?

C. Give me a 10 percent discount and I'll give you an order today.

1. I always quote my best price.
2. If you give me an order for 10, I can give you a 10 percent discount. Would you like to order 10?
3. [Prospect's name], we build your product up to a certain quality and service standard—not down to a certain price. We could produce a lower-priced item, but our experience shows it isn't worth it. This is a proven product that gives 100 percent satisfaction—not 90 percent.

D. You've got to do better than that.

1. Why?
2. What do you mean by *better*?
3. Do you mean a longer service warranty? A lower price? Extended delivery? Tell me exactly what you want.

until you can compare it to product benefits. If you successfully postpone the price discussion, you must eventually return to it because your prospect seldom forgets it. Some prospects are so preoccupied with price that they give minimal attention to your presentation until the topic reemerges. Other prospects falsely present price as their main objection to your product, which conceals their true objection.

By observing nonverbal signals, asking questions, listening, and positively responding to the price question when it arises, you can easily handle price-oriented objections.

Many salespeople think that offering the lowest price gives them a greater chance of sales success. Generally, this is not the case. Once you realize this, you can become even more successful. You might even state that your product is not the least expensive one available because of its benefits and advantages and the satisfaction it provides. Once you convey this concept to your buyer, price becomes a secondary factor that usually can be handled successfully.

Do not be afraid of price as an objection; be ready for it and welcome it. Quote the price and keep on selling. It is usually the inexperienced salesperson who blows this often minor objection into a major one. If the price objection becomes major, prospects can become excited and overreact to your price. The end result is losing the sale. If prospects overreact, slow down the conversation; let them talk it out and slowly present product benefits as they relate to cost.

See the box, "Selling Tips, Money Objections" for ways to respond to the money objection. One way to view the money objection concerns the price/value formula.

The Price/Value Formula

The price objection is a bargaining tool for a savvy buyer who wants to ensure the best, absolutely lowest price. But there is often more to it than shrewd bargaining.

If the buyer is merely testing to be sure the best possible price is on the table, it's a strong buying signal. But perhaps the prospect sincerely believes the price is too high.

Let's define why one buyer might already be convinced the product is a good deal—fair price—but is just testing to make sure it's the best price, whereas another buyer may sincerely believe the asking price is more than the goods are worth.

Remember that cost is what concerns the buyer, not just the price. Cost is computed in the buyer's mind by considering what is received compared with the money paid.

In other words, price divided by value equals cost:

$$\frac{\text{Price}}{\text{Value}} = \text{Cost}$$

What seems fair to you may not seem fair to others.

In this price/value formula, the value is what the prospect sees the product doing for them and/or their company. *Value* is the total package of benefits you have built for the prospect. Value is the solution you provide to the buyer's problems.

The price will not change. The company sets that price at headquarters. The company has arrived at the price scientifically—computers were used—based on costs, competition, and other salient factors. It is a fair price, and it's not going to change. So, the only thing to change is the prospect's perception of the value. For example, assume the buyer viewed the cost as follows:

$$\frac{\text{Price } 100.}{\text{Value } 90.} = \text{Cost } 1.11$$

The price is too high. You have to solve the prospect's problem with the product by translating product benefits into what it will do for the buyer. You have to build up the value:

$$\frac{\text{Price } 100.}{\text{Value } 110.} = \text{Cost } .90$$

Now that is more like it. The cost went down because the value went up.

The price/value formula is not the answer to "Your price is too high." It is only a description of the buyer's thinking process and an explanation of why the so-called price objection is heard so often. It tells us what we must do to answer the price objection.

The salesperson is usually the one who identifies a statement or question from the prospect as an objection. Rarely does the prospect say, "This is my objection." So, you need to ask, "Why did the buyer say that?" If you ask that question, you can ask the prospect to say more about why he or she made the objection.

Remember, at one extreme, the buyer may be sold on the product and is simply testing to see if there is an extra discount. At the other extreme, the buyer may not see any benefit in the product or service but only see the price. When this is the case, "it costs too much" is a legitimate objection to be overcome by translating features into advantages into benefits for the buyer. Use the SELL Sequence technique.

SELLING TIPS

Handling Product Objections

A. Your competitor's product is better.

1. You're kidding! [Act surprised.]
2. Better in what way? [Have customer list features liked in the other product; then show how your product has the same or better features.]
3. I'm interested in hearing your unbiased opinion of the two products.
4. You've had a chance to look at their product. What did you see that impressed you?
5. Are you referring to quality, service, features, or the product's value after five years of use?

B. The machine we have is still good.

1. I understand how you feel. Many of my customers have said that before they switched over. However, they found that the reason a new model makes an old model obsolete is not that the old one is bad, but that the new one is so much more efficient and productive. Would you like to take a look at what these businesses found?
2. That's exactly why you should trade now. Since your machine is still good, you still have a high trade-in value. When it breaks down, your trade-in value will go down, too. It's less expensive to trade in a workable machine than to wait for it to fail.

C. I'll buy a used one.

1. When you buy a used product, you take a high risk. You buy something that someone else has used and

probably abused. Do you want to pay for other people's mistakes?

2. You may save a few dollars on your monthly payments, but you'll have to pay much more in extra service, more repairs, and downtime. Which price would you rather pay?
3. Many of our customers thought about a used product before they decided to buy a new one. Let me show you why they decided that new equipment is the best buy. The cost comparisons will make it clear.
4. I understand you want to save money. I like to save money. But, you have to draw the line somewhere. Buying a used product in this field is like shopping for a headache. Perhaps you should consider the smaller model for starters. At least you won't have any worries about its reliability!

D. I don't want to take risks.

1. You feel it's too risky? We rarely hear that. What do you mean by risky?
2. "Risky" compared to what?
3. What could we do to make you feel more secure?
4. [Prospect's name], it may be more risky for you not to buy. What is the price you may pay for low productivity in your plant?

The Product Objection

All salespeople encounter **product objections** that relate directly to the product. Everyone does not like the best-selling product on the market. At times, most buyers have fears about risks associated with buying a product—they are afraid that the product will not do what the salesperson says it will do, or that the product is not worth either the time and energy required to use it or the actual cost.

You also sell against competition. The prospect either already uses a competitive product, has used one, would like to use one, has heard of one, or knows people who have used one. Your reaction to a product objection must use a positive tone. The use of a guarantee, testimonial, independent research results, and demonstrations helps counter the product objection. See the box, "Selling Tips, Handling Product Objections" for ways to respond to the product objection.

The Source Objection

The **source objection** is the last major category of objections salespeople typically face. Source objections relate loyalty to a present supplier or salesperson. Also, the prospect may not like you or your company.

SELLING TIPS

The Source Objection

A. I'm sorry; we won't buy from you.

1. Why not?
2. You must have a reason for feeling that way. May I ask what it is?
3. Are you not going to buy from us now or forever?
4. What could we do to win your business in the future?
5. Is there anyone else in your company who might be interested in buying our cost-saving products? Who?
6. I respect the fact you aren't buying from us this one time. However, I suspect that as you hear more about our fantastic products in the news and from customers, you will buy something from us in the future. Do you mind if I stop by periodically to update you on our new products?
7. Would you like to work with someone else in our company?
8. Is there anything about me that prevents you from doing business with our company?

B. I want to work with a more established company. We've done business with . . . for five years. Why should I change?

1. I understand how safe you feel about a relationship that goes back five years. And yet, I saw your eyes light up when you looked at our products. I can see that you're giving serious consideration to diversity. Just out of curiosity, could we compare the pros and cons of the two choices? Let's take a piece of paper and list the reasons for and against buying from us. The first reason against us is that we haven't worked with you for the past five years. What are some reasons for giving us a chance to prove ourselves?
2. I can only say good things about my competitor, and if I were you, I would go with him or her—unless, of course, you want a better product at a better price.

Prospects often discuss their like for a present supplier or salesperson. They may tell you that they do not like your company. Seldom, however, will someone directly say, "I don't want to do business with you."

Usually, handling a source objection requires calling on the prospect routinely over a period. It takes time to break this resistance barrier. Get to know the prospect and the prospect's needs. Show your true interest. Do not try to get all of the business at once—go for a trial run, a small order. It is important to learn exactly what bothers the prospect. Some examples are shown in the "Selling Tips, The Source Objection." Choose one of these responses to handle the objection illustrated in Exhibit 12.6.

TECHNIQUES FOR MEETING OBJECTIONS

Having uncovered all objections, a salesperson must answer them to the prospect's satisfaction. Naturally, different situations require different techniques; several techniques shown in Exhibit 12.7 apply in most situations. You can:

- Dodge.
- Pass up the objection.
- Rephrase the objection as a question.
- Postpone the objection.
- Boomerang the objection.
- Ask questions regarding the objection.
- Directly deny the objection.
- Indirectly deny the objection.
- Compensate for the objection.
- Obtain a third-party answer to the objection.

EXHIBIT 12.6

Imagine that this customer says, "I like your proposal but we are happy with our present supplier." What would you say?

EXHIBIT 12.7

Techniques for meeting objections.

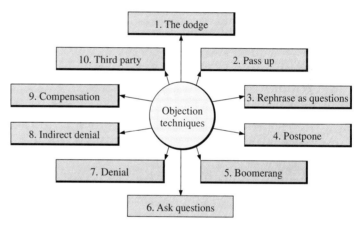

Objection techniques

1. The dodge
2. Pass up
3. Rephrase as questions
4. Postpone
5. Boomerang
6. Ask questions
7. Denial
8. Indirect denial
9. Compensation
10. Third party

The Dodge Neither Denies, Answers, nor Ignores

Central Michigan University students in Professor Dean Kortge's personal selling class created a new communication technique for handling a sales objection. Here's how. When the buyer said, "I think your price is a little high," Scott Dodge replied, "Before you decide to buy let me tell you about the value that goes with this product." It is called the **dodge** because the salesperson neither denies, answers, nor ignores the objection, but simply temporarily dodges it.

Notice how the phrase is structured in a positive manner: "Before you decide to buy. . . ." This positive communication technique now allows the seller to effectively make a smooth transition into a proper response to the buyer. Done in a calm, natural manner it is a very professional technique.

We discuss the *dodge* as the first objection-handling technique because you could use it by itself or in combination with one of the other techniques, such as the pass up, rephrase, postpone, boomerang, or third party. As you study the following objection handling techniques, see if you could first use the phrase, "Before you decide to buy. . . ." You would use it only once in a presentation.

Don't Be Afraid to Pass Up an Objection

Occasionally, you may have a prospect raise an objection or make a statement that requires not addressing it. After introducing yourself, for example, a prospect may say, "I'm really not interested in a service such as yours."

You have two options. First, you can say, "Well, if you ever do, here is my card. Give me a call." Or second, you could take the **pass up** approach used by top salespeople and say something that allows you to move into your presentation, such as immediately using the customer benefit approach or simply asking "Why?"

EXHIBIT 12.8

Examples of rephrasing objections as a question.

Facts Are Incorrect	Facts Are Incomplete	Facts Are Correct	Based on Bad Personal Experience
■ Acknowledge viewpoint.	■ Acknowledge their viewpoint.	■ Acknowledge their viewpoint.	■ Thank the prospect for telling you.
■ Rephrase objection.	■ Rephrase the objection.	■ Rephrase the objection.	■ Acknowledge their viewpoint.
■ Obtain agreement.	■ Obtain an agreement.	■ Obtain an agreement.	■ Rephrase the objection.
■ Answer question providing information supported by proof—a third party.	■ Answer the question by providing the complete facts.	■ Answer the question, outweigh it with benefits.	■ Obtain an agreement.
■ Ask for their present viewpoint.	■ Ask for a present viewpoint.	■ Ask for a present viewpoint.	■ Answer the question.
■ Return to the selling sequence.	■ Return to the selling sequence.	■ Return to the selling sequence.	■ Return to the selling sequence.

As you gain selling experience, you will be confident in knowing when to pass or to stop and respond to the objection. If you pass up an objection and the prospect raises it again, then treat this as an important objection. Use your questioning skills to uncover the prospect's concerns.

Rephrase an Objection as a Question

Since it is easier to answer a question than to overcome an objection, **rephrase** an objection **as a question** when you can do so naturally. Most objections are easily rephrased. Exhibit 12.8 presents examples of several procedures for rephrasing an objection as a question. Each procedure, except the objection based on a bad previous experience with the product by the prospect, has the same first three steps: (1) acknowledging the prospect's viewpoint, (2) rephrasing the objection into a question, and (3) obtaining agreement on the question. Here is an example:

Buyer: I don't know—your price is higher than your competitors'.

Salesperson: I can appreciate that. You want to know what particular benefits my product has that make it worth its slightly higher price. [Or, What you're saying is that you want to get the best product for your money.] Is that correct?

Buyer: Yes, that's right.

Now discuss product benefits versus price. After doing so, attempt a trial close by asking for the prospect's viewpoint to see if you have overcome the objection.

Salesperson: Do you see how the benefits of this product make it worth the price? [Trial close.]

A variation of this sequence is sales training consultant Bruce Scagel's Feel-Felt-Found method, where he first acknowledges the prospect's viewpoint, saying, "John, I understand how you *feel.* Bill at XYZ store *felt* the same way, but he *found,* after reviewing our total program of products and services, that he would profit by buying now."

Scagel refers to rephrasing the objection to a question as his Isolate and Gain Commitment method. He gives as an example: "Mary, as I understand it, your only objection to our program is the following. . . . If I can solve this problem, then I'll assume that you will be prepared to accept our program."

EXHIBIT 12.9

Suppose you show your prospect your business proposition, and the prospect ask, "How much does this software cost?" What would you say?

Scagel knows that he can solve the problem or he would not have asked the question. When Mary says yes, he has isolated the main problem. He is not handling an objection; he is answering a question. He now shows her how to overcome the problem and then continues selling. If Mary says no, Bruce knows he has not isolated her main objection. He must start over in uncovering her objections. He might say, "Well, I guess I misunderstood. Exactly what is the question?" And now, when Mary responds, it usually will be a question. "Well, the question was about. . . ." Involve the customer and find out what is happening internally. You can do this with the proper use of questions.

Postponing Objections Is Sometimes Necessary

Often, the prospect may skip ahead of you in the sales presentation by asking questions that you address later in the presentation. (See Exhibit 12.9.) If you judge that your customary method will handle the objection to your prospect's satisfaction, and that the prospect is willing to wait until later in the presentation, you politely **postpone the objection.** Five examples of postponing objections are

Prospect: Your price is too high.

Salesperson: In just a minute, I'll show you why this product is reasonably priced, based on the savings you will receive compared to what you presently do. That's what you're interested in, savings, right? [Trial close.]

or

Salesperson: Well, it may sound like a lot of money. But let's consider the final price when we know the model you need. OK? [Trial close.]

or

Salesperson: There are several ways we can handle your costs. If it's all right, let's discuss them in just a minute. [Pause. This has the same effect as the trial close. If there is no response, continue.] First, I want to show you. . . .

or

Salesperson: I'm glad you brought that up [or, I was hoping you would want to know that.] because we want to carefully examine the cost in just a minute. OK? [Trial close.]

or

Salesperson: High? Why, in a minute I'll show you why it's the best buy on the market. In fact, I'll bet you a Coke that you will believe it's a great deal for your company! Is it a deal? [Trial close.]

Tactfully used, postponing can leave you in control of the presentation. Normally, respond to the objection immediately. However, occasionally it is not appropriate to address the objection. This is usually true for the price objection. Price is the primary objection to postpone if you have not had the opportunity to discuss product benefits. If you have discussed the product fully, then respond to the price objection immediately.

Send It Back with the Boomerang Method

Always be ready to turn an objection into a reason to buy. By convincing the prospect that an objection is a benefit, you have turned the buyer immediately in favor of your product. This is the heart of the **boomerang method.** Take, for example, the wholesale drug salesperson working for a firm like McKesson and Robbins, who is selling a pharmacist a new container for prescription medicines. Handling the container, the prospect says:

Prospect: They look nice, but I don't like them as well as my others. The tops seem hard to remove.

Salesperson: Yes, they are hard to remove. We designed them so that children couldn't get into the medicine. Isn't that a great safety measure? [Trial close.]

Or, consider the industrial equipment salesperson who is unaware that a customer is extremely dissatisfied with a present product:

Prospect: I have been using your portable generators and do not want to use them anymore.

Salesperson: Why?

Prospect: Well, the fuses kept blowing out and causing delays in completing this project! So get out of here and take your worthless generators with you.

Salesperson: [with a smile] Thank you for telling me. Say, you and our company's design engineers have a lot in common.

Prospect: Oh yeah? I'll bet! [Sarcastically.]

Salesperson: Suppose you were chief engineer in charge of manufacturing our generators. What would you do if valued customers—like yourself—said your generators had problems?

Prospect: I'd throw them in the trash.

Salesperson: Come on, what would you really do? [With a smile.]

Prospect: Well, I would fix it.

Salesperson: That's why I said you and our design engineers have a lot in common. They acted on your suggestion—don't you think? [Trial close.]

You have used reverse psychology. Now, the prospect is listening, giving you time to explain your product's new features and to make an offer to repair the old units. You are ready to sell more products, if possible.

Be Positive in Discussing Price

All prospects are sensitive to how price is presented. This is a typical list of negative and positive ways to deal with price issues during the business proposition phase:

Negative Words:
- This costs $2,300.
- Your down payment . . .
- Your monthly payment . . .
- You can pay the purchase price over a series of months.
- How much would you like to pay us every month?
- We'll charge you two points above the prime rate.
- We'll take off $6,700 to trade in your used car.

Positive Words:
- This is only $2,300.
- Your initial investment . . .
- Your monthly investment . . .
- We would be happy to divide this investment into small monthly shares.
- What monthly investment would you feel comfortable with?
- Your rate will be only prime plus two.
- We are offering you $6,700 to trade your existing model.

Another example is the industrial salesperson who responds to the prospect's high price objection by saying, "Well, that's the very reason you should buy it." The prospect was caught off guard and quickly asked, "What do you mean?" "Well," said the salesperson, "for just 10 percent more, you can buy the type of equipment you really want and need. It is dependable, safe, and simple to operate. Your production will increase so that you will pay back the price differential quickly." The prospect said, "Well, I hadn't thought of it quite like that. I guess I'll buy it after all."

Boomeranging an objection requires good timing and quick thinking. Experience in a particular selling field, knowledge of your prospect's needs, a positive attitude, and a willingness to stand up to the objection are necessary attributes for successful use of this technique.

Ask Questions to Smoke Out Objections

Intelligent questioning impresses a prospect in several ways. Technical questions show a prospect that a salesperson knows the business. Questions relating to a prospect's particular business show that a salesperson is concerned more with the prospect's needs than with just making a sale. Finally, people who ask **intelligent questions,** whether they know much about the product, the prospect's business, or life in general, are often admired. Buyers are impressed with the sales professional who knows what to ask and when to ask it. Examples of questions are

Prospect: This house is not as nice as the one someone else showed us yesterday.

Salesperson: Would you tell me why?

or

Prospect: This product does not have the [feature].

Salesperson: If it did have [feature], would you be interested?

[This example is an excellent questioning technique to determine if the objection is a smoke screen, a major or minor objection, or a practical or psychological objection. If the prospect says no to the response, you know the feature was not important.]

or

Prospect: I don't like your price.

Salesperson: Will you base your decision on price or on the product offered you . . . at a fair price?

[If the prospect says "Price," show how benefits outweigh costs. If the decision is based on the product, you have eliminated the price objection.]

Five-Question Sequence Method of Overcoming Objections

Buyers state objections for numerous reasons. From time to time, all salespeople sense that a buyer will not buy. As you gain sales experience, you will be able to feel it. It may be the buyer's facial expressions or a tone of voice that tips you off. When this occurs, find out quickly why a prospect doesn't want to buy. To do this, consider using a preplanned series of questions as shown in Exhibit 12.10.

Let's assume you have finished the presentation. You try to close the sale and see that the buyer will not go further in the conversation. What do you do? Consider using the following **five-question sequence.**

First, use this question: "There must be some good reason why you're hesitating to go ahead now; do you mind if I ask what it is?" When the buyer states a reason or an objection, immediately double-check the objection with one more question by using question number two: "In addition to that, is there any other reason for not going ahead?" The buyer may give the real reason for not buying, or the buyer may give the original objection. No matter what the customer says, you have created a condition for buying.

Just supposing you could convince yourself that. . . . Then would you want to go ahead with it?

Now, use question number three, a "just suppose" question: "Just suppose you could. . . . Then you'd want to go ahead?" If the answer is yes, discuss how you can do what is needed. If you receive a negative response, use question number four: "Then there must be some other reason. May I ask what it is?" Respond with question number two again. Then ask, "Just suppose. . . . You'd want to go ahead?" If you receive another negative response, use question number five by saying, "What would it take to convince you?"

What often happens will surprise you. The buyer often will say, "Oh, I don't know. I guess I'm convinced. Go ahead and ship it to me." Or, you might be asked to go back over some part of your presentation. The important point is that this series of questions keeps the conversation going and reveals the real objections, which increases your sales. Imagine you are the salesperson in this example:

EXHIBIT 12.10

Five-question sequence method of overcoming objection.

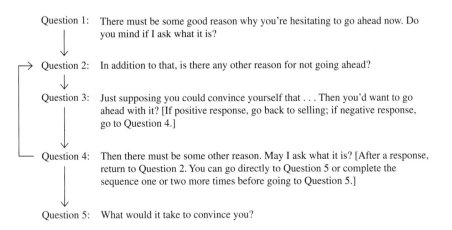

Question 1:   There must be some good reason why you're hesitating to go ahead now. Do you mind if I ask what it is?

Question 2:   In addition to that, is there any other reason for not going ahead?

Question 3:   Just supposing you could convince yourself that . . . Then you'd want to go ahead with it? [If positive response, go back to selling; if negative response, go to Question 4.]

Question 4:   Then there must be some other reason. May I ask what it is? [After a response, return to Question 2. You can go directly to Question 5 or complete the sequence one or two more times before going to Question 5.]

Question 5:   What would it take to convince you?

Salesperson: Should we ship the product to you this week or next?

Buyer: Neither; see me on your next trip. I'll have to think about it.

Salesperson: You know, there must be some good reason why you're hesitating to go ahead now. Would you mind if I asked what it is? [Question 1]

Buyer: Too much money.

Salesperson: Too much money. Well, you know, I appreciate the fact that you want to get the most for your money. In addition to the money, is there any other reason for not going ahead? [Question 2]

Buyer: No.

Salesperson: Well, suppose that you could convince yourself that the savings from this machine would mean it pays for itself in just a few months, and that we could fit it into your budget. Then you'd want to go ahead with it? [Question 3]

Buyer: Yes, I would.

Now, return to selling by discussing the return on investment and affordable payment terms. You went from the first objection to the double-check question. ("In addition to the money, is there any other reason for not going ahead?") Then, you used the just suppose question. You met the condition, the machine's cost. Then, you used the convince question. The buyer said yes, so you can keep selling. Now, let's role-play as if the buyer had said no. (Again, you are the salesperson.)

Buyer: No, I wouldn't go ahead.

Salesperson: Well, then there must be some other reason why you're hesitating to go ahead now. Do you mind if I ask what it is? [Question 4]

Buyer: It takes too much time to train my employees in using the machine.

Salesperson: Well, you know, I appreciate that. Time is money. In addition to the time, is there any other reason for not going ahead? [Question 2]

Buyer: Not really.

Salesperson: Suppose that you could convince yourself that this machine would save employees time so that they could do other things. You'd find the money then, wouldn't you? [Question 3]

Buyer: I'm not sure. [Another potential negative response]

Salesperson: Money and time are important to you, right?

Buyer: Yes, they are.

Salesperson: What would it take for me to convince you that this machine will save you time and money? [Question 5]

Now you have to get a response. The buyer has to set the condition. You, as the salesperson, are in control. The buyer is answering the questions. Remember, you want to help the person buy. When you get an objection, it tells you what you must do to make the sale happen. So do not fear objections; welcome them!

Use Direct Denial Tactfully

You will face objections that are often incomplete or incorrect. Acknowledge the prospect's viewpoint; then answer the question by providing the complete or correct facts:

Prospect: No, I'm not going to buy any of your lawn mowers for my store. The Bigs-Weaver salesperson said they break down after a few months.

Salesperson: Well, I can understand. No one would buy mowers that don't hold up. Is that the only reason you won't buy?

Prospect: Yes, it is, and that's enough!

Salesperson: The BW salesperson was not aware of the facts, I'm, afraid. My company produces the finest lawn mowers in the industry. In fact, we are so sure of our quality that we have a new three-year guarantee on all parts and labor. [Pause.]

Prospect: I didn't know that. [Positive buying signal.]

Salesperson: Are you interested in selling your customers quality lawn mowers like these? [Trial close.]

Prospect: Yes, I am. [Appears that you have overcome the objection.]

Salesperson: Well, I'd like to sell you 100 lawn mowers. If even one breaks down, call me and I'll come over and repair it. [Close.]

As you see by this example, you do not say, "Well, you so-and-so, why do you say a thing like that?" Tact is critical in using a direct denial. A sarcastic or arrogant response can alienate a prospect. However, a **direct denial** based on facts, logic, and politeness can effectively overcome the objection.

If I say to you, "You're wrong. Let me tell you why," what happens to your mind? It closes! So, if I tell you that you are wrong and this closes your mind, what would I have to tell you to open your mind? That you are right! But, if what you said was wrong, do I tell you it was right? No, instead, do what the example illustrated by saying, "You know, you're right to be concerned about this. Let me explain." You have made the buyer right and kept the buyer's mind open. Also, you could say, "You know, my best customer had those same feelings until I explained that. . . ." You have made the customer right.

A mind once stretched by a new idea, never regains its original dimensions.

The Indirect Denial Works

An **indirect denial** is different from a direct denial in that it initially appears as an agreement with the customer's objection but then moves into a denial of the fundamental issue in the objection. The difference between the direct denial and the indirect denial is that the indirect denial is softer, more tactful, and more courteous. Use the direct denial judiciously, only to disconfirm especially damaging misinformation.

The typical example of indirect denial is the "yes, but" phrase. Here are several examples:

- Yes, but would you agree that it takes information, not time, to make a decision? What kind of information are you really looking for to make a good decision?
- I agree. Our price is a little higher, but so is our quality. Are you interested in saving $1,200 a year on maintenance?
- Sure, it costs a little more. However, you will have the assurance that it will cost much less over its lifetime. Isn't that the way your own products are made?

- Your point is well taken. It does cost more than any other product on the market. But why do you think we sell millions of them at this price?
- I appreciate how you feel. Many of our customers made similar comments prior to buying from me. However, they all asked themselves: "Can I afford not to have the best? Won't it cost me more in the long run?"

The indirect denial begins with an agreement or an acknowledgment of the prospect's position: Yes, but; I agree; Sure; Your point is well taken; and I appreciate how you feel. These phrases allow the salesperson to tactfully respond to the objection. Done in a natural, conversational way, the salesperson will not offend the prospect.

Try this yourself: when a friend says something you disagree with, instead of saying, "I don't agree," say something like "I see what you mean. However, there's another way to look at it." See if this, as well as the other communication skills you have studied, helps you to better sell yourself—and your product.

Compensation or Counterbalance Method

Sometimes a prospect's objection is valid and calls for the **compensation method.** Several reasons for buying must exist to justify or compensate for a negative aspect of making a purchase. For example, a higher product price is justified by benefits such as better service or higher performance. In the following example, it is true that the prospect can make more profit on each unit of a competing product. You must develop a technique to show how your product has benefits that will bring the prospect more profit in the long run.

Prospect: I can make 5 percent more profit with the Stainless line of cookware, and it is quality merchandise.

Salesperson: Yes, you are right. The Stainless cookware is quality merchandise. However, you can have an exclusive distributorship on the Supreme cookware line, and still have high-quality merchandise. You don't have to worry about Supreme being discounted by nearby competitors as you do with Stainless. This will be the only store in town carrying Supreme. What do you think? [Trial close.]

If the advantages presented to counterbalance the objection are important to the buyer, you have an opportunity to make the sale.

Let a Third Party Answer

An effective technique for responding to an objection is to answer it by letting a **third party answer** and using someone else's experience as your proof of testimony. Salespeople use a wide range of proof statements today. You might respond to a question in this way: "I'm glad you asked. Here is what our research has shown," or, "EPA tests have shown," or, "You know, my best customer brought that point up before making the purchase . . . but was completely satisfied." These are examples of proof statement formats. If you use a person or a company's name, be sure to obtain their approval first.

Secondary data or experiences, especially from a reliable or reputable source, are successful with the expert or skeptical prospect. If, after hearing secondary testimony, the prospect is still unsure about the product, one successful equipment salesperson asks the buyer to contact a current user directly:

Salesperson: I still haven't answered your entire question, have I?

Buyer: Not really.

Salesperson: Let's do this. Here is a list of several people currently using our product. I want you to call them up *right now* and ask them that same question. I'll pay for the calls.

A salesperson should use this version of the third-party technique only when certain that the prospect is still unsatisfied with how an objection has been handled, and that positive proof will probably clinch the sale. This dramatic technique allows the salesperson to impress a prospect. It also shows a flattering willingness to go to great lengths to validate a claim.

TECHNOLOGY CAN EFFECTIVELY HELP RESPOND TO OBJECTIONS!

Providing buyers the necessary information to make a decision can frequently overcome objections. Data stored in handheld computers or laptops, or obtained using a telephone modem or satellite transmission, can provide information to overcome buyers' objections.

Frito-Lay salesperson June Steward frequently uses her computer to show buyers their past purchases of products and to project future sales. Using his laptop computer while in the buyer's office, Fisher Electronic's salesperson, John Berry checks with his warehouse daily on available products and shipment schedules. Merrill Lynch salesperson Sandy Lopez uses Lotus software to display her client's present investments, past earnings, and recommendations on how much money should be put into stock and bond mutual funds.

Technology can be incorporated easily into most, if not all, of the techniques for meeting objections. Anytime you need to provide information to buyers, you can create a technological method of presenting data in an accurate and dramatic manner.

AFTER MEETING THE OBJECTION— WHAT TO DO?

As shown in Exhibit 12.11, your prospect has raised an objection that you have answered and overcome; now what? First, as shown in Exhibit 12.12, use a trial close, then either return to your presentation or close the sale.

EXHIBIT 12.11

Imagine your are this pharmaceutical salesperson and you just answered this medical doctor's objections. What should you do now?

A Strategy for Handling Objections

One of the biggest hurdles to success for salespeople is handling objections. Here is a strategy top salespeople use to draw out, understand, and overcome objections:

1. Plan for objections.
2. Anticipate and forestall objections when needed.
3. Handle objections as they arise.
4. Be positive.
5. Listen to objections—hear them out.

6. Understand objections—ask questions to clarify.
7. Meet the objection by selecting methods or techniques to use in responding to the objection.
8. Confirm that you have met the objection—use a trial close.
9. Where am I? Decide if you need to keep selling, handle another objection, or close the sale.

EXHIBIT 12.12

The procedure to follow when a prospect raises an objection.

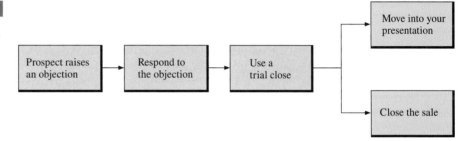

First, Use a Trial Close—Ask for Opinion

After meeting an objection at any time during the interview, you need to know if you have overcome the objection. If you have not overcome it, your prospect may raise it again. Whether it resurfaces or not, if your prospect believes that an objection was important, your failure to handle it, or your mishandling of it, will probably cost you the sale. Ideally, all objections raised should be met before closing the sale. So, after responding to the objection, use a trial close to determine if you have overcome the objection. Ask questions such as these:

- That clarifies this point entirely, don't you agree?
- That's the answer you're looking for, isn't it?
- With that question out of the way, we can go ahead—don't you think?
- Do you agree with me that we've covered the question you raised and given you a way to handle it?
- Now that's settled entirely, isn't it?
- That solves your problem, doesn't it?

Once you have confirmed overcoming an objection, immediately go to the next SELL Sequence step. To signal that the last step is over, and that you are moving on, use body language as you speak. That is, make an appropriate gesture, look in a new direction, turn the page of your proposal, or shift in your chair—make some physical movement. Now, do one of two things (assuming you have handled the objection): either return to your presentation or close the sale.

Move Back into Your Presentation

When you have answered and overcome an objection, make a smooth transition back into your presentation. As you nonverbally signal that the last step is over, let the prospect know you are returning to your presentation with a phrase such as, "As we were discussing earlier." Now, you can continue the presentation.

ETHICAL DILEMMA

A University Sets a Condition

You are a salesperson for a large, national company that publishes and sells college textbooks. Three days ago you talked with Dr. Bush, the department head, about adopting one of your books in a sophomore course of 2,000 students. He said the book is a good one but there were three others that were just as good.

Before leaving, Dr. Bush said the department would use your book if the publisher donates $1,000 and provides a new computer and printer to the English department. You tell your boss about this and she says, "Do it, but keep it quiet so none of your other schools hear of it. This will be a $100,000 sale. The home office will approve this expense if we don't do it for too many schools."

What would be the most ethical action to take?

1. Tell your boss that you do not think that the situation is fair but go ahead and do it anyway—it is ultimately her call in the end.
2. Tell your boss that you are uncomfortable making that type of sale and that you no longer want to be involved. It is not only unfair to your customers, but also unfair to you by asking you to keep it quiet.
3. Go ahead—take the sale and donate the computer and the money.

Move to Close Your Sale

If you had finished your presentation when the prospect raised an objection, and the prospect's response to your trial close indicates that you overcame an objection, your next move is to close the sale. If the objection was raised during your close, then it is time to close again.

As you move on to the close with a gesture, you might summarize benefits discussed previously with a phrase such as, "Well, as we have discussed, you really like. . . ." Then, again ask the prospect for the order. Chapter 13 gives you other ideas on how to ask for the order.

If You Cannot Overcome the Objection

If you cannot overcome an objection or close a sale because of an objection, be prepared to return to your presentation and concentrate on new or previously discussed features, advantages, and benefits of your product. If you determine that the objection your prospect raises is a major one that cannot be overcome, admit it, and show how your product's benefits outweigh this disadvantage.

If you are 100 percent sure that you cannot overcome the objection and that the prospect will not buy, go ahead and close. *Always ask for the order.* Never be afraid to ask your prospect to buy. The buyer says no to the product—not you. Someone else may walk into the prospect's office after you with a product similar to yours. Your competitor also may not be able to overcome this person's objection, but he or she may get the sale nonetheless just by asking for it!

IN ALL THINGS BE GUIDED BY THE GOLDEN RULE

Please remember, in all things be guided by the Golden Rule. It is your moral compass guiding you in your primary purpose in sales and business. You are in someone's business to help that person. Review "The Tree of Business Life" section at the beginning of this chapter to remind yourself why you would press on when faced with objections from a buyer. The only reason to use the many communication techinques in this chapter is to serve others from your heart, not your pocketbook.

These time-tested selling techniques are to be used for the good of others. This is a new way of selling for many. Start your career selling with the Golden Rule. It will lead you to the good life.

THE *Golden* RULE

SUMMARY OF MAJOR SELLING ISSUES

People want to buy, but they do not want to be misled, so they often ask questions or raise objections during a sales presentation. Your responsibility is to be prepared to logically and clearly respond to your prospect's objections whenever they arise.

Sales objections indicate a prospect's opposition or resistance to the information or request of the salesperson. Basic points to consider in meeting objections are to (1) plan for them, (2) anticipate and forestall them, (3) handle them as they arise, (4) listen to what is said, (5) respond warmly and positively, (6) make sure you understand, and (7) respond using an effective communication technique.

Before you can successfully meet objections, determine if the prospect's response to your statement or close is a request for more information, a condition of the sale, or an objection. If it is a real objection, determine whether it is minor or major. Respond to it using a trial close, and if you have answered it successfully, continue your presentation based on where you are in the sales presentation. For example, if you are still in the presentation, then return to your selling sequence. If you have completed the presentation, move to your close. If you are in the close and the prospect voices an objection, then you must decide whether to use another close or return to the presentation and discuss additional benefits.

Be aware of and plan for objection. Objections are classified as hidden, stalling, no-need, money, product, and source objections. Develop several techniques to help overcome each type of objection, such as stalling the objection, turning the objection into a benefit, asking questions to smoke out hidden objections, denying the objection if appropriate, illustrating how product benefits outweigh the objection drawbacks, or developing proof statements that answer the objection.

Welcome your prospect's objections. They help you determine if you are on the right track to uncover prospects' needs and if they believe your product will fulfill those needs. Valid objections are beneficial for you and the customer. A true objection reveals the customer's need, which allows a salesperson to demonstrate how a product can meet that need. Objections also show inadequacies in a salesperson's presentation or product knowledge. Finally, objections make selling a skill that a person can improve constantly. Over time, a dedicated salesperson can learn how to handle every conceivable product objection—tactfully, honestly, and to the customer's benefit.

MEETING A SALES CHALLENGE

Before handling an objection, it's important to find out what the *exact* objection is. Is price a stall or bona fide reason for changing suppliers? Is the competitor's cheaper price attractive, or does the problem exist with the salesperson and the possible inability to sell a high-priced line? There could be many problems, so before you answer the objection, do some probing and find out what the real one is. A good question would be, "Would you mind telling me exactly why you're considering this move?" Then continue to probe until you totally understand the buyer's reasoning for wanting to change suppliers.

Listen carefully to what the buyer says. This person may be a tough negotiator wanting to see if you will lower your prices. Nonnie Young may be happy with your prices.

KEY TERMS FOR SELLING

sales objection	376	dodge	391
condition of the sale	380	pass up	391
negotiation	380	rephrase as a question	392
practical objection	381	postpone the objection	393
psychological objection	381	boomerang method	394
hidden objection	382	intelligent questions	395
stalling objection	383	five-question sequence	396
no-need objection	386	direct denial	398
money objection	386	indirect denial	398
product objection	389	compensation method	399
source objection	389	third-party answer	399

SALES APPLICATION QUESTIONS

1. Halfway through your sales presentation, your prospect stops you and says, "That sounds like a great deal and you certainly have a good product, but I'm not interested now; maybe later." What should you do?

2. Assume you are a salesperson for the Japan Computer Corporation. You have finished your computer presentation, and the purchasing agent for Gulf Oil says, "Well, that sounds real good and you do have the lowest price I have ever heard of for a computer system. In fact, it's $200,000 less than the other bids. But we have decided to stay with IBM, mainly because $200,000 on a $1 million computer system is not that much money to us." Let's further assume that you also know that other than price, IBM has significant advantages in all areas over your product. What would you do?

3. When a customer is not receptive to your product, there is some objection. In each of the following situations, the customer has an objection to a product:

   a. The customer assumes she must buy the whole set of books. However, partial purchases are permitted.

   b. The customer does not like the color and it's the only color your product comes in.

   c. The customer doesn't want to invest in a new set of books because she doesn't want to lose money on her old set. You have not told her yet about your trade-in deal.

   In which of these situations does the objection arise from a misunderstanding or lack of knowledge on the customer's part? In which situation(s) does the product fail to offer a benefit that the customer considers important?

4. Which response is best when you hear the customer reply, "I'd like to think it over"? Why?

   a. Give all the benefits of using the product now.

   b. If there is a penalty for delaying, mention it now.

   c. If there is a special-price deal available, mention it now.

   d. None of the above is appropriate.

   e. Depending on the circumstances, the first three choices are appropriate.

5. Cliff Jamison sells business forms and he's regarded as a top-notch salesperson. He works hard, plans ahead, and exhibits self-confidence. One day, he made his first presentation to a prospective new client, the California Steel Company.

"Ladies and gentlemen," said Jamison, "our forms are of the highest quality, yet they are priced below our competitor's forms. I know that you are a large user of business forms and that you use a wide variety. Whatever your need for business forms, I assure you that we can supply them. Our forms are noted for their durability. They can run through your machines at 60 per minute and they'll perform perfectly."

"Perfectly, Mr. Jamison?" asked the California Steel executive. "Didn't you have some trouble at Ogden's last year?"

"Oh," replied Jamison, "that wasn't the fault of our forms. They had a stupid operator who didn't follow instructions. I assure you that if our instructions are followed precisely you will have no trouble.

"Furthermore, we keep a large inventory of our forms so that you need never worry about delays. A phone call to our office is all that is necessary to ensure prompt delivery of the needed forms to your plant. I hope, therefore, that I can be favored with your order."

Did Jamison handle this situation correctly? Why?

6. One of your customers, Margaret Port, has referred you to a friend who needs your Hercules Shelving for a storage warehouse. Port recently purchased your heavy-duty, 18-gauge steel shelving and is pleased with it. She said, "This will be an easy sale for you. My friend really needs shelving and I told him about yours."

Port's information is correct and your presentation to her friend goes smoothly. The customer has asked numerous questions and seems ready to buy. Just before you ask for the order, the customer says, "Looks like your product is exactly what I need. I'd like to think this over. Could you call me next week?" Which of the following would you do? Why?

a. Follow the suggestion and call next week.

b. Go ahead and ask for the order.

c. Ask questions about the reason for the delay.

FURTHER EXPLORING THE SALES WORLD

1. A national sales company is at your school wishing to hire salespeople. What are some objections that such a company might have toward hiring you? How would you overcome them during a job interview?

2. Visit three different types of business (such as a grocery store, a hardware store, and a stereo shop), and pick out one product from each business. If you were that store's buyer, think of the major objections or questions you would ask a product salesperson if you were asked to buy a large quantity and promote it. Now, as that salesperson, how would you overcome those objections?

STUDENT APPLICATION LEARNING EXERCISES (SALES)

Sales objections are defined as opposition or resistance from the buyer. To make SALE 6

1. List three objections a buyer might give you. See example of various types of objections on pages 382–390. Make certain you use objections that relate to your product. Do not use general objections, such as "I do not like it." The objection should be specific, such as "I do not like the color."

(Sales 6 of 7)

Objection 1:

Objection 2:

Objection 3:

2. Select a different technique for handling each of the above objections. Write the technique's name below. See pages 390–400.

Technique 1: _____

Technique 2: _____

Technique 3: _____

3. Write the buyer–seller dialog for each objection. State the buyer's objection and then your response to it. Each time you respond to an objection use a trial close (see pages 392–394) to determine if you have overcome the objection or correctly answered the buyer's concern or question. After your trial close, label it using parentheses (Trial Close).

Buyer's objection 1:
Your response:
Buyer's objection 2:
Your response:
Buyer's objection 3:
Your response:

Role-play the buyer giving you the above objections and your response. If possible, use a tape recorder to play back the dialogue. Does what you say sound natural and conversational to you? If not, adjust it. If it does, go with it.

CHAPTER 12

Welcome Your Prospect's Objections

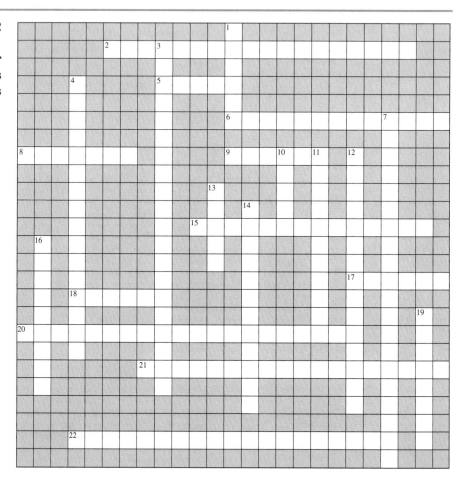

Across

2. The method of offsetting negative product aspects with better benefit aspects.
5. The prospect's opposition or resistance to the salesperson's information or request. This is a _____ objection.
6. A hidden objection based on the prospect's attitudes is known as a _____ objection.
8. A _____ objection relates directly to the product.
9. A _____ objection disguises the actual objection with either silence or triviality.
15. An apparent agreement with the prospect used by the salesperson to deny the fundamental issue of the objection.
17. In a _____ objection the prospect declares he or she does not need the product and implies the end of the selling effort, but this may actually be either a hidden or a stalling objection.
18. A _____ objection is a loyalty-related objection by which the prospect states a preference for another company or salesperson, and may specify a dislike for the salesperson's company or self.
20. The five-step process of overcoming objections in which facts, logic, and tact are used.
21. A situation in which an objection becomes a condition of the sale such that if the condition is met, the prospect will buy.

22. A question in which the salesperson rephrases what the prospect has said in order to clarify meaning and determine the prospect's needs.

Down

1. The option of a salesperson not to pursue a presentation or sale or not to respond to an objection.
3. The option of a salesperson to respond to an objection later during the sales presentation.
4. The technique of responding to an objection with testimony from authoritative sources.
7. Questions relating to a prospect's business that show the salesperson's concern for the prospect's needs.
10. Neither denies, answers, nor ignores the objection, but simply temporarily dodges it.
11. The buyer and the seller reach a mutually satisfactory agreement.
12. The process of turning an objection into a reason to buy.
13. A price-oriented objection or _____ objection.
14. The method of overcoming objections through the use of facts, logic, and tact.
16. A _____ objection is based on real or concrete causes.
19. A _____ objection delays the presentation or the sale.

This is your fourth call on Ace Building Supplies to motivate them to sell your home building supplies to local builders. Joe Newland, the buyer, gives every indication that he likes your products.

During the call, Joe reaffirms his liking for your products and attempts to end the interview by saying: "We'll be ready to do business with you in three months—right after this slow season ends. Stop by then and we'll place an order with you."

Questions

1. Which one of the following steps would you take? Why?
   a. Call back in three months to get the order as suggested.
   b. Try to get a firm commitment or order now.
   c. Telephone Joe in a month (rather than make a personal visit) and try to get the order.
2. Why did you not choose the other two alternatives?

George Wynn is a salesperson for EGC whose primary responsibility is to contact engineers in charge of constructing commercial buildings. One such engineer is Don Snyder, who is in charge of building the new Texas A&M College of Business Administration facility. Don's Houston-based engineering firm purchased three new EGI portable generators for this project. George learned that Don's company will build four more buildings on the Texas A&M campus, and he felt that Don might buy more machines.

Salesperson: Don, I understand you have three of our new model electric generators.

Buyer: Yeah, you're not kidding.

Salesperson: I'm sure you'll need additional units on these new jobs.

Buyer: Yeah, we sure will.

Salesperson: I've gone over the building's proposed floor plans and put together the type of products you need.

Buyer: They buy down in Houston; you need to see them!

Salesperson: I was just in there yesterday and they said it was up to you.

Buyer: Well, I'm busy today.

Salesperson: Can I see you tomorrow?

Buyer: No need; I don't want any more of your lousy generators!

Salesperson: What do you mean? That is our most modern design!

Buyer: Those so-called new fuses of yours are exploding after five minutes' use. The autotransformer starter won't start. . . . Did you see the lights dim? That's another fuse blowing.

Questions

George Wynn feels pressured to sell the new EGI. Don Snyder's business represents an important sale both now and in the future. If you were George, what would you do?

a. Have EGC's best engineer contact Don to explain the generator's capabilities.
b. Come back after Don has cooled down.
c. Get Don to talk about problems and then solve them.

Closing Begins
the Relationship

LEARNING OBJECTIVES

If everything has been done to properly
develop and give a sales presentation, then
closing the sale is the easiest step in the
presentation. After studying this chapter,
you should be able to

- Explain when to close.

- Describe what to do if your prospect
  asks for more information, gives an
  objection, or says no when you ask for
  the order.

- Explain why you must prepare to close
  more than once.

- Discuss the 12 keys to a successful
  close.

- Present, illustrate, and use several
  techniques for closing the sale in your
  presentation.

- Construct a multiple-close sequence.

John made his presentation for in-office coffee service to the office manager. As he neared the end of it, the office manager asked, "What's your price?" John quoted the standard price, and immediately the manager said, "Way out—your competitor's price is $10 cheaper!"

As Lisa, who represented a medical laboratory equipment company, finished her presentation, the pathologist asked her about the cost. She stated the list price and heard, "Your price is too high. I can get the same type of equipment for a lot less."

Ralph, selling a line of office copying machines, was only halfway through his presentation when the director of administration asked for the cost. When Ralph quoted the price on the top-of-the-line model the administrator closed off the interview with the familiar phrase, "Your price is too high."

John, Lisa, and Ralph are facing a real challenge. Their buyers said, "Your price is too high," indirectly saying, "No, I'm not interested." In each situation, what would you do now?

This chapter wraps up our discussion of the main sales presentation elements. We discuss when to close, showing examples of buying signals, and discussing what makes a good closer. Next we discuss the number of times you should attempt to close a sale, along with some problems associated with closing. Eleven closing techniques are presented, followed by an explanation of the importance of being prepared to close several times based on the situation.

To be a good closer, you must be able to handle objections. Objections frequently arise as the salesperson nears the end of the presentation, as in the case of John, and after the close, as Lisa experienced. However, as Ralph found out, price objection can pop up anytime. This chapter and the previous chapters on objections will help you solve the "Sales Challenge" above.

THE TREE OF BUSINESS LIFE: CLOSING

You have spent hours preparing your sales presentation. The discussion of your product, marketing plan, and business proposition went well. You feel it is now time to ask the person to buy. Before you ask someone to buy, you should answer an important question: "Should the person buy this product?" The traditional salesperson will sell it to the person even if she or he does not need it (refer back to Exhibit 1.3). The Golden Rule salesperson would like to know if this product fulfills their need or solves their problem. If not, the salesperson may say something like, "You may know something I do not, Mr. Buyer, but it does not appear this product is what you need?" The buyer may reply, "I feel it fits my needs, I want to buy." Would you believe a very small number of salespeople would not sell the product to the person? Most people would. What would you do? A book cannot say what to do in all situations, since all facts are not known. You are asked to remember the purpose of contacting the customer in making your decision.

Take a look at the title of this chapter. Let's say you close the sale and the person buys. Soon the buyer will know if what you said is true. Will the correct product be received on time at the agreed-upon price? Will the product do what you promised? Your relationship begins with this first sale and continues on into the future.

Have you had someone you trusted lie to you? Have you had someone you trusted cheat you? Why did the person lie or cheat you? How did it make you feel? It is hard to forgive, isn't it? Well, in industry you lie and lose the sale, maybe your job, and

EXHIBIT 13.1

Close when the prospect is
ready.

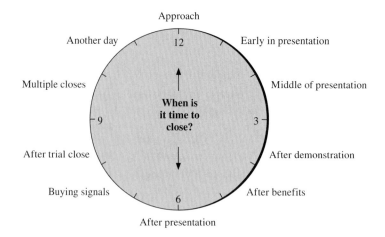

possibly go to jail. But some people use unethical practices to sell—usually motivated
by greed. They are hopeful of not getting caught. But in the end the customer wins!

In closing, it is extremely important to think about the purpose of the sales call—
unselfish service to the other person. Placing the other person's interest first builds
long-term relationships. The question is, "When should you pop the question?"

WHEN SHOULD I POP THE QUESTION?

In baseball you'll always miss 100 percent of the balls you do not swing at.

Closing is the process of helping people make a decision that will benefit them. You
help people make the decision by asking them to buy. As successful salespeople
know, there are no magic phrases and techniques to use in closing a sale. It is the
end result of your presentation. If everything has been done to properly develop a
sales presentation, closing the sale is the next step in a logical sequence.

Although it seems obvious, some salespeople forget that prospects know that the
salesperson is there to sell them something. So, as soon as they meet, the prospect's
mind already may have progressed beyond the major portion of the salesperson's
presentation. At times, the prospect may be ready to make the buying decision early
in the interview.

So when should you attempt to close a sale? Simply, *when the prospect is ready!*
More specifically, when the prospect is in the conviction stage of the mental buying
process. A buyer can enter the conviction stage at any time during the sales
presentation. As Exhibit 13.1 shows, you might ask someone to buy as early as the
approach stage or as late as another day. Much of the time, however, the close comes
after the presentation. The ability to read a prospect's buying signals correctly helps
a salesperson decide when and how to close a sale.

READING BUYING SIGNALS

After prospects negotiate each stage of the mental buying process and are ready to
buy, they often give you a signal. A **buying signal** refers to anything that prospects
say or do indicating they are ready to buy. Buying signals hint that prospects are in
the conviction stage of the buying process. Prospective buyers signal readiness to
buy when they

- **Ask questions**—"How much is it?" "What is the earliest time that I can receive
it?" "What are your service and returned goods policies?" At times, you may

EXHIBIT 13.2

Answering a prospect's buying signal question with a question.

Buyer Says:	Salesperson Replies:
■ What's your price?	■ In what quantity?
■ What kind of terms do you offer?	■ What kind of terms do you want?
■ When can you make delivery?	■ When do you want delivery?
■ What size copier should I buy?	■ What size do you need?
■ Can I get this special price on orders placed now and next month?	■ Would you like to split your shipment?
■ Do you carry 8-, 12-, 36-, and 54-foot pipe?	■ Are those the sizes you commonly use?
■ How large an order must I place to receive your best price?	■ What size order do you have in mind?
■ Do you have Model 6400 in stock?	■ Is that the one you like best?

respond to a buying signal question with another question, as Exhibit 13.2 shows. This helps determine your prospect's thoughts and needs. If your question is answered positively, the prospect is showing a high interest level and you are nearing the close.

■ **Ask another person's opinion**—The executive calls someone on the telephone and says, "Come in here a minute; I have something to ask you." Or the husband turns to his wife and says, "What do you think about it?"

■ **Relax and become friendly**—Once the prospect decides to purchase a product, the pressure of the buying situation is eliminated. A state of visible anxiety changes to relaxation because your new customer believes that you are a friend.

■ **Pull out a purchase order form**—If, as you talk, your prospect pulls out an order form, it is time to move toward the close.

■ **Carefully examine merchandise**—When a prospect carefully scrutinizes your product or seems to contemplate the purchase, this may be an indirect request for prompting. Given these indications, attempt a trial close: "What do you think about . . . ?" If you obtain a positive response to this question, move on to close the sale.

A buyer may send verbal or nonverbal buying signals at any time before or during your sales presentation (remember Exhibit 13.1). The accurate interpretation of buying signals should prompt you to attempt a trial close. In beginning a trial close, summarize the major selling points your prospect desires. If you receive a positive response to the trial close, you can move to Step 9 and wrap up the sale (see Exhibit 13.3). A negative response should result in a return to your presentation, step 4, or to determine objections, Step 6. This is illustrated in Exhibit 13.3. In any case, a successful trial close can save you and your prospect valuable time, while a thwarted trial close allows you to assess the selling situation.

WHAT MAKES A GOOD CLOSER?

In every sales force, some individuals are better than others at closing sales. Some persons rationalize this difference of abilities by saying, "It comes naturally to some people," or, "They've just got what it takes." Well, what does it take to be a good closer?

Good closers have a strong desire to close each sale. They have a positive attitude about their product's ability to benefit the prospect. They know their customers, and they tailor their presentations to meet each person's specific needs.

EXHIBIT 13.3

A positive response to the trial close indicates a move toward the close; a negative response means return to your presentation or determine the prospect's objections.

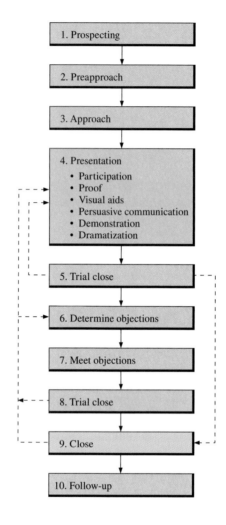

1. Prospecting

2. Preapproach

3. Approach

4. Presentation
- Participation
- Proof
- Visual aids
- Persuasive communication
- Demonstration
- Dramatization

5. Trial close

6. Determine objections

7. Meet objections

8. Trial close

9. Close

10. Follow-up

Always be closing.

Good closers prepare for each sales call. They take the time to carefully ascertain the needs of their prospects and customers by observing, by asking intelligent questions, and most of all, by earnestly listening to them. To be successful, salespeople should know their ABCs. ABC is an acronym for *Always Be Closing*. Be alert for closing signals and close when the prospect is ready to buy.

The successful salesperson does not stop with the prospect's first no. If a customer says no, determine the nature of the objection and then return to the presentation. After discussing information relative to overcoming the objection, use a trial close to determine if you have overcome the objection, and then determine if there are other objections. If resistance continues, remain positive and remember that every time you attempt to close, you are closer to helping the prospect make a decision. In addition, always ask for the order and then be silent.

Ask for the Order and Be Quiet

No matter when or how you close, remember that when you ask for the order, it is important to be silent. Do not say a word. If you say something—anything—you increase the probability of losing the sale.

You must put the prospect in a position of having to make a decision, speak first, and respond to the close. If you say anything after your close, you take the pressure off the prospect to make that decision.

Imagine this situation: The salesperson has finished the presentation and says, "Would you want this delivery in two or four weeks?" The average salesperson cannot wait more than two seconds for the prospect's reply without saying something like, "I can deliver it anytime," or starting to talk again about the product. This destroys the closing moment. The prospect does not have to make the decision. There is time to think of reasons not to buy. By keeping quiet for a few seconds, the prospect cannot escape making the decision.

All individuals experience the urge to say no, even when they are not sure of what you are selling or when they may want what you propose. At times, everyone is hesitant in making a decision. To help the prospect make the decision, you must maintain silence after the close.

The professional salesperson can stay quiet all day, if necessary. Rarely will the silence last more than 30 seconds. During that time, do not say anything or make a distracting gesture; merely project positive nonverbal signs. Otherwise, you will decrease your chances of making the sale. This is the time to mentally prepare your responses to the prospect's reaction.

It sounds simple, yet it is not. Your stomach may churn. Your nerves make you want to move. You may display a serious look on your face instead of a positive one. You may look away from the buyer. Worst of all, you may want to talk to relieve the uncomfortable feeling that grows as silence continues. Finally, the prospect will say something. Now, you can respond based on the reaction to your close.

Constantly practice asking your closing question, staying silent for 30 seconds, and then responding. This will develop your skill and courage to close.

Get the Order— Then Move On!

Talking also can stop the sale after the prospect has said yes. An exception would be if you ask the customer for names of other prospects. Once this is done, it is best to take the order and move on.

In continuing to talk, you may give information that changes the buyer's mind. So, ask for the order and remain silent until the buyer responds. If you succeed, finalize the sale and leave.

HOW MANY TIMES SHOULD YOU CLOSE?

Courtesy and common sense imply a reasonable limit to the number of closes a salesperson attempts at any one sitting. But you say, "I'm afraid to ask the person to buy the first time. I'm certainly not going to ask again." Yet what if you think the product is exactly what the customer needs? When the customer says, "I don't think so," do you say "OK" and leave? Are you unselfishly helping by taking the first "No" and leaving? To help others by selling your product, you must be able to use multiple closes. If needed, you should come back another day to present and close again. This is why salespeople need to be persistent.

Keep in mind that three closes is a minimum for successful salespeople. Three to five well-executed closes should not offend a prospect. Attempting several closes in one call challenges a salesperson to employ wit, charm, and personality in a creative manner. So, always take at least three strikes before you count yourself out of the sale.

"I will persist until I succeed."

OG MANDINO

CLOSING UNDER FIRE

To close more sales effectively, never take the first no from the prospect to mean an absolute refusal to buy. Instead, you must be able to close under fire (see Exhibit 13.4). In other words, you must be able to ask a prospect who may be in a bad mood or even hostile toward you to buy.

MAKING THE SALE

A Mark Twain Story

Mark Twain attended a meeting where a missionary had been invited to speak. Twain was deeply impressed. Later he said, "The preacher's voice was beautiful. He told us about the sufferings of the natives and pleaded for help with such moving simplicity that I mentally doubled the fifty cents I had intended to put in the plate. He described the pitiful misery of those savages so vividly that the dollar I had in mind gradually rose to five. Then that preacher continued. I felt that all the cash I carried on me would be insufficient. I decided to write a large check. Then he went on," added Twain, "and on and on about the dreadful state of those natives. I abandoned the idea of the check. Again, he went on, and I was back to five dollars. As he continued, I went to four, two, and then one dollar. Still, he persisted to preach. When the plate finally came around, I took ten cents out of it."[1]

EXHIBIT 13.4

Closing under fire.

You can tell this customer is unhappy with your product or you. How do you save the sale and close her?

The salesperson was your author.

Take the experience of a consumer goods salesperson who suggested that a large drug wholesaler should buy a six-month supply of the company's entire line of merchandise. Outraged, the purchasing agent threw the order book across the room. The salesperson explained to the furious buyer that the company had doubled its promotional spending in the buyer's area and that it would be wise to stock up because of an increase in sales. The salesperson calmly picked up the order book, smiled, and handed it to the buyer saying, "Did you want to buy more?"

The buyer laughed and said, "What do you honestly believe is a reasonable amount to buy?" This was a buying signal that the prospect would buy, but in a lesser quantity. They settled on an increased order of a two-month supply over the amount of merchandise normally purchased. This example illustrates why it is important for the salesperson to react calmly to an occasional hostile situation. That salesperson was me. I will never forget that day!

DIFFICULTIES WITH CLOSING

Closing the sale is the easiest part of the presentation. It is a natural wrap-up to your sales presentation because you solidify details of the purchase agreement. Yet, salespeople sometimes have difficulty closing the sale for several reasons.

One reason salespeople may fail to close a sale and take an order is that they are not confident in their ability to close. Perhaps some earlier failure to make a sale has caused this mental block. They may give the presentation and stop short of asking for the order. The seller must overcome this fear of closing to become successful.

Second, salespeople often determine that the prospect does not need the quantity or type of merchandise, or that the prospect should not buy. So, they do not ask the prospect to buy. The salesperson should remember that *it is the prospect's decision and responsibility whether or not to buy*. Do not make the decision for the prospect.

Finally, the salesperson may not have worked hard enough in developing a customer profile and customer benefit plan—resulting in a poor presentation. Many times, a poorly prepared presentation falls apart. Be prepared and develop a well-planned, well-rehearsed presentation.

ESSENTIALS OF CLOSING SALES

Although there are many factors to consider in closing the sale, the following items are essential if you wish to improve your chances:

- Be sure your prospect understands what you say.
- Always present a complete story to ensure understanding.
- Tailor your close to each prospect. Eighty percent of your customers will respond to a standard close. It is the other 20 percent of customers that you need to prepare for. Prepare to give the expert customer all facts requested, to give the egotistical customer praise, to lead the indecisive customer, and to slow down for a slow thinker.
- Consider the customer's point of view in everything you do and say.
- Never stop at the first no.
- Learn to recognize buying signals.
- Before you close, ask a trial close. Once the buyer says "No," it is hard to change the person's mind. A famous proverb says "A fool finds no pleasure in understanding but delights in airing his own opinions." This can mean that once the prospect adopts an objection, the person tends to defend it and builds on it rather than seeking the truth. If you close too early and you have not answered the objection, the prospect may say "No," and there will be no way to change the person's mind. So you come back another day!
- After asking for the order—be silent.
- Set high goals for yourself and develop a personal commitment to reach your goals.
- Develop and maintain a positive, confident, and enthusiastic attitude toward yourself, your products, your prospects, and your close.

Don't think or say "I." Think and say "we."

PETER F. DRUCKER

Before we discuss specific techniques on how to ask for the order or close the sale, remember that you will increase your sales closings by following 12 simple keys to success. The keys are shown in Exhibit 13.5.

As you see from these 12 keys, a successful close results from a series of actions that you have followed before asking for the order. Closing is not one giant step.

MAKING THE SALE

Closing Is Not One Giant Step

Too many salespeople regard the close as a separate and distinct part of the sales call. "I've discussed benefits, advantages, and features, answered some objections, handled price, and now it's time to close."

Chronologically, of course, the close does come at the end. However, you must close all along. Closing is the natural outgrowth of the sales presentation. If the rest of the sales call has been a success, closing simply means working out terms and signing the order.

What about the salesperson who says, "I always have trouble closing. Everything's fine until it's time to close the sale." Chances are, there's no basis for the sale. "Everything's fine . . ." may merely be a way of saying. "I stated my case and the prospect listened. At least she never told me to pack up and go."

EXHIBIT 13.5

Twelve keys to a successful closing.

1. Think *success!* Be enthusiastic.
2. *Plan* your sales call.
3. Confirm your prospect's *needs* in the approach.
4. Give a *great* presentation.
5. Use *trial closes* during and after your presentation.
6. Smoke out a prospect's *real* objections.
7. *Overcome* real objections.
8. Use a *trial close* after overcoming each objection.
9. Summarize *benefits* as related to a buyer's *needs*.
10. Use a *trial close* to confirm Step 9.
11. Ask for the *order* and then *be quiet*.
12. Leave the door *open*. Act as a professional.

The race is not always won by the swift but by those who keep on running.

Should you not make the sale, always remember to act as a professional salesperson and be courteous and appreciative of the opportunity to present your product to the prospect. This allows the door to be open another time. Thus, Key 12 cannot be overlooked—always remember to leave the door open!

Often, salespeople believe that there is some mystical art to closing a sale. If they say the right words in the appropriate manner, the prospect will buy. They concentrate on developing tricky closing techniques and are often pushy with prospects in hopes of pressuring them into purchasing. Certainly, salespeople need to learn alternative closing techniques. However, what they need most is a thorough understanding of the entire selling process and of the critical role that closing plays in that process.

A memorized presentation and a hurriedly presented product will not be as successful as the skillful use of the 12 keys to a successful close. A close look at the 12 keys illustrates that a lot of hard work, planning, and skillful execution of your plan occurs before you reach number 11 and ask for the order. The point is that if salespeople understand how each of the 12 applies to them and their customers, and if they perform each successfully, they earn the right to close.

In fact, many times the close occurs automatically because it has become the easiest part of the sales presentation. Often, the prospect will close for the salesperson, saying: "That sounds great! I'd like to buy that" (see Exhibit 13.6). All

EXHIBIT 13.6

Often the seller does not have to close.

In this case, the product sold itself. After examining the business proposition, the prospect bought without the salesperson asking for an order.

the salesperson has to do is finalize the details and write up the order. Often, though, the prospect is undecided on the product after the presentation, so the skillful salesperson develops multiple closing techniques.

PREPARE SEVERAL CLOSING TECHNIQUES

To successfully close more sales, you must determine your prospect's situation, understand the prospect's attitude toward your presentation, and be prepared to select instantly a closing technique from several techniques based on your prospect. For example, suppose you profiled the prospect as having a big ego, so you planned to use the compliment closing technique. You find the prospect is eager to buy, so you switch to using your standing-room-only closing technique. By changing to a closing technique that fits the situation, you can save the sale and keep your customer satisfied.

Successful salespeople adapt a planned presentation to any prospect or situation that may arise. Some salespeople have up to 11 closing techniques, each designed for a specific situation. Following are 11 common closing techniques:

- Alternative-choice close.
- Assumptive close.
- Compliment close.
- Summary-of-benefits close.
- Continuous-yes close.
- Minor-points close.
- T-account or balance-sheet close.
- Standing-room-only close.
- Probability close.
- Negotiation close.
- Technology close.

Whatever product is sold, whether an industrial or consumer product, these closing techniques can be used to ask a prospect for the order (see Exhibit 13.7).

The Alternative-Choice Close Is an Old Favorite

The **alternative-choice close** was popularized in the 1930s as the story spread of the Walgreen Drug Company's purchase of 800 dozen eggs at a special price. A sales trainer named Elmer Wheeler suggested to the Walgreen clerks that when a customer

Techniques for closing the sale:
Which close should be used?

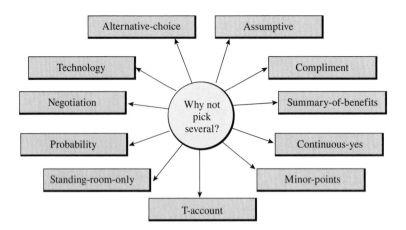

asked for a malted milk at a Walgreen fountain, the clerk should say, "Do you want one egg or two?" Customers had not even thought of eggs in their malteds. Now, they were faced with the choice of *how many eggs*—not whether or not they wanted an egg. Within one week, all 800 dozen of the eggs were sold at a profit. Two examples of the alternative close are

- Which do you prefer—one or two neckties to go with your suit?
- Would you prefer the Xerox 6200 or 6400 copier?

As you see, the alternative choice does not give prospects a choice of buying or not buying, but asks which one or how many items they want to buy. It says, "You are going to buy, so let's settle the details on what you will purchase." Buying nothing at all is not an option.

Take, for example, the salesperson who says: "Would you prefer the Xerox 6200 or 6400?" This question: (1) assumes the customer has a desire to buy one of the copiers; (2) assumes the customer will buy; and (3) allows the customer a preference. If the customer prefers the Xerox 6400, you know the prospect is ready to buy, so you begin the close. A customer who says, "I'm not sure," is still in the desire stage, so you continue to discuss each product's benefits. However, you see that the customer likes both machines. Should the prospect appear indecisive, you can ask: "Is there something you are unsure of?" This question probes to find out why your prospect is not ready to choose.

If used correctly, the alternative-choice close is an effective closing technique. It provides a choice between items, never between something and nothing. By presenting a choice, you either receive a yes decision or uncover objections, which if successfully met, allow you to come closer to making the sale.

The Assumptive Close

With the **assumptive close,** the salesperson assumes the prospect will buy (see Exhibit 13.8). Statements can be made such as, "I'll call your order in tonight," or, "I'll have this shipped to you tomorrow." If the prospect does not say anything, assume the suggested order has been accepted.

Many times the salesperson who has called on a customer for a long time can fill out the order form, hand it to the customer, and say, "This is what I'm going to send you," or, "This is what I believe you need this month." Many salespeople have earned customer trust to such an extent that the salesperson orders for them. Here, the assumptive close is especially effective.

After completing the presentation on a new antibiotic, this pharmaceutical salesperson says, "I appreciate your using Ebiotic for your patients with an ear infection, Dr. Smith." What type of close is he using?

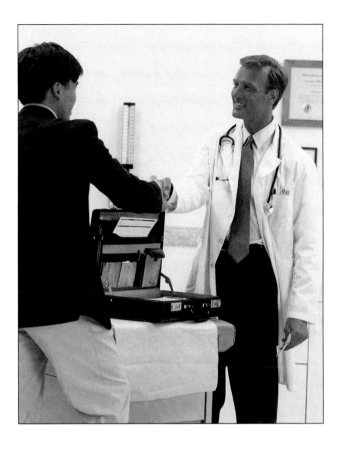

The Compliment Close Inflates the Ego

Everyone likes to receive compliments. The **compliment close** is especially effective when you talk with a prospect who is a self-styled expert, who has a big ego, or who is in a bad mood. Would-be experts and egotistical prospects value their own opinions. By complimenting them, they listen and respond favorably to your presentation. The prospect with low self-esteem or one who finds it difficult to decide also responds favorably to a compliment. Here is an example of a housewares salesperson closing a sale with a grocery retail buyer.

> **Salesperson:** Obviously, you know a great deal about the grocery business. You have every square foot of your store making a good profit. Ms. Stevenson, our products also will provide you with a good profit margin. In fact, our profit will exceed your store's average profit-per-square-foot. And, they sell like hotcakes. This added benefit of high turnover will further increase your profits—which you have said is important to you. [He pauses, and when there is no response, he continues.] Given the number of customers coming into your store, and our expected sales of these products due to normal turnover, along with our marketing plan, *I suggest you buy* [he states the products and their quantities]. This will provide you with sufficient quantities to meet your customers' demands for the next two months, plus provide you with the expected profit from your products. [Now he waits for the response or again asks for the order using the alternative choice or assumptive close.]

All buyers appreciate your recognition of their better points. Conscientious merchants take pride in how they do business; customers entering the retail clothing

Kind words are short and easy to speak, but their echoes are truly endless.

MOTHER TERESA

store take pride in their appearance; people considering life insurance take pride in looking after their families. So compliment prospects relative to something that will benefit them as you attempt to close the sale. Remember, always make honest compliments. No matter how trusting you may think people are, nearly anyone can detect insincerity in a compliment. When a compliment is not in order, summarize the benefits of your product for a specific customer.

The Summary-of-Benefits Close Is Most Popular

During the sales presentation, remember the main features, advantages, and benefits of interest for the prospect and use them during the close. Summarize these benefits in a positive manner so that the prospect agrees with what you say; then ask for the order.

Here is an example of using the **summary-of-benefits close** on a prospect. Assume that the prospect indicates during your sales presentation that she likes your profit margin, delivery schedule, and credit terms.

Salesperson: Ms. Stevenson, you say you like our profit margin, fast delivery, and credit policy. Is that right? [Summary and trial close.]

Prospect: Yes, I do.

Salesperson: With the number of customers in your store and our expected sales of the products due to normal turnover, along with our marketing plan, *I suggest you buy* [state the products and their quantities]. This will provide you with sufficient quantities to meet customer demand for the next two months, plus provide you with the profit you expect from your products. I can have the order to you early next week. [Now wait for her response.]

You can easily adapt the FAB statements and SELL Sequence for your summary close. The vacuum cleaner salesperson might say, "As we have discussed, this vacuum cleaner's high speed motor [feature] works twice as fast [advantage] with less effort [advantage], saving you 15 to 30 minutes in cleaning time [benefit] and the aches and pains of pushing a heavy machine [benefit of benefit]. Right? [trial close. If positive response, say:] Would you want the Deluxe or the Ambassador model?"

The sporting goods salesperson might say, "As we have said, this ball will give you an extra 10 to 20 yards on your drive [advantage], helping to reduce your score [benefit] because of its new solid core [feature]. That's great—isn't it? [trial close. If positive response, say:] Will a dozen be enough?"

The air-conditioning salesperson could say, "This air conditioner has a high efficiency rating [feature] that will save you 10 percent on your energy costs [benefit] because it uses less electricity [advantage]. What do you think of that? [Trial close. If positive response, say:] Would you want it delivered this week or do you prefer next week?"

The summary close is possibly the most popular method to ask for the order. Emmett Reagan, sales trainer at the Xerox Training Center, says the major closing technique taught consists of these three basic steps of the summary close: (1) determine the key product benefits that interest the prospect during the presentation, (2) summarize these benefits, and (3) make a proposal. The summary-of-benefits technique is useful when you need a simple, straightforward close rather than a close aimed at a specific prospect's personality.

The Continuous-Yes Close Generates Positive Responses

The **continuous-yes close** is like the summary close. However, instead of summarizing product benefits, the salesperson develops a series of benefit questions that the prospect must answer.

Like an athlete train hard and run well, remembering the reward that lies ahead, helping someone.

Salesperson: Ms. Stevenson, you have said you like our quality products, right?

Prospect: Yes, that's right.

Salesperson: And you like our fast delivery?

Prospect: Yes, I do.

Salesperson: You also like our profit margin and credit terms?

Prospect: That's correct.

Salesperson: Ms. Stevenson, our quality products, fast delivery, profit margin, and good credit terms will provide you with an excellent profit. With the large number of customers you have coming into your store, [salesperson completes the close as done in the summary-of-benefits close].

In this example of the continuous-yes close, the salesperson recognized four product benefits that the prospect liked: (1) the product's quality, (2) fast delivery, (3) profit margin, and (4) favorable credit terms. After the presentation, the salesperson used three questions to give the prospect the opportunity to agree that she was impressed with each of the four product benefits. By stacking these positive questions, the salesperson kept the prospect continually saying, "Yes, I like that benefit."

The prospect has placed herself in a positive frame of mind. Her positive stance toward the product makes it likely that she will continue to say "yes" when asked to buy.

Realize, of course, that some prospects may want to be cute and relish the thought of seeing the look of surprise on your face when, after they agree to all of your product benefit statements (yes . . . yes . . . yes), they respond to your order request with an unexpected no. Also, suspicious prospects may view your continuous-yes close as trickery or as an insult to their intelligence rather than aiding a purchase decision. In either case, calmly handling the situation reflects a sales professionalism that both surprises the trickster and impresses the suspicious person.

The Minor-Points Close Is Not Threatening

It is sometimes easier for a prospect to concede several minor points about a product than to make a sweeping decision on whether or not to buy. Big decisions are often difficult for some buyers. By having the prospect make decisions on a product's minor points, you can subtly lead into the decision to buy.

The **minor-points close** is similar to the alternative-choice close. Both methods involve giving the buyer a choice between two options. The alternative-choice close asks the prospect to make a choice between *two* products, which represents a high-risk decision to some people that they may prefer not to make. However, the minor-points close asks the prospect to make a low-risk decision on a minor, usually low-cost element of a *single* product such as delivery dates, optimal features, color, size, payment terms, or order quantity.

Single- or multiple-product element choices may be presented to the prospect. The stereo salesperson says, "Would you prefer the single or multiple disc player for your car stereo system?" The Xerox Business Products salesperson asks, "Are you interested in buying or leasing our equipment?" The automobile salesperson asks, "Would you like to install a cellular telephone?"

This close is used widely when prospects have difficulty in making a decision or when they are not in the mood to buy. It is also effective as a second close. If, for example, the prospect says no to your first close because of difficulty in deciding whether or not to buy, you can close on minor points.

The T-Account or Balance-Sheet Close Was Ben Franklin's Favorite

The **T-account close** is based on the process that people use when they make a decision. Some sales trainers refer to it as the Benjamin Franklin close. In his *Poor Richard's Almanac,* Franklin said, "You know, I believe most of my life is going to be made up of making decisions about things. I want to make as many good ones as I possibly can." So, in deciding on a course of action, his technique was to take pencil and paper and draw a line down the center of the paper. On one side, he put all the pros and on the other side he put all the cons. If there were more cons than pros, he would not do something. If the pros outweighed the cons, then he felt it was a good thing to do; it was the correct decision.

This is the process a customer uses in making a buying decision, weighing the cons against the pros. At times, it may be a good idea to use this technique on paper. Common column headings are pros and cons, debits and credits, or to act and not to act. For example, on a sheet of paper, the salesperson draws a large T, placing *to act* (asset) on the left side and *not to act* (liability) on the right side (debit and credit, in accounting terms). The salesperson reviews the presentation with the prospect, listing the positive features, advantages, and benefits the prospect likes on the left side and all negative points on the right. This shows that the product's benefits outweigh its liabilities, and it leads the prospect to conclude that now is the time to buy. If prospects make their own lists, the balance-sheet close is convincing. Here is an example:

Salesperson: Ms. Stevenson, here's a pad of paper and a pencil. Bear with me a minute and let's review what we have just talked about. Could you please draw a large T on the page and write "To Act" at the top on the left and "Not to Act" on the right? Now, you said you liked our fast delivery. Is that right?

Life is like a field of newly fallen snow; where I choose to walk, every step will show. Tell the truth.

To Act	Not to Act
Fast delivery	Narrow assortment
Good profit	
Good credit	

Prospect: Yes.

Salesperson: OK, please write down "fast delivery" in the To Act column. Great! You were impressed with our profit margin and credit terms. Is that right?

Prospect: Yes

Salesperson: OK, how about writing that down in the left-hand column? Now is there anything that could be improved?

Prospect: Yes, don't you remember? I feel you have a narrow assortment with only one style of broom and one style of mop. [Objection.]

Salesperson: Well, write that down in the right-hand column. Is that everything?

Prospect: Yes.

Salesperson: Ms. Stevenson, what in your opinion outweighs the other—the reason to act or not to act? [A trial close.]

Prospect: Well, the To Act column does. But it seems I need a better assortment of products. [Same objection again.]

Salesperson: We have found that assortment is not important to most people. A broom and mop are pretty much a broom and mop. They want a good quality product that looks good and that holds up continuously. Customers like our products' looks and quality. Aren't those good-looking products? [Trial close showing broom and mop.]

Prospect: They look OK to me. [Positive response—she didn't bring up assortment so assume you have overcome objection.]

Salesperson: Ms. Stevenson, I can offer you a quality product, fast delivery, excellent profit, and good credit terms. I'd like to suggest this: Buy one dozen mops and one dozen brooms for each of your 210 stores. However, let's consider this first: The XYZ chain found that our mops had excellent drawing power when advertised. Their sales of buckets and floor wax doubled. Each store sold an average of 12 mops. [He pauses, listens, and notices her reaction.] You can do the same thing.

Prospect: I'd have to contact the Johnson Wax salesperson and I really don't have the time. [A positive buying signal.]

Salesperson: Ms. Stevenson, let me help. I'll call Johnson's and get them to contact you. Also, I'll go see your advertising manager to schedule the ads. OK? [Assumptive close.]

Prospect: OK, go ahead, but this stuff had better sell.

Salesperson: [Smiling] Customers will flock to your stores [he's building a picture in her mind] looking for mops, polish, and buckets. Say, that reminds me, you will need a dozen buckets for each store. [Continuous-yes, keep talking.] I'll write up the order. [Assumptive.]

Some salespeople recommend that the columns of the T-account be reversed so that the Not to Act column is on the left and the To Act column is on the right. This allows the salesperson to discuss the reasons not to buy first, followed by the reasons to buy, ending the presentation on the positive side. This decision depends on a salesperson's preference.

Modified T-Account or Balance-Sheet Close

Some salespeople modify the T-account close by only listing reasons to act in one column. They do not want to remind the prospect of any negative reasons not to buy as they attempt to close the sale. This is similar to the continuous-yes close. The only difference is that the product benefits are written on a piece of paper.

This is a powerful sales tool because the prospects are mentally considering reasons to buy and not to buy anyway. Put the reasons out in the open so that you can participate in the decision-making process.

While this close can be used anytime, it is especially useful as a secondary or backup close. For example, if the summary close did not make the sale, use the T-account close. A contrary idea in the prospect's mind is like steam under pressure—explosive. So, when you remove the pressure by openly stating an objection, opposition vaporizes. An objection often becomes minor or disappears. Remember, however, if the customer says, "Well, I'm going to buy it," do not say, "Well, let's first look at the reasons not to buy." Instead, finalize the sale.

The Standing-Room-Only Close Gets Action

What happens if someone tells you that you cannot have something that you would like to have? You instantly want it! When you face an indecisive prospect or if you want to have the prospect purchase a larger quantity, indicate that if they do not act now they may *not* be able to buy in the future. Motivate the prospect to act immediately by using the **standing-room-only close:**

- I'm not sure if I have your size. Would you want them if I have them in stock?
- My customers have been buying all we can produce. I'm not sure if I have any left to sell you.
- Well, I know you are thinking of ordering *X* amount, but we really need to order (a larger amount) because we now have it in stock and I don't think we will be able to keep up with demand and fill your summer order.
- The cost of this equipment will increase 10 percent next week. Can I ship it today, or do you want to pay the higher price?

For the right product, person, and situation, this is an excellent close. Both retail and industrial salespeople can use this technique to get the prospects so excited that they cannot wait to buy. However, it should be used honestly. Prospects realize that factors such as labor strikes, weather, transportation, inflation, and inventory shortages could make it difficult to buy in the future. Do them a favor by encouraging them to buy now using the standing-room-only close.

The Probability Close

When the prospect gives the famous, I want to think it over objection, or some variation, try saying, "Ms. Prospect, that would be fine. I understand your desire to think it over, but let me ask you this—when I call you back next week, what is the probability, in percentage terms, out of a total of 100, that you and I will be doing business?" Then pause, and don't say another word until the prospect speaks.

The prospect's response will be from three possible categories:

1. *More than 50 percent but less than 85 percent for buying.* If your prospects respond in this range, ask what the remaining percent is against buying, then pause and be silent. When you become skilled in this technique, you will see prospects blink as they focus on their real objections.

   Many times, we hear that prospects want to think it over. It is not because they want to delay the decision; it is because they don't fully understand what bothers them. The **probability close** permits your prospects to focus on their real objections. Once you have a real objection, convert that objection with a persuasive sales argument.

2. *Above 85 percent but not 100 percent for buying.* If they're in this range, recognize that there is a minor probability against you. You might want to say, "As it is almost certain that we'll do business together, why wait until next week? Let's go ahead now; and if you decide in the next couple of days that you want to change your mind, I'll gladly tear up your order. Let's get a running start on this project together."

   When prospects indicate a high percentage of probability, you can use their statements as a lever to push them over the top.

3. *Less than 50 percent for buying.* This is a signal that there is little, if any, chance that you will ever close this particular sale. The only appropriate tactic is returning to square one and starting the reselling process. It is amazing how many professional salespeople in a closing situation expect the prospect to say 80–20 as a probability in their favor, and instead they hear "80–20 against."

What is the probability we will be doing business?

Your Prospect's Name Is a Powerful Closing Tool

Dale Carnegie, author of *How to Win Friends and Influence People,* taught his students, "If you remember my name, you pay me a subtle compliment; you indicate that I have made an impression on you." Your prospect's name is one of the most powerful closing tools because most of us are more interested in ourselves than anyone else.

Repeat your prospect's name several times—but don't overdo it—during your sales call. *Connect your prospect's name with the major benefit statements:*

- "This automatic dialing feature, Jim, will save you a lot of time."
- "Our warranty is designed to give you peace of mind, Susan."

Your prospect will not know that you are using a powerful psychological strategy referred to as *learned association* or *positive pairing.* If you have connected your prospect's name with three or four prominent product benefits, your customer will expect to hear something positive when you merely mention his or her name. When you approach the close, remember to use your prospect's name. Chances are that the sound of her or his name will again evoke positive feelings. By using this little-known secret of master sales closers, you will improve your chances of making the sale.

The probability close permits prospects to focus on their objections. It allows the true or hidden objections to surface. The more prospects fight you and the less candid they are about the probability of closing, the less likely they will buy anything.

The Negotiation Close

Every sale is a negotiation. Most sales negotiations focus on two major themes: value and price. Customers often demand more value and lower prices. In their quest for more value at a lower cost, prospects often resort to unfair tactics and put heavy pressure on the salesperson. The purpose of a good sales **negotiation close** is not to haggle over who gets the larger slice of pie, but to find ways for everyone to have a fair deal. Both the buyer and seller should win. Here are two examples of a salesperson using a negotiation close:

- If we could find a way in which we would eliminate the need for a backup machine and guarantee availability, would you be happy with this arrangement?
- Why don't we compromise? You know I can't give you a discount, but I could defer billing until the end of the month. That's the best I can do. How does that sound?

When you hit a tennis ball over the net, the kind of spin put on the ball determines the type of return shot received. In a negotiation, the attitude that you project determines the attitude you receive. Be positive! Be helpful! Be concerned! Show your interest in helping the prospect.

The Technology Close

Picture this! You have just completed the discussion of your product, marketing plan, and business proposition. You summarize your product's main benefits to your customer. Now you bring out your laptop computer, placing it on the buyer's desk so she can see the screen or you prepare to project the computer screen onto the wall. Using graphs and bar charts, you show the buyer past purchases and sales trends.

Then you call up your recommended purchase suggestion. If appropriate, you can show payment schedules considering different quantity discounts. This **technology close** is very impressive to buyers.

The exact use of technology in closing a sale depends on the type of product and customer you're selling. Without a doubt, incorporating technology into your presentation will help you close more prospects and customers.

PREPARE A MULTIPLE-CLOSE SEQUENCE

By keeping several different closes ready in any situation, you are in a better position to close more sales. Also, the use of a multiple-close sequence, combined with methods to overcome objections, enhances your chance of making a sale.

For example, you could begin with a summary close. Assuming the buyer says no, you could rephrase the objection and then use an alternative close. If again the buyer says no and would not give a reason, you could use the five-question sequence method for overcoming objections, repeating it two or three times.*

It takes courage to stay the course when life gets hard.

Exhibit 13.9 gives an example of a multiple-close sequence that was developed by Jane Martin, who works for an electrical wholesaler. Notice that she uses both methods to overcome objections and closing techniques. First, she uses the summary-of-benefits close and then waits for a response. Martin does not rush. She realizes it is a big decision and is prepared to handle resistance and ask for the order several times. The buyer is sending out green signals, so Martin does not stop; she continues to respond to the buyer.

Notice that the buyer finally gave the real reason for not buying when he said, "No. My supervisor will not let me buy anything." By professionally handling John's objections and politely continuing to close, Jane is in a position to talk with the real decision maker—John's boss.

CLOSE BASED ON THE SITUATION

Since different closing techniques work best for certain situations, salespeople often identify the common objections they encounter and develop specific closing approaches designed to overcome these objections. Exhibit 13.10 shows how to use different closing techniques to meet objections.

Assume, for example, that a buyer has a predetermined belief that a competitor's product is needed. The salesperson could use the T-account approach to show how a product's benefits are greater than a competitor's product. In developing your sales presentation, review your customer profile and develop your main closing technique and several alternatives. By being prepared for each sales call, you experience increased confidence and enthusiasm, which results in a more positive selling attitude. You can help the customer *and* reach your goals.

RESEARCH REINFORCES THESE SALES SUCCESS STRATEGIES

Although it is difficult to summarize all sales success strategies discussed throughout this book, one research report reinforces several key procedures that improve sales performance. This research sought to examine two key questions all salespeople frequently ask themselves: What makes one sales call a success and another a failure? Do salespeople make common mistakes that prevent success?

*See Chapter 12 for correct procedures on overcoming objections.

EXHIBIT 13.9

Multiple closes incorporating techniques for overcoming objections.

Salesperson: John, we have found that the Octron bulb will reduce your storage space requirements for your replacement stock. It offers a higher color output for your designers, which reduces their eye fatigue and shadowing. Should I arrange for delivery this week or next week? [Close 1—Summary-of-benefits close.]

Buyer: Well, those are all good points, but I'm still not prepared to buy. It's too costly.

Salesperson: What you're saying is, "You want to know what particular benefits my product has that make it worth its slightly higher price." Is that correct? [Rephrase as question.]

Buyer: Yes, I guess so.

Salesperson: Earlier, we saw that considering the extended life of the lamps and their energy savings, you can save $375 each year by replacing your present lamps with GE Watt-Misers. This shows, John, that you save money using our product. Right? [Trial close.]

Buyer: Yes, I guess you're right.

Salesperson: Great! Do you prefer installation this weekend or after regular business hours next week? [Close 2—Alternative close.]

Buyer: Neither, I need to think about it more.

Salesperson: There must be some good reason why you're hesitating to go ahead now. Do you mind if I ask what it is? [Question 1 in sequence.]

Buyer: I don't think I can afford new lighting all at one time.

Salesperson: In addition to that, is there another reason for not going ahead? [Question 2 in sequence.]

Buyer: No.

Salesperson: Just supposing you could convince yourself that group replacement is less expensive than spot replacement. . . . Then you'd want to go ahead with it? [Question 3.]

Buyer: I guess so.

Salesperson: Group replacement is not a necessity; however, it does allow you to realize immediate energy savings on all of your fixtures. It saves you much of the labor costs of spot replacement because the lamps are installed with production-line efficiency. See what I mean? [Trial close.]

Buyer: Yes, I do.

Salesperson: Do you feel that installation would be better at night or on the weekend? [Close 3—Minor-points close.]

Buyer: I'd still like to think about it.

Salesperson: There must be another reason why you're hesitating to go ahead now. Do you mind if I ask what it is? [Question 1.]

Buyer: We just don't have the money now to make that kind of investment.

Salesperson: In addition to that, is there any other reason for not going ahead? [Question 2.]

Buyer: No. My supervisor will not let me buy anything.

Salesperson: You agree you could save money for your company on this purchase—right?

Buyer: Yes.

Salesperson: Well, John, how about calling your supervisor now and telling her about how much money we can save in addition to reducing your storage space and the eye fatigue of your employees? Maybe both of us could visit your supervisor. [Close 4—Summary-of-benefits close.]

To answer these questions, Xerox Learning Systems enlisted a team of observers to monitor and analyze more than 500 personal sales calls of 24 different sales organizations. The products and services sold ranged from computers to industrial refuse disposal.

Mike Radick, the Xerox senior development specialist overseeing the study, stated that the average successful sales call lasted 33 minutes. During that call, the salesperson asked an average of 13.6 questions and described 6.4 product benefits and 7.7 product features. Meanwhile, the customer described an average of 2.2 different needs, raised 1.0 objection, made 2.8 statements of acceptance, and asked 7.7 questions.

EXHIBIT 13.10

Examples of closing techniques
based on situations.

Situation \ Closing approach	Alternative	Compliment	Summary	Continuous-yes	Minor-points	Assumptive	T-account	Standing-room-only	Probability	Negotiation	Reason why
Customer is indecisive	X		X	X	X		X	X	X	X	Forces a decision
Customer is expert or egotistical		X					X		X	X	Lets expert make the decision
Customer is hostile		X	X						X	X	Positive strokes
Customer is a friend						X			X	X	You can take care of the small things
Customer has predetermined beliefs							X		X	X	Benefits outweigh disbeliefs
Customer is greedy, wants a deal								X	X	X	Buy now

THE *Golden* RULE

The observers noted that it does not seem to matter whether the salesperson is 28 or 48 years old, male or female, or has 2 or 20 years of experience. What matters is the ability to use certain skills and avoid common errors. These six common mistakes have prevented successful sales calls: By using these research findings you are following the Golden Rule of Selling:

■ **Tells instead of sells; doesn't ask enough questions.** The salesperson does most of the talking. Instead of asking questions to determine a customer's interest, the salesperson charges ahead and rattles off product benefits. This forces the customer into the passive role of listening to details that may not be of interest. As a result, the customer becomes increasingly irritated.

For example, a person selling a computerized payroll system may tell a customer how much clerical time this service could save. However, if clerical time is not a concern, then the customer has no interest in learning how to reduce payroll processing time. On the other hand, the same customer may have a high need for more accurate recordkeeping and be extremely interested in the computerized reports the system generates.

■ **Overcontrols the call; asks too many closed-end questions.** This sales dialogue resembles an interrogation, and the customer has limited opportunities to express needs. The over-controlling salesperson steers the conversation to subjects the salesperson wants to talk about without regard to the customer. When the customer does talk, the salesperson often fails to listen or respond, or doesn't acknowledge the importance of what the customer says. As a result, the customer is alienated and the sales call fails.

■ **Doesn't respond to customer needs with benefits.** Instead, the salesperson lets the customer infer how the features will satisfy his or her needs. Consider the customer who needs a high-speed machine. The salesperson responds with information about heat tolerance, but doesn't link that to how fast the equipment manufactures the customer's product. As a result, the customer becomes confused, loses interest, and the call fails.

Research shows a direct relationship between the result of a call and the number of different benefits given in response to customer needs; the more need-related benefits cited, the greater the probability of success.

■ **Doesn't recognize needs; gives benefits prematurely.** For example, a customer discussing telephone equipment mentions that some clients complain that the line is always busy. The salesperson demonstrates the benefits of his answering service, but the customer responds that busy lines are not important since people will call back. In this case, the customer is not concerned enough to want to solve the problem.

■ **Doesn't recognize or handle negative attitudes effectively.** The salesperson fails to recognize customer statements of objection (opposition), indifference (no need), or skepticism (doubts). What isn't dealt with effectively remains on the customer's mind, and left with a negative attitude, the customer will not make a commitment. The research also shows that customer skepticism, indifference, and objection are three different attitudes. Each attitude affects the call differently; each one requires a different strategy for selling success.

■ **Makes weak closing statements; doesn't recognize when or how to close.** In one extreme case, the customer tried to close the sale on a positive note, but the salesperson failed to recognize the cue and continued selling until the customer lost interest. The lesson is that successful salespeople are alert to closing opportunities throughout the call.

The most powerful way to close a sales call involves a summary of benefits that interest the customer. Three out of four calls that included this closing technique in Radick's study were successful.

KEYS TO IMPROVED SELLING

How is the bridge from average to successful salesperson made? Xerox found that it involves learning and using each of the following skills:

■ Ask questions to gather information and uncover needs.
■ Recognize when a customer has a real need and how the benefits of the product or service can satisfy it.
■ Establish a balanced dialogue with customers.
■ Recognize and handle negative customer attitudes promptly and directly.
■ Use a benefit summary and an action plan requiring commitment when closing.[2]

Learn and use these five selling skills, use the other skills emphasized throughout the book, and develop your natural ability and a positive mental attitude to become a successful, professional salesperson.

THE BUSINESS PROPOSITION AND THE CLOSE

For some salespeople, the discussion of the business proposition provides an excellent opportunity to close. The business proposition, as discussed in Chapter 6's appendix, is the discussion of costs, markups, value analysis, or a return-on-investment (ROI) profit forecast. It follows the discussion of a product's FABs and marketing plan. Remember, the marketing plan explains the following:

1. For wholesalers or retailers, how they should resell the product.
2. For end users, how they can use the product.

The product's FABs and marketing plan justify your suggested order. The business proposition is the third step within the presentation and very important to closing the sale.*

Use a Visual Aid to Close

The use of the visual aid works well in discussing the business proposition and when closing. Immediately after discussing the marketing plan for Cap'n Crunch cereal, the salesperson pulls out the profit forecaster shown in Exhibit 13.11. Notice it is personalized by writing the account's name at the top.

The salesperson discusses each item on the profit forecaster. Then the salesperson says, "Based on your past sales, the profits you will earn, and our marketing plan, I suggest you buy 100 cases for your three stores." The suggested order is written on the profit forecaster.

Now the salesperson remains silent. The buyer will respond with either yes, no, or that is too much to buy. While waiting, the salesperson should mentally go over what to say for each response that can be made by the buyer.

CLOSING BEGINS THE RELATIONSHIP

When you make a sale for the first time, you change the person or organization from a prospect to a customer. You have helped the customer. You have contributed to the customer's welfare. Yes, you should feel good about the sale because you have served someone. What a wonderful feeling!

Now, how do you earn the opportunity to sell the customer in the future? You do it by making sure you have followed the Golden Rule in selling the correct product for the customer's need, and providing exceptional service. It is now that the customer will find out if you told the truth about what the product will do, gave the best price, delivered on time, and provided great service.

The enjoyment you receive from selling is equal to the service you put into it.

Revisit Exhibit 1.11 and the personal characteristics needed to sell for building long-term relationships. Hopefully you can see more clearly why today's salesperson needs these personal characteristics. "Which is the most important?" you might ask. All are important; yet if there is one that is most important, it is the "caring for the customer" characteristic. Did you place the customer's interests before yours? Do you truly care that what you sold will benefit the customer? The strong desire to help the customer is the most important ingredient to building a long-term relationship. All of the other eight personal characteristics will occur if you truly "care."

WHEN YOU DO NOT MAKE THE SALE

A group of purchasing agents were asked their biggest gripes about poor sales procedure. One item on their list was this: "They [salespeople] seem to take it personally if they don't get the business, as though you owe them something because they are constantly calling on you."[3]

Although you should try, you cannot always sell everyone. When you have done the best you can to persuade prospects or customers to make a purchase, and they

*The three steps are discussed in Chapters 8 and 10.

EXHIBIT 13.11

Example of a personalized
visual.

Using a visual is an excellent way to close. After discussing the financial information
on the visual, close by suggesting what and how much should be ordered.

still will not buy or do what you wish, remember there is always tomorrow. Act as
a professional, adult salesperson, and do not take the buyer's denial personally, but
recognize it as a business decision that the buyer must make given the circumstances.
Be courteous and cheerful; be grateful for the opportunity to discuss your product
(see Exhibit 13.12).

The proper handling of a no-sale situation actually helps build a sound business
relationship with your customers by developing a spirit of cooperation. Ask why
you lost out. At the end of each day, review why you did or did not close the sale.
Use this information to strengthen your presentation. Learn from your successes and
your no-sales.

ETHICAL DILEMMA

I'll Buy If . . .

You have been seated in the president's office of a large bank in your town for an appointment you had worked six months to obtain. The president begins your meeting by saying that he is in the market for more insurance and that he had spoken with one of your competitors earlier in the day.

After your presentation and proposal, you begin to close, and he tells you that he is convinced and you get the sale. But, there is one condition. He will only accept a policy with preferred nonsmoker rates. A dirty ashtray is on his desk, and he is obviously at least 25 pounds overweight. You know it is impossible to obtain preferred nonsmoker rates for him if you complete the application truthfully. You also know your company relies on the information you send them when it underwrites the policy.

Purposely submitting false information on an application is grounds for agent termination. If the client dies during the policy's two-year contestable period, death benefits are reduced to the amount of premiums paid if the application had been submitted falsely.

However, if he dies you can say that he told you he did not smoke. He also has to take a physical, so you can blame it on the doctor. This is a big sale, with high commissions. You know he will buy and that you can get away with falsifying the application. If you do not do it, someone else will.

What would be the most ethical action to take?

1. Tell the customer that you will fill out the preferred nonsmoker application if he agrees to try to quit smoking. However, let him know that if the doctor disagrees with your application type, you will have to go with the doctor's recommendation.
2. Go ahead with the preferred nonsmoker application, falsifying information where you need to. Chances are that no one will find out and you can get the commission.
3. Tell the customer that you cannot submit the preferred nonsmoker application. You might lose the sale, but at least you did not compromise your job or your values.

EXHIBIT 13.12

Sometimes the salesperson will not make the sale, but it is important to leave the door open.

If this software salesperson had not made a sale, he would have left the door open for a return sales call by being just as friendly leaving as when he came.

SUMMARY OF MAJOR SELLING ISSUES

Closing is the process of helping people make decisions that will benefit them. You help people make those decisions by asking them to buy. The close of the sale is the next logical sequence after your presentation. At this time, you finalize details of the sale (earlier, your prospect was convinced to buy). Constantly look and listen for buying signals from your prospect to know when to close. It is time to close the sale any time the prospect is ready, whether at the beginning or end of your presentation.

As you prepare to close the sale, be sure you have presented a complete story on your proposition and that your prospect completely understands your presentation. Tailor your close to each prospect's personality and see the situation from the prospect's viewpoint. Remember that you may make your presentation and close too early, which causes a prospect to say no instead of "I don't understand your proposition and I don't want to be taken advantage of." This is why you should never take the first no. It is another reason to use a trial close immediately before the close. But, no matter when or how you close, do so in a positive, confident, and enthusiastic manner to better serve your prospect. Learn and follow the 12 steps to a successful closing.

Plan and rehearse closing techniques for each prospect. Develop natural closing techniques or consider using closes such as the alternative, compliment, summary, continuous-yes, minor-decision, assumption, T-account, or the standing-room-only close. Consider the situation and switch from your planned close if your prospect's situation is different than anticipated.

A good closer has a strong desire to close each sale. Rarely should you accept the first no as the final answer. If you are professional, you should be able to close a minimum of three to five times.

Do not become upset or unnerved if a problem occurs when you are ready to close. Keep cool, determine any objections, overcome them, and try to close again—you can't make a sale until you ask for the order!

MEETING A SALES CHALLENGE

Lisa had finished her presentation. John and Ralph had not. At least Lisa was able to tell her whole story. John and Ralph should have postponed discussing price. They may have lost all hope of making the sale.

In all three cases, the prospect said, "Your price is too high." Many buyers learn or are trained to say this to see if the seller will decrease the price.

When the buyer said, "What's your price?" John could have said, "It will depend on the type of service you need and the quantity purchased. Let's discuss that in just a minute." When the buyer said, "Way out—your competitor's price is $10 cheaper!" John could say, "I quoted you our base price. Your actual price will depend on the quantity purchased. We can meet and beat that price (the competitor's price)."

Lisa needs to find out more, such as what specific equipment and from whom. Equipment is different. So are service, terms, and delivery.

When Ralph's buyer said, "Your price is too high," he needs to find out what the buyer is comparing his price to. Ralph's buyer may not need his top-of-the-line model. So he must get back to a discussion of the buyer's needs before determining the model and price.

KEY TERMS FOR SELLING

closing 412
buying signal 412
alternative-choice close 419
assumptive close 420
compliment close 421
summary-of-benefits close 422
continuous-yes close 422

minor-points close 423
T-account close 424
standing-room-only close 426
probability close 426
negotiation close 427
technology close 428

SALES APPLICATION QUESTIONS

1. A salesperson must use a closing technique that is simple and straightforward, and ask the prospect only to buy rather than something in addition to buying. In which of the following examples, if any, is the salesperson suggesting something to the buyer that is a close, rather than something the buyer must do in addition to buying?

   a. If you have no objection, I'll go out to the warehouse now to see about reserving space for this new item.

   b. To get this promotion off right, we should notify each of your store managers. I've already prepared a bulletin for them. Should *I* arrange to have a copy sent to each manager, or do *you* want to do it?

   c. To start this promotion, we should notify each of your store managers. I've already prepared a bulletin for them. On my way out, I can drop it off with the secretary.

   d. We should contact the warehouse manager about reserving a space for this new item. Do you want to do it now or after I've left?

2. Buying signals have numerous forms. When you receive a buying signal, stop the presentation and move in to close the sale. For each of the following seven situations, choose the appropriate response to your prospect's buying signal that leads most directly to a close.

   a. "Can I get it in blue?" Your best answer is:
      (1) Yes.
      (2) Do you want it in blue?
      (3) It comes in three colors, including blue.

   b. "What's your price?" Your best answer is:
      (1) In what quantity?
      (2) To quote a specific price.
      (3) In which grade?

   c. "What kind of terms do you offer?" Your best answer is:
      (1) To provide specific terms.
      (2) Terms would have to be arranged.
      (3) What kind of terms do you want?

   d. "How big an order do I have to place to get your best price?" Your best answer is:
      (1) A schedule of quantity prices.
      (2) A specific-size order.
      (3) What size order do you want to place?

   e. "When will you have a new model?" Your best answer is:
      (1) A specific date.
      (2) Do you want our newest model?
      (3) This is our newest model.

   f. "What is the smallest trial order I can place with you?" Your best answer is:
      (1) A specific quantity.
      (2) How small an order do you want?
      (3) A variety of order sizes.

   g. "When can you deliver?" Your best answer is:
      (1) That depends on the size of your order. What order size do you have in mind?
      (2) A specific delivery date.
      (3) When do you want delivery?

3. Which of the following is the most frequently committed sin in closing? Why?
   a. Asking for the order too early.
   b. Not structuring the presentation toward a closing.
   c. Not asking for the order.
4. Is a good closing technique to ask the customer outright (but at the right time), "Well, how about it? May I have the factory ship you a carload?" Why do you agree or disagree?
5. After completing a presentation that has included all of your product's features, advantages, and benefits, do not delay in asking the customer, "How much of the product do you wish to order?" Is this statement true or false? Why?
6. Each visual aid you use during your presentation is designed to allow the customer to say yes to your main selling points. What should your visual aids include that allows you to gauge customer interest and help move to the close? What are several examples?
7. "Now, let's review what we've talked about. We've agreed that the Mohawk's secondary backing and special latex glue make the carpet more durable and contribute to better appearance. In addition, you felt that our direct-to-customer delivery system would save a lot of money and time. Shall I send our wall-sample display or would you be interested in stocking some 9 by 12s?"
   a. The salesperson's closing statement helps ensure customer acceptance by doing which of the following:
      (1) Summarizing benefits that the customer agreed were important.
      (2) Giving an alternative.
      (3) Assuming that agreement has been reached.
   b. The salesperson ends the closing statement by
      (1) Asking if the customer has any other questions.
      (2) Asking if the product will meet the customer's requirements.
      (3) Requesting a commitment from the customer.
8. "Assuming agreement has been reached" reflects the kind of attitude you should project when making a closing statement. When you make a close, nothing you say should reflect doubt, hesitation, or uncertainty. Which of the following salesperson's remarks assume agreement?
   a. If you feel that Munson is really what you want.
   b. Let me leave you two today and deliver the rest next week.
   c. Well, if you purchase.
   d. Well, it looks as if maybe.
   e. We've agreed that.
   f. When you purchase the X-7100.
   g. Why don't you try a couple, if you like.
9. A good rule is, "Get the order and get out." Do you agree? Why?
10. The real estate salesperson is showing property to a couple who look at the house and say, "Gee, this is great. They've taken good care of this place and the rugs and drapes are perfect. Do you think they'd be willing to leave the rugs and drapes?" What should the salesperson do or say? Why?

FURTHER EXPLORING THE SALES WORLD

1. Assume you are interviewing for a sales job and there are only five minutes remaining. You are interested in the job and know if the company is interested, they will invite you for a visit to their local distribution center and have you

work with one of their salespeople for a day. What are several closing techniques you could use to ask for the visit?

2. Visit several retail stores or manufacturing plants in your local area and ask their purchasing agents what they like and do not like about the closing when they are contacted by salespeople. See if they have already decided to buy or not to buy before the salesperson closes. Ask how a salesperson should ask for their business.

3. Develop a complete sales presentation that can be given in eight minutes. Include the buyer–seller dialogue. Make sure the appropriate components in Exhibit A are contained in the presentation. Use one of the three approaches shown in Exhibit A depending on your situation. For example, use the SPIN approach if this is the first time you have called this prospect. Use the SPIN or summary-of-benefits approach if this is a repeat sales call on a prospect or customer.

Your presentation must use several SELL Sequences and should contain a minimum of one proof statement; two similes, metaphors, or analogies; and a demonstration of important benefits. The marketing plan also must incorporate one or more SELL Sequences that tie the marketing plan back to the information uncovered in the approach and the first SELL Sequence.

The business proposition is last and contains the appropriate discussion on price and value. Relate the business proposition to the information uncovered earlier in the presentation. Develop visuals for presenting your benefits, marketing plan, and business proposition. Anywhere within the presentation prior to the close, use a minimum of one objection and answer one of the buyer's questions with a question.

Now, ask for the order using a summary-of-benefits close that includes a suggested order if appropriate for your product or service. Use a minimum of three closes. This requires you to develop a *multiple-close sequence* since the buyer has raised an objection or asked for more information after each close. Use three different closes, the first being the summary-of-benefits close. Also, use different methods of handling objections. In the presentation, be sure to (1) have a professional appearance; (2) firmly shake hands and use direct eye contact before and after the presentation; (3) project positive nonverbal signs; and (4) use a natural level of enthusiasm and excitement in conversation.

STUDENT APPLICATION LEARNING EXERCISES (SALES)

Now it's time to ask for the order! Frequently, questions and objections arise when you ask someone to buy. Thus, you should anticipate questions and/or objections and be prepared to use several different closing and objections-handling techniques. To make **SALE 7**

(SALE 7 of 7)

1. List the main benefits discussed in your presentation.

2. Select a closing technique, such as the summary-of-benefits close on page 422. Write out your close and label it with the name of the closing technique in parentheses. Use a trial close after completing the close to verify that these benefits are important to the buyer. Write out your trial close and label it using parentheses as shown on page 422 (trial close).

3. Create a visual aid showing your suggested order. See page 432 for an example. This visual aid may be similar to the one you developed for discussing your price(s).

4. Now you are ready to construct your multiple-closing sequence. First carefully study Exhibit 13.3 on page 414. Now look at the example of a multiple-closing

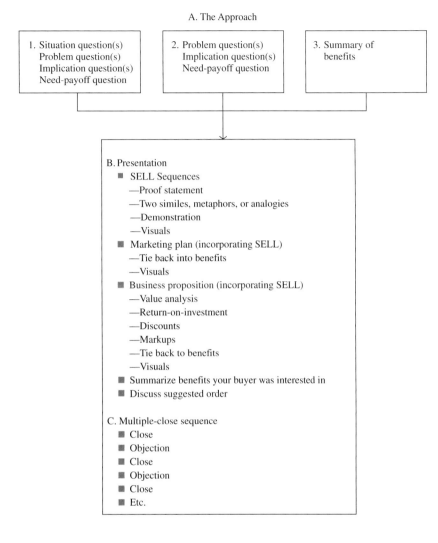

EXHIBIT A

Format of your sales presentation.

A. The Approach

1. Situation question(s)
   Problem question(s)
   Implication question(s)
   Need-payoff question

2. Problem question(s)
   Implication question(s)
   Need-payoff question

3. Summary of benefits

B. Presentation
   ■ SELL Sequences
      —Proof statement
      —Two similes, metaphors, or analogies
      —Demonstration
      —Visuals
   ■ Marketing plan (incorporating SELL)
      —Tie back into benefits
      —Visuals
   ■ Business proposition (incorporating SELL)
      —Value analysis
      —Return-on-investment
      —Discounts
      —Markups
      —Tie back to benefits
      —Visuals
   ■ Summarize benefits your buyer was interested in
   ■ Discuss suggested order

C. Multiple-close sequence
   ■ Close
   ■ Objection
   ■ Close
   ■ Objection
   ■ Close
   ■ Etc.

sequence on page 429. The multiple-closing sequence should be composed of the following:

a. Your summary-of-benefits close.

b. Your trial close.

c. Your suggested order.

d. Use the assumptive or alternative close.

e. Have the buyer ask a question or give an objection.

f. Respond using another objection-handling technique.

g. Ask a trial close to see if you successfully handled the objection.

h. Ask for the order again using an unused closing technique. Don't be pushy. Use a calm, laid-back, friendly, conversational style.

i.   The close–objection–close–objection sequence can be repeated if appropriate.

5. To complete **SALE 7**, write up the above *a–i* in a script format. Role-play this dialogue until it sounds natural to you. This may require replacing the used techniques with new ones. Once the manuscript is finalized, type it and turn it in to your instructor.

CHAPTER 13

**Closing Begins
the Relationship**

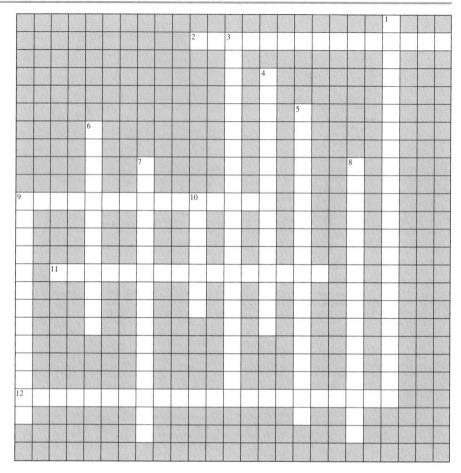

Across

2. A type of close that assumes the prospect will buy.
9. A close in which the seller uses technology to present information.
11. A close in which buyer and seller find ways for everyone to have a fair deal.
12. A close in which the salesperson summarizes the benefits of the product in a positive manner so that the prospect agrees with what the salesperson says.

Down

1. Gives the prospect a choice between two alternatives.
3. A close by which a salesperson suggests that if a prospect does not act now, he or she may not be able to buy in the future, thus motivating the prospect to act immediately.
4. A close in which the salesperson ends with a compliment to the prospect.
5. A kind of close by which the salesperson develops a series of benefit questions that the prospect must answer.
6. Anything that prospects say or do indicating they are ready to buy.
7. A close that permits the prospect to focus on his or her real objections, which a salesperson attempts to reverse with a persuasive sales argument.
8. A close in which the salesperson asks the prospect to make a low-risk decision on a minor element of a product.

9. A close that is based on the process that people use when they make a decision by weighing the pros against the cons.

10. The process of helping people make a decision that will benefit them by asking them to buy.

CASE 13-1
Skaggs Omega

Skaggs Omega, a large chain of supermarkets, has mailed you an inquiry on hardware items. They want to know about your hammers, screwdrivers, and nails. On arrival, you make a presentation to the purchasing agent, Linda Johnson. You state that you had visited several of their stores. You discuss your revolving retail display, which contains an assortment of the three items Johnson had mentioned in her inquiry, and relate the display's advantages and features to benefits for Skaggs.

During your presentation, Johnson has listened but has said little and has not given you any buying signals. However, it appears she is interested. She did not object to your price nor did she raise any other objections.

You approach the end of the presentation and it is time to close. Actually, you have said everything you can think of.

Questions

1. What is the best way to ask Johnson for the order?
   a. How do you like our products, Ms. Johnson?
   b. What assortment do you prefer, the A or B assortment?
   c. Can we go ahead with the order?
   d. If you'll just OK this order form, Ms. Johnson, we'll have each of your stores receive a display within two weeks.
2. Discuss the remaining alternatives from Question 1, ranking them from good to bad, and state what would happen if a salesperson responded in that manner.

CASE 13-2
Central Hardware Supply

Sam Gillespie, owner of Central Hardware Supply, was referred to you by a mutual friend. Gillespie was thinking of dropping two of its product suppliers of home-building supplies. "The sale should be guaranteed," your friend had stated.

Your friend's information was correct and your presentation to Gillespie convinces you that he will benefit from buying from you. He comments as you conclude the presentation: "Looks like your product will solve our problem. I'd like to think this over, however. Could you call me tomorrow or the next day?"

Questions

1. The best way to handle this is to
   a. Follow his suggestion.
   b. Ignore his request and try a second close.
   c. Probe further. You might ask: "The fact that you have to think this over suggests that I haven't convinced you. Is there something I've omitted or failed to satisfy you with?"
2. What would be your second and third choices? Why?

CASE 13-3
Furmanite Service Company—A Multiple-Close Sequence

Chris Henry sells industrial valves and flanges, plus tapes and sealants. He is calling on Gary Maslow, a buyer from Shell Oil, to sell him on using Furmanite to seal all of his plant's valve and flange leaks. Chris has completed the discussion of the product's features, advantages, and benefits, plus the marketing plan and the business proposition. Chris feels it is time to close. Chris says:

Salesperson: Let me summarize what we have talked about. You have said that you like the money you will save by doing the repairs. You also like our response time in saving the flanges so that they can be rebuilt when needed. Finally, you like our three-year warranty on service. Is that right?

Buyer: Yes, that is about it.

Salesperson: Gary, I suggest we get a crew in here and start repairing the leaks. What time do you want the crew here Monday?

Buyer: Not so fast—how reliable is the compound?

Salesperson: Gary, it's very reliable. I did the same service for Mobil last year and we have not been back for warranty work. Does that sound reliable to you?

Buyer: Yeah, I guess so.

Salesperson: I know you always make experienced, professional decisions, and I know that you think this is a sound and profitable service for your plant. Let me schedule a crew to be here next week or maybe in two weeks.

Buyer: Chris, I am still hesitant.

Salesperson: There must be a reason why you are hesitating to go ahead now. Do you mind if I ask what it is?

Buyer: I just don't know if it is a sound decision.

Salesperson: Is that the only thing bothering you?

Buyer: Yes, it is.

Salesperson: Just suppose you could convince yourself that it's a good decision. Would you then want to go ahead with the service?

Buyer: Yes, I would.

Salesperson: Gary, let me tell you what we have agreed on so far. You like our online repair because of the cost you would save, you like our response time and the savings you would receive from the timely repair of the leaks, and you like our highly trained personnel and our warranty. Right?

Buyer: Yes, that's true.

Salesperson: When would you like to have the work done?

Buyer: Chris, the proposition looks good, but I don't have the funds this month. Maybe we can do it next month.

Salesperson: No problem at all, Gary; I appreciate your time, and I will return on the fifth of next month to set a time for a crew to start.

Questions

1. Label each of the selling techniques Chris used.
2. What were the strengths and weaknesses of this multiple-closing sequence?
3. Should Chris have closed again? Why?
4. Assume Chris felt he could make one more close. What could he do?

CASE 13-4

Steve Santana: Pressured to Close a Big Deal

Video

Case

Steve Santana works for a pharmaceutical manufacturer. Steve's company is pressuring his division to increase sales. Presently Steve is working on closing a big deal with the Danson HMO. This sale would be huge for the company. Not only would the sale allow Steve to reach his sales goals, but also his entire sales division's sales quota.

Rob, the divisional sales manager and Steve's boss, is understandably anxious about making the sale to Claire Manford, Danson's purchasing agent. In their conversation about Claire, Rob suggests Steve go around Claire and talk with Danson's chief medical advisor. This might help close the sale. Steve is against this suggestion. Rob then suggests they place Claire on their consulting board, which pays a nice fee to board members. Rob feels this would help close the deal. However, Steve is against this idea.

After meeting with Rob, Steve calls on Claire at her business. During their visit, Claire mentions her son is learning disabled and she is the new fund-raising chairperson for an information and referral center for the learning disabled. Her fund-raising group will need $100,000 just to get the center started. As Steve is getting ready to leave, Claire also says that she likes Steve's proposal but his prices seem a little too high.

That afternoon Steve visits with Rob about his sales call on Danson and the conversation with Claire. When Rob hears about her interest in the learning disabled center he immediately suggests that their company make a $10,000 donation. Rob feels this would greatly increase the probability of making the sale. Again, Steve is reluctant and thinks this is bad business. However, Steve can see Rob is very nervous. At the end of their meeting Rob says, "Steve I rarely let someone in your position handle such a big sale. But I am going to leave this up to you. It is your responsibility."

Questions

1. What are the main ethical issues, if any, in the Santana case? Describe each ethical issue.
2. What are Santana's options?
3. How do the three levels of moral development relate to Perry's situation?
4. What would you do?

Service and Follow-Up for Customer Retention

LEARNING OBJECTIVES

Providing service to the customer is extremely important in today's competitive marketplace. After studying this chapter, you should be able to

- State why service and follow-up are important to increasing sales.

- Build friendships.

- Discuss how follow-up and service result in account penetration and improved sales.

- List the eight steps involved in increasing sales to your customer.

- Explain the importance of properly handling customers' returned goods requests and complaints in a professional manner.

As a construction machinery salesperson, you know that equipment malfunctions and breakdowns are costly to customers. Your firm, however, has an excellent warranty that allows you to replace a broken piece of equipment with one of your demonstrators for a few days while the equipment is repaired. King Masonry has called you four times in the past three months because the mixer you sold them has broken down. Each time you have cheerfully handled the problem, and in less than two hours they have been back at work. Your company's mixer has traditionally been one of the most dependable on the market, so after the last breakdown, you let King Masonry keep the new replacement in hopes of solving any future problems.

The owner, Eldon King, has just called to tell you the newest mixer has broken down. He is angry and says he may go to another supplier if you cannot get him a replacement immediately.

If you were the salesperson, how would you handle this situation?

The last but not least cliché applies to this chapter, which ends our discussion of the elements of the selling process. Follow-up and service to customers is the salesperson's most important activity for future sales. Planning the sales presentation may take hours, days even. Giving the sales presentation may take only minutes. Follow-up and service never end.

Many salespeople's interest declines after the sale. Yet their customer's interest in the product and wanting to interact with the salesperson increases. This is one of the reasons service after the sale is so important to the seller–buyer long-term relationship. Please pay close attention to the discussion of this important chapter.

THE BUSINESS TREE OF LIFE: SERVICE

Sales is hard work. It is not about you but about taking care of the customers. Often customers are difficult, like Eldon King in the above "Facing a Sales Challenge." Salespeople do not earn the big bucks for nothing. If all you had to do was give a presentation and they bought, everyone would be in sales. The fact is many people do not make it in sales because they do not have the ability to put someone's interests before their own needs for money, power, and influence. All they want to do is make the sales and move on to the next conquest.

Sales is not for everyone. Some in sales should not be in the job. They are the ones giving all salespeople a bad name. This is why the majority of people do not trust salespeople.

The illustration in Exhibit 14.1 is again used to show the gap often found between buyer and seller. Only through truth can trust be supported to bridge the gap between people—seller and buyer. Truth that is without distortion due to personal feelings or prejudices is the center-pole supporting trust.

Closing begins the relationship with your customer. Service and follow-up after the sale show you truly care. The customer sees if the product does what you said it would. When you promise someone something and deliver, your integrity, trustworthiness, character, and values shine like a star in the night sky. Selling guided by the Golden Rule leads to ethical daily actions, actions to habits, habits to character, character to your destiny. By providing outstanding service you place the interest of the customer before your self-interest. Ethical service truly does build long-term relationships.

EXHIBIT 14.1

Only through truth can trust be supported to bridge
the gap between people.

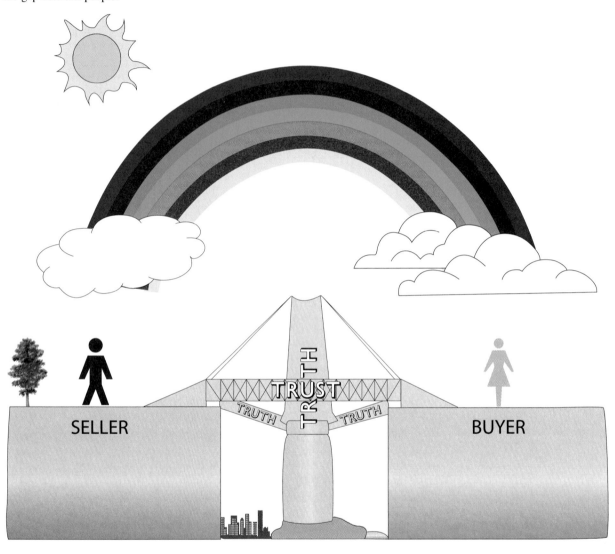

THE IMPORTANCE OF SERVICE AND FOLLOW-UP

In Chapter 1 we defined service as making a contribution to the welfare of others and we defined service as part of a product, such as insurance or advertising. Most of the book refers to service in the context of helping others, and that is the emphasis of this chapter. How does a salesperson help customers? **Follow-up** by maintaining contact with a customer (or prospect) in order to evaluate the effectiveness of the product and the satisfaction of the customer is the answer.

Ideas about taking care of customers have developed over the years. Let's think about several of the more important words of sales wisdom that all salespeople should understand.

Words of Sales Wisdom

Salespeople are often guided by their eagerness to sell. Some salespeople view selling as a competitive sport. They have to win. After all, salespeople are only human. They want to be successful. They have bills to pay and people to support. Many feel under pressure to sell and others are driven by greed. "Yes, I am here to help," said a saleswoman, but "I am here mainly to sell."

This book, however, offers sales wisdom the reader can use to learn how to help others through the purchase of their products rather than how to sell in pursuit of their own self-interest. Caring for people is the beginning of sales wisdom. The purpose of this book is to teach people how to attain wisdom in order to do what is right and just and fair. This book strives to help new salespeople gain knowledge and discretion and to help seasoned salespeople add to their learning.

Sales Proverbs

A **proverb** is a short, wise, easy-to-learn saying that calls a person to think and act. The following are a few proverbs of sales wisdom:

- Customer choice between suppliers has never been greater.
- You lose X percent of sales or customers per year.
- People do not care how much you know until they know how much you care.
- You do business with the one you trust and you trust the one you know.
- 80 percent of your profits comes from about 20 percent of your customers.
- Obtaining new customers and selling more products to present customers are the ways to increase sales.
- Like a ripple in water, satisfied customers will tell others about their positive experiences.
- It is always easier to sell a satisfied customer than an unsatisfied one or a prospect.
- The cost of acquiring a new customer is higher than keeping a present customer.

What does this mean to the salesperson? Take excellent care of your current customers!

Knowledge versus Wisdom

This knowledge is good, but there is a vast difference between **knowledge** (having these facts) and **wisdom** (applying these facts to taking care of customers). We may amass knowledge, but without wisdom, our knowledge is useless. We must learn how to live out what we know. In this age of information, knowledge is plentiful, but wisdom is scarce. Wisdom means far more than simply knowing a lot. It is a basic attitude that affects every aspect of life. The foundation of knowledge is to honor and respect people. All people!

Wisdom Is Learned

In sales, one gains wisdom through a constant process of growing. First, we must trust and honor people. Second, we must realize that our purpose is to help people. Third, we must make a lifelong series of right choices and avoid moral pitfalls. Fourth, we must learn from our errors and recover. People do not develop all aspects of sales wisdom at once. The sales career involves both science and art that takes time to learn.

EXHIBIT 14.2

If customers are truly important, their needs come first. Sellers should care about customers as much as themselves.

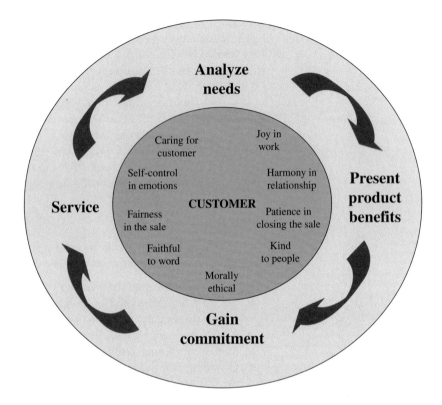

Exhibit 14.2 helps illustrate the importance of follow-up and service. The business relationship begins after you sell someone. This is referred to in Exhibit 14.2 as commitment. If the salesperson is to have the privilege of selling again, the customer must answer positively to questions like these:

1. Can I trust this person?
2. Did the product and salesperson do what was presented?
3. Does the salesperson truly care about me?

If the customer answers "yes" to these questions, certainly he or she will allow the salesperson to make future presentations. Will the customer always buy? No. But if the customer feels the salesperson is trustworthy and cares, the customer often will give the salesperson the benefit of the doubt and buy rather than taking a chance on another salesperson.

True Caring Builds Relationships and Sales

What is the purpose of the sales call? Is it solely to make a sale? Or is the sales call meant to help someone? There is a big difference! The potential buyer can often see this difference.

Exhibit 14.2 shows that the salesperson first analyzes the prospect, customer, or organization's needs. This can take time. Yet it is critical. It is somewhat like a medical doctor getting someone to have X-rays and blood analysis before determining the exact problem and prescribing a course of action. Once the prospect feels the salesperson understands needs, confidence improves in what the salesperson recommends.

After the sale, customers look to see if you are the same as before the sale. People like to buy and be remembered, not sold and forgotten. A relationship should be stronger, not weaker, after the sale. This is why Chapter 1 pointed out that to-day's salespeople need personal characteristics allowing them to

- Care for the customer, take joy in work, and find harmony in the relationship.
- Have patience in closing the sale, kindness to all people, and moral ethics.
- Be faithful to one's word, fair in the sale, and self-controlled in emotions.

Do these success characteristics describe you? Do you have all, or part, of them? Can you develop the missing ones?

Caring Is Seen!

Caring about the customer is more than simply warm feelings; it is an attitude that reveals itself in action. How can sellers care about a customer as much as them-selves? By helping when it is not convenient, by giving the best price, by devoting energy to their welfare, by making sure the customer is satisfied. These are just a few ways the seller shows caring for the customer.

Caring Is Hard to Do!

This kind of caring is hard to do. That is why people notice when the seller does it. This is how customers know the salesperson places their welfare first. This is how customers know the seller can be trusted. This is how a long-term relationship be-gins and extends into the future. Through caring comes exceptional service to the customer, which in turn brings peace to the relationship. Buyer and seller care for and trust each other. Wow!

BUILDING A LONG-TERM BUSINESS FRIENDSHIP

Today's sales professionals strive to create long-term business relationships with customers, which implies that a personal relationship with clients is formed. And in fact, salespeople often develop more than just a casual relationship with the client; they frequently develop business friendships.

What Is a Business Friendship?

The relationship between a salesperson and client that revolves around business-related issues is referred to as a **business friendship.** A good business friendship is a relationship much like any of your personal friendships.

How to Build a Business Friendship

Do you build a friendship with a business client, or do you expect it to just happen? Most of the time salespeople are in too big a hurry to make a sale and move on to the next customer. Even after calling on the same person over a long period of time, the salesperson may not know the customer.

The answer is that you build a business friendship in much the same way that you build a personal friendship. Think about your present friends. You consider some better friends than others. Usually we have one of three levels of relationships with both business and personal friends: acquaintances, friends, and intimate friends. (See Exhibit 14.3.)

Level 1. **Acquaintances** are people whose names you know, whom you see occa-sionally, and of whom you may know little about even if you've known them for a

Trust and wisdom in a relationship grow over time. Years may pass before an intimate friendship develops between buyer and seller.

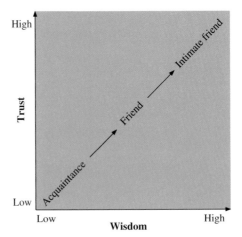

long time. This is where all friendships must start. Usually these people turn out to be friends we meet along the way in our life. In the business world, as well as in one's personal life, acquaintances are viewed as having low levels of wisdom and trust.

Level 2. **Friends** are people whom we spend more time with and with whom we share common interests and/or hobbies. We know not only who they are, but also what they are about. These people are good for a long walk in our life. In industry, business friends are trusted. They have earned loyalty by demonstrating their caring for the customer over time.

Level 3. **Intimate friends,** often called "best friends," are the people we know on a deeper level. We know about their family. We know many of their deepest thoughts and feelings. They confide in us. They ask our advice. We may have shared personal hardships. We share deep mutual interests. These wonderful people are friends for our life's journey. In the customer-seller relationship, personal interests of each other and their families have top priority.

Building any friendship takes time, especially in the business world. It can often take three years or more to build a truly good, level 2 friendship. Usually several things happen between people before they become friends:

- Self-disclosure—sharing a few things about yourself and allowing your client to share a few things about him- or herself. If your client is not immediately responsive to your efforts, don't worry. Remember, building friendships takes time.
- Acknowledgment—Take time to listen to your client. Everyone has a desire to be heard, acknowledged, and understood. Remember these three steps to acknowledgment:

  Step 1: Repeat back—You might want to repeat, in a summarized fashion, what your client tells you.

  Step 2: Don't invalidate—Avoid telling or making your clients feel that they are wrong.

  Step 3: Don't try to change—Do not attempt to change clients' minds on an issue. Simply listen to what they say and formulate a solution based on their perceived problems.

■ Attending—Pay attention, or attend, to your client. Your eyes, ears, body, and thought should all be focused on them and what they are saying. Make eye contact to show your client that you are really listening to what he or she has to say.

■ Talking—The foundation for any relationship is good communication. This means that to develop a good business friendship with your client, you must be a great listener. Share information and allow information to be shared.

The previous steps provide a good start to building a friendship with your business client. But once a relationship has begun, it must be maintained. To maintain a good friendship requires structure, not trying to control or out-do your client, and not attempting to pressure your friend to buy.

Structure for Survival

A good relationship needs structure to survive. Define your and your business friend's responsibilities, expectations, and roles at the outset and follow them accordingly. What responsibilities will you or won't you take on? What can your client reasonably expect from you, and what can you reasonably expect from her or him? What role will you play in his or her life? These questions are important to answer early in the relationship and to continually reaffirm in order to avoid confusion.

Avoid Control and One-Upmanship

There is often a tendency for one person to take control in a relationship. This can be damaging, and it should be avoided. Do not try to control your client, and do not allow yourself to be controlled. Allow your client his own point of view, and listen to it.

Another tendency in relationships is to try to out-do, or one-up, your friend. This creates tension and can cause your client to feel threatened, neither of which adds to a healthy, productive business relationship. Try to avoid this snag by listening to your client and responding in terms of potential solutions to their problem.

Do You Pressure a True Friend?

Would you pressure a true friend to buy from you? If you do, whose interest is first, your self-interest or your business friend's needs? Would you be tempted to pressure your friend to buy? Most of us would. Yet to maintain a healthy and lasting business relationship, the needs of the people you serve should come before your own self-interest. However difficult it may be in practice, you should never abandon the effort to put others' interests before yours. Does this relate to any of your personal relationships?

What Is Most Important? Refer again to Exhibit 14.2 to review the nine personal characteristics needed to build long-term business relationships. The most important ingredients in building a lasting friendship are truly caring for the other person and placing their interests before your interests. Friendship is based on their needs, not on your needs. Otherwise it will not work. Why?

If a friendship is based on your needs, at times you will take advantage of your so-called friend. True friendship, instead, is based upon how you can help the other person. This makes it possible to build a relationship! Am I this person's friend because I need something from him or her? If so, at times your feelings may be hurt, such as when the person buys from a competitor. This is why you want to be a friend without expecting something in return.

How Many Friends?

A wise old proverb says a person with too many friends comes to ruin. If you have many friends, your friendships become broad but not deep. In this case, when the going gets tough, they get going. Will they stick by you no matter what? Will you stick by them no matter what?

Friends are wonderful! Real friends are one of the greatest assets you have in your life. Yet three true, intimate business friends may be all you can handle and have time for. This is not talking about casual business acquaintances, but true intimate friendships.

RELATIONSHIP MARKETING AND CUSTOMER RETENTION

Salespeople deal directly with customers. Others in the salespeople's organization usually do not, and thus they think in general terms about customers. There are three levels of customer relationship marketing:

- *Transaction selling:* the salesperson sells to customers and does not contact them again.
- *Relationship selling:* after the purchase the seller finds out if the customer is satisfied and has future needs.
- *Partnering:* the seller works continually to improve the customer's operations, sales, and profits.

Take a moment to compare transaction selling, relationship selling, and partnering to the three levels of business friendship. Do you see any similarities? Becoming a partner takes time just as developing an intimate friendship does. It takes time to build a personal, sales, and marketing friendship between seller and buyer. Let's take a moment to review relationship marketing in an effort to better understand the importance of follow-up and service, ways of keeping customers, methods of helping customers increase sales, and how to handle customer complaints.

Relationship Marketing Builds Friendships

Relationship marketing is the creation of customer loyalty and retention. Organizations use combinations of products, prices, distribution, promotions, and service to achieve this goal. Relationship marketing is based on the idea that important customers need continuous attention.

An organization using relationship marketing is not seeking simply a sale or a transaction. It has targeted a major customer that it would like to sell to now and in the future. The company would like to demonstrate to the customer that it has the capabilities to serve the account's needs in a superior way, particularly if a *committed relationship* can be formed. The company's goal is to get customers and more important, to retain customers. Customer relationship marketing provides the key to retaining customers.

THE PRODUCT AND ITS SERVICE COMPONENT

When a customer buys a product, what is being purchased? Remember from Chapter 2 that a product (good or service) is a bundle of tangible and intangible attributes, including packaging, color, and brand, plus the services and even the reputation of the seller. People buy more than a set of physical attributes. They buy want-satisfaction such as what the product does, its quality, and the image of owning the product.

Please note the phrase *plus the services.* Buyers usually believe an organization ought to deliver a certain level of service to the customers when they purchase something. Here are several expected services:

- Product—the product purchased has no defects.
- Price—fair value for the price.
- Place—the product is available when and where needed and promised.
- Promotion—correct, honest information in advertisements, from salespeople, and on product labels.
- Exchange transaction—handled correctly, quickly, and professionally the first time.
- After the sale—warranty honored, repairs or exchanges made cheerfully; written information or company representative available to discuss how to put together, hook up, or use the product.

When buying something, you have certain expectations of what you are receiving for your money. So do organizations. Did the customer receive what was expected? The answer to this question determines the level of service quality perceived by the buyer.

Customer service refers to the activities and programs the seller provides to make the relationship satisfying for the customer. The activities and programs add value to the customer's relationship with the seller. Warranties, credit, speedy delivery, invoices, financial statements, computer-to-computer ordering, parking, gift wrapping, and having items in stock are services designed to satisfy customers.

Expectations Determine Service Quality

The quality of service an organization and its salespeople provide must be based on its customers' expectations. Customers expect a certain level of service from the seller. Their expectations frequently are based on information the salesperson provides, past experiences, word of mouth, and personal needs.

When buyers perceive service received as what they expected, or more, they are satisfied. Thus, service quality must match the customers' perception of how well the service provided meets their expectations.

CUSTOMER SATISFACTION AND RETENTION

Customer satisfaction also relates to met expectations. **Customer satisfaction** refers to feelings toward the purchase. As illustrated in Exhibit 14.4, perceived purchase satisfaction reflects the customer's feelings about any differences between what is expected and actual experiences with the purchase. If satisfied, chances of selling to the customer in the future increase. If satisfied with repeat purchases, customers tend to continue to buy from the salesperson.

EXHIBIT 14.4

Customer retention occurs when the buyer is satisfied with purchases over time.

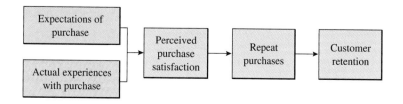

Satisfaction can result in a customer so loyal that it is very difficult for another seller to get the business. Thus, customer retention is critical to a salesperson's long-run success.

EXCELLENT CUSTOMER SERVICE AND SATISFACTION REQUIRE TECHNOLOGY

Providing good service to customers in today's competitive marketplace is not enough—service must be excellent. Excellent service often requires technology and automation. Here is an example of how companies are improving customer service.[1]

For the Livingston Group, a Toronto-based logistics company that sells such services as freight forwarding and distribution to importers and exporters, the question was how to spend no more than $80,000 to make their eight salespeople more effective in working with their customers. The division's goals were (1) to make account executives accessible to customers and each other no matter where they were; (2) to create presentations on the road that could be shared internally; and (3) to be sure account executives could manage their accounts easily while eliminating the administrative tasks that take up considerable selling time.

InteGain set up the following integrated application for Livingston Group: Each account executive received an IBM Thinkpad, loaded with GoldMine for Windows Software (produced by ELAN Software Corporation of Pacific Palisades, California), Microsoft Windows for WorkGroups 3.11, WinFax Pro 4.0, and WinCIM (which allows access to CompuServe). They each also received a Hewlett-Packard DeskJet portable printer and a Nokia portable telephone. Each account executive was equipped with the MyLine telephone service from Call America Business Communications based in San Luis Obispo, California. This service provides account executives with their own 800 numbers and directly connects inbound calls to them wherever they are via their portable or home office phones.

The program works like this: At the end of each business day, account executives use their laptops to send new data or presentations collected and created during the day to a CompuServe mailbox. As part of an automated process, a system at Livingston Trade Technologies' home office automatically dials into this CompuServe mailbox, retrieves the uploaded information, consolidates it, prepares reports, and redistributes the consolidated information to each of the executives in several minutes. InteGain's integrated application is called TARGET.

Automating allows salespeople to work independently out of their cars and to spend less time on administrative tasks. And, because management is kept informed, it can make quick decisions on facts relating to customer service.

SO, HOW DOES SERVICE INCREASE YOUR SALES?

Take a look at Exhibit 14.5. By now you are very familiar with it! Now what's the answer to the heading question?

You—the salesperson—increase sales by obtaining new customers and selling more products to present customers. What is the best method for obtaining new customers? For many types of sales, customer referrals are best! Customers provide referrals when they are satisfied with the salesperson. So how important is it to your success and livelihood to take care of your customers? Even though it is last in the selling process, step 10 is extremely important to a salesperson's success.

What has occurred after you have completed Step 9 of Exhibit 14.5 and are no longer with the customer? You have either made or not made a sale. Now what do

EXHIBIT 14.5

Sales come from present and new customers, Salespeople are constantly involved in follow-up and service, plus planning their next sales call on the customer; they also spend time prospecting.

1. Prospecting

2. Preapproach

3. Approach

4. Presentation

5. Trial close

6. Determine objections

7. Meet objections

8. Trial close

9. Close

10. Follow–up

The circular relationship in managing a sales call.

you do? You evaluate why you made the sale or did not make the sale. Why? It prepares you for making the next sales call.

Salespeople are continually planning, implementing, and evaluating their purpose, plans, and success for contacting each customer. Wow, is this important to your success in sales and in the classroom!

As also illustrated in Exhibit 14.5, after Step 10 of the selling process the salesperson moves back to the second step, or preapproach, when it's time to plan the next sales call on a customer or prospect. Meanwhile, the salesperson also is prospecting if needed in his or her type of sales. Thus, the salesperson is involved in the ongoing process of finding new customers and taking care of present customers. With this review in mind, let's discuss several service and follow-up techniques next.

TURN FOLLOW-UP AND SERVICE INTO A SALE

High-performing salespeople can convert follow-up and service situations into sales (see Exhibit 14.6). Jack Pruett of Bailey Banks & Biddle, a jewelry retailer, gives several examples:

I send customers a thank-you card immediately after the sale, and after two weeks, I call again to thank them and see if they are pleased with their purchase. If the purchase is a gift, I wait on contacting the customer or contact the spouse. This has been a key to my success in building a relationship and in farming or prospecting. Very often I get a lead.

Here is how it works. In two weeks they have shown it around to someone who has made a comment. I start with, "Is everything OK?" Then I say. "Well, I know

Follow-up is critical for
ensuring that the customer is
satisfied.

Here, a sales rep follows up her sale with a fax describing additional uses for the
product before catching her plane to meet another customer.

*If you don't take care
of the customer . . .
somebody else will.*

STANLEY MARCUS

Judy [or Jack] is real proud of it, and I'm sure she's [he's] shown it to someone—
parents, family, friends. I was curious if there is anyone I could help who is
interested in something. I'd like to talk to them or have you call and see if they'd
like me to call them." If I've done a good job, the customer feels good about letting
me call this individual and will help me. If I wait too long to call, they say. "Well,
someone was asking about it, but I've forgotten who it was."

My biggest sale to a single customer was $120,000. It took about two weeks.
A man initially called asking for 12 diamonds to give 2 stones to each of his children.
In handling this, I found some other pieces I felt were good for him—a ruby ring,
a 4.62 sapphire ring, a gold and diamond bracelet, and two other rings. He bought
everything. Thus, much of my success comes from follow-ups, suggestion selling
[when someone comes in for something and they buy other things], or service
situations. Once you realize you can turn routine situations into sales, retail selling
becomes exciting and challenging.[2]

Pruett realizes follow-up and service help satisfy the needs of his customers.
Another way to help customers involves account penetration.

ACCOUNT PENETRATION IS A SECRET TO SUCCESS

Follow-up and service create goodwill between a salesperson and the customer,
which increases sales faster than a salesperson who does not provide such service.
By contacting the customer after the sale to see that the maximum benefit is derived

from the purchase, a salesperson lays the foundation for a positive business relationship. Emmett Reagan of Xerox says:

> Remember that there is still much work to be done after making the sale. Deliveries must be scheduled, installation planned, and once the system is operational, we must monitor to assure that our product is doing what is represented. This activity gives us virtually unlimited access to the account, which moves us automatically back to the first phase of the cycle. We now have the opportunity to seek out new needs, develop them, and find new problems that require solutions. Only this time, it's a lot easier because, by now, we have the most competitive edge of all, a satisfied customer.[3]

The ability to work and contact people throughout the account, discussing your products, is referred to as *account penetration.* Successful penetration of an account allows you to properly service that account by uncovering its needs and problems. Achieving successful account penetration is dependent on knowledge of that account's key personnel and their situation. If you do not have a feel for an account's situation, you reduce chances of maximizing sales in that account.

Tailor the presentation to meet buyers' objectives and benefit them. By knowing your buyers, their firms, and other key personnel, you uncover their needs or problems and develop a presentation that fulfills the needs or solves the problems. Account penetration is determined by several factors:

- Your total and major-brand sales growth in an account.
- Distribution of the number of products in a product line, including sizes used or merchandised by an account.
- Level of cooperation obtained, such as reduced resale prices, shelf space, advertising and display activity, discussion with their salespeople, and freedom to visit with various people in the account.
- Your reputation as the authority on your type of merchandise for the buyer.

As a general rule, the greater your account penetration, the greater your chances of maximizing sales within the account. Earning the privilege to move around the account freely allows you to better uncover prospect needs and to discuss your products with people throughout the firm. As people begin to know you and believe that you are there to help, they allow you to take action that ultimately increases sales, such as increasing shelf space or talking with the users of your industrial equipment in the account's manufacturing facilities. A good sign that you have successfully penetrated an account is when a competitor dismally says, "Forget that account; it's already sewn up." You have created true customer loyalty.

SERVICE CAN KEEP YOUR CUSTOMERS

You work days, weeks, and sometimes months to convert prospects into customers. What can you do to ensure that they buy from you in the future? After landing a major account, consider these six factors:

Some succeed because they are destined to. Most succeed because they are determined to.

1. Concentrate on improving your account penetration. As discussed earlier, account penetration is critical in uncovering prospect needs or problems and consistently recommending effective solutions through purchasing your products. This allows you to demonstrate that you have a customer's best interests at heart and are there to help.
2. Contact new accounts frequently and on a regular schedule. In determining the frequency of calls, consider

Can Someone Please Help Me?

Customer: May I speak to Frank, please? I want to reorder.

Supplier: Frank isn't with us anymore. May someone else help you?

Customer: What happened to Frank? He has all my specs; I didn't keep a record.

Supplier: Let me give you Roger; he's taken over Frank's accounts.

Customer: Roger, you don't know me, but maybe Frank filled you in. I want to reorder.

Salesperson: You want to reorder what?

Customer: I want to repeat the last order, but increase your number 067 to 48.

Salesperson: What else was in the order?

Customer: Frank had a record of it. It's got to be in his file.

Salesperson: Frank isn't here anymore, and I don't have his records.

Customer: Who does?

Salesperson: I don't know. I'm new here, so you'll have to fill me in on your requirements. Are you a new customer?

Customer: Does four years make me new?

Salesperson: Well, sir, you are new to me. How long ago did you place your order?

Customer: Last month.

Salesperson: What day last month?

Customer: I don't remember; Frank always kept track of it. Maybe I could speak to the sales manager?

Salesperson: You mean Mort?

Customer: No, I think his name is Sam.

Salesperson: Sam left us about the same time as Frank. I can ask Mort to call you, but I'm sure he doesn't have your file either.

Customer: Roger, have you ever heard that your best prospect is your present customer?

Salesperson: Is that true?

Customer: I don't think so.

Multiply this conversation by the millions of times it happens each year, and you have the biggest deterrent to sales in America.

- Current sales and/or potential future sales to the account.
- Number of orders expected in a year.
- Number of product lines sold to the account.
- Complexity, servicing, and redesign requirements of the products the account purchases.

Because the amount of time spent servicing an account may vary from minutes to days, be flexible in developing a call frequency for each customer. Typically, invest sales time in direct proportion to the actual or potential sales represented by each account. The most productive number of calls is reached at the point at which additional calls do not increase sales to the customer. This relationship of sales volume to sales calls is referred to as the *response function* of the customer to the salesperson's calls.

3. Handle customers' complaints promptly. This is an excellent opportunity to prove to customers that they and their businesses are important, and that you sincerely care about them. The speed with which you handle even the most trivial complaint shows the value you place on that customer.

4. Always do what you say you will do. Nothing destroys a relationship with a customer faster than not following through on promises. Professional buyers do not tolerate promises made and subsequently broken. They have placed their

Advertising helps inform customers of the service salespeople provide.

faith (and sometimes reputation) in you by purchasing your products, so you must be faithful to them to ensure future support.

5. Provide service as you would to royalty. By providing your client with money-saving products and problem-solving ideas, you can become almost indispensable. You are an advisor to listen to rather than an adversary to haggle with. Provide all possible assistance. As State Farm insurance agent Catherine Irons says in Exhibit 14.7, "We're there to help."

6. Show your appreciation. A buyer once said to a salesperson, "I'm responsible for putting the meat and potatoes on your table." Customers contribute to your success, and in return, you must show appreciation. Thank them for their business and do them favors. Here are several suggestions:

- Although you may be hundreds of miles away, phone immediately whenever you've thought of something or seen something that may solve one of your customer's problems. See Exhibit 14.8.
- Mail clippings that may interest your customers even if the material has no bearing on what you're selling. They could be items from trade journals, magazines, newspapers, or newsletters.
- Write congratulatory notes to customers who have been elected to office, promoted to higher positions, given awards, and so on.
- Send newspaper clippings about your customers' families such as marriages, births, and activities.

EXHIBIT 14.8

Three fast and inexpensive tools for customer follow-up and service are the fax machine, the telephone, and e-mail.

- Send holiday or special-occasion cards. If you limit yourself to just one card for the entire year, send an Easter card, Fourth of July card, or a Thanksgiving card. This makes a big impression on customers.
- Send annual birthday cards. To start this process, subtly discover when your prospects were born.
- Prepare and mail a brief newsletter, perhaps quarterly, that keeps customers informed on important matters.
- Fax and/or e-mail information to prospects and buyers (see Exhibit 14.8).

These are just a few of the many practical, down-to-earth ways you can remember customers. The important point is to personalize whatever you send.

Specifically, it doesn't take much thought, energy, or time to send a card, newspaper clipping, or copy of an article. The secret to impressing customers is to personalize the material with a couple of sentences in your handwriting. Be sure it's legible!

YOU LOSE A CUSTOMER—KEEP ON TRUCKING

Build bridges, not walls.

All salespeople suffer losses, either through the loss of a sale or an entire account to a competitor. Four things can win back a customer:

1. Visit and investigate. Contact the buyer and your friends within the account to determine why the customer did not buy from you. Find out the real reason.
2. Be professional. If you have lost the customer to a competitor completely, let the customer know you have appreciated past business, that you still value the customer's friendship, and that you are still friendly. Remember to assure this lost account that you are ready to earn future business.
3. Don't be unfriendly. Never criticize the competing product that your customer has purchased. If it was a bad decision, let the customer discover it. Sales is never having to say, "I told you so!"
4. Keep calling. Treat a former customer like a prospect. Continue to make calls normally; present your product's benefits without directly comparing them to the competition.

Like a professional athlete, a professional salesperson takes defeat gracefully, moves on to the next contest, and performs so well that victories overshadow losses.

One method of compensating for the loss of an account is to increase sales to existing accounts.

RETURNED GOODS MAKE YOU A HERO

One of the best ways to help customers is through careful examination of merchandise you have sold in the past to see if it is old, out-of-date, or unsalable due to damage. If any of these conditions exist, the salesperson should cheerfully return the merchandise following the company's returned goods policies.

HANDLE COMPLAINTS FAIRLY

Customers may be dissatisfied with products for any number of reasons:

- The product delivered is a different size, color, or model than the one ordered.
- The quantity delivered is less than the quantity ordered—the balance is back-ordered (to be delivered when available).
- The product does not arrive by the specified date.
- Discounts (trade or promotional payment, see Chapter 6) agreed on are not rendered by the manufacturer.
- The product does not have a feature or perform a function that the customer believed it would.
- The product is not of the specified grade or quality (does not meet agreed-on specifications).

Whenever you determine that the customer's complaint is honest, make a settlement that is fair to the customer. Customers actually may be wrong, but if they honestly believe they are right, no amount of haggling or arguing will convince them otherwise. A valued account can be lost through temperamental outbursts.

IS THE CUSTOMER ALWAYS RIGHT?

So you might ask, "Is the customer always right?" Many academics and industry people feel the answer to the question is "yes." What do you think? Is the customer always right? You might say "yes" because this book has stressed that the salesperson put the interest of the customer first.

Always is the key word in this phrase. What if the customer wanted the salesperson to do something illegal or unethical? What if a customer demanded that a seller provide illegal price kickbacks? What if a customer requested terms that would produce results harmful to the employer, yet beneficial to customer?

Salespeople are often placed in positions of determining what is right and what is wrong. As discussed in Chapter 3, it is critically important to have a fixed frame of reference for making morally ethical decisions. While others will disagree, your author feels the customer is *not* always right.

This Customer Is Not in the Right!

Occasionally, a dishonest customer may require you and your company not to honor a request. Retailer A once purchased some of my firm's merchandise from Retailer B, who had a fire sale and eventually went out of business. Retailer A insisted he purchased it from me and that I return close to $1,000 of damaged goods to my company for full credit. He actually had paid 10 cents on the dollar for it at the fire sale. I told Retailer A that I would have to obtain permission from the company to return such a large amount of damaged goods.

That afternoon, a competitive salesperson told me that Retailer A had asked him to do the same thing. I informed my sales manager of the situation. He investigated the matter and found out about Retailer B, who sold most of his merchandise to Retailer A—who happened to be my customer. I went back and confronted Retailer A with this and said it was company policy only to return merchandise that was purchased directly from me. This was a rare situation; yet you must occasionally make similar judgments considering company policy and customer satisfaction.

Customers should get the benefit of the doubt. Always have a plan for problem solving. Some procedures you can use include these:

- Obtain as much relevant information from your customer as possible.
- Express sincere regret for the problem.
- Display a service attitude (a true desire to help).
- Review your sales records to make sure the customer purchased the merchandise.
- If the customer is right, quickly and cheerfully handle the complaint.
- Follow up to make sure the customer is satisfied.

Take care of your customers—especially large accounts. They are difficult to replace and are critical to success. When you take care of accounts, they take care of you. However, the salesperson does need to be prepared to handle the demands of a dishonest customer.

Dress in Your Armor

Use a double-edged sword with customers.

Each day before leaving for work, the salesperson should prepare to meet a few unethical and dishonest people. This requires a person to have tough skin, even armor. To withstand the attacks of unethical prospects and customers requires speaking the truth, being prepared to do what is right, readiness to discuss what is the ethical action, and trust that you are doing right. These traits will save the salesperson from doing something that is illegal or unethical.

The salesperson is often required to use a double-edged sword in dealing with customers. One edge represents dealing with the ethical customer. It is used to cut through the red tape that might hinder proper servicing of the customer, such as speeding up delivery.

You may need to use the other edge of the sword to cut ties to dishonest or morally unethical customers. Occasionally a prospect or customer may lie, cheat, steal, or want the seller to do something that is morally wrong or unethical. The salesperson's attitudes and actions should exemplify the proper way to do business. The salesperson serves as a role model to all encountered during the day. By conducting oneself so as to set an example worthy of imitation by your spouse, children, grandmother, and others, you will be seen as a person of integrity and character. This helps build professionalism.

BUILD A PROFESSIONAL REPUTATION

This book stresses the concept of sales professionalism. Sales professionalism directly implies that you are a professional person—due the respect and ready for the responsibilities that accompany the title. In speaking before a large class of marketing students, one sales manager for a large college textbook publishing company continually emphasized the concept of sales professionalism. This man stated that a professional sales position is not just an 8-to-5 job. It is a professional and responsible position promising both unlimited opportunity and numerous duties.

This veteran sales manager emphasized that a sales job is an especially good vocational opportunity because people are looking for "someone we can believe in; someone who will do what she says—a sales professional."

To be viewed as a professional and respected by your customers and competitors, consider these eight important points:

- First, be truthful and follow through on what you tell the customer. Do not dispose of your conscience when you start work each day. See Exhibit 14.9.
- Second, maintain an intimate knowledge of your firm, its products, and your industry. Participate in your company's sales training and take continuing education courses.
- Third, speak well of others, including your company and competitors.
- Fourth, keep customer information confidential; maintain a professional relationship with each account.
- Fifth, never take advantage of a customer by using unfair, high-pressure techniques.
- Sixth, be active in community affairs and help better your community. For example, live in your territory, be active in public schools, and join worthwhile organizations such as the Lions Club, the Chamber of Commerce, environmental organizations, and so forth.
- Seventh, think of yourself as a professional and always act like one. Have a professional attitude about yourself and your customers.
- Eighth, provide service "above and beyond the call of duty." Remember that it is easier to maintain a relationship than to begin one. What was worth attaining is worth preserving. Remember, when you do not pay attention to customers, they find someone who will. The professional salesperson never forgets a customer after the sale.

DOS AND DON'TS FOR BUSINESS SALESPEOPLE

What do purchasing agents expect of business salespeople? A survey of purchasing agents showed that they expect results. The following list shows the most important traits that purchasing agents found in their top business salespeople:

- Willingness to go to bat for the buyer within the supplier's firm.
- Thoroughness and follow-through after the sale.
- Knowledge of the firm's product line.
- Market knowledge and willingness to "keep the buyer posted."
- Imagination in applying one's products to the buyer's needs.
- Knowledge of the buyer's product line.
- Preparation for sales calls.

EXHIBIT 14.9

A super sales success secret.

■ Think positively	. . . and follow up
■ Plan carefully	. . . and follow up
■ Present thoroughly	. . . and follow up
■ And follow up	. . . and follow up
. . . and follow up	. . . and follow up
. . . and follow up	. . . and follow up
. . . and follow up	. . . and follow up

I Appreciate Your Business

People buy from you for many reasons but primarily because of your excellent products and the service you and your company provide to customers. You follow the GOLDEN RULE: "Do unto others as you would have done unto you." You feel customers put the meat and potatoes on your table. They are responsible for the good income you earn. You appreciate that and always try to show how much you appreciate their trust and business.

You occasionally have been taking one of your customers, whom you like personally, out to lunch. Recently, this customer's purchases have increased from $50,000 to $650,000 a year. You want to show your appreciation by buying your customer two season tickets for the local professional basketball team. The buyer and his spouse are great basketball fans. However, if your other clients and co-workers find out, they may view the gift as unprofessional.

What would be the most ethical action to take?

1. Get a season ticket for yourself and for your client. That way, you can always justify it as a "business meeting" if people ask.

2. Buy your client and his wife the season tickets. You are just trying to show your appreciation for his business.

3. Do not buy the season tickets. It is unprofessional to mix work and social ties. Instead, write your client a nice thank-you letter stating that you appreciate his continued business.

- Regularity of sales calls.
- Diplomacy in dealing with operating departments.
- Technical education—knowledge of specifications and applications.

The survey also asked purchasing agents what they did not like salespeople to do during sales calls. The results, shown in Exhibit 14.10, are "The Seven Deadly Sins of Industrial Selling."[4] Purchasing agents want salespeople to act professionally, to be well trained, to be prepared for each sales call, and to keep the sales call related to *how the salesperson can help the buyer.*

Professional selling starts in the manufacturer's firm. A professional attitude from the manufacturer reinforces professionalism among the sales force. One such company is B. J. Hughes, a division of the Hughes Tool Company. B. J. Hughes manufactures and sells oil-field equipment and services to companies in the oil and gas industry. Exhibit 14.11 presents Hughes's checklists of *dos* and *don'ts* for their salespeople. By providing these checklists, the company encourages them to act professionally.[5]

THE PATH TO SALES SUCCESS: SEEK, KNOCK, ASK, SERVE

Seek, knock, ask, serve.

Selling is hard. Selling is not for everyone. Yet for those who have a pure heart to serve and hear the call to be a salesperson, it is a wonderful way of life. To follow the Golden Rule of Selling allows a person to serve others in a wonderful manner. So in any type of sales, please remember to:

1. Seek customers to serve and you will find them.
2. Knock and people will open their doors.
3. Ask and people will buy.
4. Provide service after the sale and customers will buy again.

EXHIBIT 14.10

The seven deadly sins of business selling.

1. *Lack of product knowledge.* Salespeople must know their own product line as well as the buyer's line or nothing productive can occur.
2. *Time wasting.* Unannounced sales visits are a nuisance. When salespeople start droning on about golf or grandchildren, more time is wasted.
3. *Poor planning.* A routine sales call must be preceded by some homework—see if it's necessary.
4. *Pushiness.* This includes prying to find out a competitor's prices, an overwhelming attitude, and backdoor selling.
5. *Lack of dependability.* Failure to stand behind the product, keep communications clear, and honor promises.
6. *Unprofessional conduct.* Knocking competitors, drinking excessively at a business lunch, sloppy dress, and poor taste aren't professional.
7. *Unlimited optimism.* Honesty is preferred to the hallmark of the good news bearers who promise anything to get an order. Never promise more than you can deliver.

Here are a few comments purchasing agents made on these deadly sins:

- They take it personally if they don't get the business; it's as though you owe them something because they constantly call on you.
- I don't like it when they blast through the front door like know-it-alls and put on an unsolicited dog-and-pony show that will guarantee cost saving off in limbo somewhere.
- Many salespeople will give you any delivery you want, book an order, and then let you face the results of their "short quote."
- They try to sell *you*, rather than the product.
- After the order is won, the honeymoon is over.
- Beware the humble pest who is too nice to insult, won't take a hint, won't listen to blunt advice, and is selling a product you neither use nor want to use, yet won't go away.

EXHIBIT 14.11

B. J. Hughes's checklists of dos and don'ts help it to be a customer-oriented company.

Salesperson's Checklist of Dos	Salesperson's Checklist of Dont's
1. Know the current products/services and their applications in your area. Look for the new techniques/services your customers want.	1. Never bluff; if you don't know, find out.
2. Maintain an up-to-date personal call list.	2. Never compromise your, or anyone else's, morals or principles.
3. Listen attentively to the customers.	3. Don't be presumptuous—never with friends.
4. Seek out specific problems and the improvements your customers want.	4. Never criticize a competitor—especially to a customer.
5. Keep calls short unless invited to stay.	5. Do not take criticisms or turndowns personally—they're seldom meant that way.
6. Leave a calling card if the customer is not in.	6. Do not worry or agonize over what you cannot control or influence. Be concerned about what you *can* affect.
7. Identify the individual who makes or influences decisions, and concentrate on that person.	7. Do not offend others with profanity.
8. Entertain selectively; your time and your expense account are investments.	8. Do not allow idle conversation to dominate your sales call. Concentrate on your purpose.
9. Make written notes as reminders.	9. Don't try to match the customer drink for drink when entertaining. Drink only if you want to and in moderation.
10. Plan work by the week, not by the clock. Plan use of available time. Plan sales presentation. Have a purpose.	10. Don't be so gung ho that you use high-pressure tactics.
11. Ask for business on every sales call.	11. Never talk your company down—especially to customers. Be proud of it and yourself.
12. Follow through with appropriate action.	12. If you smoke, never do so in the customer's office unless invited to smoke.

Hardship creates character.

Selling takes faith, focus, and follow-through—the three Fs. Never give up. Always continue to seek more knowledge, patience, wisdom, caring, and understanding of others' situations. Focus on caring for others' needs. This takes the spotlight off your challenges and struggles. Consider all hardships as character builders. Your character will grow as you endure the ups and downs of the sales life. If you take care of your character, your reputation will grow. In the end, you will be rewarded. It takes courage to stay the course when life gets hard and sales do not come. Yet success comes to the people who get up, even when they feel they cannot go on.

SUMMARY OF MAJOR SELLING ISSUES

Salespeople increase sales by obtaining new customers and selling more product to current customers. Customer referrals are the best way to find new prospects. Thus, it's important to provide excellent service and follow-up to customers. By building a relationship and partnership, you can provide a high level of customer service.

Customers expect service. When you deliver service, customers are satisfied and continue to buy; this results in retention and loyalty. Providing service to customers is important in all types of selling. Follow-up and service create goodwill between salesperson and customer that allows the salesperson to penetrate or work throughout the customer's organization. Account penetration helps the salesperson to better service the account and uncover its needs and problems. A service relationship with an account leads to increases in total and major brand sales, better distribution on all product sizes, and customer cooperation in promoting your products.

To serve customers best, improve account penetration. Contact each customer frequently and regularly; promptly handle all complaints. Always do what you say you will do, and remember to serve customers as if they were royalty. Finally, remember to sincerely thank all customers for their business, no matter how large or small, to show you appreciate them.

Should customers begin to buy from a competitor or reduce their level of cooperation, continue to call on them in your normal professional manner. In a friendly way, determine why they did not buy from you, and develop new customer benefit plans to recapture their business.

Always strive to help your customers increase their sales of your product or to get the best use from products that you have sold to them. To persuade a customer to purchase more of your products or use your products in a different manner, develop a sales program to help maximize sales to that customer. This involves developing an account penetration program; increasing the number and sizes of products the customer purchases; maintaining proper inventory levels in the customer's warehouse and on the shelf; achieving good shelf space and shelf positioning; clear communication with persons who directly sell or use a product; a willingness to assist wholesale and retail customers' salespeople in any way possible; a willingness to help customers; and an overall effort to develop a positive, friendly business relationship with each customer. By doing these eight things, your ability to help and properly service each customer increases.

Today's professional salesperson is oriented to service. Follow-up and service after the sale maximize your territory's sales and help attain personal goals.

MEETING A SALES CHALLENGE

What a tough situation! You have to keep servicing the equipment if you want to keep King Masonry as a customer. If the customer is misusing the mixer, causing it to break down, you must train the operators of the mixer and explain to Eldon King what is happening. Before saying anything to King, get his permission to talk with the mixer operators. Find out why the machine is breaking down.

KEY TERMS FOR SELLING

follow-up   446
proverb   447
knowledge   447
wisdom   447
business friendship   449
acquaintances   449

friends   450
intimate friends   450
customer service   453
customer satisfaction   453

SALES APPLICATION QUESTIONS

1. Compare the relationships between customer service and follow-up to a business relationship. Include in your answer why the customer's interest should come before the seller's.
2. What is account penetration? What benefits can a salesperson derive from it?
3. List and briefly explain the factors salespeople must consider to ensure that customers buy from them in the future.
4. What must a salesperson do after losing a customer?
5. A good way for a salesperson to create goodwill is by helping customers increase their sales. What steps should the salesperson attempting to increase customer sales take?
6. This chapter discussed several reasons why a salesperson must project a professional image. Why is being a sales professional so important?
7. Return to Exhibit 14.10, the seven deadly sins of business selling. Think of an experience you had with a salesperson who displayed a poor sales image. How did the salesperson's attitude affect your purchase decision?
8. You have just learned that one of your customers, Tom's Discount Store, has received a shipment of faulty goods from your warehouse. The total cost of the merchandise is $2,500. Your company has a returned-goods policy that only allows you to return $500 worth of your product at one time unless a reciprocal order is placed. What would you do?

   a. Call Tom's and tell them you will be out to inspect the shipment in a couple of days.
   b. Ask Tom's to patch up what they can and sell it at a reduced cost in an upcoming clearance sale.
   c. Send the merchandise back to your warehouse and credit Tom's account for the price of the damaged goods.
   d. Go to Tom's as soon as possible that day, check the shipment to see if there are any undamaged goods that can be put on the shelf, take a replacement order from Tom's manager, and phone in the order immediately.
   e. Call your regional sales manager and ask what to do.

FURTHER EXPLORING THE SALES WORLD

1. Contact the person in charge of the health and beauty aids department of a local supermarket. In an interview with this person, ask questions to determine what service activities salespeople perform in the department. For example, do

they build product displays, put merchandise on the shelves, straighten products on the shelves, and keep a record of how much product is in the store? Also, determine how the department head feels salespeople can provide the best service.

2. Contact the person in charge of marketing in a local bank. Report on the role that service plays in attracting and retaining bank customers.

SELLING EXPERIENTIAL EXERCISE

Providing excellent customer service often requires a special person—someone who quietly enjoys interacting with people even when they are upset. To help you better understand yourself, respond to each statement by placing the number that best describes your answer on a separate sheet of paper.

1 Never   2 Rarely   3 Sometimes   4 Usually   5 Often

What's Your Attitude toward Customer Service?

1. I accept people without judging them.
2. I show patience, courtesy, and respect to people regardless of their behavior toward me.
3. I maintain my composure and refuse to become irritated or frustrated when coping with an angry or irate person.
4. I treat people as I would want them to treat me.
5. I help others maintain their self-esteem, even when the situation requires negative or critical feedback.
6. I do not get defensive when interacting with other persons, even if their comments are directed at me.
7. I realize that my attitude toward myself and others affects the way I respond in any given situation.
8. I realize that each person believes his or her problem is the most important and urgent thing in the world at this time, and I attempt to help each one resolve it immediately.
9. I treat everyone in a positive manner, regardless of how they look, dress, or speak.
10. I view every interaction with another person as a golden moment, and I do everything in my power to make it a satisfactory win–win situation for both of us.

Total Score

Total your score: If your score is more than 40 you have an excellent service attitude; if it is 30–40, you could use improvement; and if you scored less than 30, you need an attitude adjustment.[6]

CHAPTER 14

Service and Follow-Up for Customer Retention

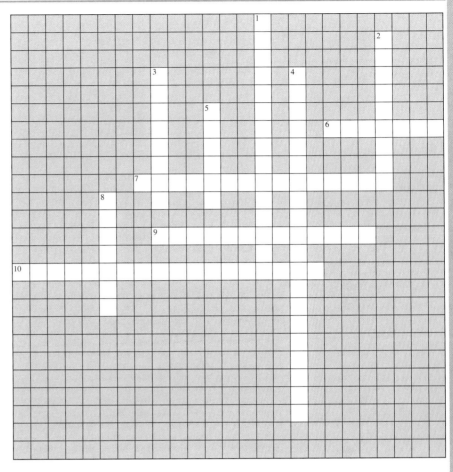

Across

6. People known for some time and with whom we share common interests and/or hobbies.

7. Activities and programs provided by the seller to make the relationship satisfying for the customer.

9. People you know little about.

10. The relationship formed between a salesperson and client that revolves around business-related issues.

Down

1. People known on a deeper, more personal level than a friend.

2. Knowing something gained through experience and/or training.

3. Maintaining contact with a customer (or prospect) in order to evaluate the effectiveness of the product and the satisfaction of the customer.

4. Feelings toward the purchase.

5. Ability to make good use of knowledge.

8. A short, wise, easy-to-learn saying that calls a person to think and act.

CASE 14-1

California Adhesives
Corporation

Marilyn Fowler recently became a sales representative for the California Adhesives Corporation and covers the states of Oregon and Washington. After completing a three-week training program, Marilyn was excited about the responsibility of reversing a downward sales trend in her territory, which had been without a salesperson for several months.

The previous salesperson was fired due to poor sales performance and had not left behind any information regarding accounts. After contacting her first 20 or so customers, Marilyn came to a major conclusion: None of these customers had seen a CAC salesperson for six to nine months; they had CAC merchandise, which was not selling, and they had damaged merchandise to return. These customers were hostile toward Marilyn because the previous salesperson had used high-pressure tactics to force them to buy, and as one person said, "Your predecessor killed your sales in my business. You said you would provide service and call on me regularly, but I don't care about service. In fact, it's OK with me if I never see anyone from your company again. Your competition's products are much better than yours, and their salespeople have been calling in this area for years trying to get my business." Marilyn was wondering if she had gone to work for the right company.

Questions

1. If you were Marilyn, what would you do to improve the sales in your territory?
2. How long would your effort take to improve sales, and would you *sell* it to your sales manager?

CASE 14-2

Sport Shoe Corporation

You are a salesperson for the Sport Shoe Corporation. At the office, there is a letter marked urgent on your desk. This letter is from the athletic director of Ball State University, and it pertains to the poor quality of basketball shoes that you sold to him. The director cited several examples of split soles and poor overall quality as his main complaints. In closing, he mentioned that since the season was nearing, he would be forced to contact the ACME Sport Shoe Company if the situation could not be rectified.

Question

What actions would be appropriate for you? Why?
a. Place a call to the athletic director assuring him of your commitment to service. Promise to be at Ball State at his convenience to rectify the problem.
b. Go by the warehouse and take the athletic director a new shipment of shoes and apologize for the delay and poor quality of the merchandise.
c. Write a letter to the athletic director assuring him that SSC sells only high-quality shoes and that this type of problem rarely occurs. Assure him you'll come to his office as soon as possible but if he feels ACME would be a better choice than Sport Shoe he should contact them.
d. Don't worry about the letter because the athletic director seems to have the attitude that he can put pressure on you by threatening to switch companies. Also, the loss in sales of 20 to 40 pairs of basketball shoes will be a drop in the bucket compared to the valuable sales time you would waste on a small account like Ball State.

CASE 14-3

Wingate Paper

Video

Case

George McGinnis, a marketer for Wingate Paper, is jogging with Tom Cagle.[7] Tom is a long-time distributor for Wingate Paper and has a good relationship with the company and its owners. George asks Tom about the status of the Orkand contract. Tom explains that he has nearly sold them on going with Wingate for all of their paper products needs, both administrative and production. George remarks that the Orkand contract could not have come at a better time. He has never seen Wingate squeeze the numbers so hard. He also states that he is counting on his bonus to pay his daughter's tuition. Tom admits that he needs this contract badly, as well, to pay off a bank loan.

In Wingate Paper's warehouse, George is talking with Kyle Cross, a new distributor. Kyle is impressed with Wingate Paper and informs Goerge that he is going after the Orkand account for Wingate and to establish himself in the business. He remarks that he knows Orkand is interested in Wingate Paper products. Kyle implies that he might win the account in part to help Orkand increase its minority contracting but that he does not want the decision to be based solely on that factor and is therefore offering them a 10 percent discount. George questions if Kyle knows that Tom Cagle has also been pitching Orkand. Kyle acknowledges that Tom is a good competitor, but he is confident of success because of the low price he offered.

A week later, Tom is complaining to George that he may lose the Orkand account because of Kyle Cross. Tom questions why George did not tell Kyle that the Orkand account was his, and George explains that Kyle is a legitimate competitor. Tom warns that Orkand may question the way Wingate Paper operates because of the two very different price quotes, but George reminds Tom that he cannot tell distributors what to charge.

Orkand has given Tom one week to meet Kyle's price, but Tom claims he cannot do it and tells George that he needs his help. First, Tom requests a price break, but George explains that he has to give all the distributors the same price. Next, Tom asks for a portion of the design fund for distributors, and George refutes this possibility, stating that the fund is only used for developing a product. Tom then wants part of the ad budget, but George explains the budget is already committed. Frustrated, Tom acknowledges that he undersands why George wants to do business with Kyle, but he threatens to take away his other accounts from Wingate Paper. George tries to salvage the situation, but Tom argues that George should remember about all the times he pushed Wingate Paper instead of other brands to help George get rid of inventory or promote a new line. George tries to express his appreciation for Tom's help, but Tom does not want appreciation, he wants money. He tells George to find a way to help him, if he really cares. George contemplates his decision.

Questions

1. What are the main ethical issues, if any, in the Wingate Paper case? Describe each ethical issue.
2. What are George's options?
3. How do the three levels of moral development relate to George's situation?
4. What would you do?

PART IV

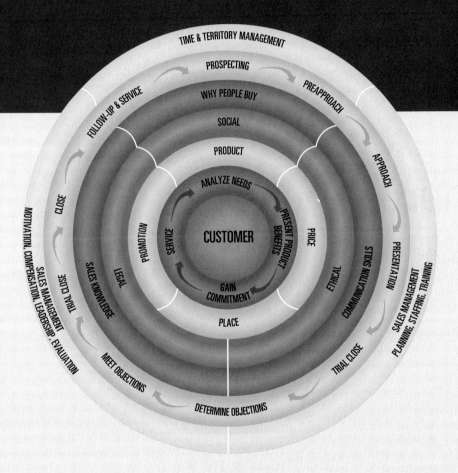

TIME & TERRITORY MANAGEMENT
PROSPECTING
PREAPPROACH
FOLLOW-UP & SERVICE
WHY PEOPLE BUY
SOCIAL
APPROACH
PRODUCT
CLOSE
ANALYZE NEEDS
PRESENT PRODUCT BENEFITS
PRICE
PROMOTION
SERVICE
CUSTOMER
SALES KNOWLEDGE
LEGAL
GAIN COMMITMENT
ETHICAL
PRESENTATION
TRIAL CLOSE
COMMUNICATION SKILLS
PLANNING, STAFFING, TRAINING
PLACE
MEET OBJECTIONS
TRIAL CLOSE
DETERMINE OBJECTIONS
SALES MANAGEMENT
MOTIVATION, COMPENSATION, LEADERSHIP, EVALUATION
SALES MANAGEMENT

MANAGING YOURSELF, YOUR CAREER, AND OTHERS

You see there is more to the sales profession than you might have imagined at the beginning of the book. You have been introduced to what it takes to be successful in sales and the many factors salespeople need to consider in serving customers. We have thoroughly covered the main steps in the selling process. By now you should be able to put together a "show and tell" sales presentation. This final part of the book introduces you to both territory and sales management. Chapter 15 discusses efficient use of time in identifying prospects and contacting customers in a sales territory. Chapters 16 and 17 provide you with an overview of what is involved in managing a sales force.

15

Time, Territory, and Self-Management: Keys to Success

MAIN TOPICS

The Tree of Business Life: Time

Customers Form Sales Territories

Elements of Time and Territory Management

LEARNING OBJECTIVES

A salesperson's ability to manage time and territory is important to success. After studying this chapter, you should be able to

■ Discuss the importance of the sales territory.

■ Explain the major elements involved in managing the sales territory.

■ Explain why salespeople need to segment their accounts by size.

■ Calculate a salesperson's break-even point per day, hour, and year.

474

"How can I manage my time to take better care of my customers?" thought Alice Jenson. "It seems each day I work I get further and further behind."

Alice had recently taken over the sales territory of Mike Batemen, who retired and moved across the country after 35 years of calling on customers. He kept all records in his head. Alice had to contact the 200 customers in the sales territory with no information other than their past sales. After several weeks, Alice had seen 95 percent of the customers once and 25 percent of them a second time. Two weeks ago, complaints started coming in that Alice had not followed up on her last calls or that she had not been back to see them.

Alice started telephoning people. That helped some, but customers wanted to see her. She almost stopped prospecting for new customers because she felt it was easier to keep a customer than get a new one. However, as sales started to decline, Alice realized customers were beginning to buy from her competitors.

Alice is in trouble and it is getting worse. What can you suggest Alice do to keep customers, have time to prospect, and increase sales?

Managing time and territory is one of the most important factors in selling. The "Facing a Sales Challenge" box illustrates that Alice is certainly having a challenging time doing all she needs to do in a day. Because of such things as the rapidly increasing cost of direct selling, decreasing time for face-to-face customer contact, continued emphasis on profitable sales, and the fact that time is always limited, it is no wonder that many companies are concentrating on improving how salespeople manage time and territory. Time is money. That is what this chapter is about—how to effectively use time.

THE TREE OF BUSINESS LIFE: TIME

Time is money because time is limited. There is only so much time in a day, week, month, year. People spend time doing what is most important in their lives. That is why living with "purpose" is the only way to really live. Everything else is just existing. You need purpose to get out of bed in the morning. You need purpose to get in your car and drive to see a stranger or someone you hardly know to try and help them. You need purpose in your life for guidance in your job.

Who am I? Do I matter? What is my purpose in life? What job is best for me? Why am I in this job? Serious questions we ask ourselves as we decide our purpose and how to spend the time in our lives and career in order to fulfill our purpose.

Today the average life span is 25,550 days. That's how long you will live if you are typical. Chances are you will work over 10,000 of those days as an adult in a full-time job. Don't you think it would be best to spend your time wisely? How you spend your time determines your life. It greatly influences the level of your success in sales—and school. Time encompasses the time spent with customers and your life activities. Using your life's time in a career to help others, and get paid for it, results in a wonderful life. Using ethical service as a guide for actions allows one to spend time doing what one loves. It allows you to find your purpose.

CUSTOMERS FORM SALES TERRITORIES

A **sales territory** comprises a group of customers or a geographical area assigned to a salesperson. The territory may or may not have geographical boundaries. Typically, however, a salesperson is assigned to a geographical area containing present and potential customers.

Why Establish Sales Territories?

Companies develop and use sales territories for numerous reasons. Next, we discuss the seven important reasons listed in Exhibit 15.1.

To Obtain Thorough Coverage of the Market

With proper coverage of territories, a company will reach the sales potential of its markets. The salesperson analyzes the territory and identifies customers. At the individual territory level, the salesperson better meets customers' needs. Division into territories also allows management to easily realign territories as customers and sales increase or decrease.

To Establish Each Salesperson's Responsibilities

The more I know, the more I realize the less I know.

Salespeople act as business managers for their territories. They are responsible for maintaining and generating sales volume. Salespeople's tasks are defined clearly. They know where customers are located and how often to call on them. They also know what performance goals are expected. This can raise the salesperson's performance and morale.

To Evaluate Performance

Performance is monitored for each territory. Actual performance data are collected, analyzed, and compared to expected performance goals. Individual territory performance is compared to district performance, district performance compared to regional performance, and regional performance compared to the performance of the entire sales force. With computerized reporting systems, the salesperson and a manager can monitor individual territory and customer sales to determine the success of selling efforts.

To Improve Customer Relations

Customer goodwill and increased sales are expected when customers receive regular calls. From the customer's viewpoint, the salesperson is, for example, Procter & Gamble. The customer looks to the salesperson, not to Procter & Gamble's corporate office, when making purchases. Over the years, some salespeople build such goodwill with customers that prospects will delay placing orders because they know

EXHIBIT 15.1

Reasons companies develop and use sales territories.

- To obtain thorough coverage of the market.
- To establish each salesperson's responsibilities.
- To evaluate performance.
- To improve customer relations.
- To reduce sales expense.
- To allow better matching of salesperson to customer's needs.
- To benefit both salespeople and the company.

the salesperson will be at their business on a certain day or at a specific time of the month. Some salespeople even earn the right to order merchandise for certain customers.

To Reduce Sales Expense

Sales territories are designed to avoid duplicating efforts so that two salespeople do not travel in the same area. This lowers selling cost and increases company profits. Such benefits as fewer travel miles and fewer overnight trips, plus regular contact with productive customers by the same salesperson can improve the firm's sales-to-cost ratio.

To Allow Better Matching of Salesperson to Customer's Needs

Salespeople are hired and trained to meet the requirements of the customers in a territory. Often, the more similar the customer and the salesperson, the more likely the sales effort will succeed.

To Benefit Both Salespeople and the Company

Proper territory design aids in reaching the firm's sales objectives. Thus, the company can maximize its sales effort, while the sales force can work in territories that allow them to satisfy personal needs, such as a good salary.

Why Sales Territories May Not Be Developed

In spite of advantages, there are disadvantages to developing sales territories for some companies, such as in the real estate or insurance industries. First, salespeople may be more motivated if not restricted by a particular territory; they can develop customers anywhere. In the chemical industry, for example, salespeople may sell to any potential customer. However, after the sale is made, other company salespeople are not allowed to contact that client.

Second, the company may be too small to be concerned with segmenting the market into sales areas. Third, management may not want to take the time, or may not have the know-how for territory development. Fourth, personal friendships may be the basis for attracting customers. For example, life insurance salespeople may first sell policies to their families and friends. However, most companies establish territories, such as the one assigned to Alice Jenson in "Facing a Sales Challenge."

ELEMENTS OF TIME AND TERRITORY MANAGEMENT

For the salesperson, time and territory management (TTM) is a continuous process of planning, executing, and evaluating the sales and service provided to customers. By completing each of the seven key elements involved in time and territory management, as shown in Exhibit 15.2, the salesperson ensures customers will be provided excellent service. Additionally, prospects will be found in the territory that many eventually become customers.

Building relationships with customers requires spending time with them. As discussed in Chapter 14, a good business friendship is like a personal friendship. Time is required to get to know each customer and his/her needs. But there is only so much time in the day, week, month, and year. This requires you to make the hard decision on how to spend your business time. Using the Golden Rule of Selling as

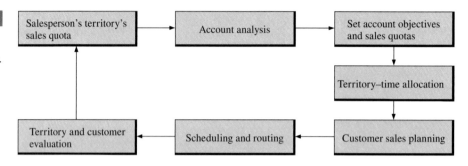

EXHIBIT 15.2

Elements of time and territory management for the salesperson.

a guide in creating your strategic plan for your territory, you will find these seven elements will help increase sales by obtaining new customers and selling more to present customers. The first step is to set goals or quotas.

Salesperson's Sales Quota

A salesperson is responsible for generating sales in a territory based on its sales potential. The salesperson's manager typically establishes the total sales quota that each salesperson is expected to reach.

Once this quota is set, it is the salesperson's responsibility to develop territorial sales plans for reaching the quota. Although there is no best planning sequence to follow, Exhibit 15.2 presents seven factors to consider in properly managing the territory for reaching its sales quota.

Account Analysis

Once a sales goal is set, the salesperson must analyze each prospect and customer to maximize the chances of reaching that goal. First, a salesperson should identify all prospects and present customers. Second, a salesperson should estimate present customers' and prospects' sales potential. This makes it possible to allocate time between customers, to decide what products to emphasize for a specific customer, and to better plan the sales presentation.

Two general approaches to **account analysis**—identifying accounts and their varying levels of sales potential—are the undifferentiated selling approach and the account segmentation approach.

The Undifferentiated Selling Approach

An organization may see the accounts in its market as similar. When this happens and selling strategies are designed and applied equally to all accounts, the salesperson uses an **undifferentiated selling** approach. Notice in Exhibit 15.3 that the salesperson aims a single selling strategy at all accounts. The basic assumption underlying this approach is that the account needs for a specific product or group of products are similar. Salespeople call on all potential accounts, devoting equal selling time to each of them. The same sales presentation may be used in selling an entire product line. The salesperson feels he/she can satisfy most customers with a single selling strategy. For example, many door-to-door salespeople use the same selling strategies with each person they contact (a stimulus–response sales presentation).

Salespeople whose accounts have homogeneous needs and characteristics may find this approach useful. The undifferentiated selling approach was popular in the past, and some firms still use it. However, many salespeople feel that their accounts have different needs and represent different sales and profit potentials. This makes an account segmentation approach desirable.

EXHIBIT 15.3

Undifferentiated selling
approach.

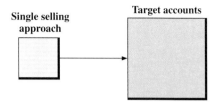

EXHIBIT 15.4

Account segmentation based on
yearly sales.

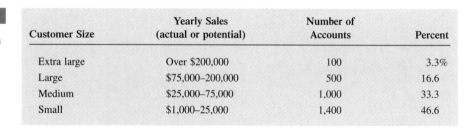

Customer Size	Yearly Sales (actual or potential)	Number of Accounts	Percent
Extra large	Over $200,000	100	3.3%
Large	$75,000–200,000	500	16.6
Medium	$25,000–75,000	1,000	33.3
Small	$1,000–25,000	1,400	46.6

The Account Segmentation Approach

Salespeople using the **account segmentation** approach recognize that their territories contain accounts with heterogeneous needs and differing characteristics that require different selling strategies. Consequently, they develop sales objectives based on overall sales and sales of each product for each customer and prospect. Past sales to the account, new accounts, competition, economic conditions, price and promotion offerings, new products, and personal selling are among the key elements in the analysis of accounts and territories.

Salespeople classify customers to identify profitable ones. This classification determines where the salesperson's time is invested. One method of segmenting accounts is by

1. Key account.
   a. Buys over $200,000 from us annually.
   b. Loss of this customer would substantially affect the territory's sales and profits.
2. Unprofitable account.
   a. Buys less than $1,000 from us annually.
   b. Little potential to increase purchases to more than $1,000.
3. Regular account.
   a. All other customers.

The salesperson would not call on the unprofitable accounts. The **key accounts** and regular accounts become target customers.

Once the accounts are classified broadly, categories or types of accounts are defined in terms such as extra large (key), large, medium, and small, which we refer to as the **ELMS system.** For example, management may divide the 3,000 total accounts in the firm's marketing plan into these four basic sales categories, as shown in Exhibit 15.4. There are few extra large or large accounts, but they often account for 80 percent of a company's profitable sales even though they represent only 20 percent of total accounts. This is known as the **80/20 principle.** The number of key accounts in an individual territory varies, as does responsibility for them. Even though the key account is in another salesperson's territory, a key account salesperson may call on the extra-large customer. Typically, this approach is taken because of the account's importance or because of an inexperienced local salesperson.

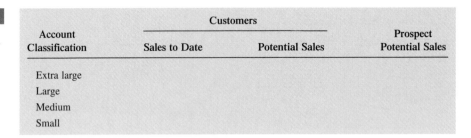

EXHIBIT 15.5

Basic segmentation of accounts.

Account Classification	Customers		Prospect Potential Sales
	Sales to Date	Potential Sales	
Extra large			
Large			
Medium			
Small			

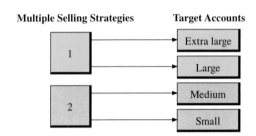

EXHIBIT 15.6

Account segmentation approach.

Accounts can be segmented whether or not the firms are actual customers or prospects. As shown in Exhibit 15.5, actual customers are further segmented based on sales to date and sales potential. Prospects also are segmented into the ELMS classification, and each account's potential sales are estimated.

Multiple Selling Strategies

Exhibit 15.6 illustrates how multiple selling strategies are used on various accounts. Salespeople know the importance of large accounts; in fact, meeting sales objectives often depends on how well products are sold to these customers. As a result, companies often develop their sales force organizational structure to service these accounts—incorporating elements such as a key-account salesperson.

As Exhibit 15.6 illustrates, selling strategies vary depending on the account. The bulk of sales force resources (such as personnel, time, samples, and entertainment expenses) should be invested in the key accounts, and the needs of these large accounts should receive top priority.

Company positioning relative to competition must receive careful consideration. Competitors also will direct a major selling effort toward these accounts. Thus, salespeople should strive to create the image that they, their company, and their products are uniquely better than the competition. One way to accomplish this is to spend more time on each sales call and to make more total sales calls during the year, thus providing a problem-solving approach to servicing accounts.

Selling larger accounts is different than selling medium and small accounts. However, these smaller accounts may generate 20 percent, and sometimes more, of a company's sales and must not be ignored.

Multivariable Account Segmentation

Multivariable account segmentation means using more than one criterion to characterize the organization's accounts. Sales organizations use segmentation because they sell to several markets and use many channel members in these markets.

EXHIBIT 14.7

Multivariable account
segmentation.

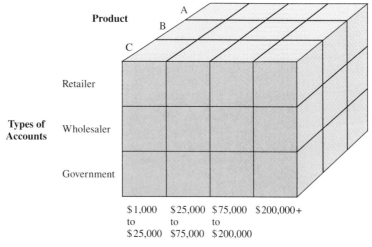

Furthermore, they may emphasize different products, product sizes, or product lines
to different channel members in various markets.

Exhibit 15.7 illustrates how firms might use several variables to segment their
accounts. This allows sales personnel to develop plans for selling various products
to specific segments of their accounts. For example, they might develop different
selling strategies for the extra-large and large accounts. There might be different
sales plans for retailers, wholesalers, and government accounts. These three types
of accounts might be further segmented. Retailers, for instance, could be segmented
into mass merchandisers and specialty stores. Furthermore, different products might
be emphasized in each account segment. The type of market, environment, account
sales potential, and sales volume are major variables for segmenting accounts.

Develop Account Objectives and Sales Quotas

The third element of time and territory management is developing objectives and
sales quotas for individual products and for current and potential accounts. Objectives might include increasing product distribution to prospects in the territory or
increasing the product assortment current customers purchase.

Increasing the number of sales calls each day and the number of new accounts obtained for the year are other examples of objectives salespeople develop to help meet
sales quotas. In recalling his early days as a salesperson, Shelby H. Carter, Jr., former
Xerox senior vice president of sales of U.S. field operations, said, "I placed a sign on
my car's visor that read, 'Calls are the guts of this business.' We lived in Baltimore,"
he recalls, "and I drove 40 miles every day to get to Annapolis. You've got to make
extra calls," he told his salespeople, "because 1 more call a day is 5 a week, 20 a month,
and 240 calls a year. If you close 10 percent of the people you contact, you have an
extra 24 sales a year. You have to be tough on yourself to make that extra call."

*Calls are the guts of
this business.*

SHELBY H. CARTER, JR.

Territory–Time Allocation

The fourth element of time and territory management is how salespeople's time is
allocated within territories. Time allocation is the time spent by the salesperson traveling around the territory and calling on accounts. These are seven basic factors to
consider in time allocation:

1. Number of accounts in the territory.
2. Number of sales calls made on customers.

3. Time required for each sales call.
4. Frequency of customer sales calls.
5. Travel time around the territory.
6. Nonselling time.
7. Return on time invested.

Get weary in your work but not of your work.

Analysis of accounts in the territory has resulted in determining the total number of territory accounts and their classification in terms of actual or potential sales. Now, the number of yearly sales calls required, the time required for each call, and the intervals between calls can be determined. Usually, the frequency of calls increases as there are increases in (1) sales and/or potential future sales, (2) number of orders placed in a year, (3) number of product lines sold, and (4) complexity, servicing, and redesign requirements of products.

Since the time spent servicing an account varies from minutes to days, salespeople must be flexible in developing call frequencies. However, they can establish a minimum number of times each year they want to call on the various classes of accounts. For example, the salesperson determines that the frequency of calls for each class of account in the territory, as shown in Exhibit 15.8, should be one contact a month for all but the small accounts.

Typically, the salesperson invests sales time in direct proportion to the actual or potential sales that the account represents. The most productive number of calls is reached at the point at which additional calls do not increase sales. This relationship of sales volume to sales calls is the **sales response function** of the customer to the salesperson's calls.

Return on Time Invested

Time is a scarce resource. To be successful, the salesperson uses time effectively to improve territory productivity. In terms of time, costs also must be accounted for. That is, what is the cost both in time and money of an average sales call?

Break-even analysis determines how much sales volume a salesperson must generate to meet costs in a territory. The difference between cost of goods sold and sales is the gross profit on sales revenue. Gross profit should be large enough to cover selling expenses. **Break-even analysis** is a quantitative technique for determining the level of sales at which total revenues equal total costs. A territory's break-even point is computed in dollars with this formula:

$$\text{Break-even point (in dollars)} = \frac{\text{Salesperson's fixed costs}}{\text{Gross profit percentage}}$$

To illustrate the formula, let us use the values shown here for sales and costs, with gross profit being the difference between a salesperson's sales revenue and

EXHIBIT 15.8

Account time allocation by salesperson.

Customer Size	Calls per Month	Calls per Year	Number of Accounts	Number of Calls per Year
Extra large	1	12	2	24
Large	1	12	28	336
Medium	1	12	56	672
Small	1*	4	78	312
Total			164	1,344

*Every 3 months.

costs of goods sold in the territory, expressed as a ratio of gross profit to gross sales in percentage form:

Sales	$200,000
Cost of goods sold	
Gross profit	$60,000
Gross profit (percentage)	(60,000 ÷ 200,000), or 30 percent

Assume the salesperson's direct costs are as follows:

Salary	$20,000
Transportation	4,000
Expenses	5,000
Direct costs	$29,000

and substitute in the formula:

$$\text{BEP} = \frac{\$29,000}{.30} = \$96,667$$

If the salesperson sells $96,667 worth of merchandise, it exactly covers the territory's direct costs. A sales volume of $96,667 means that the salesperson produces a gross margin of 30 percent, or $29,000. Sales over $96,667 contribute to profit.

Assume that the salesperson works 46 out of 52 weeks (considering time off for vacations, holidays, and illness) for 230 days each year; also assume a five-day week and an eight-hour day in which six calls are made. There are 1,840 working hours per year and 1,380 sales calls (230 × 6 calls) made each year in the territory. To determine a salesperson's cost per hour, divide direct costs ($29,000) by yearly hours worked (1,840 hours). The cost per hour equals $15.76. The break-even volume per hour is as follows:

$$\frac{\text{Break-even}}{\text{volume per hour}} = \frac{\text{Cost per hour}}{\text{Gross profit percentage}} = \frac{\$15.76}{.30} = \$52.53$$

Thus, the salesperson must sell an average of $52.53 an hour in goods or services to break even in the territory. Carrying this logic further, the salesperson must sell an average of $420.24 each day or $70.04 each sales call to break even.

This simple arithmetic shows that a sales territory is a cost- and revenue-generating profit center, and because it is, priorities must be established on account calls to maximize territory profits.

The Management of Time

"Time is money" is a popular saying that applies to our discussion because of the costs and revenue the individual salesperson generates. This is particularly evident with a commission salesperson (see Exhibit 15.9). This salesperson is a territory manager who has the responsibility of managing time wisely to maximize territorial profits. Thus, the effective salesperson consistently uses time well. How does the effective salesperson manage time?

You reap what you sow.

Plan by the Day, Week, and Month. Many salespeople develop daily, weekly, and monthly call plans or general guidelines of customers and geographical areas to be covered. The salesperson may use them to make appointments with customers in advance, to arrange hotel accommodations, and so forth. Weekly plans are more specific, and they include the specific days that customers will be called on. Daily planning starts the night before, as the salesperson selects the next day's prospects, determines the time to contact the customer, organizes facts and data, and prepares sales presentation materials.

"In our initial training we teach people how to be organized, set a list of priorities and plan their activities, and we encourage them to think outside of the box. They need to think about tomorrow, next week, down the road and to set objectives and anticipate needs before they occur," explains Jeff DeRoux, information and technology manager for the Preston, Washington-based SanMar Corporation. DeRoux believes that good organization, long- and short-range planning, and setting priorities are absolutely necessary in eliminating time wasting.[1]

Exhibit 15.10 is an illustration of a daily plan, and Exhibit 15.11 shows the location of each account and the sequence of calls.

"It's been said," says Tupperware's Terry Fingerhut, "21 days make a habit—good or bad. In three weeks, the results of the work I did or didn't do today will show up. If I spent my time well, three weeks from today I'll have positive results. If I wasted my time, three weeks from today, I'll have negative results. The conclusion—each day, every day—is produce *now* at your best. In three weeks and every week thereafter you'll have a string of truly positive results."

Qualify the Prospect. Salespeople must be sure that their prospects are qualified to make the purchase decision, and they must determine whether sales to these accounts are large enough to allow for an adequate return on time invested. If not, they do not call on these prospects.

Alvin Perez, sales executive with Total Graphics in Norwalk, Connecticut, feels that the biggest time waster of all is spending time with a prospect who isn't qualified.[2] "It's important that you gather, within reason, as much information as

EXHIBIT 15.10

Daily customer plan.

Hours	Sales Calls		Service Customers
	Customers	Prospects	
7:00–8:00 A.M.	Stop by office; pick up Jones Hardware order		
8:00–9:00	Travel		
9:00–10:00	Zip Grocery		
10:00–11:00	Ling Television Corp.		
11:00–12:00	Ling Television Corp.		
12:00–1:00 P.M.	Lunch and delivery to Jones Hardware		
1:00–2:00	Texas Instruments		
2:00–3:00		Ace Equipment	
3:00–4:00	Travel		
4:00–5:00			Trailor Mfg.
5:00–6:00	Plan next day—do paperwork		

EXHIBIT 15.11

Location of accounts and sequence of calls.

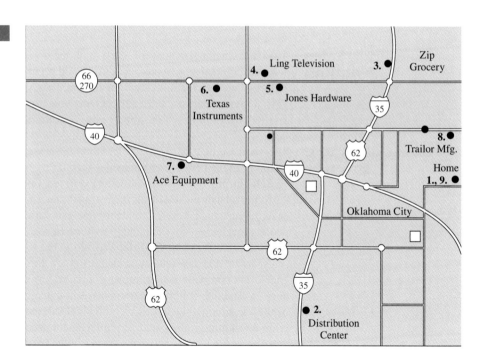

possible about prospects and determine whether they are serious about doing business with you," he says. "After all, in the sales business, time is money."

Use Waiting Time. Have you seen salespeople waiting to see buyers? Have you ever noticed their actions? Top salespeople do not read magazines. They work while waiting: studying material about their products, completing call reports, or organizing material for the sales presentation. Also, they quickly determine whether buyers they wait for will be free within a reasonable time. If not, they contact other customers.

Time is a present.
Use it wisely.

Have a Productive Lunchtime. Salespeople often take prospects to lunch. However, the results of one study show that the business lunch does not lead directly to a sale, but to the buyer and seller knowing each other better, which builds confidence and trust. In turn, this may lead to sales in the long run.

During a business lunch, salespeople must keep an eye on the clock and not monopolize too much of the buyer's time. They should not have a lunchtime cocktail. Although it is customary for some people to have a drink at lunch, the salesperson will be less alert in the afternoon as a result. In fact, in some companies, a luncheon cocktail or any use of alcohol or other drugs is against company policy. A salesperson's lunch is time to review activities and further plan the afternoon. It is a time to relax and start psyching up for a productive selling afternoon.

Records and Reports. Records and reports are a written history of sales and of the salesperson's activities. Effective salespeople do paperwork during nonselling times; evenings are best. Many companies note these records and reports in performance evaluations of salespeople, and the salesperson should keep them current. The company, however, should hold paperwork to a minimum.

So you see, time is important for salespeople. Yesterday's the past, tomorrow's the future, but today is a *gift*. That's why it's called the *present*. Life is like the sands of time slipping through the hourglass. Use yours wisely!

Customer Sales Planning

The fifth major element of time and territorial management is developing a sales-call objective, a customer profile, and a customer benefit program, including selling strategies for individual customers.* You have a quota to meet, have made your account analysis, have set account objectives, and have established the time you will devote to each customer; now, develop a sales plan for each customer.

Scheduling and Routing

The sixth element of time and territory management is scheduling sales calls and planning movement around the sales territory.

Scheduling refers to establishing a fixed time (day and hour) for visiting a customer's business. **Routing** is the travel pattern used in working a territory. Some sales organizations prefer to determine the formal path or route that their sales people travel when covering their territory. In such cases, management must develop plans that are feasible, flexible, and profitable to the company and the individual salesperson, and satisfactory to the customer. In theory, strict formal route designs enable the company to (1) improve territory coverage; (2) minimize wasted time; and (3) establish communication between management and the sales force in terms of the location and activities of individual salespeople.

"You've got to be careful if you don't know where you're going cause you might not get there!"

YOGI BERRA

In developing route patterns, management needs to know the salesperson's exact day and time of sales calls for each account; approximate waiting time; sales time; miscellaneous time for contacting people such as the promotional manager, checking inventory, or handling returned merchandise; and travel time between accounts. This task is difficult unless territories are small and precisely defined. Most firms allow considerable latitude in routing.

Typically, after finishing a workweek, the salesperson fills out a routing report and sends it to the manager. The report states where the salesperson will work (see Exhibit 15.12). In the example, on Friday, December 16, she is based in Dallas and plans to call on accounts in Dallas for two days during the week of December 26. Then, she plans to work in Waco for a day, spend the night, drive to Fort Worth

---

* Refer to Chapter 8 for further discussion of customer sales planning.

EXHIBIT 15.12

A weekly route report.

Today's date December 16		**For week beginning** December 26
Date	**City**	**Location**
December 26 (Monday)	Dallas	Home
December 27 (Tuesday)	Dallas	Home
December 28 (Wednesday)	Waco	Holiday Inn/South
December 29 (Thursday)	Fort Worth	Home
December 30 (Friday)	Dallas	Home

early the next morning and make calls, and be home Thursday night. The last day of the week, she plans to work in Dallas. The weekly route report is sent to her immediate supervisor. In this manner, management knows where she is and, if necessary, can contact her.

Some firms may ask the salesperson to specify the accounts to be called on and at what times. For example, on Monday, December 26, the salesperson may write, "Dallas, 9 A.M., Texas Instruments; Arlington, 2 P.M., General Motors." Thus, management knows where a salesperson will be and what accounts will be visited during a report period. If no overnight travel is necessary to cover a territory, the company may not require any route reports because the salesperson can be contacted at home in the evening.

Carefully Plan Your Route

"We're lost, but we're making good time!"

YOGI BERRA

At times, routing is difficult for a salesperson. Customers do not locate themselves geographically for the seller's convenience. Also, there is the increasing difficulty of traveling throughout large cities. Another problem is accounts that can see you only on certain days and hours.

In today's complex selling situation, the absence of a well-thought-out daily and weekly route plan is a recipe for disaster. It's impossible to operate successfully without it. How do you begin?

Start by locating your accounts on a large map. Mount the map on some corkboard or foamboard from an office supply store or picture-framing shop. Use a road map for large territories or a city map for densely populated areas. Also, purchase a supply of map pins with different colored heads. Place the pins on the map so that you can see where each account is located. For example, use

- Red pins for extra-large (**EL**) accounts.
- Yellow pins for large (**L**) accounts.
- Blue pins for medium (**M**) accounts.
- Green pins for small (**S**) accounts.
- Black pins for best prospects.

Once all pins are in place, stand back and take a look at the map. Notice first where the **EL** accounts are located. This helps determine your main routes or areas where you must go frequently.

Purpose produces passion.

Now, divide the map into sections, keeping the same number of **EL** accounts in each section. Each section should be a natural geographic division, that is, roads should be located in a way that allows you to drive from your home base to each section, as well as to travel easily once you are there. Generally, your **L, M,** and **S** accounts will fall into place near your **ELS,** with a few exceptions.

For example, if you work on a monthly or four-week call schedule for **ELS,** then divide your territory into four sections, working one section each week. In this way, you will reach all **ELS** while having the flexibility needed to reach your other accounts regularly.

Section 1	Section 2	Section 3	Section 4
7 EL	9 EL	5 EL	10 EL
15 L	12 L	15 L	15
35 M	25 M	35 M	25 M
40 S	35 S	49 S	36 S

By creating geographical routes this way, you could call on all **EL** accounts every four weeks, half of your **L** and **M** accounts (an 8-week call cycle) and 25 percent of your **S** accounts (a 16-week call cycle) in that period. Also, allow time for calls on prospective customers too. Use the same procedure as for regular customers. The only difference is that in most cases prospects would be contacted less frequently than customers.

There is no right number of sections or routes for all salespersons. It depends on the size of your territory, the geographical layout of your area, and the call frequencies you want to establish. Design your travel route so that you can start from home in the morning and return in the evening—or, if you have a larger territory, make it a Monday to Friday route or a two-day (overnight) route. Remember that the critical factor is travel time—not miles. In some cases, by using major nonstop highways, your miles may increase but your total travel time may decrease.

The actual routes followed each day and within each section are important to maximize your prime selling hours each day. For this reason, make long drives early in the morning and in the late afternoon, if possible. For example, if most accounts are in a straight line from your home, leave early and drive to the far end of your territory before making your first call, then work your way back so that you end up near home at the end of the day, which is called the *straight-line method*. Exhibit 14.13 illustrates three ways to route yourself.

Using the Telephone for Territorial Coverage

The telephone can be a great time-waster or time-saver, depending on how it is used. The increasing cost of a personal sales call, and the increasing amount of time spent traveling to make personal calls are reasons for the efficient territory manager to look to the telephone as a territory coverage tool.

With field sales costs still rising and no end in sight, more companies are developing telephone sales and marketing campaigns to supplement personal selling efforts. These campaigns utilize trained telephone communicators and well-developed telephone marketing techniques. Usually, they require a companywide effort.

Although each salesperson has to decide the types of calls and accounts that lend themselves to telephone applications, most people benefit from adopting the following practices as minimal territory coverage:

- Satisfy part of the service needs of accounts by telephone.
- Assign smaller accounts that contribute less than 5 percent of business to mostly telephone selling.
- Do prospecting, marketing data gathering, and call scheduling by telephone.
- Carefully schedule personal calls to distant accounts. If possible, replace some personal visits with telephone calls.

EXHIBIT 15.13

Three basic routing patterns.

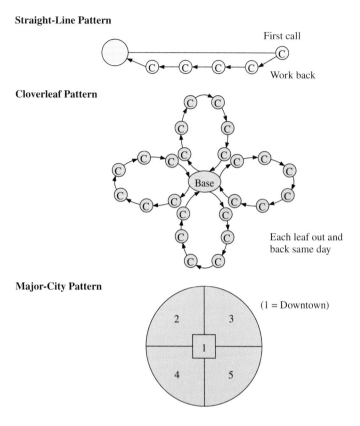

Straight-Line Pattern

First call

Work back

Cloverleaf Pattern

Base

Each leaf out and
back same day

Major-City Pattern

(1 = Downtown)

2	3
1	
4	5

The telephone and the computer are important selling tools for salespeople. Many sales jobs require extensive travel. Out of the office, traveling salespeople can keep in contact with their offices, access computer files containing customer information, and record customer information.

Territory and Customer Evaluation

Territorial evaluation is the establishment of performance standards for the individual territory in the form of qualitative and quantitative quotas or goals. Actual performance is compared to these goals for evaluation purposes. This allows the salesperson to see how well territory plans were executed in meeting performance quotas. If quotas were not met, new plans must be developed.

Many companies routinely furnish managers and individual salespeople with reports on how many times during the year salespeople have called on each account and the date of the last sales call. Management can monitor the frequency and time intervals between calls for each salesperson.

As an example, a national pharmaceutical company supplies its sales force with a net sales by customer and call report shown in Exhibit 15.15. The report lists each customer's name, address, and medical specialty. The desired number of monthly calls on a given customer and the actual number of calls to date are noted. Net sales are broken down into last year's sales, the current month's sales, and year-to-date sales. Finally, the date the salesperson last called on each customer is reported.

Using the report, one can see that H. L. Brown is a Houston physician in a general practice. He should be called on twice a month, and for the past four months, he has been seen eight times. He purchased $60 worth of merchandise this month, and his purchases so far are $50 more than last year. He was last called on

ETHICAL DILEMMA

A Breakdown in Productivity

You are a hard worker, often putting in 60 hours a week. On your first sales job and with the company only five months, you realize the importance of getting off to a good start. You have sold an average of 30 percent over your sales quota for the past three months. One reason is your hard work. Another reason is that the salesperson that preceded you in this territory either neglected accounts or just renewed old orders, never striving to upgrade current accounts. Most customers complained that they hadn't seen a salesperson from your company for months before you began to call on them.

Last month one of the older salespeople jokingly suggested that you slow down—you are making everyone look bad. You have noticed a breakdown in productivity among your fellow salespeople who seem to be goofing off to extremes. Although it doesn't affect you directly, it will ultimately have an adverse impact on the department's productivity. Your boss likes good news and frequently asks you for ideas on how to increase sales in other territories. Because you are new and have not yet established yourself as a loyal employee, you have kept quiet in the past, hoping to win the trust of your co-workers. Tomorrow you have a meeting with your boss about your territory's productivity and you are sure he is expecting input about the other territories.

What would be the most ethical action to take?

1. Tell your boss nothing. State that your territory must be particularly active right now and that you think the other territories must just be slow right now. It does not affect you, so why should you get involved?

2. Tell your boss that your numbers have been so high because you have been working very hard and putting in long hours. Let him know that you have noticed that the other sales people have been slacking and, in fact, have told you to "slow down." After all, it isn't right that they are abusing their positions and hurting the company's profits.

3. Suggest to your boss that he have some type of new sales incentive plan. This way, maybe the other sales people will stop "goofing off" and you don't have to say anything.

The telephone is an effective tool that keeps salespeople connected to sales operations no matter where they travel.

EXHIBIT 15.15

Net sales by customer and call frequency: May 1, 2005.

	Brown (GP, Houston)	Peterson (Pediatrics, Galveston)	Gilley (GP, Galveston)	Bruce (GP, Galveston)	Heaton (GP, Texas City)
Calls					
Month	2	1	1	0	2
Year-to-date	8	4	4	4	9
Last call	4/20	4/18	4/18	3/10	4/19
Net sales in dollars					
Current month	60	0	21	0	500
Year-to-date:					
This year	350	200	75	1000	2000
Last year	300	275	125	750	1750
Entire last year	2000	1000	300	1000	5000

April 20 of the current year. Using this type of information, which might include 200 to 300 customers for each salesperson, management and salespeople can continually review sales-call patterns and customer sales to update call frequency and scheduling.

SUMMARY OF MAJOR SELLING ISSUES

How salespeople invest their sales time is a critical factor influencing territory sales. Due to the increasing cost of direct selling, high transportation costs, and the limited resource of time, salespeople have to focus on these factors. Proper time and territory management is an effective method for the salesperson to maximize territorial sales and profits.

A sales territory comprises a group of customers or a geographical area assigned to a salesperson. It is a segment out of the company's total market. A salesperson within a territory has to analyze the various segments, estimate sales potential, and develop a marketing mix based on the needs and desires of the marketplace.

Companies develop and use sales territories for a number of reasons. One important reason is to obtain thorough coverage of the market to fully reach sales potential. Another reason is to establish salespeople's responsibilities as territory managers.

Performance can be monitored when territories are established. A territory may also be used to improve customer relations so that customers receive regular calls from the salesperson. This helps to reduce sales expenses by avoiding duplicated effort in traveling and customer contacts. Finally, territories allow better matching of salespeople to customer needs and ultimately benefit salespeople and the company.

There also are disadvantages to developing sales territories. Some salespeople may not be motivated if they feel restricted by a particular territory. Also, a company may be too small to segment its market or management may not want to take time to develop territories.

Time and territory management is continuous for a salesperson; it involves seven key elements. The first major element is establishing the territory sales quota. The second element is account analysis, which involves identifying current and potential customers and estimating their sales potential. In analyzing these accounts, salespeople may use the undifferentiated-selling approach if they view accounts as similar; or, if accounts have different characteristics, they use the account-segmentation approach.

Developing objectives and sales quotas for individual accounts is the third element. How salespeople allocate time in their territories is another key element. Salespeople have to manage time, plan schedules, and use spare time effectively.

The fifth element of time and territorial management is developing the sales-call objective, profile, benefit program, and selling strategies for individual customers. Salespeople have to learn everything they can about customers and maintain records on each one. Once this is done, they can create the proper selling strategies to meet customers' needs.

Another major element is scheduling sales calls at specific times and places and routing the salesperson's movement and travel pattern around the territory. Finally, established objectives and quotas are used to determine how effectively the salesperson performs. Actual performance is compared to these standards for evaluation purposes.

MEETING A SALES CHALLENGE

How Alice Jenson manages her time will determine her productivity. Alice should tell her boss the situation. Then she should analyze her accounts to classify them according to past sales and sales potential. Now she can allocate her time by concentrating on her extra-large and large accounts, contacting each as often as necessary. The medium-sized customers might be seen every one to two months, and the small ones less frequently or contacted by telephone. If needed, her boss could be asked to contact some customers. Alice's situation illustrates why companies require salespeople to do so much record keeping. After each sales call, Alice needs to develop a customer profile, as shown in Chapter 8, to have up-to-date information on all customers.

KEY TERMS FOR SELLING

sales territory 476
account analysis 478
undifferentiated selling 478
account segmentation 479
key accounts 479
ELMS system 479
80/20 principle 479
sales response function 482

break-even analysis 482
scheduling 486
routing 486

SALES APPLICATION QUESTIONS

1. How could you use technology to better manage your customers and your territory? Explain how you could use technologies such as management software, e-mail, and cellular telephones to manage a sales territory.
2. What is a sales territory? Why do firms establish sales territories? Why might sales territories not be developed?
3. Briefly discuss each of the elements of time and territory management and indicate how these seven elements relate to one another.
4. What is the difference between the undifferentiated selling approach and the account segmentation approach for analyzing accounts? When might each approach be used?

5. Assume a sales manager determines that in a given territory each salesperson sells approximately $500,000 yearly. Also, assume that the firm's cost of goods sold are estimated to be 65 percent of sales and that a salesperson's direct costs are $35,000 a year. Each salesperson works 48 weeks a year, eight hours a day, and averages five sales calls per day. Using this information, how much merchandise must each salesperson sell to break even?
   a. For the year?
   b. Each day?
   c. Each sales call?
6. What is a key account?
7. What are the factors to consider when a salesperson allocates time?
8. What is the purpose of customer sales planning?
9. Define *scheduling*. Define *routing*.

FURTHER EXPLORING THE SALES WORLD

1. Visit a large retailer in your community and ask a buyer or store manager what salespeople do when they make a sales call. Determine the number of times the retailer wants salespeople to visit each month. Are calls from some salespeople preferable to others? If so, why?
2. Contact a salesperson or sales manager and report on each one's philosophy toward managing time and territory. Ask each person to calculate how much it costs to contact one prospect, and on the average, what amount must be sold each day just to break even.

SELLING EXPERIENTIAL EXERCISE

Make a chart similar to the one on page 494 and record the time you spend on various activities for one week. Each day, place codes on your chart to indicate the time spent on each activity. Some codes are suggested here; add any codes you need. At the end of the week, write your total hours in that column. If any activity takes up a great deal of time—such as personal—subdivide it by assigning such additional activities as television, phone, or partying. Now that you have a good idea of how you spend your time, decide if you want to make some changes.

Name _____ Week beginning _____

(Date)

	Mon	Tue	Wed	Thur	Fri	Sat	Sun
7:00–7:30 A.M.							
7:30–8:00							
8:00–8:30							
8:30–9:00							
9:00–9:30							
9:30–10:00							
10:00–10:30							
10:30–11:00							
11:00–11:30							
11:30–12:00							

Activity	Code	Total Hours
Class	CL	_____
Sleep	SL	_____
Study	SU	_____
Work	W	_____
Personal	P	_____
_____	_____	_____
_____	_____	_____

	Mon	Tue	Wed	Thur	Fri	Sat	Sun
12:00–12:30 P.M.							
12:30–1:00							
1:00–1:30							
1:30–2:00							
2:00–2:30							
2:30–3:00							
3:00–3:30							
3:30–4:00							
4:00–4:30							
4:30–5:00							

	Mon	Tue	Wed	Thur	Fri	Sat	Sun
5:00–5:30 P.M.							
5:30–6:00							
6:00–6:30							
6:30–7:00							
7:00–7:30							
7:30–8:00							
After 8:00*							

*Note: If you need to, make another sheet.

CHAPTER 15

Time, Territory, and Self-Management: Keys to Success

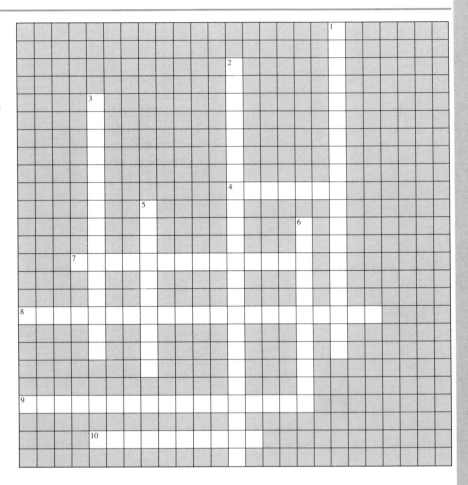

Across

4. The travel pattern used in working a sales territory.
7. The group of customers or a geographic area assigned to a salesperson.
8. The relationship between sales volume and sales calls.
9. A quantitative technique for determining the level of sales at which total revenues equal total costs.
10. The establishment of a fixed time for visiting a customer's business.

Down

1. The process of applying different selling strategies to different customers.
2. The process of applying and designing selling strategies equally to all accounts.
3. The process of analyzing each prospect and customer to maximize the chances of reaching a sales goal.
4. The process of dividing customers into varying sizes.
6. Customers the loss of whom would greatly affect sales and profits.

CASE 15-1

Your Selling Day: A Time and Territory Game*

Your sales manager is working with you tomorrow only, and you want to call on customers with the greatest sales potential (see Exhibit A). Because you are on a straight commission, you will also have the opportunity to maximize your income for that day. The area of your territory that you want to cover contains 16 customers (see Exhibit B). To determine travel time, allow 15 minutes for each side of the square. Each sales call takes 30 minutes. You can leave your house at 8:00 A.M. or later. If you take time for lunch, it must be in 15-minute time blocks (15, 30, 45, or 60 minutes). Your last customer must be contacted by 4:30 P.M. to allow you enough sales time. Your customers do not see salespeople after 5:00 P.M. You travel home after 5:00 P.M.

Questions

1. Develop the route that gives the highest sales potential for the day your boss works with you.
2. For the next day, develop the route allowing you to contact the remaining customers in this part of the territory.

EXHIBIT A

Customers' sales potential.

Customer	Sales Potential	Customer	Sales Potential
A	$4,000	I	$1,000
B	3,000	J	1,000
C	6,000	K	10,000
D	2,000	L	12,000
E	2,000	M	8,000
F	8,000	N	9,000
G	4,000	O	8,000
H	6,000	P	10,000

EXHIBIT B

A partial map of your sales territory.

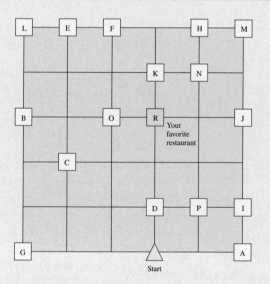

*Case copyright © 2000 by Charles M. Futrell.

CASE 15-2

Sally Malone's District—Development of an Account Segmentation Plan

Sally Malone sat listening to her boss talk about the new time and territory management program being implemented by her company. Her boss was saying, "Since we wish eventually to establish priorities for our accounts in order to make time-investment decisions, we must classify the accounts into categories. A simple A, B, C, D, E designation of categories is the most commonly used approach, with A accounts the most valuable.

"The basis for setting the values or limits for each category is the distribution of sales or concentration patterns in most industries. In general, business in our company is distributed approximately as shown in Exhibit A. Generally, the top 10 percent of the accounts will generate 65 percent of sales, and the top 30 percent will generate 85 percent of the sales in any given territory. Salespeople may use this rule-of-thumb breakdown of accounts in determining the classification system for their accounts." Once the potential for all their accounts has been calculated, their territory should break down like this:

- A accounts = top 10 percent of the accounts
- B accounts = next 20 percent of the accounts
- C accounts = next 50 percent of the accounts
- D accounts = next 10 percent of the accounts
- E accounts = last 10 percent of the accounts

"Sally, I want you to have each of your salespeople take a close look at his or her sales-call cycles. As I have explained, a call cycle is a round of calls in which all A accounts are called on at least once and some, but not all, B, C, D, and E accounts are called on. When a salesperson has visited all of his or her A accounts, the cycle is completed. Then, a new cycle begins and the series of calls repeats. Since not all B, C, D, and E accounts are called on in every cycle, the specific accounts to be seen in these classifications differ from cycle to cycle. A call cycle, therefore, is established around the call frequency patterns of A accounts."

Suppose that a group of accounts is classified in this way:

Accounts	Expected Value
A	$100,000 and over
B	50,000–100,000
C	30,000–50,000
D	20,000–30,000
E	Under $20,000

Distribution of sales.

Customer Classification	Percentage of Customers	Percentage of Total Sales Volume
A	10%	65%
B	20	20
C	50	10
D	10	3
E	10	2
	100%	100%

The call frequency patterns, therefore, based on potential and return on time invested, may be as follows:

Accounts	Weeks between Calls	Number of Accounts
A	2	10
B	4	20
C	6	45
D	8	12
E	10	10

Thus, a call cycle in this territory will cover two weeks. This means that in every two-week cycle the salesperson will call on these accounts:

- All of the *A*s.
- Half of the *B*s.
- One-third of the *C*s.
- One-fourth of the *D*s.
- One-fifth of the *E*s.

Questions

1. Develop a table showing a salesperson's call cycle using the call frequency patterns.
2. Discuss why this should be done.

Planning, Staffing, and Training Successful Salespeople

LEARNING OBJECTIVES

Many salespeople strive to move up to management positions in their organizations. Typically, this is the job of sales manager. After studying this chapter, you should be able to

- Discuss the relationship between a firm's marketing plan, sales force, and sales force's budget.

- Describe the organization of a sales force.

- Explain the two major elements involved in staffing the sales force—personnel planning and employment planning.

- Discuss what is involved in training the sales force.

You promoted John Scott, a top sales producer, to district sales manager, with 12 sales-people reporting directly to him. Now, you see warning signs of serious problems in the district. Sales figures are falling off too rapidly. When you visit the district office, you are aware that attitudes have changed from high-key enthusiasm and cheerfulness to low-key activity, and John appears unable to handle pressure. Further, absenteeism has risen alarmingly high in his district. Overall productivity has fallen, threatening your department's ability to make its quota, and several of the district's salespeople have asked for transfers or leaves of absence. One quit, and now John wants to fire another for insubordination—the first such act for your department.

Salespeople need timely decisions, but John is a procrastinator. He puts off making decisions, sometimes until it is too late to reduce risks or increase opportunities. In sales meetings, John does all the talking, inhibiting his salespeople's initiative. Also, his reports are no longer exceptionally clear; they no longer analyze risks and opportunities, stating facts, data, figures—information needed for sales planning.

Your own manager wants to know why the district is doing so poorly and what you plan to do about it. Your options do not include firing John. What option do you choose and why?

Sales managers are responsible for planning, staffing, training, directing, and evaluating their sales forces' activities, strategies, and tactics to generate sales that meet corporate objectives.[1] Chapters 16 and 17 examine these five job functions of the sales manager. This chapter discusses the planning, staffing, and training functions so important for the success of a sales manager. Let's begin by considering the personal characteristics required of a sales manager.

THE TREE OF BUSINESS LIFE: MANAGEMENT

Caring, joy, harmony, patience, kindness, moral ethics, faithful, fair, self-controlled.

Do you like sports? If so, you know professional sports teams have players and coaches. Both coaches and players are paid to entertain fans and win games. The success of the team depends on the performance of the coaches, especially the head coach.

Managers of sales personnel are somewhat similar to coaches of a professional sports team. They are paid to make sure the sales team sells and keeps the customer happy. Wow, is this a challenging and rewarding career. Sales managers are the "spark plugs" that ignite salespeople to high performance levels.

Chapter 1 reviewed the characteristics needed for the salesperson. These same characteristics are required of today's sales leaders. Sales managers must be caring, joyful in helping others, and intent on having harmony within the sales group and with customers. Patience, kindness, and moral ethics help build the relationship between boss and subordinate.

The manager who cares, likes people, is good to work with, and is patient, kind, and morally ethical is certainly someone who will be faithful in taking care of salespeople and customers. This leader will be fair to all, treating them according to what is the right thing to do as described in Chapter 3's discussion of the principle of moral development level. Finally, the leader must be able to control emotions, passions, and desires when leading people to higher sales levels. These nine characteristics comprise the **Golden Rule of Sales Management** of unselfishly treating salespeople as you would like to be treated.

As I consider these leadership requirements I think, "Wow, it is hard enough managing my own life. How could I be expected to manage others?" Well, the demand for outstanding sales leaders is enormous. There are few people with all of the personal traits. Many people quickly drop out of leadership positions. Why? They cannot make the transition from salesperson to sales manager.

TRANSITION FROM SALESPERSON TO SALES MANAGER

What happens when a salesperson is promoted into a management position? Often, the qualities that make a good sales manager are significantly different from those needed by a salesperson, particularly in attitude toward the job and responsibility. Many changes accompany a promotion from subordinate to boss. Some of these changes are immediate and apparent to everyone: a private office, a new title, a secretary, a new supervisor. The more significant differences between the new and old jobs are less obvious and take longer to adjust to.

What Changes Occur?

The process of feeling comfortable with these changes is what learning to think like a manager is all about. The following are major changes that occur when a person becomes a new manager.

Perspectives Change

Most salespeople are largely concerned with doing a good job at their assigned tasks and planning how to get ahead. Managers, however, must keep the big picture in mind. They make plans and decisions by considering their impact on the goals and well-being of the group (sales district) and the organization as a whole.

Goals Change

A manager's primary concern is meeting the organization's goals. In contrast, a salesperson's focus is on meeting personal goals.

Responsibilities Change

A manager must supervise and speak for a group of people, in addition to completing administrative tasks. As a person moves up in the management ranks, more and more time is spent achieving results through others than on doing the selling itself.

Satisfaction Changes

Because a manager does less of the actual sales and customer work, satisfaction comes from watching others succeed rather than from the work itself.

Job Skill Requirements Change

Being technically competent is important for managers, but possessing additional skills is vital to success. Managers must become proficient at communicating, delegating, planning, managing time, directing, motivating, and training others.

Relationships Change

New relationships with former peers, other managers, and a new supervisor must be developed. People quickly change how they act toward the new manager, whether or not the manager alters his or her behavior toward them.

The Experience of Being Promoted

A new manager does not make an overnight transformation from thinking and behaving like a subordinate to thinking and behaving like a boss. Instead, in making the transition from one role to the other, the manager passes through several predictable stages. Although people seldom move neatly from one phase to the next, they generally experience all seven phases.

Phase 1

Immobilization. The person feels overwhelmed by the changes he or she is facing.

Phase 2

Minimizing or denial of change. This phase allows the individual time to regroup and fully comprehend the change.

Phase 3

Depression. Awareness sets in regarding the magnitude of the changes that must be made in one's habits, customs, and relationships.

Phase 4

Acceptance of reality. Feelings of optimism return and the person is ready to let go of the past.

Phase 5

Testing. This is a time of trying out new behaviors and ways of coping with the new situation.

Phase 6

Searching for meanings. The person's concern shifts to trying to understand both how and why things are different now.

Phase 7

Internalization. In this final phase the person incorporates the new meanings into his or her behavior.

Problems New Managers Experience

One of the biggest problems facing most new managers is their lack of preparation for the job. There are several reasons why this happens. For example, a salesperson often is selected for promotion to a management position because of outstanding performance in their present job. The skills and abilities that help a person develop into a salesperson, however, are quite different from the skills needed by a manager.

As a result, the new manager must acquire new attitudes, behaviors, and skills to succeed at managing others.

Adding to new managers' difficulties is the fact that companies generally expect them to step into the job and function effectively immediately. This expectation exists even though many organizations offer them little help or support. Even formal training programs that teach essential new skills are not always offered until several months after a person is promoted into management. The sink-or-swim philosophy is still prevalent.

Finally, the new manager often lacks an immediate peer group. Former peers no longer regard the manager as one of them. Other managers may be hesitant to consider this person a member of their group until he or she has demonstrated the ability to think and act like management. This leaves the new manager belonging to neither group at a time when support from others is badly needed.

Given these and other problems, many new managers often feel inexperienced, uncertain, and overwhelmed by their new responsibilities. For example, Quaker Oats' Linda Slaby-Baker said, "The first week I started my new position [as district manager] I had to create a complete new district, train four new employees, and set up my district office."

The Key to Making a Successful Transition

One key to making a successful transition into management is for the new manager to have a *learning attitude:* being willing to learn, change, adapt, and seek help when needed. Managers with this attitude find the going much smoother than those who expect things to remain relatively unchanged (see Exhibit 16.1).

Having realistic expectations about what it is like to be in management plays a large part in determining how quickly new managers adjust to the position. These newcomers can expect to face unfamiliar situations. They can expect their previous job expertise to be useful in some, but not all, situations. They also can expect to make mistakes, as this is an unavoidable part of learning a new job.

New managers must leave the old job behind and get off to a good start with peers, subordinates, and superiors. This means learning what responsibilities go with

Successful new managers adopt a learning attitude going into a new situation.

the new job, not just continuing to work at one's old job. It takes hard work—and a lot of listening—to gain the loyalty and support of other people. A trap to avoid is making a lot of changes right away. This will likely cause resentment among subordinates, and the changes may become inappropriate once the manager has gained a better understanding of the operation.

Finally, new managers would do well to remember one fact: they are the ones who have assumed a new role. They—not subordinates, other managers, or the surroundings—need to make the initial adjustments.

TECHNOLOGY IS NEEDED IN THE JOB

Face it, you need technology to be an effective manager in the 21st century. For example, when any of the 42,000 employees of Aetna Life & Casualty want to communicate with their leader—to ask a question, register a complaint, or make a suggestion—they face no complex management hierarchy, no daunting series of memos in triplicate, no door, and no protective secretary. Instead, they need only to turn to their personal computers, stroke a few keys, and send their thoughts via e-mail.

Chances are CEO Ron Compton will get back to them by the next day, if not sooner. "I check my e-mail constantly," says Compton, who has received as many as 40 messages in a single day, "and I answer every one." He even takes his laptop on weekend sailing excursions.

Is Compton's behavior compulsive, or merely the evidence of good management? Perhaps both. He admits to being addicted to computer technology: With his PC he orders clothes, keeps lists of movies he wants to see, and even prints his own checks. But he has also realized that the computer is a powerful leadership tool, one of the most potent in the management arsenal. "It's the best communication instrument I know," he says, calling his PC "absolutely essential. On a needs scale of 1 to 10, it's a 10."

Many other executives are concurring, developing their high-tech skills to discover the various ways a computer can enhance their ability to communicate, coach, convince, and compete.[2]

BEING A FIRST-LINE SALES MANAGER IS A CHALLENGING JOB

Being a first-line sales manager is a challenging and always demanding job. As Exhibit 16.2 shows, the district sales manager is the link between the salespeople and the manager's immediate boss—the regional sales manager. Thus, to be effective in the job, the manager must be effective in managing salespeople and influencing the boss.

Generally, the first-line management position in any organization is one of the most challenging of all management jobs, especially in sales jobs. The great responsibility of generating sales for the company, plus the many facets and activities of the job, requires a talented person.

WHAT IS THE SALARY FOR MANAGEMENT?

Why do people strive to achieve management positions? One reason is the personal reward of operating and managing an organization. The second reason is financial reward. A sales job is often a stepping-stone to higher positions. The assumption is that the larger a company's revenues, the heavier the responsibility

EXHIBIT 16.2

The district sales manager links salespeople to the company.

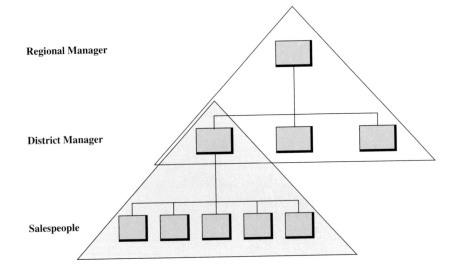

Regional Manager

District Manager

Salespeople

of the chief executive, and thus the larger the compensation. Salary is usually related to

- Annual sales volume of units managed.
- Number of salespeople supervised.
- Length of experience in sales.
- Annual sales volume of the firm.

Leaving aside compensation at the top echelons, both corporate and field sales managers typically receive higher salaries than production, advertising, product, or personnel managers at the same organizational level. Moreover, salary is just one part of compensation. For example, many firms offer elaborate packages that include extended vacation and holiday periods; pension programs; health, accident, and legal insurance programs; automobiles and compensation for auto expenses; payment of professional association dues; educational assistance for themselves and sometimes for their families; financial planning assistance; company airplanes; home and entertainment expenses; and free country club membership. The higher the sales position, the greater the benefits offered.

OVERVIEW OF THE JOB

The demand for top sales managers is much too great to be satisfied by people born with extraordinary talent.

PETER F. DRUCKER

Sales management is the attainment of sales force goals in an effective and efficient manner through planning, staffing, training, directing, and evaluating organizational resources. Sales managers work with and through individuals and groups in the company, in the sales force, and outside the firm to accomplish their goals. The sales manager's main goal is to achieve the levels of sales volume, profits, and sales growth desired by higher levels of management.

The factor underlying a manager's success in achieving this goal is the ability to influence the behavior of all parties involved. This includes the ability to influence salespeople to do things that they would not do on their own. The manager must recruit good people and provide proper motivation and effective leadership. The sales manager is held responsible for the success of her or his salespeople. Consequently, sales managers are performance oriented. They look for ways to make salespeople efficient and effective.

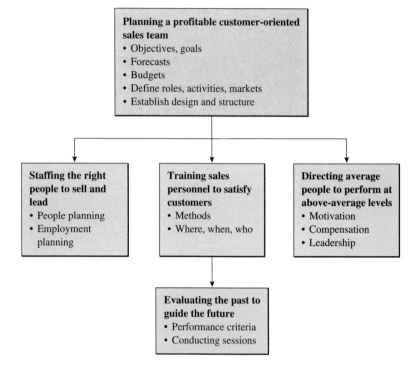

EXHIBIT 16.3

The basic sales management functions.

SALES MANAGEMENT FUNCTIONS

Whether in a top, middle, or first-line managerial position, the sales manager fulfills five basic functions as indicated in Exhibit 16.3. These are

Planning—Establishing a broad outline for goals, policies, and procedures that will accomplish the objectives of the organization—including forecasting and developing budgets, as discussed in Chapter 1—plus establishing the organizational design and structure.

Staffing—Attracting, hiring, and retaining an effective sales force within an organization.

Training—Deciding which methods to use, plus whom to train, where, and when.

Directing—Dealing with people positively and persuasively from a leadership position regarding motivation and compensation.

Evaluating—Comparing actual performance to planned performance goals to determine whether to take corrective action if goals are not achieved, or to continue using the same methods if goals are met.

First-line managers, such as district sales managers who hire salespeople, spend more time directing salespeople than higher-level managers. In comparison, top-level sales managers spend more time planning and organizing.

SALES FORCE PLANNING

A firm's corporate management, including the national sales manager, develops sales goals for the company. As discussed in Chapter 2, the marketing department develops plans, strategies, and tactics that allow the company to reach its sales objectives. In turn, the sales force also develops plans, strategies, and tactics for meeting their sales objectives and quotas. Two additional important elements of planning are the development of sales forecasts and budgets.

Sales Forecasting

Sales forecasting is one method used to predict a firm's future revenues when planning the company's marketing and sales force activities. Since customer satisfaction is the purpose of every business, the forecast of customer needs is of primary importance. Forecasting is an integral part of planning that contributes to overall organizational effectiveness.

Uses of Sales Forecasts

Sales forecasting involves the prediction of events that may influence the demand for a firm's goods or services. Total industry sales, total company sales, industry product categories, company product lines, and individual products are major elements that must be noted in estimating future demand. These forecasts are made for customer, sales territory, region, division, the entire country, and sometimes world sales. Forecasts are made for short-range (three to six months), medium-range (six months to one or two years), and long-range (over two years) demand. As illustrated in Exhibit 16.4, computer software has simplified analyzing the past to forecast future sales.

The firm's sales forecast depends on many factors. The planned marketing activities of the firm have a major impact on the level of sales obtained in the marketplace. The firm's marketing plans have an influence on sales forecasts and budgets. Marketing plans can increase sales, which can increase budgets and quotas. From sales forecasts, sales goals are generated for products and product lines, individual salespeople, or company divisions. Typically, sales goals are slightly higher than sales forecasts. Once plans have evolved into sales forecasts, the company develops its sales budgets.

The Sales Manager's Budget

The **sales force budget** is the amount of money available or assigned for a definite period, usually one year. It is based on estimates of expenditures during that time and proposals for financing the budget. Thus, the budget depends on the sales

EXHIBIT 16.4

Computer software has revolutionized the process of analyzing the past to forecast future sales. This greatly simplifies creating budgets.

forecast and the amount of revenue expected to be generated for the organization during that period. The budget for the sales force is a valuable resource that the sales manager reassigns among lower-level managers. Budget funds must be appropriated wisely to properly support selling activities that allow sales personnel and the total marketing group to reach performance goals.

Methods of Developing Sales Force Budgets

How much money does the sales manager receive to operate the sales force? Although there are no fixed financial formulas to use in appropriating funds, there are three general methods for determining how money should be allocated. First, some firms use an arbitrary percentage of sales. Second, other firms may use executive judgment. Third, a few companies estimate the cost of operating each sales force unit, along with costs of each sales program over a specified time to arrive at a total budget.

In Exhibit 16.5, some typical costs in operating a sales force are listed. Whatever method is chosen, the actual amount budgeted will be based on the organization's sales forecast, marketing plans, projected profits, top management's perceived importance of the sales force in reaching corporate objectives, and the sales manager's skills in negotiating with superiors. Budgets usually are modified several times before the final dollar figures are determined.

> Never ask of money spent
> Where the spender thinks it went.
> Nobody was ever meant
> To remember or invent
> What he did with every cent.
>
> —*Robert Frost*

Organizing the Sales Force

The operation of a sales force requires the coordination of numerous interacting or interdependent groups and activities. In deciding on the organizational design and structure of a sales force, we

- Examine our customers in each market.
- Determine the types of sales jobs needed to serve a market.
- Note the job activities salespeople must do in each job.
- Design sales jobs around customers.
- Set up the sales-force organizational structure, which includes the various sales jobs and geographic territories.

EXHIBIT 16.5

Operating costs for the sales force.

- Base salaries
  Management
  Salespeople
- Commissions
- Other compensation
  Social Security
  Retirement plan
  Stock options
  Hospitalization
- Special incentives
- Office expenses
- Product samples
- Selling aids
- Transportation expenses
- Entertainment
- Travel

EXHIBIT 16.6

Multiple factors determine the design of the sales force.

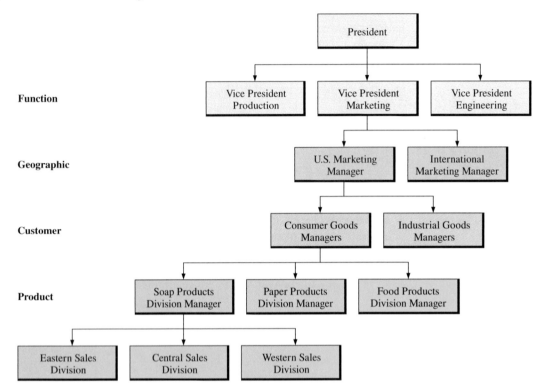

Organizational design refers to the formal, coordinated process of communication, authority, and responsibility for sales groups and individuals. An effectively designed sales organization is one in which its framework enables the organization to serve its customers. Sales personnel know what their responsibilities are and to whom they report, and thus can concentrate on the activities needed to do their various jobs.

Organizational structure is the relatively fixed, formally defined relationship among jobs within the organization. Structure is reflected in a company's organizational chart. Many companies organize on the basis of some combination of function, geography, product, or customer design. Exhibit 16.6 illustrates a company with production, marketing, and engineering functional specialists; the firm sells consumer and industrial products in both U.S. and foreign markets. The consumer-goods division sells three categories of products through three geographically organized sales force divisions.

STAFFING:
HAVING THE
RIGHT PEOPLE
TO SELL

Staffing refers to activities undertaken to attract, hire, and maintain effective sales force personnel within an organization. As shown in Exhibit 16.7, staffing comprises two elements: people planning and employment planning. As you will see, these two elements involve the entire process of determining how many people to hire, whom to hire, selection—matching these people to the right sales jobs—and placing them in the right sales territory.

EXHIBIT 16.7

Activities involved in managing the human resources of a sales force.

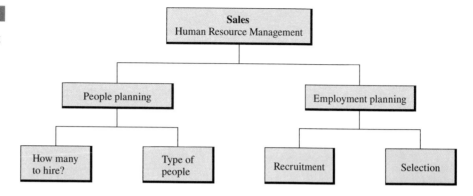

People Planning

People are the most important ingredient in developing a successful sales force. "Your people," says IBM's Matt Suffoletto, "are more important than anything else, including training and compensation. If you don't have the right people, no amount of training and money can turn a 'sow's ear into a silk purse.'"

Why is planning necessary? To develop a successful sales team, management should carefully plan for its sales personnel needs. **People planning** involves how many and what type of people to hire.

Sales Force Size

Deciding on the size of the sales force is an important decision affecting the organization's sales and profits. A small bank may employ one outside salesperson, whereas large firms such as IBM, Xerox, Procter & Gamble, or Allstate Insurance have thousands. Sales force size depends on several factors such as the nature of the job, intensity of market coverage—intensive, selective, or exclusive distribution—and type of products sold. One popular method of deciding sales force size is the breakdown approach; see the Selling Tips box.

Type of People

Life is like a box of chocolates. You never know what you are going to get.

FORREST GUMP, THE MOVIE

After the number of salespeople to be hired is decided, it is necessary to determine the type of salesperson to recruit for each sales job. Accordingly, sales managers analyze their salespeople's jobs, develop job descriptions, and create job specifications.

A **job analysis** is the definition of a sales position in terms of specific roles or activities to be performed, and the determination of personal qualifications suitable for the job. **Job descriptions** are formal, written statements describing the nature, requirements, and responsibilities (e.g., sales volume, territory, product line, customers, supervisory duties) of a specific sales position. They officially establish what the salesperson will do, how it will be done, and why these duties are important, as well as indicate the salary range for the position.

Job Specifications

Job specifications convert job descriptions into the people qualifications (e.g., abilities, behavior, education, skills) the organization feels are necessary for successful job performance. Often, management determines job specifications in compliance

SELLING TIPS

The Breakdown Approach: Three Steps for Determining Sales Force Size

There are numerous methods for determining sales force size. They range from the personal judgment of a sales executive to having a computer determine the size and shape of territories and the location of salespeople. Here is a simple three-step procedure frequently used today:

Step 1:

Forecast Sales and Determine Sales Potentials. The firm forecasts sales for its total market and each geographic region. Sales potentials also are considered.

Step 2:

Determine Sales Volume Needed for Each Territory. Next, management determines the level of sales needed to support each territory. Consideration must be given to all costs associated with the territory, including the salesperson's salary and expenses.

Step 3:

Determine Number of Territories. There are several ways to determine the number of territories needed to sell and service a firm's market. The breakdown approach is the simplest. The breakdown approach uses factors such as sales, population, or number of customers. Assume that a firm forecasts sales of $18 million. It believes that each territory must generate $1 million. Using the following formula, 18 territories are needed:

$$\text{Sales force size} = \frac{\text{Forecasted sales}}{\text{Average sales per salesperson}} =$$

$$\text{Sales force size} = \frac{\$18,000,000}{\$1,000,000} = 18$$

Number of customers and population are frequently used to determine number of territories. The Houston sales district of companies such as Quaker Oats has a guideline of one salesperson for every 100 to 120 retail stores. The population of an area determines the number of retail grocery stores. Thus, sales, population trends, and number of retail stores help a district manager estimate the number of territories needed in the sales unit.

---

with governmental regulations. This includes qualifications for initial employment and for training as a successful salesperson. Increasingly, however, statistical analyses also assist in generating job specifications. By this method, the relation of successful sales performance to certain personal characteristics, such as education, specific aptitudes, communication skills, personality type, and experience is statistically determined.

Job Specifications for Successful Salespeople

Sales managers often express frustration over the difficulty of selecting potential salespeople. Typical comments include the following: "What are the characteristics necessary for successful salespeople in my industry and my company? If I knew," states one sales manager, "I'd have fewer staffing problems." "We think we know," says another sales manager. "We hire them. Some do well; others don't." Another manager said: "The company gives us job specifications but they are difficult to use. I have to hire in a short time. I find the best people I can in the job market at that time who have good personality characteristics, background, and potential, and hire them. I don't really use job specifications."

Does character matter to success?

Let us review the desirable characteristics to include in job specifications. We know the selling job is people-oriented. Thus, salespeople must deal with people positively and effectively.

The successful salesperson should have the proper empathy and ego drive for a specific sales job. Empathy is needed for identifying and understanding the other person's situation. Ego drive is the desire to make the sale, to overcome lack of

EXHIBIT 16.8

Selected characteristics of successful salespeople. Which are most important?

- High energy levels
- High self-confidence
- Need for material things
- Hard working
- Requires little supervision
- High perseverance
- Competitive
- Good physical appearance
- Likable
- Self-disciplined
- Intelligent
- Achievement oriented
- Good communication skills

sales, and to continue calling on customers. Other reported desirable characteristics appear in Exhibit 16.8. A point can be made that the individual company should determine the job specifications and sales personnel characteristics necessary for successful performance. They must be updated continually. Most sales managers say the minimum components of a successful salesperson are

1. *Education.* The individual should be an above-average student.
2. *Personality.* A good salesperson is achievement oriented, tactful, mature, self-confident, a self-starter with a positive outlook on life. The salesperson also has a realistic career plan.
3. *Experience.* A good salesperson works hard and goes beyond the call of duty; if a recent graduate, this person will have participated in school organizations and developed above-average class projects.
4. *Physical attributes.* A good salesperson has a neat appearance, good personal habits, is physically fit, and makes a good first impression.

Employment Planning

Employment planning refers to the recruitment and selection of applicants for sales jobs. Recruitment begins with the initiation of a search (i.e., prospecting for applicants). Once all of the activities leading up to and including the actual decision by the applicant to accept or reject the final job are over, the recruitment process ends for the individual applicant. In essence, recruiters attempt to close sales by getting applicants to accept employment offers. On the other side, applicants attempt to sell themselves to the prospective employer, while searching for a job that will fulfill their needs and expectations.

Typically, candidates complete a job application form and undergo an initial interview. If applicants appear to be good candidates, they go through several in-depth interviews. Some companies have applicants work with salespeople to show them what the job is like.

Tests are frequently given to applicants to determine their intelligence and aptitude for sales jobs. Applicants submit names of people who can provide character references, which are checked. The final step is the physical examination.

Both the applicant and the sales manager have the option to say no at any of the six steps in the selection process. During the process, the applicant and the sales manager collect enough information about each other to make a decision.

Legal Framework for Employment

The sales manager faces an increasing number of laws governing employment practices. Although a number of federal agencies are involved, the **Equal Employment Opportunity Commission (EEOC)** is the principal government agency responsible for monitoring discriminatory practices. As such, the EEOC has a major influence on sales force staffing. Changing social values, attitudes toward minorities and women entering the workforce, recognition of the traditional advantages enjoyed by white males, and an increasing number of government regulations necessitated creation of the commission.

The legislation affecting employment practices ranges from the Constitution to more recent laws such as the 1964 Equal Pay Act, which specifically prohibits sex discrimination in pay. The provisions of this act were broadened under the 1972 Education Amendments Act, which states that "Any employee employed in a bona fide executive, administrative, or professional capacity . . . or in the capacity of outside salesman" is entitled to equal pay. The most far-reaching recent legislation in this context is the Civil Rights Act of 1964, especially Title VII of the act as amended by the Equal Employment Opportunity Act of 1972, which prohibits discrimination based on race, gender, religion, or national origin. A law influencing sales hiring is the **Americans with Disabilities Act (ADA),** which defines a disability as a physical or mental impairment that substantially limits one or more major life activities. Discrimination is prohibited under this law if the disabled person can do the job.

Laws were created because industry was not following the Golden Rule.

Remember that what might be labeled discrimination is allowed if an employer can show that a given action is "reasonably necessary to the operation of that particular business or enterprise" and that the employment decision is based on a "bona fide occupational qualification." Included in this context are such factors as age, testing, and inquiries into preemployment background. However, there are few cases in which this argument can stand up against charges of discrimination.

The government has many ways of influencing employment practices. Consequently, the sales manager must have continually updated information on government regulations and must have specific guidelines to follow. Broadly speaking, the equal employment opportunity criteria are based on two questions:

1. Are the employment practices equally applied and do they have the same effect on all potential employees, regardless of race, gender, religion, or national origin?
2. Are the employment practices job related?

Sales managers must understand laws related to their jobs—especially as the sales force becomes more diverse.

Diversity of the Sales Force

Today diversity refers to far more than skin color and gender. **Diversity** refers to all kinds of differences among people. As Exhibit 16.9 shows, these differences include religious affiliation, age, disability status, military experience, sexual orientation, economic class, educational level, and lifestyle in addition to gender, race, ethnicity, and nationality.

The real me is on the inside not the outside.

Although members of different groups (white males, Vietnam veterans, Hispanics, Asians, women, blacks, etc.) share within their groups many common values, attitudes, and perceptions, there is also much diversity within each of these categories. Every group is made up of individuals who are unique in personality, education, and life experiences. There may be more differences among, say, three Asians from Thailand, Hong Kong, and Korea than among a Caucasian, an African-American, and an Asian, all born in Chicago. And not all white males share the same personal or professional goals and values or behave alike.

EXHIBIT 16.9

The sales force is becoming diverse.

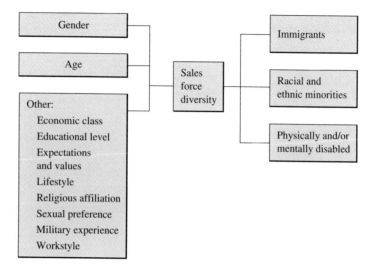

EXHIBIT 16.9

The sales force is becoming diverse.

The Multicultural Sales Organization

To capitalize on the benefits and minimize the costs of a diverse workforce, organizations can strive to become **multicultural.** This term refers to the degree to which an organization values cultural diversity and is willing to utilize and encourage it.

Multicultural organizations fully integrate gender, racial, and minority group members both formally and informally. The multicultural organization is marked by an absence of prejudice and discrimination and by low levels of intergroup conflict. Such an organization creates an environment in which all members can contribute to their maximum potential; thus, the advantages of diversity are fully realized.

Recruitment— Finding the Right People

Recruitment involves searching for, finding, and interviewing people for the job. Recruitment of salespeople takes the proper recruiters, budget, and amount of time to attract and hire quality individuals. Recruiting is typically the responsibility of the sales manager rather than the personnel department.

College recruiting, though an expensive process, is a major source of high-quality applicants. Many companies work hard to get top students into their interviews. Applicants are attracted by the type of sales job, the company's image, word of mouth, and salaries.

Selection—Choose the Best Available!

Selection refers to the process of selecting the best available person for the job. The selection process is no longer based on intuitive feelings; it involves a series of steps designed to test whether a person is right for a company and vice versa (see Exhibit 16.10). The application form is the most common tool used in hiring. Data collected include such information as education, work experience, and physical and personal characteristics.

The personal interview is an important part of the selection process. Although it is a good method for obtaining factual information, it is often too subjective; however, it remains the most popular tool used by managers in building a sales force. People who meet the minimum job qualifications in the initial interview are asked back for several in-depth interviews and often work with salespeople for a day in the field. This gives applicants a realistic preview of what to expect from the job.

EXHIBIT 16.10

Major steps in sales personnel
selection process. Not all
companies take every step.

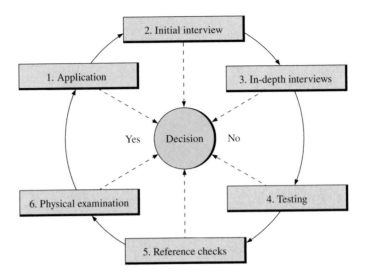

Certain employment tests also can be used in selecting personnel. Some firms have assessment centers where qualified applicants can be evaluated in a comprehensive manner. Employment references and physical examinations are two additional steps used to gather information on an applicant. The applicant can be hired or rejected at any step in the selection process.

A Sales Manager's View of the Recruit

The following is a sales manager's views of the recruit and the recruiting process. This person's description is fairly typical of how all leaders approach selection of salespeople. This particular sales manager had 20 years' experience recruiting for a manufacturer of computer equipment. The following discussion is based on a tape recording of a talk given to a graduate class in sales management.

Is Sales the Right Job for the Applicant?

The search for the sales job begins with the applicant. To obtain any job, applicants must sell themselves. If applicants are excited and enthusiastic about the future, recruiters will be, too.

Applicants should ask themselves what they look for in a job. They should be honest and realistic. They need to ask themselves:

- What are my past accomplishments and future goals?
- Do I want the responsibility of a sales job?
- Do I mind travel? How much travel is acceptable?
- How much freedom do I want in the job?
- Do I have the personality characteristics for the job?

These are questions recruiters attempt to answer about the applicant during the interview.

What Recruiters Look for

Applicants need to determine which industries, types of products or services, and specific companies they are interested in. Find out what recruiters from different companies may look for in an applicant to better prepare yourself.

MAKING THE SALE

Finding the Right Sales Position

For the job seeker, a job search can be just as daunting as the recruiting problem is for the company. When Robert Roland, sales manager with Shannon Corporation of Grand Prairie, Texas, started looking for a new job three years ago, he tried various sources for information on available positions. The Internet, he said, seemed to be filled with ads for either entry-level people or CEOs. He fell in the middle and found nothing there.

He turned to a professional recruiting agency. The recruiter first listened to what he wanted. Roland was looking for a position either in sales or middle management with a manufacturer in a specific geographic area. The recruiter then had him take a series of tests that measured aspects of his personality, values, and job competence. The counselor also guided him in preparing his résumé and application letter. Based on test information, the recruiter gave him a list of positions that best fit his needs and abilities. That list led him to Shannon.

Roland is very happy with the result. He has been with Shannon for three years and was recently promoted from salesperson to sales manager, an indication that he was an excellent match for the company.

"I would recommend that salespeople looking for jobs find a good employment counselor," he says. "It certainly worked for me."[3]

Recruiters look for outstanding applicants who are mature and intelligent. They must handle themselves well in the interview, demonstrating good interpersonal skills. They should have well-thought-out career plans and discuss them rationally. They must have friendly, pleasing personalities. A clean, neat appearance is a must. They should have positive attitudes, be willing to work hard, be ambitious, and demonstrate interest in the employer's business field. They should have good grades and other personal, school, and business accomplishments. Finally, they must have clear goals and objectives in life. The more common characteristics on which applicants for our company are judged are appearance, self-expression, maturity, personality, experience, enthusiasm, and interest in the job.

The Application Letter

The application letter introduces the applicant to the prospective employer. It should not totally rehash the information in the résumé. It should be neat and personalized. The letter should begin by mentioning the job for which the person is applying. In the next paragraph, the applicant states reasons for interest in the position and the company. It indicates knowledge of the company. If currently in school, applicants must explain how their education qualifies them for the position. The same should be done with school activities and work experience. In the third paragraph, the résumé can be mentioned, possibly pointing out the relevant factors not previously discussed (e.g., grade point average, honors, graduation date). The last paragraph should ask positively for an interview at a time and place convenient to the company.

The Résumé

The application letter serves to arouse the recruiter's interest and develops the desire to review the résumé. Again, neatness is a must. Printed copies may be made

MAKING THE SALE

I Want to Hire the Four Horsemen

In 1924, the Four Horsemen led the Fighting Irish to their first national football championship and a victory over Stanford in the Rose Bowl. That was Notre Dame's only bowl appearance until the school administration permitted postseason trips again in 1970.

The backfield of that team was immortalized by the late sports writer Grantland Rice when he wrote:

Outlined against a blue-gray October sky, the Four Horsemen rode again. In dramatic lore, they were

known as famine, pestilence, destruction, and death. But these are only aliases. Their real names are Stuhldreher, Miller, Crowley, and Layden.

I believe at times all sales managers dream that one day their salespeople will be equivalent to the Four Horsemen. They will all be all-Americans, all-stars, people who achieve Olympic gold medal performance levels.

with a picture attached. There are many résumé formats, but, in general, they should contain information such as

- **Personal data**—including address and phone number.
- **Job objective.**
- **Education**—listing most recent degree first.
- **Work experience**—listing most recent job first.
- **Activities.**
- **Reference section**—stating that references will be furnished on request.

This information summarizes the applicant's life in one to two pages. In a few minutes, the recruiter should have a good idea of the applicant's background. Recruiters are busy people. If the résumé is mailed and there has not been a response in one to two weeks, the applicant should call and/or write the company.

The Interview

Be a person of 100% truth, not 99% truth. The % proof is in your word.

Applicants should be prepared. They should anticipate interview questions, prepare for them, and practice. Be prepared for questions such as

- What can you tell me about yourself?
- Why do you want to be in sales?
- What do you know about my company?
- Why do you want to work for my company?
- What problems have you had and how have you solved them?
- Where do you want to be in five years?

Some recruiters may ask the applicant to sell them something, for example, an ashtray or a pencil. The applicant cannot always prepare for everything. However, the recruiter knows when the applicant is prepared. When being interviewed, it is important to be early to review plans for the interview. The recruiter should be addressed by name. See Exhibit 16.11.

Be as prepared as possible for your job interview—but be aware that the interviewer may ask questions you have not anticipated.

Applicant: Create a Performance Portfolio

The next time you go on an interview to land a lucrative sales job, walk in armed with more than a résumé. Add an "I do good work" portfolio that gives details of your positive performance. This sales tool can back up your claims of top performance with solid evidence.

If you are currently in sales, each Friday before you leave the office write down five things you—not necessarily others—believe you did well this week, even if they represent common tasks. Perhaps you returned all phone calls, leaving no loose ends to tie up at the end of the week. Or maybe the details you provide in your sales reports enabled you to find additional product fits for the client. Any letters from happy customers or e-mails thanking you for solving a problem should go right in your folder. Cold calling that led to new customers and servicing existing customers with special attention should also go in your folder. Be sure to include sales awards and any positive letters from your manager.

Tuck that list away and continue this weekly exercise for the entire month. At the end of the month, narrow the four or five lists to 10 accomplishments that stand out to you. At the end of the year, review the 120 items and cull them to 25. Formalize the language that describes those 25 achievements and print them out in an organized manner on résumé paper along with your references.

If you are someone with no sales experience, and even very little work experience such as some college students, create your portfolio with projects you have completed in your school courses, membership with an organization, church, community activities, and work experience.

When someone asks, "What do you bring to this organization?" you won't merely reply, "I'm good with people," You'll hand that sales manager or HR person "proof." See the "Sell Yourself" exercise at the back of this textbook for other interview tips.

Interview Follow-up

A letter immediately following the interview is not always necessary. However, if the recruiter has set a time for notifying the applicant of a decision and if that time has passed, a follow-up letter or call is appropriate.

The Second Interview

An applicant invited for a second interview has passed the first major step in the job search. The recruiter feels that this individual may be what the company seeks in a salesperson. Now, the applicant should prepare for this visit by doing everything from reviewing information to planning what to wear.

Job Offers

If a company offers a job, the applicant should respond positively in one of three ways. First, accept the offer and stop interviewing. Second, reject the offer tactfully but give the reasons for your decision; this should be done as soon as possible. Third, request more time to either complete the job search or consider the offer.

No Job Offer

If the recruiter feels that there is no match and does not make a job offer, the applicant may write a letter of appreciation for the opportunity to be interviewed. If still interested in the job, the applicant can express hope for future consideration.

TRAINING THE SALES FORCE

Sales training is the effort put forth by an employer to provide the opportunity for the salesperson to acquire job-related attitudes, concepts, rules, and skills that result in improved performance in the selling environment.

John H. Patterson, founder of the National Cash Register Company and known as the father of sales training, used to say, "At NCR, our salespeople never stop learning." This philosophy is the reason that even today successful companies thoroughly train new salespeople and have ongoing training programs for experienced sales personnel, in which even the most successful salespeople participate.

Basically, sales training changes or reinforces behavior to make salespeople more efficient in achieving job goals. Salespeople are trained to perform activities they would not normally undertake. In addition, training reinforces successful sales practices.

Purposes of Training

Companies are interested in training primarily to increase sales, productivity, and profits. As the chair and chief executive officer at United States Steel expressed it:

> We support training and development activities to get results. . . . We're interested in specific things that provide greater rewards to the employee, increased return to the stockholder, and enable reinvestment to meet the needs of the business. In other words, [we're interested in] those things that affect the "bottom line." Although you cannot always evaluate training as readily as some other functions, as people improve their performance, it is reflected in on-the-job results as well as all aspects of their lives.

Edward G. Harness, a past chair of the board of Procter & Gamble, says: "We grow our own managers, and it starts with finding the right people through an extremely intensive selection process, followed by continuing on-the-job training." There are specific purposes for training other than improving general sales volume. They relate to the type of training offered and include these goals:

- Helping salespeople become better managers.
- Orienting the new salesperson to the job.
- Improving knowledge in areas such as product, company, competitors, or selling skills.

- Lowering absenteeism and turnover.
- Positively influencing attitudes in such areas as job satisfaction.
- Lowering selling costs.
- Informing salespeople.
- Obtaining feedback from the salespeople.
- Increasing sales in a particular product or customer category.

Yet, the primary purpose of training is to invest in the sales organization's most valuable resource—its salespeople. Training is an ongoing process and the responsibility of the trainee, the trainer, and the organization.

Training Methods

The three basic training methods are discussion, role playing, and on-the-job training.

Discussion

The discussion approach to sales training can be used in several ways, including case studies and/or discussion groups. Case studies are usually included in presession assignments. At a session, small discussion groups may be formed to further analyze the case and to report findings to the group. Lectures incorporating discussion and demonstration are the most common and effective method of training. Filmed or videotaped cases are more effective than written cases.

Role Playing

In **role playing,** the trainee acts out the sale of a product or service to a hypothetical buyer. Often the trainee's presentation is videotaped and replayed for critique by a group, the trainee, and the trainer. The role-playing procedure is generally a variation of the following:

1. *Define the sales problem.* The trainee is told the company is coming out with a new shaving cream.
2. *Establish the situation.* The trainee is asked to think about, and then describe, the largest potential account and its buyer.
3. *Cast the characters.* The trainer or a trainee is selected to play the buyer.
4. *Brief the participants.* Each person learns a role. In addition, the buyer may be briefed separately from the salesperson and given certain specific objections to raise.
5. *Act out the buyer–seller situation.* The salesperson goes through a sales presentation with interaction from the buyer.
6. *Discuss, analyze, and critique the role-playing.* This is important to the learning process. If videotaped, the presentation is shown to the group. Trainers often ask the group for their comments first. Then, the participants discuss the situation. A critique from the trainer is next. Trainees may be asked to repeat the exercise.

On-the-Job Training

On-the-job training may take several forms. New salespeople may accompany their managers and observe sales calls. At first, the manager makes all sales presentations for some period. Then, typically, a customer is selected who will be easy to call on, and the trainee makes a first sales presentation with little or no assistance. This is an exciting and important time for the trainee, and the experience must be critiqued in a positive manner to establish a good relationship between salesperson and manager.

On-the-job training includes observation and curbside counseling by the sales manager. This way, the salesperson gets immediate feedback. When the manager and salesperson leave the customer's office, the manager can critique the sales presentation. If needed, corrections are made. Imagine yourself making six sales presentations in the presence of your manager and having each critiqued. The next day, you are prepared to use what you have learned to make more effective sales presentations.

There are many variations in critiquing the salesperson. Some managers prefer to have salespeople critique themselves. For example, "Judy, that was a very good sales presentation. Can you think of anything that should have been changed or improved on?" Then, the manager asks whether the trainee would like any help toward becoming more successful, such as more selling aids and samples, or having the manager make the next presentation so that the salesperson can watch and learn.

Where Does Training Take Place?

A salesperson may receive some form of training any place, any time of day or night (see Exhibit 16.12). Sales training is continuous. In a broad sense, training occurs any time the superior does things such as commenting on a salesperson's reports, talking on the phone to the salesperson, working in the field with the salesperson, or conducting a meeting. The two broad categories of sales training are centralized and decentralized training. Companies often are divided on whether training should be totally centralized, using corporate staff trainers, or both centralized *and* decentralized.

Centralized Training

Training at a central location is primarily intended for instruction of salespeople from all geographical areas served by the company. Programs typically are held at or close to the home office/manufacturing plant, in a large city, or at a resort.

EXHIBIT 16.12

Technology allows salespeople to receive excellent training at home.

Centralized training programs supplement the basic training done by sales personnel in the field. A survey of selling costs shows that 100 percent of the business products managers questioned use their home office as a training site, while 93 percent of the consumer products and 71 percent of service companies use home office sites.

A salesperson may attend a centralized training program when first starting work, after six months to a year of employment, or at stipulated intervals. The new salesperson may initially be trained in the field, then after one year, be sent to the home office for training and to tour the firm's manufacturing facilities. There may be further training at the home office every five years.

Centralized training programs usually involve excellent facilities and equipment such as classrooms, videotapes, closed circuit television, and sales laboratories designed for role playing. Trainees get to know each other and corporate executives. Because they are away from home, they can concentrate on learning. Training content can be standardized so that the entire sales force has a common body of knowledge.

Decentralized Training

Are you teachable!?

The main form of sales force instruction, **decentralized training,** may be conducted anywhere. It can be done in a branch office, in the salesperson's car, at the customer's place of business, in a motel room, or at the salesperson's home.

There are numerous advantages to decentralized training. For one thing, costs are usually lower. For example, if a branch office is used as the training site, travel costs are less. The sessions are typically shorter, saving on motel and meal expenditures. Salespeople's geographical territories are such that often they see one another only during meetings and training programs. Many sales managers feel their salespeople receive as much knowledge and motivation from their peers in informal sessions as in regular training. Salespeople can informally discuss their problems in making sales and how they overcome sales resistance. The success stories particularly benefit the inexperienced salesperson. Of course, these informal talks also occur when salespeople attend centralized training sessions. Finally, supplies, samples, and tools can be provided to take home after the session.

There are several disadvantages to either type of training. A potential major weakness in decentralized training is that a branch manager may not be an able trainer, which can hurt salespeople. On the other hand, centralized training is expensive due to the cost of travel, meals, and facilities. Also, it is expensive for salespeople to be out of their territories, and trainees may not want to be away from their families for a prolonged time. Common disadvantages include the fact that salespeople may come to the meeting unprepared, really only wanting to get away from regular work. Trainers understand this, and overcome it by having training sessions that are well prepared, interesting, and informative and that encourage participation. Finally, customer sales may be lost. The cost of lost sales must be offset by increasing productivity and efficiency through training.

When Does Training Occur?

For new sales personnel, training begins the first day they report to work. Basic company, product, and selling skill information is usually given to the trainee to study. In a recruiting brochure, Procter & Gamble states: "Your training begins the day you join us and will continue throughout your career, regardless of your responsibility or job level." The firm gives new salespeople a two-day orientation conducted by an immediate supervisor. Company, product, and customer information is presented. Salespeople also receive a company car, equipment, and supplies. After the orientation session, salespeople call on customers with their managers. This procedure is common for persons selling consumer goods.

Training does not end with this initial session, but continues throughout the professional salesperson's career. Some firms want their salespeople to be thoroughly trained before they are assigned a sales territory. Conversely, some firms believe that new employees can relate to and retain more from training if they have been in the sales territory for a short time.

Companies provide training for experienced salespeople through periodic sales meetings. Many companies have regular sales meetings once every month or two. In addition, materials are mailed to the homes of sales personnel. Training involves working with a manager in the sales territory. Salespeople also periodically attend training programs at company headquarters.

Who Is Involved in Training?

Typically, the three basic kinds of sales trainers are corporate staff personnel, regular sales force personnel, and specialists from outside the company. These are shown in Exhibit 16.13.

Corporate Staff Trainers

Staff trainers are responsible for the creation, administration, and coordination of a firm's sales management and sales force training and development programs. Typically, the training manager and staff are separate from the personnel department. They have an ongoing relationship with all staff departments and the field organization. The training manager usually reports to someone at the upper corporate level, such as the vice president of sales.

The duties and responsibilities of the training manager can be narrow or broad, depending on the size of the organization and the importance placed on centralized training. The following are some major duties:

- The foremost duty of the manager and the manager's staff is to assist sales management in identifying training needs and developing programs to meet those needs.
- They organize, coordinate, and schedule the training.
- They determine who will conduct the training and, if needed, provide them with support material.
- The training manager may help evaluate the training and report results to corporate and field management.
- The trainer often coordinates and administers follow-up training.
- The trainer prepares an annual budget to meet the goals and needs of each training program.

EXHIBIT 16.13

Basic sources of sales training.

Sales Trainers Include

Corporate staff trainers | Regular sales force personnel | Outside training specialists

ETHICAL DILEMMA

Customers Complain of Poor Service

As district sales manager, you have been assigned to work with a problem salesperson with the agreement that "if you can't turn him around in 60 days, then you must terminate him." The action will depend solely on your recommendation. However, he must improve—quickly!

For the past six months, customers have been calling into the distribution center complaining about this person. His smaller accounts never see him. His larger customers complain that he frequently fouls up their the order, even at times forgetting to call or e-mail orders into the office.

Now his 60 days are up. Although you cannot honestly document any change, you know positive change has taken place, and you need more time.

However, each time you work with him, you wonder why he was ever hired. Even though your personality and his clash, customers seem to get along with him; some even like him. Tomorrow you are scheduled to give your recommendation to the regional sales manager.

What would be the most ethical action to take?

1. Tell your regional sales manager that although you cannot document any substantial change thus far, you know there has been some improvement. Recommend that he be put on probation for the next 60 days instead of being terminated at this point.
2. Tell your regional sales manager your opinion (that you cannot document any significant change and that you don't know why he was ever hired). Let him make the decision. You don't want to have to terminate somebody on your own recommendation.
3. Tell your regional sales manager that you really do not see any improvement. You are sure that the company can find a better salesperson that you will get along with and you do not want your reputation connected in any way with his.

Sales Force Personnel

Senior sales representatives and district and regional sales managers are the primary trainers of the sales force. These people bring to the training program years of sales experience that help the trainee relate quickly to the instructor and the material. The sales manager possesses power and authority, which aids in getting the sales personnel to cooperate and to exert greater effort in training sessions. The manager is in a position to train salespeople in the best methods of working and selling. A good rapport between the manager and the sales force can be established if the salesperson sees the trainer as imparting knowledge and teaching skills that aid the trainee in obtaining personal sales goals.

Management must provide sales force personnel with adequate time, support, and rewards to do training. Otherwise, training personnel may not perform adequately, which can create low morale among salespeople and decrease effectiveness of the training program. Often, the trainer receives support from the home office personnel (for example, product managers or technical support personnel who discuss product strategies or product information).

The trainer must be an effective salesperson and a competent teacher. A company should choose a senior salesperson as a trainer not on the basis of sales ability but because of effective communication skills. People with both sales and teaching abilities can usually be found, but management must seek them out. An assignment at the corporate level as a trainer can be a step up the career ladder for the salesperson in the field.

Outside Training Specialists

Trainers drawn from outside the company may be consultants specializing in sales training or representatives of programs such as Toastmasters, Dale Carnegie Sales Courses, and the Xerox Sales Learning Programs. Some universities also offer courses for salespeople and sales managers.

Often, the company pays all or part of the cost when the salesperson completes a college-level sales methods course. One endorsement of such sales training courses came from a vice president of engineering in the A. T. Cross Company: "As a result of taking the course, our people have new, positive attitudes toward their jobs, along with a better understanding of the company's goals. They also have a better appreciation of one another's problems, and they show better teamwork in resolving day-to-day situations."

Smaller firms may rely heavily on outside trainers. This practice affords them the training without the cost of maintaining a training staff. The courses may be standardized or customized for the company. A company must carefully select outside trainers based on individual needs.

Combination of Training Sources

Firms large and small use a combination of training sources. A firm may use its sales force personnel to do a large percentage of the training with a sales training director and staff. The latter organize and coordinate training efforts among the staff and trainers. The training director might arrange for a product manager to attend a sales meeting to give technical information and discuss future promotional plans for the product. Firms often hire consultants, such as university professors, to put on in-house seminars dealing with such subjects as the psychological aspects of why industrial buyers purchase goods or effective selling techniques.

SUMMARY OF MAJOR SALES MANAGEMENT ISSUES

A salesperson who is promoted to sales manager becomes involved in sales planning, staffing, training, directing, and evaluating sales force activities. This chapter discussed the need to understand how to make sales forecasts and budgets, how to determine the number of salespeople to hire, how to recruit and train salespeople, and the legal aspects of staffing. The sales manager uses this knowledge to achieve the sales volume, profits, and growth higher levels of management desire.

Today, firms structure their organizations to best serve their customers. Small companies use a simple line organizational design, whereas large firms design specialized structures based on geography, the products they market, customers, or a combination of these elements.

Sales managers are frequently involved in forecasting their firm's sales. They are also involved in developing budgets and allocating money to various sales units, all of which ultimately serve as input into planning and aid in coordinating and controlling sales unit activities.

The contemporary sales manager is knowledgeable in personnel practices involving the recruiting and hiring of salespeople. Government laws need to be considered so that the firm can abide by EEOC guidelines. The staff function involves both personnel planning—the determination of the kind and number of needed salespeople—and employment planning—the locating, recruiting, evaluation, and hiring of applicants for the sales job.

Once the hiring is done, the sales manager becomes involved in training salespeople on things such as product knowledge and selling skills. Training begins immediately, usually in the salesperson's territory and at company training facilities.

The sales manager is a salesperson first, but also something of a jack-of-all-trades due to the various functions required for the job. The next chapter discusses directing and evaluating functions.

MEETING A SALES CHALLENGE

Start with a private conversation with John Scott, focusing on the visible problem of falling sales performance as the effect of some cause. With his help, try to determine the cause or causes. Let John know that you believe in him, that his abilities could lead to his promotion. If John is confused or anxious about the responsibilities you assigned, encourage him to directly ask for your guidance while his managerial skills and self-confidence are maturing.

This course of action demonstrates your efforts to be objective and impersonal, and it shows that you possess a healthy combination of task and people orientation. Also, it shows you have a feeling of sharing responsibility for the present situation and concern for John's welfare and future, as well as for the bottom line of sales data.

By encouraging his suggestions, ideas, and thoughts, he will respond in his former way—analytically, prudently, and articulately. The reason for the change is that you are satisfying one of the most important of all human needs—personal recognition. By modeling two-way communication, you're also enhancing the prognosis for long-term success.

KEY TERMS FOR MANAGING

Golden Rule of Sales Management 501
sales management 506
planning 507
staffing 507
training 507
directing 507
evaluating 507
sales forecasting 508
sales force budget 508
organizational design 510
organizational structure 510
people planning 511
job analysis 511
job descriptions 511

job specifications 511
employment planning 513
Equal Employment Opportunity
  Commission (EEOC) 513
Americans with Disabilities Act
  (ADA) 514
diversity 514
multicultural 515
recruitment 515
selection 515
sales training 520
role playing 521
centralized training programs 523
decentralized training 523

SALES APPLICATION QUESTIONS

1. What is the main bottom-line responsibility of a sales manager?
2. Discuss the difference between organizational design and organizational structure. How do design and structure relate to a firm's organizational chart?
3. Discuss the relationship among a firm's marketing plan, sales forecast, and sales force budget.
4. What are the two major elements of the sales manager's staffing function? Discuss each of these elements.
5. In applying for a sales job, what are the important things an applicant must do?

FURTHER EXPLORING THE SALES WORLD

1. In interviewing for a job, you have to sell yourself. Develop a job interview presentation in the same way that you would develop a product sales presentation. Use your résumé as a visual aid. How would you open and close the interview? What are the main benefits of hiring you? What objections might arise?

2. Contact one or more sales managers in your community and ask about the steps they use in their recruiting process.

SELLING EXPERIENTIAL EXERCISE

How well do you understand people, observe their behavior, and address their personal and professional growth? This self-test can help you see your skills. On a separate sheet of paper, write your score for each question. Write 4 if you strongly agree, 1 if you strongly disagree, or 2 or 3 if your feelings are somewhere in between.

What Are Your People Skills?

Strongly Agree			Strongly Disagree
4	3	2	1

1. I think that people often are unaware of their true motivation.
2. Psychological factors often play more of a role in job performance than the job's required skills.
3. I make a conscious effort to understand the basic needs of others.
4. I am able to empathize with other people, even when I don't share their viewpoints.
5. I consciously try to organize my thinking around others.
6. People often reveal themselves by small details of behavior.
7. I am usually aware of people's strengths and weaknesses.
8. Most people aren't easy to read.
9. I notice when someone gets a new haircut, eyeglasses, or clothes.
10. After a meeting, I can usually accurately report how others responded to the discussion.
11. People may present themselves in a certain way that doesn't show who they really are.
12. I try not to read my own attitudes into other people's behavior.
13. I often think about the implications of my past impressions of people on the job.
14. When dealing with others, I try to consider how different they may be from me.
15. I don't judge someone until I have enough information to form a sound judgment.
16. I often think about ways to foster other people's personal and professional growth.
17. I see people for their potential—not how they can be of use to me, but how they can fulfill their life goals.
18. You can't change someone else.
19. When making decisions about people, I deliberately consider a wide range of factors.

20. I consciously try to help people play to their strengths and address their weaknesses.

Total Score _____

What were your skills? If your score was

- **75–80**—you're probably strong in solving people problems.
- **61–74**—you have potential strengths in this area.
- **40–60**—you have potential weaknesses in this area.
- **20–39**—you have weaknesses to work on in solving people problems.

Now relate what you've learned to your work experiences by setting goals and intermediate targets. Then adjust![4]

CHAPTER 16

Planning, Staffing, and Training Successful Salespeople

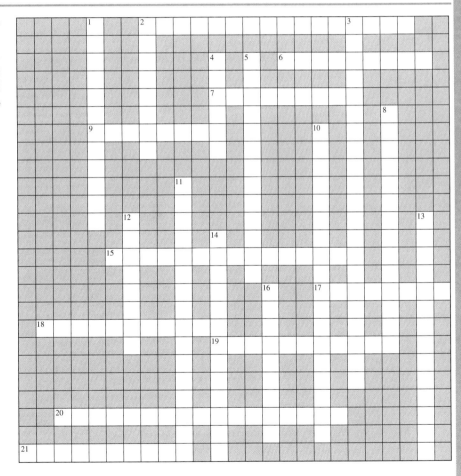

Across

2. The amount of money available or assigned for a definite period.

6. The action of dealing with people positively and persuasively from a leadership position.

7. The process of selecting the best available person for a sales job.

9. Establishing a broad guideline for goals, policies, and procedures that will accomplish the objectives of the organization.

15. The attainment of sales force goals in an effective and efficient manner through planning, staffing, training, directing, and evaluating organizational resources.

17. Deciding which methods to use, plus whom to train, when, and where.

18. The process of searching for, finding, and interviewing people for the sales job.

19. A process whereby a sales trainee acts though the sale of a product of service to hypothetical buyer.

20. The conversion of job descriptions into those people qualifications the organization feels are needed for successful job performance.

21. Comparing actual performance to planned performance goals to determine whether to take corrective action if goals are not achieved, or to continue using the same methods if goals are met.

Down

1. Formal, written statements describing the nature, requirements, and responsibilities of a specific position, known as job ___.

2. Activities undertaken to attract, hire, and retain effective sales force personnel within an organization.

3. Training that comprises the main form of sales instruction.

4. The formal, coordinated process of communication, authority, and responsibility for sales groups and individuals is ___ design.

5. The degree to which an organization values diversity and is willing to utilize and encourage it.

8. Planning how many and what type of people to hire.

10. The recruitment and selection of applicants for the job.

11. One method used to predict a firm's future revenues when planning the company's marketing and sales force objectives.

12. A job ___ defines a sales position in terms of specific roles or activities to be performed along with the determination of personal qualifications suitable for the job.

13. The relatively fixed, formally defined relationship among jobs within the organization is ___ structure.

14. The effort put forth by an employer to provide the opportunity for the salesperson to acquire job-related attitudes, concepts, rules, and skills that result in improved performance in the selling environment.

16. The difference between people due to age, religion, race, gender, and so on.

CASE 16-1

The Wilson Company: Is a Sales Manager's Job Really for Me?

Joy Gresham was still at her desk at 6 P.M. trying to tie up some loose ends with the hope that tomorrow might be a more productive day. Joy is the western regional sales director (a middle management position) in the Wilson Company. Wilson is a manufacturer of a well-known line of sporting goods. As she reads the mail she still has to answer and stacks the phone messages she still has to return, she wonders if being a middle manager is really her kind of job. Selling products, traveling, and meeting with clients seemed much more to her liking than the routine of her present job.

Today is a good example. Joy went to the office early so she could call Lewis Jackson, the eastern regional sales director, to confer on a joint sales forecast they are trying to prepare. Working with Lewis isn't the easiest of tasks. Compromise just isn't a word in Lewis's vocabulary. She also needs to call the production managers of two of the company's eastern plants to find out what is causing the delay in the receipt of the new product lines. Those production people don't seem to realize that a large inventory is needed to keep up sales. The new product lines were promised two weeks ago and still aren't here. The phone calls take longer than expected, but by midmorning Joy is finally able to settle into the major project she has planned for the day. After several days of perusing sales reports of the past several years, she concluded that total sales, as well as productivity of individual salespersons, can be improved if the region is redesigned and the territories of each salesperson are adjusted. This is a major project, and she must present it to her district sales managers at her monthly meeting tomorrow afternoon.

Joy is away from the office a little longer than expected because of lunch. When she returns she finds a half dozen phone messages, including an urgent call from the corporate vice president of personnel, Wayne McDaniel. She returns Wayne's call, and, much to her dismay, she finds she is going to have to allocate a good portion of tomorrow's sales meeting to presenting the company's new benefits program. Wayne assures her that all the materials she needs will arrive late this afternoon and stresses the need for its immediate dissemination and explanation. After trying unsuccessfully to return several of the other phone calls, she returns to the territory redesign project. She finishes that project just before the 3 P.M. appointment she has with a candidate for district sales manager. Joy spends more than an hour with the candidate and is impressed enough with him to immediately make some follow-up phone calls.

Joy looks at her watch and realizes she hasn't enough time to make all the calls she'd planned. The whole day seems to have gotten away from her. She still has the materials from Wayne to review, and she has to prepare the agenda for tomorrow's meeting. She just has to figure a way to motivate better performance from those sales managers. The redesign of the territory was only a partial solution. Joy wonders what else she can do. "Oh," she thinks to herself. "I better call and cancel my date for tonight. It has been over three weeks since I've had any life other than work, and it feels like the only time I ever leave this office is to eat lunch!"

Questions

1. Compare Joy's present job to what you think her previous job as a salesperson was. How are they similar? How are they different?
2. What managerial skills are depicted in the case? Which skill is the most important for Joy to possess? Why?
3. Why do you feel Joy might be disenchanted with her present job?

CHAPTER 17

Motivation, Compensation, Leadership, and Evaluation of Salespeople

MAIN TOPICS

The Tree of Business Life: Management

Motivation of the Sales Force

The Motivation Mix: Choose Your Ingredients Carefully

Compensation Is More Than Money

The Total Compensation Package

Nonfinancial Rewards Are Many

Leadership Is Important to Success

Performance Evaluations Let People Know Where They Stand

Sales Managers Use Technology

LEARNING OBJECTIVES

Motivation, compensation, leadership, and evaluation of salespeople are four of the most important parts of the sales manager's job. After studying this chapter, you should be able to

- Present and discuss the five elements of the motivation mix.

- Explain the basic methods of compensating salespeople.

- Review three approaches to leadership and suggest leadership techniques for improving the sales manager's effectiveness.

- Discuss why salespeople must be evaluated, who should evaluate them, when they should be evaluated, what performance criteria should be evaluated, and how evaluations should be conducted.

Judy Carter bounces from underachievement to overachievement. On the average, her sales results, in spite of her on-again, off-again behavior, are very high. But the start-and-stop approach to work keeps you on the edge of your managerial seat—especially toward the end of the month when you have to file your report on actual bookings versus budget. The rest of the sales group shares your frustration.

You believe that Judy is afraid of failure and that her self-esteem is as low as her fear of failure is high. She may feel that risk is a path to failure, rather than to success. If she were not a high producer, you would transfer her and restore stability to your work as sales manager. The sales group shows displeasure with Judy's work habits, and others outside the group are aware of Judy's ups and downs, which are quite visible in the sales summaries. The situation is not fixing itself. You need to intervene and make it better.

If you were Judy's boss, what would you do? What options do you have?

As discussed in Chapter 16, training salespeople is an invaluable part of sales management. Beyond training a salesperson comes the task of directing and evaluating his or her performance. This can be very challenging. It is very easy to work with high-performing salespeople. But how do you motivate the low and marginal performers? How do you help the high performers maintain their enthusiasm and hard work from month to month?[1]

THE TREE OF BUSINESS LIFE: MANAGEMENT

If any person in a organization needs integrity, trust, and good moral character, it is a sales manager. The sales leader impacts the lives of his or her salespeople and their families. The sales manager determines people's salary raises, promotions, and if they keep their jobs. The power to reward or discipline following the Golden Rule can only come from a person with a caring heart.

The self-centered sales leader driven by gaining personal power, influence, and wealth (PIW) is preoccupied with his or her own well-being. The needs of others are clouded by selfish concerns. This type of person should not be in management.

Once someone is hired and trained, their future relies on their performance. The sales manager should do all in his or her power to make the person successful. Even the leader who places others' interest first is responsible for each salesperson's performance.

The type of person hired for sales is critical. This person needs the ability and motivation to learn and work hard; otherwise, no amount of training and financial incentives will result in top sales performance. This chapter discusses the main ingredients used to motivate salespeople. Let's begin by understanding what is meant by the term *motivation*.

MOTIVATION OF THE SALES FORCE

Sales managers are concerned with motivating salespeople at two levels. The first is the motivation of the individual salesperson and the second is the motivation of the entire sales force. At both levels, managers should determine how much motivation is needed if the sales personnel are to successfully accomplish their assigned job goals, and they should determine the methods of motivation best for the situation at hand. Finally, they should develop a well-designed motivation program that is coordinated with other sales management activities.

Motivation is a term originally derived from the Latin word *movere*, which means "to move," but it has been expanded to include the various factors by which human behavior is activated. Let us define **motivation** as the arousal, intensity, direction, and persistence of effort directed toward job tasks over a period. The sales manager strives to increase the motivation of salespeople toward performing their job activities at a high level through the development of a motivation mix.

THE MOTIVATION MIX: CHOOSE YOUR INGREDIENTS CAREFULLY

What can the sales manager do to motivate salespeople? A review of sales management literature reveals five broad classes of factors referred to as the **motivation mix.** Sales managers use these factors, shown in Exhibit 17.1, to motivate salespeople. Examples of each factor follow:

The Basic Compensation Plan

- Salary.
- Commissions.
- Fringe benefits.

Special Financial Incentives

- Contests.
- Bonuses.
- Trips.

Nonfinancial Rewards

- Achievement awards.
- Challenging work assignments.
- Psychological rewards.
  - ★ Praise.
  - ★ Recognition.

Leadership Techniques

- Style.
- Personal contact methods (feedback).
  - ★ National, regional, district meetings.
  - ★ Individual meetings.
  - ★ Letters, telephone calls.
  - ★ Joint sales calls.

Management Control Procedures

- Performance evaluation.
- Quotas.
- Reports.

EXHIBIT 17.1

Sales manager's motivation mix.

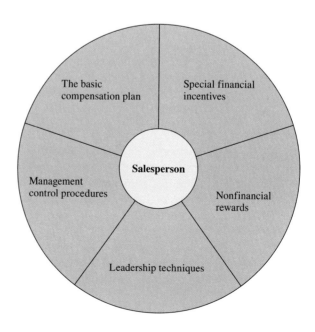

Of the five ingredients in the motivation mix, which is most important to you? "Money," you say. Easy guess. Well, let's start the discussion of the motivational mix with the various financial rewards used to motivate salespeople to high levels of performance.

COMPENSATION IS MORE THAN MONEY

Nothing that happens in a sales force has a more telling impact on its success than the behaviors that are rewarded. The design and implementation of an effective sales reward system are directly related to the sales force's level of success.

Sales performance can be rewarded in three fundamental ways. All three should be used by any type of sales organization. These interrelated elements are

1. Direct financial rewards, such as merit salary increases, bonuses, commission, contests, retirement programs, insurance, and other forms of financial incentives.
2. Career advancement, such as being reassigned to larger accounts and sales territories, promotions upward in the organization, and personal development opportunities such as training and night school.
3. Nonfinancial compensation such as recognition dinners, small gifts, a certificate of achievement, features in sales newsletters, trophies, and membership in a special group (e.g., the million dollar club).

Although a sales reward system is not the only means of motivating salespeople, it is the most important. To measure sales performance but not properly reward it severely limits the level of achievement for salespeople. Money can be an extremely powerful performance motivator if used with the right compensation program. The three basic plans are (1) straight salary, (2) straight commission, or (3) a combination of salary and incentives, such as commissions, bonuses, or contests.

Straight Salary Plans

Of all compensation plans, the **straight salary plan** is the simplest. The salesperson is paid a specific dollar amount at regular intervals, usually weekly, semimonthly, or monthly. For example, as shown in Exhibit 17.2(A), the salesperson earns $22,000 annually regardless of whether that person sells $100,000 or $500,000 in merchandise.

Advantages to the Salesperson

The straight salary plan provides the sense of security that a person may require for effective selling because it ensures a regular income. In theory, pay is independent of sales performance in the short run (a month, three months). However, if performance is low for a prolonged period, the company can take corrective action to improve sales or replace the salesperson. High sales performance can be rewarded by a periodic salary increase (every 6 to 12 months). New recruits and younger salespeople with little sales experience often prefer a compensation plan that gives them a known income.

Advantages to Management

From management's point of view, the plan is simple and economical to administer. Salespeople can be directed toward tasks the company believes are important much more easily than if they were on a straight commission plan. Management can direct selling duties that may not immediately result in sales, such as contacting

EXHIBIT 17.2

Examples of various salary plans.

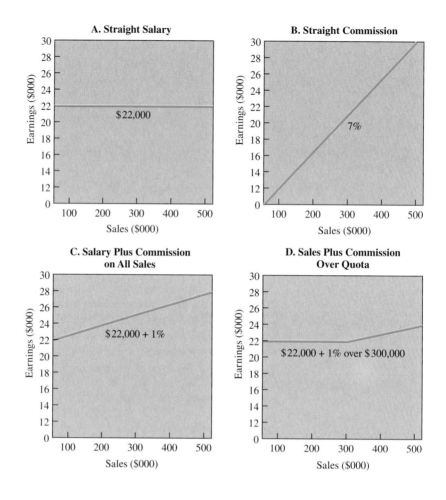

Worry is the darkroom in which negatives can develop.

nonproductive accounts or routinely calling on customers who purchase the company's products from a distribution center or wholesaler outside the territory.

Management usually finds less resistance to reassignments of accounts and personnel transfers with this arrangement. Salespeople are less likely to use high-pressure tactics or to overload customers with merchandise that may bring rewards to the salesperson, but may not be best for the buyer or the company. Finally, management can project compensation expenses for several years in the future because sales costs are relatively fixed. This can make salary budgeting much more accurate. However, because there is no direct relationship between salary and sales performance, it is difficult to estimate salary expenses as a percentage of sales.

Disadvantages of the Straight Salary Plan

The straight salary plan has several potentially undesirable features. The major disadvantage is the lack of direct monetary incentive. The salesperson who meets certain job goals is rewarded by an increase in salary. However, salary adjustments are usually made at specified intervals, so that the increase may be given long after the goal was met. In addition, salary adjustments are not always based on specific performance. Often, everyone is given the same salary increase or there is little difference in the pay adjustment that the higher performers and the lower performers receive. Because salaries are usually kept secret, even if the top performers were given substantially higher raises, they may not perceive them as rewards for good performance. This lack of incentive may cause better salespeople to change jobs.

A straight salary plan can lower work norms within the sales group. Salespeople often perceive that they are in competition with other salespeople and not with their firm's competitors. This is because their performance is compared with other salespeople in their sales district. They may want to do only an average job and meet or not greatly exceed sales quotas. This arrangement can thus favor the less productive salespeople. If not closely supervised, salespeople may accomplish their monthly goals quickly—for example, in three weeks—and not work the rest of the month.

Another problem with the plan is that salary is not distributed in proportion to sales made. One salesperson may sell $500,000 of merchandise and be paid $22,000, whereas another sells $1 million and earns $22,000. Also, since salaries are a fixed expense for the firm, they cannot be adjusted for downturns in the economy. This can increase direct selling costs as compared with other plans. When sales decline, the firm may have to dismiss people. Salespeople who are kept on often have the most job tenure and receive the larger salaries. However, they may not necessarily be the best salespeople. Another problem of using a straight salary compensation plan is that salespeople may over emphasize products that are easiest to sell, especially if this allows them to meet their sales quota.

Many companies increase the number of sales managers to offset these problems. Each manager has fewer salespeople to supervise, helping to ensure that each salesperson works at maximum capacity. However, this approach usually results in an increase in sales expenses rather than a selling effort. The amount of supervision has less effect on performance than on supervision quality.

When to Use Straight Salary Plans

A straight salary plan is best for jobs in which a high percentage of the workday is devoted to nonselling activities, and for which management finds it cannot effectively evaluate performance. Straight salary can be used effectively for routine selling jobs (selling milk, bread, or beverages), extensive missionary and educational sales (pharmaceutical selling), or sales jobs requiring lengthy presale and postsale service and negotiations (selling technical and complex products). Firms sometimes use this method when the person is in training. For example, some insurance firms pay a salary the first year. After one year, the salesperson is placed on a straight commission.

Straight Commission Plans

The **straight commission plan** is a complete incentive compensation plan. If you do not sell anything, you do not earn anything. There are two basic types of commission plans: straight commission and draw against commission.

There are three basic elements of the straight commission plan. First, pay is related directly to a performance unit such as a dollar of sales, a type or amount of product sold, a dollar of profit, type of purchaser, credit terms, or season of the sales. Second, a percentage rate of commission is attached to the unit. Third, a level at which commissions begin or change is established.

Exhibit 17.2(B) shows a 7 percent commission on all sales. The salesperson must generate approximately $314,000 in sales to earn the same $22,000 earned by the person under the straight salary plan.

In addition to the single commission plan, multiple commission rates are sometimes used. For example, a 10 percent commission may be paid on the first

If you do not stand for something, you will fall for anything.

He who angers you controls you.

$100,000 of sales and 12 percent on sales over that amount in the same year. A person who sold $300,000 would receive $34,000 in commission [($100,000 × .10) + ($200,000 × .12) = $34,000]. When the commission rate increases, it is a progressive commission plan.

On the other hand, some companies use a regressive plan, in which commission rates decrease as sales increase, such as paying 12 percent on the first $100,000 and 10 percent on sales over that amount. For sales of $300,000, the salesperson would receive $32,000. The regressive system is used to help place an upper limit on a salesperson's earnings to encourage top producers to accept management positions if they want to increase their earnings beyond the level attainable in a sales job. In some companies, a top salesperson can earn more than a boss, and even more than the president of the company.

Drawing Accounts

One version of the straight line commission plan is known as the drawing account. It combines the incentive of a commission plan with the security of a fixed income. The firm establishes a monetary account for each salesperson. The amount may be based on the individual needs of the salesperson; a base level set by the company; or a base level that considers the individual salesperson's needs, background, and selling potential.

The salesperson may believe that $2,000 a month is needed to meet base expenditures for that period. Thus, at the beginning of the month, a draw or advance of $2,000 against commission for that month is given. If sales for a particular month resulted in commissions of $2,100, at the end of the month, the company would pay $100 in commissions. Conversely, if commissions earned for that month amounted to only $1,300, the salesperson would owe the company $700.

Management must monitor each salesperson closely to prevent a negative balance on salary from becoming so large that it is difficult, if not impossible, to repay it. Should the balance become large, the possibility of repayment may be so discouraging that the salesperson might feel compelled to quit the job. Though many firms have contractual agreements calling for repayment of negative balances against a drawing account, collecting an overdraft can be difficult. Some firms use a guaranteed drawing account plan in which the salesperson does not have to pay back overdrafts. Such a plan is actually a salary plus commission.

Advantages of Straight Commission Plans

Many sales managers believe that the commission plan provides maximum incentive for salespeople. They know that earnings are contingent on selling the firm's products. This expectancy of reward based on performance should direct salespeople to use their sales time wisely and to perform at maximum capacity. It is the reason many people are attracted to commission sales jobs. Only their abilities limit earning potential, and management cannot make arbitrary earnings decisions (see Exhibit 17.3).

Salespeople often think that they are in business for themselves. This is a benefit. If they are fired or leave their employer voluntarily, often they can continue the same business relationship with their customers after taking a job with another company. In addition, more people are attracted to part-time commission sales jobs, such as selling real estate or consumer products (e.g., Mary Kay Cosmetics), because of the earning potential. They can call on people that they feel are productive, determine their work schedules, and set their own hours.

EXHIBIT 17.3

Straight commission provides
a maximum incentive and the
opportunity to earn big money.

Real estate, financial investments, automobiles, business and
medical equipment—these often let your earnings be
determined by your ability.

Many organizations prefer to use the commission plan because it is simple to administer and selling costs are kept in proportion to sales. This is important to a new
firm that cannot afford to pay a portion of its salespeople a salary if they are not
profitably productive, or during an economic recession that could cause sales costs
to severely affect profits. The firm with limited capital can hire as many salespeople
as needed and have no salary costs until sales are made.

Payment is made to the salesperson at time of the sale, when the order is shipped,
or when the order is paid for. For some sales, the salesperson may continue to receive payment in the future as long as the consumer continues to purchase the product or service. Commissions for life insurance policy premiums are an example.

Disadvantages of the Commission Plan

Straight commission plans have several potential disadvantages. Particularly for the
person who has never sold before, one drawback is the uncertainty and insecurity
of the plan. The salesperson must sell to be paid. This is fine for the company, but
may discourage people from seeking sales careers.

With some big sales volume items, a long time may elapse before a person makes
a sale. For example, in commercial real estate, it is common for a person to make only
one, two, or three sales a year. These sales often result in large commissions, but the
individual must have enough funds to live on between commissions. The uncertainty

*Never give the devil a
ride, he will always
want to drive.*

and insecurity of straight commission sales jobs can lead to high turnover and high
expenses and sales costs for recruiting, selection, and training of new salespeople.

Some salespeople on commission develop little loyalty for the company. While
believing that they are in business for themselves can have benefits for salespeople, the
company may have difficulty in controlling or channeling salespeople's efforts. Salespeople on commission select their customers and their products, and sometimes use
high-pressure techniques to close sales because they will not see their customers again.

Under the straight commission plan, salespeople are much more reluctant to split
territories or move from their present territory to another territory. They may have spent
time building a rapport with their customers and do not want to relinquish it. This can
pose difficulties for the employer. In addition, with straight commission, service after
the sale may be neglected unless service is directly tied to making a future sale.

The cost of sales may be somewhat greater with a straight commission plan even
though it produces a greater sales volume. Salespeople can earn more pay per dollar of sale on straight commission than they can on salary plans. Commissions can
fluctuate greatly. In good times, salespeople may earn large commissions, but in an
economic recession, their earnings may drop drastically.

Because of the disadvantages of the straight commission plan for employees,
sales managers often take for granted a high turnover of sales personnel. Such
turnover may make it challenging to build an experienced sales force. Sales managers may hire salespeople quickly, without thorough selection and recruitment, because they realize that if the people do not produce, they will not be with the company
for long. This lack of recruitment, training, and supervision results in an increase
in sales costs and loss of potential sales.

The firm using the straight commission plan must work with the salespeople to set
realistic sales goals that allow the salesperson and the firm to meet their objectives.
Because performance or sales activities to some extent are dictated by the marketplace
and the salesperson's customers, management must reward the behavior or selling activities it seeks from the sales force. For example, different commission rates on different products deter the salesperson from concentrating on the easy-to-sell,
low-profit-margin items. A lower commission rate could be placed on easy-to-sell
products and higher commission rates paid on harder-to-sell products. Bonuses also
could be established for the products that the company wants the sales force to
concentrate on or a higher commission rate could be placed on these products.

Administrative Problems with the Commission Plan

*People become
successful by doing
things they do not
want to do.*

With today's complex distribution channels and exchange processes, the proper
allocation of commissions to salespeople can be a problem. The company must carefully examine the process through which the sales exchange is made to determine its
commission compensation policies. Administrative policies must be developed for
each of these circumstances to provide proper compensation of sales personnel and
to prevent morale problems. For example, if two or more salespeople are involved in
a sale, the fair distribution of commissions can be a problem. Should two salespeople
put an equal amount of time and effort into the sale, the commission can easily be
split on a 50–50 basis. However, if the two salespeople differ in their perception of
each person's input, a dispute may arise over the percentage each should earn. One
solution is for management to base all commissions made by two or more salespeople
on the number of sales in which they were involved during that period.

Another potential problem is what to do when there are bad debts. A salesperson
may have sold a product or products to a customer who is unable to pay or goes

bankrupt. If the salesperson is not directly responsible for the extension of credit to accounts, most firms will not withdraw a commission. The same is true for sales returns. If a small number of items sold are returned, the company may not deduct money from commissions. However, many firms look at net sales. If, for example, a salesperson sold $11,000 worth of merchandise this month and had returns of $1,000, the company would pay a commission based on sales of $10,000.

Combination Plans

Under a **combination salary plan,** a proportion of the salesperson's total pay is guaranteed while some of it can come from commissions. The most commonly used percentage split is 80 percent base salary and 20 percent incentive. A 70/30 and 60/40 split are the next most common combinations.

Various combinations of salary plan incentives can be used by a company. The more popular plans are the following:

- Salary and commission.
- Salary and bonus: individual bonus or group bonus.
- Salary, commission, and bonus: individual bonus or group bonus.

Companies using salary-plus-incentive plans say that their chief advantages are that they (1) motivate the sales force, (2) attract and hold good people, and (3) can direct the sales force efforts in a profitable direction. Such a plan's main purpose is to provide a salary for directing behavior and an incentive for motivating salespeople.

Exhibit 17.2(C) and (D) illustrate the two popular versions of a combination plan. Exhibit 17.2(C) shows earnings of $22,000, plus 1 percent commission on all sales. Sales of $300,000 earn the salesperson an extra $3,000. Exhibit 17.2(D) illustrates a salary plus commission over a sales quota. In this example, the salesperson who sells $300,000 earns 1 percent on all additional sales. The quota of $300,000 may be based on meeting last year's actual sales or it may represent a sales quota above last year's actual sales.

Bonus: Individual or Group

In addition to combination plans based on salary and commissions, many firms use a bonus system. Bonuses can be used with any basic compensation plan. A **bonus** is something given in addition to what the salesperson usually earns. Typically, it is money earned over an extended period, such as one year.

Across-the-Board Bonus

One type of bonus includes the Christmas or year-end bonus given to all salespeople, regardless of their productivity. An equal sum of money may be paid to each salesperson, or the bonus may be based on current salary and tenure with the organization. For example, a company may pay a Christmas bonus of 1.5 percent of their annual salary to salespeople who have been with the firm for one to two years and 2 percent to those who have been with the firm for two or three years. The percentage may go as high as 8 percent. The bonus is paid on an individual basis and is not directly related to employee performance.

Performance Bonus

The second type of bonus is related to performance. Numerous bonus plans of this type can be devised, but they fall into two general categories according to whether they are awarded on an individual or group basis. Bonuses can be awarded not only

*Be a person of the light
(truth) not the dark.*

on the basis of sales or units sold but also on the basis of gross profit margins, on sales performance appraisals, on new accounts acquired, on company or geographical sales unit earnings or sales, and on sales of specific products.

A sales region may be given a bonus amount based on its performance as compared with that of other sales regions in the organization. The regional sales manager would then allocate a certain amount to each sales district according to performance. The district manager could distribute the district bonus equally among all salespeople or use a merit system based on individual performance.

Sales Contests

Another compensation variable for influencing salespeople's performance is the sales contest. **Sales contests** are special sales programs offering salespeople incentives to achieve short-term sales goals. The incentives may include items that indicate recognition of achievement (e.g., certificates, cash, merchandise, or travel). Occasionally, contests may run for as long as a year; examples include the insurance or real estate industry's million dollar club. The incentives are given in addition to regular compensation.

Billions are spent on sales contests each year. Industry typically spends 35 percent on sales incentives, 78 percent on merchandise awards, and 22 percent on incentive travel programs. In the past, there was little use of incentive travel programs. However, as corporations attempted to find means of motivating salespeople to top the previous year's performance, travel was used increasingly to glamorize sales programs. Offering merchandise and cash keeps such programs flexible.

The sales contest is an effective incentive method that intensifies, directs, and makes salespeople more persistent in their work over time. Salespeople work harder to meet contest goals and thereby earn rewards. Management can direct salespeople to sell specific products or to perform activities they would not normally do through contest incentives. Contests also cause salespeople to work harder for longer periods (persistence) to achieve the contest goals and earn extra rewards. As one executive in the cosmetics industry stated, "Our incentive program allows us to apply no direct sales pressure while motivating the salespeople, and to reward those who reach company-approved goals. Contests have helped this company increase sales from $7.8 million to over $31 million in five years."

Sales contests can have several indirect influences on salespeople. Many sales managers feel that these contests, as well as bonuses, can increase the team spirit of their sales groups, interest in the job, and job satisfaction and can discourage absenteeism and turnover.

THE TOTAL COMPENSATION PACKAGE

People choose a sales career for both nonfinancial and financial reasons. The salesperson receives numerous forms of financial compensation. Exhibit 17.4 illustrates the dollar value one company places on its total compensation for the beginning salesperson.

Monthly salary, including fringe benefits, equals $4,183.33, which is $1,183.33 a month above the base salary of $3,000. Also, the salesperson participates in an incentive bonus plan, plus 10 additional benefits. Thus, it is not surprising that a sales career is attractive to thousands of people.

EXHIBIT 17.4

Salary and fringe benefits for a new representative (based on starting salary of $3,000 per month, with automatic increases to $3,500 at training completion).

Starting Salary before Completion of Training (annual):

$36,000.00	($3,000.00/month)—base salary
3,600.00	Company contribution to pension plan for future service only (10 percent)
3,000.00	Company contribution to group health insurance, major medical and life insurance plans
1,100.00	Telephone allowance
5,500.00	Estimated value of having a company car
$50,200.00	Total salary
$4,183.33	Monthly salary including fringe benefits

Plus, an incentive bonus plan determined on relative attainment of sales forecast. Additional benefits that are not measured in dollars, but contribute materially to standard of living, security, and development:

1. Under 5 years, two weeks' vacation; after 5 years, three weeks' vacation; after 15 years, four weeks' vacation; after 25 years, five weeks' vacation.
2. Seven paid holidays.
3. Christmas furlough.
4. Pension plan rated as one of the best in the industry.
5. Group health insurance and major medical plan cover not only the representative but also spouse and unmarried children under 19, and student children to age 26. Continuance of 20 percent of life insurance after retirement at age 60 or later without cost to employee.
6. Liberal sick pay plan.

Total Period Covered

Years of Service	Full Base Pay (weeks)	Half Base Pay (weeks)
Less than 5 years	4	12
Over 5 years	8	12
Over 10 years	10	12
Over 15 years	12	12
Over 21 years	16	12

7. New long-term disability (LTD) plan. LTD provides financial security for you and your family for period of continuous total disability extending beyond the benefits provided under the sick and accident plan or the company worker's compensation supplement.
8. Employees' education fund pays half of tuition for approved courses successfully completed, if the representative is employed less than one year; 75 percent of tuition after one year.
9. Twenty weeks' intensive training followed by constant supervision and guidance by district sales manager.
10. Regular reviews of job performance for salary consideration.

NONFINANCIAL REWARDS ARE MANY

Nonfinancial rewards are effective in motivating salespeople. The sales manager can reward a salesperson for achieving sales goals with bonuses and other awards. Achievement or recognition awards are commonly presented at sales meetings. Although there are usually no financial benefits associated with achievement awards, winning salespeople receive recognition from their managers and other salespeople, motivating them to work harder.

Salespeople who do well may be transferred to larger, more challenging sales territories or promoted to key account managers. This recognizes their contribution to the company and serves as further motivation. Furthermore, little personal things such as a sales manager's praise can motivate a salesperson to improve performance.

It is up to the manager to develop ways of creating a work environment in which performing well is a rewarding experience to the salesperson, even though no pay raise, bonus, or contest is involved. Good job performance should give the salesperson a feeling of accomplishment and satisfaction. Special nonfinancial awards, certificates, medals, and praise are an important part of the manager's motivational mix.

LEADERSHIP IS IMPORTANT TO SUCCESS

In a recent survey, nearly 500 sales and marketing managers working for some 450 companies of all sizes ranked the most important factors in managing their firms' sales forces. Leadership was ranked first. The second most important factor was the sales manager's ability to motivate salespeople.[2]

Leadership is the process by which the sales manager attempts to influence the activities of salespeople. What makes a person a successful leader? Indications are that the manager should exhibit both task and relationship behavior in different situations.

The Leader's Task and Relationship Behavior

The study of leadership has identified two forms of behavior leaders can use to influence their salespeople. **Task behavior** involves the leader in describing the duties and responsibilities of an individual or group. This includes telling people what to do, how to do it, when to do it, where to do it, and who is to do it. In addition, the person is closely supervised to make sure the job is done correctly.

Relationship behavior is people oriented. It involves the extent to which the leader uses two-way communication, not one-way as in task behavior. It includes listening, providing clarification, getting to know the individual's motives and goals, and giving positive feedback to help reinforce such things as a person's self-image, confidence, and ego. Relationship behavior can exhibit a very high degree of delegation of the authority and responsibility to salespeople in developing their own goals and how they will meet these goals. The sales manager is available to assist and give guidance if necessary. However, it is up to the salesperson to accomplish the job's various goals. This is a very democratic leadership approach toward motivating people.

To help illustrate the use of leadership styles in different situations, four different styles have been identified, based on past research. These four styles form the leadership continuum shown in Exhibit 17.5. On one extreme, the leadership approach is task oriented and on the other extreme, people oriented.

Next, four quadrants were developed to position these four basic leadership styles (see Exhibit 17.6). The following examples illustrate different situations in which these styles can be used.

Style 1—Tells

A telling leadership style is characterized by above-average levels of task behavior and below-average levels of relationship behavior.

- **Example of an appropriate use:** A new salesperson is unsure of how to develop a sales presentation.
- **Example of an inappropriate use:** An experienced, high-performing salesperson is told how to develop a sales presentation.

The sales manager makes all the decisions here, exhibiting task behavior.

Style 2—Persuades

A persuading leadership style is characterized by above-average amounts of both task and relationship behavior. The sales manager makes the decision; however, the

EXHIBIT 17.5

Four basic leadership styles a sales manager can select from to influence salespeople.

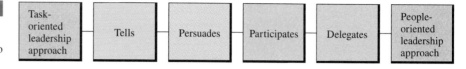

EXHIBIT 17.6

A sales manager can choose one of these leadership styles based on the salesperson and the situation.

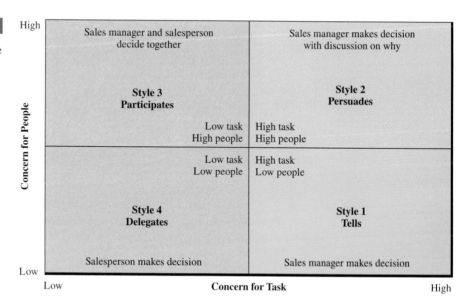

salesperson's cooperation is sought by explaining what needs to be done and then persuading the salesperson to carry out the decision.

- **Example of an appropriate use:** A salesperson is promoted to a key account position and is motivated to do the new job but is currently unable to carry out the job's various activities.
- **Example of an inappropriate use:** A new product will be introduced on the market. The salespeople are experienced at selling new products. However, at the sales meeting the manager instructs people on the procedures they should use to sell the new product and gives them an opportunity to ask questions and clarify the instructions.

Style 3—Participates

A participating leadership style is characterized by above-average levels of relationship behavior and below-average levels of task behavior.

- **Example of an appropriate use:** A salesperson needs to do more service work in the sales territory but does not see how it will improve sales. The manager provides reasons for increased service and discusses the idea with the salesperson. The salesperson presents his viewpoint and, based on what is discussed, is allowed to continue present activities without increasing the level of service work.
- **Example of an inappropriate use:** Salespeople are experiencing declining sales due to the introduction of a competitor's new product. At a sales meeting,

EXHIBIT 17.7

This manager compares the salesperson's actual sales against her quotas.

the manager asks people how to handle the problem, praises their past work, and encourages their future efforts. The manager provides little direction and has few suggestions on what should be done to improve sales.

Style 4—Delegates

A delegating leadership style is characterized by below-average levels of both task behavior and relationship behavior.

- **Example of an appropriate use:** The salesperson is a high-performing, seasoned veteran who is highly motivated to be a top performer. The sales manager lets the person do the job with little direction.
- **Example of an inappropriate use:** A newer salesperson asks for help in selling several customers and is unsure of the best way to routinely contact customers within the territory. The manager says, "You handle it. It is your responsibility."

The delegating type of leadership provides little direction, low levels of personal contact, and little supportive behavior. Styles 3 and 4 are different from Styles 1 and 2, in which the sales manager provides the directions and makes the decisions. As you can see, quite often the leadership style of choice is based on the salesperson.

Choosing a Leadership Style

Although there is no one best way to lead salespeople in all situations, these leadership techniques can improve a manager's effectiveness:

- Be familiar with each salesperson's territory, customers, and personal circumstances to properly diagnose the person's situation.
- Have the flexibility to be task or people oriented when dealing with a salesperson, based on the situation—for example, be people oriented with the high-performing salesperson and task oriented with the low performer.
- Clearly show salespeople the way to reach their goals (see Exhibit 17.7).
- Play the role of a coach whose aim is to aid salespeople to reach their personal and territorial goals.
- Develop technical, human, and conceptual skills.

Leaders are like eagles, they don't flock, you find them one at a time.

ROSS PEROT

How do managers lead or influence when their salespeople are not around? Managers have to go out into the field and work with salespeople. Effective sales managers lead by example through on-the-job coaching.

On-the-Job Coaching

Coaching has been described as the single most important training technique available to the sales manager. Coaching is also an important leadership activity. **Coaching** refers to training someone on the job intensively through instruction, demonstration, and practice. The purpose of coaching is to help the person be more efficient. Nothing improves performance more than regular on-the-job coaching by the manager.

Coaching involves special objectives and techniques. It is specifically planned for strengthening selling skills, reemphasizing or reinforcing formal training exposure, and pointing out opportunities to improve or expanding on selling skills already developed. Coaching, then, is a very important link in the continuous training process discussed in Chapter 16.

The main element of a coaching session is the **joint sales call.** This means the manager accompanies a person on a sales call. By observing what went on face-to-face with customers, the manager can discuss strengths and opportunities to improve immediately after the sales call. With regular coaching sessions, the manager can reinforce good selling habits and improve selling skills.

PERFORMANCE EVALUATIONS LET PEOPLE KNOW WHERE THEY STAND

Achieving acceptable levels of performance is essential for the organization to stay in business and for the salesperson to reach personal goals. A major part of the manager's job is to lead and motivate salespeople to perform at an acceptable level. At the end of each performance period, such as the end of the year, the manager evaluates each salesperson's performance. This creates a **management control system** that establishes performance goals, evaluates the salesperson's accomplishments compared to those goals, and then rewards or penalizes the individual based on the performance level.

Performance Evaluation—What Is It?

The performance evaluation is a time of reflection on the past and hope for the future. This time of decision may have lasting consequences on an individual's career and life. **Performance evaluation** refers to a formal, structured system of measuring and evaluating a salesperson's activities and performance. Management compares the results of a person's efforts with the goals set for the person.

Reasons for Performance Evaluation

Performance evaluations are done for three reasons: (1) to appraise a salesperson's past performance; (2) to develop a sales plan to increase the salesperson's future sales; and (3) to motivate salespeople to improve their performance. Sales managers' evaluations provide the basis for numerous decisions on salary, promotions, transfers, demotions, and dismissal.

Appraisal sessions involve giving face-to-face feedback to the salespeople on quality of performance, getting to know each other better, and gaining an understanding of what each person expects from the other.

Who Should Evaluate Salespeople?

The primary evaluator should be the salesperson's immediate superior because this person has direct knowledge about sales performance. The manager has actually worked with the salesperson. In some companies, the immediate superior completes the entire evaluation, including recommendations for pay raises and promotions. The

EXHIBIT 17.8

Quantitative and qualitative
performance criteria.

Quantitative Criteria	Qualitative Criteria
■ Sales volume	■ Selling skills
Percentage of increase	Finding selling points
Market share	Product knowledge
Quotas obtained	Listening skill
■ Average sales calls per day	Obtaining participation
■ New customers obtained	Overcoming objections
■ Gross profit	Closing the sale
Product	■ Territory management
Customer	Planning
Order size	Utilization
■ Ratio of selling costs to sales	Records
■ Sales orders	Customer service
Daily number of orders	Collections
Total	Follow-up
By size, customer classification, and product	■ Personal traits
Order:sales call ratio	Attitude
Goods returned	Empathy
	Human relations
	Team spirit
	Appearance
	Motivation
	Care of car
	Self-improvement

Can you critique someone and still be friends?

evaluations and recommendations are sent to the manager's immediate superior for final approval. The manager's superior accepts the recommendations without question.

In the majority of organizations, several managers evaluate each salesperson. The simplest approach is for the district manager and the regional sales manager to arrive at an evaluation together. For a few companies, other district managers in the region also may express their opinions when the region's entire management group gets together periodically for performance appraisals.

Many companies use the entire region's management group and a home office personnel specialist to evaluate salespeople's work, as shown in Exhibit 17.8. The specialist presents the home office viewpoint by making sure that the evaluation procedures are followed and that each person is treated fairly.

When Should Salespeople Be Evaluated?

Salespeople should be evaluated at the end of each performance cycle. A performance cycle is a period related to specific product goals and/or job activities. For example, consumer goods manufacturers typically have certain products they want to emphasize periodically. They may have six performance cycles during the year. Every two months, the sales force is given specific sales goals for 5 to 10 different products. It is necessary to compare goals to results after each cycle. In addition, salespeople are monitored monthly in terms of the other products they sell.

These periodic performance evaluations provide the input for semiannual and/or annual performance evaluations. These performance evaluations provide important feedback to both management and salespeople. A minimum of one formal evaluation should be completed yearly for each salesperson.

Performance Criteria

What is a **performance criterion?** The dictionary defines it as a standard on which a judgment or decision may be based. In our case, companies examine their salespeople's jobs; determine the important parts of the job; and develop performance criteria based on their findings. These performance criteria serve as the basis for evaluating a salesperson's performance. They are of two types—quantitative and qualitative.

Quantitative Performance Criteria

Of the two categories of performance criteria, **quantitative performance criteria** are best for effectively evaluating performance. This category represents end results or bottom-line objective data, such as shown in Exhibit 17.8.

Qualitative Performance Criteria

Many organizations use **qualitative performance criteria** because they represent the salesperson's major job activities, and they indicate why the quantitative measures look as they do. Care should be taken to minimize the evaluator's personal biases and subjectivity in evaluating qualitative performance criteria. Examples are also shown in Exhibit 17.8.

One sales manager said, "Qualitative performance criteria help explain quantitative performance results. If, for example, a salesperson's volume is low, poor methods used to close the sale may be the reason. Only by working with salespeople can I determine what's causing their numbers."

Conducting the Evaluation Session

Typically, the company sets up procedures for who will do the evaluation and how it will be done. The performance criteria for evaluation have been decided and materials, such as evaluation forms, are available. Basic guidelines for an effective performance evaluation follow.

Both Manager and Salesperson Should Be Prepared for the Interview

The manager should collect all information on the performance of the salesperson. The manager should then contact the salesperson and establish a time and place for the evaluation. The salesperson should be asked to review past performance using the evaluation forms, and to review the job description. This takes place before the formal meeting. Quantitative data should be used when possible.

Be Positive

Even if you're on the right track, you'll get run over if you just sit there.

WILL ROGERS

Both the manager and salesperson should believe that the evaluation is a positive method of helping the salesperson do the job better. The salesperson may feel required to defend rather than explain past performance. The following examples illustrate negative and positive approaches to evaluation.

Manager: Well, Larry, it's that time of the year again.

Salesperson: Yes, Amy, I'm looking forward to it!

Manager: I didn't have time to review your file, Larry, but I know you really messed up this year on the Goodyear account.

Salesperson: Well?

Manager: Well nothing! I really got chewed out by the regional manager over that.

Salesperson: Did you look at my total performance, Amy? Sales were up 5 percent above the district average.

Manager: All right, all right, so you're doing OK, but why did you lose the Goodyear account?

Amy, the manager, was not prepared to talk to Larry, and he was on the defensive from the beginning. It is no wonder neither of them looks forward to this confrontation. Compare this negative approach to a performance evaluation to a positive one:

Manager: Larry, it's great we can get together and discuss your achievements and your goals.

Salesperson: Yes, Amy, I'm looking forward to it!

Manager: You know I'm pleased with your sales. You're 5 percent above the district average. That's great! You're doing a good job in managing your territory.

Salesperson: I'm glad you noticed. You know, I often feel I'm out there all by myself.

Manager: Well, Larry, you're not! Is there anything I can do to help you?

Salesperson: Well, things are going good.

Manager: What about the Goodyear account?

Salesperson: I sure hated to lose them. My competitor got their business with a low price. But they aren't happy with the service or the products. I'll have that account back in my pocket before you know it!

Manager: I know you will, Larry; we are here today to develop ways to make you the best salesperson in the best district, and this is the best district the company has.

Salesperson: Sounds great to me, Amy. What can I do?

Manager: Did you use the forms I sent you to evaluate your performance?

Salesperson: Sure did.

Manager: What did you find out?

Salesperson: Well, there are a few areas I need to look at.

Manager: OK, but before we get to those, remember we are here to evaluate your performance to help you. You and I will work out a plan for this coming year that will allow you to continue to do the good job that you want to do. How does that sound?

Salesperson: In other words, ways I can make more money and maybe earn a promotion.

Manager: That's right. Ways for you to grow and prosper with our company.

> *Performance is a discipline learned through persistence.*
>
> PETER F. DRUCKER

These examples point to the need for both people to have a positive attitude toward the evaluation. Amy should believe in the positive effects this meeting will have on Larry's future performance and attitude toward his job. She has sold Larry on the purpose of their meeting. Both the manager and the salesperson have prepared for the evaluation and agreed on its purpose.

Actually Review Performance

Again, the manager should be sincere and positive in discussing each of Larry's performance criteria. There will be disagreements. Research has shown that people tend to evaluate themselves better than their superiors do. It is important to

EXHIBIT 17.9

This performance evaluation session is a time for Amy and Larry to discuss his past accomplishments and future plans. Both the manager and the salesperson must be prepared for the session.

- Freely discuss each performance criterion.
- Ask salespeople to discuss their performance.
- Ask salespeople to evaluate their performance.
- Give the manager's view of performance.

As Exhibit 17.9 shows, the manager has prepared for the session. Larry's past and present sales results are out on the table for a full discussion, and he has the opportunity to fully discuss his results and future plans with Amy, his manager.

Finalize the Performance Evaluation

The manager should now review each performance area with the salesperson. It is preferable to begin by reviewing the high ratings and work down. The salesperson should understand clearly what has been decided. If there are disagreements, the manager should explain carefully why the salesperson receives a low evaluation in a particular performance area. Serious differences of opinion can occur when the salesperson does not fully understand what was expected.

Summarize the Total Performance Evaluation

The salesperson should be told how the manager views past performance. For example: "Susan, you have done above average work this year. You are continuing to improve year after year, and will receive a good raise. If you continue this level of performance, in a few more years you will be ready for a management position."

"Sam, this is the second year in a row your sales have decreased while the district's have increased. This has to change if you are to stay with the company. I don't want to do this, but you have six months to get your territory turned around."

Ethical and moral decisions can not be made without using your moral compass. Otherwise it is just opinion.

Develop Mutually Agreed-On Objectives

Performance and career objectives can be established now. Both manager and salesperson provide input.

ETHICAL DILEMMA

Cheating on the Expense Account

You have been a sales manager for a small regional manufacturing firm for just over a year. By accident you overheard two salespeople discussing how much they had padded their expense reports for that month. These two salespeople have been with the company for several years, are very successful in their jobs, and are well liked by the rest of the sales staff. You know that the firm has strict rules regarding sales expense reporting and that this policy would require that the two salespeople be severely reprimanded or fired.

What would be the most ethical action to take?

1. Do nothing. It is not your responsibility to turn them in. Besides, you never would have known if you didn't "accidentally" hear.
2. Without mentioning particulars, let your boss know that you have heard people were padding their expense reports and that he/she might want to review them more carefully.
3. Tell your boss about the conversation you heard and who was involved. It is not right of them to take advantage of the company—they should expect whatever punishment comes to them.

Formalize Evaluation and Objectives

Immediately after the evaluation session is over, the manager should write a letter to the salesperson restating the results of the performance evaluation and the objectives. A copy is sent to the manager's superior to go into the salesperson's permanent personnel file.

SALES MANAGERS USE TECHNOLOGY

As you have learned, today's salespeople and their managers have so much to do in their jobs that the use of technology is essential. Take Tim Mathes, a regional sales manager in Gillette Company's retail division. His territory includes more than 1,300 retailers in upstate New York, Connecticut, Vermont, Massachusetts, New Hampshire, and Maine. Here's how Mathes uses technology to manage customers and salespeople.

To Manage Customers

To take care of all those accounts, Mathes has two market managers, 20 reps, and a fairly sizable amount of computing power. Although only a few companies have sales forces working with pen-based computers, Gillette chose this technology because its salespeople work on their feet. They are constantly traveling around, collecting information, and grabbing a few moments of a busy store buyer's time. Gillette's reps need flexibility, agility, and convenience. Mathes finds pen-based computers are more efficient and easier to use in these situations than hunt-and-peck keyboards.

Information gathering is one of the most important tasks Gillette's salespeople perform. Their first step on a sales call is to collect data on how Gillette's product is doing. Reps do not necessarily have to conduct an in-depth inventory, but rather look for very specific pieces of information. Foremost are out-of-stocks, Mathes says, referring to bare shelves. The software in the pen-based computer also asks whether floor stands are up or new items are in the store. "The GRiD tells the sales reps which items the store is to carry. They go through and check if it's out of stock or if there are pieces on the shelves. That way we can analyze the out-of-stock level," Mathes says.

To Manage Salespeople

Information collected by the salespeople on their pen-based computers is transmitted to a central database each night. Mobile computers are updated on a daily basis, according to Phil Druker, senior applications manager at Gillette. Salespeople come home, plug their units into electrical outlets to recharge and then into the Internet to transmit. "Once you get home, there's very little time invested in it, probably about five minutes," Druker says. "There are programs that take over and draw information off your computer."

Over the months, the system creates a statistical picture of product trends and store activity for each store and downloads it to the salespeople to help convince store buyers to purchase more. "When you can show store managers they've had out-of-stocks on certain product sizes for the past four months, they almost get overwhelmed," Mathes says. Computers allow salespeople to present lots of data without slowing down their presentations significantly.

As a result of the new system, Gillette gains a clear vision of how products are moving. "We can be sitting with a buyer on Wednesday and tell him down to the store level what occurred in his chain's stores on Monday," says division Vice President John Conley.

"Customer data show a clear picture of each salesperson's sales. Sales managers receive a sales report on each salesperson weekly, plus [a report on] how our major products are selling. They receive almost instant feedback on how each salesperson is performing," says Mathes.[3]

SUMMARY OF MAJOR SALES MANAGEMENT ISSUES

An important challenge of the sales manager is to motivate salespeople using financial and nonfinancial methods. Salary, commissions, contests, bonuses, and travel awards are common financial motivators. Achievement awards, challenging work assignments, recognition, leadership techniques, and performance evaluations are nonfinancial methods used as motivators.

Today, salespeople are paid by several methods, but most firms use a combination of salary and financial incentives rather than straight salary or straight commission plans. This provides salespeople with a guaranteed salary and helps motivate them to reach their sales goals to earn commissions and bonuses or to win contests.

The sales manager needs to understand the principles of leadership and apply them to salespeople based on their individual personalities and territorial situations. Managers need to be people oriented and job oriented toward salespeople to help them reach sales goals. This ultimately helps to reach the manager's goals.

The performance of sales personnel is evaluated by comparing their quotas and objectives to actual sales and job activities to determine their success. The salesperson's immediate manager implements periodic evaluations each year using both quantitative and qualitative performance criteria.

To effectively evaluate salespeople, managers should develop procedures to ensure fair treatment. By being prepared for the interview and having a positive attitude, the salesperson will be receptive to the manager's critique. The manager should evaluate each performance criterion and explain the evaluation to the salesperson. A discussion of the salesperson's past performance concludes the interview. Future performance quotas and objectives can now be established to serve as goals to reach for the upcoming sales period.

This chapter concludes the discussion of the challenging fundamentals of selling and sales management.

MEETING A SALES CHALLENGE

There is a good chance that once Judy Carter understands the situation, she will straighten out. The first step in problem solving is awareness. People with problems can't do anything about solving them until they know and accept that they have problems. It's up to you to help Judy see the full effect of her erratic pace. It hurts her, her peers, and the company. And it doesn't help you do your job.

Without any threats, implied or explicit, you can discuss the situation with her, as calmly and impersonally as possible. That won't be easy because the situation is so serious. However, there are some good things going for both of you. Intelligent and bright, the acceptance of her peers is important to her. Of course, only Judy can actually change her undesirable work habits. But you can be the catalyst for that change by helping her understand what she is doing—or not doing—and by helping her learn how to improve overall performance. Those changes will make her a very welcome member of the sales team.

KEY TERMS FOR MANAGING

motivation　534
motivation mix　534
straight salary plan　535
straight commission plan　537
combination salary plan　541
bonus　541
sales contests　542
leadership　544
task behavior　544

relationship behavior　544
coaching　547
joint sales call　547
management control system　547
performance evaluation　547
performance criterion　549
quantitative performance criteria　549
qualitative performance criteria　549

SALES APPLICATION QUESTIONS

1. What is meant by motivation? What can a sales manager do to motivate salespeople?
2. What are the major methods used to compensate salespeople? Discuss each method's advantages and disadvantages.
3. Discuss why salespeople's performance should be evaluated, who should evaluate their performance, when they should be evaluated, and proper procedures for evaluating performance.
4. A company is considering the following three compensation plans. Which of these will be the most expensive? Which will be the least expensive? Is the monetary cost the only consideration that a company should have?

   Plan A—Give each salesperson a commission of 10 percent on the first $250,000 worth of sales made each year and 12 percent on the next $250,000.

   Plan B—Give each salesperson a salary of $10,000 a year and 5 percent commission on all sales made each year.

   Plan C—Give each salesperson a salary of $25,000 a year and a bonus of 4 percent commission on all sales made over $250,000 in a year.

5. Imagine yourself a manager with a 54-year-old salesperson who consistently had poor performance for the past two years. This person has worked for the company 25 years. The person has two children in high school and one in college. The person's spouse recently quit work due to bad health. How would you handle this situation?
6. Discuss what kind of leadership style a sales manager should use in working with a highly motivated new salesperson and a veteran salesperson. Why?

FURTHER EXPLORING THE SALES WORLD

Visit a sales manager of a local real estate firm and a sales manager of a national corporation and compare how each company motivates their salespeople. Ask each sales manager about the company's leadership style. Finally, determine the performance criteria and procedures each manager uses to evaluate salespeople.

SELLING EXPERIENTIAL EXERCISE

A Failure to Communicate?

"What we have here is a failure to communicate," goes a line from the movie *Cool Hand Luke*. In reality, managers label a lot of issues communications problems that are not. For example:

- **Disagreement:** "My subordinates do not agree with the new pricing strategy," a vice president lamented. "I guess we have a communication problem." In this case communication was not the problem. Subordinates understood the strategy; they simply thought it was a bad idea. To call disagreements communication problems only confuses others.
- **Distrust:** "My manager tells me one thing and does another," an employee complained. "We just don't communicate." No amount of communication could improve this relationship. It is a matter of trust, not communication. To improve relationships, the manager must work on improving trust among subordinates. A beginning step is to be open and direct with people.
- **Information overload:** From a manager: "I don't know why our people complain about communication. We provide them with stacks of reports." This organization bombarded employees with tons of data, but employees could have cared less about most of the details. The few things of interest were often buried deep. Again, more communication does not reduce frustration. But a newly designed, more effective management information system would probably help.

SALES MANAGEMENT QUIZ

Assume that you have 10 points to allocate to each of the following pairs of statements. Assign the points so they indicate the strength of your belief; write your answers on a separate sheet of paper.

1A.   Communication is a major problem.
1B.   Communication is a symptom of other issues.

2A.   Words are more important than actions.
2B.   Actions are more important than words.

3A.   Listening is more important than telling.
3B.   Telling is more important than listening.

4A.   Human relations is more important than logic.
4B.   Logic is more important than human relations.

5A.   Effective communication is persuasive.
5B.   Effective communication is understanding.

6A.   Disagreements represent communication problems.
6B.   Disagreements represent conflict problems.

Total the points allocated to the following: 1B, 2B, 3A, 4A, 5B, 6B. If you have a score of 40 or more, you have an effective communication philosophy.[4]

CHAPTER 17

Motivation, Compensation, Leadership and Evaluation of Salespeople

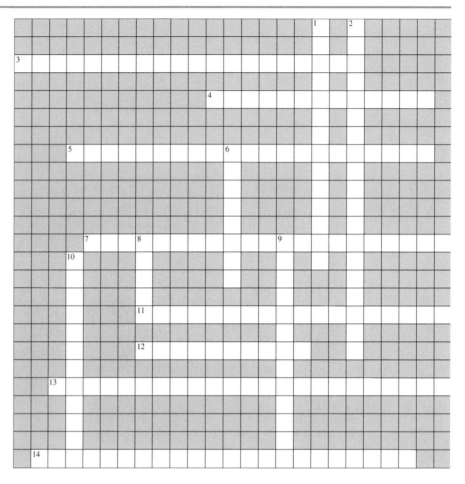

Across

3. A kind of leadership that is people oriented; it involves use of two-way communication.

4. Five broad classes of factors used to motivate salespeople.

5. The formal, structured system of measuring and evaluating a salesperson's activities and performance.

7. A plan wherein a proportion of the salesperson's total pay is guaranteed while a portion of it can come from commissions.

11. A compensation plan whereby the salesperson is paid a specific dollar amount at regular intervals.

12. The arousal, intensity, direction, and persistence of effort directed toward job tasks over a period of time.

13. A process wherein a manager evaluates each salesperson's performance, comparing it to performance goals, and rewarding or penalizing a salesperson based on that comparison.

14. A complete incentive compensation plan in which earnings accrue only if sales take place.

Down

1. A sales call that takes place when the manager accompanies a salesperson on the call.

2. Bases for evaluating a salesperson's performance.

6. Intensive on-the-job training through instruction, demonstration, and practice.

8. Additional compensation given to the salesperson that is over what is usually earned.

9. Special sales programs offering salespeople incentives to achieve short-term goals.

10. Behavior that involves the leader describing the duties of an individual or group.

CASE 17-1

Baxter Surgical Supplies Incorporated*

The marketing vice president for Baxter Surgical Supplies Incorporated (BSSI), a manufacturer and distributor of medical supplies and equipment, was reviewing the company's method of compensation at the end of 1998. BSSI was second in the industry in total sales to American Hospital Supplies. The company's main offices were located in Richmond, Virginia, with plants in Florida, Texas, California, and Michigan. The sales force consisted of more than 600 people supervised by 60 sales managers.

BSSI had a variety of products that required different levels of selling skills. Its equipment line consisted of such items as X-ray machines, cast saws, therapeutic equipment, and prosthesis parts. The medical supplies line included all types of medicines, cast material, bandages, splints, and syringes. To sell both lines, the salesperson had to receive good training. These products were sold to hospitals and to physicians with medical practices.

The Role of the Salespeople. The salesperson was expected to search for new accounts, service existing accounts, and maintain goodwill between the company and its clients. A typical day might find the salesperson calling on a hospital in the morning. There, she would check on emergency room needs, the material supplies office, and administrative offices. Afterward, she might set up a display at the hospital, next to the doctor's parking lot. Later, the salesperson might begin making calls on offices located in the immediate area. Usually, a salesperson could make several individual calls because the private offices were generally located near the hospitals. A call might be made to introduce new products to the doctor or it might simply be to check with the nurses about replenishing supplies. If the former was the case, a special time might be scheduled. Major products often required selling on the weekends.

A few products could cost as much as $60,000, whereas other products might not cost more than $1. Generally, the individual accounts placed orders for supplies that would last about two weeks. However, hospital accounts, because of the larger storage rooms, normally ordered monthly. In addition, the hospitals, which had staffs in charge of their inventory, would usually send in their order forms without the help of a salesperson. BSSI policy was to check with these people regularly whether or not they needed any additional help.

Sales Force Compensation. Bill Woodson, a marketing vice president, had the idea of examining the firm's sales force compensation. He believed two areas involving sales personnel needed improvement—sales force turnover and number of sales calls.

Sales managers did some occasional selling, but their primary responsibility was supervision and training of the sales force. Each manager had from 9 to 11 salespeople

---

* This case was developed by Rich Knight, under the supervision of Professor Charles M. Futrell. The company name and geographical location have been changed. Mr. Knight is now president of BSSI.

reporting to him. They were paid a straight salary that depended on their length of time with BSSI. In addition, a bonus was paid to the sales manager at the end of the year depending on how well the district had done. Salaries for all sales managers averaged $90,400 with a range of $79,000 to $117,000.

The sales personnel were paid a straight salary their first year. BSSI management felt that the first-year salesperson knew so little about selling and contributed such a small portion to profits relative to experienced sales personnel that a straight salary would benefit them more. These first-year salespeople were paid $43,000 in 1998. They are typically placed in smaller territories with relatively low sales. As they gained experience, they were paid a larger base salary that depended on the length of time they had been with the company. They also received a bonus at the end of each year according to the district's performance. The bonus equals up to 10 percent of their sales. Sales managers and sales personnel were reimbursed for all expenses incurred while selling. BSSI was proud of the fact that most of its sales force had at least bachelor's degrees, with several members having MBAs.

As Woodson looked over the sales personnel compensation policy, he wondered why his turnover rate was so high. Turnover for people working less than 18 months was 35 percent. After this turnover dropped to 8 percent. It appeared to him that many of the salespeople would get training from BSSI and then run off to competitors. He also felt that because the salespeople were unsupervised so much, they often took off early in the afternoon and possibly did not even work on some days. Woodson understood that there would be several people who would try to take advantage of this freedom. However, he believed that there was just not enough incentive to hunt for those extra sales or spend after-hours time with clients. It appeared to him that the compensation method was benefiting only persons who had been with the firm for some time. He felt there was not enough incentive to keep the really good performers. The aggressive salespersons could earn more in other companies without having to wait. For example, both American Hospital and Stevens Hospital Supply paid 100 percent commission—even for new salespeople.

Woodson considered the three basic compensation plans—straight salary, straight commission, and a combination of salary and incentives. Then he called Bill Jones, BSSI's national sales manager, to discuss the alternatives.

Questions

1. What are the advantages and disadvantages of a straight salary for Baxter Surgical Supplies?
2. Is the compensation plan causing a problem? How?
3. What would you do to correct the situation, if anything?

CASE 17-2
The Dunn Corporation*

Robert Head, the newly appointed sales manager for the Dunn Corporation, completed a review of the sales force that he inherited. He knew that he had an important decision facing him regarding one of his sales representatives, John Little.

Company Background. The Dunn Corporation, with headquarters in Tuscaloosa, Alabama, produced and sold asphalt roofing products and other building materials throughout the southeastern United States. The primary market area consisted of the

* This case was developed by Professor James L. Taylor, Department of Management and Marketing, University of Alabama. The company name has been changed.

states of Alabama, Tennessee, Georgia, Florida, and Mississippi. There were also selected accounts in Kentucky, Indiana, and South Carolina. Five sales representatives covered the primary marketing area, with each representative having one state assigned as a territory. The selected accounts were assigned to the sales representatives at the sales manager's discretion.

Historically, the management of Dunn had pursued a conservative growth strategy with particular emphasis on achieving maximum return on investment. To keep costs down, capital expenditures for replacement of worn-out or obsolete equipment were given low priority. This led to a drop in production efficiency at the company's Tuscaloosa plant such that production was unable to keep pace with demand. Thus, from 1999 to 2003, company sales were limited by the availability of the product. However, despite these difficulties, the company was profitable and had an excellent reputation in the construction industry for service and quality.

The company initiated successful capital improvement programs during 2002 and 2003; consequently, the company's production capacity had increased greatly. No longer would Dunn's sales performance be hindered by lack of product availability. Robert Head recognized that this increase in production capacity would require some revisions in the sales representatives' duties. More time would have to be spent seeking new accounts to fully realize this new sales potential.

One of the first tasks that Head undertook as sales manager was a review of the field operations and performance of each sales representative. Head traveled with the sales representatives for a week to obtain as much information on each representative as possible. Head also spent two days with each person compiling a territorial analysis. This analysis broke each representative's district into trade areas that were analyzed in terms of established accounts, competitive accounts, potential of the trade territory, market position of competitive manufacturers, and selection of target accounts. Head believed that a properly prepared territorial analysis could reveal whether the sales representatives really knew and worked their districts. Some pertinent statistics uncovered by the analysis are reported in Exhibits A and B.

John Little's Performance. Head concluded, after reviewing the results of the territorial analysis, that John Little's sales performance could be improved. Little had been with the company for over 20 years. A tall, handsome individual with a polished, articulate manner, he appeared to be a perfect salesperson, yet his performance never seemed to equal his potential.

Sales performance of the individual sales representatives, 2004–2005.

Sales Representative	Sales Volume	
	2004	2005
Peters	$2,732,464	$2,636,832
Little	1,366,232	1,315,916
Homer	1,639,420	1,879,880
Cough	2,368,136	2,443,844
Stiles	1,001,903	1,127,928
Totals:	$9,108,216	$9,399,402

EXHIBIT B

Results of territorial analysis.

Sales Representative	Number of Accounts	New Accounts in 2002	Average Daily Calls
Peters	63	3	4
Little	34	0	2
Homer	52	2	5
Cough	78	4	2
Stiles	47	2	3
Averages:	54.8	2.2	3.2

While evaluating Little's accounts, call reports, and expense accounts, Head uncovered a pattern of infrequent travel throughout Little's district. Little sold only 34 active accounts, well below the company average of approximately 55. With the low number of accounts and a daily call rate of two, it appeared that Little was not working hard. When Little's sales performance was compared to his district's estimated potential, it appeared that Little was realizing only about 60 percent of the potential sales of his area. When compared with the other territories, Little's district ranked last in sales volume per 1,000 housing starts and sales volume per 100,000 population.

Head questioned Little concerning coverage in his Georgia district. Head recalled part of their conversation:

Head: John, it appears that you are not calling on the potential customers in the outer areas of your district. For example, last month you spent 12 out of 20 days working in Atlanta. I know you live in Atlanta, and there is a tendency to work closer to home, but I believe that we are missing a lot of business in your area simply by not calling on people.

Little: Look, I have been selling roofing for a long time, even when the plant couldn't produce and ship it. Why get upset when we have a little extra product to sell?

Head: Look, John, we have increased production by 20 percent. You will have all the product you can sell. This means extra income to you, better services to your accounts, and more profit to the company. I will be happy to assist you in working out a plan for coverage of your district.

Little: Bob, don't you ever look at the volume of our customers? If you did, you would know that the Republic Roofing Supply in Atlanta is the second largest account of Dunn. Upchurch, the owner of Republic, is very demanding concerning my servicing Republic on ordering, delivery, and product promotion. It has taken a long time, but I have gained the trust and respect of Upchurch. That is why he looks to me to take care of the account. The reason that we have not lost the account to our competitors is that I give the type of service demanded by Upchurch.

Head: John, I agree that service to all of our accounts is extremely important. However, service does represent a cost, not only in terms of an outlay of money but also in the potential loss of business from other accounts. I seriously question the profitability of spending approximately 40 percent of your time with one account.

Little: What do you mean, profitability? My district has always made money. Just because we have new management, why does everything have to change?

Head continued the conversation by suggesting that he and Little meet at some future date to lay out a travel schedule. It was Head's intention to structure the schedule so that Little could make a minimum of four calls per day. Little, however, refused to consider setting a schedule or to increase the number of calls per day. His refusal was based on the contention that he needed at least two days a week to service Republic properly. Little further stated that if Dunn would not allow him the two days a week to service Republic, other roofing manufacturers would.

Robert Head pondered his decision regarding John Little and the Georgia territory. He felt that he had three options. First, he could simply fire Little with the possibility of losing the Republic account. Because Republic was Dunn's second largest account, Head realized that this might be a dangerous course of action. Second, Head considered rearranging Little's district by transferring some of the outer counties to other sales representatives. Finally, Head realized that he could simply accept the situation and leave things as they were now. He remembered once being told by a close friend with years of management experience that sometimes a don't-rock-the-boat strategy is the best way to handle difficult situations.

Question

What should Robert Head do regarding John Little and his Georgia territory?

Appendix A: Sales Call Role-Plays

How would you like to take a computer class without ever using a computer? To learn, you need an instructor, a textbook, and a computer. To learn to sell, you need an instructor, a textbook, and one or more role-plays. Role-plays are where the true learning takes place, where you see how to use all of the classroom instruction materials your instructor and textbook provided.

I have worked with thousands of people to help them develop role-plays similar to those presented in a sales training class. The following role-plays have been created from actual organizations' sales information provided to their salespeople. The names of the companies and their products have been changed to provide anonymity.

ROLE-PLAY ONE: CONSUMER SALES

You are a salesperson for a multibillion-dollar consumer goods manufacturer. Today you will be calling on Amy, the cereal buyer for ABC Grocery Stores. ABC is a chain of 20 large grocery stores. You have known Amy since last year about this time, when she became the buyer. Since then you have called on Amy about every month to sell her your various new items, talk about reordering your other products ABC currently carries, and create marketing plans for your major items.

Amy's office is in the largest city in your area. ABC currently carries about 100 different products of yours, with each of these 100 products available in various sizes and flavors. Thus ABC has 450 SKUs (stock-keeping units) of yours that it sells. (Each item carried in the store is given a tracking, or stock-keeping, number referred to as an SKU.)

You will be selling Amy one size of a new ready-to-eat cereal. For your role-play choose any cereal in your favorite grocery store to use in this exercise. Carefully analyze the features, advantages, and benefits of the cereal you select. Incorporate the FABs into your presentation as if this were a new cereal. The following information relates to the role-play's product, promotion, pricing, and sales objectives.

Product Description

Select any ready-to-eat (RTE) cereal of your choice to use in your role-play.

- Ready-to-eat cereal is the largest dry grocery category, with sales of $8 billion.

Category/Segment Performance

The following information is based on AC Nielsen information and test markets.

- 93 percent of consumers will buy your cereal in addition to their normal cereal.
- Your cereal focuses on people nine years of age to older adults.

Item Fit and Uniqueness

- 60 percent of category growth comes from new cereal products.
- Your product attracts your key consumer group—households with kids.
- 67 percent of households that tried your cereal in test markets said that it would be their first or second favorite cereal.
- 61 percent of households with kids said they would buy your cereal in test markets.

Introductory Promotional Period (IPP)

- 95 percent of adults 18 to 49 years of age will see your cereal's advertising an average of 10 times.
- 64 percent of kids age 9 to 14 will see your cereal an average of six times.
- Advertising, consumer promotions, and a public relations blitz will run for two and one-half months, beginning in two months; $16 million will be spent on advertising, with over 50 percent of spending in network prime time: three FSIs (free-standing inserts) will appear, one every other week, with a high coupon value.
- Trade promotion pricing is available two months from today.

Normal Pricing		Introductory Pricing Promotion*	
Case pricing	$33.24	Case pricing	$33.24
Net unit	2.77	Introductory discount rate	−13.56
Suggested retail	3.39	Net case cost	19.68
Normal store price	3.40	Net unit cost	1.64
% Margin	18%	Suggested retail	1.99
		Margin	18%

*Requires feature and display.

- 12 boxes of cereal in each case.
- Estimated number of cases the average individual grocery store will sell: 7 cases for three-day special at a featured price of $1.79; 20 cases per two-week promotion at a featured price of $1.99; 2 cases per average week with no promotion at a normal store price of $3.40.

Sales Objectives

- Purchase enough cereal for a three-day special with feature price of $1.79; two-week special with feature price of $1.99; and four-week normal sales period with a $3.40 suggested retail price.
- Have an in-store aisle display and $1.79 shelf-talker for the three-day special.
- Have an in-store shelf-talker showing the $1.99 price for two weeks.
- For either the three-day or the two-week period have one advertisement in ABC's weekly in-store printed ad newspaper.
- Have a normal store price of $3.40.

You feel certain Amy will buy from you today. Both you and Amy know your organization will withdraw future special pricing deals if ABC buys the new cereal at the low introductory price and does not reduce the initial price and promote it. You feel Amy will buy some cereal to promote. The question is, How much?

Your goal is to sell her on the idea of running two price specials. This will allow you to sell her more product, plus the grocery stores' customer will buy more, resulting in a large reorder once the four-week supply of cereal is sold.

ROLE-PLAY TWO: DISTRIBUTOR SALES

You are a new sales representative for Creative Solutions, Wireless Division. The Wireless Division is a distributor of wireless technology and software for sale to businesses. Creative Solutions' primary clients include businesses that maintain a large sales force, require constant communication, and demand the latest technology.

You are taking over for Alex Jones, who recently moved on to a management position. This afternoon you have your first appointment with one of Creative Solutions' largest clients, Greg Johnson. Mr. Johnson is a regional manager for a large commercial real estate firm, Urban Properties. He is responsible for managing 15 sales representatives in three states. Mr. Johnson is concerned with maintaining the most prepared sales force while keeping costs to a minimum.

The material Alex Jones collected on this account follows. Use this material to prepare your first sales call on Mr. Johnson. He has allowed only 10 minutes of his busy schedule to meet with you.

Information on Greg Johnson

Greg Johnson is a regional manager with Urban Properties, one of the nation's largest commercial real estate firms. He maintains a sales force of 15 people spread over three states and understands the importance of effective and efficient communication. Mr. Johnson is interested in having his sales force use new technology to improve performance. He has recently expressed concerns about the increasing costs of travel for his salespeople.

Mr. Johnson used Creative Solutions' products in the past because he thought they were high quality. His main interest has been in communication tools and mobile office technology. He was a salesperson before his advancement to regional manager and loves the tools of the trade. In fact, he takes pride in the quality of the technology his sales force uses.

Mr. Johnson likes to be given all the information on a product. He is interested in hearing the benefits of a product, rather than just being told about a long list of available products. He likes salespeople who get straight to the point. Mr. Johnson is a very busy man. His relationship with the previous Creative Solutions' salesperson, Alex Jones, was a good one.

Annual Call Report Summary (*Prior Year*) Sales Representative: Alex Jones Client: *Greg Johnson (Urban Properties*)

Month 1

Spoke to Mr. Johnson for 25 minutes to introduce our Infrared Modem Kits designed for wireless Internet connections. I mentioned the savings on large purchases for his sales force. No purchase was indicated.

Month 2

Talked with Mr. Johnson for about 10 minutes. Answered some questions about compatibility of the Infrared Modem Kit with PCs or handheld computers. He indicated some interest in the kits for his salespeople.

Month 3

The special on Infrared Modem Kits was about to end. I tried to sell Mr. Johnson one more time. He was impressed with the simple and instant connection but decided his budget was too tight this month.

Month 4

Spent about 15 minutes discussing PC Cards for wireless Internet connections. PC Cards (Air Card 510) allow you to connect to the Internet or send e-mail from any mobile location without the need for a mobile phone or land-line. He was very interested in the convenience and quality over Infrared Modem Kits. He mentioned he would like to know more about the PC Cards. A sale is getting closer.

Month 5

Stopped in to talk with Mr. Johnson for 10 minutes. Discussed the mobility features of the Air Card 510 for Notebooks. His salespeople can log on to the Internet or send e-mails from anywhere in the world from their mobile offices by simply plugging a card into their computer. This interested him, so we began discussing price. A decision would be made next month.

Month 6

Met with Mr. Johnson for 35 minutes. We agreed that the convenience and quality of the new Air Card 510 were worth the price. He purchased 15 PC Cards for $5,700.

Month 7

Mr. Johnson met with me for 20 minutes this morning. He was impressed with the improved mobility and communication with the PC Cards. I solved a couple of technical problems with one of the cards.

Month 8

Mr. Johnson was on a business trip for the month. I stopped by his office to drop off some donuts for his secretaries.

Month 9

Spent 15 minutes with Mr. Johnson this morning. He seemed especially interested in a way to cut down on travel costs to visit potential properties. He frequently travels with his salespeople to look at commercial real estate property. Mr. Johnson said he would like to spend more time in the office but still be able to approve new real estate ventures. He asked about any new video technologies that might help him out. I mentioned our Digital Recorder, designed especially for Internet video transfer. The Digital Recorder has the capability of quickly sending real-time, streaming video over the Internet.

Month 10

Spent 30 minutes with Mr. Johnson this afternoon. I mentioned the convenience and compatibility of our Digital Recorder when used with the PC Cards he bought in July. He liked the fast transfer of video over the Internet to view potential properties. Apparently, traveling to view properties is getting expensive, and the Digital Recorder is the best alternative to being there. He wanted to wait a few months because of new computer hardware they were purchasing soon. I left him some information on the new Digital Recorder. I plan to discuss it with him again in a few months, once their new computer system is in place.

Month 11

Spent about 15 minutes discussing the new computer system Urban Properties was setting up. I mentioned installing our Act! Software on his new system. He was very interested in the ability to keep detailed records of his meetings and calls with customers and prospects. He mentioned he would like to try out the software on his new computer system. I told him I'd get him a demo disk.

Month 12

Stopped by Mr. Johnson's office in the morning and dropped off some donuts for his secretaries. I talked to Mr. Johnson for about five minutes, just long enough to drop off the ACT! demo software. He seemed very excited about the new software.

Creative Solutions— Product Information

MPEG-4 Digital Recorder www.sharpe-usa.com

World's first streaming video camcorder offers the fastest way to send video by e-mail or over the Internet. The recorder produces moving picture files that are small in size and easy to send anywhere.

- Great for a mobile office.
- Quick and easy sharing of video.
- Immediate—real-time viewing over the Internet.
- Excellent way to show clients a property.
- Good way for management to view a property.
- Reduces costs/expenses to view properties.

ACT! www.act.com

The ultimate tool for managing and growing your business relationships.

- Easily identify all contacts and activities related to each account.
- Sales forecasting.
- Sales training.
- Share ACT! Calendar with Microsoft Outlook.
- Synchronize your laptop with your Palm Pilot and cellular phone.
- Manage tasks.
- Preparation and organization lead to increased sales.
- Reduces administrative time and costs.
- Compatible with existing hardware and software.

Air Card 510 www.sierrawireless.com

Connects laptops directly to the Internet and e-mail without the need for a wireless phone or land-line connection.

- Great convenience for mobile offices.
- Works with Windows 95, 98, NT, and 2000.

- Offers simplicity, mobility, and freedom.
- Patented internal antenna for maximum mobility.

Infrared Modem Kit www.ericsson.com

Allows user to send data from a PC or PDA with an infrared port.

- Conveniently connects to mobile phone.
- Line up the mobile phone with the infrared port for a quick and easy wireless connection.
- Great for mobile offices.
- No cables.
- No clutter.

Product Comparison Data			
Feature	AirCard 510	Acme AirCard	MCA Card
Laptop compatiable	Yes	No	No
Handheld compatible	Yes	Yes	Yes
Windows 95, 98, NT, and 2000 compatible	Yes	No	No
Transfer speed	1.5 MB	75K	24K
Cost	$399.00	$301.00	$375.00

Product Price List (per unit)			
Product	1–4 Units	5–14 Units	15+ Units
Infrared Modem Kit	$215.00	$199.95	$195.00
PC Card 510	399.00	399.00	380.00
ACT!	400.00	350.00	300.00
Digital Recorder	699.95	685.00	600.00

ROLE-PLAY THREE: BUSINESS-TO-BUSINESS

Friday before last was your first day on the job.[1] Last week you completed your initial one-week training course. Your boss now wants you to make several sales calls this week before you attend their four-week sales training program beginning next week. She feels this will help you relate better to the class materials.

You talked with Chris Hammond, owner of Travel Xpress, for about five minutes last week when he was called into the district sales office. You mentioned to your boss that you would like to call on Chris. She said, "Go for it!" The following are some of the main things you learned from talking to Chris.

Travel Xpress—A Small Business

Travel Xpress (TX) is a personalized travel agency located in your town. TX has been in business since 1990. Chris bought the agency from the original owner in 1996. He worked at the agency as a part-time (college student) employee since its beginning. He makes all business decisions for the company.

TX has one full-time and one part-time employee. The full-time employee is going to have a child and will shortly become a part-time worker. In today's prosperous economy, Chris has had trouble getting good part-time help. Right now the part-timer is a 17-year-old student. Most part-timers stay about three months because the job demands customer service skills and a detail orientation.

Business has been growing for Chris. Two years ago sales were about $5,000 per week. Last year, sales increased to $10,000 per week because Chris opened a Web site. This year's sales are expected to be about $12,000 per week.

Four years ago, Chris purchased a Futrell 300. Its cost was $675. At that time Chris had just purchased the agency. Sales were about $1,500 per week. Although the Futrell works well for incidental copying, it is a bit slow (six copies per minute). In addition, the Futrell can only print single copies—so Chris or the employee has to stand by the machine to make multiple copies. Since TX has begun group sales, it is often necessary to issue multiple itineraries. In addition, Chris now provides multiple-page information sheets to customers and to attendees at travel seminars. He has begun to send out multiple-page work to Kinko's. However there is a $50 processing fee on each Kinko's job (pick-up/delivery and order handling). Chris estimates he makes about 5,000 copies a month.

Chris has called DataMax, the Futrell dealer, several times about upgrading his machine. DataMax encouraged Chris to deal with a telemarketer who specializes in small businesses. The telemarketing representative talked with Chris for about 10 minutes. The representative sent Chris a bid on another Futrell machine. However, the bid did not mention the toner cost or copy speed. The representative stressed that the machine was lightweight and easy to use. The bid price is $595. Chris likes this price! Chris asked the representative how long he could expect the copier to last and was told about five years.

Chris is concerned with the copy quality and durability. Last year, Chris had to send the copier out for repairs three times. One time the copier shut off and would not restart. The auto shut-off mode had short circuited. That repair took three days and cost TX about $400. On another occasion, a customer got upset with Chris's full-time employee because the copy the customer was given was too light to read. The customer threw a fit, screaming at the full-time employee and telling the other customers on site that TX was a "rinky-dink, small-time operation." Shortly thereafter, the full-time employee indicated that she would go part-time after the birth of her child.

Three weeks before, the copier jammed late one evening. Chris decided to fix it. After opening the copier case with a screwdriver. Chris failed to dislodge the jammed paper. Chris was unable to reassemble the copier. Paul, owner of Office Machine Repair told Chris that it would cost more to fix the Futrell 300 than the machine was worth.

So Chris is stuck with a dead, four-year-old copy machine. Chris wants to buy another machine but is skeptical about all copiers.

Preparation for the Sales Call

Excited, yet nervous, about making your first sales call, you wonder how to prepare for meeting Chris. Your boss suggested you find the answer to these three questions:

1. How many copies does Chris make a year? Chris told you he makes about 60,000 copies a year.
2. How many years does Chris think he will keep the copier? You guess about five years.
3. What are the costs associated with the copier you will recommend and the Futrell copier? A bottle of Futrell copier's toner lasts for 1,600 copies and costs $100.95. Your machine's toner costs $14.50 and produces 1,500 copies.

You also create a table showing how your Minolta copier compares with the Futrell copier on six items. Your biggest challenge is to overcome the initial price objection. Also, you feel, maybe wrongly, that Chris will not want to know about all the items in your comparative analysis. However, you need to be prepared to discuss all items Chris may consider in his buying decision.

Your sales manager said that getting a small business owner to part with $1,000 is sometimes harder than getting a purchasing agent of a large corporation to pay $100,000 for equipment. Small business owners seldom look past actual price, whereas buyers for large businesses will.

| | Competitive Information | |
	Minolta	Futrell
Price	$2,295	$595
Type		
Mfn Rec Mo/vol	500 to 2,500 copies	Up to 500 copies
Configuration	Desktop, stationary	Desktop, moving
Toner	Dry, dual component	Dry, monocomponent
Optics	Lens and mirror	Fiber optics
Speeds		
First copy	5.9 sec	15 sec
Multicopy	13 cpm	Single sheet
Warm-up	30 sec	None
Paper		
Paper feed	Single tray	User feeds single sheets
Paper capacity	250 sheets	Single sheets
Maximum original size	8½″ × 14″	8½″ × 11″
Supplies		
Copy toner yield	1,500 copies	1,600 copies
Toner price	$14.50	$100.95
Imaging cartridge (drum)	$365 for 21,500 copies	Included in toner price
Comments	Can produce up to one set of 50 copies; imaging unit contains organic drum, cleaning blade, remote meter reading.	Maintenance-free—user replaces PC cartridges, no warm-up time, portable, desktop unit with pop-up carrying handle.
Specifications		
Dimensions (H × W × D)	14″ × 25″ × 21″	14⅛″ × 15½″ × 4¼″
Weight	70 lb	17 lb
Power requirements	120V, 11A	115V, 6A

ROLE-PLAY FOUR: BUSINESS-TO-BUSINESS

You are an outside salesperson for Ferguson Enterprises, Inc. Ferguson (www.ferguson.com) is one of the country's leading distribution companies of plumbing supplies; pipe, valves, and fittings (PVF); and heating and cooling (HVAC) equipment. One of your customers is the Centex Corporation.

Centex Corporation

Established in 1950, Centex Corporation (www.centex.com) has annual revenues exceeding $5 billion. It is a publicly held firm with over 13,000 full-time associates and is the nation's leader in contracting and construction services, investment real estate, and home building. Centex is headquartered in Dallas, Texas.

Centex has been a trade customer for Ferguson for many years. In the past, Ferguson supplied a limited amount of the plumbing-related materials for Centex's projects. In an effort to gain more of their business, we have targeted an upcoming large project recently awarded to Centex.

Centex is currently in the material-acquisition phase of an upscale multifamily condominium complex in downtown Houston. There will be a total of 30 buildings with 24 units in each building. Each of the units will have two bathrooms, one in the master suite and one secondary. The architects and designers have specified that all finished products (plumbing fixtures) must have a brand name and be of the highest quality. The focal point of the master bath suite is specified to be a 66-by-66-inch corner whirlpool.

Jacuzzi Products

Based on its experience in the past, Centex has used Jacuzzi products (www.jacuzzi.com) on most of its projects. Because they have been very satisfied with Jacuzzi from all aspects of doing business (quality, product offering, and price points), you want to encourage them to try other Jacuzzi products. As a Ferguson outside sales representative, your focus for this call will be to secure orders for the Jacuzzi whirlpool bath, lavatory, toilet, and kitchen sink.

Suggested Purchase Order

Based on conversations with Centex, you know that the project will go in phases and that they intend to build one or two buildings at a time. With this schedule in mind, it will be your recommendation that they order the whirlpools two buildings at a time. This will allow Centex to take advantage of the truckload quantity discount Jacuzzi has extended to them on this project. You should suggest they purchase the following for each condo:

- One Fiore whirlpool bath
- One Nicolo kitchen sink
- Two Gallery Suite pedestal lavatories
- Two Gallery Suite two-piece toilets

For information on these four products, go to Jacuzzi's website. Print out all information available for each product. Other selling points that you should offer Centex include these:

- There is limited storage space on the job.
- Purchasing in this quantity will reduce shrinkage on the project (preventing theft from the job site.)

Ferguson Price List					
			Quantity Discounts		
Flore Whirlpool Bath	**List Price**	**Builder Price**	**0–10**	**11–29**	**30+**
Per-unit price	$6,441	$5,796	$5,796	$5,475	$4,509
Savings		$645	$645	$966	$1,932
			Quantity Discounts		
Gallery Suite Pedestal Lavatory	**List Price**	**Builder Price**	**0–10**	**11–20**	**21–40**
Per-unit price	$540	$486	$486	$459	$432
Savings		$54	$54	$81	$108

(continued)

Nicolo Kitchen Sink	List Price	Builder Price	Quantity Discounts		
			0–10	11–20	21–40
Per-unit price	$399	$359	$359	$339	$319
Savings		$40	$40	$60	$80

Gallery Suite 2-Piece Toilet	List Price	Builder Price	Quantity Discounts		
			0–10	11–20	21–40
Per-unit price	$450	$400	$400	$375	$350
Savings		$50	$50	$75	$100

Appendix B: Personal Selling Experiential Exercises

ACT! EXPRESS   This assignment will teach you how to use ACT!'s contact management software to manage yourself and sales territory. You will learn how to enter contact information, schedule meetings, plan phone calls, and record important tasks. Weekly activities will have you record sales information and generate letters, reports, and graphs. The following sections explain the scenario, setup, and expectations of this assignment.

Scenario   You are a salesperson for Soothsayer Corporation, an information management software provider. Your sales manager has requested that you begin using ACT! Express, a type of customer contact management software that helps one manage interactions with clients. ACT! provides its users with easily accessible customer contact information, a daily task planner, and many other account management tools. Salespeople use ACT! to track prospects and clients through the selling process and to generate sales reports and graphs for clients and managers. ACT! enables salespeople to keep track of customer information and automates many administrative tasks to better serve customers.

About the Company   Soothsayer Corporation designs, develops, markets, and supports computer software products. The company's software products are classified into two types: systems software and Internet business applications software. Systems software includes applications designed for the Internet and corporate Intranets to create, access, and change data stored on a computer system. Internet business applications software allows users of any computer with an Internet browser to access information and automates business data-processing functions. Both software products are priced at $399.

Setup   Instructions are provided on how to install ACT! Express on your computer. Installation should take no more than 15 minutes if you choose to use your own computer.

The Weekly Activities   A list of specific tasks and activities will be sent to you on a weekly basis by your instructor (sales manager). The activities include such things as scheduling meetings and phone calls, entering new sales, and generating sales graphs and letters. Each week you will generate printouts based on the completed activities. Special instructions and printing directions will guide you through each week's activity.

Deliverables   The final deliverable will be an organized collection of weekly activities. You will turn in the assignment bound in either a half-inch ringed binder or a folder. Tabs should separate and clearly reference each activity.

How to Install ACT!

(Installation will take 5 to 10 minutes.)

1. Insert the ACT! for Windows CD into the CD-ROM drive. The CD starts automatically, and the ACT! installation screen appears. If the CD does not start up, double click the My Computer icon on the Windows desktop. Locate the CD-ROM drive in the window, double click the drive letter to display the contents of the CD, and double click SETUP.EXE.
2. Click Install ACT!
3. Follow the on-screen instructions.

   - Agree to the license agreement.
   - Enter user information (personal information about you).
   - Select destination location (use the recommended destination).
   - Choose country version.
   - Select program folder (use the recommended folder).
   - Select placement of ACT! icons. (This is a personal preference. It is up to you.)
   - Verify if your information is correct.

When installation is complete, register your copy of ACT! You can register online, by mail, or fax. Registration is optional but recommended.

How to Set Up a Database

- Follow the on-screen instructions.

List of Weekly Activities

Activity 1: Week 1

Objective: Get familiar with the features of ACT! Express.

To Do

- Enter in 10 new contacts (supplied by sales manager). Press the "Insert" key on your keyboard to enter in new contacts. Press the "Insert" key after each entry to enter a new contact.

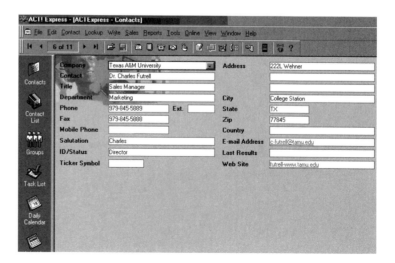

You may edit your contact list by clicking the mouse in the desired location. Pressing the tab key will control movement between fields.

Schedule

- Meeting with Joe Burns at Interact Software next week:
- 9:00 Monday
- Duration 15 minutes

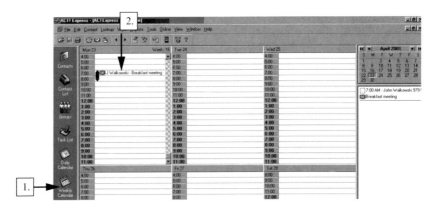

- Regarding "sales call"

Meeting with Chris Hammond at Travel Xpress next week:

- 11:00 Wednesday
- Duration 1 hour
- Regarding "contract negotiations"

How to Schedule a Meeting or Activity

1. Click on the Weekly Calendar icon.
2. Double click on appropriate date and time from weekly calendar.
3. Fill out schedule activity.

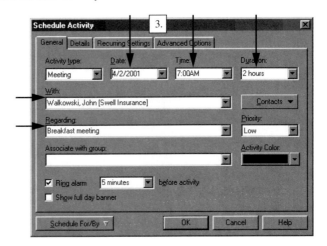

Sales This Week

- 75 units of Internet Business Software to Crystal Corporation on Wednesday.
- 15 units of Systems Software to Tractor Company on Wednesday.

1. **To record a sale:** Click on the "Contacts" icon. From the Contacts page toolbar, select the specific contact and click on "Sales" in the toolbar. Next click

"New Sales Opportunity" and type in the product name. (Systems software or Internet Business Software). Type in the number of units and the unit price ($399). Select the appropriate contact and click on "Complete the Sale." Be sure to select the appropriate "Actual Close Date." Finally, click "OK."

2. *To change a sale:* Go to the contacts page and select the contact to which you sold the product. At the bottom of this screen you should see the sale. Click on the sale and select "Reopen Sale" at the bottom left of the sales window. From there you should be able to edit the date.

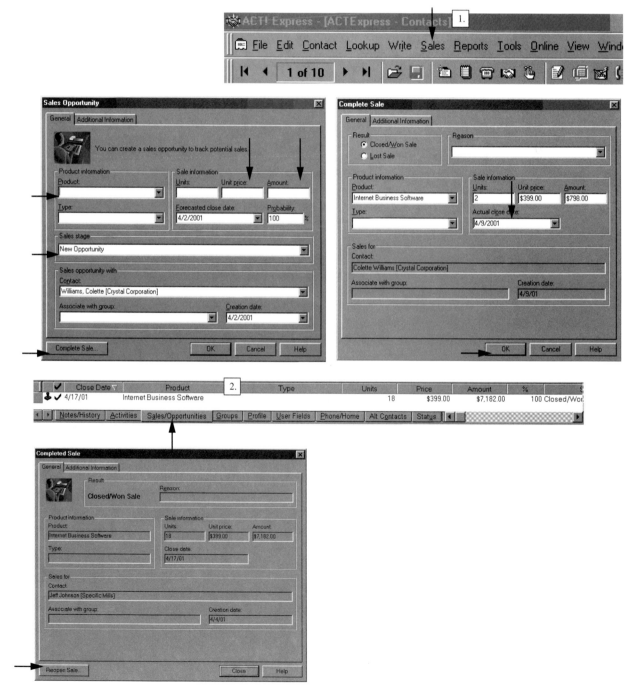

Printouts

1. Contact directory. From the toolbar select "Reports," "Contact Directory," "All Contacts," and "All Users."
2. Next week's schedule. First, select the Weekly Calendar icon from the sidebar. Then, from the toolbar, select "File," "Print," and "Plain Letter Full Page (P) (2 Col)."

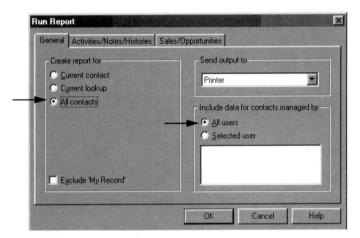

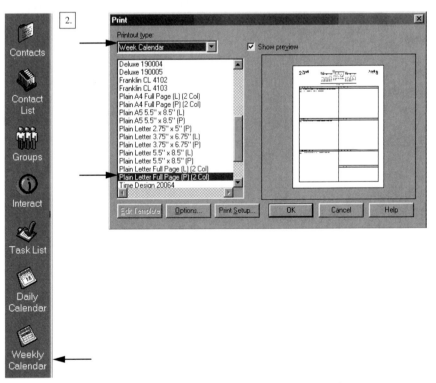

Activity 2: Week 2

To Do

- Generate a sales list after you close your two sales for the week.

Schedule

Weekly sales team meeting:

- Sales meetings occur Thursdays at 7:00 A.M. and last two hours.
- Schedule the meeting with your sales manager (instructor).
- Select "Recurring Settings" and complete the options for a weekly Thursday meeting.
- This meeting should occur once a week for the next six months. Make sure you select the appropriate time under "Until."

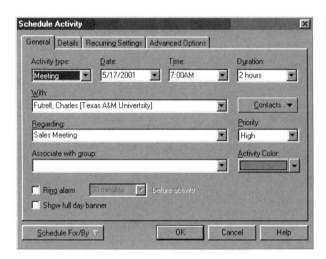 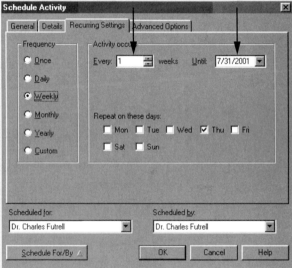

Meeting with Amy Samuel at XYZ Grocery next week:

- 9:00 Monday
- Duration 45 minutes
- Regarding "Presentation"

Meeting with Jeff Johnson at Specific Mills next week:

- 10:00 Tuesday
- Duration 45 minutes
- Regarding "sales call"

Meeting with Crystal Goodman at P&Q Financial next week:

- 2:00 Tuesday
- Duration 1 hour
- Regarding "sales call"

Phone call with Greg Johnson at Urban Properties next Monday morning to schedule a meeting.

- 8:00 Monday

Phone call with Colette Williams at Crystal Corp next Monday morning to schedule a meeting.

- 8:30 Monday

Schedule a "to do" reminder next Monday to prepare a presentation for the meeting with Specific Mills.

- 4:00 Monday

Sales This Week

- 100 units of Internet Business Software to Interact Software on Monday.
- 150 units of Internet Business Software to Travel Xpress on Wednesday.

Printouts

1. Next week's schedule.
2. Sales list. From the toolbar, select "Reports," "Sales Reports," and "Sales List." The Sales List should cover all sales from the past two weeks.

Activity 3: Week 3

To Do

- Write two letters, one to Interact Software and one to Travel Xpress, thanking them for the sale. The letter is generated by selecting "Write" in the toolbar.

Schedule

Meeting with Greg Johnson at Urban Properties next week:

- 10:00 Tuesday
- Duration 45 minutes
- Regarding "demonstration"

Meeting with Colette Williams at Crystal Corp next week:

- 3:00 Tuesday
- Duration 1 hour
- Regarding "sales call"

Schedule a "to-do" reminder on next Wednesday to prepare sales graphs.

Sales This Week

- 100 units of Systems Software to XYZ Grocery on Monday.
- 7 units of Systems Software to P&Q Financial on Tuesday.
- 18 units of Internet Business Software to Specific Mills on Tuesday.

Printouts

1. Next week's schedule.
2. Letter to Interact Software.
3. Letter to Travel Xpress.

Activity 4: Week 4

To Do

- Generate graph on closed/won sales for the entire month by amount after this week's sales.
- Generate graph on closed/won sales for the entire month by units after this week's sales.

Meetings to Schedule

- Performance review with sales manager (instructor): anytime next week.

Sales This Week

- 200 units of Internet Business Software to Urban Properties on Tuesday.
- 200 units of Systems Software to Crystal Corp on Tuesday.

Printouts

1. Next week's schedule.
2. Print out closed/won sales graphs:
   A. Click on the "Contacts" icon. From the Contacts page toolbar, select "Sales," "Sales Graph," "All Contacts," "All Users," "Graph by Week" and "Value in Units."
   B. Next, print a similar graph by "Amount."

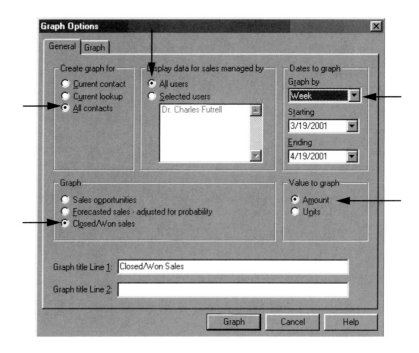

SELL YOURSELF ON A JOB INTERVIEW

You will play the roles of a sales job applicant and a recruiter.[1] You may interview any organization, but the hope is you will choose to interview an organization with which you would like to interview for a job sometime in the future. For your role as an applicant, develop a one- to two-page professional-looking résumé. Before you are to be interviewed, turn in a copy of the résumé to your instructor to give to your interviewer to go over before the meeting. Also give the instructor a one- to two-page description of the company at which you are applying for a beginning sales job. Assume this is your first interview with the company and you have never met the recruiter. It will last approximately five to eight minutes.

Recruiter   Create a business card to give to the applicant sometime during the interview.

Résumé   Bring an original copy of the résumé with you to the interview (see page 585). During the interview, be prepared to point out one or more selling points in the résumé that relate to the interviewer's question(s) or to major point(s) you will discuss about yourself during the interview.

Personal Business Card   Here are several format ideas for your business card. On the left side have a head and shoulder photograph of yourself. This should be a professional pose. On the right side have your name in bold. Underneath your name, have your address, telephone number, and e-mail address in a regular typeface. Now skip a line and have the name of your school in bold, followed by your degree, such as B.B.A. in Marketing, and graduation date. On the card's back have a bulleted list of items such as your overall and major GPA, courses relating to job, and main job(s). You are creating a creative mini-résumé.

Portfolio   Create a bound portfolio of school projects you have completed during your work career and coursework (see page 591). At the appropriate time during the interview, go over one or more of the projects that best relate to this job. If you have no projects, use a fake portfolio. Make up facts related to the project(s) for discussion with the recruiter.

The résumé and course portfolio serve as visuals that aid in creating the image of you as a creative, highly motivated person who has thoroughly prepared for this interview and is very interested in obtaining a job with the organization. You will leave both the résumé and the portfolio with the interviewer. They will be returned to you after the interview. You are encouraged to develop other creative elements for your presentation.

I Want the Job
Before the interview is over, consider letting the recruiter know "you are very interested in this job." The interviewer may not feel this is true if you do not show knowledge about the organization and the job. However, if you can demonstrate in-depth knowledge about the company, the job, products, and customers, such a statement will be taken positively by the recruiter. Some organizations will not hire someone unless that person states: "I want this job." If true, you would declare this in a later interview.

Grade Beginning and Ending
Your grade for this exercise begins when you shake hands for the greeting and ends when you shake hands to end the interview. You should act in a professional manner the entire time.

Follow-up
After the interview, create a professional "thank you" letter (see page 589). In order to know the interviewer's address, ask for a business card sometime during the interview. Within one day after the interview, mail or e-mail the "thank you" letter to your instructor. For the letter's inside address and salutation, use the recruiter's name as shown on the business card. If you send a thank you by e-mail, consider sending an electronic greeting card "thank you." Bluemountain, Amazon, Hallmark, and others have free electronic greeting cards on the Internet you can use for this part of the assignment. Select a professional "thank you" card to e-mail your recruiter.

Two weeks after the interview send a follow-up e-mail to your recruiter (see page 589). Use the recruiter's name in the e-mail (To: Mr. Smith). The e-mail actually goes to your instructor. Assume you have not heard anything back from the recruiter after the interview, and you want to know if the recruiter has received your follow-up letter and has any other questions to ask you. Also, assume that you are interested in being further considered for the sales job and that the recruiter said she or he would let you know if you are still being considered for the job within two weeks after the interview.

You Are Selling
Whether you are an applicant or an interviewer, imagine that you have been placed in a sales situation. As an applicant you are selling yourself. As an interviewer you are selling not only yourself but also your company and the sales job as well.

Interviewers are looking for indications that the applicant can sell or can be trained to sell. How can you—the applicant—apply basic selling procedures to the job interview situation?

You can look, dress, and groom like, and have the attitude of a successful person. Showing the interviewer you have prepared for the interview indicates how you might prepare to make a sales call on a customer. Using the résumé and portfolio during the interview helps distinguish you from others interviewing for the job. Finally, you should "close" the sale by asking for the order (job).

Sales Call Objective

An applicant typically goes through several interviews before being offered a job. Consider this your first interview. What is your sales call objective for the first interview? It is to be asked back for a second interview! The end of the interview is an excellent time for you to illustrate your sales skills.

Futrell's Closing Sequence

One way to demonstrate your sales skills is by using "Futrell's Two-Question Interview Closing Sequence." At the end of most first interviews the recruiter will ask something like, "Do you have any questions?" You should respond as follows:

- "Yes, I have two questions. What is the next step in the interview process?" Wait for the reply. Then ask,
- "Based on my background, my résumé, and what we have talked about today, what is my chance of being asked back for a second interview?"

Should the interviewer not ask if you have a question, you should say something such as "I have two questions," or "May I ask two questions before I go?"

Plan Your Interview Appearance

After your interview, complete the Interview Appearance Questionnaire. Give the completed questionnaire to your instructor.

Name: _____

The most successful people in customer-contact jobs claim that mental sharpness means communicating a positive self-image. Like an actor or actress, interacting with others requires you to be on stage at all times. Creating a good first impression is essential. Also important is understanding the direct connection between your attitude and how you look to yourself. The better your self-image is when you encounter customers, clients, or guests, the more positive you are.

Rate yourself on each of the following grooming areas. If you write 5, you are saying improvement is not required. If you write a 1 or 2, you need considerable improvement. Be honest.

	Excellent	Good	Fair	Weak	Poor
Hairstyle, hair grooming, fingernails (appropriate length and cleanliness)	5	4	3	2	1
Personal cleanliness habits (body)	5	4	3	2	1
Clothing, piercings, and jewelry (appropriate to the situation)	5	4	3	2	1
Neatness (shoes shined: clothes clean, well pressed, etc.)	5	4	3	2	1
Fragrances, tattoos, and makeup	5	4	3	2	1
General grooming: Does your appearance reflect professionalism on the job?	5	4	3	2	1

When it comes to appearance on the job, I would rate myself as follows:
___Excellent   ___Good   ___Need improvement

RÉSUMÉ, FOLLOW-UP LETTER, E-MAIL

There are many formats of résumés to chose from that will best highlight your qualifications and experience. No matter which of these you decide to use, there are some things that should be included in any format. The following is a checklist of these necessary items.

Résumé Checklist

- Personal Data: Include your name, permanent and local addresses, phone number and e-mail address.
- Career Objectives: May include the skills you want to use and goals you would like to reach. Use phrases—indicate position desired or areas of interest. Avoid using general statements and terms such as opportunity for promotion, a challenging position, a position dealing with people, a progressive company.
- Education: Begin with the most recent school attended. List the name and location of college or university (city and state are sufficient) degree received, your major and minor, and dates of attendance or month and year graduating. Include your GPA. May include relevant course work (six to eight important classes). Include honors achieved, such as dean's list, class rank, awards, and scholarships. Include special training, licensure, or certifications.
- Experience: Begin with the most recent. List full-time, part-time, internship and co-op jobs. Do not include part-time work unless it's particularly relevant. Include dates of employment, company or organization name, city, and state of location, and your job title. Describe your duties using phrases, beginning with action verbs, in present or past tense, depending on the time of the experience.
- Activities: List your professional affiliations, clubs/organizations, campus activities, and dates of involvement. Include any offices you held or committees you chaired. You may want to briefly describe the activity and what you did using action verbs.
- Skills: Include any technical skills, such as computer software applications, hardware, and/or languages. List any language fluencies.
- Personal Categories: These sections can be used to demonstrate valuable attributes, for example, military experience, publications and presentations, relevant projects completed, and major accomplishments.
- Miscellaneous: Optional information includes willingness to relocate, willingness to travel, dates of availability, and/or special interests.
- References: A statement "References available upon request" is common. However, if space is limited, this statement is not necessary. Rule of thumb: For the interview, have references available on a separate sheet.

Other Tips

- Arrange categories/sections in order of relevance, presenting your most marketable information first.
- Use brief descriptive phrases instead of complete sentences. Avoid using personal pronouns—I, me, my, their.
- Have someone critique your résumé to check for spelling and/or grammatical errors.

Appearance Checklist

- Always buy good-quality paper for résumés—at least 50 percent cotton.
- Select a subdued-colored paper: white, pale beige, light gray. Résumés are traditionally white. Print the résumé in *black ink* only.
- Limit résumé to one page unless a second page is essential for relevant details and extensive work experience.

Action Verbs

Use action verbs when describing your experiences/accomplishments on your résumé, in your letters, and during your interview. Skills you will bring to an employer will consist of three basic types: people, things, and ideas. The following are common verbs used to describe these skills.

- People: administered, conducted, motivated, promoted, directed, coordinated, supervised, advised, explained, affected, managed, taught, activated, programmed, organized, conducted, stimulated, accomplished, adapted, adjusted, advertised, analyzed, accomplished, assisted, catalogued, collaborated, calculated, consulted.
- Things: built, constructed, compiled, specified, designed, changed, improved, prepared, calculated, completed, invented, created, programmed, revised, expedited, drafted, edited, enlarged, established, evaluated, examined, expanded, facilitated, familiarized, formulated, generated, governed, guided.
- Ideas: established, wrote, proposed, coordinated, illustrated, modified, analyzed, adapted, investigated, explained, defined, devised, innovated, implemented, created, educated, synthesized, initiated, integrated, interviewed, maintained, manipulated, marketed, monitored, negotiated, obtained, persuaded, presented, presided.

Résumé Formats

There are many different types of résumés. The most common type of résumé used is the Chronological, which focuses on work history and experiences. A second type, which will become more widely used as technology expands, is the Scannable. The Scannable Résumé is printed ready to be read by a computer. Here are suggestions for both of these types.

Chronological Résumés

The Chronological Résumé is the most common format and the one that is most familiar to employers (see Exhibit 1). It focuses on work history and experience and is organized by type of experience. Examples of categories of experience are education, technical experience, work experience, and activities.

This type of résumé has advantages and disadvantages. It can provide prospective employers with a clear and concise assessment of your experience. It also highlights most students' major asset: their education. On the downside, if you do not have a steady or relevant work history, this will be emphasized in the Chronological Résumé.

To write this type of résumé, first list your education, work experience, and activities. Then go beyond just listing the experiences and write what you gained in each experience that proves you have qualities that the employer desires.

Scannable Résumé

As technology advances, an increasing number of employers are requesting scannable résumés (see Exhibit 2). In many cases, your résumé will no longer be initially reviewed by an employer, but rather by a computer. **Remember: Computers read résumés differently than people do!** To make sure that no important information about you is lost in the scanning process and to increase your chances of being electronically selected, the following are suggested guidelines for writing a scannable résumé:

- Use plain, white paper—8½″ × 11″
- Do not fold—use large envelopes
- Use no borders, graphics, or landscape printing
- Select an unembellished typeface (such as Arial, Courier, Helvetica, ITC Bookman, ITC Avante Garde Gothic, New Century Schoolbook, Optima, Palatino, Times, Univers)
- Avoid *italics* and <u>underlining</u>
- Use **bold** sparingly, and preferably not on key words
- Put name and address on each page
- Clearly state functional and geographic preferences

EXHIBIT 1

Example undergraduate résumé.

Jane Smith

Current Address:		**Permanent Address:**
234 Your Street		5678 Your Street
College Station, TX 77840		Hometown, TX 75555
(979)555-7775		(903)555-6789
janesmith@email.com		

OBJECTIVE

Sales in the fashion industry.

EDUCATION

Bachelor of Business Administration Degree in Marketing May 20xx

Texas A&M University, College Station, Texas

GPA: 3.0 overall; 3.2 major

RELATED COURSEWORK

Introduction to Marketing

Personal Selling

Sales Management

TECHNICAL EXPERIENCE

Microsoft Word, PowerPoint, Excel, Access

WORK EXPERIENCE

Department of Marketing, Texas A&M University

Student Worker, January 20xx–May 20xx

■ Worked for different professors within the department

■ Duties included grading papers, making copies, typing, and editing

Recreational Center, Texas A&M University

Personal Trainer, January 20xx–December 20xx

■ Scheduled appointments with clients

■ Met with individual clients on a weekly basis

■ Planned a workout schedule for each client to help client reach fitness goals

Payless Shoes, Houston, Texas

Buying Office Intern, May 20xx–September 20xx

■ Analyzed sales trends and markdowns

■ Correlated with vendors the sending of samples and shipping orders

■ Created and presented advertisements for newspapers and magazines

■ Keyed and processed orders and distributions

LEADERSHIP ACTIVITIES

American Marketing Association, 20xx–present

Retailing Society, 20xx–20xx

Intramural Sports, 20xx–20xx

Business Students Society, 20xx–20xx

HONORS

Alpha Mu Alpha, National Marketing Honor Society

Marketing Department Distinguished Student, Fall 20xx

References available upon request.

EXHIBIT 2

Example scannable résumé.

Jane Smith
1234 Your Street
College Station, Texas 77840
Phone: (979)555-7775
E-mail: janesmith@email.com

EDUCATION
Bachelor of Business Administration Degree in Marketing May 20xx
Texas A&M University, College Station, Texas
GPA: 3.0 overall; 3.2 major

COMPUTER SOFTWARE SKILLS
Microsoft Word, PowerPoint, Excel, Access

WORK EXPERIENCE
Department of Marketing, Texas A&M University
Student Worker, January 20xx–May 20xx
Worked for different professors within the department. Duties included grading papers, making copies, typing, and editing.
Recreational Center, Texas A&M University
Personal Trainer, January 20xx–December 20xx
Scheduled appointments with clients. Met with individual clients weekly to help them achieve their fitness goals.
Payless Shoes, Houston, Texas
Buying Office Intern, May 20xx–September 20xx
Analyzed sales trends and markdowns. Correlated with vendors the sending of samples and shipping orders. Created and presented advertisements for newspapers and magazines.
Keyed and processed orders and distributions.

ACTIVITIES & AFFILIATIONS
American Marketing Association
Retailing Society
Intramural Sports
Business Students Society

OTHER INFORMATION
Financed most of my college expenses, past 2 years 100%
Strong interest in languages and travel; willing to relocate

- Include degrees, majors, GPAs
- List computer software and hardware skills
- Include job titles, employers, dates, accomplishments, as usual, and additional sections for activities, honors, and the like.

You can also insert a summary paragraph near the beginning of your résumé. You should include important key words and other qualifications in this summary. Once it is identified by a computer search, a person will read your résumé.

Letter Writing Is an Excellent Sales Tool

It may be necessary to write many letters during your job search. Some companies may prefer that you correspond by e-mail, and proper e-mail formats will also be discussed. Your best bet is to follow the lead of the recruiter in regards to communication. If you are unsure of whether to send an e-mail or a letter, it is always best to send a professional, typed letter.

You should always address letters to a specific person and include that person's job title. They should only be one page in length and printed on the same type of paper as your résumé. There are several different styles of letter writing, but the favorite is the Block Style because it is the easiest. In Block Style, all lines begin at the left margin. Professional-looking business letters are very organized and contain standard parts (see Exhibit 3).

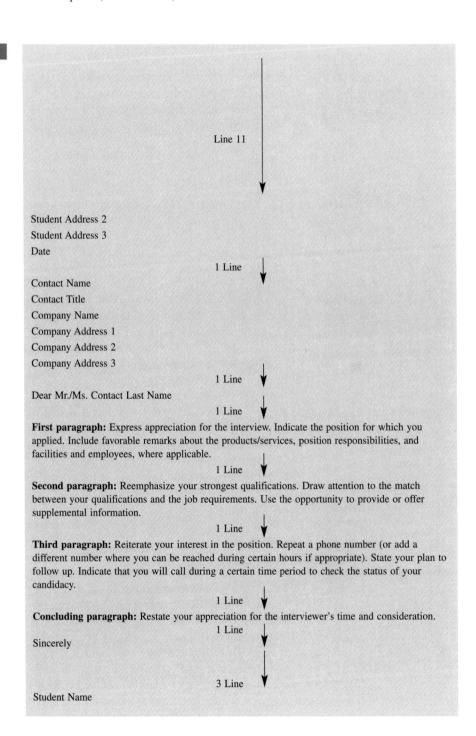

Line 11

Student Address 2
Student Address 3
Date

1 Line

Contact Name
Contact Title
Company Name
Company Address 1
Company Address 2
Company Address 3

1 Line

Dear Mr./Ms. Contact Last Name

1 Line

First paragraph: Express appreciation for the interview. Indicate the position for which you applied. Include favorable remarks about the products/services, position responsibilities, and facilities and employees, where applicable.

1 Line

Second paragraph: Reemphasize your strongest qualifications. Draw attention to the match between your qualifications and the job requirements. Use the opportunity to provide or offer supplemental information.

1 Line

Third paragraph: Reiterate your interest in the position. Repeat a phone number (or add a different number where you can be reached during certain hours if appropriate). State your plan to follow up. Indicate that you will call during a certain time period to check the status of your candidacy.

1 Line

Concluding paragraph: Restate your appreciation for the interviewer's time and consideration.

1 Line

Sincerely

3 Line

Student Name

Return Address   In this section, beginning on line 11, you should type your street address and city, state, and ZIP code. Do not type your name as part of the address. On line 13, the next line after your address, you should type the date. Do not use abbreviations, except for the two-letter state abbreviation.

Inside Address   This part of the letter is where you type the address of the person receiving your letter. You should include the person's name and position in the organization. Be careful with the spelling of the recipient's name and always include a courtesy title such as Mr., Ms., or Mrs.

Salutation   You should place the salutation two lines below the inside address. You should type "Dear" followed by the person's courtesy title and last name. In Block Letter Style, you do not add a colon after the person's name, unless you are on a first-name basis with that person.

Body   This portion of the letter should be single-spaced with double line spacing between paragraphs.

Complimentary Close   The complimentary close should come two lines after the last line of the letter. For a formal letter you should use a closing such as "Sincerely" or "Cordially."

Signature   Three to four lines below the complimentary closing, you should type your name. Sign the letter in the space above your typed name.

Enclosure Notation   If you are including something with your letter, such as your résumé, you should make a note of this two lines below your typed name. This serves as a reminder to the recipient to look for your attachment. You may type out the word "Enclosure" or "Attachment," or you can abbreviate it by typing "Enc." or "Att." You may indicate the number of attachments by adding a colon after the notation, for example. "Enclosure: 1 Résumé."

Thank-You Letters Are Important   Every time you meet with a recruiter, you should follow up with a thank-you letter (see Exhibit 4). If you are interviewed by more than one person, then each person should be written or thanked individually in a letter sent to the main contact person. A thank-you letter can be the final factor in the decision-making process. For example, if you and another recruit have practically the same skills and qualifications, and you sent a thank-you letter and the other recruit did not, chances are you will get the job. Your letter should reflect your desire to work for the organization and should once again highlight the skills and attributes that make you the best candidate for the job.

E-Mail Messages   In today's "e-world," some of the corresponding you do with future employees may be done by e-mail (see Exhibits 5 and 6). Because e-mail is constantly developing as a communications medium, its formatting and usage are always changing. The following suggestions are just a basic guide to help you construct your e-mail messages when you are unaware of the format the particular organization you are corresponding with uses.

To Line   In this portion of the e-mail, you should include the receiver's e-mail address. You may personalize this line by typing the name of the receiver first, followed by the receiver's e-mail address in angle brackets: John Smith <johnsmith@email.com>.

EXHIBIT 4

Example thank you letter.

1234 Your Street
College Station, TX 77840
April 3, 20xx

Mr. John Doe
Manager of Human Resources
Industry Fashions
555 Main Street
Austin, TX 77543

Dear Mr. Doe

Thank you for the interview for the position of sales representative. Industry Fashions is a dynamic company with outstanding products. I would love to work as a sales rep for such a wonderful organization.

The interview strengthened my enthusiasm for the position and interest in working for Industry Fashions. Industry Fashions seeks only the most qualified recruits, and I believe that my education and experience are a good match for your company.

Hearing back from you would be very exciting. The phone number is 979/555-3418. Please call at your convenience.

Thank you again for your time and consideration.

Sincerely

Jane Smith

EXHIBIT 5

Example e-mail follow-up.

From:	**Student Name <student@email.com>**
Sent:	**March 1, 20xx**
To:	**Recipient Name <recipient@email.com>**
Cc:	

Subject: **Type a concise but interesting subject here.**

Dear Mr./Ms. Contact Last Name

First paragraph: Express appreciation for the interview. Indicate the position for which you applied. Include favorable remarks about the products/services, position responsibilities, and facilities and employees, where applicable.

Second paragraph: Reemphasize your strongest qualifications. Draw attention to the match between your qualifications and the job requirements. Use the opportunity to provide or offer supplemental information.

Third paragraph: Reiterate your interest in the position. Repeat a phone number (or add a different number where you can be reached during certain hours if appropriate). State your plan to follow up. Indicate that you will call during a certain time period to check the status of your candidacy.

Concluding paragraph: Restate your appreciation for the interviewer's time and consideration. Make sure your message is not longer than two screens in length.

Sincerely
Student Name

EXHIBIT 6

Example e-mail thank-you
letter.

From:	Jane Smith <janesmith@email.com>
Sent:	March 1, 20xx
To:	John Doe <johndoe@industryfashions.com>
Cc:	

Subject: Thank you for the interview.

Dear Mr. Doe

Thank you for the interview for the position of sales representative. Industry Fashions is a dynamic company with outstanding products. I would love to work as a sales rep for such a wonderful organization.

The interview strengthened my enthusiasm for the position and interest in working for Industry Fashions. Industry Fashions seeks only the most qualified recruits, and I believe that my education and experience are a good match for IF.

Hearing back from you would be very exciting. The phone number is 979/555-3418. Please call at your convenience.

Thank you again for your time and consideration.

Sincerely
Jane Smith

From Line   This section contains your e-mail address and is automatically inserted by most systems.

Cc   Cc is an acronym for carbon copy or courtesy copy. The single c for any kind of copy is becoming the most common used copy notation. You should type the e-mail address, or addresses, of the people who need to receive a copy of the message in this line. There is also a Bcc function, which stands for blind carbon copy. This allows you to send a copy of your e-mail message to someone without the receiver's knowledge.

Subject   In this line you should briefly state the subject of your message. Include enough information so that the receiver will understand why you are writing and will be interested in reading what you have sent.

Salutation   You may include a brief greeting at the beginning of your message. Some writers use a salutation much like that of a letter, such as "Dear Mr. Smith." You may choose to include the receiver's name in the first line instead of using a salutation, for example, "Thanks, Mr. Smith, for meeting with me last week." There is a division in the way to treat an e-mail message: Some treat them more like letters (with a salutation), whereas others write them as if they were memos (with no salutation).

Message   Cover only one topic in your message. You should try to keep your message very concise and no more than two screens in length. To help you with this, many systems have features such as cut, copy, paste, and word-wrap. Do not get too carried away with formatting because the receiver's system may not support different fonts or colors.

Closing   You should close your message as you would a letter, with a closing followed by your name and e-mail address. If you do not include your e-mail address, and your system does not transmit your address to the recipient, then they will not be able to reply to you.

HOW TO CREATE A PORTFOLIO

A portfolio is a binder or book that shows off your work and abilities. It goes beyond a cover letter and a résumé. A portfolio is a job-hunting tool that you develop that gives employers a picture of who you are: your experience, your education, your accomplishments, and your skills. Not only does it show the employer who you are, it displays what you have the potential to become. It is designed to do one thing: **support you as you market yourself!**

Top Six Reasons to Have a Portfolio

1. Distinguish yourself from the competition.
2. Turn the interview into an offer.
3. Increase the salary offer by impressing the interviewer.
4. Offer tangible proof of your abilities.
5. Potentially help you get promoted.
6. Help you find the position that is right for you!

Where to Begin

You should start developing your portfolio by first doing a self-assessment. Evaluate what you have to offer and what the best ways are to market your assets. You should decide which of your skills and experiences will relate to the needs of the interviewer, or what you would most like the interviewer to see. If you don't have much work experience—most students don't—you'll need to mine your schoolwork, volunteer work, and hobbies for evidence of the relevant skills you know you have. For example, if you did event promotions for a campus organization, include a copy of a flyer or poster you designed.

The following is a list of items you may want to include:

- **Table of contents** (for easy reference).
- **Career summary and goals:** A description of what you stand for (such as work ethic, organizational interests, and management philosophy) and where you see yourself in two to five years.
- **Traditional résumé:** A summary of your education, achievements, and work experience, using a chronological or functional format.
- **Scannable résumé:** A text-only version of your résumé should be included.
- **Skills, abilities, and marketable qualities:** A detailed examination of your skills and experience. This section should include the name of the skill area; the performance or behavior, knowledge, or personal traits that contribute to your success in that skill area; and the background and specific experiences that demonstrate your application of the skill.
- **Samples of your work:** A sampling of your best work, including reports, papers, studies, brochures, projects, and presentations. Besides print samples, you can include CD-ROMs, videos, and other multimedia formats.
- **Testimonials and letters of recommendation:** A collection of any kudos you have received from customers, clients, colleagues, past employers, professors, and so on. Some experts suggest including copies of favorable employer evaluations and reviews.
- **Awards and honors:** A collection of certificates of awards, honors, and scholarships.
- **Conferences and workshops:** A list of conferences, seminars, and workshops you've participated in and/or attended.
- **Transcripts, degrees, licenses, and certifications:** A description of relevant courses, degrees, licenses, and certifications.
- **Test results:** Professional or graduate school testing results (such as GRE subject test results).
- **Newspaper clippings:** Articles and/or photos that address your achievements.

- **Military records, awards, and badges:** A description of your military service, if applicable.
- **References:** A list of three to five people (including full names, titles, addresses, and phone/e-mail) who are willing to speak about your strengths, abilities, and experience. At least one reference should be a former manager.

Organize Your Portfolio

1. Keep your portfolio in a professional three-ring binder.
2. Come up with an organizational system of categories to put your items together. Sample categories are as follows: Work Experience, Education, Awards and Certificates, Special Skills, Personal Accomplishments, Background. Use tabs or dividers to separate the categories.
3. Your portfolio should be no more than 25 pages. The shorter it is the better, because an employer will really absorb only 6 to 10 samples.
4. Every page should have a title, a concise caption, and artifact. Captions should explain the process you went through and the resulting benefits, such as: "This is a flyer I designed for the promotion of the American Marketing Association Membership drive. We gained over 50 new members that year." Use the same type of action verbs you would use in a résumé.
5. Photocopy full-page samples to a smaller size, if needed.
6. Make the layout and design consistent, and don't get overly decorative—keep it clean and use lots of white space.
7. You may also consider including a disk or CD with samples of your work. An online portfolio is another option.
8. Once you have put together your portfolio, you should create a title page, a table of contents, and an introduction. The introduction provides an opportunity to tie together your portfolio contents and summarize your qualifications.

Finishing Touches

- Have a faculty member or someone at the career center review and critique your portfolio.
- Develop a condensed version of your portfolio that contains your most important accomplishments to leave with your interviewer. It could be in an inexpensive report cover or folder. This provides something physical to remind the interviewer that you were there. It also provides an occasion for an additional contact in a week or so to arrange for its pickup. Make sure you do not include original materials of which you only have one copy!
- Mention that you have a portfolio in the reference section of your résumé as well as in your cover letter.

How Do I Use My Portfolio during the Interview Process?

- Bring the condensed version of your portfolio with you to the interview and be prepared to present all the information within it to the interviewer. You may not always want to leave a condensed version of your portfolio. Level of interest in the position and cost should help you decide.
- Announce at the beginning of the interview that you have a portfolio and would like to present it at some point during the interview.
- You can use your portfolio to support your responses. For example, the interviewer might say, "I see that you have worked on your school newspaper. What were your favorite writing assignments?" You might reply, "My favorite assignments include this article (turn portfolio toward the interviewer and show the interviewer the article in the portfolio), which required a lot of research, and this creative writing piece (show article), which I wrote for a special edition."
- If you are unable to present it during the interview, begin the time allotted for questions by mentioning that you would like to present your portfolio.

SALES TEAM BUILDING

You and your sales team were flying from Chicago, Illinois, to Fairbanks, Alaska, when your plane crash-landed in the woods somewhere in the Canadian Yukon. It is 10 A.M. on a day in January. The single-engine plane and the bodies of the pilot and co-pilot were completely destroyed except for the airplane's frame. No one in your sales team was injured.

The plane was struck by lightning, causing it to crash instantly. The pilot was unable to radio for help. The storms in the region caused the plane to change course several times. Immediately before the plane was struck by lightning, the pilot announced the plane was about 90 miles from the nearest town.

You are in a wooded area with numerous lakes, rivers, and mountains. It is −10°F now, and night-time temperatures are expected to be −30°F. The group is dressed in casual clothes appropriate for living in a city—jeans, shirts, street shoes, and overcoats.

Before the plane caught fire, your group was able to salvage the 15 items listed in Exhibit A. You are to rank these 15 items in order of their importance to your survival, from 1 as the most important to 15 as the least important.

You can assume the number of survivors is the same as the number on your team, the team has agreed to stick together, and all items are in good condition.

Assignments

- First, on his or her own, each member of the sales team is to individually rank each item in order of importance to survival.
- Second, rank each item as a team. It is critical that no one change his or her individual rankings once discussion starts within the group.

WHAT'S YOUR STYLE—SENSER, INTUITOR, THINKER, FEELER?

Individuals differ in the way they interact with others and the way they gather and evaluate information for problem solving and decision making. Four psychological functions identified by Carl Jung are related to this process: sensation, intuition, thinking, and feeling.[2]

Before you read further, complete the Problem-Solving Diagnostic Questionnaire (Part A) and then check the scoring key that appears in Part B.[3] It has no right or wrong answers; just read each item carefully and then give your answer.

Part A: Questionnaire to Determine Your Style

Indicate your responses to the following questionnaire on a separate sheet of paper. None of these items has right or wrong responses.

  I. Write down the number and letter of the response that comes closest to how you usually feel or act.
   1. I am more careful about
      a. People's feelings.
      b. Their rights.
   2. I usually get along better with
      a. Imaginative people.
      b. Realistic people.
   3. It is a higher compliment to be called
      a. A person of real feeling.
      b. A consistently reasonable person.
   4. In doing something with many people, it appeals more to me
      a. To do it in the accepted way.
      b. To invent a way of my own.

EXHIBIT A

Items	Step 1 Your Individual Ranking	Step 2 The Team's Ranking	Step 3 Survival Expert's Ranking	Step 4 Difference between Steps 1 and 3	Step 5 Difference between Steps 2 and 3
Compress kit					
Ball of steel wool					
Cigarette lighter					
.45-caliber pistol					
Newspaper					
Compass					
Ski poles					
Knife					
Sectional air map					
Piece of rope					
Chocolate bars					
Flashlight					
Whiskey					
Shirt and pants					
Shortening					
Totals (The lower the score, the better)					
				Your Score (Step 4)	Team Score (Step 5)

Please complete the following steps and insert the scores under your team's number.	Team Number					
	1	2	3	4	5	6
Step 6 Average Individual Score—Add up all the individual team members' scores (Step 4) and divide by the number on the team.						
Step 7 Team Score (Step 5 above)						
Step 8 Gain (Loss) Score—The difference between the Team Score and the Average Individual Score. If the Team Score is lower than Avg. Ind. Score, gain is "+"; if higher, gain is "−".						
Step 9 Percentage Change—Divide the gain (loss) by the Average Individual Score.						
Step 10 Lowest Individual Score—on the team.						
Step 11 Number of Individual Scores—lower than the team score.						

5. I get more annoyed at
   a. Fancy theories.
   b. People who do not like theories.
6. It is higher praise to call someone
   a. A person of vision.
   b. A person of common sense.
7. I more often let
   a. My heart rule my head.
   b. My head rule my heart.
8. I think it is a worse fault
   a. To show too much warmth.
   b. To be unsympathetic.
9. If I were a teacher, I would rather teach
   a. Courses involving theory.
   b. Fact courses.

II. Write down the letters of the words in the following pairs that appeal to you more.
   10. *a.* compassion   *b.* foresight
   11. *a.* justice   *b.* mercy
   12. *a.* production   *b.* design
   13. *a.* gentle   *b.* firm
   14. *a.* uncritical   *b.* critical
   15. *a.* literal   *b.* figurative
   16. *a.* imaginative   *b.* matter of fact

According to Jung, only one of the four functions—sensation, intuition, thinking, or feeling—is dominant in an individual. However, the dominant function is usually backed up by one of the functions from the other set of paired opposites. Part C shows the four problem-solving styles that result from these matchups.

Part B: Scoring Key to Determine Your Style

The following scales indicate the psychological functions related to each item. Use the point-value columns to arrive at your score for each function. For example, if you answered *a* to the first question, your *Ia* response in the feeling column is worth 0 points when you add up the point-value column. Instructions for classifying your scores follow the scales.

Sensation	Point Value	Intuition	Point Value	Thinking	Point Value	Feeling	Point Value
2b___	1	2a___	2	1b___	1	1a___	0
4a___	1	4b___	1	3b___	2	3a___	1
5a___	1	5b___	1	7b___	1	7a___	1
6b___	1	6a___	0	8a___	0	8b___	1
9b___	2	9a___	2	10b___	2	10a___	1
12a___	1	12b___	0	11a___	2	11b___	1
15a___	1	15b___	1	13b___	1	13a___	1
16b___	2	16a___	0	14b___	0	14a___	1
Maximum Point Value:	(10)		(7)		(9)		(7)

Classifying Total Scores

- Write *intuition* if your intuition score is equal to or greater than your sensation score.
- Write *sensation* if your sensation score is greater than your intuition score.
- Write *feeling* if your feeling score is greater than your thinking score.
- Write *thinking* if your thinking score is greater than your feeling score.

Part C: The Four Styles and Their Tendencies

Personal Style	Action Tendencies
Sensation–thinking	Emphasizes details, facts, certainty Is decisive, applied thinker Focuses on short-term, realistic goals Develops rules and regulations for judging performance
Intuitive–thinking	Shows concern for current, real-life human problems Is creative, progressive, perceptive thinker Emphasizes detailed facts about people rather than tasks Focuses on structuring organizations for the benefit of people
Sensation–feeling	Prefers dealing with theoretical or technical problems Is pragmatic, analytical, methodical, and conscientious Focuses on possibilities by using interpersonal analysis Is able to consider a number of options and problems simultaneously
Intuitive–feeling	Avoids specifics Is charismatic, participative, people oriented, and helpful Focuses on general views, broad themes, and feelings Decentralizes decision making; develops few rules and regulations

According to Jung, gathering information and evaluating information are separate activities. People gather information by either *sensation* or *intuition* but not by both simultaneously. People using *sensation* would rather work with known facts and hard data and prefer routine and order while gathering information. People using *intuition* would rather look for possibilities than work with facts and prefer solving new problems and using abstract concepts.

Information evaluation involves making judgments about the information a person has gathered. People evaluate information by *thinking* or *feeling*. These represent the extremes in orientation. *Thinking* individuals base their judgments on impersonal analysis, using reason and logic rather than personal values or emotional aspects of the situation. *Feeling* individuals base their judgments more on personal feelings, such as harmony, and tend to make decisions that result in approval from others.

Questions

1. Look back at your scores. What is your personal problem-solving style? Read the action tendencies. Do they fit?
2. Studies show that the sensation–thinking (ST) combination characterizes many managers in Western industrialized societies. Do you think the ST style is the best fit for most jobs in today's society?
3. Also look at Chapter 4's Exhibit 4–9: Guidelines to Identifying Personality Style. Compare yourself and others you know to the guidelines. Do you find a match between you and the individual style? What about your roommate, spouse, parents, or siblings?
4. How can you use this information to improve your communication ability?

Appendix C:
Comprehensive Sales Cases

Juan Mendez, president of Zenith Computer Terminals (ZCT), has recently promoted Rob Zwettler to be his assistant. Rob has been a salesperson and then a sales manager for the past four years. Rob's main job is to work at different levels of the organization to help implement the firm's objective-setting process. Rob has to work with each department manager to assist them in determining their objectives.

In brief, Mendez's major corporate objective for next year is to increase profits to $1 million (before taxes). It is now late December; a simplified profit-and-loss statement for the current year (including a projection for the balance of the year) follows:

Sales		$10,000,000
Less Expenses:		
Sales	$1,500,000	
Production	6,000,000	
Marketing	1,300,000	
Administration	500,000	
Service	250,000	−9,550,000
Net Profit		$ 450,000

In discussions with the president and five department managers, Rob has learned a great deal that should help him in establishing budget (expense) objectives for each department.

First, Mendez feels that sales must be raised to the $12 million level if the profit objective is to be met. All of the department managers concur and think this a realistic and challenging objective for next year. They have also committed to freeze their salaries and those of their staff for the year to meet the profit objective.

THE SALES DEPARTMENT

In conversations with the national sales manager, Rob has learned the following facts, which should aid him in determining an objective for the sales department budget:

- Currently there are 20 sales reps in the sales force.
- A sales rep costs an average of $75,000 per year for salary, travel expenses, and the cost of supervision.
- Last year, each rep produced, on average, $500,000 in sales. A new rep, while costing the same as an experienced one, will produce about $300,000 the first year. Obviously, the sales force must be expanded to meet targeted sales of $12 million.

■ In a normal year (next year is projected to be normal), the sales volume from sales reps will grow at a rate of 10 percent, assuming the sales manager can work with each rep at least four days per year.

While the major objective of the sales department relates to attaining sales volume within its budget, supporting objectives must be set by the sales manager, with your help. In addition to the background information previously supplied, here are some other facts Rob uncovered:

■ Hiring a sales rep normally takes about a month. It is desirable to recruit and hire all the new sales reps at one time.
■ Training of new reps takes four weeks of classroom time followed by a month of on-the-job coaching in the field. The sales manager must handle the classroom segment but can delegate three of the field training weeks to senior sales reps, as long as he personally handles at least one week of coaching during the new sales reps' first month in the field.
■ The sales manager must not neglect his existing sales staff on a long-term basis. Ideally, the sales manager should average four days a year with each rep, supporting his or her efforts and upgrading performance.

THE PRODUCTION DEPARTMENT

Rob also met the production department and learned some significant facts about the operations and projections for the future. Last year, production turned out 10,000 units (computer terminals) at a total production cost of $6 million. To achieve the new sales goal of $12 million, production will have to be increased to 12,000 units. At present, ZCT has four production lines, which can produce 2,500 units each per year. New production equipment to support additional production will cost $400,000 (amortized cost for next year) plus an additional $125,000 for labor costs and $325,000 for materials used in production. The fifth production unit will also be able to produce 2,500 units.

Because of the late date for setting objectives for the coming year (remember, it is now December), a problem has been created in ordering the necessary equipment for the production line. The equipment order cannot be placed until January 1, and it will take three months for delivery and installation. However, the production target for the year must be achieved, regardless. The production manager feels that this can be accomplished by running the existing four production lines on a second eight-hour night shift (in addition to the day shift) for as long as necessary to compensate for the delay of the new production line. From a budget standpoint, the cost of paying overtime can be absorbed by the savings of not having to purchase the equipment for three months.

Two weeks will be needed to recruit and select 10 additional workers for the new production line, and another two weeks will be needed to train them on existing equipment. The necessary production equipment and materials will be automatically ordered by purchasing administration.

As far as objective-setting is involved, neither Rob nor the production manager need to be concerned about the 1,000 new terminals that will be sold during the fourth quarter. Even though the terminals may be booked during the fourth quarter, they will not be produced and delivered until the first quarter of the following year.

THE MARKETING DEPARTMENT

Rob's meeting with the marketing manager to discuss the department's needs was equally productive. The marketing department is responsible for advertising, promotion, and new product development. The marketing manager has a staff of 15 people with a related overhead (projected for next year) of $600,000. In addition, the manager normally budgets about 5 percent of projected sales for direct mail and advertising to support the sales force activities. Further plans call for the introduction of a new terminal by the fourth quarter of next year. (The president stressed that this is critical and hopes to sell 1,000 units before the year ends.)

The following new product budget is required during the year:

- $250,000 for product development
- $25,000 for sales aids
- $25,000 for training and introduction

The training will be budgeted through the marketing department, but the sales department will plan and implement a one-week workshop in late September to introduce the new terminal to the sales reps.

One of the most important functions of the marketing department is providing direct-mail support for the sales force. Last year the direct-mail efforts produced 6,000 leads (inquiries for the sales staff) as a result of doing 12 monthly mailings, each consisting of 50,000 pieces of direct mail. This represents a 1 percent return, which probably cannot be improved on. However, the size of the mailings must be increased to accommodate both the enlarged sales objective (20 percent) and the expanded sales force.

A second important item on the marketing manager's agenda is the development of a new product. This is normally done on a contract basis with an outside consulting firm, and the new product has been tentatively named the Alpha Terminal. Basically, the consultant will modify one of the existing products, updating both the design and styling to meet or exceed competition. Two months will be needed to select a vendor for this, and about six months' lead time will be required to develop a production model. A sales brochure to accompany this introduction cannot be started until the new product is about one-third finished, and this brochure will require three to four months to write and print.

THE ADMINISTRATION DEPARTMENT

The following is what Rob learned from the administration manager regarding the department's needs. Based on an efficiency study, three clerical jobs can be safely eliminated, and Rob has convinced the administration manager that the payroll should be cut accordingly. Last year's budget breakdown looked like this:

7 managers	$240,000
12 clericals	200,000
General overhead	+ 60,000
	$500,000

The administration department literally services the other departments at ZCT, handling finances, paperwork, and providing internal systems backup. The administration manager, while agreeing to the suggested cutback in clerical staff, felt that it would be desirable to stagger the release so that a heavy strain is not incurred at one time; this would also permit other people to be trained to pick up the slack. Rob agreed to this but emphasized the need for all changes to take place as soon as possible. About two weeks of on-the-job training will be needed for the staff to absorb the tasks and assignments being handled by each of the three clerical staff scheduled to be let go.

Further, one of the seven managers in the administration department is considered marginal at this time. The manager in question, Joe Wallace, has been aboard for about a year and has failed to meet expectations. His weaknesses may become a big liability as these clerical cutbacks take place, and a decision about him should be made as soon as possible. If necessary, a plan should be made to replace him immediately. This evaluation should take about a month.

To support the new sales growth, Juan Mendez feels that the entire administrative function must be computerized during the next two years. Consequently, he has asked the administration manager to do an internal study, with a task force from the staff, and to present a report by December 1 of the coming year. Based on Rob's discussions, he estimates that the task force will need a month for each of the four other departments, a month for interviewing computer vendors, and two months to write a comprehensive report.

THE SERVICE DEPARTMENT

Rob's final conference was with the service manager to discuss the objectives for the coming year. Basically, the service manager feels a strong need to increase service support to the sales force. Customer complaints are on the rise because the service staff growth has not kept pace with sales. Each of five service reps is budgeted at $40,000 for salary and travel expenses. Supervision and other expenses run about $50,000. In the past, a four-to-one ratio of sales to service reps was adequate, but now that the terminal population has grown, the service manager wants the ratio to be three to one and is determined to implement this strategy next year. Rob tends to agree with him. In addition to the above expenses, the service manager estimates that he will need $30,000 for new servicing tools and equipment.

One of the big problems facing the service department manager is the heavy load of service calls that must be handled within 24 hours, especially with increased sales projected. This could be alleviated by additional service reps.

The service manager feels that, in addition to staffing up, the total number of calls can be cut significantly by having the staff sell maintenance contracts to customers. This will provide some additional revenue, but a planned maintenance program will head off service calls before they occur and, equally important, will enable the staff to plan their schedules more efficiently. Right now, the service manager's staff is handling about 7,400 calls per year, and this will rise in proportion to the projected sales increase. However, if the sales manager can achieve this new maintenance program and get it implemented, he feels strongly that the overall number of calls required can be cut by 25 percent.

The sales manager anticipates needing about six months to design the program and get it kicked off. The manager is also planning on hiring the new service people immediately; about a month will be needed to hire and train them.

Questions

1. Develop a new budget based on how the ideal profit and loss statement should look if it reflects the president's bottom-line objective for ZCT. Justify your expenses for each of the five budgeted expense areas.

2. What would be the net profit if sales
   a. remained at $10 million and budgeted expenses increased to the projected levels?
   b. increased to $14 million and budgeted expenses increased to the projected levels?
3. Determine the four most important objectives for each department. Be specific by detailing what should be done and the time frame for reaching the objective.
4. Write up your recommendations to Juan Mendez, the president, in a memorandum format.

CASE 2

Wallis Office Products: Defining New Sales Roles

As he looked across the desert horizon from his Phoenix sales office, John Stevens, vice president of sales for the Southwest region of Wallis Office Products (Wallis) felt good about his latest results.[1] "This has been a good year," he thought. "O'Brien will do cartwheels when she sees these year 2000 sales numbers." As John closed the third-quarter report, Margaret O'Brien, Wallis's national sales manager, passed John's door. "Maggie!" John shouted. "Come get a look at these numbers. With the bonus I'm delivering you this year, you'll be able to buy back the old St. Louis Cardinals and bring them home."

"That football team hasn't won a thing since they came to Phoenix anyway," said O'Brien as she walked into John's office. "And with the news I just got, you may want to save your sales for January."

O'Brien had just spoken with Wallis's president and CEO, Phillip Plimpton, about the company's 2001 sales goal. "He gave me some of that corporate babble about the stockholders and return on investment," said O'Brien, "and then he laid a $1.5 billion sales goal on me! That's up 25 percent from this year, . . . and we'll do well to make this year's number!"

John joked about squeezing water from a stone, but O'Brien was in no mood to joke and was rushing out to get her flight back to St. Louis. On the way to the airport, she called John to voice her appreciation for the year he was having. "You do another $350 million, plus 50 percent next year, and I'll give you your own football team," said O'Brien, knowing she would need John to have a great 2001 for her to reach $1.5 billion.

After O'Brien's call, John began thinking what his region's sales goal would be if Wallis had to do $1.5 billion in 2001—and he didn't like the numbers he came up with. His region had been having a good year, in fact, the best year since he had been promoted to vice president of sales for the Southwest four and a half years ago. He knew that in a few weeks O'Brien was going to give him and the other four regional vice presidents their 2001 sales goals. "Now I know why they never ask us for our input," thought John. "The regional VPs would never volunteer $1.5 billion."

COMPANY BACKGROUND

A sister and brother from Missouri, Phyllis and George Clemens, founded Wallis Office Products in 1948. The company began to thrive in the mid-1950s, and built a reputation in the Midwest as a quality producer of a variety of business forms. Phyllis handled the creation and production of the forms, and George did the selling. In the early 1960s, George attended a trade show on the future of the forms business. There he met a young entrepreneur, Roberto Martinez, who sold George on an idea.

Roberto believed that American business was "fed up with you and all your forms." He told George that growth in the forms business was going to slow down once technology took off, and that new ideas would be needed if the Clemenses were going to continue to grow their business. Roberto proposed a new service for Wallis Office Products: document storage and record keeping. "Essentially," said Roberto, "the business will remotely store documents electronically that aren't needed regularly. When someone needs a stored document, you'll retrieve it and send it to the customer."

Roberto believed that this service would eliminate thousands of file cabinets in government offices and large companies, and it would free employees to spend their time on more valuable work than moving old files and archiving unneeded documents. In return, companies would pay for each document stored and a monthly storage charge.

In 1962, Phyllis and George Clemens were persuaded by Roberto Martinez and made an agreement that changed Wallis Office Products forever. Roberto joined the company, and growth in Wallis Office Products' document storage business in the 1960s shot up faster than an Apollo rocket.

Over the next 30 years, the business grew to become a billion-dollar corporation. Its core business became document storage and record keeping. In the mid-1980s, the U.S. Supreme Court ruled that film document reproductions were acceptable as court evidence, and this contributed to the growth of the electronic document storage business. Wallis Office Products divested itself of the forms business because of declining margins and slow market growth and concentrated on document storage. The company had national distribution, with an account base of over 900 customers. In 2000, revenues were expected to be $1.2 billion. Wallis had over 8,000 employees in 32 offices (primarily sales and local operations). Headquarters remained in St. Louis, where most functions were centralized, including finance, human resources, and marketing. Regional sales and operations offices were in New York, Atlanta, Phoenix, San Francisco, and St. Louis.

PRODUCTS AND SERVICES

In 2000, Wallis's core product was a relatively manual, paper- and microfilm-based document storage service. Typical contracts (which were renewed annually) called for Wallis to provide the following:

- Document pickup.
- Document indexing.
- Document storage (which could include microfilm, paper copies, or both).
- Document retrieval on demand (i.e., companies called an 800 number to request specific paper copies of documents).

Customers pay Wallis based on two types of fees:

- Processing fees per new document (i.e., the number of picked up, indexed, and retrieved pages).
- Storage based on the volume of documents stored and document format (paper, microfilm, or both).

Annual revenues per customer range from $100,000 to $10 million, with most accounts generating between $500,000 and $1.5 million in revenue. With some customers, up to 85 percent of Wallis's revenues are storage charges.

Wallis offers multiple "value-added services" on top of the plain vanilla offering (e.g., reporting services relative to retrieval, consultative document management services, and the like). The add-on services have been very lucrative for Wallis—they produce 10 percent of revenues and 13 percent of profits—and management is looking into ways to expand this market. In 2000, Margaret O'Brien estimated that 88 percent of Wallis's sales revenue would come from a version of the traditional business (excluding value-added services). Although 2000 was shaping up to be a good year, O'Brien knew that the market wasn't growing as quickly as it had in the late 1980s, and it was only a matter of time before Wallis's traditional product could no longer meet the company's growth goals.

In 1997, Wallis introduced an automated document retrieval system called SARS (Safe Automated Retrieval System) 1000. The system is computer based and offers customers online, real-time document retrieval. In addition to providing document pickup and storage services, SARS 1000 gives customers immediate access to all their stored documents. The system requires a significant investment in computer hardware and software for the user (up to $100,000). In 2000, Wallis introduced a more powerful version of SARS called Document Flash, which has online storage capability in addition to retrieving documents.

Sales have been disappointingly slow for SARS 1000. O'Brien had forecast $50 million in sales for this product in 2000 (by converting 15 existing buyers and selling 10 new customers), but actual sales were only projected to be $20 million. Strong sales of the traditional product and another good year in the Southwest looked like they would get O'Brien to her goal. But O'Brien knew her future success was tied to SARS 1000.

BUSINESS OBJECTIVES

In 1983, Wallis Office Products made its initial public offering (IPO). After 35 years as a family-held business, Wallis quickly became a hot stock on Wall Street. On the one-year anniversary of Wallis's IPO, the Supreme Court ruling sent the company's stock soaring to $40 per share, 250 percent of its initial price.

Since the company went public, Wallis had promised stockholders a 20 percent annual return on their investment. It has met this goal every year except 1992. That was the year Phyllis Clemens retired as CEO and chairman of Wallis. Pushed by Wall Street analysts, Wallis hired an outside executive, Philip L. Plimpton, to replace Clemens. Plimpton wasted no time putting his mark on the company, reorganizing the management team and cutting costs throughout the organization. The field sales organization was reduced from eight regions to five (at that time John Stevens gained responsibility for Southern California as part of the Southwest), and Margaret O'Brien was put under increased pressure to grow the business's top line.

Plimpton's objective was to grow profits 8 to 10 percent in 1999, 2000, and 2001. He knew he met his goal in 1999, based on the cost cutting completed in 1997–98 and the company's record of retaining 83 percent of its customers. In 2000 and 2001, however, Plimpton was counting on revenue growth of 25 percent each year, for $1.5 billion and $2 billion goals, respectively. Plimpton believes the market for his traditional document storage services is mature and fully penetrated. Since he feels growth in the traditional business is flat, he believes Wallis needs new product sales (e.g., SARS 1000 and the Document Flash product being introduced in 2000) and value-added services to meet his revenue goals. In addition, Plimpton is not convinced that the sales and marketing organizations have used effectively the available distribution channels, which will be necessary in order to reach these goals.

SOUTHWEST REGION

John Stevens is one of the rising stars of Wallis. First as an account executive and now as a vice president of sales in Southwest, he consistently exceeds the goals the company gives him. Plimpton is impressed by John's ingenuity and willingness to try new ideas.

John's organization consists of 14 account executives and 16 service representatives in six offices. His account executives average 10 years of industry experience and are very knowledgeable about traditional document storage services and the marketplace. John and his organization have been particularly effective in retaining customers, which he believes is the key to his success. John is so committed to this strategy that he established on-site service for his largest customers. His is also the only region that has more service representatives than account executives. John is concerned, however, that his sales organization has sold only five SARS 1000 systems.

John's market is large in comparison with other regions, by both customer numbers and sales revenue. With the addition of the Los Angeles, Orange County, and San Diego territories, John estimated sales of $350 million (versus a goal of $310 million) in 2000 on a base of 253 customers. Many of his customers are government agencies, law firms, and financial services companies. Unlike the other regions, John proactively targets specific industry accounts. Of John's 253 customers, many represent a single site or department. In 2000 his region lost only 21 customers, most of whom generated less than $1 million in revenues.

As John thought about the sales target O'Brien would give him for 2001, he wondered how she would determine the final number. He figured he would be penalized for having a great 2000 and be asked to do more than his fair share in 2001. "I've got to figure out a better way to deploy my people," John thought, "not only to increase their sales productivity but to improve the sales of the new products and services."

Questions

1. Formalize the sales strategy and quantify the sales opportunities that exist.
2. Map out the sales process associated with the different products/services and the roles of current sales and service personnel in the process.
3. Use the five Ws (who, what, where, when, and why) to determine if the sales process requires different sales roles for the process.
   a. Who is the customer?
   b. What is it that you are offering?
   c. Where can customers purchase the products?
   d. When do customers buy, and how frequently do they make purchases?
   e. Why should a customer purchase your product? What is the value proposition?
4. Determine the gaps that exist between the current sales process and the desired sales process.
5. Formulate and implement new sales roles to fill the gaps.

CASE 3

United Cosmetics, Inc.: Creating a Staffing Program

It was Al Kantak's first day on the job, and he was anxious to get started. Al knew that what he needed to do would be one of the biggest challenges of his life. Al's job title was Field Sales Employment Manager for United Cosmetics, Inc. (UCI). UCI is a national manufacturer and marketer of consumer goods sold primarily to retail grocery stores.

As Al began unloading boxes in his new office, the telephone rang. "Al, this is Sparky [the company's executive vice president of sales]. Come on up to my office, and let's discuss some ideas to help you get started, and let's talk about the employment information received this morning from our regional sales managers."

As soon as Al entered the office, Sparky started in. "Al, as you know, I asked our four regional managers to send in a report on employment activities and costs for their areas. You'll find this interesting.

"We have sales territories sitting vacant for a great deal of time while the district managers go out and recruit, hire, and train new people. This year, I calculated that there will be 2,700 days of vacant territories. Someone said this represents as much as $10 million in lost sales opportunities. I just cannot believe that, but I do feel we are losing sales due to having vacant territories.

"This year we will have 68 new hires, with 55 found through employment agencies. This is costing us $5,000 for each person. That's too much money to spend on these people. Many of them quit after a short time.

"I feel the worst thing about all of this is the drain on the DMs' time and the way people are trained to take over their new territories. Each time someone leaves, the DM has to recruit, hire, and train an individual. With the number of new hires we have each year, many of the DMs are spending too much time training the new people. Managers are not spending enough time working with others in their district. Some salespeople are complaining that their managers work with them only a few times a year. The new person is often left to 'sink or swim' after being trained, and many people are quitting because of this.

"We don't have a centralized training program. We could have 10 managers individually training 10 people at the same time in 10 locations. This is inefficient and costly and results in some salespeople not being properly prepared to operate their sales territory.

"Al, I'm not even sure our DMs know how to properly screen and interview people. They get almost no training in this area. Maybe this is the reason for so much turnover. I'm not sure. I do know that sales are rapidly increasing, and we need to begin expanding the size of our sales force.

"This is what I want you to do. [Sparky began writing this list on a blackboard.] As quickly as humanly possible,

- Begin to decrease the cost per hire.
- Establish a uniform recruitment program.
- Increase the quality of new hires.
- See that our managers spend less time recruiting.
- Decrease the number of vacant territory days per year.
- Eliminate our dependence on employment agencies.

"Al, don't waste any time getting started, we need a new employment program yesterday. We may be losing millions of dollars in sales each year due to vacant territories. The cost of recruitment, training, and our managers' time also may run into the millions. I'm afraid to calculate that figure.

"If I can help you in any way, if you need more money, let me know. Your program will have a direct impact on our bottom line. Keep me up to date on your progress. We have a meeting of the regional sales managers in three weeks. I want you to present your ideas on what we should do."

"Sparky," Al said, "I can't do this overnight. It is too big a project. What I have in mind is to develop a five-year plan. At the end of five years we will have accomplished everything you have asked for and more. However, we will see major results in just a few years. To hire the number of people needed, we'll have to recruit primarily on college campuses throughout the United States. To plan and implement a national sales employment program is a big undertaking."

"OK, OK, OK," said Sparky. "I understand. But at this meeting I want you to outline what we will do. We'll get input from the regional managers and see what they think. The field sales managers will have to believe in this program or it will be a hard row to hoe."

When Al got back to his office, he asked his assistant to hold all of his telephone calls. He might as well start outlining his new sales employment program.

Question

Assume you are Al Kantak. What would be your recommended college recruitment program?

CASE 4
Mead Envelope Company—Is a New Compensation Plan Needed?

Mead Envelope Company, a $100 million division of a large, diversified paper products company, manufactures and markets standard and customized envelopes.[2] It is a real company, but we have changed the name, the industry, and certain identifying details. Mead sells to both direct accounts—banks, insurance companies, utilities, direct-mail services—and distributors. Until 1997, the division achieved relatively steady sales growth, in the range of 5 to 6 percent per year. Top management believes, and marketing research supports the opinion, that the division could achieve annual sales growth in the 10 to 12 percent range.

As a first step to that growth, management hired a new vice president of sales, Hal Jones. Jones toured the field to meet with key customers and the sales force to learn firsthand why the company was growing at only about half the rate of the estimated potential. Jones observed the following.

CUSTOMER VISITS

The customers he visited, particularly the large accounts, said they were pleased with Mead's product quality and customer service and with the relationship with their account executive.

ACCOUNT EXECUTIVES

Mead has 45 geographically deployed account executives who call on customers of widely different sizes, ranging from community banks to large direct-mail marketers. The company has no national or major accounts program. The salespeople told Jones that their account planning is "informal," and Mead offers no training in how to develop complete account plans for customers, regardless of size. Overall, the account executives appear to be working hard in the face of the competition from both national and local competitors. Mead compensates account executives with a salary and a sales commission. On average, their W-2 earnings are 50 percent salary, and 50 percent commission. The company pays a commission at the rate of 3 percent of all sales over a base. The firm defines the base as the prior year's actual sales plus an upward adjustment for price increases. The average account executive earns $70,000 in total compensation, while the annual pay among all salespeople ranges from $40,000 to $150,000.

CUSTOMER SERVICE REPRESENTATIVES

Fifteen customer service representatives handle accounts that account executives cannot reach on a regular basis, either because they are too busy or because there does not appear to be enough business in the account to justify on-premises sales calls. Typically, these accounts call the customer service representatives to reorder, to ask about incomplete orders and billing problems, or to inquire about new products. Some customer service representatives told Jones they did not have enough to do so they are telephoning customers that their account executive has turned over to them. Mead pays customer service representatives a salary; it does not include them in the sales commission plan.

FIELD SALES MANAGERS

The three field sales managers spend the majority of their time working with account executives on major sales opportunities. They spend a relatively small amount of time on sales analysis and planning. They appear to be good trainers, motivators, and coaches for their people. Two of the field sales managers told Jones they believe sales results would be higher if their people specialized in certain types of accounts: direct-mail companies, for example, or utilities. The company pays field sales managers a salary plus a 1 percent commission (that is, an override) on the sales of their people over the sales base. The W-2 earnings for the field sales managers averaged $125,000 last year.

WHAT DOES THE PRODUCT MANAGER THINK?

When Jones returned from his field tour, he asked Mead's product manager to meet with him. The product manager for the standard product line indicated that the current sales "run rate" was on target for the year, and she was satisfied with the sales force's efforts this year and last. The product manager for the customized product line was not satisfied. He noted that sales results for his products were, on average, 50 percent below target. He pointed out that Mead made significant investments last year in manufacturing and envelope design capabilities to support the sale of customized products. This product manager was concerned that the sales force is not comfortable with computer-based envelope design—an essential part of the sales process—for accounts for which significant new sales have been booked. He pointed out that in virtually every large account for which Mead has won new, customized business, he has had to play a role in the sale, particularly in analysis of the need, design of the solution, and the business case for the pricing.

A Brief Analysis of Sales

After meeting with the product managers, Jones looked over his sales numbers for the year and the growth projections that top management had given his predecessor for next year. What he saw was discouraging. The sales force was well behind its $106 million goal for the year. Standard product sales, which represented

80 percent of the business, appeared to be on target; but customized product sales, projected to be $21 million, were well below target. In fact, as the product manager had pointed out, actual sales were running at about half of the year's goal. What Jones found particularly disturbing was that while customized projects were projected to be 20 percent of the current year's business, next year's forecast showed they were supposed to be 30 percent of the business, and the total goal for the business was set at $118 million. This meant that the customized product sales goal would be $35 to $36 million, or slightly more than three times greater than the current sales rate.

With his previous employer, Jones found everyone felt that any sales performance problems were always related to compensation. At least today, Hal is unsure of the way to improve sales. "I do not see how pay is the problem here," thought Jones. Just then the telephone rang in Hal's office. It was his boss's secretary saying that he wanted to see Jones next Monday at 9 in the morning. Hal was hired to improve sales growth. What is he going to tell his boss?

Questions

1. Why is a new compensation plan needed at Mead, and what are the positive outcomes of a successful sales compensation plan?
2. What are the reasons that compensation plans fail?

CASE 5

McDonald Sporting Goods Company: Determining the Best Compensation Program

The annual sales volume of the McDonald Sporting Goods Company (MSG) for the past three years had ranged between $7,200,000 and $7,650,000.[3] Although profits continued to be satisfactory, Hudson McDonald, president and chief operating officer, was concerned because sales had not increased appreciably from year to year. Consequently, he asked a consultant in New York City and the officers of the company to submit proposals for improving the salespeople's compensation plan, which he believed was the basic weakness in the firm's marketing operations.

THE PRODUCTS

MSG's factory and warehouse were located in Albany, New York, where the company manufactured and distributed sporting equipment, clothing, and accessories. Hudson McDonald had organized it in 1990, when he learned that the market for sporting goods would grow because of the predicted increase in leisure time and the rising level of income in the United States.

Products of the company, approximately 700 items, were grouped into three lines: (1) fishing supplies, (2) hunting supplies, and (3) accessories. The fishing supplies line, which accounted for approximately 40 percent of the company's annual sales, included nearly every item needed to fish, such as fishing jackets, vests, caps, rods and reels of all types, lines, flies, lures, landing nets, and creels. The hunting supplies line contributed 30 percent of annual sales; it consisted of hunting clothing of all types, safety garments, shell holders, whistles, calls, and gun cases. The accessories line, which made up the balance of the company's annual sales volume, included items such as compasses, cooking kits, lanterns, hunting and fishing knives, hand warmers, and novelty gifts. Although the sales of the hunting and fishing lines were very seasonal, they tended to complement each other. The January–April period accounted for the bulk of the company's annual volume in fishing items, and most sales of hunting supplies were made during the months of May through August. Typically, the company's sales of all products reached their lows for the year during the month of December.

The MSG sales volume is $7,529,806 for the current year, with products manufactured by the company accounting for 35 percent of this total. Imported products, which come primarily from Taiwan, comprise 50 percent of the company's volume. Items manufactured by other domestic producers and distributed by MSG account for the remaining 15 percent of total sales.

McDonald reported that wholesale prices to retailers were established by adding a markup of 50 to 100 percent to MSG cost for the item. This practice is followed on products manufactured by MSG as well as on items purchased from other manufacturers. The resulting average markup across all products is 70 percent of cost.

THE SALES FORCE

The MSG market area consisted of the New England states, New York, Pennsylvania, Ohio, Michigan, Wisconsin, Indiana, Illinois, Kentucky, Tennessee, West Virginia, Virginia, Maryland, Delaware, and New Jersey. The area over which MSG could effectively compete was limited to some extent by shipping costs, because all orders were shipped from the factory and warehouse in Albany.

MSG salespeople sold to approximately 6,000 retail stores in small and medium-sized cities in its market area. Analysis of sales records showed that the firm's customer coverage was very poor in the large metropolitan areas. Typically, each account was a one- or two-store operation. McDonald stated that he knew for a fact that MSG's share of the market was very low. For all practical purposes he felt the company's sales potential was unlimited. McDonald believed that, with few exceptions, MSG's customers had little or no brand preference, and in the vast majority of cases, they bought hunting and fishing supplies from several suppliers.

McDonald felt that the pattern of retail distribution for hunting and fishing products had been changing during the past 10 years as a result of the growth of discount stores. He thought that the proportion of retail sales for hunting and fishing supplies made by small and medium-sized sporting goods outlets had been declining as compared with the percentage sold by discounters and chain stores. An analysis of company records revealed that MSG had not developed business among the discounters, with the exception of a few small discount stores. Some of MSG's executives felt that the lack of business with discounters might have been due in part to the company's pricing policy and in part to the pressures that current customers had exerted on company people to keep them from calling on the discounters. No one knows if people would buy their products through the mail or over the Internet.

MSG's sales force for the current year totaled 11 people full-time. Their ages ranged from 23 to 67, and their tenure with the company from 1 to 10 years. Salespeople, territories, and sales volume for the previous year and the current year are shown in Exhibit 1. Duvall, Edwards, and Logan's territories were created when all territories were redesigned around state geographical boundaries.

The company's sales force played the major role in its marketing efforts, since MSG did not use magazine, newspaper, or radio advertising to reach either the retail trade or consumers. One advertising piece that supplemented the work of the salespeople was MSG's merchandise catalog. It contained a complete listing

EXHIBIT 1

McDonald Sporting Goods sales
force.

Salesperson	Age	Years of Service	Territory	Sales ($)	
				Previous Year	Current Year
Allen	45	2	Illinois and Indiana	371,548	370,368
Campbell	62	10	Pennsylvania	1,341,216	1,552,770
Duvall	23	1	New England	—	466,488
Edwards	39	1	Michigan	—	471,842
Gatewood	63	5	West Virginia	403,344	403,370
Hammond	54	2	Virginia	466,802	466,570
Logan	37	1	Kentucky and Tennessee	—	638,684
Mason	57	2	Delaware and Maryland	725,662	928,224
O'Bryan	59	4	Ohio	611,920	643,942
Samuels	42	3	New York and New Jersey	829,152	927,532
Wates	67	5	Wisconsin	417,050	384,976
Salespeople terminated in previous year				2,057,418	
House account				289,556	275,040
Total				7,513,668	7,529,806

of all the company's products and was mailed to retailers who were either current accounts or prospective accounts. Typically, store buyers used the catalog for reordering.

Most accounts were contacted by a salesperson two or three times a year. The salespeople planned their activities so that each store would be called on at the beginning of the fishing season and again prior to the hunting season. Certain key accounts were contacted more often.

THE COMPENSATION PLAN

The salespeople were paid straight commissions on their dollar sales volume for the calendar year. The commission rate was 5 percent on the first $675,000, 6 percent on the next $225,000, and 7 percent on all sales over $900,000 for the year. Each week, the salespeople could draw all or a portion of their accumulated commissions. McDonald encouraged the salespeople to draw commissions as they accumulated, because he felt the salespeople were motivated to work harder when they had a very small or zero balance in their commission accounts. These accounts were closed at the end of the year, so the salespeople began the new year with nothing in their accounts.

The salespeople provided their own automobiles and paid their traveling expenses, of which all or a portion were reimbursed per diem. Under the per-diem plan, each salesperson received $101.25 per day for Monday through Thursday and $47.25 for Friday, or a total of $452.25 for the normal work week. No per diem was paid for Saturday or Sunday nights in the territory.

In addition to the commission and per diem, the salespeople could earn cash awards under two sales incentive plans that were begun two years earlier. Under one, called the Annual Sales Increase Awards plan, a total of $23,400 was paid to the five salespeople who had the largest percentage increase in dollar sales volume over the previous year. To be eligible for these awards, the salespeople had to show

EXHIBIT 2

Earnings and incentive awards for the current year.

	Sales ($)		Annual Sales Increase Awards		Weekly Sales Increase Awards	
Salesperson	Previous Year	Current Year	Percentage Increase in Sales	Award ($)	Total Accrued ($)	Earnings[a]
Allen	371,548	370,368	—		2,307	$45,000[b]
Campbell	1,341,216	1,552,770	15.773	6,750(2nd)	5,049	92,943
Duvall	—	466,488	—	—	5,049	45,000[b]
Edwards	—	471,842	—	—	—	45,000[b]
Gatewood	403,344	403,370	.007	900(5th)	2,484	20,169
Hammond	466,802	466,570	—	—	957	45,000[b]
Logan	—	638,684	—		—	45,000[b]
Mason	725,662	928,224	27.914	9,000(1st)	7,749	49,230
O'Bryan	611,920	643,942	5.233	2,250(4th)	3,402	32,193
Samuels	829,152	927,552	11.865	4,500(3rd)	2,925	50,796
Wates	417,050	384,976	—	—	1,377	19,251
Totals:	$5,166,694	$7,254,786		$23,400	$31,299	$489,582

[a]Exclusive of incentive awards and per diem.
[b]Guarantee of $900 per week, or $45,000 per year.

sales increases over the previous year. The awards were made at the January sales meeting, and the winners were determined by dividing the dollar amount of each salesperson's increase by his or her volume for the previous year, with the percentage increases ranked in descending order. Earnings under this plan for the current year are shown in Exhibit 2.

Under the second incentive plan, the salespeople could win Weekly Sales Increase Awards for every week in which their dollar volume in the current year exceeded their sales for the corresponding week in the previous year. Beginning with an award of $9 for the first week, the amount of the award increased by $9 for each week in which the salespeople surpassed their sales for the comparable week in the previous year. If a salesperson produced higher sales during each of the 50 weeks in the current year, he or she received $9 for the first week, $18 for the second week, and $450 for the fiftieth week, or a total of $11,475 for the year. The salesperson had to be employed by the company during the previous year to be eligible for these awards. A check for the total amount of the awards accrued during the year was presented to the salesperson at the sales meeting held in January. Earnings under this plan for the current year are shown in Exhibit 2.

The company frequently used "spiffs" to promote sales of special items. The salesperson was paid a spiff, which usually was $18 for each order obtained for the items designated in the promotion.

For the past three years, in recruiting salespeople, McDonald had guaranteed the more qualified applicants a weekly income while they learned the business and developed their respective territories. During the current year, five salespeople—Allen, Duvall, Edwards, Hammond, and Logan—had a guarantee of $900 a week, which they drew against their commissions. If the year's cumulative commissions for any of these salespeople were less than their cumulative weekly drawing accounts, they received no commissions. The commission and drawing accounts were closed on December 31, so each salesperson began the year with a zero balance in each account.

The company did not have a stated or written policy specifying the maximum length of time a salesperson could receive a guarantee if his or her commissions continued to be less than his or her draw. McDonald felt that the five salespeople who currently had guarantees would quit if these guarantees were withdrawn before their commissions reached $45,000 per year.

McDonald was convinced that MSG's salespeople's annual earnings had fallen behind earnings for comparable selling positions, particularly in the past six years. As a result, he felt that the company's ability to attract and hold high-caliber, professional salespeople was being adversely affected. He felt strongly that each salesperson should be earning $90,000 annually.

In December of the current year, McDonald met with his comptroller and production manager, who were the only other executives of the company, and solicited their ideas concerning changes in the company's compensation plan for salespeople.

The comptroller pointed out that the salespeople who had guarantees were not producing the sales that had been expected from their territories. He was concerned that the annual commissions earned by four of the five salespeople on guarantees were approximately half of or less than their drawing accounts. Furthermore, according to the comptroller, several of the salespeople who did not have guarantees were producing a relatively low volume of sales year after year. For example, annual sales remained at low levels for Gatewood, O'Bryan, and Wates, who had been working four to five years in their respective territories.

The comptroller proposed that guarantees be reduced to $450 per week, plus commissions at the regular rate on all sales. The $450 would not be drawn against commissions, as was done under the existing plan, but would be in addition to any commissions earned. In the comptroller's opinion, this plan would motivate the sales force to rapidly increase sales, because incomes would rise directly with sales. The comptroller calculated the incomes of the five salespeople who had guarantees in the current year as compared with the incomes they would have received under his plan (Exhibit 3).

From a sample check of recent shipments, the production manager had concluded that the salespeople tended to overwork accounts located within a 75-mile radius of their homes. Sales coverage was extremely light in a 100- to 150-mile radius of the salespeople's homes. The coverage seemed to result from the desire of the salespeople to spend most evenings during the week at home with their families.

He proposed that the per diem be increased from $101.25 to $121.50 per day for Monday through Thursday, $47.25 for Friday, and $121.50 for Sunday if the salesperson spent Sunday evening away from home. He reasoned that the per diem of $121.50 for Sunday would act as a strong incentive for the salespeople to drive to the perimeters of their territories on Sunday evenings rather than use Monday morning for traveling. Further, he believed that the increase in per diem would result in a more uniform coverage of the sales territories and an overall increase in sales volume.

The consultant from New York City recommended that the guarantees and per diem be retained on the present basis, and he proposed that McDonald adopt what he called a Ten Percent Self-Improvement Plan. Under the consultant's plan, each salesperson would be paid, in addition to the regular commission, a monthly bonus commission of 10 percent on all dollar volume over sales in the comparable months of the previous year. For example, if a salesperson sold $90,000 worth of merchandise in January of the current year and $81,000 in January of the previous year, he or she would receive a $900 bonus check in February. For salespeople on guarantees, bonuses would be in addition to earnings. The consultant reasoned that the bonus commission would motivate the salespeople, both those with and those without guarantees, to increase their sales.

He further recommended discontinuing the two sales incentive plans currently in effect. He felt the savings from these plans would nearly cover the costs of his proposal.

Question

Which of these plans, if any, should the company use to compensate its salespeople? Why?

Appendix D: Selling Globally

Imagine an American salesperson, Harry Slick, starting out on his overseas business trip. The following events occur on his trip:

1. In England, he phones a long-term customer and asks for an early breakfast business meeting so that he can fly to Paris at noon.
2. In Paris, he invites a business prospect to have dinner at La Tour d'Argent and greets him with, "Just call me Harry, Jacques."
3. In Germany, he arrives 10 minutes late for an important meeting.
4. In Japan, he accepts the business cards of his hosts and, without looking at them, puts them in his pocket.

How many orders is Harry Slick likely to get? Probably none, although his company will face a pile of bills.

International business success requires each businessperson to understand and adapt to the local business culture and norms. Here are some rules of social and business etiquette that managers should understand when doing business in other countries.

France	Dress conservatively, except in the south where more casual clothes are worn. Do not refer to people by their first names—the French are formal with strangers.
Germany	Be especially punctual. An American businessperson invited to someone's home should present flowers, preferably unwrapped, to the hostess. During introductions, greet women first and wait until they extend their hands before extending yours.
Italy	Whether you dress conservatively or go native in a Giorgio Armani suit, keep in mind that Italian businesspeople are style conscious. Make appointments well in advance. Prepare for and be patient with Italian bureaucracies.
United Kingdom	Toasts are often given at formal dinners. If the host honors you with a toast, be prepared to reciprocate. Business entertaining is done more often at lunch than at dinner.
Saudi Arabia	Although men kiss each other in greeting, they never kiss a woman in public. An American woman should wait for a man to extend his hand before offering hers. When a Saudi offers refreshment, accept; declining it is an insult.
Japan	Don't imitate Japanese bowing customs unless you understand them thoroughly—who bows to whom, how many times, and when. It's a complicated ritual. Presenting business cards is another ritual. Carry many cards, present them with both hands so your name can

be easily read, and hand them to others in descending rank. Expect Japanese business executives to take time making decisions and to work through all of the details before making a commitment.[1]

SELLING GLOBALLY
Customer Gift Giving
in Japan

The highly ritualized practice of exchanging presents is paramount to cultivating long-lasting relationships in Japan. Gifts are exchanged with customers, between companies doing business together, and between employees and superiors within Japanese companies. As important as the gifts may be, so are the decorative wrappings and even the stores where the items are purchased.

As for presents, IBM's Vince Matal rules "the more lavish the better." Matal claims that he learned his lesson the hard way after a few buying missions when he offered totally inappropriate items, such as books, which are generally deemed too practical or unimpressive for the gift swap. Matal finds luxuries to be more on target, such as French chocolates, fine wine, or hard-to-come-by treats, such as the honeydew melon he once presented to a client. "It was a $55 melon," Matal says, "It was an imported melon from—possibly California—I don't know. But they sure don't grow them in Japan. It came in a beautiful wooden crate. And then we gave them a beautiful bottle of very nice sake. Another $90. So we gave a $150 gift, easily, and that was regular."[2]

SELLING GLOBALLY
Respecting the Traditions
of India

Lisa Hendrick walked briskly through the low door; the sound of her heels was muffled by the soft, thick rugs on the floor. She greeted her customer, Babu Jagjivan, with a wide smile and an outstretched hand. Babu Jagjivan was clad in a long, khaki cotton shirt with swirls of white cloth wrapped around his legs. He took her hand rather tentatively and gestured her to take a seat. Hendrick sat on the nearest available chair and crossed her legs. She was ready to negotiate prices with the help of her interpreter, who spoke Hindi. However, Babu Jagjivan did not appear ready to conduct business. Instead, he summoned a boy with a clap of his hands. Immediately, the boy brought two steel containers filled with hot, steaming tea. Being a hot, summer day with temperatures soaring to the 100s, Hendrick declined the tea. Babu Jagjivan seemed to be extremely reluctant to talk let alone negotiate a deal. Hendrick was puzzled. She had thought she was adjusting to India very well. Only yesterday, she had negotiated a good contract with Mr. Rajan in Bangalore, a large metropolitan city in south India. But here, in Kanpur (a major city in north India), she was not meeting with much success. Hendrick wondered what could be wrong.

In India, customers vary from Westernized, urban sophisticates like Mr. Rajan to the earthy Babu Jagjivan. Although people always seek to maximize economic benefits from a contract, the subtleties of negotiation and social mores cannot be overlooked. Babu Jagjivan was uncomfortable dealing with a woman. In the more traditional areas of India, it is not customary to shake hands with women—the traditional gesture of folding one's hands in respect (*namaste*) is the norm. The golden rule is to give the customer the pleasure of playing host, by accepting his tea and indulging in social pleasantries before getting down to business. Salespersons in India, as elsewhere, try to adapt to their customers by identifying with their customs. Hence, in urban India, the preferred language for business is English and customers are more apt to be familiar with Western customs. In smaller towns, customers are more comfortable in the regional language (there are 15 official languages in India). People would be distrustful of salespersons who do not respect their customs. Certain weekdays (usually Fridays) are considered auspicious for signing business contracts, although this may vary from one region to another. For instance, even though people in many parts of south India would not commence new business on Tuesdays, this may not be true in the north.[3]

A new minority is in demand in corporate America and overseas. Colgate-Palmolive Company calls these people *globalites*. In Europe, they are known as *Euro-managers*. Regardless of the name, corporations around the world are scrambling to locate and nab the brightest and best candidates for global management.

Competition is intense. Colgate-Palmolive's program, introduced in 1987, attracts 15,000 applicants for 15 slots. The need for global managers also has spawned several succesful executive search firms. Top international headhunters such as Korn/Ferry, Egon Zehnder International, and Russell Reynolds Associates, Inc., recruit multilingual executives with wide experience and the ability to deal with other cultures.

Could you qualify? Do you have enough international knowledge to answer these questions? A smiling fish is (*a*) a term used in the Middle East or (*b*) a dish served in China. During meals in Belgium, you should (*a*) keep your hands off the table or (*b*) keep your hands on the table. Eye contact and gestures of openness are important when discussing business in (*a*) Mexico or (*b*) Saudi Arabia. When they're talking, Americans stand closer than do South Americans or Africans: (*a*) true or (*b*) false. In England, to table an issue mean to (*a*) put it aside or (*b*) bring it up for discussion. (The correct answer for each question is *b*.)

Global corporations have initiated and promoted management programs to help employees overcome their cultural blunders. A program at General Electric's aircraft engine unit encourages foreign language and cross-cultural training for midlevel managers and engineers. American Express regularly transfers junior managers to overseas units. PepsiCo, Raychem, Honda of America, and GM are among the growing number of companies with global management training programs. As one international human resource manager pointed out, "Knowing how to conduct business in foreign cultures and to grasp global customers' different needs is the key to global business."

Multilingual skills aren't enough; corporations seek candidates with highly developed human skills. "We tend to look for people who can work in teams and understand the value of cooperation and consensus," said the chairman of Unilever. Successful globalization requires teamwork and overcoming national, racial, and religious prejudice. That minority of managers who quickly grasp global skills will increasingly find themselves on the fast track to success.[4]

- The workday begins around 8:15 or 8:30 A.M. Men wear suits and ties; women wear appropriate business attire.
- Travel is by taxi to most appointments. Many use bicycles for personal transportation but chaotic traffic makes this hazardous.
- Mostly you call on men; women hold about 10 percent of the senior advisory or management positions.
- Use English on most business calls (it's the international business language) although Mandarin or Cantonese (in the southern part of China) are required on some. It's not necessary for foreigners to know the many Chinese regional dialects.
- When taking taxis, get someone to write out directions to your destination in Chinese. Negotiate the fare before you leave. If your prospect's office is off

the beaten path, or if your call is late in the day, pay extra to have the taxi wait for you. On-call taxis take hours to arrive and you may have a long hike back to a main street to flag one down.

■ Expect to conduct business at your client's office or at your office and after hours on the golf course, over cocktails, or at dinner. If you must conduct business at your office, send a car to call for your prospect or customer. However, if your customers prefer meeting in your office, sending a car is not necessary.

■ Appearances can be deceiving; senior managers may show up at a trade show wearing overalls. One-on-one sales calls are not the norm. Expect to meet with two or more people. The Chinese are genuinely curious about your company and product line. They all want to learn more.

■ Get right down to business. Although meetings can begin with personal discussions about your experiences in Asia, the Chinese are not prone to idle chitchat.

■ Meals are important and can include 12 courses. If you plan to meet through lunch, you will likely send out for (surprise!) Chinese. Evening meals are divided equally between Asian and Continental cuisine.

■ Sales calls usually last from 30 to 45 minutes; depending on the industry, they can last up to several hours. Because of traffic, four calls a day—two in the morning and two in the afternoon—make a great day. Group your calls geographically.

■ Companies used to doing business with the West or Japan are fully automated with computers and faxes, although they use much older models than you are used to seeing. Not too many people carry portable phones or pagers, but this is changing almost hourly.

■ Show your company is serious about staying in China by printing bilingual order forms. Shaking hands and thanking the customer for the order are normal. Bowing is not required unless your customer is Japanese.

■ The business of business cards is serious. Take your customer's card in both hands, look at it carefully, remark on something you see. Offer your card first at the beginning of the meeting. If you will be in China for longer than one meeting, print bilingual business cards. If you smoke, offer a cigarette. If the meeting is at your office, offer tea or coffee immediately.

■ Business hours end at 6:30 P.M. but days end around 10 or 11 P.M. with dinner and then time at a club. Understand your customer's normal routine. Customers may transport key personnel to and from work in a company bus or other scheduled transportation. Don't get caught at closing with two-thirds of your meeting hurrying out to catch their group ride home.

■ Be patient, with yourself and the host country. Study before you go so you won't be caught with egg foo yung on your face.[5]

SELLING GLOBALLY
Little Cold Calling in Japan

Since it's customary in Japanese companies for a sales representative to be formally introduced to a prospect, the purpose of initial calls is understood but not discussed. The decision to do business together, if it occurs, results from the subtlety and patience of relationship building. "In America," says Chuck Laughlin, co-author of *Samurai Selling: The Ancient Art of Service in Sales,* "we may be into the middle of the sales process within days, hours . . . where a Japanese selling person can spend a year building the relationship before he begins to introduce his product."

"It's all a matter of time," says IBM's Vince Matal. Then, after thinking again, he adds, "Proportion, I guess is what I'm saying. Where we might be 20 percent relationship, rapport, that kind of thing, and 80 percent selling the product, they're the opposite."

Now back in the United States as a consulting marketing representative for IBM in Raleigh, North Carolina, Matal remembers the rules from his early days in sales. "You always try to develop a relationship and service your customers," he says; "but [the Japanese] do it to the exclusion—in my opinion—of actually trying to sell the product."

With years of relationship building before any deals get done, how do salespeople earn a living? The answer—a flat salary—is unusual in the United States, but standard procedure in Japan. This compensation arrangement, which goes hand-in-hand with the tradition of lifetime employment, was the inspiration for the term *salarymen,* the unglamorous description of employees in a workforce that was once predominantly male.[6]

SELLING GLOBALLY
Chinese Culture: Don't Shy Away from Negotiating

To the Chinese, negotiation can be sport. "Negotiating? It's not esoteric," says former U.S. Ambassador to China James Lilley, who is now a business consultant. "There's no arcane world of Chinese deviousness. Once you figure out what they want—and they telegraph their punches—you can make your deal. You've got to be willing to go to the brink. You've got to be willing to use them against each other. You've got to be willing to come in on top and bring pressure to bear." (In other words, use high-level pressure developed through relationships.)

The tough-love approach is suggested again and again: Be respectful; don't fly off the handle, but be resolute. Jim Stepanek, who spent years negotiating in China for Honeywell and other U.S. companies, says: "The only universal language is pain and anger. When they push down your price, and you calmly say no, they are going to delay the meeting another day and push you some more. When you finally get upset, and you ask to leave the room to control yourself because your blood vessels are popping out, and you come back a half hour later with steam still coming out your ears, then they know it is your lowest price."

There are advantages to negotiating in China rather than Japan, suggests Craig McLaughlin. "When you are negotiating with a Japanese organization, even when what you are presenting is totally unacceptable to the individual or company, they may not tell you. That is not a problem in China. They will be very direct. They're more likely to try and get you to negotiate against yourself. Instead of giving you a counterproposal they say, 'Go home and think about it, and come back with a better offer.'

"Another trait," continues McLaughlin, "is that quite often the people with whom you are negotiating do not have the authority to reach a compromise. The delegation of authority in China is not totally spelled out. Your best move? Tell them that there is little point in going further with the meeting unless they are willing to reveal their chain of command. They may not necessarily give you a straight answer, and sometimes they may not even know themselves, but it is a step in the right direction."[7]

SELLING GLOBALLY
Salespeople Are Making It Happen in China

Today thousands of American companies are competing to take advantage of the booming market in China. Avon is selling cosmetics door to door. Texaco has opened gas stations. AST computers hum away in schools and factories while Keystone valves are finding their way into infrastructure projects. Boeing keeps its assembly lines at peak capacity through lucrative aircraft sales to China. Experts estimate that China will purchase 50 to 60 large aircraft per year for the next three years to meet the rapidly growing demand. Motorola built a plant in China that produces 10,000 pagers a week that retail for $200 with a one-year service contract. The market for pagers is estimated at 4 million a year.

AT&T has publicly stated that its Chinese business may eclipse its U.S. business in the early part of this century. While most of the country's 400,000 entrepreneurs view cellular telephones as a necessity, 95 percent of the people in China look with envy at the communication toys their rich cousins use.

The insurance giant AIG has hired 140 salespeople who are knocking on doors in Shanghai. According to *The Wall Street Journal,* in eight months they sold more than 12,000 policies.

A few years ago, Diebold Inc., an Ohio-based manufacturer of banking equipment, learned that China was in the process of upgrading 100,000 bank branches. The company sent a lone sales representative, Edgar Petersen, on a two-week trip to China. He visited a number of banks, found a need for safe-deposit boxes, and returned with orders for safe-deposit boxes equal to a year's worth of Diebold's manufacturing capacity. Today, Diebold has captured 60 percent of China's ATM market. Diebold's chairman, Robert W. Mahoney, estimates the Chinese market for ATMs will grow to 5,000 units per year within a short time. (That's about one-half the size of the U.S. market.)[8]

SELLING GLOBALLY
Watch Out in Russia and China—They May Bug Your Room to Find Out Your Secrets

Computerized banking services are, at long last, coming to Russia and China—thanks in no small part to Hurston Anderson at Arkansas Systems Inc. in Little Rock. Over the course of several months in the early 1990s Anderson, vice president of sal es and marketing, and his colleagues worked out deals to supply the Central Bank of Russia and the People's Bank of China with software that will help bring their banking systems into the 20th century. Arkansas Systems beat out a number of competitors, mostly foreign. In Russia and China, says Anderson, there's still "this idea that because it's American, it's the best."

Negotiating in these countries can be dicey, says Anderson. "They bug your hotel rooms, for one thing," he says. But then again, the stakes are huge. While the initial deals have been in the six-figure range, the long-term payoff could reach into the tens of millions.

One new deal is for automated teller machine software and a check-clearing system in Siberia. In an earlier ATM deal in Moscow, recalls Anderson, "the guy from Central Bank pulled $130,000 out of a valise and wanted to pay us that way!"

The Chinese project includes check-clearing systems at 10,000 branch banks in three Chinese banking regions. Though the initial contract is for $500,000, Anderson notes that there are no fewer than 77 banking regions in China. "And 77 times $500,000 is what? About $40 million, I'd say. Boy, I hope they don't try delivering all that in a valise."[9]

SELLING GLOBALLY
French versus American Salespeople

Gerhard Gschwandtner, editor of *Personal Selling Power* (PSP) magazine, interviewed Jean-Pierre Tricard, a French sales trainer. The following excerpts from this interview discuss three important areas of a salesperson's job:

1. Differences between French and American salespeople:

PSP: How do you see the differences between French salespeople and American salespeople?

Jean-Pierre Tricard: As you know, there are significant cultural differences between our two countries. For example, in our culture, the one thing that we tend to be afraid of is to talk about money. While the French are embarrassed to talk about how much money they make, Americans consider money as a concrete measure of success. In France, people who brag about how much money they make are looked on as thieves.

PSP: How does this impact a sales negotiation?

Tricard: When French salespeople get to the point of discussing the price, they start to panic. They literally don't know how to deal with that because they have not been trained to talk about money. In my opinion, American salespeople are better equipped to talk about price.

2. French salespeople focus on solving customer problems:

PSP: Let's talk about the strong points of French salespeople.

Tricard: First, most French salespeople love their company. They tend to love their product more than their bosses give them credit for. They tend to work hard for their company. Also, they have a great desire to be well thought of by their clients.

PSP: How would you describe their relationship with their clients?

Tricard: They go out of their way to help a customer solve a problem even when the problem has nothing to do with the sale. In other words, their aim is to be of service. Salespeople in France see themselves more as the client's team. For example, if a reseller has an inventory problem, the salesperson will help the customer move the inventory.

3. How Americans appear to the French:

PSP: What is a difference in selling between the two countries?

Tricard: One difference would be that American salespeople are very direct. When you want something, you ask for it directly. In France, we're following different customs. We don't want to risk offending someone and we're afraid to show bad manners. As a result, we skirt the issues—beat around the bush and it takes us much longer to make a request. Therefore, French salespeople tend to make more sales calls than necessary. They're often afraid of leading the prospect to the close.

PSP: So you are saying that American salespeople who sell to a French prospect should plan on spending more time. . . .

Tricard: Yes, more time to listen to their clients, encouraging them to talk more, trying to get them relaxed and comfortable. French customers don't like to be pushed to a conclusion.[10]

SELLING GLOBALLY
Israel—The Home Court Advantage

Rita Hunter was sent to Israel during the 1994 peace process to establish a beachhead for her company in a region that finally seemed prepared to live up to its market potential.

After two weeks and three broken appointments at one company, she had begun to wonder if she would ever get her foot in the door. The next day she mentioned the problem to a local friend of hers, Sarit; she was surprised when Sarit called back to say that the appointment was set up for the following week. Hunter asked Sarit how she had arranged the appointment; Sarit explained her husband served in the same reserve unit as a manager at her target company. This manager set up the appointment for Hunter; and because the request came from in-house, the appointment was kept.

Getting an appointment in Israel is not always this easy. However, given the geographical density, close family ties, local friendliness, military reserve duty, and workforce mobility, sometimes it is not too difficult to find somebody to act as a contact in an organization, either to set up an appointment or to find out who can set up the appointment.

Most Israelis are very social and friendly people. Their desire to be helpful enables them to assist others just for the intrinsic satisfaction of being able to help. They tend to make everybody's business their own, so that they can offer a solution. Perhaps one of the key reasons for this is the feeling that all Israelis face the same problems, and if they can't help each other, who else will help? On the other hand, their generosity and courtesy are not always extended to foreigners; thus a local contact can ease the difficulty.

Not everyone, however, is willing to act as a go-between because this implicitly suggests an obligation. Although Israelis will usually go out of their way for friends, making friends locally is not always easy for a foreigner. Finding the right contact can sometimes consume more time than it is worth, and salespeople are encouraged to try the frontal approach as well.[11]

SELLING GLOBALLY
Working a Deal in the Arab World

Buyers in the Arab world are very hospitable and favorably disposed toward salespersons. Decisions there are frequently based on personal impressions supplemented by facts. The business climate and the tone of communication are very important. Arabs consider business transactions as social events; bargaining is an enjoyable and integral part of life.

Salespeople must respect all the religious and cultural customs of their Arab partners. They should remember that during the course of negotiations the Arabs may not be available at all times because of their religious customs.

One particularly aggravating thing to American businesspeople is that an Arab counterpart never says no directly; this custom avoids any loss of face on either side. By being aware of this, an American can respond accordingly.

At the end of the negotiation, an Arab counterpart signals agreement orally and commits himself firmly by giving his word. If circumstances change, however, an Arab buyer feels free to renegotiate a modification of the agreement.[12]

SELLING GLOBALLY
The Japanese Take Relationship Selling Seriously

The selling rules between Japanese clients and company representatives are highly ritualized. For instance, the president of one company might make a formal request of the president of another to introduce his sales manager, setting in motion the long process of establishing a relationship. But some concessions are being made in these recessionary times.

"You hear stories about Japanese companies just saying, 'Okay, it's a done deal and the price doesn't mean anything because it's just based on relationship,'" says Daniel Wong, a salesperson for Japan Database. "Well, I think that's changing even now, because of the economic situation as it is."

A sales rep isn't likely to be able to break into a Japanese company without a proper introduction. "There are no hard-and-fast rules about anything," Wong says, "but [if you try it], your chances of success are limited. If you call on a traditional Japanese company, and you just cold call—I mean, myself [being a foreigner], I would have no chance whatsoever."

Because maintaining a relationship with a client is central to the Japanese concept of service, accounts and territories are not generally shifted around, according to IBM's Vince Matal. In fact, it's the opposite. "Quite frequently," he says, "if there's a key account that [a sales rep] had a relationship with," the same rep will continue to call on the client as he moves up the corporate ladder, "even though [the original rep doesn't] have direct responsibility for the revenue from that account anymore."[13]

SELLING GLOBALLY

Europe and IBM—Changes
Had to Be Made

On a crisp, sunny September morning, Lucio Stanca, the new chief of IBM Europe, greeted his top 100 managers in the basement of the company's Paris headquarters. The 52-year-old Italian promised to give all his energy and passion to speeding change. Between the lines, the message was clear: Anyone who lagged behind just might be left there.

Following the abrupt departure of IBM Europe chief Hans-Olaf Henkel, Stanca and his top executives at the Paris operation were racing to implement Chief Executive Louis V. Gerstner, Jr.'s vision of a more nimble global company. Deadlines to create a new management organization had been pushed forward and efforts to think globally redoubled.

Stanca's first job was to assuage wounded egos and get IBM's troops marching together. "The biggest challenge is getting everyone sorted out and creating a new mind-set," said Robert Dies, an executive vice president at IBM Europe.

There's no way IBM could have avoided a serious shakeup. The old model of doing business—local operations complete with a chairman and board, financial staff, sales force, a full complement of technical experts, and unquestionable say over all aspects of the company—was passé. Now a debilitated Big Blue struggled to control costs, to cater to a global clientele, and to serve its markets across industry groups and regions. That meant breaking down its once sacrosanct national boundaries.

It also meant shifting clout from country managers to the centralized groups of experts, each focused on a key region of the world. According to Dies, 70 to 80 percent of IBM Europe's business would be handled by new industry sector teams.

The main goal of the remake was to globalize control over product development, sales, and marketing. Before, multinationals found it impossible to do business with IBM as a single entity. Now, a single contract could cover the world. "Getting a global buying arrangement remains one of the hardest problems," says William R. Hoover, chairman of Computer Sciences Corp., an IBM customer.

One reason for Gerstner's sense of urgency was to improve IBM's overseas performance. The previous year, European revenues fell 12.8 percent to $21.85 billion. Europe showed a profit on operations of $714 million but posted a net loss of $1.7 billion as a result of charges for restructuring. In Japan, IBM lost $240 million on sales of $12.6 billion. In 1993, both regions were up 18 percent, but efforts to cut expenses abroad lagged those in the United States. Gerstner's new team in Europe said he left the execution up to them. They'll need Stanca's passion—and more—to make it work.[14]

Appendix E: Answers to Crossword Puzzles

Chapter 1—The Life, Times, and Career of the Professional Salesperson

Across

7. Order getter
10. Conceptual skill
12. Rule
13. Personal selling
14. Career path
15. Customer contact person

Down

1. Human skill
2. Technical skill
3. Wholesale salesperson
4. Direct sellers
5. Service
6. Territory manager
8. Retail salesperson
9. Sales process
11. Order taker

Chapter 2—Relationship Marketing: Where Personal Selling Fits

Across

1. Partnering
3. Advertising
5. Service
6. Price
7. Publicity
9. Top to top
10. Relationship gap
13. Mix
16. Eighty twenty principle
18. Transaction
22. Distribution
24. E sales call
25. Exchange
26. Added
27. Consumer
28. Government
30. Good
31. Long term ally

Down

1. Product
2. Reseller
4. Sales promotion
8. Consultative
11. Household
12. Personal selling
14. Buying teams
15. Marketing
17. Team selling
19. Concept
20. Leader
21. Business
23. Industrial
29. Firm

Chapter 3—Ethics First . . . Then Customer Relationships

Across

5. Reciprocity
6. Stakeholder
8. Love
11. Preconventional
15. Code of ethics
18. Committee
19. Clayton
20. Cooling off laws
22. Green River
24. Tie in sale
25. Social responsibility

Down

1. Principled
2. CCC GOMES
3. Behavior
4. Fixed point of reference
7. Cooperative acceptance
9. Conventional
10. Price discrimination
12. Discretionary
13. Misrepresentation
14. Breach of warranty
16. Employee
17. Cornerstone
21. Ombudsman
23. Ethics

Chapter 4—The Psychology of Selling: Why People Buy

Across

2. Personality
6. Retention
9. Feature
10. Wants
13. Ideal self
16. Collect information
18. Conscious
20. Arousal
21. Real self
24. LOCATE
25. Satisfaction
27. Extensive
28. Image
29. Routine decision making
30. Black box
31. Purchase dissonance

Down

1. Purchase
2. Perception
3. Attitude
4. Information evaluation
5. Unconscious
7. Need
8. Concept
11. Preconscious
12. Benefit selling
14. Limited
15. Belief
17. Economic needs
19. SELL sequence
22. Exposure
23. Benefit
24. Learning
26. Advantage

Chapter 5—Communication for Relationship Building: It's Not All Talk

Across

1. Personal space
5. Persuasion
7. Medium
10. Communication
14. Listening
15. Receiver
16. Empathy
18. Source
20. Space threat
22. Noise
24. Disagreement signals
25. KISS
26. Space invasion

27. Territorial space
28. Memory
29. Caution signals

Down

2. Probing
3. Feedback
4. Public space
6. Intimate space
8. Enthusiasm
9. Decoding process
11. Encoding process
12. Proof statements
13. Acceptance signals
17. Hearing
19. Social space
21. Credibility
23. Message

Chapter 6—Sales Knowledge: Customers, Products, Technologies

Across

2. Shelf positioning
6. Flaming
7. Shelf facings
9. Cooperative
11. Mobile offices
14. Netiquette
16. Retail
18. Web page
20. Links
22. Direct mail
23. Premium
24. National
25. Surfing the Internet

Down

1. Contact management
3. Point of purchase displays
4. Personal productivity
5. Consumer sales promotion
8. Calendar management
10. Price

12. Internet
13. Electronic mail
15. Trade
17. Sales training
19. World Wide Web
21. Industrial

Chapter 6 Appendix—Sales Arithmetic and Pricing

Across

5. Trade discounts
11. FOB shipping point
12. Return on investment
13. Gross profit
14. Zone price

Down

1. Value analysis
2. Consumer discounts
3. FOB destination
4. Markup
6. Cash discounts
7. Net price
8. Net profit
9. Unit cost
10. List price

Chapter 7—Prospecting—The Lifeblood of Selling

Across

6. Sales process
8. Referral
9. Prospect
12. Lead
13. Parallel referral sale
14. Center of influence method
15. Networking
16. Orphaned customers
17. Prospecting

Down

1. Prospect pool
2. Telephone prospecting

3. Qualified prospect
4. Direct mail prospecting
5. Observation method
7. Customer service
8. Referral cycle
10. Telemarketing
11. Call reluctance

Chapter 8—Planning the Sales Call Is a Must!

Across

1. Success
6. Prospects mental steps
8. Sales call objective
10. Attention
12. Customer profile
14. Sales presentation
15. Sales call purpose
17. Conviction

Down

2. Sales call planning
3. Customer benefit plan
4. Desire
5. Purchase or action
7. Creative problem solver
9. Interest
11. Preapproach
13. Strategic
16. Plan

Chapter 9—Carefully Select Which Sales Presentation Method to Use

Across

3. Need development
4. Sales presentation
5. Memorized presentation

Down

1. Formula presentation
2. Need fulfillment
3. Need awareness

Chapter 10—Begin Your Presentation Strategically

Across

1. Customer benefit approach
3. Direct question
5. Multiple question approach
10. Complimentary approach
13. Approach
14. Nondirective question
16. Product
17. Introductory approach

Down

2. Referral
4. Creative imagery
6. Redirect question
7. Rephrasing question
8. Showmanship
9. Curiosity approach
11. Premium
12. Opinion
15. Shock

Chapter 11—Elements of a Great Sales Presentation

Across

3. Dramatization
6. Logical reasoning
10. Visuals
13. Prestige suggestions
14. Analogy
15. Counter suggestion
16. Simile

Down

1. Suggestive propositions
2. Demonstration
4. Indirect suggestion
5. Paul Harvey dialogue
7. Sales presentation mix
8. Proof statements
9. Metaphor

11. Direct suggestion
12. Autosuggestion

Chapter 12—Welcome Your Prospect's Objections

Across

2. Compensation method
5. Sales
6. Psychological
8. Product
9. Hidden
15. Indirect denial
17. No need
18. Source
20. Five question sequence
21. Condition of the sale
22. Rephrase as a question

Down

1. Pass up
3. Postpone the objection
4. Third party answer
7. Intelligent questions
10. Dodge
11. Negotiation
12. Boomerang method
13. Money
14. Direct denial
16. Practical
19. Stalling

Chapter 13—Closing Begins the Relationship

Across

2. Assumptive close
9. Technology close
11. Negotiation close
12. Summary of benefits close

Down

1. Alternative choice close
3. Standing room only close
4. Compliment close

5. Continuous yes close
6. Buying signal
7. Probability close
8. Minor points close
9. T account close
10. Closing

Chapter 14—Service and Follow-up for Customer Retention

Across

6. Friends
7. Customer service
9. Acquaintances
10. Business friendship

Down

1. Intimate friends
2. Knowledge
3. Follow up
4. Customer satisfaction
5. Wisdom
8. Proverb

Chapter 15—Time, Territory, and Self-Management: Keys to Success

Across

4. Routing
7. Sales territory
8. Sales response function
9. Break even analysis
10. Scheduling

Down

1. Account segmentation
2. Undifferentiated selling
3. Account analysis
5. ELMS system
6. Key accounts

Chapter 16—Planning, Staffing, and Training Successful Salespeople

Across

2. Sales force budget
6. Directing
7. Selection
9. Planning
15. Sales management
17. Training
18. Recruitment
19. Role playing
20. Job specifications
21. Evaluating

Down

1. Descriptions
2. Staffing
3. Decentralized training
4. Design
5. Multicultural
8. People planning
10. Employment planning
11. Sales forecasting
12. Analysis
13. Organizational
14. Sales training
16. Diversity

Chapter 17—Motivation, Compensation, Leadership, and Evaluation of Salespeople

Across

3. Relationship behavior
4. Motivation mix
5. Performance evaluation
7. Combination salary plan
11. Straight salary plan
12. Motivation
13. Management control system
14. Straight commission plan

Down

1. Joint sales call
2. Performance criteria
6. Coaching
8. Bonus
9. Sales contests
10. Task behavior

A

acceptance signals: Signs that your buyer is favorably inclined toward you and your presentation.

account analysis: The process of analyzing each prospect and customer to maximize the chances of reaching a sales goal.

account segmentation: The process of applying different selling strategies to different customers.

acquaintance: People you know little about.

advantage: The performance characteristic of a product that describes how it can be used or will help the buyer.

advertising: The nonpersonal communication of information paid for by an identified sponsor, for example, an individual or an organization.

alternative-choice close: Gives the prospect a choice between two alternatives.

Americans with Disabilities Act (ADA): Prohibits discrimination against people who are physically or mentally impaired but are capable of doing the job.

analogy: A comparison between two different situations that have something in common.

approach: Opening of the presentation from first talk with person to discussion of product.

assumptive close: A type of close that assumes the prospect will buy.

attention: The first step in the prospect's mental steps. From the moment a salesperson begins to talk, he or she should try to quickly capture and maintain the prospect's attention.

attitude: A person's learned predisposition toward something.

autosuggestion: A kind of suggestion that attempts to have prospects imagine themselves using the product.

B

belief: A state of mind in which trust or confidence is placed in something or someone.

benefit: A favorable result the buyer receives from the product because of a particular advantage that has the ability to satisfy a buyer's need.

benefit selling: A method of selling whereby a salesperson relates a product's benefits to the customer's needs using the product's features and advantages as support.

black box: The unobservable, internal process taking place within the mind of the prospect as he or she reaches a decision whether or not to buy.

bonus: Additional compensation given to the salesperson that is over what is usually earned.

boomerang method: The process of turning an objection into a reason to buy.

breach of warranty: A legal cause of action on which an injured party seeks damages. It arises when a salesperson makes erroneous statements or offers false promises regarding a product's characteristics and capabilities.

break-even analysis: A quantitative technique for determining the level of sales at which total revenues equal total costs.

business consultant: A salesperson who gives advice and service.

business friendship: The relationship formed between a salesperson and client that revolves around business-related issues.

buying signal: Anything that prospects say or do indicating they are ready to buy.

buying teams: Composed of multifunctional specialists who ensure that their organizations accurately convey their complex needs to the seller and thoroughly assess the accuracy of suppliers' recommendations.

C

calendar management: Scheduling appointments, telephone calls, or "to do" lists.

call reluctance: Not wanting to contact a prospect or customer.

career path: The upward sequence of job movements during a sales career.

cash discounts: Discounts earned by buyers who pay bills within a stated period.

caution signals: Signs that a buyer is neutral or skeptical toward what the salesperson says.

CCC GOMES: Acronym for the eight important stakeholders of an organization: customers, community, creditors, government, owners, managers, employees, suppliers.

center of influence method: A method of prospecting whereby the salesperson finds and cultivates people who are willing to cooperate in helping to find prospects.

centralized training programs: Centrally located instruction of salespeople that supplements training conducted in the field.

character: Made up of an organization or salesperson's integrity and trust. Example: who you are when no one is looking and what you are willing to stand for when someone is looking.

Clayton Act: Prohibits the practice of tie-in sales when they substantially lessen competition.

closing: The process of helping people make a decision that will benefit them by asking them to buy.

coaching: Intensive on-the-job training through instruction, demonstration, and practice.

code of ethics: A formal statement of the company's values concerning ethics and social issues.

cold canvass prospecting method: A method whereby the salesperson contacts as many leads as possible with no knowledge of the business or individual called upon.

collect information: The process by which buyers visit retail stores, contact potential suppliers, or talk with salespeople about a product's price, size, advantage, and warranty before making a decision regarding buying.

combination salary plan: A plan wherein a proportion of the salesperson's total pay is guaranteed while a portion of it can come from commissions.

communication: The act of transmitting verbal and nonverbal information and understanding between seller and buyer.

compensation method: The method of offsetting negative product aspects with better benefit aspects.

compliment close: A close wherein the salesperson ends with a compliment to the prospect.

complimentary approach: An approach that opens with a compliment that is sincere and therefore effective.

computer-based presentations: Using the computer to present information to prospects and customers.

conceptual skills: The ability to see the selling process as a whole and the relationship among its parts.

condition of the sale: A situation wherein an objection becomes a condition of the sale, such that if the condition is met the prospect will buy.

conscious need level: A state of mind in which buyers are fully aware of their needs.

consultative selling: The process of helping the customer achieve strategic short- and long-term goals through the use of the seller's good or service.

consumer discounts: One-time price reductions passed on from the manufacturer to channel members or directly to the customer.

consumer products: Products produced for and purchased by, households or end consumers for their personal use.

consumer sales promotion: A promotion that includes free samples, coupons, contests, and demonstrations to consumers.

contact management: Automated listing of all customer contacts a salesperson makes in the course of conducting business.

continuous-yes close: A kind of close whereby the salesperson develops a series of benefit questions that the prospect must answer.

conventional moral development level: The second level of an individual's moral development. At this level, an individual conforms to the expectations of others, such as family, employer, boss, and society, and upholds moral and legal laws.

conviction: In the conviction step of the prospect's mental buying process, the salesperson should strive to develop a strong belief that the product is best suited to the prospects' specific needs. It is established when no doubts remain about purchasing the product.

cooling-off laws: Laws that provide a cooling-off period during which the buyer may cancel the contract, return any merchandise, and obtain a full refund.

cooperative acceptance: The right of employees to be treated fairly and with respect regardless of race, sex, national origin, physical disability, age, or religion, while on the job.

cooperative advertising: Advertising conducted by the retailer with costs paid for by the manufacturer or shared by the manufacturer and the retailer.

cornerstone: The essential component of a building's foundation which for the organization is love of others.

counter suggestion: A suggestion that evokes an opposite response from the prospect.

creative imagery: A relaxation and concentration technique that aids in stress management, in which a salesperson envisions successful coping in various sales situations.

creative problem solver: A person with the ability to develop and combine nontraditional alternatives in order to meet specific needs of the customer.

credibility: A salesperson's believability, established through empathy, willingness to listen to specific needs, and continual enthusiasm toward his or her work and the customer's business.

cumulative quantity discounts: Discounts received for buying a certain amount of a product over a stated period.

curiosity approach: An approach whereby the salesperson asks a question or does something to make the prospect curious about the product.

customer benefit approach: An approach whereby the salesperson asks a question(s) that implies that the product will benefit the prospect.

customer benefit plan: A plan that contains the nucleus of information used in the sales presentation.

customer contact person: Another name for a salesperson.

customer profile: Relevant information regarding the firm, the buyer, and individuals who influence the buying decision.

customer satisfaction: Feelings toward the purchase.

customer service: Activities and programs provided by the seller to make the relationship a satisfying one for the customer.

D

decentralized training: Training that comprises the main form of sales instruction.

decoding process: Receipt and translation of information by the receiver.

demonstration: The process of showing a product to a prospect and letting him or her use it, if possible.

desire: The third step in the prospect's mental buying process. It is created when prospects express a wish or wanting for a product.

direct denial: The method of overcoming objections through the use of facts, logic, and tact.

direct-mail advertising: Advertising that is mailed directly to the customer or industrial user.

direct-mail prospecting: The process of mailing advertisements to a large number of people over an extended geographical area.

direct question: A question that by and large can be answered with a yes or no response or at most by a very short response consisting of a few words.

direct sellers: Sellers who sell face-to-face to consumers—typically in their homes—who use products for their personal use.

direct suggestion: An approach that suggests prospects buy rather than telling them to buy.

directing: The action of dealing with people positively and persuasively from a leadership position.

disagreement signals: Signs that the prospect does not agree with the presentation or does not think the product is beneficial.

discretionary responsibility: Actions taken by a company that are purely voluntary and guided by its desire to make social contributions not mandated by economics, law, or ethics.

distribution: The channel structure used to transfer products from an organization to its customers.

diversity: The difference between people due to age, religion, race, gender, and so on.

dodge: Doesn't deny, answer, or ignore the objection, but simply temporarily dodges it.

dramatization: The theatrical presentation of products.

E

economic needs: The buyer's need to purchase the most satisfying product for the money.

eighty/twenty principle (80/20): A situation in which a few key or large accounts bring in 80 percent of profitable sales although they represent only 20 percent of total accounts.

electronic mail: Allows information to be sent electronically through a system that delivers the message immediately to any number of recipients.

ELMS system: The process of dividing customers into varying size accounts.

empathy: The ability to identify and understand another person's feelings, ideas, and circumstances.

employee rights: Rights desired by employees regarding their job security and the treatment administered by their employers while on the job, irrespective of whether those rights are currently protected by law or collective bargaining agreements of labor unions.

employment planning: The recruitment and selection of applicants for sales jobs.

encoding process: One of the eight elements of the communication process. This is the conversion by the salesperson of ideas and concepts into the language and materials used in the sales presentation.

endless chain referral method: A method of prospecting whereby a salesperson asks each buyer for a list of friends who might also be interested in buying the product.

enthusiasm: A state of mind wherein a person is filled with excitement toward something.

Equal Employment Opportunity Commission (EEOC): The principal governmental agency responsible for monitoring discriminatory practices.

E-sales call: A sales call in which the seller and the customer meet using the computer screen.

ethical behavior: Behavior demonstrating a willingness to treat others fairly and that shows one to be honest and trustworthy and that exhibits loyalty to company, associates, and the work for which one is responsible.

ethics committee: A group of executives appointed to oversee company ethics.

ethics ombudsman: An official given the responsibility of corporate conscience who hears and investigates ethical complaints and informs top management of potential ethical issues.

ethics: Principles of right or good conduct, or a body of such principles, that affect good and bad business practices.

evaluating: Comparing actual performance to planned performance goals to determine whether to take corrective action if goals are not achieved, or to continue using the same methods if goals are met.

exchange: The act of obtaining a desired product from someone by offering something in return.

exhibitions and demonstrations: A situation in which a firm operates a booth at a trade show or other special-interest gathering staffed by salespeople.

extensive decision making: Decision-making characteristic of buyers who are unfamiliar with a specific product and who must therefore become highly involved in the decision-making process.

F

FAB selling technique: A presentation technique stressing features, advantages, and benefits of a product.

feature: Any physical characteristic of a product.

feedback: Verbal or nonverbal reaction to communication as transmitted to the sender.

firm: An organization that produces goods and services.

five-question sequence: The five-step process of overcoming objections in which facts, logic, and tact are used.

fixed point of reference: Something that provides the correct action to take in any situation and never gets tailored to fit an occasion.

flaming: Flaming is the equivalent of a verbal lashing on the Internet.

FOB destination: The point at which the seller pays all shipping costs and title passes on delivery.

FOB shipping point: The shipping process in which the buyer pays transportation charges for goods, the title for which passes to the customer when the goods are loaded onto the shipping vehicle.

follow-up: Maintaining contact with a customer (or prospect) in order to evaluate the effectiveness of the product and the satisfaction of the customer.

formula presentation: A presentation by which the salesperson follows a general outline that allows more flexibility and tries to determine prospect needs.

four P's of marketing: (product, price, place and promotion) aid the salesperson's selling efforts.

friends: People known for some time and with whom we share common interests and/or hobbies.

G

geographic information systems: View and manipulate customer and/or prospect information on an electronic map.

Global Positioning System (GPS): A worldwide radio-navigation system formed from a constellation of satellites circling the earth and their ground stations.

Golden Rule of Personal Selling: The sales philosophy of unselfishly treating others as you would like to be treated.

Golden Rule of Sales Management: The management philosophy of a leader unselfishly treating salespeople as the leader would like to be treated.

good: A physical object for sale.

government: An organization that provides goods and services to households and firms, and that redistributes income and wealth.

Green River ordinance: This type of ordinance protects consumers and aids local firms by making it more difficult for outside competition to enter the market.

gross profit: Money available to cover the costs of marketing the product, operating the business, and profit.

H

hearing: The ability to detect sounds.

hidden objection: An objection that disguises the actual objection either with silence or triviality.

household: A decision-making unit buying for their personal use.

human skills: The seller's ability to work with and through other people.

I

ideal self: The person one would like to be.

indirect denial: An apparent agreement with the prospect used by the salesperson to deny the fundamental issue of the objection.

indirect suggestion: A statement by the salesperson recommending that the prospect undertake some action while making it seem that the idea to do so is the prospect's.

industrial advertising: Advertising aimed at individuals and organizations who purchase products for manufacturing or reselling other products.

industrial products: Products sold primarily for use in producing other products.

information evaluation: A process that determines what will be purchased as the buyer matches this information with needs, attitudes, and beliefs in making a decision.

integrity: Being honest without compromise or corruption.

intelligent questions: Questions relating to a prospect's business that show the salesperson's concern for the prospect's needs.

interest: The second step in the prospect's mental buying process. It is important for the salesperson to capture the prospect's interest in their product. If this link is completed, prospects usually express a desire for the product.

Internet: A global network of computers.

intimate friends: People known on a deeper, more personal level than a friend.

intimate space: A spatial zone up to two feet, about an arm's length, from a person's body that is reserved for close friends and loved ones.

introductory approach: The most common but least powerful approach; it does little to capture the prospect's attention.

J–K

job analysis: The definition of a sales position in terms of specific roles or activities to be performed along with the determination of personal qualifications suitable for the job.

job descriptions: Formal, written statements describing the nature, requirements, and responsibilities of a specific position.

job specifications: The conversion of job descriptions into those people qualifications the organization feels are needed for successful job performance.

joint sales call: A sales call that takes place when the manager accompanies a salesperson on the call.

key accounts: Accounts the loss of which would greatly affect sales and profits.

KISS: A memory device standing for Keep It Simple, Salesperson.

knowledge: Knowing something gained through experience and/or training.

L

lead: A person or organization who might be a prospect.

leadership: The process by which a sales manager attempts to influence the activities of salespeople.

learning: Acquiring knowledge or behavior based on past experiences.

limited decision making: Decision-making characteristic of a buyer who invests a moderate level of energy to the decision to buy because, although the buyer is not familiar with each brand's features, advantages, and benefits, the general quality of the good is known to him or her.

links: Pointers to other pages of information on the World Wide Web.

list price: A standard price charged to all customers.

listening: Ability to derive meaning from sounds that are heard.

L-O-C-A-T-E: An acronym for methods to uncover important needs: Listen, observe, combine, ask questions, talk to others, empathize.

logical reasoning: Persuasive techniques that appeal to the prospect's common sense by applying logic through reason.

long-term ally: A salesperson who helps customers reach long-term goals.

looking-glass self: The self that people think other people see them as.

love: The strong affection, desire, or devotion to people.

M

management control system: A process wherein a manager evaluates each salesperson's performance, comparing it to performance goals, and rewarding or penalizing a salesperson based on that comparison.

manufacturer's sales representative: A person who works for an organization that produces a product.

marketing: The process of planning and executing the conception, pricing, promotion, and distribution of goods, services, and ideas to create exchanges that satisfy individual and organizational objectives.

marketing concept: A philosophy of business maintaining that the satisfaction of customer needs and wants is the economic and social reason for a firm's existence and that the firm should therefore direct its activities toward fulfilling those needs and wants, yielding, at the same time, long-term profitability.

marketing mix: The four main elements used by a marketing manager to market goods and services. These elements are product, price, distribution or place, and promotion.

markup: The dollar amount added to the product cost to determine its selling price.

medium: The form of communication used in the sales presentation and discussion, most frequently words, visual materials, and body language.

memorized presentation: A type of presentation in which the salesperson does 80 to 90 percent of the talking, focusing on the product and its benefits rather than attempting to determine the prospect's needs.

memory: The ability to recall information over time.

message: Information conveyed in the sales presentation.

metaphor: An implied comparison that uses a contrasting word or phrase to evoke a vivid image.

minor-points close: A close in which the salesperson asks the prospect to make a low-risk decision on a minor element of a product.

misrepresentation: A legal cause of action on which an injured party seeks damages. It arises when a salesperson makes erroneous statements or offers false promises regarding a product's characteristics and capabilities.

mobile offices: Vehicles converted to mobile offices.

money objection: A price-oriented objection.

morals: A person's adherence to right or wrong behavior and right or wrong thinking.

motivation: The arousal, intensity, direction, and persistence of effort directed toward job tasks over a period of time.

motivation mix: Five broad classes of factors used to motivate salespeople.

multicultural: The degree to which an organization values diversity and is willing to utilize and encourage it.

multiple-question approach (SPIN): An approach in which the salesperson uses three types of questions—situation, problem implication, and need-payoff—to get a better understanding of the prospect's business.

N

national advertising: Advertising designed to reach all users of the product, whether customers or industrial buyers.

need arousal: A situation in which a salesperson triggers a psychological, social, or economic need in the buyer.

need awareness: The stage at which the salesperson is aware of the buyer's needs and takes control of the situation by restating those needs to clarify the situation.

need development: In a need-satisfaction sales presentation, the stage at which the discussion is devoted to the buyer's needs.

need fullfillment: The last phase of a need-satisfaction sales presentation. Here, the salesperson shows how the product will satisfy mutual needs.

need-satisfaction presentation: A flexible, interactive type of presentation in which a prospect's needs are thoroughly discussed.

needs: The desire for something a person feels is worthwhile.

negotiation: The process by which the buyer and the seller reach a mutually satisfactory agreement.

negotiation close: A close in which buyer and seller find ways for everyone to have a fair deal.

netiquette: Etiquette used on the Internet.

net price: The price after allowance for all discounts.

net profit: Money remaining after costs of marketing and operating the business are paid.

networking: The continuous prospecting method of making and utilizing contacts.

no-need objection: An objection in which the prospect declares he or she does not need the product and implies the end of the selling effort, but which may actually be either a hidden or a stalling objection.

noise: Factors that distort communication between buyer and seller, including barriers to communication.

noncumulative quantity discounts: Discounts received for buying a certain amount of a product over a stated period.

nondirective question: A question that opens up two-way communication by beginning the question with who, what, where, when, how, and why.

nonprofit clients: Recipients of money and/or services from a nonprofit organization.

nonverbal communication: Unspoken communication such as physical space, appearance, handshake, and body movement.

O

observation method: The process of finding prospects by a salesperson constantly watching what is happening in the sales area.

opinion approach: An approach whereby a salesperson shows that the buyer's opinion is valued.

order-getter: Salespeople who get new and repeat business using a creative sales strategy and a well-executed sales presentation.

order-taker: Salespeople who only take orders by asking what the customer wants or waiting for the customer to order. They have no sales strategy and use no sales presentation.

organizational design: The formal, coordinated process of communication, authority, and responsibility for sales groups and individuals.

organizational structure: The relatively fixed, formally defined relationship among jobs within the organization.

organizing: Setting up an administrative structure through which work activities are defined.

orphaned customers: Customers whose salesperson has left the company.

P

parallel referral sale: Not only selling a product but also selling the idea of giving prospects names as well.

partnering: When the seller works continually to improve the customer's operations, sales, and profits.

pass-up: The option of a salesperson not to pursue a presentation or sale, or not to respond to an objection.

Paul Harvey dialogue: The process of incorporating methods of speech and delivery to make talk come alive rather than sounding dull and memorized.

PDA: A tiny fully functional computer that works as an extension of a desktop or laptop computer.

people planning: Planning how many and what type of people to hire.

perception: The process by which a person selects, organizes, and interprets information.

performance criteria: Bases for evaluating a salesperson's performance.

performance evaluation: The formal, structured system of measuring and evaluating a salesperson's activities and performance.

personal productivity: Technology to help a salesperson increase productivity through more efficient data storage and retrieval, better time management, and enhanced presentations.

personal selling: Personal communication of information to unselfishly persuade a prospective customer to buy something—a good, service, idea, or something else—that satisfies that individual's needs.

personal space: An area two to four feet from a person; it is the closest zone a stranger or business acquaintance is normally allowed to enter.

personality: A person's distinguishing character traits, attitudes, or habits.

persuasion: The process of changing a person's belief, position, or course of action.

plan: A method of achieving an end.

planning: Establishing a broad outline for goals, policies, and procedures that will accomplish the objectives of the organization.

point-of-purchase (POP) displays: Displays that allow a product to be easily seen and purchased.

postpone the objection: The option of a salesperson to respond to an objection later during the sales presentation.

practical objection: An overt objection based on real or concrete causes.

preapproach: Planning the sales call on a customer or prospect.

preconscious need level: The level at which needs are not fully developed in the conscious mind.

preconventional moral development level: The first level of an individual's moral development. At this level, an individual acts in his or her own best interest and thus follows rules to avoid punishment or receive rewards. This individual would break moral and legal laws.

premium: An article of merchandise offered as an incentive to the user to take some action.

premium approach: An approach in which the salesperson offers a prospect something as an inducement to buy.

prestige suggestions: A technique in which the salesperson has the prospect visualize using products that people whom the prospect trusts use.

price: The value or worth of a product.

price discrimination: The act of selling the same quantity of the same product to different buyers at different prices.

principled moral development level: The third level of an individual's moral development. At this level, an individual lives by an internal set of morals, values, and ethics, regardless of punishments or majority opinion.

probability close: A close that permits the prospect to focus on his or her real objections, which a salesperson attempts to reverse with a persuasive sales argument.

probing: The act of gathering information and uncovering customer needs using one or more questions.

problem–solution presentation: A flexible, customized approach involving an in-depth study of a prospect's needs, requiring a well-planned presentation.

product: One of the four main elements of the marketing mix, it is a bundle of tangible and intangible attributes, including packaging, color, and brand, plus the services and even the reputation of the seller.

product approach: An approach in which the salesperson places the product on the counter or hands it to the customer, saying nothing.

product objection: An objection relating directly to the product.

promotion: One of the four main elements of the marketing mix, it increases company sales by communicating product information to potential customers.

proof statements: Statements that substantiate claims made by the salesperson.

prospect: A qualified person or organization that has the potential to buy a salesperson's good or service.

prospecting: The process of identifying potential customers.

prospect pool: A group of names, gathered from various sources, that are prospective buyers.

prospect's mental steps: In making a sales presentation, quickly obtain the prospect's full attention, develop interest in your product, create a desire to fulfill a need, establish the prospect's conviction that the product fills a need, and finally, promote action by having the prospect purchase the product.

proverb: A short, wise, easy-to-learn saying that calls a person to think and act.

psychological objection: A hidden objection based on the prospect's attitudes.

public space: Distances greater than 12 feet from a person.

publicity: The nonpersonal communication of information that is not paid for by an individual or organization.

purchase decision: A buyer's decision to purchase something.

purchase dissonance: Tension on the part of a buyer regarding whether the right decision was made in purchasing a product.

purchase or action The final step in the prospect's mental steps. Once the prospect is convinced, the salesperson should plan the most appropriate method of asking the prospect to buy or act.

purchase satisfaction: Gratification based on a product that supplies expected, or greater than expected, benefits.

purpose: A constant truth that guides your business life.

Q

qualified prospect: A prospect who has the financial resources to pay, the authority to make the buying decision, and a desire for the product.

qualitative performance criteria: Criteria that represent the salesperson's major job activities and indicate why the quantitative measures look as they do.

quantitative performance criteria: Criteria that represent end results or bottom-line objective data.

R

real self: People as they actually are.

receiver: The person a communication is intended for.

reciprocity: An agreement whereby a person or organization buys a product if the person or organization selling the product also buys a product from the first party.

recruitment: The process of searching for, finding, and interviewing people for the sales job.

redirect question: A question that guides the prospect back to selling points that both parties agree on.

referral: A prospect who has been referred to a salesperson by another person.

referral approach: An approach that uses a third person's name as a reference to approach the buyer.

referral cycle: Provides guidelines for a salesperson to ask for referrals in four commonly faced situations experienced by salespeople.

relationship behavior: A kind of leadership that is people-oriented; it involves use of two-way communication.

relationship gap: The difference between the buyer and the seller's postsale level of concern for each other.

relationship marketing: The creation of customer loyalty.

relationship selling: When the seller contacts the customer after the purchase to determine if the customer is satisfied and has future needs.

rephrasing question: A question in which the salesperson rephrases what the prospect has said in order to clarify meaning and determine the prospect's needs.

reseller: Resellers purchase products and sell to organizations and/or individuals.

retail advertising: Advertising used by a retailer to reach customers within its geographic trading area.

retail salesperson: This individual sells goods or services to customers for their personal, nonbusiness use.

return on investment (ROI): The additional sum of money expected from an investment over and above the original investment.

Robinson-Patman Act: An act that allows sellers to grant quantity discounts to larger buyers based on savings in manufacturing costs.

role playing: A process whereby a sales trainee acts through the sale of a product or service to a hypothetical buyer.

routine decision making: The process of being in the habit of buying a particular product so attitudes and beliefs toward the product are already formed and are usually positive.

routing: The travel pattern used in working a sales territory.

rule: A prescribed guide for conduct or action.

S

sales call objective: The main purpose of a salesperson's call to a prospect or customer.

sales call planning: The process of preparing to approach a prospect attempting to make a sale.

sales call purpose: Sales call purpose is to make a contribution to the welfare of a person or organization.

sales contests: Special sales programs offering salespeople incentives to achieve short-term goals.

sales force budget: The amount of money available or assigned for a definite period.

sales forecasting: One method used to predict a firm's future revenues when planning the company's marketing and sales force activities.

sales management: The attainment of sales force goals in an effective and efficient manner through planning, staffing, training, directing, and evaluating organizational resources.

sales objection: The prospect's opposition or resistance to the salesperson's information or request.

sales presentation: The actual presentation of the sales message to the prospect.

sales presentation mix: The key communication elements used by the salesperson in the presentation.

sales process: A sequential series of actions by the salesperson that leads toward the prospect taking a desired action and ends with a follow-up to ensure purchase satisfaction.

sales promotion: Activities and materials used to create sales of goods and services.

sales response function: The relationship between sales volume and sales calls.

sales territory: The group of customers or a geographical area assigned to a salesperson.

sales training: The effort put forth by an employer to provide the opportunity for the salesperson to acquire job-related attitudes, concepts, rules, and skills that result in improved performance in the selling environment.

scheduling: The establishment of a fixed time for visiting a customer's business.

selection: The process of selecting the best available person for a sales job.

selective distortion: The altering of information when it is inconsistent with a person's beliefs or attitudes.

selective exposure: The process of allowing only a portion of the information revealed to be organized, interpreted, and permitted into awareness.

selective retention: The act of remembering only the information that supports one's attitudes and beliefs.

self-concept: A person's view of him- or herself.

self-image: How a person sees him- or herself.

SELL Sequence: A sequence of things to do and say to stress benefits important to the customer: show the feature, explain the advantage, lead into the benefit, and let the customer talk by asking a question about the benefit.

service: Making a contribution to the welfare of others.

service: The product which is an action or activity done for others for a fee.

service quality: A subjective satisfaction assessment customers arrive at by comparing the service level they believe an organization ought to deliver to the service level they perceive as being delivered.

shelf facings: The number of individual products placed beside each other on the shelf.

shelf positioning: The physical placement of the product within the retailer's store.

shock approach: An approach that uses a question designed to make the prospect think seriously about a subject related to the salesperson's product.

showmanship approach: An approach that involves doing something unusual to catch the prospect's attention and interest.

simile: A direct comparison statement using the word *like* or *as*.

social responsibility: The responsibility to profitably serve employees and customers in an ethical and lawful manner.

social space: A zone that is 4 to 12 feet from a person and is the area normally used for sales presentations.

source: The origin of a communication.

source objection: A loyalty-related objection by which the prospect states a preference for another company or salesperson, and may specify a dislike for the salesperson's company or self.

space invasion: A situation in which one person enters another person's personal or intimate space.

space threat: A situation in which a person threatens to invade another's spatial territory.

staffing: Activities undertaken to attract, hire, and retain effective sales force personnel within an organization.

stakeholder: Any group within or outside the organization that has a stake in the organization's performance.

stalling objection: An objection that delays the presentation or the sale.

standing-room-only close: A close whereby a salesperson suggests that if a prospect does not act now he or she may not be able to buy in the future, thus motivating the prospect to act immediately.

stimulus–response: A model of behavior that describes the process of applying a stimulus (sales presentation) that results in a response (purchase decision).

straight commission plan: A complete incentive compensation plan in which earnings accrue only if sales take place.

straight salary plan: A compensation plan whereby the salesperson is paid a specific dollar amount at regular intervals.

strategic: Programs, goals, and projects of great importance.

strategic customer relationship: A formal relationship between the seller and customer with the purpose of being a joint pursuit of mutual goals.

success: Setting a goal and accomplishing it.

suggestive propositions: Propositions that imply that the prospect should act now.

summary-of-benefits close: A close wherein the salesperson summarizes the benefits of the product in a positive manner so that the prospect agrees with what the salesperson says.

surfing the Internet: Exploring the different sites found within World Wide Web links.

T

T-account close: A close that is based on the process that people use when they make a decision by weighing the pros against the cons.

task behavior: Behavior that involves the leader describing the duties of an individual or group.

team leader: The salesperson who coordinates all of the information, resources, and activities needed to support the customers before, during, and after the sale.

team selling: Brings together the appropriate people and resources needed to make the sales call.

technical skills: The understanding of and proficiency in the performance of specific tasks.

technology close: A close in which the seller uses technology to present information.

telemarketing: A marketing communication system using telecommunication technology and trained personnel to conduct planned, measurable marketing activities directed at targeted groups of consumers.

telephone prospecting: The process of reaching potential customers over the phone.

termination-at-will rule: The employer's right to terminate sales personnel for poor performance, excessive absenteeism, unsafe conduct, and poor organizational citizenship.

territorial space: The area around oneself that a person will not allow another person to enter without consent.

territory manager: A person who plans, organizes, and executes activities that increase sales and profits in a given territory.

third-party answer: The technique of responding to an objection with testimony from authoritative sources.

tie-in sale: Prohibited under the Clayton Act, it occurs when a buyer is required to buy other, unwanted products in order to buy a particular line of merchandise.

top-to-top: The top executives from the seller's company meet with the customer's or prospect's top executives.

trade advertising: Advertising undertaken by the manufacturer and directed toward the wholesaler or retailer.

trade discounts: Discounts on the list retail price offered to channel members.

trade sales promotion: A promotion that encourages resellers to purchase and aggressively sell a manufacturer's products by offering incentives like sales contests, displays, special purchase prices, and free merchandise.

training: Deciding which methods to use, plus whom to train, when, and where.

transaction: A trade of values between two parties.

transaction selling: When a customer is sold a product and not contacted again.

trial close: A close that checks the attitude of your prospect toward the sales presentation.

true: Something or someone who is consistent with fact or reality.

trust: From integrity flows confidence that one can trust the other.

truth: Facts needed to make ethical and moral decisions.

U

unconscious need level: The level at which people do not know why they buy a product.

undifferentiated selling: The process of applying and designing selling strategies equally to all accounts.

unit cost: A small component price of a product's total cost.

V

value-added: Benefits received that are not included in the purchase price of the individual good or service.

value analysis: An investigation that determines the best product for the money.

values: Are moral codes of conduct toward others; created through integrity, trust, and character.

visuals: Illustrative material that aids a prospect in increasing memory retention of a presentation.

W–Z

wants: Needs that are learned by a person.

Web page: Each computer screen of information on the Internet.

wholesale salesperson: A person who sells products to parties for resale, use in producing other goods or services, or operating an organization.

wisdom: Ability to make good use of knowledge.

word processing: Computerized written communication.

World Wide Web: The part of the Internet that houses Web sites—providing text, graphics, video, and audio information.

worldview: People's different beliefs about the world around them.

zone price: The price based on geographical location or zone of customers.

Notes

Chapter 1: The Life, Times, and Career of the Professional Salesperson

1. www.business2.com, March 2002.

2. www.Gallup.com, November 26–27, 2001.

3. Saying from Jeff Reeter, Northwestern Mutual Financial Network, Houston, Texas.

4. Lee Strobel, *God's Outrageous Claims,* Grand Rapids MI: Zondervan Publishing House, 1997, p. 155.

5. For further discussion on direct selling see, Robert A. Peterson and Thomas R. Wotruba, "What Is Direct Selling?— Definition, Perspectives, and Research Agenda," *The Journal of Personal Selling,* Fall 1996, pp. 1–16 and Richard C. Bartlett, *The Direct Option* (College Station, TX: Texas A&M University Press, 1994).

6. Author unknown.

7. www.cooperwellness.com

8. DeAun Woosley and Derith Hibbetts, *ACSM Exercise Guidelines,* Texas A&M University, 2002.

9. David Jeremiah, *Fruit of the Spirit,* San Diego: CA, Turning Point, 1995, p. 84.

10. Author unknown.

11. Excerpts from Xerox Corporation sales literature.

12. Conversation between Carl Sewell and author, January 2000.

13. George Meadow, "Selling Has Changed," *Sales & Marketing Management,* July 2000, pp. 23–26.

14. Adapted from Cynthia Barmun and Netasha Wolninsky, "Why Americans Fail at Overseas Negotiations," *Management Review,* October 1989, pp. 55–57.

15. *Webster's Ninth New Collegiate Dictionary* (Springfield, Massachusetts: Merriam-Webster, 1973), p. 1076.

16. Kay Author on the radio program *Focus on the Family,* July 1, 2002.

17. Joel Champion, Colorado Christian University, 2002.

18. E. Dean Gage, "The Biblical Character Traits of Leadership," presentation at Texas A&M University, 2002.

19. Adapted from www.interviewwithGod.net.

20. www.scruples.org/web/seminars/pssb/chapter2/purpose.htm

Chapter 2: Relationship Marketing: Where Personal Selling Fits

1. See Paul Hawken, *The Ecology of Commerce* (New York: HarperBusiness, 1993) for a further discussion.

2. Peter D. Bennett, *Dictionary of Marketing Terms* (Chicago, IL: American Marketing Association, 1988), p. 115.

3. For further discussion, see Thomas L. Powers, Warren S. Martin, Hugh Rushing, and Scott Daniels, "Selling Before 1900: A Historical Perspective," *Journal of Personal Selling & Sales Management,* November 1987, pp. 1–7; and Thomas R. Wotruba, "The Evolution of Personal Selling," *Journal of Personal Selling & Sales Management,* Summer 1991, pp. 1–12.

4. Based upon the work of William J. Stanton.

5. R. M. Kanter, " Collaborative Advantage: The Art of Alliances," *Harvard Business Review,* July/August 1994, pp. 96–108.

6. Adapted from Bill Fromm and Len Schlesinger, *The Real Heroes—of Business—And Not A CEO Among Them* (New York, N.Y.: Doubleday, 1994), pp. 112–113.

7. Adapted from Richard L. Daft, Management, Fort Worth, Texas: The Dryden Press, 2000, p. 321.

8. Malcolm Fleschner, "Anatomy of a Sale," *Selling Power,* January/February 1999, 79–82, 84.

Chapter 3: Ethics First... Then Customer Relationships

1. Adapted from discussion of Robert D. Hay, University of Arkansas, Fayetteville, Arkansas.

2. Weld F. Royal, "It's Not Easy Being Green," *Sales & Marketing Management,* July 1995, pp. 84–90.

3. For an in-depth discussion of worldview see Charles Colson and Nancy Pearcey, *How Now Shall We Live?* (Nashville, TN: LifeWay Press, 1999).

4. David Jeremiah, *The New Spirituality* (San Diego, CA: Turning Point, 2002), p. 114. This information is based upon a February 12, 2002 national poll by researcher George Barna of the Barna Research Group (www.barna.org).

5. Yogi Berra and Dave Kaplan, *What Time Is It? You Mean Now?* (New York: Simon & Schuster, 2002), p. 33.

6. Barna Research Group, February 12, 2002 (www.barna.org).

7. Author unknown.

8. The concept of a fixed pint of reference separate from oneself comes from a speech made by Frank Peretti entitled "What We Believe." A tape recording of the speech can be obtained from Dr. James C. Dobson, Focus on the Family (www.family.org).

9. Sam Todd, "World-Changing Lay Ministry," *Texas Episcopalian,* February 2002, p. 8.

10. Laura P. Hartman, *Perspectives in Business Ethics* (Burr Ridge, IL: McGraw-Hill/Irwin, 2002), p. 76.

11. President George W. Bush, *Remarks by the President on Faith-Based Initiative,* April 11, 2002, usinfo.state.gov/usa/faith/s041102.htm.

12. Also see Thomas R. Wotruba, "A Comprehensive Framework for the Analysis of Ethical Behavior, with a Focus on Sales Organizations," *Journal of Personal Selling & Sales Management,* Spring 1990, pp. 29–42; and Michael A. Mayo and Lawrence J. Marks, "Empirical Investigation of a General Theory of Marketing Ethics," *Journal of the Academy of Marketing Science,* Spring 1990, pp. 163–72.

13. Shay Sayre, Mary L. Joyce, and David R. Lambert, "Gender and Sales Ethics: Are Women Penalized Less Severely than Their Male Counterparts?" *Journal of Personal Selling & Sales Management,* Fall 1991, pp. 50–65.

14. *Fair Employment Report,* August 2, 1996, p. 123.

15. Also see Leslie M. Fine and Janice R. Franke, "Legal Aspects of Salesperson Commission Payments: Implications for the Implementation of Commission Sales Programs," *The Journal of Personal Selling & Sales Management,* Winter 1995, pp. 53–68.

16. Richard F. Beltramini, "Exploring the Effectiveness of Business Gifts: A Controlled Field Experiment," *Journal of the Academy of Marketing,* Winter 1992, pp. 87–91.

17. Adapted from "Strange Tales of Sales," *Sales & Marketing Management,* June 3, 1995, p. 46.

18. Bristol Voss, "Eat, Drink, and Be Wary," *Sales & Marketing Management,* January 1991, pp. 49–54.

19. Anne M. Phaneuf, "Is It Really Better to Give?" *Sales & Marketing Management,* September 1995, pp. 95–104.

20. Author unknown.

21. Author unknown.

22. John Jobs, "Watch Those Buyers," *Sales & Marketing Management,* October 1997, pp. 34–38.

23. Les Andrews, "Watch What You Say," *Distribution,* April 1997, p. 23.

24. Charles H. Schwepker, Jr., O. C. Ferrell, and Thomas N. Ingram, "The Influence of Ethical Climate and Ethical Conflict on Role Stress in the Sales Force," *Journal of the Academy of Marketing Science,* Spring 1997, pp. 99–108.

25. Art idea adapted from Gerhard Gschwandtner, "Job 1: What's the Heart of Your Brand?" *Selling Power,* April 2002, pp. 72–76.

26. Adapted from a talk by Dr. E. Dean Gage, 2003.

27. Based on Bart Victor and John B. Cullen, "The Organizational Bases of Ethical Work Climates," *Administrative Science Quarterly,* 33 (1988), 101–125.

28. "Honesty," in *The Forbes Book of Business Quotation,* Ted Goodman, ed. (New York: Black Don and Leventhal, 1997), p. 408.

29. Adapted from John C. Maxwell, *There's No Such Thing as "Business Ethics"* (New York: Warner Books, 2003), pp. 19–20.

Chapter 4: The Psychology of Selling: Why People Buy

1. Developed by Professor John C. Hafer of the University of Nebraska at Omaha.

2. Adapted from J. R. Schermerhorn, J. G. Hunt, and R. N. Osborn, *Managing Organizational Behavior* (New York, NY: John Wiley, 1991), p. 123.

Chapter 5: Communication for Relationship Building: It's Not All Talk

1. Gerhard Gschwandtner, *Nonverbal Selling Power,* (Englewood Cliffs, NJ: Prentice Hall, 1995), p. 3.

2. Author unknown.

3. Dorothea Johnson, "Five Tips for International Handshaking," *Sales & Marketing Management,* July 1997, p. 90.

4. Also see, Dana Ray, "Every Guest Leaves Satisfied," *Selling Power,* April 1997, p. 37 and Robert A. Peterson, Michael P. Cannito, and Steven P. Brown, "An Exploratory Investigation of Voice Characteristics and Selling Effectiveness," *The Journal of Personal Selling & Sales Management,* Winter 1995, pp. 1–16.

5. Text of figure reproduced from the sales training course, "The Languages of Selling," by Gerhard Gschwandtner & Associates, (Falmouth, VA). Photos by Professor Futrell.

6. "The Four Tongues," *Life Application Study Bible: New International Version Large Print Edition,* (Wheaton, Illinois: Tyndale House Publishers, Inc. and Grand Rapids, Michigan: Zondervan, 1991), p. 1335.

7. Adapted from Bruce Barton, *The Man Nobody Knows: A Discovery of the Real Jesus,* (Indianapolis: The Bobbs-Merrill Company, 1924), pp. 150–151.

8. Adapted from Ethel C. Glenn and Elliot A. Pood, "Listening Self-Inventory," Reprinted by permission of the

publisher from *Supervisory Management,* January 1996, pp. 12–15.

9. Adapted from *Marketplace Ethics: Issues in Sales and Marketing* (Westport, CT: J/S Productions, 1990), pp. 73–92. Used with permission.

Chapter 6: Sales Knowledge: Customers, Products, Technologies

1. Also see, Sanjay K. Dhar and Stephen J. Hoch, "Price Discrimination Using In-Store Merchandising," *Journal of Marketing,* January 1996, pp. 17–30.

2. Karen Starr, "Blue Ribbon Training: Dupont Merck's Formula for Technology Training Wins Awards," *Personal Selling Power,* October 1996, pp. 22–23.

3. Portions of this section were adapted from George W. Colombo, *Sales Force Automation,* (New York, NY: McGraw-Hill, 1994).

4. Kate Griffin, "Telephone-fax, Beeper—E-mail Address," *Marketing News,* September 1994, pp. 7–8.

5. Charles R. Swindoll, Job, (Nashville, Tennessee: W Publishing Group, 2004), pp. 239–240.

6. Andy Cohen, "Going Mobile, Part 2," *Sales & Marketing Management,* June 1994, p. 5.

7. Shari Couldron, "Virtual Manners," *Workforce,* February 2000, pp. 31–32.

8. Marjorie Brody, "Etiquette for the New Millennium," *Successful Meetings,* March 2000, pp. 81–84.

9. Julie Hill, "Confronting the Ring of Rudeness," *Presentations*, March 2000, p. 13.

10. Susan Golding, "City of San Diego Mayor's Press Release," July 10, 2000.

11. Adapted from Elwood N. Chapman, *Sales Training Basics* (Menlo Park, CA: Crisp Publications, 1992), p. 11.

12. Adapted from *Marketplace Ethics: Issues in Sales and Marketing* (Westport, CT: J/S Productions, 1990), pp. 55–72. Used with permission.

Chapter 7: Prospecting—The Lifeblood of Selling

1. Also see, Malcolm Fleschner, *Selling Power,* January/February 1997, p. 60.

2. Al Paul Lefton, Jr., "The Lucky Seven: How to Roll into Sales," *Business Marketing,* August 1987, pp. 86–89; and David H. Sandler, "Prospecting… for Profit," *Personal Selling Power,* September 1990, p. 40.

3. Donald L. Brady, "Determining the Value of an Industrial Prospect: A Prospect Preference Index Model," *Journal of Personal Selling & Sales Management,* August 1987, pp. 27–32; and Roger Pell, "It's a Fact…Qualified Referrals Bring More Sales in Your Company," *Personal Selling Power,* March 1990, p. 30.

4. "Trade Shows: Creating Sales Leads," *Marketing Communications,* November 1993, pp. 36–40.

5. Also see Herbert E. Brown and Roger W. Brucker, "Telephone Qualifications of Sales Leads," *Industrial Marketing Management,* August 1987, pp. 185–90; and Sandler, "Prospecting for Profit."

6. Portions of this section adapted from Scott Krammick, *Expecting Referrals: The Resurrection of a Lost Art* (Fredericksburg, VA: Associate Publishing, 1994).

7. Also see George W. Dudley and Shannon L. Goodson, *Earning What You're Worth? The Psychology of Sales Call Reluctance* (New York, NY: Behavioral Sciences Research Press, 1992).

8. Ibid.

9. Adapted from Donald R. Rice, *What I Think About Selling* (Menlo Park, CA: Crisp Publications, 2000), p. 33.

Chapter 8: Planning the Sales Call Is a Must!

1. L. Carroll, *Alice's Adventures in Wonderland* (New York: Knopf, 1983), p. 72.

2. Adapted from *Marketplace Ethics: Issues in Sales and Marketing* (Westport, CT: J/S Productions, 1990), pp. 35–54. used with permission.

Chapter 9: Carefully Select Which Sales Presentation Method to Use

1. Adapted from G. M. Grikscheit, H. C. Cash, and W. J. E. Crissy, *Handbook of Selling: Psychological, Managerial, and Marketing Bases* (New York: Wiley, 1981).

2. Example provided by Professor Richard D. Nordstrom, California State University—Fresno.

3. Adapted from Grikscheit, Cash, and Crissy, *Handbook of Selling: Psychological, Managerial, and Marketing Bases.*

4. Ibid.

5. Example provided by Professor Richard D. Nordstrom, California State University—Fresno.

6. David Fitzpatrick, IBM Executive in Residence, Howard University, Washington, D.C., and Charles M. Futrell, 2004.

7. Also see Tony Alessandra, Phil Wexler, and Rich Barrera, *Nonmanipulative Selling* (Englewood Cliffs, N. J.: Prentice Hall, 1997).

8. David Fitzpatrick, IBM Executive in Residence, Howard University, Washington, D.C., and Charles M. Futrell, 2001.

9. Dale Carnegie, *How to Win Friends and Influence People* (New York, NY: Simon and Schuster, 1936), p. 208.

10. Adapted from Robert B. Maddax, *Successful Negotiation* (Menlo Park, California: Crisp Publications, Inc., 1988), p. 19.

11. Exercise provided by Professor Richard D. Nordstrom, California State University—Fresno.

12. Dru Conant, "Business Selling," *Business,* Spring, 1995, p. 16.

Chapter 10: Begin Your Presentation Strategically

1. Philip Proctors, "A Well-Bread Sale," *Selling Power,* September 2000, p. 20.

2. For a complete discussion, see Neil Rackham, *SPIN Selling* (New York, NY: McGraw-Hill, 1988).

3. Dennis DeMaria, "Keep Quiet and Get the Order," *Personal Selling Power,* March/April 1993, p. 17.

4. Adapted from Joseph P. Smith, *Dress for Business* (Menlo Park, CA: Crisp Publication, 1997), p. 23.

Chapter 11: Elements of a Great Sales Presentation

1. Rosemary P. Ramsey and Ravipreet S. Sohi, "Listening to Your Customers: The Impact of Perceived Salesperson Listening Behavior on Relationship Outcomes," *Journal of the Academy of Marketing Science,* Spring 1997, pp. 127–137.

2. Patricia M. Doney and Joseph P. Cannon, "An Examination of the Nature of Trust in Buyer–Seller Relationships," *Journal of Marketing,* April 1997, pp. 35–51.

Chapter 12: Welcome Your Prospect's Objections

1. Adapted from Tom Hopkins, *How to Master the Art of Selling* (New York: Warner Books, 1994), p. 191.

Chapter 13: Closing Begins the Relationship

1. Adapted from John L. Johnston, *Works of Mark Twain* (New York, N.Y.: Harper & Row, 1989), p. 133.

2. Gerhard Gschwandtner, "How to Sell in France," *Personal Selling Power,* July/August 1991, pp. 54–60.

3. Mike Radick, "Training Salespeople to Get Success on Their Side," *Sales & Marketing Management,* August 15, 1993. Also see Neil Rackham, *SPIN Selling* (New York, N. Y.: McGraw-Hill, 1988).

Chapter 14: Service and Follow-Up for Customer Retention

1. Melissa Campanelli, "Starting from Scratch," *Sales & Marketing Management,* November 1994, p. 55.

2. Charles M. Futrell, *ABC's of Relationship Selling Through Service* (Burr Ridge, IL: Irwin, 2005), p. 418.

3. Ibid., p. 67.

4. James Lewis, "These Sins Will Kill a Sale," *Selling,* October 1997, p. 6.

5. Reprinted with permission of B. J. Hughes, Inc.

6. Adapted from Richard F. Gerson, *Beyond Customer Service: Keeping Customers for Life* (Menlo Park, CA: Crisp Publications, 1992), p. 79.

7. Adapted from *Marketplace Ethics: Issues in Sales and Marketing* (Westport, CT: J/S Productions, 1990), pp. 15–35. Used with permission.

Chapter 15: Time, Territory, and Self-Management: Keys to Success

1. William F. Kendy, "Time Management," *Selling Power,* July/August 2000, pp. 34–36.

2. Ibid.

Chapter 16: Planning, Staffing, and Training Successful Salespeople

1. For an in-depth discussion of topics in Chapter 16, see Charles M. Futrell, *Sales Management: Teamwork, Leadership, and Technology* (Mason, Ohio: South-Western Thompson Learning 2001).

2. Dick McNeal, "Sales and Technology," *Sales & Marketing Management,* January 1997, pp. 159–61.

3. G. Berton Latamore, "Perfect Match," *Selling Power,* September 2000, p. 152.

4. Aubrey Penny, "People Skills," *Personnel Magazine,* February 1997, pp. 33–36.

Chapter 17: Motivation, Compensation, Leadership, and Evaluation of Salespeople

1. For an in-depth discussion of topics in Chapter 17, see Charles M. Futrell, *Sales Management: Teamwork, Leadership, and Technology* (Mason, Ohio: South-Western Thompson Learning, 2001).

2. John Lewis, "What Does It Take To Be a Leader?" *Sales & Marketing Management,* September 7, 1997, pp. 23–27.

3. Tony Seideman, "On the Cutting Edge," Part 2, *Sales & Marketing Management,* June 1997, pp. 18–23.

4. Leslie Stark, "Sales Communication," *Sales Bulletin,* January 1995, pp. 15–16.

Exercises, Technology, and Integrative Cases

Appendix A

1. This exercise created by Professor Jeffrey K. Sager of the University of North Texas, Richard Langlotz of Minolta

Business Systems, and Professor Charles M. Futrell of Texas A&M University.

Appendix B

1. This exercise was created by Professors Charles M. Futrell of Texas A&M University and George Wynn of James Madison University. Copyright 2000.

2. Carl Jung, *Psychological Types* (London: Routhledge and Kegan Paul, 1923).

3. Adapted from I. Myers, *The Myers-Briggs Type Indicator* (Princeton, NJ: Educational Testing Service, 1962).

Appendix C

1. Reprinted from COMPENSATING NEW SALES ROLES by Jerome A. Colletti, et al. Copyright © 1999 The Alexander Group, Inc. Reprinted by permission of AMACOM, a division of American Management Association International, New York, NY. All rights reserved. http://www.amanet.org.

3. Reprinted from COMPENSATING NEW SALES ROLES by Jerome A. Colletti, et al. Copyright © 1999 The Alexander Group, Inc. Reprinted by permission of AMACOM, a division of American Management Association International, New York, NY. All rights reserved. http://www.amanet.org.

4. Based upon the work of Zarrell V. Lambert, Professor of Marketing, Southern Illinois University at Carbondale, and Fred W. Kniffin, Professor Emeritus of Marketing, University of Connecticut.

Appendix D

1. Adapted from Susan Harte, "When in Rome, You Should Learn to Do What the Romans Do," *Atlanta Journal Constitution,* January 22, 1996, pp. D1, D6. Also see Lufthansa's *Business Travel Guide/Europe,* 1995, and Betsy Cummings, "Selling Around the World," *Sales & Marketing Management,* May 2001, p. 70.

2. Paula Champ, "How to Sell in Japan," *Selling,* December 1993, pp. 30–47.

3. Developed by Pushkala Raman.

4. Joann S. Lublin, "Companies Use Cross-Cultural Training to Help Their Employees Adjust Abroad," *The Wall Street Journal,* August 4, 1997.

5. Arne J. DeKeijzer, "China: The Sales Doors Open," *Personal Selling Power,* January–February 1994, pp. 12–22.

6. Paula Champa, "How to Sell in Japan," *Selling,* December 1993, pp. 39–47.

7. Arne J. DeKeijzer, "China: The Sales Doors Open," *Personal Selling Power,* January–February 1994, pp. 12–22.

8. Arne J. DeKeijzer, "China: The Sales Doors Open," *Personal Selling Power,* January–February 1994, pp. 12–22.

9. John Anderson, "Pulling Off a Six-Figure Bank Job," *Selling,* May 1994, p. 14.

10. Gerhard Gschwandtner, "How to Sell in France," *Personal Selling Power,* July–August 1991, pp. 54–60.

11. Written by Moshe Davidow, University of Haifa, Israel.

12. Adapted from Sergy Frank, "Global Negotiation," *Sales & Marketing Management,* May 1997, pp. 64–69.

13. Jackie Hill, "Globally Service Counts," *Executive Travels,* January 1997, pp. 11–14.

14. Ira Sager, "Big Blue Wants the World to Know Who's Boss," *Business Week,* September 26, 1994, p. 78.

644

A

B

Word processing, 196
Words, listening to, 163–164
Workers' compensation, 84
Worldview, 75
World Wide Web, 198–199
WyndMail for Windows, 246
Wynn, George, 355–356, 363

X

Xerox, 26, 29, 95, 184, 226–227, 229, 457, 511
Xerox Sales Learning Programs, 526
Xerox Training Center, 422

Y

Yahoo, 229

Z

Zenith Computer Terminals (ZCT), 597–601
Zone price, 207